UNDERAGE WARRIORS

Over 600 Stories about the Courage and
Hardship of Children, Ages Seven to Fourteen,
Who Fought in the American Revolution

Jack Darrell Crowder

HERITAGE BOOKS
2017

HERITAGE BOOKS
AN IMPRINT OF HERITAGE BOOKS, INC.

Books, CDs, and more—Worldwide

For our listing of thousands of titles see our website
at
www.HeritageBooks.com

Published 2017 by
HERITAGE BOOKS, INC.
Publishing Division
5810 Ruatan Street
Berwyn Heights, Md. 20740

Copyright © 2017 Jack Darrell Crowder

All rights reserved. No part of this book may be reproduced or transmitted in any form or by any means, electronic or mechanical, including photocopying, recording or by any information storage and retrieval system without written permission from the author, except for the inclusion of brief quotations in a review.

International Standard Book Number
Paperbound: 978-0-940-90716-4

This book is dedicated to my 4th great-grandfather
Sergeant Matthew David Scott

He served in the 8th Virginia Regiment
of the Continental Army
in the cause of American Independence
during the Revolutionary War.

The book is also dedicated to the
men, women, and children who fought and aided
this cause for freedom.

Table of Contents

Preface……………………………………………..vii

Introduction…………………..…………………….ix

Underage Children…………………………………1

Bibliography……………………………………..809

Name Index………………………………………811

Preface

While researching the American Revolution for another book, I kept reading about young boys serving with the various units. I began to look into this and discovered that there were many boys as young as seven serving in the military. Many were drummers, played the fife, or served as waiters. However, I also found many of these young people were in the middle of battles. Not only did they serve as soldiers, but also as spies and scouts. I became curious as to the reason they would join the army and put their lives at risk. After all, they were exempt from military service, and they received little or no pay for their service.

Most of these boys applied for a pension in the early 1800's, and by that time they were in their forties or fifties, so their memories were still very clear about events during their service. It was fascinating to read in their pension applications the descriptions of battles, military life, and famous participants in the war.

These young boys have an important story to tell, but for the most part are forgotten soldiers in the early history of our country. The sacrifice and hardships that these boys endured needs to be preserved and recognized.

Much of the information obtained on these soldiers come from their own words in their pension applications. Their words are the original wording and spelling, and they have not been changed. Some of the information is from sources written over a hundred years ago and out of print. These stories provide a unique insight to the lives of these men.

Introduction

"When I volunteered under Captain Nailor I heard no inquiry made about my age, they wanted volunteers and I was in the service I presumed I was considered a good volunteer. I never knew anyone refused to be received who was able to raise a musket."

James Kidd - age 14 Virginia Militia

****

Nowadays most people are repulsed with the thought of young children going to war. Killing and dying in battle is work for adults and until recently the work of adult men only. However, in the American colonies in 1775 the concept of youth was entirely different in society.

The journey to adulthood was much shorter in Colonial America. By the age of 5 or 6 children were starting to be treated as young adults. They worked alongside their parents doing chores on the farm. Few children had the time to attend school or engage in meaningless play. They were also needed to help defend the family farm from Indian attacks. Girls married young, which was usually 16 to 18 years old. Boys were considered men at 16 and were even required to start paying taxes.

The Continental Army was not established until two months after the battles at Lexington and Concord. The minimum age for enlistment was 16, but with parental consent a boy could enlist at 15. Boys younger than 15 were sometimes allowed to serve as drummers and fifers, waiters to officers, or they were used to do chores around camp.

During the early part of the war very few boys under the age of 18 served in the army. This was because of the hard life of a soldier. Mortality rates were high due to shortages of food and diseases such as small pox. Also, the Continental Army suffered many defeats in battle, and parents would find reasons to keep their young boys at home rather than permit them to join the army. As the war progressed, a shortage of soldiers for the army forced the Continental Congress in 1778 to ask the states to draft men from their militias to serve one year in the Continental Army. States were given manpower quotas to fill. When the quotas were hard to fill, the recruiting officers were willing to turn a blind eye and sign an underage recruit. As a result, some officers began to complain about the number of boys in their units that were small and too weak to do the duties required of a soldier.

Many young boys were more likely to join the local militia. This enabled a boy to play soldier for a few days and return back home. The colonies required military service in the militia for males between 16 and 60. The exceptions were clergy, college students, slaves, and in some cases free blacks.

Many fathers encouraged their sons under the age of 16 to serve in their place in the militia. This enabled the father to stay and work the land and protect his family from Tory or Indian attacks. An underage boy, who was large for his size or had proved himself in battle with Indians, would be allowed to join the militia. Once the call went out for the militia to form, the commanders would pay little attention to the size or age of their men. If you brought food and a musket, then you could stay and fight.

What was the difference between the Continental Army and the militia?

During the Revolutionary War the American military forces consisted of a combination of state militias, especially trained militia units such as the Minutemen, and a small professional force created by Congress called the Continental Army. The militia received only a few days training during the year. Men of the required age, or their substitutes, were expected to answer the alarm call. They would return to their homes once the threat or battle was over. Their supplies consisted of what they could carry, and hunting for food was most of their training. They received no pay for their service.

Militia forces were much less reliable than the professional army, and commanders found it difficult to plan their moves. They never knew exactly how many men would show up and how long they might stay. One militia unit apparently left the field immediately before the 7 October, 1777 battle at Saratoga. At Camden, South Carolina on 16 August, 1780 the bulk of American forces were militia. British regulars charged the colonials with bayonets fixed, and the militiamen panicked. Many dropped their loaded muskets and never fired a shot in one of the most decisive American defeats of the war.

Ultimately, however, the militias played a critical role in helping the colonists to defeat the British. They supplied enough men to keep the Continental Army going, and they provided on very short notice large numbers of armed men for brief periods of emergency service.

The Continental soldiers received supplies, uniforms, and some training. Each soldier was issued a musket, bayonet, cartridge box, and tools necessary to keep his weapons working. When a soldier signed up for an enlistment period, which could be up to three years, they were promised a bounty at the end of the time. This bounty would be in the form of money or land. They also received a monthly salary of $6.00 if they were a private. In some cases they had to buy their own uniforms and gear. Congress authorized an army of 75,000 men. At its peak General Washington's main force never had more than 18,000 men. At its height the patriots had 35,000 Continentals and 44,000 militia against 56,000 British troops and 30,000 Hessians.

How were the Americans divided during the war?

Patriots: also known as rebels, Continentals, or Whigs consisted of about 40% of the population. They were actively in favor of independence from British rule. The *New York Journal* in 1775 defined a Tory as: *"A thing with a head in England, a body in America, and a neck that needs stretching."*

Tories: who were known as royalists or loyalists consisted of about 20% of the population and supported the British King.

Neutral: were the remaining colonists. Sometimes they supported whichever army was in the area.

Many members of minority groups remained loyal to the King, because they needed his protection against local majority groups. Throughout the war some colonists would change their minds and switch from one side to another. People would choose a side that would help their various needs.

The war became a bitter struggle between neighbors and families. The savagery between the Patriots and Tories in battle even shocked the British and Hessian troops. In 1776 Josiah Brandon, age 15 of North Carolina, volunteered for duty in the militia. For the next 3 years he served several short tours while in the militia. Most of his fights were against the local Tories. His father was a loyalist and served with the British. His father finally asserted his authority and forced his son to join the loyalist side with him. After his father was killed at the battle of Kings' Mountain, Josiah switched sides and rejoined the militia for another 3 years.

Why did young boys enlist?

What would compel a boy to leave the comfort and safety of his home to serve and face hardships and possible death? In many cases it was probably the allure of adventure and excitement. The following boys give their reasons for joining from their pension applications.

The reason that **Nicholas Hill** and his brother **Henry** joined the army at the young ages of 10 and 8 occurred in 1774. Their father Henry, a fearless patriot, made a remark in the presence of British military officers, which was construed by them as disrespectful to their King. For that remark Henry was overpowered and unmercifully whipped in the presence of his wife and his two sons. The boys swore vengeance, and they enlisted the first chance they got.

John Jenks couldn't wait to get away from his guardian who he apparently did not like. So he ran away and enlisted at age 12.

Nicholas Johnston, at age 14 deserted the British Army and floated down the Hudson River in the winter to join the American Army.

Drury Logan said he enlisted at age 14 *"because the area was overrun by the Tories and Indians and every person that was a friend to Independence and able to bear arms had to do so for his own safety."*

It was very inconvenient for his father to leave home so **Elisha Lyman** at age 13 asked Captain Blip to take him as a substitute, which the Captain agreed to do.

Joshua Prewett said, *"After I arrived at the age of thirteen years when my father married a second wife, I being unwilling to come under the government of a Step Mother deserted my father and went to the Garrison at Louisville and in the month of March 1779 I did enlist."*

George Hofstalar joined at age 14 because, *"I was miserable when I was sent to live with relatives in North Carolina when my father died."*

Dan Granger at the age of 13 walked into the American camp in Boston and talked the officer in charge into letting him take the place of his brother. Dan's brother was ill, and he feared that his brother might die if he did not return home.

Some boys signed on for financial reasons. States in need of filling quotas would pay a signing bonus of $10.00 or higher if you joined. A man drafted could avoid military duty by paying a substitute to go in his place. Many times young boys would receive this money and give it to their families.

Simeon Justice enlisted at the age of 12 along with, *"....my father John Justice and my brother John Justice, on the first day of June 1777 enlisted or volunteered under Captain Benjamin Tutt -- who paid each of us $30 in Cash as bounty money."*

Joseph David enlisted at the age of 13 for William Pepper who was not willing to leave home, so William hired Joseph to take his place.

William Wills was 14 when, *"My Father offered me if I would take his place he would give me a Negro girl. I declined having been so young not exceeding 14 years. My father however told me that I should stay and perform the duty assigned him."*

Frederick Unsell at age 14 said, *"I enlisted as a private soldier & took the bounty money."*

Dangers in Battle

Many of these young boys were in the thick of battle. When the fighting started they received no mercy from the British troops because of their age.

Nicholas Boom enlisted at the age of 14 and was injured on a scouting party. *"I left the service in the year 1782 having received a wound in consequence of which wound I have lost my right leg."*

John McGregory served with **Lemuel King**, who enlisted at the age of 14. John wrote, *"While I was here I saw Lemuel King who was dreadfully wounded & then lay languishing with his wounds & in this condition Doctor Hamilton a Surgeon of Somers in Connecticut was sent down to see and assist King."*

Asa Gillett enlisted at the age of 13 and wrote, *"I was severely wounded at Valentines Hill about eight miles north of White Plains about eight miles north of White Plains. I stopped to load my musket and while in the act of loading and partly facing the enemy I received a musket ball in my left leg on the inside just above the ankle joint which passed through the bone and splintered it badly. The surgeon of the Regiment Dr. Branson proposed immediate amputation but in my protesting he decided from amputation."*

Nathaniel Hodges at age 14 in the Massachusetts militia said, *"I was wounded in the head by a musket ball & two buck shot which may have contributed to my present Idiotic condition. I have been for so many years Idiotic & insane that I cannot give any distinct amount of the term."*

Children in the Navy

At the start of the revolution England ruled the seas. They had 60 ships of war sailing around the American coast, plus nearly 200 merchant ships bringing a steady stream of supplies and troops to America. The Continental Navy of the United States was formed in 1775. The first vessel to sail under an American flag was the *Hannah* launched on 5 September, 1775. At the same time the British navy had over 200 warships. By 13 December, 1775 Congress authorized the construction of 13 new frigates. Only eight of them made it to sea and nearly all were captured or sunk by 1781.

Many boys served aboard as privateers. If a privateer captured an enemy ship the proceeds from the sale of the captured ship and its cargo would be shared among the privateer ship's owners and crew. The privateers were given Letters of Marque, which gave the privateer permission from the government to capture the enemy's ship during wartime. During the war it is estimated that more than 70,000 men served as privateers, while about 4,000 men served in the navy. On a good voyage a young boy could return to port in several months hundreds of dollars richer than when he left. If he served in the army, he would be lucky to receive $8 a month.

Many young boys from New England and the Mid-Atlantic states joined the navy or privateers during the Revolutionary War. Their reasons for joining were usually to get away from an unhappy home, for adventure, or the chance to make some money. Many of the wharfs had recruiting officers trying to make the life on the sea alluring, especially to the young. They would draw crowds with wit and speeches of patriotism and their zeal for freedom.

The boys would usually sign-on as cabin boys, powder boys, boatswains, and midshipmen. Young boys that served as powder boys or powder monkeys would carry gunpowder from small cramped spaces below deck to the cannons. This would be a very dangerous job if the ship was under attack.

The boys that served as cabin boys had numerous duties. They would help the cook by carrying buckets of food from the kitchen to where the seamen ate. They would also carry messages throughout the ship between the officers. They might have to climb up the rigging if the sails had to be trimmed. Some of the boys were the personal waiters for the ship's captain or other officers. The boatswains were involved in all the activities of running the ship and making it sea worthy. The young boys that served in the navy as midshipmen were training as officer cadets. They would be taught the various aspects of sailing a ship.

Children as Spies

Children were used as spies in the American Revolution because they had such an innocent appearance. They could play around British camps or buildings and gather information without bringing attention to themselves. Sometimes they would carry secret messages sewn inside the buttons or linings of their clothing.

On the frontier young boys would be used as Indian spies, because they would draw little attention to themselves. Because they were small and light their horses could carry them longer distances and at a faster pace than a larger man. A frontier Indian spy led a hard life. They were expected to sleep on the ground, live off the land, and live in constant danger of being caught. Their job was to warn the settlers of an Indian attack, so they could prepare for defense.

If the spy was caught by the British it would probably mean prison and possibly death. If an Indian spy was caught, it would probably mean torture and death. Even knowing the dangers involved, many children both male and female were willing to put their lives at risk.

Young women in the war

Women lost property and legal rights once they got married. Marriage and having children were the main goals for women. As a result they were not expected to take part in the war. However, they did participate. They sewed uniforms, gathered supplies for the soldiers, and nursed the wounded. When the husband was away fighting they took over running the farm. Like the men, women held protest against British goods. For example, they renounced drinking British tea and wearing clothes made of British cloth.

Some were camp followers, who accompanied their husbands or family members when they enlisted. Some of these women sought adventure or were in search of a living. Most were involved in cooking, nursing, or doing wash. Occasionally, they fought alongside the men and were usually dressed as men. Even though they were dressed as men, they did not pass themselves off as males. There was no doubt in anyone's eyes that they were females dressed as males.

Some women, however, went a step further. They disguised themselves as men and fought along with the soldiers. They knew that if they were discovered, they would be removed from the ranks and could face jail time.

Nancy Bailey enlisted in 1777 under the name of Samuel Gay. She served in the 1st Massachusetts Regiment, and in just a few weeks she was promoted to the rank of Corporal. After 3 weeks, for reasons known only to her, she deserted. Her company commander, Captain Abraham Hunt, swore out a warrant for her arrest. She was soon captured and discovered to be a woman. She was fined by a civilian court for "appearing in men's clothing" and was sentenced to two months in prison.

A young New Jersey woman enlisted as a male in 1778 and was discovered almost at once. She was ordered to march through town while being humiliated by soldiers and townspeople. Sally St. Clair disguised herself as a man and served in a South Carolina Regiment. It was reported that she fought alongside either her husband or boyfriend. They were both killed in the same battle. Her true identity was not discovered until her death.

The most famous female soldier was Deborah Sampson who, disguised as a man, served in the army for 17 months. She was wounded in battle and her secret was later discovered when she became ill. She was honorably discharged at West Point and later received a pension.

Young People of Color in the War

When the Revolutionary War began General Washington was very vocal about not supporting enlistment of African Americans, both free and especially slaves as soldiers. Most of the slave owners in the south and some in the north were afraid that training and arming the slaves could lead to a rebellion. By the start of the war both George Washington and Thomas Jefferson both owned over 130 slaves each.

Days after taking command of the army General Washington issued orders that no black, free or slave, could be recruited to fight. He was, as a southerner, reacting to the fear in the south of an armed slave rebellion. He said that African Americans serving in the north would be able to finish their term of service. Then, he would have his all white army. However, his and Jefferson's views on slavery would change as the war progressed.

The first colonial armies were the state militias. As tensions with the British grew the militias in the north were not very particular who joined. In order to fill local quotas, they were willing to accept African Americans and underage children to their ranks. For example, in Massachusetts over 1,000 African Americans joined the militia. Many were assigned to support roles like digging ditches, but many were also engaged in battle. Both free African Americans and slaves enlisted in New England. Later, when they began to enlist in the south, it became common that they enlisted and served in place of their owners. In many cases their signing bonuses and pay went straight to their masters.

At the beginning of the war the British saw an excellent opportunity to divide the colonies over the issue of African Americans. The last royal governor of Virginia, Lord Dunmore, offered freedom to slaves and indentured servants if they would bear arms for the British. This promise was only for slaves owned by the rebels, and not slaves owned by Loyalists.

During the winter at Valley Forge enlistments were down, and there was fear that by spring there might not be an effective American army. Rhode Island complained that they could not, like some of the other colonies, fill the enlistment quotas. Desperate for additional troops Washington finally agreed to accept African Americans into the army.

The government of Rhode Island promised to free all black, Indian, and mulatto slaves who enlisted in the new 1st Rhode Island Regiment. The government did offer to compensate their owners. More than 140 black men enlisted in the new regiment. The 1st Rhode Island had white officers and separate companies designated for black and white soldiers. The rest of the army was fully integrated.

The town of Boston raised an all-black regiment called the "Bucks of America". The regiment was commanded by Colonel Middleton, a black man. A third black regiment was formed, which was made up of 545 black Haitian volunteers who came to America to fight for the Americans. The mixture of black and white soldiers caused a French staff officer to refer to them as "speckled."

No one is sure how many African Americans served in the Revolutionary War. Estimates range from 4,000 to 8,000 depending on which history book you read. The majority of African American troops came from the northern states. South Carolina and Georgia prohibited the enlistment of blacks, but they did use them as auxiliaries. Some historians maintain that if those two states had sent their slaves into battle, the extra 15,000 to 20,000 men could have shortened the war.

African Americans took part in every major battle of the war and were present at Valley Forge. When the war began on 19 April, 1775 at Lexington, the last American to be wounded there was an African American named Caesar Augustus. At the Battle of Bunker Hill 150 African Americans stood shoulder to shoulder with over 1,000 Americans who faced the British. A black man named Salem Poor, who had purchased his freedom several years before, was cited by Colonel William Prescott for his heroism.

One young soldier, sixteen year old John Greenwood, on his way to the battle at Bunker Hill made this observation and entered it into his journal. *"Just as I came near the place, a negro man, wounded in the back of his neck, passed me and, his collar being open and he not having anything on except his shirt and trousers, I saw the wound quiet plainly and the blood running down his back. I asked him if it hurt him much as he did not seem to mind it; he said no, that he was only going to get a plaster put on it, **and meant to return**. You cannot conceive what encouragement this immediately gave me. I began to feel brave and like a soldier from that moment and fear never troubled me afterward during the whole war."* ---The Revolutionary Services of John Greenwood of Boston and New York 1775-1783, 1923, pages 12-13.

When the Treaty of Paris was signed on 3 September, 1783 it officially ended the American Revolution. It was now time to address the promises made to the African Americans by the British and the Americans. The Revolution did help start a movement for emancipation in the North. Northern states abolished slavery by law or in their new constitutions. However, in the South slavery became further entrenched and the issue would not be settled until the Civil War.

Many of the African Americans that were under British or Loyalist control eventually ended up back in bondage. Loyalists left the colonies for plantations taking thousands of slaves with them. Other African Americans were resettled in Canada, West Indies, West Africa, or parts of the British Empire.

Most of the slaves who fought for the Americans remained the property of their masters after the war. State legislatures in some states, such as Connecticut and Massachusetts, banned all blacks, free or slave, from military service. In 1792 the United States Congress formally excluded African Americans from military service, and they allowed only free able-bodied male citizens to enlist. By the time the government offered pensions to the black veterans of the Revolutionary War, most of the black soldiers were dead.

As for Native Americans there are none included in this book, because although they served it was not possible to certify their ages because of limited information on their birth dates. Many Native Americans wished to remain neutral and saw no advantage to selecting a side to support. Most of the ones that did engage in the war took the side of the British.

The British side was chosen for several reasons. Native American towns and villages were often attacked by patriot militias, and sometimes without regard to which side the Native American belonged. Most Native Americans felt a greater threat from encroachment of their land from the Americans than they did from the British. For some Native American tribes a continued British presence would restrain American westward expansion.

In a few cases religion played a part in deciding which side the Native Americans chose. The Oneida and Tuscarora tribes fought for the Americans, because they were converted to Christianity by Samuel Kirkland who was a strong supporter of American independence. The Mohawks were converted to Christianity by John Stuart who was an Anglican and a supporter of the British.

Promises to the Indians were not kept by either side that wanted their support. In 1783 under the terms of the Treaty of Paris, Britain handed over to the United States all its territory east of the Mississippi, south of the Great Lakes, and north of Florida. Much of that land was not British according to its treaties with the various native tribes.

In conclusion, the Revolution gave the African Americans a strong argument for their freedom from slavery. It began the long journey toward their legal emancipation in all parts of the United States. For the Native Americans it began their journey toward the destruction of their way of life. Rebecca Tanner was a Mohegan Indian who lost all five sons in the cause of liberty.

Pension Applications

Revolutionary War pensions can contain a wealth of information to researchers or genealogists. You can find names, birthdates, death dates, marriage dates of husbands, wives, and names of children. Also, information on a soldier's rank, officers, enlistment, battles, and family member information is available. Most of the information is easy to read, while some can be a challenge.

Fires in 1800 destroyed the earliest Revolutionary War pension application records. As a result, pension application papers on file at the National Archives begin after 1800. Estimates are that 20,485 soldiers were granted pensions in 1818, and 1,200 in 1828, and 33,425 in 1832.

On March 18, 1818 the first service pension act was passed, which provided that every resident of the United States who had served in the Revolutionary War, until its close or for the term of 9 months or longer, at any period of the war, on the Continental establishment or navy, and who was by reason of his reduced circumstances in need of assistance, should receive a pension. If the man was an officer he would receive twenty dollars a month, if he was a private he would receive eight dollars a month.

Congress passed the Act of 1832, which provided a yearly grant to every man who had served more than 6 months, and widows married at that time were also eligible. 33,000 claims were submitted by vets and nearly 23,000 additional claims by widows.

To qualify for a pension they had to indicate the time and place of service, names of units, and officers and engagements in which they participated. The narratives were presented and sworn in open court of law and had to be supported by two character witnesses. Men that applied for a pension had to prove their need of assistance. They were required to list the value of all their property and debts that they had. Many of the men could do very limited work because of age, injury, or illness. In 1848 Congress provided for life pensions for widows of veterans, if they were married before 2 January, 1800.

This book is about the underage soldiers that served in the American Revolution. Much of the information will be in their own words as reported to others and recorded in their pension applications. Four out of five among the applicants for pensions in the 1830's had been teenagers in the Revolutionary War. Many of them claimed to be older than they really were, so that they could receive benefits.

The majority of the stories of the young people were taken from their pension applications filed in the early 1800's. The vast majority of these applications have been well preserved and are fairly easy to read.

The author has recorded their statements in the first person, just as they told it to the official who wrote it down. The author made no changes in grammar or spelling. Pension numbers that start with an S were made by the soldier. Pension numbers that start with a W were filed by the widow of the soldier.

At times the author stated that the soldier later in life owned slaves. This was not mentioned to pass any judgement. Slave ownership and the number of slaves indicated the amount of wealth, since very few farmers could afford a slave.

Underage Children

William Addison age 14

William Addison was born on 29 December, 1766 in Fairfield County, South Carolina, and he died 20 May, 1853 in Todd County, Kentucky. His first wife was unknown, and he married his second wife, Nancy Mobley, in 1797 in South Carolina. He had a total of nineteen children.

"I was born in Fairfield County in the State of Carolina on the 29th day of December 1766. I entered the service of the United States in the Year 1780 to the best of my recollection, when I was just a boy as a substitute for my brother Christopher Addison who had just returned from a long Campaign. I rendezvoused at Winnsborough in said County of Fairfield in the State of South Carolina and was attached to a company of Militia commanded by one Captain Camp Strother. The name of the Lieutenant was Jedidiah Kirkland the name of the other officers in said company I cannot now recall. Colo Hunter was the commander of the whole of the troops which Rendezvoused at this place from hence we marched to Campden: it was completed when I joined the army that I would Join the army in Charlston but after being at Campden for three weeks and before the army which lay at Campden was ready to march to the relief of Charleston news reached us of the surrender of General Lincoln and we was discharged and sent home. Soon after my return home which was to the best of my recollection in the last of the Spring or first of the Summer of the year 1780 I again entered the Service of the United States in said County of Fairfield in the State of South Carolina as a private in the company of Rangers or Mounted Militia commanded by Captain John Gray, Andrew Gray his brother was Lieutenant in said company and after the promotion of his brother John, was appointed Captain and commanded the company. James Kincaid was the Lieutenant and Francis Kirkland was ensign. Some time after the company organized we were ordered down to the Congaree River to a place called Fords ferry. Here we were joined by two other companies one of which was a company of Cavalry commanded by Captain John McCool. After remaining here

perhaps a month or more we were marched to a place called four hole bridge in Deans Swamp. We joined a Considerable body of South Carolina militia in the command of Colo Joseph Kirkland here we lay incamped about a month from here We marched to Santee River to a place called Managills ferry. Here we caught two British soldiers and a troy, who made his escape the night after he was taken, by knocking down an old Dutchman by the name of Buoly who was standing guard over him. We were stationed here three or four weeks from here we marched back to Fairfield there being at this time a small collection of tories in the neighbor. We were told by a woman that they would cross brand River at Lyles ferry. We put off in pursuit of them and came to the bend of the river when the Tories had got about half over, we fired upon them as they retreated from us. We continued to beat about the country in the neighborhood of Fairfield County until we received orders to join General Greens Army some short time before the Battle of Eutaw Springs. I was attached to General A. Pickens command and was within a few paces of the general when I received a wound in my left breast buckle from a spent ball. We joined General Pickens about fourteen miles from the battle grounds the day before the Battle. We continued in the fight until it was over and some short time after the battle we returned to the neighborhood of Fairfield County but continued in the said company and in the service of the United States until the army was disbanded."

William later moved to Kentucky and served about nine weeks in Captain Jacob Starns' Company, in Colonel Trotter's regiment. During this time they went against the Northwestern Indians. They marched to St. Joseph's River, and a few days after arriving there they were in the battle in which General Harmar was defeated. Shortly after the battle William returned home and was discharged after nine weeks of service.

General Harmar in 1790 was sent out against the Indians and remaining British in the Northwest Territory. His force of Federal soldiers were defeated by a tribal coalition led by Little Turtle. This battle became known as Harmar's defeat.

William applied for and received a pension of $80.00 a year for his service. A few months after his death in 1853 his 88 year old widow applied to receive his pension. On the application she could not recall the date of their marriage but could recall the name of the preacher, Thomas Williams, which married them. After sending in the paperwork for the pension, she was told she had not proved her marriage because she had no date or any other evidence. After people that knew her wrote to the pension bureau, she was finally approved to receive her husband's pension.

Sources: 1. Census of 1790, 1820, 1830, 1840, and 1850. 2. U.S. Pensioners 1818-1872. 3. Tombstone. 4. Roster of South Carolina Patriots in the Revolutionary War. 5. History of Kentucky—Revolutionary Soldiers. 6. U.S. Pension Roll of 1835. 7. Pension Papers W5599.

****

Obadiah Albee age 13

Obadiah Albee was born on 19 August, 1763 in Wiscasset, Maine and, he died there on 8 December, 1853. He married Abigail Huntoon in 1790.

"In April of 1776 I enlisted as a private in the war of the revolution for one year in that company and regiment, and served out that period as a waiter to the captain and was verbally discharged in April 1777."

Obadiah enlisted in May of 1777 as a marine for six months on a Brig of War with sixteen guns and was involved in one battle on the Saint Lawrence River. In April of 1781 he enlisted as a private for one year under the command of Captain Jordan Parker and Colonel Samuel McCobb of the Massachusetts Line. He later stated that he was a sergeant in Captain Lemon's Company, but he did not give a date.

Sources: 1. Wiscasset in Powalborough: a History of the Shire town and the Salient Historical Features of the Territory. 2. U.S. Pensioners 1818-1872. 3. Pension Application S29578.

****

Cyrus Allen age 10

Cyrus Allen was born 14 October, 1771 in Ashford, Windham County, Connecticut, and died 28 March, 1851 in Troy, Orleans County, Vermont. He joined the 3rd Connecticut Infantry and served as a waiter to his father Captain Daniel Allen. He qualified for a soldier's pension, because he was able to prove that he had been a regular soldier. In his pension application and the testimony of another soldier, Eber Robinson, he proved that he had done some of the duties of a regular soldier.

In 4 February, 1834 pension application statement of Eber Robinson: *"Cyrus Allen a son of Capt. Allen served that year as waiter to his father and although he was not required to stand guard or go out on* scouting parties as he was a waiter he would frequently from choice perform that service and although he was but a youth of about twelve years of age I at that time had rather have him with me as a scouting party that one half of the soldiers take them as they would ride and one instance as we were going out on a scouting party to watch the cow boys I said to him Cyrus you had better not go for they will kill you, he replyed I am so small they will not be half so likely to kill me as they are to kill you..."

He further stated on 26 August, 1834: *"In the spring of 1782 I was appointed as Ensn in Capt. Danl Allens Company...Cyrus Allen son of Capt Allen then a stout boy of between 10 and twelve years old...he served principally as his Fathers Waiter but that at times he did company duty as I assisted his Father...I know that he drew his pay as a soldier in said company and I further say that I am very certain that Cyrus Allen now of Troy in Orleans co is the same identical person that then served in his Fathers company."*

In his pension statement Cyrus Allen stated: *"That in the year 1782 in the month of March or April I entered the service as a waiter to my Father Capt. Daniel Allen and served as I always supposed..."* He said that his father was credited 24 pounds, 9 shillings, and 4 pence for his son's wages.

His brother-in-law, David Carpenter, 11 years older than Cyrus, testified in support of his pension application that he had discouraged Cyrus before his enlistment about going into the service so young.

Aruba Carpenter, the sister of Cyrus Allen, wrote in his pension application in September of 1834: *"Cycrus Allen now of Troy, VT is my brother and was my fathers oldest son. That I well recollect my fathers being absent in the Service in the Revolutionary war-in the last part of the war-recollect distinctly his going from home and his return-That I also recollect that my brother Cyrus Allen...went with him from home, as his waiter. That they left home in the Spring and were abroad the following winter-that I had conservations with my said brother after his return about what he had seen and where he had been. He was younger than me and I should think must have been between ten and twelve when he went from home."*

This is an excerpt of a letter dated 20 July, 1782 from Daniel Allen to his wife: *Dearest, I have the privilege to inform you that I am well. Cyrus is well and makes a harty soldier, he has been on guard twice. He says he can eat thwice as much as when he lived at home."*

In 1801 Cyrus married Eleanor Fitch. They lived in Haverhill, N.H. according to the 1830 census and later moved to Troy Vermont. Cyrus was a farmer and had at least 5 children.

Sources: 1.Connecticut Revolutionary War Military Lists, 1775-83. 2. Vermont, Vital Records, 1720-1908.3.Tombstone. 4. Pension application and widow's application. 5. Children and Youth in a New Nation by James Marten. 6. History of the Town of Haverhill, NH, William F Whitcher, The Rumford Press, 1919. 7. Census of 1830.

****

Andrew Anderson age 13

Andrew Anderson was born in Sussex County, New Jersey on 21 August, 1763, and he died after 1833. He enlisted in the army in March of 1777.

"I was living in the state of New Jersey in the year 1776, when my father William Anderson was killed by the enemy in a battle fought near Philadelphia. I then moved with my mother into York County in the state of Pennsylvania, where, in the spring of 1777, I enlisted in the Pennsylvania line of the state troops. I belonged to the company commanded by Captain John Rippy and the regiment commanded by Colonel James Ross. I marched to Lancaster, in Pennsylvania. When we arrived there, I was informed by Joseph Reed, forage master, that there was a driver wanted for one of the United States teams and he, the said Reed, being acquainted with me, agreed to procure me that situation. Accordingly, when the officers our names for the purpose of entering them upon regular roll, the said Joseph Reed had my name entered upon his roll, and he assigned me the charge of a team the continuation of the war. I was employed hauling grain to the mills, flour and meat to the storehouses and commissary stores of the army until the summer of 1783, where I gave up the team at Lancaster and the said Joseph Reed procured me a discharge from the commanding officer, who signed my discharge. I left the service having been in the actual service six years."

Source: Pension Papers S201.

****

James Anderson age 12

James Anderson was born 18 August, 1763 in Cecil County, Maryland and died in 1835 in Bedford County, Tennessee. In 1787 he married Elizabeth Heater in Virginia.

He states in his pension application, *"I entered the service of the United States as a volunteer under Captain David Looney in the spring of 1776 to assist guarding a Fort on Holston River called Looney's Fort on the frontiers of the White Settlement then making on that River.....but my the permission of my Father and the promise of Captain Looney that as he understood and was well acquainted with the use of the rifle..."*. James served for about two months and was discharged in the summer.

In 1724 Robert Looney and his wife came to America and settled in Augusta County, Virginia on the James River. Because of the constant threat of Indian attacks, a fort was built in 1755 around the site of the Looney homestead. Fort Looney was visited in 1756 by Colonel George Washington. Captain David Looney was the son of Robert.

James volunteered again in 1778 and served under Captain Thomas Caldwell for about two months. *"...we marched to a Fort at the mouth of Big Creek on Holston River, and was told by my captain that the object in going to said Fort was to meet a suppose attack, by some white families, that stated they were from North Carolina and intended going down Holston River, but was suppose to be friendly with the Cherokee Indian Enemies at that home to the Americans."*

Unlike most of the Cherokee Nation, which decided to stay neutral in the Revolution, the Chickamaugan Cherokee sided with the British. One of the first attacks against American settlers came at Fort Watauga near Sycamore Shoals on the Holsten River in July, 1775. For the next 25 years violence occurred across much of Tennessee. Only when the Chickamaugans moved west did the fighting end.

James again volunteered in December 1779 to fight the Cherokee Indians. He served under Colonel George Maxwell's Company of mounted gunmen, commanded by Colonel Arthur Campbell and Colonel Joseph Martin.

James Anderson describes his service against the Cherokee Indians, *"We marched into the Cherokee nation, and what was called the Tennessee River, to a little town called the beloved Town, and at that place was engaged in a skirmish with the Indians in which engagement or skirmish only one American wounded and several horses. Afterwards I was in another skirmish at an Indian Town called Tellico, where the Americans killed five Indians, and lost Captain Elliot, who was shot through the head."*

After destroying several Indian towns, James marched back home and was discharged. Around the first of August 1780 he joined Captain Mosey Looney's Company of militia under the command of Colonel Isaac Shelby and Colonel Anthony Bledsoe. They marched up Though River and crossed the yellow Mountain and Blue Ridge then through Lincoln into South Carolina, crossed over Santee, and joined General Francis Marion. They arrived a few days after the Battle of Camden, South Carolina had taken place.

James describes what he saw after the battle, *"I saw the sills of house still on fore that were burnt at that battle and particularly the sills of a mill that was burnt down near the Town."* While with General Marion's army, *"A British Hospital was taken by our troops and I think about thirty or forty prisoners taken."* After serving for about five months he returned home by Christmas. For his service in the revolution James Anderson received a yearly pension of $30.00.

Sources: 1. Southern Indians in the American Revolution by James O'Donnell. 2. Soldiers of Fincastle County, Virginia 1774 compiled by Mary B. Kegley. 3. Virginia Militia in the Revolutionary War by J.T. McCallister. 4. Pension for James Anderson S1786.

****

James Anderson age 14

James Anderson was born 25 March, 1763 in Chester County, Pennsylvania, and he died 6 March, 1850 in Highland City, Ohio. He married Rachel Hopkins on 2 May, 1801 in Maryland and they had 12 children. His father was Captain Patrick Anderson who fought in the French and Indian War and the Revolution. James grew up on the family farm just a few miles from Valley Forge. His older brother, Isaac, served as a Lieutenant in the Revolution. James received a pension of $30 a year for his service. Rachel received a widow's pension of $96 a year.

"I went into the service as a volunteer in the month of March 1777 at Chester County Pennsylvania. I was in the company commanded by Captain Nathan Musgrave in the regiment commanded by Major Henry Garett and Colonel Morgan. After I volunteered I marched to Wilmington in the state of Delaware where the regiment remained about 6 months when said regiment marched to the neighbor of Philadelphia. We joined the main body of the American army near the crossing of Brandywine when the battle was fought between the Americans and the British. I was engaged in that battle and a few days after that was also engaged in the

battle at Germantown. After serving nine months I was verbally discharged."

Sources; 1. Maryland Marriages. 2. Tombstone 3. Census of 1810, 1820, 1840, & 1850. 4. U.S. Pensioners 1818-1872. 5. Pension Papers W513.

****

Elkanah Andrews age 12

Elkanah was born in Virginia in 1765, and he died on 17 September, 1844. He enlisted aboard a galley ship called the *Accomack* for a term of three years in 1777. This ship was a patrol craft and commissioned on 30 May, 1777. The Captain was William Underhill and the ship had a crew of 53. It was ordered to the eastern shore during the British invasion of Pennsylvania by 30 August, 1777 in company with other forces.

He wrote in his pension application, *"I served onboard said Galley as a Seaman or Sailor until she was dismantled & her crew discharged which was sometime in the winter of 1780-82. The said Gally cruised mostly in the Chesapeake Bay & on the sea side of the peninsula whilst in Service. The said Gally was built principally for the defense of the counties of Accomack and Northampton & was stationed mostly in the waters of those counties & was never in any battle."*

He filed for a pension and received 100 acres land bounty and $10.00 a month pension. His papers were approved and he had a letter from his clergyman, William Lee who testified that Elkanah was in the navy during the Revolution. Everything was filled out and approved, and yet this author found a letter that said his petition was rejected and to see the letter dated 24 July, 1824. This author found no such letter, and I did find much proof that he did receive a pension.

Sources: 1. Revolutionary War Records Virginia Section I Virginia State Navy. 2. Ships and Shipbuilding in the Chesapeake Bay and Tributaries by Arthur Pierce Middleton, in Chesapeake Bay in the American Revolution, Ernest M. Eller Editor. 3. U.S. Pensions 1815-1872. 4. Pension Application for Elkanah Andrews S6507. 5. 1820 and 1840 Census. 6. The History of Virginia Navy in the Revolution. 7. Historical Register of Virginians in the Revolution.

****

Israel Anthony age 14

Israel Anthony was born on 17 December, 1760 in Fishkill, New York, and he died on 23 October, 1835 in Troy, New York. He married Elizabeth Van Arnhem in 1787 in Albany, New York. He received a yearly pension of $61.11. Israel served in the Albany County Militia off and on for 7 years.

"*I entered the service in February 1775. In the month of February 1775 I went on Service as far as Johnstown and Canajoharie & was out one week. In the Spring of the year 1776 I was marched with my regiment to Fort Ann and Fort Edward, by the way of Saratoga and was out three weeks. In the later part of July the regiment was again marched to Fort Ann & Fort Edward and I served on that tour two weeks and more. In the fall of the same year 1776 we were again marched to Saratoga & I served on that tour two weeks.*"

"*In the Spring of the year 1777 we again marched to Fort Edward & Fort Ann & I served on that tour three weeks. In the summer of the same year about harvest time we were again marched to the same place & were engaged at that time in breaking up the road and bridges for the purpose of retarding the progress of the enemy & I served on that tour four weeks. In the fall of the year 1777 we were at Stillwater with the American troops at the time Burgoyne surrendered & I served on that tour thirty three days.*"

"*In the month of May in the year 1778 we were marched to the West to German Flats & Fort Hunter, & I served on that tour three weeks. In the Summer time, about harvest, we were marched to Schoharie & I served on that tour three weeks. In the fall of the same year we again marched to Schoharie and I served on that tour four weeks and five days.*"

"*After the year 1778 and during the year 1779-80-81 & 82 my company was divided into four classes & we served by classes, the class to which I belonged was marched four times each year to Schoharie and I went with them, and I served on each of those tours two weeks at least and we were out sometimes rather longer than two weeks making the whole time I served in this manner eight weeks each year and in the whole four weeks thirty two weeks. Beside my service in my class during these <u>four years being the musician</u> of my company and of the regiment.*"

Israel also said he marched to Fort Plain and then met Colonel Henry Van Resselaer's Unit of Levies, and later they were inspected by

Brigadier General Peter Gansevoort at Poor Meadow. In 1778 he helped in removing people in Beaver Dam to Greenbush. He stated that once in 1779 his company was sent to capture the Loyalist Walter Meyers and his men from Canada, but he did not find them. He said that while marching to Cherry Valley in November of 1778 they were attacked by the British.

Sources: 1. The Bloodied Mohawk: The American Revolution in the Words of Fort Planks Defenders and Other Mohawk Valley Partisans by Kenneth D. Johnson. 2. New York City Marriages 1600-1800. 3. U.S. Pension Roll of 1835 4. Pension Papers W20607.

****

Asher Applegate age 14

Asher Applegate was born on 13 May, 1762 in Hightstown, New Jersey, and he died there on 2 March, 1834. He married Sarah Higby on 30 March, 1786. He received a yearly pension of $53.33.

"Sometime in the year 1776 was drafted in the New Jersey Militia in the company commanded by Capt. Jonathan Combs. Generally a month at each tour. Was principally engaged in guarding the then around Amboy."

Asher served several short tours from 1776 to 1781. He served a total of seventeen and a half months, and he may have been at the Battle of Monmouth in June of 1778. He later served in the War of 1812 and was stationed at Sandy Hooks, New Jersey.

Sources: 1. D.A.R. Lineage Book Vol. 116. 2. Pension Papers S846.

****

Daniel Wiggins Applegate age 11

Daniel Applegate was born in 1768 in Albany, New York, and he died 11 February, 1826 in St. Louis, Missouri. He married Rachael Lindsay on 10 June, 1790 in Kentucky. He received a pension of $8 a month and a hundred acres of land for his service.

When Daniel's mother died his father joined the army and he placed Daniel in the home of a Dutch farmer. Daniel was not happy with this so he ran away and tried to find his father. Unable to find his father, eleven year old Daniel was allowed to join the 2nd New Jersey Regiment under Colonel Israel Shreve as a drummer, fifer, and a color bearer in January, 1780. Colonel Shreve taught Daniel the military music he needed to know. After the war Daniel went to sea, some say with the son of Colonel Shreve.

> "I enlisted in the state of New Jersey at a place called Bottle hill in Morris County in the month of January 1780 in the company Commanded by Capt Ballard of the 2nd Jersey regt. Commanded by Col Israel Shreve belonging to Genl Maxwells Brigade of Lord Stirling Division of the Jersey Continental line and I continued to serve in said Corps or in the Service of the united States as a fifer until the 5th day of June 1783 when I was discharged at Snake hill. I was at the Siege of Yorktown in Virginia."

Daniel may have been part of the Battle of Connecticut Farms in New Jersey on 7 June 1780. Colonel Shreve wrote that this *"Action was the warmest that has Ever Happened since the war with Our Brigade."* When Daniel was at the Siege of Yorktown his regiment was under the 2nd Division commanded by Lafayette. On the night of 14 October, 1781 the Jersey Infantry took part in the assault and capture of Redoubt Number 10.

Sources: 1. Sons of the American Revolution Application. 2. Kentucky Marriages 1802-1850. 3. U.S. Pension Roll of 1835. 4. A Narrative of the Life of Daniel Applegate by his son Lisbon written about 1870. 5. Pension Papers S34628. 6. The Applegate Families in America by Hugh E. Voress.

****

Archibald Armstrong age 13

Archibald Armstrong was born in 1765 in Herkimer County, New York, and he died from the effects of a rattlesnake bite on 29 January, 1847 in Saline, Michigan. He married (1) Ruth, (2) Lydia, and (3) Sabra Pritchard on 29 April, 1839. Sabra applied for a widow's pension. Archibald enlisted in January of 1779, which means he was probably 13 years old. He was discharged in June of 1783 and received $96 a year for his service.

> "I enlisted in the Company Commanded by Captain Hicks with the 1st New York Regiment Commanded by Col Van Schaick in the month of January 1779. I continued to serve in the said Corps until the month of June 1783 when I was discharged from Service at Newburg in the state of New York. I was at the taking of Cornwallis."

Archibald and his two brothers, John and Adam, served through the war in the 1st New York Regiment. Archibald was a drummer and the other two were fifers. Archibald was a drummer at the execution of Major

John Andre and drummed in his death march. He also sounded the salute when Cornwallis surrendered. The discharge papers of the three brothers was probably signed by George Washington since Adam's paper is in the National Archives. Besides the surrender at Yorktown, Archibald probably served during the Sullivan Expedition. The 1st New York disbanded on 15 November, 1783.

Archibald was described as a rough character in later life. He had great physical strength and was seldom beat in physical contests. It was said that at times his brother-in-law was able to thrash him. The brother-in- law, Alexander Porter, married Archibald's sister Catherine. During the revolution Catherine was taken prisoner by Indians near Fort Stanwix and taken to Canada. After three years she was brought back by a relative that was a British officer who knew her. After her return, she and other prisoners were provided with dinner by General Washington, while he was visiting Albany.

According to a relative, while Archibald was in the service a hostile Indian was killed and skinned and his hide was given to Archibald. He tanned the hide and made a drum-head of it, and on Lafayette's visit to this country in 1825 Archibald took his drum and showed it to him. The General recalled the circumstance and at once recognized Archibald, with whom he was acquainted with in the army.

Sources: 1. Tombstone. 2. U.S. Pensioners 1818-1872. 3. Pension Papers W1355. 4. Past and Present of Washtenaw County. 5. History of Yates County. 6. Earliest Armstrong Ancestor by Kathy Alvis Patterson. 7. Ontario Repository and Messenger, 29 January, 1868 The Reminiscences of Archibald Armstrong's Son. 8. A History of Herkimer County including the Upper Mohawk Valley: from the earliest period to the present time.

****

Isaac Arnold age 12

Isaac Arnold was born on 20 May, 1764 in Mansfield, Connecticut and he died on 30 January, 1841 in Mansfield. In his pension application he states that he was 13 when he enlisted, however, the birth and enlistment dates he gives would make him 12 at the time he enlisted. He received a yearly pension of $88.

"About the first of September 1776 then in the 13th year of my age I enlisted for a term of three months in the Continental State Levies and served as a Drummer in the Company Commanded by Capt. Lemuel Clark of said Mansfield—Phinehas Allen of said Mansfield was Ensign—Col Experience Storrs of Said Mansfield commanded the Regiment to which I

belonged—I marched to Kingsbridge N.Y.—was encamped near Fort Washington until about the middle of October following—I then marched with the army to White Plains, when we introduced ourselves into the expectation of an attack from the Enemy—Gen Washington was there—the Enemy came out (I believe from N. York) then was at that time some fighting in detached parties—after a while, the Enemy withdrew to York Island—the Regiment to which I belonged was discharged about the 1st of Dec 1776—I returned home."

The Battle of White Plains was fought on 28 October, 1776 and it involved several regiments of General Washington's army. The fighting was intense and the Americans suffered over 200 killed or wounded before they withdrew.

There are several origins of where Washington Irving came up with his headless horseman in the book "The Legend of Sleepy Hollow". Some people say it was based on an actual Hessian soldier who was decapitated by a cannonball during the Battle of White Plain and has since been riding around looking for his head.

"About the first of July 1778 I again enlisted in the said United States, under Capt John Arnold of Covington in Tolland County—Lient Dunham of Mansfield—and Ensign Coy of Windham—I served as a Drummer in said company for the term of two months—I first marched to New Haven where I remained about 8 or 10 days some of the Continental troops passed through New Haven while I was there, being on their way to Rhode Island—the company to which I belonged was ordered to Rhode Island—we marched by the way of Hartford & Providence and arrived in the Island the fore part of August—Gen Sullivan was commander-in-chief of the Expedition—I came off from the Island about the first of September, was discharged and returned home."

Isaac Arnold did not take part in the Battle of Rhode Island on 29 August, 1778. The militia units from Massachusetts did not arrive until the first part of August. Two regiments of the Massachusetts Continental Line did take part in the battle.

"In October of the same year (1778) I enlisted for the term of one month in the State Service, under Capt Eleazer Huntington of said Mansfield—Lieut Huntington of Lebanon and Ensign Philipps of Trenton—I marched to New London & there performed duty—In November 1778 I was dismissed & returned to Mansfield."

"I again enlisted for the term of Eight months, as a Drummer in Capt James Dana's Company of State Troops—John Arnold Jr. of said Mansfield was Ensign of Said Company--I resided in said Mansfield at the time of my enlistment, which was about the first of July 1779. I marched to New London then joined Col. Levi Wells Regiment --I continued in New London till about the first of December following--we marched to West Haven Connecticut for winter quarters & then remained till about the first of March 1780--was then dismissed and again returned to Mansfield."

"About the first of March 1781--then residing in the town of Mansfield I enlisted into the State Service for the term of one year, as a Drummer in Capt James Dana's Company—Newet of Franklin, was Ensign, part of the time Major Shipman commanded the Regiment which under Gen Waterbury who commanded the division. I joined the Regiment at Stamford, Connecticut, I continued through the summer season in Stamford & vicinity, in Horse Neck—Rye--White Plains &c--I was in a Battle at Frog point I do not recollect the date. In the fall of the year, we built a fort on Stamford heights for winter quarters there I continued till sometime in the Month of March 1782 when I was dismissed—having served the full term of one year—and returned home."

Isaac said he was at the Battle of Frog Point. This battle is also known as the Battle of Pell's Point or Battle of Pelham which was fought on 18 October, 1776. The area is a narrow piece of land that sits between the East River and Long Island Sound. The battle involved a skirmish between some of Washington's troops and the British. From there General Washington took his troops to White Plains, Isaac being among them. Isaac gives a short description of the battle:

"I recollect that the British left three men upon the ground--two were dead--and the other Mortally wounded—the Americans had 3 wounded--one of whom died--We were at the time so near to the British Shipping that some of their Balls reached us."

Amos Clark served a tour with Isaac and wrote about Isaac in a letter to the pension bureau verifying their service together. *"I very well remember him on account of his being but a small lad."*

Sources: 1. "Halloween History; the Legend of Sleepy Hollow", New York Historical Society Museum & Library. History Detectives. Jacqueline Smith, October 25, 2013. 2. Yearbook of the Connecticut Sons of the American Revolution 1899. 3. Connecticut Deaths & Burial Records 1650-1934. 4. Pension Papers S31526.

****

John Ash age 14

John Ash was born on 2 February, 1762 in Charlestown, Rhode Island, and he died on 13 July, 1843 in Conewango, New York. He married Priscilla Frink on 28 May, 1782 in Connecticut. He received a yearly pension of $47.77 for his service.

"In the Spring of the year 1776 my father whose name is also John Ash and I lived at that time in the town of Exeter in the State of Rhode Island enlisted into Captain John Carr's Company of Rhode Island Troops (my Lieutenants name was potter) and in Colonel Crarys Regiment."

"In the month of June or July '76 I took the place of my father as his substitute in the same company, he being aged and infirm, I was enrolled by the name of John Ash __?__. And was in my 15th year [actually 14th year]. *I marched in said Company after my enrollment to a place called Warwick Neck, R. I. and while stationed there a British armed Frigate lay in the Bay and was in the habit of Sending a watering party with a small guard onto Patience Island for a supply of fresh water every morning. In July or August Captain Carr volunteered with a party of his company (myself being among them) to take the party; we proceeded in the night and lay in ambush near the watering place, and in the morning when the party arrived we rose from our ambush, and after a short skirmish, in which one man, was killed on each side, and one of the enemy wounded we took them prisoner and escaped from the Island."*

"We remained at Warnick Neck where General Cornwall [Cornwallis] *had the command until near Winter, when we removed to what was then called Bristol Ferry where we remained until sometime in the winter following, when myself with the whole company was discharged, having been in the service Nine Months term for which my father enlisted."*

"About the first of March 1777 I enlisted at Exeter under Captain George Wait Babcock in the Privateering Service and went to Boston, and on the 8th day of March I went on board a Privateer called the "General Mifflin" carrying twenty-six pounders, and maned with 130 men and boys. I was in the Marine Service under Joseph Holly Captain of Marines."

In 1777 General Washington had about 11, 000 men in his army. In that same year there were around 11,000 American privateers. When John Ash joined as a privateer it meant that the ship he was on was authorized by the government to attack foreign vessels and take them as a prize. The ships and its cargo could be sold, and the privateers and the ship's owners could divide the prize money. A crew member could earn as much as a $1,000 for one voyage, while the average pay at that time was $9.

"We immediately sailed on a cruise of the Bay of Fundy and on the 8th of Mat as I now believe we fell in with said captain off East of the Islands of St. Johns, called the "Tartar", after a sharp Engagement of an hour and thirty minutes, she mounted twenty six, six pounders. In this engagement we had fourteen men killed, and eighteen or twenty wounded: The Enemy lost twenty seven killed and a number of wounded. We took our prisoners on board, sent the "Tartar" to Boston and proceeded on our cruise: on the 16th of May we fell in with, and after a short engagement: captured the "Elephant" from New York armed with 14 Guns, and Sent her also into Boston. The "Tartar" while on her way to Boston fell in with and captured a British Vessel Laden with fish: In a few days after the capture of the "Elephant" we captured a British Brig from Antiqua Laden with Tar and Indigo, and sent her also to Boston. In a short time after this we fell in with and captured a transport from Great Britain bound to Dublick Laden with Provisions, Arms, Ammunition and sent her also to Boston: We continued on our cruise until we had nearly reached the Bay of Biscay; when we fell in with a British Letter of marque* [A letter of marque was a government license authorizing a privateer to attack and capture an enemy vessel] and after an engagement of near two hours in which our vessel was very much injured and we lost a number of men She over __?__ us. We sailed into the mouth of which empties into the Bay of Biscay (France) we also run to Lowson and Penbross repaired the "General Mifflin"" and enlisted a few recruits and again sailed to the Bay of Biscay and in our way we took a British Vessel Landen with Sperm Oil. We soon sailed again for the Banks of New found land and on our way captured a Vessel Laden with Sugar and Salt which we brought into Boston in the fall of 1777 having been in this service Eight Months."

"As soon as I returned home I took the place of Joseph Reynolds, as a substitute in Captain Jonathan Bates Company in Col Potters Regiment, as I now think, and in General Spencers Division, we marched to Rehoboth on the East side of Rhode Island where we __?__ twenty days, when I was dismissed & returned home."

"In August 1778 I entered the service as a substitute for my father John Ash under the command of Captain Walter Clark in Colonel Charles Dyus Regiment in General Sullivans expedition against the enemy at

Rhode Island had our engagement lasted several hours, our troops shortly after this retreated from the Island and I was discharged after serving at that time about twenty days."

"In the fall of 1778 I again entered the service as a substitute for Thomas Fainer in Colonel Christopher Greens regiment and under Captain John Olden we rendezvoused at East Greenwich from thence we marched to Providence where we remained until discharged which was four months."

Sources: 1. U.S. Pensioners 1818-1872. 2. Tombstone 3. Early Connecticut Marriages. 4. Pension Papers S6547.

****

Daniel Ashcraft age 13

Daniel Ashcraft was born on 13 March, 1768 in Pennsylvania, and he died on 5 June, 1849 in Richland County, Illinois. He married Salloy Dye on 2 October, 1793 in Kentucky. He received a yearly pension of $30.

"That about the 1 of April 1781 I volunteered as an Indian Spy under the command of Captain John Vertrees who was stationed in Soverns Valey about 40 miles south of the Falls of the Ohio River, the settlement of said valey being forted from the Indians and the government kept up a guard to guard said forts and settlements of Soverns Valey during this Summer I served as an Indian spy about five months and during the time I was on a campaign against the Indians on the Northwest of the Ohio River and on the Wabash, I was then under the command of Colo. Patrick Brown, that in the year 1782 I volunteered as an Indian Spy under the command of Capt Joseph Friend and spyed for Indians about the settlement & forts aforesaid and stood as a guard for said forts and settlement during the whole of the Summer, and during the time I went on a volunteer campaign under the command of Colo John Butler against southern Indians on the Tennessee River, during this summer I was in service about four months and that in the year 1783 I again volunteered as an Indian Spy and guarded the forts and settlements aforesaid and spyed for indians and during the summer I volunteered and went on a campaign against the Indians on the North West of the Ohio River under the command of Colo. John Hardin, on this campaign we killed 12 or 13 Indians and took two prisoners and retook some horses which had been stolen by the Indians in the summer I was in service as aforesaid about five months."

On 24 June, 1833 Daniel made the following statement as an amendment to his original pension statement in February of 1833.

"That about the 1 of April 1781 I volunteered as an Indian Spy under the command of Captain John Vertrees in the militia of Virginia, that we were stationed in Soverns Valey about 40 miles south of the Falls of the Ohio River then in the State of Virginia, the settlement of said valey being forted from the Indians and the government kept up a guard to guard said forts and settlement of Soverns Valey and during the time of my service this summer I went on a Campaign against the Indians on the north west of the Ohio River and on the Wabash, I was then under the command of Colo Patrick Brown of the Militia of Virginia that in this sumer going on the campaign and spying for indians and guarding the forts I was in service of the United States at least five months. That in the Spring of the year 1782 I volunteered in the militia of Virginia as an Indian spy under the command of Captain Joseph Friend and was stationed at the Forts in Soverns Valey aforesaid and guarded the forts and settlement and spyed for Indians during the most of the spring & summer and during the time I went on a campaign under the command of Colo. John Butler (of the militia of Virginia) against the Southern Indians on the Tennessee River, during this tour I was in service at least four months in this service we had a skirmish with the Indians and I was wounded and killed seven indians. That in the year 1783 I again volunteered as an Indian Spy and guarded the forts and settlements aforesaid and spyed for Indians and during the summer I volunteered and went on a campaign against the Indians on the north west of the Ohio River under the command of Captain Ballard and of Colo. John Hardin of the Virginia Militia. On this Campaign we killed 12 or 13 Indians & took two prisoners and retook some horses which had been stolen by the indians that during this spring & summer I was in the service aforesaid at least five months."

The following statement was made on 15 August, 1840. It is unusual because it is in his own handwriting. The spelling is very rough and can make reading the statement difficult. It is the story of how he settled in Kentucky. It gives a good description of the dangers faced in the backwoods during this period.

"August the 15 1840 this morning I Daniel ashcraft of lawrence County and State of Illinois Set down to make out a short memorial of my first setling in Cantucky we landed at the mouth of baregrass [sic: Beargrass Creek] by Lewisvill the 15 of Jenuary 1780 and mov'd. sixty miles to South of lewisville and setled on violin waters of green river. and

the indians soon found us out and was in Rold in Captin John virtres Company it was then Jefferson County the Curnel lived at lewisville and the indians was so trobleson he had to Rase a Cumpany of Rangers to gard the forts and settlement between the ohio and forts and I was one of the Cumpaney and that was our imployment Every Summer from march tel the falling of the leves and in that time I went fore Campanes three against the waubash indianes and under Captain bur and Curnel brown and one under Curnel John harden and one under General wilkeson and one under Curnel butler a gainst the Cherokee indianes and in Eighty Eight we was out between the ohio and settlement and struck a trale of River indianes Cuming in to doomistled and persud them and over took them neere the settlement and kild nine laust one man kild and too wounded my self was shot through the thigh and sholder and I feel the affects to this day and my wife that now is in Eighty too was shot through the leg and has been a Cripple ever sence and my father in settling Cantuck was kild by the indianes and three uncles and one aunt my memorial I sent from kentucky to Congress only Extended to Eighty three which the pople in the County teles me if I had sent a morial of all my sarvises I should of Drade three times what I do now Mr Rian if you will be so good as to take this and transcribe it in form and send it on by Mr Cacy and Direct him to Call on willis green and albert y hass both from kentuky they will asist mr Rian if you will undertake for me and send on to Congress....." [the last sentence is in the fold of the paper and is difficult to read].

Sources: 1. Kentucky Marriages, 1802-1850. 2. Tombstone 3. Historical Register of Virginians in the Revolution. 4. U.S. Pensioners 1818-1872. 5. Pension Papers W23466.

****

Ebenezer Atwood age 14

Ebenezer Atwood was born on 14 August, 1766 in Thompson, Connecticut, and he died in New York on 16 March, 1854. He had a twin sister named Leah. After the death of his parents he lived in the home of his guardian, John Younglove, who gave his consent to enlist. When he returned home he enlisted again for one year.

"I enlisted for six months as a private in a company of Infantry in Colonel Willis' Regiment, Gen. Parson's Brigade of the Connecticut Line of the Continental Army. The company was commanded by Lieutenant Heath and was called Colonel's Company. I served in the said company under the said officers six months and was discharged at the Highlands in

the state of New York in the month of December 1780 from the winter Quarters of the Regiment."

"In March of 1781 (I cannot recollect the day of the month) with the consent of my guardian I again enlisted at Thompson in the Connecticut State Troops for one year as a private in a company under Captain Moulton of Windham, Lieutenant Root Ensign Cutter. The company belonged to a Battalion commanded by Major Dana (I think was his name) and to a Brigade consisting of their Battalion and another commanded by Major Humphrey. The Brigade was under the command of Gen Waterbury. I marched with the other recruits from Thompson to White Plains in New York then joined the Brigade I was stationed during the summer at White Plains _____ Brigade was stationed a part of the time a body of French Troops, principally cavalry I believe. In the fall of the year 1781, I marched with the Brigade to the town of Stamford in the state of Connecticut, and there built redoubts and barracks for winter quarters. I was stationed at Stamford until March 1782 where I was discharged with the whole Brigade."

The troops stationed in this area were there to protect the area from the British troops that were still in New York. Even though Cornwallis had surrendered months earlier, the British and Tories were still a threat. Many of the Tories were involved in stealing cattle in the area.

Ebenezer received a pension of $57.00 a year for his service. When he died in 1854 his wife Damaris Wilson applied for a widow's pension. To prove that they were married, her sister and brother wrote to the Pension Bureau to vouch for their marriage. Her brother was only 10 at the time but remembered that a Baptist preacher, John Martin, married them at her father's house in Thompson on 3 February, 1791.

Sources: 1. Children & Youth in a New Nation edited by James Marten. 2. Census of 1830, 1840, and 1850. 3. Heroes of the Revolution, St. Lawrence County, D.A.R. 4. U.S. Revolutionary Rolls 1775-1783. 5. Pension Papers W23469.

****

James Ayres age 12

James Ayres was born on 6 January, 1761 in Cumberland County, Virginia, and he died c. 1831 in Pickens County, South Carolina. His mother strongly objected to her son joining the army but her husband, Daniel, was anxious for his son to be active.

"When I was twelve years of age as well as I recollect my Father Enlisted me in what was called the minute Service, called to Guard the frontier of Georgia, my Enlistment was I believe for 18 months I served out this Tour Eighteen months under Captain William Ayres---Col. John Stewart and was discharged by them. I am certain that I did serve at this time not less than eighteen months and was employed most of the time on the frontier of Georgia & South Carolina against the Indians and was discharged in Augusta Ga. In the year 1775 as well as I recall."

Shortly after he returned home he volunteered and served under Capt. William Nettles and Colonel John Marshall. He marched to Savannah and was discharged two months later. In 1778 he enlisted with a friend, James Kelly, and served under Captain James Dunkins of the 4th Virginia commanded by William Drennon. They joined up with General Nathaniel Green and marched to Petersburg and then to Norfolk. James said he was at the Battle of Eutaw Springs fought on 8 September, 1781. He was discharged about the time of the Battle of Cowpens fought on 17 January, 1781. (If he was discharged before the Battle of Cowpens then he could not have fought at the Battle of Eutaw Springs nine months later.

His pension application was rejected even though he had several people write about his service and good character. The reason for rejection was given as, *"Period, length, grade, station, marches, and names of company and field officers required."*

Sources: 1. Roster of South Carolina Patriots in the American Revolution. 2. Pension Papers R334. 3. Children & Youth in a New Nation edited by James Marten.

****

John Baldwin age 12

John Baldwin was born in 1763 in Washington County, and he died in 1838 in Harrison County, Indiana. He served in a company of frontier rangers from 1775 to 1783.

Source: 1. D.A.R. Lineage Book, Vol. 57.

****

Robert Ballard age 12

Robert Ballard was born outside of Medford, Massachusetts in 1763. His father James joined the local militia under the command of Colonel William Prescott in 1775. James thought that he would be gone only a few days and it would be safe, so he allowed his 12 year old son Robert to join him. The militia joined with a larger American force and engaged the British at Breed's Hill. This battle later was known as the Battle of Bunker Hill.

Robert witnessed the horror and death associated with battle which impacted him forever. After he learned of the death of his father he returned home and refused to join any military unit or participated in the war. He never set foot in Boston again. When the War of 1812 began he refused to allow it to be discussed in his home.

Source: 1. Voices of the American Revolution by Kendall Haven.

****

George Bailey age 14

George Bailey was born on 21 February, 1762 in Albany, Pennsylvania, and on he died 16 March, 1854 at Codorus, Pennsylvania. He married Catharine Eberhart on 9 June, 1800. He joined the Pennsylvania Militia on 1 July, 1776. He received $20.00 a year for his service.

"I was drafted in York County about the 1st of July 1776 in Captain Long's company of militia in Colonel Swope's battalion for three months in the revolutionary war, and marched from York to Lancaster, from thence to Philada [Philadelphia] *and to Trenton and Brunswick, from thence to Amboy and then Newark, the state OF New Jersey, and duly served out the time for which I was drafted, and was Honorably discharged at Newark in the month of October in the year 1776."*

"In the fall of the year 1782, I was again drafted to serve in Captain Furry's company in the county of York under Major Austin to guard watch and secure the British prisoners taken with Genl Cornwallis at a place called Camp Security in the county aforesaid and served three months, and was Hon. Discharged by Captain Furry about the first of December in the same year."

Camp Security was a prison camp built in 1781 to hold British troops surrendered by General Burgoyne at Saratoga, New York. Prisoners captured at Yorktown arrived later. It housed over one thousand British and Canadian prisoners of war between the summer of 1781 and the spring of 1783. The camp consisted of log huts and a large stockade.

Source: 1. 1790 Census. 2. Pennsylvania and New Jersey, Church & Town Records 1708-1985. 3. Pennsylvania Pensioners 1835. 4. Pension papers S23523.

****

Casparus Bain age 14

Casparus Bain was born on 15 September, 1763 in Columbia, New York, and he died on 20 October, 1835 in Argyle, New York. He married (1) Maria Clum and (2) Mary Gillespie. Mary received his pension of $80.00 a year after his death in 1835.

"In the spring of 1777 I volunteered in Livingston's Manor, County of Columbia & state aforesaid for the purpose of protecting lives & property of the Whigs from the depredations of the Tories & other enemies & continued upon Sentry every other night during that season until the capture of Burgoyne in the fall of 1777 and doing actual duty for the term of six months as a common soldier."

"That in 1778 I entered the service for three months tour as a volunteer for a class of fifteen (of which I was one) who were to stand a draft for one man out of that number--Mister & in Livingston's Manor under Captain John Shaver in the month of August 1778. From thence moved to Claverack and from thence marched by the way of Albany & joined the Regiment at Fort Plain at the Mohawk River under Coln. Robert Van Rensselaer, where I remained doing duty the three months."

"I again entered the service in the Spring (I think in April) of 1779 as a volunteer for a class of fifteen as above stated, for a six months tour—mustered again in Livingston's Manor aforesaid under Captain Gausbeck, marched from thence to ____, moved up the _____ creek some 15 or 18 miles where they were stationed in the vicinity of a Block House for about three months, from thence I was transferred to Captain Shaver again, Where I remained doing duty until the end of the six months."

"I then in the year 1780 joined a militia company commanded by Captain Philip Smith, Lieutenant Casparus Shults & Ensign Bartel Hendricks, all of Livingston's Manor aforesaid, and continued with the company doing duty whenever we were called, until the British evacuated the City of New York—during this period of three years upwards my Col. Was Samuel Ten Broeck. My service during this period were not located for any great length of time at any one point, being often called out in various directions on short tours to quell the Indians. I remember in the Fall of the year, I think 1782 of a party of about twenty picked men, sent

from the regiment at Stillwater north to Argyle for procuring cattle, from whence we returned with a number for the use of the Regiment."

After the war he married and joined the Washington County militia. In 1797 he was promoted to Lieutenant, and in 1803 he was made a Captain of his own militia company.

<small>Sources: 1. U.S. Revolutionary Rolls 1775-1783. 2. Census of 1790, 1800, 1810, 1820, and 1830. 3. Landholders of Northeastern New York, 1759-1802. 4. Military Minutes of the Council of Appointment of the State of New York 1783-1821. 5. New York Pensioners 1835. 6. History of Washington County, New York. 7. Pension Papers W1125.</small>

****

Jeremiah Baker age 14

Jeremiah Baker was born on 22 May, 1761 in Dedham, Massachusetts, and he died there on 12 September, 1855. He married Fanny Whiting on 9 November, 1786 in Massachusetts. Like General Washington, Jeremiah was a Mason. Jeremiah did not receive a pension because his service was less than six months.

He was a private on the Lexington Alarm Roll of Captain Daniel Draper's Company in Colonel Davis's Regiment. Jeremiah marched on this alarm on 19 April, 1775. If Jeremiah was at the Battle of Lexington he would have had over a five hour march from his home in Dedham.

Jeremiah enlisted for about two weeks in the militia on 23 March, 1778 in Captain Abel Richard's Company under the command of Colonel McIntosh. He enlisted for fifteen days in July, 1778 to guard the stores at Watertown, Massachusetts.

<small>Sources: 1. Register of the California Society of the Sons of the American Revolution. 2. Massachusetts Marriages 1633-1850. 3. Sons of the American Revolution Application. 4. Massachusetts Mason Membership Cards 1733-1990.</small>

****

Jonathan I. Baker age 14

Jonathan Baker was born on 17 February, 1764 in Westfield, New Jersey, and he died there on 19 March, 1844. He received $8 a month for his service

"I enlisted at Elizabeth Town in the state of New Jersey in the company commanded by captain Daniel Baldwin in Col Matthais Ogden being the first Jersey Regiment in May 1778--I continued to serve in the

said corps or in the service of the United States until February following having served <u>nine months</u> when I was discharged at Elizabeth Town. I was in the Battles of Monmouth and Elizabeth Town."

At the age of 22 Matthais Ogden was named Lieutenant Colonel of the 1st New Jersey, also known as the "Jersey Line". In March of 1776. Jonathan served in the 8th Company of the 1st New Jersey Regiment. At the Battle of Monmouth the regiment was under the command of Major General Charles Lee. Lee called for a retreat from the field of battle and was admonished publically by Washington who then removed him from command.

This author believes that when Jonathan said he was at The Battle of Elizabethtown he must have meant The Battle of Springfield. The Battle of Elizabethtown was fought in June of 1780 and he would have already been discharged from the army. He enlisted in May of 1778 and served only nine months.

Sources: 1. Tombstone 2. New Jersey Births & Christenings Index 1660-1931. 3. Pension Papers W1210.

****

Asa Ballou 14

Asa Ballou was born on 31 September, 1762 in Glocester, Rhode Island, and he died on 4 August, 1834 in Burrillville, Rhode Island. He married Rhoda Williams on 3 November, 1780 in Rhode Island. He served as a Private, Sergeant, First Lieutenant, Lieutenant Commander, and Captain during the years 1776, 1777, 1780, and 1781 in the Rhode Island Militia. After the war he served in the 4th Regiment of Glocester Rhode Island Militia as a Lieutenant and Captain in the years 1792 to 1797.

Sources: 1. Census 1790, 1810, & 1830. 2. Massachusetts Soldiers and Sailors in the Revolutionary War. 3. Tombstone 4. DAR Patriot Index NSDAR 1967.

****

Edward Barber age 13

Edward Barber was born in October 1761 in Massachusetts, and he died on 19 April, 1775. As the British were retreating after the Battles of Concord and Lexington earlier in the day, they were being shot at from behind trees and stone walls along the road to Boston. This 20 mile retreat to Boston became known as Battle Road. As the British neared

Charlestown, word was sent to the residents that no harm would come to them unless the British troops were fired upon. As they entered the town around dusk reports say that a careless excited Negro boy fired his musket, and in an instant the British returned fire.

Edward Barber was inside his house looking out the window when the firing began. Perhaps a British soldier saw the boy's face in the window, and it may have looked threatening. The thirteen year old boy was shot, and he became the first child killed when the actual fighting of the American Revolution began.

This was not the first time in New England when an impulsive action of a white person was blamed on the actions of a "careless negro." The person that fired on the British that evening is unknown. Edward's death is significate, because it represents all the young children that would die during the American Revolution.

Source: 1. The Beginnings of the American Revolution, Vol. 3 by Ellen Chase.

****

Josiah Barker age 13/14

Josiah Barker was born on 7 May, 1763 in Marshfield, Massachusetts, and he died on 23 September, 1847 in Charlestown, Massachusetts. He married Penelope Hatch on 9 December, 1787. He received a monthly pension of $8.

"The Company was raised for a year and was stationed at the gurnet [lighthouse] at the entrance of Plymouth Harbor--a part of the company went down I think about the 1st of Jany. Of that year [1777] I enlisted into and joined the company in the early part of the spring of that year. We were employed in guarding the Fort. I staid there nine months, as I think, and returned home about Jany. 1778 Only one company was there; not attached to any Regiment."

"I had been home but a short time when in Jany. Or Feby. Of A.D. 1778 a company was raised in Pembroke, and the adjoining towns of Duxbury and Mansfield to guard at the Fort at Nantucket Capt Josiah Cushing commanded the company. I enlisted into his company for six weeks. We were employed in guard duty at the Fort. I remained there until the expiration of my time and returned home."

"I had been home a very short time, when in Spring of A.D. 1778 my father, Ebenezer Barker, again received a commission as a Lieutenant

in Capt Griffiths Company. I enlisted in the company for a year. Capt James Hatch [possibly his future father-in-law] *of Pembroke was Muster Master. I marched to ___?__ Rhode Island where I joined the company and was employed in guard duty til about August when we marched across Howlands Ferry to Butts Hill, at which time we experienced a very severe storm. We staid there a few days and then proceeded to a place about two miles from New-Port where we were attacked by the British and driven off the Island on to the Main, and were stationed at Trenton and performed guard duty in the winter of 1778-79 and served as I think about ten months."*

Josiah was part of the Massachusetts militia at the Battle of Rhode Island or Siege of Newport on 29 August, 1778. Large numbers of Massachusetts militia joined the militias from New Hampshire and Rhode Island and engaged the British troops and the Royal Navy. The Americans had abandoned their siege on Newport and were retreating to Aquidneck Island when they encountered the British. The battle ended in a draw but was a British strategic victory.

"In summer of A.D. 1780 my father had removed from Pembroke to Bridgewater where a company was raised to go to Rhode Island. I enlisted for three months and went to Rhode Island, was stationed at Butts Hill where we were employed in building a Fort and doing guard duty. Capt Packard commanded the company one waterman the Lieutenant and Col Jacobs command the Regiment. I staid on this tour three months and returned home to Bridgewater."

"Previous to A.D. 1782 my father had died and my mother had removed to Pembroke I joined The Frigate in Boston Harbor as a marine at this time I was under the command of Capt Nickolson, but before we sailed he resigned and Capt Manly took the command of her. The name was changed to The Hague. We lay in Boston Harbor till about August of that year, when we sailed on a cruise among the West India Island. The first stop made was St. Luce in Martinique—afterwards The Frigate was chased by the British Fleet into ___?__ We cruised about till the Spring of 1783 we returned home and Peace was declared. I served two months on The Frigate."

Josiah served on *The Hague* under Captain John Manley, who was one of the outstanding captains in the American Navy. Manley had recently returned from a long imprisonment in England. While in the West Indies they made a spectacular escape from a 36 hour chase by a 50 gun

British ship. In January Captain Manley captured the last major prize of the war, *The Baille*.

Sources: 1. U.S. Pensioners 181801872. 2. Census 1810 & 1840. 3. Massachusetts Town & vital Records 1620-1988. 4. Sons of the American Revolution Application. 5. Massachusetts Marriages 1633-1850. 6. Tombstone 7. Pension Papers S30257. 8. Year book of the Sons of the Revolution in the State of New York 1899. 9. A Naval history of the American Revolution, Vol. 2 by Gardner Weld Allen.

****

Shadrack Barnes age 14

Shadrack Barnes was born on 6 February, 1764 in Culpepper County, Virginia, and he died on 31 December, 1844 in Gallatin County, Kentucky. On 18 May, 1786 in Culpepper County he married Frances Mozingo. After the war he moved to Bourbon County, Kentucky and eventually to Gallatin County. He was a successful farmer, because the 1830 census reported that he owned two slaves.

Shadrack enlisted in the Virginia militia on 1 March, 1778, which was just a month after turning 14 years old. He enlisted for two months as a substitute for his father, Francis. He served under Captain John Higginbotham and Colonel Taylor. During this time he was stationed at the Albemarle barracks. He continued substituting two months or more until June of 1780. During much of this time he was involved in no fighting, but instead he guarded prisoners at Albemarle barracks.

"I again joined the army having been selected by my division to serve a three months tour. I entered and served as a private in the Virginia militia. I joined my company under Captain Pollard in Culpepper County & marched near Petersburg where we joined the Army commanded by General Mulenburg and Genl Stuban. Colonel James Slaughter commanded the Regiment to which I belonged. Sometime after I had joined the army at Petersburg we had a skirmish with the British & retreated."

The skirmish that Shadrack refers to is called the Battle of Petersburg, which was fought on 25 April, 1781. The Virginia militia led by General Peter Muhlenberg, under the command of General Baron von Steuben, were outnumbered by the British 2 to 1. The British troops were led by the traitor Benedict Arnold. The British, however, were surprised at the stiff resistance the militia put up, and continuous fire on the Americans by the British artillery forced an American retreat to be called. The Americans made an orderly and disciplined retreat by crossing a bridge and reaching safety. The last companies to cross the bridge removed the planks as they went, which helped to delay the British from pursing them.

Shadrack's and the rest of the troops retreated to Richmond and remained there a few days before marching to the Malvern Hills just below Richmond. There they joined with Lafayette's army, and together they marched to Culpepper County where they joined with the army of General Anthony Wayne. Shadrack's three month term was now up, and he promptly enlisted for another tour. As each three month tour ended, he rejoined for another tour.

"In June 1781 I entered and served a tour under Capt Reed for three months. In September the same year, I entered Capt Yancy for the last time & was during this tour at the siege of York & was finally discharged verbally in November 1781 near Westchester Barracks by Capt Yancy."

After serving nearly three years and fighting in two battles, twenty-one year old Shadrack Barnes was ready to return home and start a new life. He received a pension of $80.00 a year for his service.

Sources: 1. 1830 Census. 2. Pension Papers S30840. 3. Sons of the American Revolution Application. 4. Virginia Marriages 1660-1800.

****

James Barron age 12

James Barron was born on 15 September, 1768 in Hampton, Virginia, and he died on 21 August, 1851 in Portsmouth, Virginia. He married (1) Elizabeth Mosely Armistead and (2) Mary Ann Wilson after the death of his first wife, Elizabeth, in 1823. There was much discussion in his pension application as to just how much he was entitled to and how much his wife would receive after his death. Part of the problem was how much time he spent in the navy during the Revolutionary War and how much his second wife was entitled to. He believed that he was entitled to more of a pension than he was granted. He received a pension of $144.00 a year for his service.

James served with his father as an apprentice for several years until he enlisted. His father was James Barron who was Commodore of the small Virginia State Navy during the Revolution. In James Barron's pension application several men wrote of his service:

"*I John S. Westwood of Elizabeth City County Virginia do hereby certify that I am well acquainted with Commodore James Barron of the United States Navy. Affiant has known him from his boyhood until the present period, and he well knows that the said James Barron, when a mere youth during the Revolutionary War, was attached to the Schooner Liberty, as a young midshipman, and served in that capacity under the command of his father Commodore James Barron, the commander in chief of the Virginia State Navy. The said Barron served as a midshipman in the said state navy until the close of the war in the year 1783. His service commenced at the close of 1780 or early in 1781. The said Barron was a young midshipman, and performed service during the said War for at least three years until the peace of 1783 he served principally in the schooner Liberty, and as an aid to his father visiting the various vessels composing the fleet."*

From Williams Jennings: *"...said Barron was a young midshipman and performed service on board of the schooner Liberty, and I think was occasionally on board of other vessels attached to the squadron commanded by his Father; he was in the service at least three years till the peace of 1783."*

"I John Cox of the town of Portsmouth do hereby certify that during the War of the Revolution I held a private commission in the service of Virginia as a Captain, and commenced service in the year 1777, and commanded for several years thereafter, many private armed vessels which were engaged in the transportation of munitions of war from the West Indies to the United States, and in performing other duties in the service of the state of Virginia – My public duties frequently required me to receive the commands and instructions of that distinguished officer Commodore James Barron, the commander in chief of the Naval forces of Virginia, and I well remember to have seen on several of these occasions young James Barron, his son (the present Commodore in the U.S.N.) as an officer performing duty in the Naval Service I was struck with his youthful appearance and the alacrity, zeal, and intelligence with which he performed service"

James served in the navy with his father before he was 12. *"I entered in the Navy of the United States in the year 1780, and served in the State Navy of Virginia, to the close of the War in 1783."* Since there is no proof when James actually entered this author will use his enlistment date of 1780 as he stated in his pension.

James entered the newly created United States Navy in 1789 as a Lieutenant aboard the *United States*. He was successful on his first tour and was promoted to Captain and given command of the frigate *Essex* in 1789. Five years later he was promoted to Commodore and given control of the USS *Chesapeake*. In 1807 his ship engaged the British ship *Leopard* resulting in the capture of his ship, USS *Chesapeake*. This battle was a major contributor to the cause of the War of 1812.

James was court-martialed and found guilty of premature surrender of his ship. He claimed that his ship was defenseless against the more powerful British ship. He was found guilty of not having his ship ready for action and suspended for five years without pay. He spent the next 10 years abroad. He returned back to the United States hoping to reenter the Navy. He was much criticized, especially by Commodore Stephen Decatur. James challenged Decatur to a duel and killed him on 22 March, 1820. James was reinstated in the Navy in 1822 but not given command of a ship. He retired in 1842.

Sources: 1. Sons of the American Revolution Application. 2. Virginians in the Revolution. 3. Pension Papers W12264. 4. American Naval Heroes 1775-1812-1861-1898 by John Howard Brown. 5. The Encyclopedia of the Wars of the Early American Republic, 1783-1812, edited by Spencer C. Tucker.

****

Samuel Bartol age 10

Samuel Bartol was born on 12 August, 1764 in Marblehead, Massachusetts, and he died on 23 January, 1835 in Salem, Massachusetts. He married Mercy Northey on 4 December, 1785 in Marblehead. He received a monthly pension of $8. His application said that he was a mariner and had a leg amputated. After the war he was a painter, when he could find work. A death record said that he died from a disordered bladder.

"On June A.D. 1775 I enlisted as a Drummer in a Company commanded by Captain Craig in the Pennsylvania Regiment of Riflemen which was then under the command of Col Thompson. I served in the said capacity of a Musician in said Regiment on the Continental establishment for the time of nine months and 5 days when I was discharged."

This raises the question, how did a young boy in Massachusetts join a Pennsylvania regiment of riflemen? After the battle of Lexington in

April of 1775, eight companies of riflemen were raised in Pennsylvania to join the Continental army near Boston. In June of 1775 the companies of Colonel James Thompson's Battalion began marching toward Massachusetts. The battalion camped outside of Cambridge at Prospect Hill. A call went out for men to join the cause, and Samuel probably walked the 19 miles to Cambridge to join up. After Samuel's discharge, he then went to sea as a cabin boy and lost his leg sometime later. This could explain why he was not drafted into the army at a later date.

Sources: 1. Lineage Book D.A.R. Vol. 38, 1902. 2. Massachusetts Town & Vital Records 1620-1988. 3. U.S. Pensioners 1818-1872. 4. Pension Papers S33974.

****

Joseph Bassett age 13

Joseph Bassett was born on 27 April, 1763 in Barnstable, Massachusetts, and died there on 7 July, 1855. He married Nancy Hawes in Barnstable on 2 April, 1808. He received a monthly pension of $8.

Most of the first page of his pension application was blackened out and could not be read. I began in the middle of the statement.

"...term of one year in the spring of 1776 in the town of Taunton Bristol county in Massachusetts in the Company commanded by Capt Perry of the Regiment commanded by Col Sargent in the Massachusetts line on the Continental establishment. I continued to serve in said corps til the expiration of my enlistment."

"Within two or three months thereafter I reenlisted in Capt Perkins Company of Col Crane's regiment in Gen Knox's Brigade of artillery on the continental Establishment for the term of three years. I served said last mentioned term and was discharged from the service at Morristown, New Jersey. I was in in the Battles of Brandywine Monmouth & Rhode Island."

Sources: 1. Massachusetts Town & Vital Records 1620-1998. 2. Sons of the American Revolution Application. 3. Pension Papers S35770. 4. Registry of the District of Columbia Society of the American Revolution 1896.

****

William Bates age 13

William Bates was born in 1766 and he enlisted in the army at Prince Edward Court House in Virginia in 1779 by John Davison. William served in the company commanded by Captain Tarpley White in the regiment commanded by Colonel William Davis. He was in the battles of Guilford Courthouse, Jamestown, and was at the surrender of Cornwallis at Yorktown.

Source: 1. Pension Application S35176.

****

Henry Baugh age 13

Henry Baugh was born on 12 April, 1762 in Virginia, and he died 9 October, 1836 in Pulaski, Kentucky. He married Margaret Phillipi on 20 March, 1786 in Virginia. He received a pension of $21.35 a year for his service. After his death his wife filed for and received a widow's pension of $33.33 a year. In Henry's will he stated that he left everything to his son Henry Jr., including any pension money now and in the future. He also stated in his will that his wife was unable to care for herself and should live with his son who would provide for her needs.

"I Volunteered in the now County of Wythe & State of Virginia my then place of residence, in the month of April, in the year 1775 in Captain Robert Davises Company. Colonel William Christy General William Preston. all of the now County of Wythe & State of Virginia aforesaid and left the same at the end of three months, and two weeks, serving two weeks over and above the time I Volunteered to serve marching from the s'd. now Wythe County Virginia through the State of North Carolina, was Station at Middle Tenn, in said State of North Carolina, and was there Discharged by my Gen'l. William Preston, after servicing as above stated, but was furnished with no written Discharge, during my servitude aforesaid, Maj'r. William Cloyed, of the Regular Army frequently visited the Troops to which I belonged, as above Described. upon being Discharged I returned home to my residence in Wythe County. – in the year 1776 I volunteered for my second tour, in the service of the United States in the Revolutionary war in the said now County Wythe & State of Virginia on the 10 day of November of that year, under Captain Henry Francis, Maj'r. William Cloyd all of the County & State afores'd. (Virginia) marching through the State of North Carolina, to the Moravian Towns, was at the battle or scurmish at the Shallow ford on the Atkin River in the said State of North Carolina against the British & Tories, and at the Moravian Towns afores'd. was discharged, by said Maj'r. William Cloyed, receiving a verbal discharge, and then together with the troops or company returned

home to my residence in the afores'd. now County of Wythe & State of Virginia."

The skirmish at the shallow ford that Henry mentioned in his pension application may have been the Battle of Shallow Ford that took place on 14 October, 1780. The Patriot militia ambushed the Tory militia as they crossed the Yadkin River. One American patriot was killed, Captain Henry Francis. If Henry Baugh was at this battle then he enlisted for a second time in 1780 and not 1776.

Sources: 1. Will of Henry Baugh. 2. Tombstone. 3. Census of 1810, 1820, & 1830. 4. U.S. International Marriage Records 1560-1900. 5. U.S. Headstone Applications for Military Veterans 1925-1963. 6. U.S. Pension Roll of 1825. 7. Pension Papers W8337.

****

Nathan Beals (Buel) age 13

Nathan Beals was born on 11 February, 1768 in Pembroke, Massachusetts, and he died on 1 August, 1851 in Kittery, Maine. He married Lucy Allen on 17 March, 1793 in Kittery, Massachusetts. He received a yearly pension of $39.90 for his service.

"On or about the tenth of September 1781 at the town of Killingworth in the county of New London and State of Connecticut I was called into the service of the United States as a "Minute Man" in a company of Militia and served as a private under Captain Daniel Palmeters. Lieutenant Ichabod Ward, which company belonged to Colonel Sylvester Grave's Regiment. I immediately marched with the company and joined the Regiment at Guilford and was there met by another Regiment commanded by General Sage. The two Regiments marched to Saybrook where the troops stopped one night and then proceeded on to East River where we remained on guard and marched from thence to New London which place had been burnt by the British. The enemy having retreated I marched from New London back through Lyme and Saybrook to Killingworth, and I was discharged."

Nathan served several more tours and he was discharged for the final time in 1783.

Sources: 1. Maine Society Sons of the American Revolution. 2. Massachusetts Town & Birth Records 1620-150. 3. Pension Papers S23558.

****

William Beck age 14

William Beck was born in Granville, North Carolina on 12 February, 1766 and died in Stokes, North Carolina on 7 February, 1845. He married Christine Huffman in North Carolina on 7 August, 1778.

"I entered the service as a substitute for my father John Beck, at the court house in the County of Granville and State of North Carolina on the 10th day of June 1780 in the company commanded by Captain Bennet, Lieutenant Crafton or Grafton as well as I recollects that with my company marched to Hillsboro in the County of Orange...."

Peter Bennet was a Captain in the Hillsboro militia under the command of Colonel Joseph Taylor. After William Beck joined the troops, they marched into South Carolina and camped a few mile from Camden. They were in hearing range of the Battle of Camden fought on 16 August, 1780.

"I was one of the guard on that day, who had charge of the baggage-wagons and some prisoners that General Caswell had commanded the North Carolina militia, my Regiment was commanded by Colonel Taylor from Hillsboro in North Carolina, after the battle we retreated back to Hillsboro where we remained a week or two, I recollect that the battle of Gates defeat was fought on the 16th day of August, from Hillsboro we marched to the Waxhaw settlement in South Carolina to six mile creek, where we remained for two or three weeks, when we retreated back as far as Salisbury in North Carolina, where I received a written discharge...sometime in the last of October or first of November 1780."

"Sometime in the month of February or March 1781 I again entered the service for the term of three months as a substitute for my father John Beck at the court house in Granville in North Carolina in the company of Captain Hicks & lieutenant Gilliam as well as I recollects their names, shortly before the battle of Guilford I was placed under Captain Hodges and Lieutenant Hester, I was in the battle of Guilford, I remember that General Green was the highest officer in command, and that my Regiment was commanded by one Colonel Taylor from Grandville, it was not the same Colonel Taylor before spoken of, I well recollect that Colonel Taylor had posted himself behind the stump of an old tree mounted upon his horse, I also remember that my Regiment retreated after one or two fires....."

General Greene had prepared his defense in three lines. The untested North Carolina militia, which William Beck was a member of, formed the first line. On their flanks were riflemen to snipe at the advancing British. One hundred yards behind the North Carolina militia was the Virginia militia. About one in the afternoon the British deployed for an attack. The British halted their advance about 150 yards from a fence where the North Carolina militia stood.

Sergeant Lamb of the North Carolina militia later noted that the militia, *"had their arms presented and resting on the picket fence...they were taking aim with nice precision."* When the first volley was fired, dozens of British soldiers fell but the rest continued the advance. When the British troops were at fifty yards, they charged the North Carolina militia. The militia dropped their personal goods and ran into the woods. The battle continued for only ninety minutes, until the Americans broke off their retreat.

The Americans had about 160 men killed or wounded while the British had over 500 killed or wounded. When the leader of the British Whig Party, Charles James Fox, heard that British General Cornwallis had declared a victory, he remarked, *"Another such victory would ruin the British Army."* After the battle, American General Greene said, *"We fight, get beat, rise, and fight again."*

After the battle and retreat, William went home for a few days and then joined the army again. During this tour he marched around the Camden area, and then he went to Charleston and from there he was discharged and returned home. He enlisted in March of 1782 for three months again as a substitute for his father. He was marched to Hillsboro, and after a months there he was discharged for the last time. For his service he received $23.33 a year.

Sources: 1. Tombstone. 2. U.S. Pensioners 1818-1872. 3. Pension Papers S2376. 4. A Battlefield Atlas of the American Revolution by Craig L. Symonds, Cartography by William J. Clipson.

****

Daniel Bedinger age 14

Daniel Bedinger was born in the winter of 1761 in Lancaster, Pennsylvania, and he died on 17 March, 1818 in Jefferson County, Virginia. In April of 1791 he married Sarah Rutherford in Berkeley County, Virginia.

In 1775 Daniel's older brothers, Henry and Michael, left the farm to join a company of riflemen to fight against the British in the Revolution. Daniel wanted to join them, but his mother was a widow and insisted that he stay behind, work the farm, and take care of his younger brothers and sisters. Later in the year the older boys returned home and shared their tales of adventure with Daniel. The two older brothers enlisted again, and like before Daniel's mother refused to let him join them.

The two brothers were in camp one night when Daniel showed up. He had run away from home, and in August of 1776 he enlisted in Captain Shephard's Company of Riflemen in the Virginia militia just a few months shy of his fifteenth birthday. The troops, including Daniel and his brother Henry, later marched to Fort Washington in New York. On 14 November, 1776 the British along with their Hessian mercenaries attacked the Americans. During the battle Daniel's brother Henry had his finger shot off by a Hessian Captain. Young Daniel, an expert marksman, was reported firing his rifle over two dozen times and often shouting, *"Take that, you bastards!"*

The outnumbered Americans were soon defeated. Of the 2,838 Americans captured that day, only 800 would survive the harsh treatment in captivity and be alive 18 months later when they would be exchanged. Daniel and his brother Henry were captured and would survive. Daniel's actions during the battle did not go unnoticed by the officers. Young Daniel was later given a promotion to ensign.

When Daniel was captured, he was not given food for four days. He was marched to the Old Sugar House on Liberty Street in New York. There he and other members of his company remained nearly dying of exposure and starvation. They had little food to eat, and what they did get was stale or rotten. They had little clothing and blankets to protect them from the cold and snow that blew in from the glassless windows. Daniel was soon moved to a prison ship, possibly the *Whitby*, in New York Harbor.

After a few months had passed Daniel had become very ill. He was not even strong enough sit or stand. By now 52 of the 79 men captured in Daniel's company had died. A prisoner exchange had been arranged, and the British officers went among the prisoners to select the ones to be exchanged. Daniel was passed over twice due to his weakened condition. The young boy begged the officer to include him in the exchange. The officer must have been moved by the boy's determination and poor health because he finally approved Daniel as one to be exchanged. Daniel was removed from the prison ship and transferred to a hospital in Philadelphia. Unfortunately, Henry was not exchanged and remained a prisoner for four years.

Daniel was found by his older brother George who took his sick brother to a friend's house to be cared for. Many years later one of Daniel's sons wrote about his father's ordeal, *"My father was taken prisoner at the battle of Fort Washington, and the privations and cruel treatment which he then underwent gave a blow to his constitution from which he never recovered. After the close of the Revolution he returned home with a constitution much shattered."*

When Daniel was strong enough to travel his brother George took him home. Once home Daniel had a relapse and nearly died. By the summer of 1777 Daniel had regained his strength, so he enlisted in the Virginia militia again and was promoted to Lieutenant. He fought at the Battle of Brandywine on 11 September, 1777. When his tour was completed he returned home again. He once again enlisted in the Virginia militia and fought at the Battle of Cowpens on 17 January, 1781. He finally ended his service on 7 May 1783. Daniel, understandably so, hated the British until his death.

Daniel received 1,000 acres of farm land in Virginia for his service in 1785. After the war he took a position in the Custom House in Norfolk. He later was appointed Navy Agent by President Thomas Jefferson, and he was placed in charge of the Gosport Navy Yard. Near the end of his life he lived on his estate, "Bedford", near Shepherdstown. He died before he could apply for a pension. His wife Sarah applied for a widow's pension on 21 August, 1838.

"I am the widow of Daniel Bedinger who was a Lieutenant in the Army of the Revolution....he was made a prisoner at Fort Washington, was afterwards made an ensign and the a Lieutenant in which latter capacity I believe he served to the end of the Revolution." Sarah received $276.00 a year for his long service.

George Bedinger, the oldest brother, became a major in the militia. After the war he served in the State Legislature, and later he served two terms in Congress. In 1808 he was chairman of the committee to prevent further importation of slaves into the United States. His widow received a pension of $75.00 a year for his service.

Henry Bedinger, who was a prisoner with Daniel, became a Captain in the 5th Virginia Regiment by the end of the Revolution. Later, in the Indian Wars he was appointed a Major. He was elected to the Virginia Assembly in 1792. For his service he received a pension of $72.50 a year.

Sources: 1. Sons of the American Revolution Application. 2. Pension Papers W8138 for Daniel, W2992 for George, and S8059 for Henry. 3. Historic Shepherdstown by Danske Dandridge. 4. West Virginians in the American Revolution by Ross B. Johnson. 5. U.S. Revolutionary War Rolls 1775-1783. 6. Historic Shepherdstown and The historic Shepherdstown Museum. 7. American Prisoners of the Revolution by Danske Dandridge.

****

Constant Beebe age 13

Constant Beebe was born on 15 June, 1778 in Sharon, Connecticut, and died 3 October, 1834 in New York. He married Jane Peck on 15 November, 1785. He served for a total of about 10 ½ months.

"I entered the service on or about the 15 June 1778. I volunteered as a private under Captain Josiah Warner and Lieut Davenport, and served as a waiter to my Uncle Major Martin Beebe, who was an inhabitant of the same neighborhood and town as I. I believe that the manner of service as waiter was understood before my engagement. I was organized at New Concord so called and Albany County. Thence marched through Albany to guard the Western frontier—was stationed at Cherry Valley for some time, was frequently on guard when not otherwise engaged as a waiter to my uncle who I think commanded the corps which went or marched from this county and district to the next. I recollect standing guard in an orchard, while at Cherry Valley, the inhabitants of which came within the guard during night for safety, and frequently when the inhabitants went to milk their cows, a guard was sent with them. Colo. Campbell and Major Dixon were at this place but I do not recollect that they had any command. Thence marched to Canajoharie from thence to Johnstown. I recall of going into the church at that place and for the first time heard Church organs. Thence marched to Albany and home where I arrived the first of August, making my term as I verily believe not less than 1 1/2 months."

Constant volunteered for the militia again on 1 June, 1779. For the next month and a half his militia unit marched around to the northwest of Albany looking for Indians and Tories. In the fall of 1779 Constant again joined the seventeenth regiment of the Albany militia and marched to Fish Kills which is about 10 mile north of West Point.

"I was there on guard and preformed the usual duties of a camp and was dismissed and returned about the start of Nov. I recollect that it was cold weather before I was dismissed. We had to and did build fire places of turf. This term of service as I verily believe was not less than 3 months".

His next tour with the same unit began on 1 May, 1780. This time he was marched north of Albany to Schenectady and scouted the area for Indians and Tories. This tour ended in the middle of June. On 1 July, 1780 he joined as a substitute for a man name Rowly and returned to Fish Kills then they marched to West Point. From there they took a sloop and sailed up the Hudson River to Albany and then marched to Fort Edward.

"A party of Indians and Tories came to Fort Edward and burned a number of buildings in sight of the Fort but did not approach so as to be reached by small arms from the Fort, during our stay me and others lay on our arms all night expecting an attack. They however decamped and disappeared without any serious injury to the small army in the Fort. I recollect that the women and children came into Fort Edward during the Enemies burning in the vicinity of Fort Ann and Fort Edward. I volunteered to stay longer than my first assignment and did stay and did not arrive at home till about the 1 of Nov."

Sources: 1. Pension Papers S14942. 2. New York in the Revolution as Colony and State. 3. Tombstone 4. Census of 1790, 1800, and 1820. 5. U.S. Pensioners 1818-1872.

****

William Beekman age 14

William Beekman was born in June of 1767 in New York, and he died on 26 November, 1845 in Sharon, New York. He married Joanna Lowe in Cooperstown, New York. William, at the age of fourteen, was chosen by Colonel Marinus Willett to accompany him to the Mohawk Valley as a private secretary. William later served as a state senator from 1799-1802.

Sources: 1. Sons of the American Revolution Application. 2. D.A.R. Lineage Book, Vol. 18. 3. The Schoharie County Democrat, 29 March, 1899.

****

Jacob Beeler age 13

Jacob Beeler was born in 1762 in Frederick County, Virginia, and moved to the frontier in North Carolina in 1770. He writes of his enlistment in his pension application:

"I settled on the Holstin River at which time the Indians were on friendly terms and so continued until breaking out of the revolutionary war and the Cherokees, about the year 1775, began to deprecate upon frontier inhabitants, and I volunteered under Captain William Buchwhannon to guard the frontier and act as a company of Ranger which service I entered in June of 1775, and continued until the month of January following, after the battle of Long Island and which was about seven months during which time I ranged the frontier & when not engaged in that duty was stationed until the arrival of Colonel Christy & his troops at the Long Island, and his Company Joined said Christy & descended the Holston River with him to the Chickamog towns, in the Cherokee country & owing to part taking themselves to fight & others coming in & proposing a treaty, their property was saved from destruction at that time the men under Colonel Christy returned again to the Long Island & I & others under Christy continued in service until after the treaty of Long Island in January being as before stated seven months service that I was then discharged verbally by Col Christy."

In July of 1776 the Cherokee War broke out across the southern backcountry of Georgia, South Carolina, Virginia, and areas we now call Tennessee. The Battle of Long Island Flats, in Tennessee, was fought on 20 July, 1776. After the battle, Jacob and the rest of the army under the command of Colonel William Christy took canoes down the Tennessee River to destroy the encampments and provisions of the Cherokees.

Once they arrived at the towns, they found them abandoned. The troops remained for a few days and the Indians returned and sued for peace. The towns who refused to sue for peace were destroyed along with their crops and property.

"I immediately afterward volunteered under Capt Elijah Robison to be stationed at the Long Island (inasmuch as but part of the Indians had treated & it was necessary to guard the frontier against the residue) I there continued for two months in that service and was dismissed. I again enrolled for a tour under Evan Shelby against the disaffected Cherokees

for one month, as a ranger, and performed that duty on the Clinch River and was dismissed at the expiration of my month's service. Again in the month of July 1778 I was called upon to perform a month's service at Ducan's Fort own clinch river which I performed and was dismissed."

"Again in the month of August of the same year, I volunteered under John Carmack a Captain to go to McIntosh's army stationed at Fort McIntosh thence went to Muskingum river Fort Lawrence against the Shawnee & Delaware Indians and was dismissed by said Carmack Berkley County Virginia on the 26th February following which discharged I obtained for the term aforesaid being about seven months."

In August of 1780 Jacob once again was called to serve with Colonel Kyle against the Indians. The next month Jacob volunteered to serve under Captain John Pemberton of the North Carolina line. Captain Pemberton was chasing the hated Major Patrick Ferguson. The Major had aggressively recruited Loyalists and was known to treat very harshly the Patriot sympathizers. The Patriot army engaged the Tory army of Major Ferguson at the Battle of King's Mountain. Major Ferguson was killed and his army defeated on 7 October, 1780.

According to rebel accounts Major Ferguson was shot from his horse, and with his foot caught in the stirrup, he was dragged to the rebel lines. The Major was approached by a soldier for his surrender and Ferguson drew his pistol and shot him. This act infuriated the patriots, and they shot the Major eight times. It was reported that the soldiers stripped the clothes from the Major's body, urinated on him, and then buried him in an ox hide.

Jacob wrote after the battle, *"We marched prisoners to Salisbury & delivered them to the militia there being about eight hundred in number which service was for three months and was discharged, verbally, Colonel Shelby & returned home. That in December following I volunteered under Captain Waring under Cols Sevier. Clark, Martin & Campbell to go against the Cherokee Indians on the night of the New Year we reached Chota on the other side of Little Tennessee & then on 2 January 200 horsemen went up to Chellowway to burn the Town & did so and we were fired upon by the Indians on their retreat thence went down the River to Tellico & their a part of the Army was left at said place & the residue went to Chestua & thence returned home having served about two months."*

Jacob again volunteered for two months and joined Captain Butler's Company against the Cherokees on Lookout Mountain. He then was drafted for three months under Captain William Blair to serve in the Cumberland. He had no documentation of his service because he was verbally discharged and had no signed papers. But because he had some witnesses that swore to his service, he received $80.00 a year pension. His pension file is extensive, and it mentions that his brother Joseph served with him at times.

Sources: 1. Some Tennessee Heroes of the Revolution, Pamphlet No. V. 2. Tombstone. 3. Pension Roll of 1835. 4. Pension Application of Jacob Beeler. 5. Southern Indians in the American Revolution by James O'Donnell. 6. Virginia's Colonial Soldiers by Lloyd DeWitt Bockstruck.

****

Isaac Oliver Benedict age 14

Isaac Benedict was born on 14 August, 1764 in Ridgefield, Connecticut, and he died on 24 October, 1845 in Butternut, New York. He married Asenath Beach in 1788. Isaac first entered the service as a substitute in November 1778 for his 16 year old brother James. At this time he served a six month term. Isaac received a yearly pension for $30.

"I enlisted at Pitts Town in the state of New York State Troops. I went with said Regiment to Fort Edward and thence to Palmer Town where I was stationed until the first of September following. Was employed building a block house on fort __?__ and thence went to Fort Stanwix and was stationed thence & was in the command of Major Huff until said term of 9 months Expired."

"I enlisted in Massachusetts in the year 1778 in Capt. Nobles Company Col Woods Regt. In Nixons brigade and served out said term chiefly in the state of New York and was discharged at Peekskill State of New York. Also in the year 1779 I served one month in Capt Vanderhoof's company at Schenectady state of New York in Militia Service."

Sources: 1. Lineage Book National Society of the Daughters of the American Revolution, Vol. 27, 1898. 2. Tombstone 3. Sons of the American Revolution. 4. Pension Papers S12156.

****

Ebenezer Benjamin age 13

Ebenezer Benjamin was born on 4 April, 1766 in Preston, Connecticut, and he died in 1855 in New York. He received a yearly pension of $66.66. He served under Captain Silas Grey of the 4th New York Line.

"In the year 1779 I volunteered in the Militia in a company called the Silver Greys and served about *four months* at about *Fish Kill*. In April 1781 I enlisted in canaan in Capt Silas Grey's Co in a regiment under the command of I think Col John McKristy. At the time of enlistment but afterwards, I think Col Millett had command for *nine months* and was stationed at Saratoga at about there on the 6th day of April 1782 I again enlisted at canaan for *nine months* in Capt Joseph Harrisons Co Col Willetts Regiment and went to Schoharie and from thence I went to Cattskill & stationed abt. Two months & then to Schoharie and I was taken sick during the rest of my enlistment & was to sick as to be able to do duty as a soldier."

Sources: 1. Census 1840 & 1850. 2. Connecticut Town Birth Records pre-1870. 3. New York Pensioners 1835. 4. Pension Papers S12151. 5. The Bloodied Mohawk: The American Revolution in the Words of Fort Planks Defenders and Other Mohawk Valley Partisans by Kenneth D. Johnson.

****

Nathan Benjamin Jr. age 10

Nathan Benjamin Jr. was born on 7 March, 1769 in Egremont, Massachusetts, and he died on 6 April, 1813 in New York. He married Ruth Seymour. In 1779 he served in Captain John Miathorn's Company in the 4th Regiment of Colonel John Hathorn in the Orange County New York Militia. Nathan's father was Captain Nathan Benjamin Sr.

Sources: 1. Sons of the American Revolution Application. 2. Year Book of the Sons of the Revolution in New York 1899.

****

Jabez Besse age 13

Jabez Besse was born on 21 October, 1762 in Wareham, Massachusetts, and he died on 9 October, 1833 in Wayne, Maine. He married Sarah Allen in 1797. He received a yearly pension of $50.

"I enlisted in July 1776 for three months, served at Roxbury near Boston and after serving out the full term of my enlistment was discharged in October. In May 1779 I again enlisted for six months in Captain __?__ company and Col Jacob's Regiment of the same troops, I served the

44

greater part of this term in Providence R.I. in guarding the town and was discharged."

"In May 1780 I enlisted for six months in Capt ___Company & Col Putman's Regiment of the same troops, during this service I served in New Jersey was present when Maj Andre was hung. Afterwards went to West Point & after serving out the full term was discharged."

Sources: 1. Maine Society Sons of the American Revolution. 2. Pension Papers W8127.

****

Adam Bicker age 13

Adam Bicker was born on 6 October, 1762 at Redstone Fort, Pennsylvania, and he died 31 August, 1843 in Clermont County, Ohio. He married Rebecca Hartman on 2 November, 1799. He was the son of German parents who were massacred by Indians in 1770. Adam and his younger brother had been away from home or they would have been killed too. The two boys were taken in by an uncle at Fort Redstone. Adam was engaged most of the time as a hunter for the garrison, which was a position of honor for someone so young.

"I enlisted in the service of the United States in March of 1776 under the following named officers, Captain Thomas Stokely (Stokeling) Leiut Henry Hanly at Greensburgh, Westmoreland County, Pennsylvania, and marched from there to Fort Crawford on the Allegheny River about 30 above Fort Pitt where I was stationed six months, to help guard the fort. At this expiration of this time, I again enlisted for three months, and marched from Fort Crawford under the Command of Captain Stokley to Fort Wallis in the State of Pennsylvania. That while at fort Wallace we were attacked by the Indians who killed 18 of our men. At the expiration of this time, I again enlisted for three months, I was dismissed by Captain Stokely but received no written discharge."

After he was discharged from the militia Adam returned to Fort Redstone. He enlisted in a company of soldiers, and in in 1785 the troops were sent to Pittsburgh where Adam was in several expeditions against the Indians. For the next several years Adam was in and out of the army.

On 20 August, 1794 he was engaged at the Battle of Fallen Timbers in Ohio. This was the final battle in the Northwest Indian War between the Native Americans and the United States. The battle was won by the United States and ended the threat by the Indians for many years.

In 1799 he married Rebecca, and they settled down in Ohio on a farm of 100 acres where they raised 9 children. Adam enjoyed hunting and even at the age of 70 he spent much time in the woods hunting. He often expressed regret that the Indians wars were over. He received a pension of $30 a year.

Sources: 1. Clermont County, Ohio Revolutionary War Veterans, Vol. 1, book H-61 by Aileen M. Whitt. 2. 1998 Edition of Bricker Roots and Sprouts by Deloris Tarvin. 3. Census of 1820, 1830, and 1840. 4. Pension Papers W2714.

****

Daniel Bissell age 10

Daniel Bissell was born on 20 July, 1768 in Hartford Connecticut, and he died 14 December, 1833 in Franklin, Missouri. He married Deborah Sebor on 21 May, 1794. In 1847 the children of Daniel and Deborah filed for Daniel's pension. Their application was granted and they divided a yearly pension of $120.

Daniel's father, Ozias, was in the French and Indian war and also served as a Captain in the revolution. He took four of his five sons with him to the Revolutionary War leaving the youngest, Daniel, behind. When Ozias would return home, Daniel would beg his father to take him to war as well. Ozias finally gave in and allowed Daniel to join the 8th Regiment of the Connecticut Militia as a fifer.

At times Daniel was assigned to carry dispatches to other units. Many times he made the journey on foot, sometimes hiding from Indians, going without food, and enduring bitter cold. He later served as an orderly sergeant in the regiments of Colonels Bradley and Swift.

Several years after the end of the revolution, Daniel again joined the army. During this time he was in several battles including St. Clair's defeat in 1791. For gallant conduct in this battle he was promoted to Ensign in the 1st Infantry Regiment. In 1794 he was promoted to Lieutenant, and then in 1799, to Captain. In 1802 he was given command of Fort Massac in Illinois. As the U. S. Army began to expand in 1808, Daniel was promoted to Lieutenant Colonel of the 1st Infantry in 1808. The next year he was given command of Fort Belle Fontaine, the first military fort west of the Mississippi River.

During the War of 1812 he was promoted Brigadier General and was in the Battle of Cook's Mill on 19 October, 1814. This was a small battle that resulted in a draw. Daniel retired from the army in 1821.

Sources: 1. The New England Historical and Genealogical Register 1847-2011. 2. Connecticut Church Record Abstracts 1630-1920. 3. Sons of the American Revolution Application. 4. U.S. Pensioners 1818-1872. 5. Tombstone 6. Visitors Guide to General Daniel Bissell's House. 7. History of Saint Louis.

****

John Bivens age 14

John Bivens was born on 15 September, 1760 in Middletown, Connecticut, and he died 24 February, 1839 in Fulton County, Illinois. He married Hannah Owens on 18 September, 1779. He received a pension of $83 a year for his service. Hannah's claim for a widow's pension was rejected, because she was not a widow at the date of the act that was passed. Most widow's when they signed their name to pension documents could not write and signed their name with an x. Hannah signed her name to correspondence.

"I enlisted for nine months in the army of the United States about the last of March 1775 under Capt—Allen—Whipple was the General Jonathan Brewer, Colonel of the regiment. I was discharged the last day of December 1775. In the same month of December a little before the first tour expired I enlisted at Prospect Hill near Boston Massachusetts for the term of a year in the service of the U. States under Capt Aaron Haynes— Joseph William half brother of mine was 1st Lieutenant and then 2nd Lieutenant was –Smith the regiment was under the command of Colonel Asa Whitecomb. I served out my year and was discharged in December of 1776 at Ticonderoga. I was in the Militia service. I was called into the service at Worthington Massachusetts as near as I can remember early in August 1777 to march to Bennington Vermont under Capt Webber. I was discharged but a day or two before the surrender of General Burgoyne. I was also drafted for three months at New Lebanon New York in the fall I think of 1779 to ___ with the militia to Fishkill New York. I believe under Capt Gideon King & I served in such militia the term of three months except a few days before the end of the term."

"During the period of my first enlistment I was with the army in the neighborhood of Boston sometimes at Cambridge but principally on Prospect Hill on the march from Cambridge to Bunker Hill on the day of the battle (June 17) with my company but not in time to share in the fight. I was in the battle of Stillwater (September 19, 1777) as a private in the militia & in no other actual engagement."

John Bivens was part of the 13th Regiment of the Massachusetts Volunteer Infantry commanded by Colonel Jonathan Brewer. The 13th Regiment took part in the Battle of Stillwater.

The American army under General Gates was encamped near Stillwater in New York. On 17 September, 1777 British General Burgoyne was encamped just 4 miles away. Each side had nearly 3,000 men take part in the daylong battle. As the day ended the two sides fought to a draw, although each side claimed a victory. At this stage in the Revolution, any time the American forces were not defeated it could be viewed as a victory for them.

Sources: 1. Sons of the American Revolution Application. 2. Pension Papers R875. 3. Connecticut Town Records pre-1870. 4. U.S. Pension Roll of 1835.

****

David Black age 14

David Black was born on 4 August, 1763 in New York, and he died on 18 October, 1832 in Madisonville, Ohio. He married Catherine Cramer on 12 April, 1787 in Ohio. He enlisted in May, 1778 a few months before his fifteenth birthday. His son David Jr. applied for his pension in 1829, because he said his father had, *"lost his mind and became insane."* David Jr. was his father's guardian and provided, in the pension application, the regiments his father served in and his length of service. His wife received a yearly widow's pension of $80.

David served for five years from May, 1778 until June 1783. He served under Colonel Philip Cortland in the 2nd New York Regiment, under Colonel James Holmes in the 4th New York Regiment, and in the 1st New York Regiment under Colonel Goose Van Schaick. David Jr could not supply the exact times he served in each Regiment or any battles his father may have participated in. David Sr. is found on the rolls of all three Regiments.

The 3rd Regiment merged with the 1st Regiment in January, 1781. Since the 1st and the 4th Regiments were at the Battle of Yorktown in 1781, it means that David was probably at that battle.

Sources: 1. New York in the Revolution as Colony & State, 2nd edition, 1898, pages 19, 29, & 48. 2. Sons of the American Revolution Application. 3. U.S. Pensioners 1818-1872. 4. Pension Papers W5835.

****

William Blacklerr Jr. age 8

William Blacklerr was born in 1767 at Marblehead, Massachusetts, and he died in 1814. He enlisted in May 1775 for eight months as a drummer boy in Captain Francis Symond's Company and Colonel John Glover's 14th Continental Regiment. William's son filed for a survivor's pension in the 1850's but it was rejected.

Source: 1. D.A.R. Lineage Book, Vol. 19.

****

John Blair age 14

John Blair was born in 1763 in Massachusetts and he died on 26 January, 1824 in Newburg, New York. He received a pension of $8 a month.

"In the month of July 1777 I enlisted in a Company commanded by Capt William Scott in the sixteenth Massachusetts Regiment commanded by Col Henry--About Eighteen months afterwards this regiment Received to the ninth commanded by Col Henry Jackson and I was attached to Capt Joseph Fox Company and I served in the same Regiment until the month of June 1783."

Sources: 1. Suffering Soldiers by John Resch. 2. Pension Papers S45296.

****

Ezekiel Bonney age 12

Ezekiel Bonney was born on 20 December, 1762 in Pembroke, Massachusetts, and he died on 29 October, 1845 in Hanson, Massachusetts. He married Zerviah Perry on 18 September, 1787 in Massachusetts. He received a yearly pension of $34.66 for his service.

"I entered the service in the Spring of 1775. I enlisted as a Musician in Capt. Hambers Company Col. Baileys Regt. in Genl. Thomas Brigade and went to Roxbury. When the Battle of Bunker hill had taken place I was guard on the Roxbury line and I served as a musician for eight months."

"In the Spring of 1778 I enlisted again as a Musician in a company commanded by Capt. Isiah Cushing of Pembroke and went with the company to Nantucket where I served in that capacity for two months."

"In the year 1778 I enlisted as a private for two months under Capt. Partridge of Roxbury Col. Whitney's Regiment and went to Rhode Island in what was called Gen. Sullivans Expedition—was present in the retreat from the Island and was present at the affair of Butts hill on our retreat and was left on the Island by night and bristol ferry and marched by way of Tiverton and Providence to __?__ on the west side of Narragansett Bay and we were discharged."

When the Americans occupied Butt's Hill in Rhode Island, the sentinels of the British and American armies were only four hundred yards apart. On 28 August, 1778 General Sullivan decided to withdraw his forces. During the day the General had tents pitched in sight of the British, and the men were pretending to fortify the camp. That night they lit campfires in view of the British. The rest of the American army was not in sight and began to retreat. By midnight the entire army had successfully retreated.

Sources: 1. D.A.R. Lineage Book, Vol. 69. 2. U.S. Pensions of 1835. 3. Pension Papers S4957.

****

Nicholas Boom age 14

Nicholas Boom was born on 23 November, 1763 in Albany, New York. Some sources state that he died in 1816. However, according to his pension application he made a statement in court on 7 July, 1820. He received a monthly pension of $8.

He enlisted in 1777 to serve for 5 years in the 1st Regiment of the New York Line under Colonel Goose Van Schaick from 1777 to 1782. He may have participated in the Battles of Saratoga, Monmouth, Yorktown, and the Sullivan Expedition. In the summer of 1782, near Fort Stanwix, he was injured on a scouting party when he ran a hemlock limb into his right leg just above the ankle.

"I entered for the term of five years in the company commanded by Col. Van Schaick in the year 1777 and left the service in the year 1782 having received a wound in consequence of which wound I have lost my right leg."

Unable to work because of losing his leg, the New York Assembly voted on a bill that would have given him a yearly payment of $75 for the rest of his life. The bill was rejected.

Sources: 1. Massachusetts Society of the Sons of the American Revolution, 1920. 2. Sons of the American Revolution Application. 3. Pension Papers S44642.

****

Jemima Boone age 13

Jemima Boone was born on 4 October, 1762 in Rowen County, North Carolina, and she died on 30 August, 1834 in Warren County, Missouri. She was the daughter of the famous Daniel Boone. The story of her capture by Indians shows the courage that young girls displayed on the dangerous frontier during the revolution.

When the Revolutionary War began hostilities between the Native Americans and the settlers in Kentucky increased. Some of problems were encouraged by the British in the area. By the spring of 1776 less than 200 settlers remained in Kentucky. They were hiding in a few fortified settlements such as Boonesborough.

On Sunday 14 July, 1776 thirteen year old Jemima, along with Betsey and Fanny Callaway, were in a canoe on the Kentucky River. A war party of two Cherokee and three Shawnee Indians captured the three teenage girls. Forced to climb the river bank, Jemima refused to move. She told the Indians that she would die before she would march barefooted. The Indians raised their tomahawks and threatened her, but showing no fear she refused to move. The Indians finally gave in and gave her a pair of moccasins. The Indians took their captives north toward the Shawnee towns across the Ohio River.

Jemima and her two friends knew that their fathers and friends would discover that they were captured and would be on the way to rescue them. Jemima and the two teenagers did everything they could to delay the Indians. At times the girls would fall down and complain that they had injured their leg or foot. Sometimes, they complained that they were too exhausted to travel further and needed to stop to rest. Since Jemima was the main one slowing the party up, the Indians stole a horse for her to ride. When they placed her on the horse she would without their knowledge kick, pinch, or prick the horse to get him to buck and throw her off. She continued to do this every time they placed her on the horse. The Indians soon gave up and set the horse free.

After the third morning of captivity, the Indians were building a fire to prepare breakfast when the rescuers showed up. One of the Indians was shot and fell into the fire, and two others were seriously wounded during the brief fight. The remaining Indians made a hasty retreat leaving behind all of their equipment. One of the rescuers remarked, *"We sent them off almost naked."*

When the girls were returned to their homes the settlers were surprised that the girls had not been abused. In fact, Jemima said that the Indians were kind to them considering the circumstances. Many years later Jemima said she bore no grudge against her kidnappers and even spoke favorably of their behavior. A few years after the rescue Jemima married one of the men that rescued her, Flanders Callaway.

James Fenimore Cooper used this event as the basis for the captivity and rescue of Alice and Cora Munro in his story *The Last of the Mohicans*. The main character of the story had a strong resemblance to Daniel Boone.

Sources: 1. Daniel Boone: An American Life by Michael Lofaro.

****

Richard Booz age 14

Richard Booz was born on 25 July, 1764 in Amelia County, Virginia. His pension was rejected because the government said he was a civilian volunteer not engaged in military service and was too young to have enlisted. They also said they could not find his name on any military records.

"In the year 1777 as well as I now recollects I entered the military service of the United States, being then about 14 years of age. I went with my father, and joined the troops stationed at Cumberland Court House, Virginia with a view to serve as a musician, but finding no vacancy as a musician, I entered the ranks, and bore arms as a soldier, and was regularly subject to military duty as a Soldier, mustered and carried a gun, and my name was called at the calling of the rolls – in the same manner as any other soldier, and was in all respects subject to military duty, as completely as any soldier in either of the companies. After continuing in the ranks for some time, I was ordered to quit the ranks, and to work in the laboratory – together with two other soldiers, (Long and Yates,) from the same company and had no option whatever, nor any contract whatever, but I was ordered to that duty, and was under the command of a sergeant, subject to military duty, and the roll called regularly every day, and his own name, in the same manner with any other soldier. He was tasked as to the quantity of work required to be done, and subject to be

flogged if the task was not performed. I drew rations while in the laboratory, as another soldier, was not permitted to leave the encampment, without a written permit, and on one occasion I recollect getting such written permit. I was entitled to the same monthly pay as another soldier, & never considered my services in the nature of a civil contract, and in fact had no contract whatever, other than my military engagement. When the detachment to which I belonged was marched from Cumberland Court-House, to New London, in Bedford County, I marched with the troops, as much subject to military discipline, and military regulations, as any soldier in the Corps, and if I had quit the troops would have been considered a deserter, and liable to be apprehended as such, as much so as any soldier in the Corps. When the roll was called on the march between those two places, my name was called as another soldier and I encamped with the troops, and was not permitted to quit the encampment at night, any more than another soldier, and if I had done so, would certainly have been punished as another soldier. When I quit the service I got a written permit, from my officers, and did not get a regular discharge for some considerable time afterwards. Before the detachment left Cumberland Ct. House I was employed in building huts for the use of the soldiery, and laboured with the other soldiers, and at the same time I was regularly mustered twice a day as a soldier, and my name regularly called whenever the roll was called, as another soldier's. And had I refused to work, would have been subject to military punishment; and had no contract for this kind of labour, different from any other soldier in the detachment. While I was employed in the laboratory, or work-shop, at New-London there were about eight or ten other soldiers under the command of Sergeant Bachelor, besides, myself, as well as I now recollects. The troops with whom I served, were partly regulars, and partly militia, but my memory does not serve me sufficiently to designate particularly, which of the officers were regulars and which were militia. but my present impression in that Captains Wiley & Lovely were regular officers, and Capt. Greer a militia officer, but I cannot speak positively."

When Richard learned that his claim had been rejected he wrote a letter to the pension office on 9 September, 1834.

"I learned with some surprise from your letter of the 11 August, to Allan C. Bryan, (who has acted as my agent and advisor,) that my claim for a pension under the law of June 7 1832, was rejected, on the ground that I was not a <u>soldier</u>, but a labourer on civil contract. It never for a moment entered my imagination that I was not as much a soldier, bound to military service, as any soldier in the camp. My memory does not serve

me sufficiently to enable me to say what portion of the troops with whom I served, were militia, and what portion were regulars, but I do not entertain any doubt of there being both kind of troops employed, and if I am not mistaken, the records will show that some of the officers named in my declaration were regulars, and others only militias – eighteen months militia men. I presume if I had joined the militia, as a volunteer and served eighteen months in the ranks as another soldier there would be no doubt of my right to the pension, subject to the rules and regulations of militia cases, for the proof of my services; and it is extremely hard indeed, because I was ordered and compelled to perform a particular kind of service, which had to be performed by some of the soldiers, that I should be deprived of the bounty or the government. As to my being a boy of only fourteen years of age, I believe that is about the age at which Gen'l. Jackson served in the Revolution, who has received the honour of being styled the hero of two wars. The printed instructions of the War Department on the subject, say the law has been construed to embrace "all persons enlisted – drafted, or who <u>volunteered</u>, and who were bound to military service." If the facts stated by me, on oath on this sheet, are to be believed, I do not see how it can be denied for a moment that I come within the description of a volunteer bound to military service. If the certificate of the magistrate, who administered the oath as to my veracity, is not deemed sufficient on the subject, I would have no difficulty in procuring additional testimonials in abundance. I flatter myself therefor that you will not find it inconsistent with your official duties, to review my case and reverse a decision, honestly made I doubt not, but under misapprehension of the facts."

Source: Pension Papers R1026.

****

Peter Borders age 14

Peter Borders was born on 14 February, 1767 in Lancaster County, Pennsylvania, and he died in 1859 in Menard, Illinois. His pension was rejected because the government said he had no proof of service, he was too young to enlist, and militia tours in the Virginia militia were for only three months.

"I entered the service in March 1781 at Loudon County Virginia as a substitute for one John May, a resident of Loudon County – and served for the period of six months as a private in a company of militia. The service in which I was employed was in guarding the prisoners who

were sent to Winchester Barracks, Frederick County Virginia. There was only a Captains command during the six months that I was at the Barracks. The officers names were Capt James Simmerel alias Simrel and Lieut Shannon who was an Irishman. There were no regular officers at the post during the time I was there – nor continental officers except those named. Just previous to our discharge General Muhlenburg with his regiment arrived at Winchester Barracks. There was no battle fought, nor was there any skirmishing – while I was with the company of Capt. Simmeral."

Sources: 1. Databases of Illinois Veterans roll 1775-1995. 2. Pension Papers R1029.

****

Nathaniel Bosworth age 10

Nathaniel Bosworth was born on 16 June, 1767 in Bristol, Rhode Island, and he died 6 April, 1853 in Pittstown, New York. He married Suriah Mason on 25 November, 1790.

Due to a shortage of men, Nathaniel was placed in charge of an ammunition wagon in his father's regiment. His father, Benjamin Bosworth, was an officer in the militia. At the age of 12 Nathaniel assisted in removing cannon at night and at the age of 13 he was a private in Captain Henry Tew's Company, Colonel John Hathaway's Regiment. The regiment marched on a Rhode Island alarm in August 1780.

Sources: 1. D.A.R. Index of the Rolls of Honor Vols. 57-59. 2. Massachusetts Society of Sons of the American Revolution, 1899. 3. History of Rensselaer Co., New York by Nathaniel Bartlett Sylvester, 1880.

****

Jacob Bovee age 14

Jacob Bovee was born on 3 July, 1763 in Hoosick, New York, and he died there on 21 August, 1853. His pension application was very hard to read. He received a yearly pension of $43.88 for his service.

"I entered the service about the last of September, 1777." Jacob served in the New York militia for five weeks in 1777 and for three months in 1778, 1779, 1780, and 1781. In 1782 he served for six weeks. He was in no battles during this time.

Sources: 1. D.A.R. Lineage Book, Vol. 70. 2. Pension Papers S23132.

****

Charles Bowles age 14 (African American)

Charles Bowles was born in 1761 in Boston, Massachusetts, and he died on 16 March, 1843 in Franklin County, New York. His father was African and his mother was a daughter of the famous Colonel Morgan who served in the Continental Army. At the age of 12 Charles was placed in the home of a Tory, which he did not like.

At the age of 14 he enlisted as a waiter in the American army. Charles served in the army as a waiter for the first two years in the 6th Massachusetts Regiment and may have participated in the Battles of Harlem Heights and Trenton. Peter Salem a freed slave, who fought at Concord and Bunker Hill was also a member of this regiment.

"I enlisted into the Army of the United states for eight weeks and served my time out and in the month of January, 1776 I enlisted for the term of one year in Captain Malicah Glensons Company in Colonel John Nixons Regiment in the Massachusetts line and served my time out and then enlisted for two months and served my time out and was honorably discharged at __?__ Pennsylvania."

"Sometime in July 1777 I enlisted for four months. The later part of March or first part of April 1778, I enlisted (as I then supposed for two years but being young and ignorant) when my two years was up I applied to Colonel Cilley for a discharge but he told me I was enlisted for 3 years and I served the term of three years. I was in Captain Emersons Company in Colonel Cilleys Regiment in General Poors Brigade in the New Hampshire line."

Charles served in the 1st New Hampshire under the command of Colonel Joseph Cilley. He probably fought at the Battle of Monmouth in the June of 1778 and participated in Sullivan's Expedition in 1779. His regiment was left to defend the Hudson Highlands when Charles was discharged in the spring of 1781.

After the war he lived in New Hampshire and engaged in farming. He married Mary Corliss his cousin, and granddaughter of Colonel Morgan. He later became a Baptist preacher.

Sources: 1. Colored Patriots of the American Revolution by William Cooper Nell. 2. Massachusetts, Mason Membership Card. 3. Pension Papers S44640.

****

James Boyd age 14

James Boyd was born on 8 May, 1763 in Bucks County, Pennsylvania, and he died on 12 March, 1846 in Patrick, Virginia. His father was drafted but was unable to march due to a severe beating he received from the Tories, so James volunteered to go in his father's place. James made an amendment to his earlier pension statement on 11 October, 1832.

He enlisted for a three month tour in 1777 with the main purpose of pursuing Tories. In September of 1778 he volunteered again, and he spent the three month tour looking for Tories. He enlisted for a third time in 1779.

"The section of Country where the residue of my services were performed was in the North western settlement lying along the East side of the blue ridge of mountains that this section of Country so much abounded with tories and robers who formed themselves in companies concealing on the west side of the county would Frequently pounce down upon the friends to liberty to kill and plunder, and off again to their places of concealment, that it became essentially necessary for the safety of the inhabitants to keep companies of men garrisoned or imbodied at given points along the East side of the mounty to prevent those depredations and if possible subdue those enemies to liberty. For this purpose Captain James Gidens and his company of militia was stationed at Asbers mills in Surry County North Carolina about ten miles from the mountain near the Virginia line. There was but two choices for men to take in this section of country. One was to join the tories and out lyres and of cours take to the woods and the other was to join the whigs take the field or garrison or both as occasion mite require. I became of age to go on the muster roll May 1779. I was accordingly enrolled in Capt James Gidens company. I was permitted to stroll where I pleased until October following—October 1779 the first day of that month to the best of my recollection I entered the service under Captain James Gidens as a private soldier during the war. Gidens was at that time stationed at asbers mills above mentioned I remained here in garrison at least two months during which time a file of men was sent out in Pursuit of Shearad Adkins and William Worton tory Robers who had taken and brought to head quarters tried and condemned to be hanged. They were marched to the gallows under guards. While their funeral was preaching only 15 minutes to live (according to orders) Colonel Shepherd arrived with a reprieve for them they were accordingly reprieved. While one of the guard was standing the breech of his gun on

the ground his hand on the muzzle the gun went off and shot the whole contents through his hand I was then given up to General Pickens as stated in my declaration."

James stayed with the troops of General Pickens in their winter quarters. During the spring, he and the other men were in pursuit of Indians around Washington County. James rejoined Captain Gidens.

"Capt Gidens took me and several others and went over the mountains in Grayson county Virginia a distance of about twenty miles in search of Burk and Adkins tory robers and with the aid of a tory who betrayed them into our hands we engaged this tour about ten days and then returned to our garrison in a short time after this a company of men was sent out in search of Adam Short another mischievious tory who caught him and hung him at Stuarts creek. I was present when he was hung but did not go in search of him. In a short time after this William Koil a leading tory with four others stole some horses belonging to John Griffeth of Surry County NC. Capt Gidens not knowing how many was with Koil sent Loeut Gidens and four others in pursuit of them who came up with them so near to our fort that the fireing if their guns was distinctly heard I with several others were sent to their aid when they reach the spot they found Lieutenant Gidens and two others ded on the ground. The others of the whigs had made their escape they also found one of the tories killed and another wounded whom Koil was attempting to heave up but was compelled to drop him on whom the work of death was soon finished they pursued Koil on up Salt petre ridge to the top of the mountain a distance of about ten miles could not over take him returned back again to the garrison Captain Gidens took as many of his company as had horses to ride and went in pursuit of Koil and his troy company I and the rest of Gedens company who stayed joined Capt Eliphas Sheltons company of Virginia militia and was ordered to the upper end of Henry county Virginia to guard the neighborhood in gidens absence. Capt Gidens in this time having returned to his station Sheltons company was marched off and I again returned to Gidens company. A short time after a man by the name of Nickols together with 3 or 4 others murdered William Letcher a whig and a worthy citizen of Henry county Virginia on the Ararat river within a few miles of our garrison."

Captain Gidens pursued William Nichols and caught him near Eutaw Springs, South Carolina and hung him. When the Captain returned he sent James and 20 or 30 others under the command of Lieutenant Thomas Carlan to watch General Cornwallis, who had been seen in the area. Soon Captain Gidens and his militia were sent to Guilford Court House and arrived there just after the battle on March 16, 1781. They stayed there until Cornwallis surrendered in October of 1781. James was discharged at the end of October of 1781. James received $43.33 a year for his service.

Sources: 1. U.S. Pension Roll of 1835. 2. Pension Papers S12269.

****

Ariel Bradley age 8

Ariel Bradley was born on 30 December, 1767 in Salisbury, Connecticut, and he died in 1857 in Mogadore, Ohio. He married Chloe Lane on 27 September, 1792 in Connecticut. He later served in the War of 1812 in Darrow's Battalion Ohio Militia.

Before the Battle of White Plains in October of 1776, he was chosen by General George Washington to enter the British lines to learn their numbers and troop distributions. He took an old horse and a bag of grain under the pretense of going to the mill. When he rode into the British camp, he was as expected arrested. Ariel showed no fear or any unusual curiosity, as he was taken to British officers for questioning. During this time he was making mental notes of the information he was sent to retrieve.

The British officers questioned Ariel, who acted unconcerned and innocent, and eventually the officers let him go. They thought him to be more of a fool than a spy. As Ariel was leaving one British officer was heard to say, *"I believe this little devil will betray us."* Ariel later returned to the camp of General Washington with the information he was sent to gather.

Sources: 1. D.A.R. Lineage Book, Vol. 143. 2. D.A.R. Plaque. 3. Sons of the American Revolution Application. 4. Ohio Historical Marker in Mogadore.

****

Richard Bradley age 14

Richard Bradley was born on 25 December, 1762 in Duplin County, North Carolina, and he died 20 August, 1827 in Tennessee. He married Catharine Taylor on 24 July, 1783 in North Carolina.

"I enlisted as a Continental soldier on the 9th day of August 1777 in the North Carolina Continental line under the command of Captain

Henry Dawson in the 7th Regt. The latter end of the same year I with several others were marched to the Northwest and joined the Army when they were in Winter Quarters at the Valley Forge, and was there turned into the first Carolina Regt. Under the command of Captain James Reed, the Regt. Was commanded by Col Thomas Clark, we marched from the Valley Forge in pursuit of the British until the battle of Monmouth in which I was, some time after they took up winter Quarters at Paramus court house, we marched from thence to west point on Hudson river, from thence we were ordered to south Carolina for the relief of Charles Town--and I was in that siege and we were all captured on the 12th of May 1780 and I remained a prisoner with the British two years and three months and made my escape from them and joined General Green at Ashley Hall about twenty mile above Charles Town and there I got my discharge in the Fall of the year 1782."

After he was discharged he served in the militia with his brother John in 1783 on a tour against the Tories in North Carolina. His son Abraham wrote about his 3 month tour in 1783. *"...during his 3 months service he was engaged in a skirmish or battle with the Tories and took some prisoners, shot one of them..."* For his service Richard received a yearly pension of $88.

Sources: 1. Census of 1790 & 1820. 2. U.S. Pensioners 1818-1872. 3. Pension Papers W896.

****

John Brasher age 10 or 11

John Brasher was born on 15 May, 1764 in New York, and he died in 1840 in Cincinnati, Ohio. He married (1) Kezia Brown in 1784 and then (2) Sarah. He served as a waiter for his father.

"I was taken by Capt Henry Brasher in the year 1775 in the summer of that year as a waiter to said Capt. Brasher in General McDouglas Brigade Col Malans Regt. Major James Abner and continued in that character and in that duty until November 1776, ending at White Plains in said State of New York."

"I was enrolled at the age of Sixteen years and stood a draft in Capt. Arthur Smiths Company of militia Col Hosbrooks Regt, Genl Clintons Brigade at Newbury after which I was employed to drive a team of oxen, for one month in the winter to hall logs to __?__ up the __?__ at Polessolls Island two mile above West Point thence held to military duty."

"The Company lay or were stationed one mile below Tarry Town on the farm of the widow Van Wart the mother of Isaac Van Wart who with Paulding and Williams captured Andre at that place and when off guard duty had much amusement at shooting at a mark, foot racing and wrestling with said Isaac Van Wart, Paulding, the son of John Paulding, and family at that time resided at the village of Tarry Town which I was drummer to the Continental company."

Isaac Van Wart, John Paulding, and David Williams, all a few years older than John Brasher, were in the local militia. They were on morning guard duty on 23 September, 1780 when they stopped John Andre.

Major Andre was a British officer and spy. Benedict Arnold had provided Andre with civilian cloths and a passport so that Andre could escape back to British lines. Andre carried hidden papers, in Arnold's handwriting, showing the British how to capture West Point. Around 9 in the morning Andre approached the three young sentries. Andre thought they were Tories because Pauling was wearing a Hessian soldier's overcoat. He had stolen the coat when he had escaped from Tories while visiting his girlfriend. The spy told the boys that he must not be detained because he was a British officer on a mission.

The boys took Andre prisoner, but Andre said he was an American officer and showed them his fake passport. The boys were now very curious so they searched him and found the incriminating papers. As luck would have it, Paulding was the only one of the three boys that could read. Andre bribed the boys by offering them his watch and horse if they would let him go. They turned down the lucrative offer and took him to their headquarters. Because of the boy's heroic efforts, Andre was hung as a spy, Benedict Arnold was removed from the army as a traitor, and West Point was saved.

Later with the recommendation of George Washington, Congress awards the three boys the first military decoration of the United States, a federal pension of $200 a year, and they are given nice farms by the state of New York. All three boys survived the war and lived long lives.

Sources: 1. The Official Roster of the Soldiers of the American Revolution Buried in the State of Ohio. 2. Sons of the American Revolution Application. 3. Census of 1820 and 1830. 4. U.S. Pension roll of 1835. 5. Pension Papers S16057 6. The Traitor and the Spy: Benedict Arnold and John Andre by James Thomas Flexner.

****

Byrd Brazil age 12

     Byrd Brazil was born in North Carolina in 1765, and died in Hancock County, Georgia in 1845. He enlisted 5 May, 1776 in Chatham County, North Carolina. He served as a private in Captain William Brinkley's Company with the 3rd Regiment commanded by Colonel William Alston.

     He stated in his pension application, *"I marched to Charleston and stayed there about three months from Charleston I marched to Savannah did not continue to Savannah long went thence to Ossabaw Island and shortly thereafter returned to Halifax North Carolina."* (Ossabaw Island is an island off the Georgia coast about twenty miles from Savannah.)

     The 3rd Regiment joined General George Washington's army at Valley Forge for the winter of 1777-1778. Due to a shortage of men several North Carolina regiments were combined and reformed into Captain Benjamin William's Company of the 2nd North Carolina Regiment under the command of Brig. General Lachlan McIntosh.

     It would be a hard winter for Byrd, because the North Carolina Regiments, were so far from home that it took a long time for their supplies to reach them. At least twice the North Carolina Regiments got first pick of some incoming supplies because of their lack of food and clothing. Only about a third of the men had shoes, and their feet were bloody from the long marches. They suffered heavy losses compared to other regiments. Out of 1,072 men 204 died that winter at Valley Forge. About 500 women, mostly relatives of the men, were in camp as cooks and nurses. Even with the exceptionally harsh conditions only a few dozen men deserted, 12 year old Byrd Brazil stayed until the spring.

     In the spring Washington's army marched with confidence after being trained as soldiers by Baron Von Steuben, They engaged and defeated the British forces at the Battle of Monmouth. Byrd wrote, *"We reached the Battle of Monmouth about the time the battle was closed, my company after the British went to New York, marched up the North River to a crossing place and came down the River and encamped near New York until I was discharged."*

     Byrd was discharged in October of 1778 near New York. From there he marched south to Virginia under Major Davidson. When he applied for his pension, which was 27 pages long, in January of 1833 he was living in Hancock County, Georgia. He received 228 acres of land for his service in the war. He married a woman named Elizabeth and they had at least six children. In the 1820 census he was listed as a farmer with 6 slaves, and in the 1830 census he had 5 slaves.

This many slaves indicated he had a very large farm. Land records indicated that he purchased many acres over the years. In 1844 he wrote his will naming four daughter, one son, and one granddaughter as his heirs.

Sources: 1. Pension application for Byrd Brazil S31571. 2. Historic Register of Officers of the Continental Army During the War of the Revolution by Francis Bernard Heitman. 3. Regiments at Valley Forge, U.S. History. org. 4. Charlotte and the American Revolution by Richard Plumer. 5. Census records 1820, 1830, and 1840. 6. U.S. Complied Service Records, Post-Revolutionary War Volunteer Soldiers, 1784-1811. 7. Will of Byrd Brazil.

****

George Breckenridge age 12

George Breckenridge was born on 24 July, 1768 in Augusta, Virginia, and he died on 12 November, 1852 in Caledonia, Missouri. He married Elizabeth Cowan on 3 March, 1797. He fought with his father Alexander at the Battle of Kings Mountain on 7 October, 1780. It was reported that young George took an active part in the battle.

Sources: 1. Tombstone 2. History of Southwest Virginia 1746-1786, Washington County 1777-1870 by Lewis Preston Summers. 3. Revolutionary Soldiers 1776-1783 Washington County, Virginia.

****

Andrew Breden age 14

Andrew Breden was born on 4 February, 1765 in Fairfax County, Virginia, and he died on 19 November, 1843 in Anderson, Tennessee. He married Dorothy McNealy on 7 February, 1793 in Montgomery County, Virginia. His father Alexander Breden served as a Captain in the Colonial Army. Andrew received a yearly pension of $20.

"I volunteered in the army of the United States in the year 1779 in the month of July or August with Col Pickensthe no of the regiment I do not now recollect, neither do I recollect the name of my Capt. I marched under Col Pickens to Haw River in North carolina, then around, as I believe, Ramsour's at which place and at the Mills of Ramsours as I believe on said River we had a battle with a few British and some tories in this engagement the enemy retreated and left the Mills, I continued with

Col Pickens in this section of the country on Haw River, Hughes or Stony creek in Guilford and orange Counties for the space of three months. I received a discharge."

"Some short length of time after I returned from this tour of duty, I volunteered under Captain Edward Gwinn and Lt. Thomas Howell, was Remarched to Haw River in North carolina, Where a body of Tories were stationed and we took possession of their station. We marched from there to Stony Creek, to a settlement called Bracken's Settlement, where a number of Tories were embodied with whom we had a battle, which the enemy fled. We then Marched to the falls or shoals on Haw River, near the residence of my captain in Guilford County, NC. We ranged the country on Haw River for several days, then marched to Stony Creek, taken 4 or 5 Tories, sent them under Lt. Howell to headquarters. I was remarched to the falls or shoals of Haw River to the Eesidence of Capt. Gwinn and were then discharged."

"I Returned home about one week, went to the station of Col Pickens on Haw River, was with him six weeks in securing the country on Haw River. I received from his colonel in orange County, North Carolinaa, I believe, a written discharge. I then went and Joined Capt. Gwinn, was under him, Ranging the counties of Guilford, orange and some adjoining counties for two months. Having now Regulated the Tories as was thought, in this section of the country, I was discharged. Captain Gwinn Raised a Company in which applicant volunteered. I marched to High's Creek in Guilford, North Carolina in order to protect the inhabitants in that location of the country from the Tory depredations. We taken after Tories, they bolted or fled, they left their position. I ranged the country under Captain Gwinn this tour, three months and was discharged at Capt. Gwinn's in the month of June or July 1780."

"In the month February or March 1781, I volunteered under Lieutenant Howell and Marched after the Tories that was stationed at Stony Creek, in Guilford or Orange County, but the company to which I belonged was thought insufficient to encounter the enemy, we then joined Captain Gwinn, marched to Stony Creek. Before the company reached that place, the enemy left the country. I served in the Revolutionary War, seventeen months at the several different terms as above stated."

Sources: 1. Census 1830 & 1840. 2. U.S. Pensioners 1818-1872. 3. Virginia Marriages 1660-1800. 4. Pension Papers W779.

****

Adam Breton age 14

Adan Breton was born on 8 May, 1763 in Hampshire County, Virginia, and he died in February, 1834 in Owen Indiana. His pension request was rejected because he only had a total of 4 months and 5 days of service. The last tours of duty occurred in 1786 and 1791 which was after the revolution.

"I was a substitute for James Lawson in a company that was drafted in what is now called Fiatt County in the State of Pennsylvania, that Thomas Brown was the commander of said company Said Company was stationed at Red Stone old Fort situate on a bluff on the Monongahela River, to guard a magazine of Powder and lead, that the officer above named was the commander of the Guard aforesaid, that the time for which said company was drafted was one month, that it was in the year 1778 I believe in the month of February in said year, that I served during said Tour of one month."

"That a second Guard like the first above named at the County of Fiatt was raised at the expiration of the months service above stated to take the placed of those whose term of service was on the eve of expiring in the month of March (as I believe) in the year 1778."

"That during this last named month I was employed as a substitute for John Purdy, and served during the last named term of <u>one month</u> as his substitute, in guarding the magazine aforesaid, that for neither of the above terms I never received a written discharge for his service or if so time has erased from my memory the recollection of the fact The magazine aforesaid was guarded to prevent its being destroyed by the tories."

"That I again entered the service of the United States in what is now called Kentucky, then Virginia in the commencement of the summer in the year 1781, that the County at the time I does not distinctly recollect, that it was in what is now called Mercer County, that the company was commanded by James Kincaid, that the term for which the company last named was drafted was for <u>one month</u>, that we were stationed at the mouth of Shawny run where it empties into the Kentucky river, that the company aforesaid was stationed at the place aforesaid for the purpose of guarding the continental buffaloe meet, that was brought there by canoes on the Kentucky river, I served during the term last aforesaid and was discharged, that the reason which induces me to believe that it was early in the summer, it that we pealed bark to sleep on during said term, that I knows it was in the summer season of that year."

"I again entered the service of the United States on the Ground where Danville now is, in what was then Virginia now Kentucky, that this was in the month of October 1782, that Samuel Kirkham was captain, Henry Grider Lieutenant of the company, that the Colonel of the regiment to which said Company belonged was by the name of Benjamin Logan, that George Rogers Clark was the General who commanded in chief we were marched across the Kentucky river, and on to the forks of Licking river, thence down Licking on the south side thereof to its mouth, thence across the Ohio, near or at the place where Cincinnati now stands – where there was a cabin, called the buckeye Cabin where the invalids were placed, thence to Old Chilacothe on the little Miami, here the indians stole some of horses among whose was our adjutant's (John Crows) thence to the Pickaway town on the big Miami, there we remained some days, a part of the army scouted over the adjoining country while we were here the indians shot across the Miami and shot one Reynolds in the hip of which wound he died as we returned home, Capt. William McCraken was also wounded and died on his return home at a big hill near where Cincinnati now is. McCracken was a captain of the light horse and Greene Clay was Lieutenant of the Light Horse. that after we left where Cincinnati now is on our return home we had no provisions save what we killed in the woods till we got home; that this tour was for five weeks, we got home in November 1782."

"That I again entered the service of the United States at what is now called Garrett County in the State of Kentucky in the month of September in the year 1786, that I was employed as a substitute for Edmund Parker Capt. John Downing – Lieut. William Montgomery, the major was by the name of James Dowing Col. Barnett, and G. R. Clark General, we were marched across the Ohio river at the falls here three soldiers were drowned in crossing, named John Brunts Macum McCullum Shaw. from thence we were marched across Blue river to vincennes. a part were sent round by water with the __?__ and provisions, I was one of those who were marched across by land, the waited at Vincennes ten days for the cannon and provisions, when we got to Vincennes two companies were sent on down the Wabash to meet the cannon and provisions. the companies that were selected were commanded by Captains Robert Saunders and Robert Floyed among whom I was taken as on of Capt. Floyed company that after we met with the boats a part of the company were marched on land as a land guard, after we returned to Vincennes. and thence crossed the Wabash and marched some distance, then recrossed, and were marched some distance further when the provisions *were about to fail, and the officers called a council, as to whether they should go further, that the officers and some of them gave out the idea that the soldiers must starve if they went on, and then voted in the Council to go on, among whom was one Capt. Baker Ewing, here a large portion of the soldiers determined to return and marched about a half mile back, when the remainder of the army came, on back and they were marched on back home by way of Vincennes that they had little or no provisions from Vincennes to the falls of the Ohio. that this tour was for six weeks, that we had no engagements, that they had but four beeves when they started back, and they were lost before we got to Vincennes that during this last tour I served as a substitute as aforesaid and for which I got a gun."*

"I was drafted and served as a substitute as above stated, for which I received no compensation from Government. I volunteered in what is now called Waynes Campaign while in Mercer County Ky – in the year 1791 under Capt. Daniel Barley, Henry Grider Lieutenant of the company Col. Caldwell commanded the regiment to which I belonged, Brig Gen'l. Thomas Barbee, Major ___?___ Scott Anthony Wayne Commander in Chief, rendezvoused at Scott County Kentucky, thence to Cincinnati, thence to Fort Recovery, thence to where the Rivers Oglaze [sic: Auglaize], and Maumee form a junction there we destroyed much corn, thence, down the river to where we had an engagement with the Indiana's after the battle was over here, we were marched back to where we built Fort Defiance, thence we marched to Greenville for provisions, thence to Fort Wayne, and from thence we were marched home by way of Cincinnati This tour was for four months, and for this I received pay."

Source: 1. Pension Papers R1178.

****

David Brewer age 13

David Brewer was born in 1762 in Framingham, Massachusetts, and died on 12 December, 1834. He received a yearly pension of $68.66.

Note: This pension was particularly had to read. Some of the pages had minor damage and the ink was very dark.

"On the 19th of April 1775 I marched from Holliston in said county to Cambridge said county on hearing of the British & all out to Concord and Lexington—I staid at five days at Cambridge doing duty as a private soldier when I enlisted in the Massachusetts Militia service for the term of eight months in Col. Doolittles regiment and Holden was my Lieut Col.

And Moore of Dartmouth in the county of Worchester was my major. John Leland of said Holliston was my captain until after the Battle of Bunker Hill when a gentleman by the name of Jacob Miller took command of the company. I did duty as a soldier on Bunker Hill in the Battle of June 17, 1775."

At the Battle of Bunker Hill fought on 17 June, 1775 David Brewer was part of the 6th Massachusetts Regiment. The day before the battle David was with several regiments on Breed's Hill building fortifications in preparation of British attacks. Early in the afternoon of the 17th the British advance up the hill toward the American fortification. The British came under "heavy and severe fire" and retreated. General Howe ordered them to attack again and they were met with the same results. During the battle Major Willard Moore of David's regiment was shot and later dies. One of his soldiers said that *"he met a soldier's death."*

The British launched a third attack and forced the Americans to retreat. Most of them were out of ammunition, since they had only about 15 shots each at the start of the battle. They also had run out of water by the start of the morning. In less than two hours the British had a victory but at the cost of 1,054 men killed or wounded.

"At the expiration of said eight months in the latter part of December I again enlisted for two months in the service and served out the whole ten months—when I was enlisted, but my gun and equipment were obtained by my officers for the service of my country—I came home in __?__ of the last day of February or the first of March 1776."

"In the last days of June 1778 I volunteered my services as a soldier being then a resident of Framingham and enlisted as a corporal for six months in Captain Simon Edgells company of the Massachusetts militia—on the first day of July following I marched with about a dozen men under me to Providence and put myself under the command of Col Wade—I think he was from Plymouth County—Capt Simon Edgell on in about ten days after me—In the latter part of July we were marched on to the Island of __?__ Island to the south of Portsmouth thence we marched and encamped before Newport which was then occupied by the British and staid there till the French fleet arrived. Soon after the __?__ of said fleet we were marched off of the island to Tiverton at the end of the term of six months we were dismissed."

"On the 16th of September 1779 I received a captain commission again in the militia of aforesaid in a company in the Regiment of Col Abner

Perry—about the last of June 1780 I was ordered by Col Perry to Rhode Island—I went under said Perry as a captain with my company John Trembridge was my Lieut Col & __?__ was my Major. In this time I served about a month."

Sources: 1. Massachusetts Society of the Sons of the American Revolution. 2. Sons of the American Revolution Application. 3. Pension Papers S4974.

****

Henry Brewer age 14

Henry Brewer was born in March of 1765, and he died in Ohio on 20 February, 1829. He married Sarah Hawke on 14 February, 1786 in Berkeley, Virginia. He served 2 years in the Virginia Militia. He first enlisted under Captain John Millen in Colonel Joseph Crockett's Regiment in December of 1779. He was discharged in December of 1781. In April of 1782 he enlisted in Captain George Shaffner's Company, under Colonel Charles Armand until the fall of 1782.

In 1779 Colonel Crockett was ordered to raise a regiment, and then to proceed down the Ohio River to Kentucky to assist George Rogers Clark. For the next 18 months the regiment was in several battles with the Northwestern Indians on the Miami River.

Sources: 1. National Genealogical Society Quarterly Vol. 33, 1945. 2. Virginia Marriages 1740-1783. U.S. Revolutionary War Rolls 1775-1783. 3. Pension Papers S42093. 4. Biographical Sketch of Colonel Joseph Crockett by John Wilson Townsend and Samuel Woodson Price.

****

William Brewster age 14

William Brewster was born in 1762 in Winchester County, New York, and he died on 19 April, 1834 in Ohio. He received $80 for his service.

"I entered the service of the United States under the following named officers and served as herein stated viz Captain Goodwin Lieutenant Benjamin Benscouter my field officers were General Heath Col Swartout the name of my Major I do not recollect at Fishkill New York in the year 1776 and from there took water and landed at Fishkill and marched from there to Kings bridge and from there to the White plains and was there during the battle but was not brought in to the engagement and some days after the battle was over marched back to the North River

to Fort Constitution and there remained until discharged having served *"Five months"* and again entered the service at a place called Continental village near Pickskill New York in the year 1777."

His last tour of duty, lasting seven months, was spent standing guard and performing other military duties. When he was discharged he enlisted again as a substitute for William Langeton. He spent the next three months serving near Continental village.

General Heath ordered the construction of barracks to shelter 1,500 to 2,000 men and named the small village "Continental Village." The village, empty at the time, and burned and its supplies looted by the British in October, 1777.

Sources: 1. The Constitution of the Society of Sons of the Revolution and By-Laws and Articles of Incorporation of the Ohio Society. 2. Pension Papers S3084.

****

George Bridges age 14

George Bridges was born on 12 February, 1762 in Elizabethtown, North Carolina, and he died 20 October, 1834 in St. Clair County, Illinois. He married Margaret Ann Edwards. George received a pension of $30 a year.

"I enlisted into the Army of the United States, in the State of North Carolina at Salisbury in Rowan County as a drummer on or about the tenth day of March in the year 1777 and was commanded as stated in his declaration of the fourth day of September 1832 and served as therein stated, and was in the service of the United States as a drummer till October 1778 when I was discharged. I was acquainted with Generals Marion, Gates & Green also with Colonel Washington & Drum Major Hervey of Marion's Brigade. He declares that he served for about nineteen months as a regular soldier and ranked as a drummer. I was drafted at Salisbury in the County & State aforesaid in the month of June 1780 and was commanded as stated in my aforesaid declaration of the 4th September 1832 and served as therein stated in said declaration and was in the service for 3 months as a private when I was discharged and returned home. I was drafted again at the same place as stated above the last of October or the first of November in the year 1780 and was commanded as stated in the said declaration of the 4th of September 1832 and served as therein stated and was out for 3 months as a private and was then regularly discharged the last of January or first of February

1781. Soon after my return from the Army the British & Tories came to Salisbury when I volunteered and went against them, and was taken a prisoner at the taking of the town and was kept for some time when I made my escape and returned home, how long I was a prisoner I do not recollect. In either the month of April or May 1781 my brother William Bridges was drafted at Salisbury in the County & State aforesaid, and I took his place and served as a private soldier and was commanded by Captain Gamble & as stated in the aforesaid declaration of the 4th of September 1832 and served as stated therein and in the Battle with Fanning the notorious Tory & as stated in the said declaration. I served not less than the periods mentioned below and in the following grades. For one year and 7 months I served as a drummer and for 6 months served as a private soldier and for 3 months I served as a substitute as a private soldier and for ___?___ service I claim a pension."

Sources: 1. U.S. Pension roll of 1835. 2. Pension Papers S32139.

****

Abner Briggs age 14

Abner Briggs was born on 16 February, 1764 in Taunton, Massachusetts, and he died on 4 February, 1839 in Portland, Maine. He received a yearly pension of $80.

"I served eight months in Col. Jacobs Regt. In the Massachusetts line in the year 1778. I then enlisted in the Rhode Island Regt. For twelve months and served the time out. In July 1780 I enlisted in the Mass. Regt. Commanded by Col. Brooks. I served six months in said Regt. I was in the engagement under General Sullivan at Quaker Hill about seven miles from New Port Rhode Island in August 1778."

Abner served in the Massachusetts Militia and was at the Battle of Rhode Island on 29 August, 1778. This battle was the first attempt of the French and Americans to fight together following France's entry into the war. Quaker Hill was one of three hills where the Americans took a stand against the British. Before they retreated the Americans held off several British attacks.

Sources: 1. Pension Papers S28656. 2. D.A.R. Lineage Book, Vol. 49.

****

Benjamin Briggs age 13

Benjamin Briggs was born 3 April, 1765 in Augusta County, Virginia, and he died in 1847 in Lincoln, Kentucky. He enlisted as a volunteer in the Virginia Militia in January of 1778, and he served under the command of Captain Benjamin Logan who became second-in-command of all the militia in Kentucky. During his two year enlistment, he stayed in and around Logan's Fort being constantly threatened by the Indians. He was in no regular battles during this time. Much of the time he performed the duties of a scout or spying the southern frontiers of Virginia.

In April of 1781 Benjamin was drafted and served one month at Samuel Briggs Station in Lincoln County under the command of Captain Robert Barnett. In 1782 he was ordered by Colonel Benjamin Logan to Estill's Station. In August of 1782 Benjamin again volunteered under the command of Colonel Logan to repel an invasion of the Shawnee Indians, and he was present at the militia's defeat at the Battle of Blue Licks on 19 August, 1782. Daniel Boone, who was present at the battle, lost his son in the fight.

Benjamin wrote in his pension application, *"That in the Month of September 1782 I again entered the service as a Draft under the command of Capt Robert Barnett William Casey was Lieutenant John Logan was Colonel & Benjamin Logan was the general & marched from Lincoln County to the mouth of Licking River where they were joined by Genl George R Clark with some regular troops & other Militia Genl Clarke assumed the command and they marched up the Miami River as high as the pickaway Towns which was taken after a Battle with the Indians & he served a Tour of Two months and was verbally discharged at the mouth of Licking River by Capt Robert Barnett."*

The battle Benjamin wrote about was between the militia and loyalists and their Indian allies. The attack and victory on the Shawnee Indian Village was the final battle of the Revolutionary War in the Ohio territory. About 16 Indians were killed including their chief and numerous supplies of the Indians were destroyed.

"In the month of November I think 1782 I again entered the service as a volunteer militiaman under Capt John Woods John Logan was the Col Benjamin Logan was Genl I do not recollect the other officers. For the purpose of guarding the Emigrants to the western country through the wilderness into the interior of Kentucky which was still infested by the Indians."

Benjamin Briggs lived the remainder of his life in Lincoln County, Kentucky. He and his wife had five children. He received a pension for $80.00 a year for his service. His name was later removed from the pension rolls and an investigation started in 1837 to restore his name. In his pension file is a letter front and back that may explain the problem. Because the ink from each side had bled into the other side, and the content could not be read.

Sources: Pension Papers S30889. 2. Historical Records of Old Crab Orchard, Lincoln County Kentucky Revolutionary War Soldiers.

****

Aaron Brister age 14 (African American)

Aaron Brister, also called Alexander, was born in 1762, and he died in August of 1821 in Wayne County, New York. He married Betsey Tolibel during the war in 1778. Because he enlisted at a young age it is very likely that he served as a substitute. This raises an interesting question. After the war did he receive his freedom in Virginia? If he received his freedom after the war it would not have been granted to his wife and children.

Aaron remained in Virginia with his wife until he moved to Palmyra, New York around 1805. The census of 1820 in Palmyra lists him as a "Free Colored Person" along with his wife and three children. This author suspects that he and his family left Virginia as fugitive slaves and ran off to New York.

After the war slaves began to travel north where they could live as free persons. Much of the north was becoming anti-slavery and allowed fugitive slaves to settle to in their states. The Fugitive Slave Act of 1793 stated that slave owners and their agents had the right to search for escape slaves within the borders of free states. Once captured they would take the slaves before a judge and provide evidence that the slaves were indeed their property. If the court agreed with the evidence presented, then the slave owners or agents could return the slaves to their home states. The law also included a $500 penalty on any person who helped or concealed an escape slave.

This act had little support of the people in the north. They did not like these slave hunters coming into their towns and making threats to the citizens. As a result most of the Northern states did not enforce the laws. Several states enacted "Personal Liberty Laws" that gave the captured slave the right to a jury trial. Needless to say the Fugitive Slave Act increased ill feelings between southern and northern states. These ill feelings increased with the Fugitive Slave Act of 1850, and the issue would later provoke a war between the two regions.

"I enlisted in the town of Dumfries in Prince William County and State of Virginia in the company commanded by Captain Thomas Helm in the 3rd Virginia Regiment commanded by Colonel Weedon for two years in 1776 and that he continued to serve in the said Corps until the expiration of the aforesaid term of time when he was discharged from service at Philadelphia that he was in the Battle at York Island and White Plains."

Arron served in the 3rd Virginia Regiment under Colonel George Weedon for one year and nine months and was discharged in the spring of 1777. This would put his enlistment date around the winter of 1775. The 3rd Regiment was raised on 28 December, 1775 in Alexandria, Virginia.

Aaron fought in the Battle of Harlem Heights during the New York campaign. The battle began on 16 September. The 3rd Virginia joined Washington's army on 13 September, 1776 and the Battle of Harlem Heights began three days later. Aaron found himself in the thick of battle in a buckwheat field around what is today 116th street. The British army proved too strong and Washington was forced to retreat.

Aaron was also at the Battle of White Plains fought on 28 October, 1776. At this battle the 3rd Virginia were mainly spectators, because most of the fighting took place on Chatterton's Hill and the majority of the regiments engaged were from New York.

When Aaron filed for a pension in 1818 he stated that he was so lame from bad knees that he could not work. He stated that he had ¾ of an acre of land and still owed some money of the bank loan. He listed his total wealth at $115. 25. He received a yearly pension of $96, and he died three years later.

When Aaron's wife Betsey filed for a widow's pension it was rejected because she could show no proof of marriage. She sent back her reply on 11 September, 1844 through her agent. *"The parties at the time of the marriage were slaves and license was issued or record made of it, as it was never done in such cases."* Friends of Betsey wrote of her good character and wrote of the fact that they knew the couple to be married. She was given a widow's yearly pension of $80.

Sources: 1. Census of 1820. 2. For Virginia and for Independence: Twenty Revolutionary War Soldiers from the Old Dominion by Harry M. Ward. 3. Becoming Men of Some Consequence: Youth and Military Service in the Revolutionary War by John A. Ruddiman. 4. Pension Paper 17341.

****

Charles Broach age 14

Charles Broach was born in 1763 in Virginia, and he died on 29 September, 1829 in King William County, Virginia. He married a woman by the name of Martha in the spring of 1784. She received a widow's pension of $100 a year for his service.

"I enlisted for the term of three years, on the 23 day of December 1777 in Essex County in the state of Virginia in the company commanded by Captain Drury Ragsdale of the Regiment commanded by Col. Charles Harrison in the line of the State of Virginia on the Continental establishment; I continued to serve in the said Corps, or in the service of the United States untill the 13 day of December 1780, when I was discharged from service near Camblin *in the State of South Carolina; that he was in the Battles of Monmouth Courthouse and Camblin."*

Charles served in the 1st Continental Artillery Regiment also known as Harrison's Continental Artillery Regiment. At the Battle of Monmouth, which Charles was in, Mary Ludwig Hays who was the wife of an American artilleryman lived near the battlefield. During the battle she brought water for swabbing the cannons and for the thirsty men. The battle took place on 28 June, 1778 and the temperatures were over a hundred degrees. The artillery men nicknamed her "Molly Pitcher", because she brought water to them from a nearby spring.

The Battle of Camden was fought on 16 August, 1780 and the 1st Artillery Regiment took part. They arrived with their 12 field pieces about 9 in the morning of the 25th amidst the cheering of the soldiers. During the battle the Americans were being pushed back, and some of the Virginia and Maryland troops scrambled to save the artillery from falling into British hands.

Sources: 1. Touring South Carolina's Revolutionary War Sites by Daniel W. Barefoot. 2. U.S. Pensioners 1818-1872. 3. Virginia Historical Index Vol. I A-K. 4. Pension Papers W5921.

****

Reuben Brooks age 14

Reuben brooks was born on 19 October, 1763 in New Haven, Connecticut, and he died on 20 October, 1843 in Pittsfield, Massachusetts.

"I entered the service of the United States at Cheshire as a Substitute for one Solomon Brooks under Sergeant Moses Bradley who went with me to __?__ in the State of New York when the company to which said Solomon Brooks belonged was stationed. Said Solomon being sick was the cause of me taking his place. One Samuel Hitchcock was a Lieutenant in said company the Colonels name as I now recollect was Jackson. I continued to Serve as a Soldier at said __?__ N. York & at Millford Hill in the State of Connecticut & other places in Said Company until about the last of March 1779 when I was discharged."

"In the first week in July 1777 I entered the service of the United States in the State Troops of Connecticut—at New Haven in said State as a Substitute for one Isaac Brooks in the Company Commanded as near as I can recollect by one Captain Abner Brunnel and Major brays Battalion and in Capt Wards Regiment—I served as a Soldier in said Company at said New Haven until some time in the first part of the month of October 1779 when I was discharged."

"In four or five days after the <u>Dark Day</u> in the month of May 1780 then residing at Cambridge aforesaid was drafted into the Service of the United States for the Term of three months in the company Commanded by Captain Woodford & Lieutenant North, Ensigns name do not recollect, one of the Sergeants name was Bowen & the Col or Generals name was Parsons—I preformed Service in said Company at New Haven in said State until the latter part of the Month of August 1780—when I was— discharged."

The "dark day" that Reuben refers to occurred on 19 May, 1780 in the sky over New England. On that day there was unusual darkening of the sky. Several days prior to the 19th the sky had turned a dirty, yellowish color. When the darkness began around noon of the 19th, animal life reacted. Birds sung their evening songs then went silent, chickens returned to their roosts, cattle began to return to their barns, and it became necessary to light candles in the homes. The cause may have been a combination of smoke from forest fires, thick fog, and cloud cover.

It caused a panic in the Connecticut Senate Chamber. Abraham Davenport arose and said, *"If it is not the Day of Judgment there is no reason to adjourn; if it is I prefer to be found doing my duty; bring in candles."*

"The same day that I was discharged in said Month of August at said New Haven I again enlisted in the service of the United States in said Company as a Substitute for my father Samuel Brooks and remained in the Service of the United States in Said company at said New Haven Three Months—longer."

"In the month of August 1780 Gen Henry Dearborn then a Major in the Continental Services came to New Haven and called for volunteers to go out from said New Haven and dislodge the British who then had possession of <u>Morris Point</u>. I was one of the volunteers and was slightly wounded by a <u>musket Ball</u> on the right side of my face during the engagement the first day on said Morris Point—the British retreated on board their Boats the Second day of the engagement when Major Dearborn returned with the volunteers to said New Haven."

"In the latter part of the month of <u>March 1781</u> on the first of April on the same year I enlisted for one year at said Cambridge into the company commanded by Captain Cushom Guttle—Lieutenant Johnathan Hart the Ensigns name I do not recall, said Company marched to Middletown thence to Litchfield in said state & then to Poughkeepsie in the State of New York, & thence to Fishkill & other places. I was discharged at said Fishkill in the month of March 1782."

"In the month of April 1782 at said Cambridge I enlisted as a minute man for the Term of 8 months by Sergeant <u>Benj Hart</u> into a Company Commanded by a Captain by the name of Wadsworth or Billings which I do not recollect in the month of May following we were ordered to Litchfield in said state under Col Adams who Commanded the Regiment—thence to Poughkeepsie and thence to Fishkill & thence down the North River till I arrived opposite West Point where I remained some time & thence to Horseneck, from thence I marched in said company back to North River about 20 or 25 miles above New York thence up by the said River to a place called Oblong according to my best recollections where I was discharged in December 1782."

Sources: 1. New England's Dark Day from the Weather Doctor Almanac, 2004. 2. U.S. Pension Roll of 1835. 3. Sons of the American Revolution Application. 4. Chapter Sketches, Connecticut D.A.R. Patriots' Daughters, 1900.

****

Austin Brown age 14

Austin Brown was born on 21 July, 1762 in Hebron, Connecticut, and he died on 26 April, 1837 in Lima, New York. He married Anna Fox on 12 October, 1786. He received a yearly pension of $80.

"I enlisted the first day of January 1777 in Hebron in the State of Connecticut in the company commanded by Captain Seth Harmon in the 1st Connecticut Regiment commanded by Col Durgee, I continued to serve in said corps until the close of the wear when I was honorably discharged."

The 1st Connecticut Regiment was organized on 1 January, 1777 at Norwich, Connecticut. The Regiment saw action at the New York Campaign and the Battle of Monmouth. The Regiment was also at Valley Forge.

Sources: 1. Lineage Book National Society of the D.A.R. Vol. 27, 1898. 2. Pension Papers W23697.

****

John Brown age 12

John Brown was born in May of 1765 in Spartanburg, South Carolina, and he died on 8 August, 1847 in Oktibbeha County, Mississippi. He married (1) Elizabeth "Red Deer Crawford" c. 1785 who was the daughter of the Cherokee Indian Little Red Dear. They had 12 children until she died in 1810. On 3 May, 1811 John married (2) Jane "Jensey" Stephenson and they had 7 children. Jane received a widow's yearly pension of $80.

During the Revolutionary War John served with his father Colonel Andrew Jackson Brown. Colonel Brown was a full blooded Cherokee Indian. His son carried the nickname "Cherokee" John Brown. John's mother was Jane Long the sister of Brigadier General Nathan Young of the British army. According to family history when General Nathan Young met his sister's husband face to face after one battle he decided he could not fight his "own family" and he resigned his commission and returned to England.

"I entered the service as a volunteer for the term of <u>six months</u> on an expedition against the Indians in the year 1777, I was then indeed very young to be received as a soldier being only 12 years & two months old, yet I was received and discharged his term of duty whether I got a written

discharge for this Tour I do not know -- my Father was with me & mostly, as a parent would act attended to my rights if my father got one I do not know it having never seen one. In this expedition I was commanded by John Goyne as Captain, John Easley was Lieutenant the Ensign not remembered. The higher Officers from the length of time I do not show well recollect, but I think that Colonel Roebuck commanded the Regiment to which I was attached."

"Directly after this service was ended my Father volunteered for six months more, & a man called Buck Smith being drafted I went into the service as his substitute, being again along with my Father. My Officers were Joseph Warford Captain, John Butler Lieutenant, David Graham Ensign. I believe that I was attached to Roebuck's Regiment. This expedition was also against the Indians. This tour I faithfully served out and immediately after that I became a substitute for six months more for one Leonard Smith under the same command of Officers, which service I faithfully performed. In this last service we were called on to destroyed the Indian Towns & burn their corn, etc. this was done, with some pretty severe skirmishing & we returned from the expedition which had been accomplished -- by I think to -- a pretty warm engagement in the pass of a Mountain while going there, and another called the Ring Battle near what was called the middle settlements of the Indians -- so called from the Indians having surrounded them, & they had to fight their way through. It so happened however that I was not upon the spot, but performing other duty not far off & ran to the fight, arriving there about the time the whites had broken the ring, soon after the Indians retreated. -- That this six months service I performed fully & returned home."

"I then, together with his father (who had been an Indian spy) enlisted for twelve months under Captain Burnett (his Christian name not distinctly remembered though I am very sure it was either James or William) Lieutenant was Robert McWhorter, Ensign __ Medlock. I do not know what regular Regiment I was attached to but General Williamson was the person from whom they mostly received orders & supplies -- Col Andrew Pickens at that time had also a command over them. The troops to which I belonged were stationed at Jewetts corner, in South Carolina, near the upper parts of Abbeville District as it now stands. While in this service which was intended to have an effect on the Indians there was no general engagement, & before the time of service had fully expired a treaty was made with the Indians at that place. And at the end of this service I received a written discharge or rather my father whose name was Andrew Brown and acted as a spy received one including me his son, which I has *often seen. But I suppose that my father removed to Tennessee a great while ago, & is now dead, took it with him, it is not in my power to procure it. After this I volunteered several times in scouring after & skirmishing with the Tories but no engagement of importance."*

Sources: 1. Alabama Revolutionary War Residents. 2. Census 1790, 1800, 1810, and 1840. 3. Revolutionary War Pensioner Census 1841. 4. Pension Papers W5906.

****

Josiah Brown age 14

Josiah Brown was born on 1 January, 1764 in Westchester County, New York, and he died on 25 February, 1843 in Hinckley, Ohio. For his service he received $34.89 a year. His widow, Molly Blake, received a widow's pension of $53.22 a year for his service.

"I went as a substitute for my father in the Spring of 1778, the day and month I cannot now remember, I served as a Private in the Company of New York Militia, commanded by Lieutenant Tucker, I joined the company at Salem in the County of Westchester, State of New York where I resided, I marched from thence to New Castle, where my company & the other troops there were stationed to guard the lines, I remained there two weeks, and then was discharged."

"That in the fall of 1779 (the month and day I cannot remember) at Peekskill in the State of New York, I enlisted into Captain Field's company in Colonel Shepard's regiment in the Massachusetts' line, for and during the war, that I remained in the service three months and then my father hired a substitute, and I was discharged."

"In the month of July 1781 in the State of north Carolina, and according to the best of my recollection in the County of Rowan, I again entered into the service of the United States, for the term of three months, as a private and a substitute for one Daniel Dial, under Major Bowen in Colonel Malmada's Regiment, I immediately marched into South Carolina, and my Regiment joined General Green's Army,(I believe) at Santee Heights, the Army then marched to meet Lord Rawdon's Army, which Army they met in the month of September, at Eutaw Springs where a general engagement took place, and that during the battle I was stationed in the front lines, that the battle was a severe one, but that the Americans were Victorious, and that I understood we took 500 prisoners, that the enemy decamped during the succeeding night, that Colonel Malmada's Regiment was ordered to guard the prisoner, I marched with

the Regiment after the battle, to Salisbury in the State of North Carolina, where we arrived safely with the prisoners, I remained stationed at that place until the period of my enlistment expired."

The 180 men of the North Carolina Light Dragoons, of which Josiah was a member, was led in battle at Eutaw Springs by Colonel Marquis Francis de Malmedy. Josiah had survived one of the hardest fought and bloodiest battles of the Revolution. More than 500 Americans were killed or wounded in the four hour battle. The British had over 700 killed, wounded, or missing.

"In the month of November or December 1781 near Winchester village in Virginia I again entered into the service as a substitute, for a person whose name I do not recollect, for a term of two months, the troops among I served were stationed there to guard Lord Cornwallis' men who were then prisoners of war, I faithfully served out the full period of my enlistment and was then discharged; immediately after the discharge, I again entered the service in ____?____ Virginia as a private and as a substitute for another man whose name I do not remember, for a term of two months; I was stationed at first at Winchester and then marched to Fredericktown in Maryland and remained a month in each place guarding Cornwallis's prisoners."

Sources: 1. Census records for 1800, 1810, 1820, 1830, and 1840. 2. Tombstone. 3. U.S. Pension Roll of 1835. 4. Pension Papers S2101.

****

Reuben Brown age 12/13

Reuben Brown was born in 1765 in Preston, Connecticut, and he died on 9 August, 1824 in New London, Connecticut. He married Ruth Park on 10 February, 1788. Reuben received a yearly pension of $88.

"I served more than nine months in the war of the revolution upon the continental establishment as a fifer."

Thomas Gallet served with Reuben and wrote a letter to the pension office attesting to the fact that Reuben did served, *"He enlisted in the spring of 1778 & until said term of three years expired. He served more than nine months. I was a member of said company…..*[a large blot of ink covers several words]*…..was a musician of said company."* Reuben served as a fifer in Captain William's Company, under Colonel Samuel Webb's Regiment in the Connecticut Line.

Sources: 1. Tombstone 2. Sons of the American Revolution Application. 3. Pension Papers W17359. 4. Lineage Book D.A.R. Vol. LXI, 1907.

****

Eleazer Bulkley age 13

Eleazer Bulkley was born on 2 February, 1763 in Fairfield, Connecticut, and he died there on 5 February, 1843. He married Mary Ogden on 22 December, 1785. He received a yearly pension of $80. His father, James, was a weaver and a trade that Eleazer disliked. From the ages of 8 to 10 Eleazer attended school, and for the next couple of years he assisted his father and received a little pay. By the age of 13 Eleazer decided to leave home for the life as a sailor.

"At the commencement of the year 1776 the Defense, an armed vessel, was fitted out at New Haven by the state of Connecticut. A goodly number of men, and boys too, enlisted in her from Fairfield, I among the latter, after receiving (reluctantly) my father's permission. We were taken from Black Rock, to the vessel then lying in New Haven Harbor, on the 13th of March, 1776, and returned in the Defense to Black Rock, when we learned of the evacuation of Boston by the British. We proceeded to Boston. Our first encounter was with a sloop and brig, and after a close contest both surrendered. The loss on their side was thirty-nine killed and wounded; on ours none killed, and a few only wounded. Colonel Campbell (captain) was taken prisoner. He was afterwards exchanged for Colonel Ethan Allen, then in England a prisoner. After this action we sailed for New London, where we were put on another vessel, to which the name of our old one was given, and in June started on a cruise. When ten or twelve days out I espyed a sail. On coming up to it we found it a British ship from Jamaica We Took oit' her crew, put a prize master on board, and ordered her back to New London. Early one morning in the last of September we left Holmes Hole for New London. For two months we remained in New London. While here I was severely bitten by a squirrel, and nearly lost my life by a fall. My skull was fractured, and it was some time before I recovered. In December our captain resigned for a more important charge, and, under command of another, we sailed for the West Indies. Through the winter we cruised about the islands, captured four prizes, which safely arrived at the several ports to which they were sent. In the following spring we returned to New Bedford, when I and a number of others applied for a discharge. Some time alter this the Defense was ordered to Boston, to be cut in two and lengthened. We were discharged, and in the early summer I returned to my parents, after an absence of

thirteen months, and for the services rendered in the Defense at this early age I am now receiving a pension."

"After remaining at home three or four months 1 found a number of my associates were joining a company in Fairfield, to go to New London to a privateer that was being fitted out, and I resolved at once to go. I knew my parents would not willingly give their consent to my going, so in the evening I bundled up a few clothes and threw them to the ground from the chamber window, mingled again with the family, and as opportunity offered walked out, took up my clothes and went to Fairfield, where I joined the company and repaired to Black Rock, thence to New London. We soon went to sea, and, as we fell in with no vessels, concluded to repair to the Western Islands and intercept vessels bound for Quebec. Shortly after we captured a British vessel bound for this port, and ordered her back to New Bedford. I was one of the crew put on board. It was thirty-nine days before we made land, and for thirteen days were in want of provisions, subsisting mostly on English damaged biscuit boiled in beer. (The arrival of the brig safely seemed almost a miracle, after passing by all the British ports, and not meeting with a single British sail.) Shortly after this I took passage in a privateer sloop for New London. Having arrived here, and ashamed to go home, having earned nothing', I enlisted in the Brig Nancy, and sailed, on the first of November, for the West Indies. After cruising for some time without success we sailed for Cayenne, on the Surinam coast. Much time was spent here. We, however, resumed the cruise on the first of January. Off Antigua we were run down by what we supposed was a British vessel, but which, proved to be the American privateer, Bunker Hill, from Boston. This unlucky mistake broke up our cruise, and we bore up for home, arriving at New London in about fifteen days, after a cruise of five months. Here we found the Defense, bound for Fairfield, and I with a number of our crew took passage in her for Black Rock, not, however, to reach the latter place in this vessel, for we went back to New London. The ship brought up on a reef and was lost, and again I started for home in a galley. Arriving at Black Rock I gathered up my clothes and started for home, with a full determination to follow some other business beside privateering for the future. I was joyfully welcomed, not- withstanding my two last years had given my parents so much trouble and anxiety. My time now was mostly employed in going to school, and taking vacancies to keep guard."

"At the beginning of the year 1779, I enlisted with a company of forty men under command of Capt. E. Thorp. The guard was stationed close to the beach on the east side of Kinsey's Point; night only required close watch. But on the 7th of July, standing alone on the place now occupied by Oliver Perry, Esq., I saw two hundred British land on the hill opposite. They at once commenced the burning of Fairfield."

"At the opening of the year 1780 my time expired, and for this land service I am receiving a pension (1841) which, with my year's sea service, is termed a full pension. In April, 1780, I sailed for Nantucket with Capt. Stephen Thorp, where I with his consent, enlisted for a cruise to the "West Indies. At Providence we found our vessel ready for sea. We sailed the 20th of April for the island of Cuba. About the middle of May, when approaching our destination, the ship brought suddenly on a sunken reef, but by the Captain's stratagem was saved, and we again made sail for Hispaniola, entering in two or three days the harbor of St. Francis. Here we repaired damages. This incessant labor caused much sickness. I was brought very low with intermittent fever. Capt. Gardiner was very kind to me, showing a father's solicitude for me. I still grew weaker, and all hopes of recovery were given up. I thought if I could be at home, I should die content, but the idea of breathing my last in a foreign land, was most painful. A physician brought on board by the Captain, left a vial with my attendant, telling him to give me a few drops in water every half hour. Upon taking the first spoonful, it seemed to me like fire through my whole system, giving new life and animation, and I recovered slowly from that very hour, and in two or three weeks could walk about deck with assistance. On the first of July we sailed for Philadelphia, and on the morning of the fifteenth arrived off Cape Henlopen. All were in high spirits, expecting to be in Philadelphia that night. While waiting for a pilot we were boarded and taken possession of by two schooners of New York. The captors offered our crew their liberty if they would assist in getting the "Sally" afloat, (for she had been aground on a place called the Sheer,) they gladly accepted the proposal. Being still feeble, I lay in my berth. One of the Refugees ordered me on deck; as I was ascending the companion way slowly the ruffian aimed a blow at me with a lynch staff which just grazed my side. About sun-down, I, with the rest of the sick, were put in a boat and shoved off from the "Sally," and landed on Cape Henlopen beach; dragging our boat across the beach into Lewiston Creek, we rowed up to Lewiston, where we arrived at 10 o'clock at night. In the morning a sailor kindly gave me a straw hat, which was very acceptable, as I had nothing to screen my head from the scorching sun. I went across the street on to an eminence, to see if I could discover any signs of the "Sally" and her captors; not one of them was to be seen. I learned afterwards, that after getting the "Sally" afloat, the refugees violated their promise to *liberate the crew, confined them in a prison ship in New York, where nearly all of them died."*

"*As I stood upon the hill looking for my lost comrades, my feelings can be better imagined than described. It was a beautiful morning, about wheat harvest, the level fields covered with grain as far as the eye could reach, the birds singing, the quails whistling, and all nature seemed joyous; I alone was miserable, enfeebled by my long sickness, without friends or money, far from home, my shipmates all gone, despair overcame me, and I burst into tears. Recovering my spirits after a while, I returned to the village; the landlady gave me a bowl of bread and milk, the first food I had tasted since leaving the ship. The pilot who brought us ashore took me with him to Cape May, where was his home, and brought me to the Pilots' hotel, kept by Mr. Buck, making known to him my circumstances. Mr. Buck welcomed me with much kindness, telling me to stay with him till I was fully recovered. I remained with him nearly three weeks, and being now quite well again, I determined to return to Philadelphia. On taking leave of Mr. Buck and his family, I expressed my fears that I might never be able to make him any return for his kindness and attention to me. He replied, "You may yet become a useful member of society, if you do, and you meet a person in distress, relieve him, and in that way you will recompense me." Some months afterwards I bought in St. Thomas, a set of China, as a present for Mrs. Buck. I sent it by one of our crew, who proved to be a thief, and never delivered it. While in Philadelphia I agreed to go with Capt. Mathews in his market boat, and made three trips with him. When being fully recovered in health, I shipped in Brig Joanna for St. Thomas, for $40 the run. After a short passage, we arrived at St. Thomas. Our return cargo was salt; each of the crew had the privilege of 4 bags (8 bushels) to be sold for their benefit in Philadelphia. After a passage of six or seven weeks we reached Philadelphia, and on discharging the cargo my bags of salt were missing. This was a serious loss to me, as it cost little, and then sold for four dollars a bushel. I afterwards learned that the same rascal to whom I entrusted the set of China for Mrs. Buck, had stolen my bags of salt, and sold them in the night. I received the wages for my last voyage, deducting the physician's bill at St. Thomas, and after a few days shipped on a brig; for Havana. With what I had saved and a month's advance, I laid out $40 for flour, cheese, and apples, on my own account. In 15 days we anchored in Havana. Our cargo was in great demand; flour $20 per barrel, cheese 75 cents a pound, and other articles in proportion. I bought from a boat having such articles for sale, a powder-horn made in the "Moro Castle," on which was a representation of the Spanish Crown, the Castle, and* vessels going in and out of the harbor of Havana, which I gave to my grand-daughter, Mary Josephine Bulkeley, in 1841, having owned it myself sixty years. We sailed from Havana, and on the 20th of February, after an absence of three months, arrived in Philadelphia. On settling up my voyage I found myself in possession of over $100. After providing myself with necessary clothing, still having $80 in silver, I turned my thoughts homewards. At Kings Ferry, fifty miles above New York, on my way home, I met an old acquaintance, Gershom Bulkeley, whom I accompanied to Mill River, arriving at home on the first of April, after an absence of a year. Remaining two weeks at home, I went to Boston with Capt. Peters, discharged cargo, and returned to Middletown, when I took my discharge, and walked to Black Rock in one day. Through the summer of 1781, I was engaged on a small Brig owned by the inhabitants of "Mill River."

"Early in 1782, I went with Capt. Stephen Thorp to Rhode Island, and continued in the same vessel through the summer. In the autumn I visited my uncle Moses Bulkeley, who lived back in the country, and bought of him the land on which I now live, (1841,) for fifty dollars. In December I joined one of the boats from Fairfield, in a projected expedition to take some British forts on Long Island.

"In April, 1783, news of peace arrived, which caused great rejoicing. Everybody was anxious to visit New York, which had been in possession of the enemy seven years. I went in April. While there, I engaged to go to New Providence in a small sloop owned by George Brown. We arrived safely in New Providence, disposed of our cargo, took in a return cargo, and started again for New York. I was now put in charge of the sloop, and sailed for Nova Scotia, taking with me Gapt. Brown and wife, and a number of his friends. A part of my passengers, and himself and wife landed at Granville, and put up temporary houses. Afterward Capt. Brown laid out a town at Beaver's Harbor, and urged me to take a lot. I declined at first, but he insisting, I accepted one, and gave James Tucker a power of attorney with ten dollars to take care of it for me, but I never went there again to claim it. In September we sailed for Boston, remained there a few days, and in October sailed again for Nova Scotia. Here the sloop was laid up for the winter, but thinking it would not do to be idle long, I made a voyage to Boston, returning to Nova Scotia in 1784, the beginning of the year. I remained three months, visiting the families I had brought here. May following made a voyage to Boston, and in July one to New York. In August, after a monthly visit in the Bay, I sailed again for New York, taking with me Capt. Brown and his family, who had sold out in Nova Scotia. We arrived in October. We sailed the same month for Jamaica; a few days out experienced severe weather. Coming up with Turks Island, as I was asleep in the cabin, I dreamed that I saw land and reefs of rocks ahead. Waking suddenly, visibly impressed with my dream, I hurried on deck, and found the vessel running directly for the land and reefs just as they had appeared in my dream. She would undoubtedly have run ashore in a few minutes had I not in this singular manner been warned of our danger. Arriving safely at Kingston, we discharged our cargo in three weeks, and in November cleared for New York, arriving there the 5th of January, 1785. On settling with the owners for my services there was due me for the last nineteen months $200, which Capt. Brown paid me in gold, one of which pieces 1 have always retained. I now returned home, where I remained six weeks, but not contented to remain longer idle, I engaged as mate with Capt. Joseph Bartram, and made a voyage in a sloop to North Carolina; returned home in April. 1 was now solicited by Miah Perry to take part of a vessel with him, which I concluded to do. On one occasion, when Mr. Perry and I were in Marblehead with a cargo of flax, we were swindled out of about $100 worth of it by one whom we thought would help us sell it. We felt quite sore at our loss, as it, was the commencement of our coasting business. 1 continued in the same business during the summer. Between Mill River, New York, and New Haven. In the autumn of this year I was married to Mary Ogden, daughter of Jonathan Ogden, who died in 1775, when she was only five years old. He would often call her to him and say. 'My poor Polly, what will become of you'."

"In the spring of 1786 I built a house, which is still standing near where I now live. In the autumn Mr. Perry and I dissolved all further connection in the way of business. Unaccustomed to idle habits, I went as mate in a brig to Point Peter, about sixty miles from Cape Francis. We lay here three months, returning to Black Rock in April, 1787. In the spring of this year I bought out Miah Perry's part of the sloop, and continued in the coasting trade the next year: sold out soon after, and bought part of another vessel. Continuing this business for a time I increased my vessel property as means would allow, and as my sons grew up placed them in business with myself, and so have continued, father and sons being equally united."

Sources: 1. Pension Papers S18336. 2. Sons of the American Revolution Application. 3. Diary of Eleazer Bulkley. 4. 6th Report of the National Society of the D.A.R., Oct. 11, 1902- Oct. 11, 1903.

****

Gurdon Bull age 14

Gurdon Bull was born on 19 May, 1767 in Harwinton, Connecticut, and he died on 26 January, 1841 in Hartford, New York. He married Mary Ann Harper in 1793. Gurdon enlisted at fourteen and served at West Point in 1781 in Canfield's Connecticut Regiment.

Sources: 1. Lineage Book D.A.R. vol. 39, 1902. 2. Tombstone

****

David Burbank age 13

David was born on 5 October, 1762 in Falmouth, Maine, and he died on 7 February, 1806 in Newfield, Maine. He married Miriam Dunnell in December of 1787. David served as a drummer with his father Captain Silas Burbank. His brother, also in this book, served in the same company as a fifer at the age of 11.

David served in the 12th Massachusetts Regiment under the command of Colonel Samuel Brewer. Colonel Brewer was dismissed from the service on 17 September, 1778, and the command was given to Lieutenant Colonel Ebenezer Sprout. The regiment was disbanded in 1781.

The Burbank family marched to Boston and served under General Washington in the siege of Boston. Their regiment was the first to march into the city after the British evacuation. They next marched to reinforce Fort Ticonderoga and later took part in the Battle of Saratoga. In 1778 the regiment marched to Pennsylvania and was quartered at Valley Forge. In June of 1778 the regiment and the Burbank family fought at the Battle of Monmouth. The remainder of their service was spent protecting West Point.

Sources: 1. D.A.R. Lineage Book, Vol 13. 2. The Harmon Genealogy, Comprising All Branches in New England by Artemas Canfield Harmon. 3. Sons of the American Revolution Application.

****

Eleazer Burbank age 11

Eleazer Burbank was born on 14 October, 1764 in Falmouth, Maine, and he died on 30 August, 1840 in Belgrade, Maine. He married Mary Brackett on 25 September, 1787 in Maine. He received a yearly pension of $88. Eleazer served as a fifer with his father Captain Silas Burbank. His brother, also in this book, served in the same company as a drummer at the age of 13.

"I enlisted on the first of January 1776 as a musician for one year and served until August of the same year when I was left in Boston sick with the small pox. In January 1777 I enlisted and did duty as a musician in Captain Silas Burbank's company for the term of three years and was discharged in December 1780."

Eleazer served in the 12th Massachusetts Regiment under the command of Colonel Samuel Brewer. Colonel Brewer was dismissed from the service on 17 September, 1778 and a command was given to Lieutenant Colonel Ebenezer Sprout. The regiment was disbanded in 1781.

The Burbank family marched to Boston and served under General Washington in the siege of Boston. Their regiment was the first to march into the city after the British evacuation. They next marched to reinforce Fort Ticonderoga and later took part in the Battle of Saratoga. In 1778 the regiment marched to Pennsylvania and was quartered at Valley Forge. In June of 1778 the regiment and the Burbank family fought at the Battle of Monmouth. The remainder of their service was spent protecting West Point.

At one point in his service Eleazer was captured and held prisoner for a month by the British. When the British soldiers asked him to play for them on his fife, he began to play Yankee Doodle. Captain Silas Burbank was one of the officers chosen to lead Major John Andre out to be executed.

In 1808 Eleazer served as the Belgrade Town Treasurer. He was a devout Quaker and donated land from his farm, so that the Quakers could build a meeting house and a burial ground. In 1818 Eleazer received his pension for his war service, which upset the Quaker congregation and dropped him from membership.

Sources: 1. D.A.R. Lineage Book, Vol 13. 2. Pension Papers W23744. 3. The Harmon Genealogy, Comprising All Branches in New England by Artemas Canfield Harmon. 4. The Eleazer Burbank House by Linda Snow McLoon. 5. Sons of the American Revolution Application.

****

Gideon Burdick age 14

Gideon Burdick was born on 6 November, 1762 in Hopkinton, Rhode Island, and he died on 5 April, 1846 in Quincey, Illinois. He married (1) Catherine Robertson who died in 1806 and (2) Jane Brown in 1814. Gideon received $40.00 a year for his service.

According to family history, Gideon was the 14 year old drummer boy in 1776 who accompanied General George Washington across the Delaware River. He replaced Washington's personal drummer boy, who had been shot in the leg. Gideon often told this story to his grandchildren. The drummer boy featured on the Bicentennial 25 cent piece is alluded to be Gideon. This has been proved to be false.

"The muffled sound of Gideon's drum encouraged the soldiers through the snow and sleet to the ice bound Delaware River. Washington and his men won the struggle with the icy currents of the Delaware, defeated the enemy and turned the tide of the American Revolution. The drummer boy's drum was no longer muffled, but beat out a signal of victory." This is from the *Ogden Standard Examiner*, on 30 June, 1975.

This author found no record of Gideon serving as a drummer under Washington in 1776. In his pension file he stated that he joined in 1780 and served off and on until 1 January, 1782. A few sources state that, according to his pension application, Gideon guarded Major Andre, the British spy. This guard duty is not mentioned in his application. Gideon does state that he was a witness to the execution of Major Andre.

Sources: 1. Pension Papers S3107. 2. New York in the Revolution as Colony and State. 3. Vital Records of Rhode Island 1636-1850. 4. U.S. Revolutionary War Rolls 1775-1783.

****

Samuel Burkes age 14

Samuel Burkes was born on 24 July, 1765 in Prince Edward County, Virginia, and he died in September of 1840 in Madison County, Missouri. He enlisted in the service in 1779.

"I entered the service in the Militia of North Carolina, as a substitute for one Daniel Weaver, for three months in the company commanded by Capt. Salathiel Martin, Leonard Keeling Bradley was first Lieutenant in the first North Carolina Regiment, I do not remember the

name of the Col who commanded. My Militia general was named Lillington. We marched into Wilkes county. Then marched to Charlotte I think in Mecklenburg County. Then marched the main road to Charlestown South Carolina where I joined the continental troops commanded by Gen Lincoln. The other regular officers there whose names I recollects, were Co. Lytle Majors Dixon & Nelson & Captains Lytle & Campbell. I was detached with the others & put under command of Col Hayne as I now recollect the name, to go on an expedition to Ashley ferry on Ashley river where the British were expected to attempt to cross, I was put under the command Capt Sloane a militia officer. The enemy attempted to cross, but were repulsed after an engagement with fore arms across the river. After which I went to Charlestown & was returned to my company, where I was discharged by Capt Martin on the 24th day of March 1780, having serving three months in the State of South Carolina."

The Battle of Ashley Ferry occurred toward the middle of March of 1780. The main force of the British Army crossed the river several miles north of Ashley Ferry. Because of this the American General Lincoln retreated with his men back to Charleston. Shortly after Samuel was discharged, the British captured the city of Charleston on 12 May, 1780. This led to a call for volunteers in North Carolina for the militia. Once again Samuel answered the call to enlist. He served in the militia under Captain Absalom Bostick. The men marched to Salisbury and joined the 1,600 man army under General Griffith Rutherford.

"We crossed Pedee & went down on the East side opposite to the Cheraw hills where there was a British Garrison on drawing near the evacuated the place & fled. We then recrossed the river & pursued them until we came to Lynchs Creek, where a skirmish ensued & they fled again, we marched then towards Camden & fell in with the army commanded by General Gates in the piny woods, marched to Rugeleys mill, the enemy then fled towards Camden, we marched on until we came to a place called Gum Swamp, there we met with the enemy who attacked the front of the army after they crossed the swamp & defeated us. We lay at the edge of the swamp that night & in the morning by light the British passed & attacked our army & defeated us. After the militia had fled Major Joel Lewis rallied about thirteen of us (I among the number) who stood about one hundred yards in the rear, until DeKalb's regulars grounded their arms, when they fled, the army totally dispersed & every man took care of himself."

The Battle of Gum Swamp is also called Gates Defeat or The Battle of Camden. At this battle on 16 August, 1780, American General Gates was badly defeated by Lord Cornwallis and his British army. Two of the best regiments ever to serve in the British Army faced the untrained Virginia militia. Soon the Virginia militia broke and ran, and the panic soon spread to other militias. A group of men, including Samuel Burkes, formed a rear guard and tried to protect the retreating Americans through the surrounding woods and swamp. But as Samuel said, *"the army totally dispersed & every man took care of himself."* Samuel also took off through the woods and returned home. He stated in his pension that there was no place of rendezvous, so he did not get a discharge.

"Afterwards there was another call for men, I do not remember the date, I entered for three months in the county of Surry the militia company commanded by Capt Samuel Hampton & Col Davidson, went to the Grindle shoals on Pacolet river & joined there Gen'l Morgan & Col Washington, continental officers major McDowel commanded the North Carolina Militia. The British moved upon us & we retreated up the river for about two days & nights until we reached Cowpens, in which battle I was. We retreated with near seven hundred prisoner."

Brig. General Daniel Morgan was in command of the American Army at Cowpens on 17 January, 1781. His army of a little over a thousand men faced a British force of equal size. The problem was that many of the Americans were militia, who had a history of running after the battle began. General Morgan knew that the British knew this, and he hoped that he could use this knowledge to defeat the British. The plan was to have the center of the American forces made up of militia. They would fire a few volleys and, as they did many times before, they would retreat. This would pull the British in, and facing them in reserve were the Continental infantry troops and dragoons ready to trap the advancing British.

The night before the battle General Morgan went around the camp explaining the plan to the men. He told the militiamen, *"Just three good volleys and the girls will kiss you when you get home."* He then visited the Continental line troops and said, *"Don't worry when the militia falls back tomorrow, they are supposed to do that."*

The next day Samuel Burkes was among the 150 riflemen of the North Carolina militia under Major McDowell in the front line facing the British army. Samuel fired his three volleys like the rest of the men, and then following orders began to retreat. The British saw the militia break and run like they had done so many times before, and sensing victory they cheered and charged after them. By the time the British realized they had been pulled into a trap it was too late. By the end of the battle most of the British were killed, captured, or wounded and the Americans had only 25 men killed.

After the Battle of Cowpens Samuel's enlistment was up, so he returned home. The Tories were creating problems in the area, so once again Samuel enlisted. He joined with General Greene's army at Guilford County. Samuel was not in the Battle of Guilford Courthouse on 15 March, 1781. *"My battalion was ordered to dismount & I was ordered to take charge of the horses. After the battle I was discharged by my Capt for a six week tour."*

When Samuel returned home, he again enlisted as a substitute for Williamson Maho for another tour. He was marched near Wilmington, where a skirmish with the British near a brick house took place. Several days later he was in another skirmish at the same brick house. The British left Wilmington, so Samuel was discharged and sent home. Soon after this Lord Cornwallis surrendered at Yorktown, Samuel again enlisted for a year's tour.

"There were many tories prowling about and skilling on the borders & in the swamps of North Carolina so I volunteered in Surry as a state ranger under Capt Alison Smith for twelve months to scour the country & defeat the designs of the tories, in which service he was many months engaged, I do not recollect the length of time precisely in which I was actually engaged in that service—but was a minute man & allways held myself in readiness whenever called on."

After his service was over Samuel moved to Pendleton, South Carolina for about eighteen years. He then moved to Missouri for about a year and then to Illinois for about eighteen months. He then moved back to Rutherford, Tennessee.

Sources: 1. Tennesseans in the Revolutionary War. 2. U.S. Pension Roll in 1835. 3. Pension Papers S16670. 4. A Battlefield Atlas of the American Revolution by Craig L. Symonds and Cartography by William J. Clipson.

****

Samuel Burney age 14

Samuel Burney was born on 30 January, 1763 in Guilford County, North Carolina, and he died on 31 March, 1849 in Lauderdale County, Alabama. He married (1) Martha Waters who died in 1840 (2) Nancy Mass in April 1844 by the Justice of the Peace John Cooper in Lauderdale County. He was one of the earliest settlers of Rogersville, Alabama.

"I Entered the service as stated in my declaration in the year 1778 as a volunteer on the 26 day of August under Captain Wallace for the Term of twelve months I was mustered into service at Jones Banaugh then in north Carolina as well as I recollect, under Col John Sevier from there we were marched across the mountains at the Bald mountain Gap passing through Charlotte and through Campden and on the Santee River, in about thirty miles of Charleston was under the command of General Marion; found my own Horse Saddle & Rifle; was in a mounted Rifle company, was in no Battle of any note, was in a skirmish where they took upwards of 100 prisoners. Served out the term & was discharged. When we arrived at headquarters we joined the Troops that were guarding the River to prevent communication between the British and Tories. The British were then in possession of Charleston Col Maham or a name sounding like that near there also, he commanded the dragoons – they took by _____? ___ Scouting the country. After I had returned there were orders to raise more men for Sending to the same place and for the same purposes, as before."

"On the 23rd day of November 1779 again volunteered for the term of 12 months under Captain Smith in the company of mounted Rifle men-- was mustered into Service at the Same place I was first mustered at under the command of Col Isaac Shelby. We were marched towards Charleston crossed the mountain at the Blue Mountains, past Ramsours Mills, passing Charlotte, Camden & headquarters on Santee in about 30 miles of Charleston under the command of General Marion, was Engaged in preventing communication with the British and Tories and guarding the country--was in no Battle of any note--remained in the service until 28th day of November 1780 being a few days over the Term of 12 months."

"Lieutenant Samuel McGaughey served with Samuel on his last tour and wrote a letter in 1835 to the Pension Bureau supporting his service. He stated in the letter, We volunteered for six months when our time was out, General Marion wished the men to stay longer. I beat up for volunteers, and Burney volunteered to stay. We remained two months longer, Burney remained with us and returned home with me when our company was discharged, he was was a true Whig and a good soldier."

"On the 23rd day of November 1779 again volunteered for the term of 12 months under Captain Smith in the company of mounted Rifle men – was mustered into Service at the Same place I was first mustered at under the command of Col Isaac Shelby. We were marched towards Charleston crossed the mountain at the Blue Mountains, past Ramsours Mills, passing Charlotte, Camden & headquarters on Santee in about 30 miles of Charleston under the command of General Marion, was Engaged in preventing communication with the British and Tories and guarding the country – was in no Battle of any note."

Sources: 1. Alabama Marriage Collection 1800-1969. 2. Census 1790 & 1840. 3. U.S. Pensioners 1818-1872. 4. Pension Papers W9374.

****

John Burns age 14

John Burns was born in 1763 in Scotland, and he died on 7 July, 1827 in Switzerland County, Indiana. He married Lucretia Vanasdal on 13 June, 1810 in Warren County, Ohio. He received $96 a year for his service.

"I Enlisted in the Continental survice in the spring of 1777 in King & Queen County in the State of Virginia in the Company commanded by Capt. Phillip Talafro of the regimente Commanded by Col Richard Parker & I continued to surve in said Corps or in the survice of the united states until May 1780 in Charles Town in South Carolina. I was at the Battle of Savannah in Georgia & in the Battle at Charles Town South Caralina."

John served during the Siege of Charleston, and this may have been where he was wounded. Thousands of Americans were captured in this defeat and John's commanding officer, Colonel Richard Parker, was killed.

In 1889 the daughter of John and Lucretia had a lawyer write to the pension department requesting information on her father's service. She stated that her father was from Scotland and referred to him as Sergeant John Burns. She said that he was a surgeon and practiced it in the army. She described him as a large man weighing around 400 pounds, and she stated that he was shot in the calf during the war.

Sources: 1. Tombstone 2. U.S. Pensioners 1818-1872. 3. Pension Papers W9372.

****

Medad Butler age 10

Medad Butler was born on 23 January, 1766 in Bradford, Connecticut, and he died on 27 February, 1847 in New York. He married Hannah Tylee on 9 December, 1794.

He and several other boys educated their pastor about the revolution in 1776. The minister of the town church was a Loyalist and avoided giving any encouragement to the people to join the rebel cause. Several of the boys in town, including Medad, were very supportive of the patriot cause, and they decided they would try and change the attitude of the pastor.

One Saturday they got possession of a cannon, loaded it, and placed it at the rear of the church pointing toward the pulpit. All of this mischief was done at night and in silence. The next morning as the pastor was entering the church, the boys pointed out the cannon to him and what it was aimed at. They told the pastor that if he failed to pray for the success of the rebel cause, the cannon would be fired while he was at the pulpit. It was reported that while in church the pastor became a supporter of the rebel cause.

Sources: 1. Sons of the American Revolution Application. 2. D.A.R. Lineage Book, Vol. 17. 3. The Life and Letters of Charles Butler by Francis Hovery Stoddard.

****

Nancy Butler teenager age unknown

Nancy Butler was born in 1765 in South Carolina, and she died there in 1854. She helped to bury murdered American soldiers, while armed enemy soldiers stood ready to shoot the first person who attempted to give them a burial.

Source: D.A.R. Lineage Book, vol. 69.

****

William Caldwell age 14

William Caldwell was born in Antrim County, Ireland on 18 May, 1763, and he died in March of 1849 in Butler County, Ohio. He came to America in 1772. In 1786 he married Mary Brown in Newbury, South Carolina. He enlisted in the mounted militia as a substitute for his father, John Caldwell, in the fall of 1777. During this tour he defended the frontiers of Georgia against the Indians.

"The first of March in the year one thousand and eighty one I volunteered to serve in a volunteer company of mounted men under Captain Lindsey, I served in said company until 7th day of May following during which time I was engaged in a skirmish with the tories on Camping Creek about 8 miles from the Saluda River in Newberry district. I was also engaged in the attack made on Williams' Fort, my regiment was at that time commanded by a young Colonel Lyle. I was in one engagement against three hundred and fifty tories upon Fair Forest river in which engagement Col Hayes had the chief command. I assisted in taking Friday's Fort sometimes called Fort Granby. I was engaged in a sharp contest with the tories at Clark's ford on Inoree river, I was there commanded by Captain Jones who was killed in the contest."

On 8 May, 1781 Colonel Joseph Hayes was sent out to attack a large Tory force on Fair Creek. He was defeated and quickly withdrew his forces. The Battle of Fort Granby occurred on May 14 and 15, 1781. Lt. Colonel Henry Lee placed his 6 pound cannon within 400 yards of the fort and at daybreak began to fire it. He then ordered William Caldwell and the rest of the troops to advance. The commander of the fort surrendered and on May 15th they vacated the fort. The Americans captured large amounts of weapons, powder, and shot.

In May William again enlisted in a company of dragoons in the South Carolina Militia under the command of Captain David Glynn and Colonel John Thomas.

"I served three months under Colonel Thomas during the siege of ninety-six. I performed but little duty there was as I was soon called away. I was then transferred to Captain Smith's company in Colonel Middleton's Regiment under the command of the last two mentioned officers. I served until the expiration of the time for which I had enlisted."

The siege of Ninety-Six was from 22 May to 18 June, 1781. Ninety-Six was a fortified village in South Carolina containing 550 Loyalists. General Greene was not successful in taking the fort, and he was forced to retreat when British troops were approaching from Charlestown.

"After the siege of Ninety-six and before the battle of Eutaw I was ordered in a command under Colonel Wade Hampton who in general commanded the dragoons belonging to General Sumter's brigade, and marched from Whetstone's Mill on the south side of the Congaree river to the quarter house six miles from Charleston. From this place the command took sixty horses belonging to the British, the horses were feeding in a

pasture guarded by fifteen British soldiers one of whom was a lieutenant, these were all taken prisoners. we also took a wagon filled with clothing and other stores belonging to the British. the command then marched and crossed the Santee at Nelson's Ferry and returned safe to the North side of the Santee and carried the booty to the main army—I was at the battle of Eutaw, during the engagement I fought under the immediate command of Colonel Wade Hampton and William Washington, the last of whom was wounded and taken prisoner by the enemy. I continued in the service until the seventh day of March 1781 when I received a written discharge."

At four in the morning on 8 September, 1781 General Greene's army began the seven mile march to Eutaw Springs. William Caldwell was one of 72 cavalry men of the South Carolina state troops under the command of Captain Wade Hampton. By the end of the day both sides claimed victory. After William was discharged he was frequently called upon to serve in the militia against the Tories. This service went on for two months.

William served a total of fifteen months and received a yearly pension of $50.82. In 1806 he moved to Butler County, Ohio.

Sources: 1. Census of 1810, 1820, 1830, & 1840. 2. Sons of the American Revolution Application. 3. U.S. Pension Roll of 1835. 4. Pension Papers S2116. 5. Lineage Book—National Society if the D.A.R., Vols. 598-60. 6. A Guide to the Battles of the American Revolution by Theodore P. Savas and J. David Dameron.

****

Thomas Campbell age 14

Thomas Campbell was born on 12 March, 1767 in Montgomery County, New York, and he died after 1852. His pension claim was rejected because *"period, duration, grade, locality & names of officers of each tour required."*

Thomas enlisted in August 1781 in Captain Garret Putman's Company in Lieutenant Colonel Marinus Willett's Regiment for four months. During this time he was at Fort Hunter, Fort Plank, Fort Clyde, and Fort Plain, which were all located around the Mohawk River. He said that he fought at the Battle of Johnstown on 25 October, 1781.

This battle began when a raiding party of British soldiers were attacked by a small American force led by Colonel Willett. After an intense fight the Americans were victorious. Soon after the battle news reached the patriots that Cornwallis had surrendered at Yorktown.

In 1782 Thomas served in Captain David McMaster's Company of the Mohawk Regiment of the Tyron County Militia. His company captured a spy named Parker who was later hanged. *"I together with Capt. McMaster, 2 other men of my company marched to Jamestown & took a man by the name of Parker, a spy, a prisoner, who was afterwards executed as a spy at Albany."*

Sources: 1. The Bloodied Mohawk: The American Revolution in the Words of Fort Planks Defenders and Other Mohawk Valley Partisans by Kenneth D. Johnson. 2. Pension Papers R1646.

****

John Cannday age 14

John Cannday was born on 21 August, 1764 in Westmoreland County, Virginia, and he died after 1837. He received a yearly pension of $96.

"I enlisted in the month August 1778 (as well as I now recollects) under Midshipman Benjamin Strother, to serve three years in the Virginia State Navy. That a short time after my enlistment, I went agreeably to orders to Frazier's Ferry, on Mattapony River, where I entered the service on board the Ship Tempest, Commanded by Capt. Celey Sanders; first Lieutenant Michael James, second Lieutenant, William Steel; first Midshipman Benjamin Strother, Second Midshipman John Robbins; Third Midshipman John Peirce, Almand Saunders Gunner & Boatswain. John Wilkinson Boatswains Mate, John McNickle Surgeon, Thomas Landrum Surgeons Mate, The said Ship sailed to the Chesapeake bay, which was her general cruizing Ground. was at Hampton Fort, where we lay some time, had a skirmish with a British Brig, off Hog Island, which we captured; The Ship Tempest mounted 21 Guns. Beside the Tempest, Capt Celey Sanders had the Command as Commodore of the Ship Dragon, commanded by Capt. Callender, and the Tartar, Commanded by Capt. William Sanders. I continued on board the Tempest, until she was blockaded in Chickahominy River in 1781, when she was deserted by her crew, to escape being taken prisoners by the enemy. Her crew remained at and about New Castle in Hanover County Va. I being there, until the siege of York, when we marched thither and assisted in the siege, till the surrender of Lord Cornwallis, when I was discharged."

Source: 1. Pension Papers S9161.

****

John Canterbury age 14

John Canterbury was born in 1760 in Prince William County, Virginia, and he died 29 October, 1842 in Monroe County, Virginia. He married Nancy Lowe on 17 October, 1787 in Greenbrier County, Virginia. His pension request was rejected due to lack of proof of service.

"I volunteered and went to Point Pleasant to assist in driving Cattle for the supply of the Army in 1774 and arrived at that place the night after the memorable Battle at the Point called Dunmores Battle, that I was then but a Boy of 14 years of age and lived in a small settlement on Holstein River in what is now Washington County Virginia."

"On the 7th day of May 1777 I volunteered to go against the Indians and went on to Blackamore Station under the command of Sergeant John Harrison with seventeen others himself making eighteen, where we remained untill the first or second day of December following; that during that summer I had no engagement or encounter with the Indians, and our entire service consisted in guarding the stations and the people while tending their corn: That we left Blackamore Station at the time aforesaid and returned to our respective homes."

"In the Spring of the year 1778 I volunteered to go against the Indians and in a small company of Twenty men under the command of one John Bell who I think was either a Lieutenant or Ensign we took up their line of March on either the 15th or 17th April of that year for a place called Blue Stone, from there we marched in the month of June following to Davis's Fort where we remained between three and four weeks and then marched on to Leslie's Station where we remained until the 15th October following when there appearing no danger to the inhabitants from the Hostile Indians and having had no skirmish with them that summer we returned home."

"I again volunteered in a company of about 70 men under one Captain Joseph Martin in the summer of 1779 and on the the 22nd day of June we set out from Holstein settlement for the Cherokee Towns on the Sciota River soon after we started we joined about one hundred and thirty men under the command of one Colonel Lewis; Colonel Sevier from Wataga had gone on a little before Colonel Lewis, had crossed the French Broad River, had a sucessful engagement with the Indians, but fearing that the Indians might receive a reinforcement retreated across the River and waited until Colonel Lewis came up that their whole force when we met Colonel Sevier I think amounted to near 400 men; late in the month of

October or in the early part of the month of November we met with when on a scouting party a number of Indians near the Sciota River, when the Indians gave way in every direction, leaving about 25 killed and wounded and about the same number of Prisoners. Shortly after this engagement, the Indians abandoned their principal town on the Sciota, when we marched into it and took possession without any interruption from the enemy; that I well remember to have been in the said Indian Town on Christmas the 25th day of December 1779 and left there I think the next day after destroying their Wigwams and such other things belonging to the Indians as might seem most valuable to them."

"Again in the fall of the year 1780 a draft was made for a tour of three months out of such men as had not volunteered the preceeding year and a man by the name of Samuel Douglass being drafted who was unwilling to go he hired as a substitute for said Douglass and on the 27th of October 1780 I set out under the command of Captain Estill for Harrods Station in Kentucky and on their way to Harrods Station we passed Logan Station, where we saw Colonel Logan who had been wounded by the Indians some short time previous; after remaining sometime at Harrods Station I think until about the first January following we returned to Logans Station where we remained until the first of February 1781 when we were discharged."

"On the 8th day of August 1781 I substituted for a man by the name of Looney who had been drafted for a three months Tour to go against the British and Tories in South Carolina; I marched this time under the command of Captain Roger Toss, Lieutenant Moses Looney and Ensign Ephraim Grimes or Graham; this company was composed of about Eighty men; we marched directly to the Swamps of Santee in South Carolina and was there under the command of General Francis Marion and Colonel Campbell I was in no engagement while on said Tour upon one occasion however when on a reconnoitering party we came upon a British Hospital and fired upon it, but the fire not being returned we marched up and took it without the effusion of blood; The Hospital I think contained in all about eight men sick and well which we made prisoners; I continued in service this tour until the first of November 1781 when the news of the Surrender of Lord CornWallis being received we were discharged, wanting eight days of fulfilling a three months tour."

Sources: 1. Tombstone 2. West Virginia Marriages Index 1785-1971. 3. Census of 1810, 1820, 1830, and 1840. 4. Pension Papers R1667.

****

Caleb Carr age 14

Caleb Carr was born 13 October, 1762 in Kent, Rhode Island, and he died 18 July, 1839 in Oakland, Michigan. He enlisted 2 November, 1776 as a private in Captain Millard's company under Colonel John Waterman. Later he was a corporal in Captain Millard's company 1st Division under Colonel Wakeman.

Sources: 1. Tombstone 2. Michigan Military Records 1775-1836. 3. Michigan historical Collections Vol. XVIII. 4. Rhode Island Births 1636-1930. 5. Sons of the American Revolution Application.

****

James Carr age 13

James Carr was born in Craven County, South Carolina in 1764, and he died on 25 August, 1840. He moved to the frontier of Virginia, and in 1776 he joined with the militia in May of that year to help build forts for protection against the Indians. He wrote in his pension papers,

"The fort that I was stationed at was called Houston's Fort. About the 1st of October in the same year I enlisted by permission of my father as a private under Leut. John Williams & was marched to the Long Island of the Holston and was attached to Capt Isaac Bledsoe Company and was stationed at the Long Islands during the winter & there done service till 1st of April 1777 at which time I was discharged."

Long Island is an island in the Holston River at Kingsport near the border with Virginia in eastern Tennessee. Houston's Fort was on the waters of Moccasin Creek which was a tributary of the Holston River. The fort was built by William Houston and his neighbors in 1774. James Carr was sent to the fort in October, because the fort was attacked by Indians two months earlier. James was discharged after six months service and returned home to Washington County, Virginia in April of 1777. Once home he discovered that Captain George Adams was stationed there to guard the settlements. Once Again James volunteered as a private and served for a little over three months. In September of 1778 he volunteered for six months to guard the frontier under Captain George Maxfield.

"Sometime in the month of June (1780) there were orders issued for a guard to go on to Kentucky to protect whites from indian hostilities. I volunteered and attached my self to Capt John Snawdies Company we marched from Washington County to whites station Kentucky and

continued to do service till we were marched back to Washington County Virginia and were dismissed."

In the later part of 1780 a horse company in the 7th Regiment of the Virginia militia, under the command of Colonel Arthur Campbell, was ordered to go against the old Cherokee Towns on the Tennessee River. Colonel Campbell was afraid his force was not strong enough to be successful, so he sent word to Captain Alexander Barnett to raise a company and join him.

"I volunteered in Washington City, County and attached myself to Captain Barnetts Companey as a private in the month of December....on the approach of our force the Indians had abandoned their towns. We were ordered and did scouer the country in pursuit of the Indians we had a great many skarmishes but no general engagement—there were some Indians killed and a number taken prisoner their towns also destroyed..."

James served this tour for two months. The Americans claimed to have destroyed 50,000 bushels of corn and 1,000 houses. Some of the Indians attacked were actually American allies. The Americans were unable to determine which Cherokee towns were allies and which were enemies.

For the next several years James moved back and forth between Tennessee and Kentucky. In 1839 he applied to have his pension transferred to Illinois where his children lived.

_{Sources: 1. Frontier Forts of Southwest Virginia by Emory L. Hamilton. 2. Pension Papers S32159. 3. The Ridge Family and the Decimation of a People by Thurman Wilkins.}

****

Isaac Carter age 13 or 14

Isaac Carter was born in 1764 in Cumberland County, North Carolina, and he died on 24 March, 1834 in Pike County, Mississippi. In 1780 he married Nancy Youngn who was described as Dutch speaking, short, dumpy, and jolly.

"I enlisted in the Army of the United States on the 5th day of February in the year 1777 with Colonel Hogan of the 7th Regiment of the North Carolina line of Regular Soldiers under the following named officers. General Francis Nash, Colonel Hogan, Major John Welch Lieutenant Robert Green and Ensign James pearl and served under the

same officers from the time of my Enlistment until after the battles of Brandywine and Germantown...."

The 7th North Carolina Regiment was formed on 16 September, 1776 under the command of Colonel John Hogun. In February of 1777 the regiment was transferred to General Washington's main army. In July of 1777 the regiment was transferred to the North Carolina Brigade, which General Francis Nash commanded. All the North Carolina regiments were small and most were under 200 men.

".....the winter after my Enlistment and was placed under Captain Robert Fenner who was commanded by Colonel Sylvanus ____?____ of the 3rd Regiment of Continentals and remained at (Valley Forge then so called) on the Schuylkill in the State of Pennsylvania where the Army remained all the winter of 1777 and in the Spring of '78 when the Army Commenced a March in pursuit of the enemy to a place called Monmouth in New Jersey where the British Army halted and another General engagement ensued from whence the British Army Retreated to New York and was pursued by the American Army some small distance until they took shipping for New York then was passing to and fro through the State of New Jersey during the summer of '78 and was marched to head quarters to a place called Morristown where the American Army in part wintered. And another part wintered at a place then called Paramus afterwards in the Spring of '79 was marched to the State of New York to a place called West Point where the American Army remained during the summer in which time General Wayne strengthen his Army by raising volunteers and Marched against a Fort of the British at Stony Point where he proved Victorious and in the fall of that year was marched from West point to South Carolina and was marching in towards Charlestown through the most part of the winter until my time of service expired having served 15 days after my term of enlistment."

Isaac Carter probably wintered with the group of soldiers at Paramus because this is where General Wayne's army spent the winter. General Washington took his troops to winter quarters at Middlebrook. Perhaps it was from a desire to impress the ladies of the area, General Wayne ordered the division, before leaving Paramus, out on parade, *"in the most soldierly manner Possible, their arms and a Coutrements in the Best order. The Quartermaster will draw flour for the men to clean their jacoots & Breches and to Powder their hair."*

The Battle of Monmouth was the last major engagement fought in the northern theater of the war, as the British holed up in New York and shifted their attention to the southern colonies. This battle is often remembered for the legend of "Molly Pitcher." During the battle temperatures on the field were over 100 degrees. Molly Ludwig Hayes was married to William Hayes an artilleryman who was at the battle.

During the battle Molly brought water to the soldiers from a spring that she found. Her husband either was wounded or dropped from heat exhaustion, so Molly took his place at the cannon. Cannons needed a constant supply of water to cool down the hot barrel and soak the sponge on the end of the ramrod used to clean out the barrel. Molly took her husband's place and continued to swab and load the cannon.

During the battle a British musket ball passed between her legs and tore off the bottom of her petticoat. She made a quick remark to the effect of *"Well if that had been higher it could have been worse."* When the battle had ended, General Washington wanted to know who the woman was that he had seen loading the cannon. He issued a warrant making her a noncommissioned officer. Years later she liked using the nickname *"Sergeant Molly."*

In her later years she was often seen in the streets of her town wearing a striped skirt, wool stockings, and a ruffled cap. The people in town liked her even though they said she *"often cursed like a soldier."* In 1822 Pennsylvania awarded her an annual pension of $40 for her service.

"About the 1st of July 1781 I entered the service again for the term of 12 months in the above mentioned place as a Balloted Soldier of North Carolina under the command of Captain Dennis Porterfield rendezvoused at Fayetteville then marched to Hillsboro, Salisbury, Guilford North Carolina thence to Charlotte then to Camden thence crossing Wateree and thence Congaree at McCord's Ferry where the company joined General Green on or about the first of September 81. There marched on to Eutaw Springs where General Greene met with the British Army and a warm engagement ensued where I was wounded in my left arm and afterwards we marched through South Carolina to Bacon's Bridge near Charleston where I was discharged."

A balloted soldier was one that was eligible to receive a land grant in North Carolina for his service during the revolution. Records of the land

and the soldiers was kept in a Balloted Book. Isaac served a total of four years and fifteen days and received $80.00 a year for his service.

Sources: 1. They Called Her Molly Pitcher by Anne Rockwell. 2. The History of Paterson & its Environs by William Nelson & Charles A. Skinner, Vol. 1, 1920. 3. U.S. Pension Roll of 1835. 4. Pension Papers S8147. 5. Sons of the American Revolution Application. U.S. Census of 1790, 1800 & 1820.

****

Philip Carter age 14

Philip Carter was born on 16 March, 1766 in Spotsylvania, Virginia, and he died in 1840 in Barren, Kentucky. In Virginia of 1791 he married Dicie Coats and they had twelve children. Philip Carter received $46. 66 for his service.

He first enlisted in the militia and served tours of two months each starting in September 1780. He first entered as a substitute for Thomas Coleman, and he served under Captain Harry Stubblefield. Philip served in the third regiment on every tour. He was discharged in November 1780 and he was met by the militia unit that relieved his regiment. Philip's father was a member of the relief troops, so Philip substituted for his father for another two month tour. During this tour he was mainly stationed around Jamestown.

Philip was discharged in January of 1781 and reenlisted as a substitute for David Lively in the Company commanded by Captain Benjamin Holliday. Two months later he was discharged and reenlisted as a substitute for Richard Dillard. This tour is the first in which Philip saw some action.

"The British shortly afterwards took possession of Williamsburg, after which Maj Armisted took command of part of the troops, of whom I was one, and attacked the British at Williamsburg, & drove in their picket guard, but the attack was unsuccessful. I afterwards marched under the command of Major Armisted to Richmond. Shortly afterwards the british marched up the South Side of James River to Manchester and burnt the ware Houses &c. About this time the marquis De Lafayette joined us on Shoco Hill. Short time after this, the two months having expired some two or three days, I was discharged."

Around the first of June 1781 Philip enlisted as a substitute for Bradley Matthews. At the end of the two month tour Philip's father was drafted, so Philip served as his substitute again. In September of 1781 Philip again was the substitute for David Lively. Once again Philip saw action.

"General La Fayette, to whose command I was attached, marched to Richmond & was there joined by Baron Steuben. The British then lay at Bacon's Bridges. They started from thence; made their course for Jamestown, our army got as far as the burnt chimneys 18 miles south of Jamestown Virginia then three or four days, when Gen La Fayette took his own Brigade, Gen'l Wayne's Brigade and the Virginia militia and attacked the British at Jamestown, but was unsuccessful. The action was severe. The American Army lost two pieces of Artillery, & Gen'l La Fayette had a horse shot under him. Shortly afterwards, Count De Grasse appearing in the Chesapeake, Corn Wallis took possession of Yorktown, Va where he was besieged, and surrendered to Gen'l Washington on the 19th of October 1781. I, after the surrender, served in guarding part of the prisoners on their way to Frederick town, Maryland, I having performed this service as far as Nowlings ferry on the Potomack, where the prisoners were received by the Maryland Militia, I was there discharged."

The attack on the British at Jamestown on 6 July, 1781 was called the Battle of Green Spring. The Americans were outnumbered at least 3 to 1 when the battle began at 3:00 in the afternoon. The Americans retreated after a few hours of fighting. This was the last major land battle of the Virginia campaign prior to the Siege of Yorktown.

Sources: 1. Census of 1820 & 1830. 2. A Roster of Revolutionary Ancestry of the Indiana Daughters of the American Revolution. 3. History of Kentucky. 4. U.S. Pension Roll of 1835. 5. Pension Papers S1184.

****

Absalom Carey age 14

Absalom Carey was born on 9 April, 1765 in Orange County, New York, and he died on 30 December, 1841 in Waverly, New York. He married Temperance Cooley on 12 August, 1786 in New York. He received a yearly pension of $80.

"In the spring 1779 I entered the service of the United States as a waggoner and fatigue man for the term of five months taking place of one Benjamin Parker who had enlisted said Parker was had to leave the

service and I accepted in his stead this was at Newborough Orange County."

Absalom was a wagoner, also called a teamster, and had a very difficult job, He would transport supplies or baggage for the army. The enemy's goal was to cut the supply lines and capture the wagons. He also was a fatigue man. This was a person that did not carry arms, but rather he worked on fortifications, carrying messages or cutting roads. This was certainly dangerous and hard work for a fourteen year old boy.

Usually, the wagons had no seats, which allowed the wagon to carry more supplies. The wagoner would walk along side of the wagon and direct the team. Some wagons had a "lazy board", a board that could be pulled out behind the left front wheels of the wagon to sit on. The lead horse and the driver were on the left of the wagon and would stay to the right side of the road when passing an approaching wagon. This is probably why we drive on the right side of the road in the United States.

"There were a number of carpenters and Blacksmiths there engaged in the public __?__ there were about two hundred as near as I can recollect."

"I staid with Colonel Mitchell was sent on express and I on one occasion by him over the river about twenty miles to a place then called Fredericksburg. I also drew wood for the use of the Fort there and Colonel Mitchell."

"I continued there under that engagement to the end of the said five months. When I first entered the service of the United States was about fourteen years of age, my father was then in the service as a carpenter."

"Immediately on the termination of the said enlistment and in November 1779 I again enlisted in the service of the United States at the same place as a waggoner or fatigue man for the term of one year. At the end of the said term of one year I again enlisted in the same service at the same place for the term of one year."

Absalom's father was in the service and probably in the same regiment. When Absalom was discharged, his certificate of discharge was given to his father.

Sources: 1. Tombstone 2. Sons of the American Revolution Application 3. Pension Papers W17590.

****

Isaac Case age 14

Isaac Case was born on 25 February, 1762 in Rehoboth, Massachusetts, and he died on 3 November, 1852 in Readfield, Maine. He married Joann Snow on 26 June, 1785 in Maine. He received a yearly pension of $30.55.

"I enlisted as a private the first part of October 1776 for three months, I served at Newport until the British fleet arrived and then completed my term of service at Bristol. The first of January I again enlisted for three months in Capt. James Hill's company in Col. Daggett's regt of the Massachusetts troops. I served in Rhode Island and was discharged in March. The first of April 1777 I again enlisted for two months in a detachment under Capt. Sherman of the Massachusetts troops to guard boats at Slade's Ferry on Taunton River."

In July of 1777 Isaac entered the service for his brother Joseph who had been drafted for six weeks. In August of the same year he was drafted and served for one month, and then he served again in the month of September.

After the war Isaac became a young Baptist minister with the reputation of being a fiery and inspirational speaker. One day he arrived to preach in Thomaston, Maine, and in a few weeks he baptized fifty-four new converts. One was the eighteen year old daughter of a prominent member of the community, Joanna Snow. Joanna and the young minister Isaac later married.

Sources: 1. U.S. Pensioners 1818-1872. 2. Census of 1850. 3. Pension Papers S31599. 4. D.A.R. Lineage Book, Vol. 45. 5. History of Thomaston, Rockland, and South Thomaston, Maine by Cyrus Easton.

****

Richard Casler age 14

Richard Casler was born on 14 April, 1767 in Little Falls, New York, and he died on 16 September, 1855 in German Flats, New York. He was married by a German minister to Margaret Casler (she may have been a cousin) on 16 September, 1781 in New York. He received a yearly pension of $30 and 160 acres of land. He was described as an unusually large robust boy, and he was much larger and stronger than other boys that were 14. In his later years he was described as a large athletic old man. He enlisted as a substitute for his father.

"I entered the service of the United States in the Spring of 1781 as a nine month man (and I think it was with the state troops of the New York line) at Fort Herkimer. The name of the officers of the company with which I entered are as follows--Captain Ellsworth--Lieutenant Bloodgood—Ensign Shaw. I cannot give the Christian names of either of the officers, nor can I possibly state the day of the month on which I enter the service as I kept no record thereof. The said company belonged to a regiment commanded by Colonel Marinus Willet. This first service was to assist in the building or repairing of a redoubt near fort Herkimer for the better defense of that place and in the building of blockhouses of that place. From fort Herkimer I went with my company to Fort Dayton repaired one and built another redoubt at that place, and I went there with my company to a place called in those days fort House which was near where the East Canada Creek empties into the Mohawk in said county of Herkimer but then county of Lyon. I was here employed as a guard to the fort of the people of the surrounding county who were at that time mostly assembled in that fort. This was, I believe, some time in the fall of 1781. About that time I went with my company by the order of Coil Willet to join a detachment under him and I met said detachment under Col Willet he proceeded to Johnston to oppose the Indians & tories & some British soldiers who were advancing toward that place, under the command of Walter Butler & Major Ross and who had come from Canada as I was informed, destroying the settlements on the said Mohawk. I was in the battle at ___?__ hall, at Johnstown. Col Willet I believe commanded the americans in that occasion. The force of the British was greatly superior to the americans & the enemy drove the Americans from the bush. After this Battle the Enemy retreated toward Canada & Col Willet & his men of __?__ I was one followed them (I think this was in the fall of 1781) & Col Willet overtook the enemy at East Canada Creek that empties into the Mohawk river. From Johnstown Willets force went to Fort HerKimer in the then county of Lyon & upon that place they went on 20 or 30 miles when they overtook the enemy. When Willets men came upon the enemy they were drying their clothes by fires & were surprised at that place. Walter Butler was killed by an indian (I believe) an Oneida indian. I was there & saw the indian who killed Butler & who had Butlers coat. The indian shot Butler from across the creek Butler's Serbeant was also killed at this place as I believe. [the next sentence is crossed out and some of it I could read] ~~I saw Butler stripped naked~~ [the rest of the words I could not read]. From this place which was named Butler's Ford Col Willet followed the enemy for a considerable distance but being unable to overtake them relinquished the pursuit & went to __?__ bush, as I believe and thence to *fort Plain. After the pursuit of Butler was abondanded the detachment separated & each company went to different places and it was the company in which I went to fort Plain. At Fort Plain the company was dismissed & I returned home."*

Walter Butler was a British Loyalist that was born near Johnstown. He was blamed for the deaths of many women and children killed in the Cherry Valley Massacre in 1778. As a result he was the most hated man in upper New York. He was killed on 30 October, 1781 by the American troops that included Richard Casler.

Richard described the events leading up to and including Butler's death. This story is supported by the pension applications of Nicholas Smith, Tall William, and Rozel Holmes, who were other soldiers present at the battle. After the death of Butler a poem was written in 1859 called the *"The Death of Walter Butler"*. The final stanza said:

> *"When was told around the campfire*
> *How the hatchet clave the brain,*
> *Oh! How joyous was the shouting*
> *Walter Butler has been slain."*

Sources: 1. A History of Wilkes-Barre, Luzerne County, Pennsylvania, Vol. 5, 1909 by Oscar Jewell Harvey. 2. Sons of the American Revolution Application. 3. Pension Papers W6637. 4. The Bloodied Mohawk: The American Revolution in the Words of Fort Planks Defenders and Other Mohawk Valley Partisans by Kenneth D. Johnson.

****

Ephrain Cassel age 14

Ephrain Cassel was born in 1765 in South Carolina. His pension was rejected because he did not serve 6 months and he provided no proof of service other than his personal statement. Ephrain wrote to the Pension Bureau after his claim was rejected. He felt that the rejection was an attack on his character and he was an honest man. He wrote, *"My feelings are seriously injured in this matter..."*

"I volunteered for six months in the month of September or October 1779 under Captain Hasel and served under the following field officers, to wit: Major Chriswell, Col. Williams, all of South Carolina. I cannot now call to mind the name of his General. I volunteered in Newberry District South Carolina. I was marched from Newberry to Camden, from thence to Bacon's Bridge on Edisto River, from thence to

Courbie Ferry on Broad River I think, from thence I was marched home to Newberry District S. C. where I was discharged."

"I then moved my residence down on Savannah River near a noted Ferry called Sisters Ferry in the Spring of 1782 and was soon after drafted under Capt. Dupon or Dusson. The following were my Field Officers Major John Lecraft, and Col. Stafford commanded, as to the Genl. if any, does not now recollect him. I was in one little Battle or skirmish at Ebenezer below the Sisters Ferry on Savannah River. I served with two other Companies alternatively until peace was procured. I was at the Battle fought at the Cowpens by General Morgan in January 1781. I left home of my own accord in consequence of Disturbances very frequent occasioned by the Tories & skirmishing parties of the British. I joined General Morgan but a few days before the Battle. Colonel Howard & Colonel Washington was there at the Battle I think But cannot recollect the names of any other officers."

Sources: 1. Roster of South Carolina Patriots in the American Revolution. 2. Pension Papers R1792.

****

Richard Caster age 14

Richard Caster was born on 28 April, 1767 in German Flats, New York, and he died there on 15 September, 1855. He married Margaret Kessler.

"I entered the service of the United States in the spring of the year 1781 as a nine months man (and I think I was with the state troops of the New York lines) at Fort Herkimer."

Richard served in the Tryon County Militia under the command of Colonel Marinus Willett. The militia was formed to provide defense of the settlements along the Mohawk Valley. Willett wrote of the militia that *"I don't think I shall give a very wild account if I say, that one third have been killed, or carried captive by the enemy; one third removed to the interior places of the country; and one third deserted to the enemy."*

"I belonged to a regiment commanded by Colonel Marinus Willett. The first service after entering the army was to assist in the building or repairing of redoubts near fort Herkimer for the better defense of that place, and in the building of blockhouse From Fort Herkimer. I went with my company to Fort Dayton called in those days Fort __?__

which was near where the East Canada Creek empties into the Mohawk in said county of Herkimer but then County of Tyron. I was here employed as a guard to the fort & the people of the surrounding country who were at that time mostly assembled in that fort."

"I proceeded to Johnstown to oppose the indians & tories & some British soldiers who were advancing under the command of Walter Butler & Major Ross and who had come from Canada, as I was informed destroying the settlements on the said Mohawk. I was in the battle at Johnstown."

"Col Willet I believe commanded the Americans on that occasion. The force of the British was greatly superior to the Americans & the Enemy drove the Americans from the bush. After this Battle the Enemy retreated towards Canada & Col Willet & his men ___can't read___ was one followed them (I think this was in the fall of 1781) & Col Willet overtook the enemy at Lost Canada Creek that empties into the Mohawk river. From Johnstown Williets forces went to Fort Herkimer in the then county of Tyron from that place they went on 20 or 30 miles when they overtook the enemy. When Willets men came upon the men they were drying their clothes by fires & were surprised at that place. Walter Butler was killed by an indian (I believe) an Oneida indian. I was there and saw the indian who killed Butler & who had butlers coat & scalp. The indians shot Butlers from across the creek Butlers Sergeant was also killed at this place as I believe."

On 25 October, 1781 the Battle at Johnstown began when a raiding party led by Major John Ross and loyalist militiamen led by Walter Butler engaged the Americans led by Colonel Willett. Butler was later killed by an Indian on 30 October, 1781. The American victory at Johnstown occurred at about the same time that word reached the area of the Surrender of Cornwallis at Yorktown.

After the regiment returned to Fort Plain Richard was discharged. He received $30 a year and 180 acres of land for his service. His wife Margaret received his pension after his death.

Sources: 1. Sons of the American Revolution Application. 2. Tombstone 3. Census of 1810 & 1840. 4. New York Pensioners of 1835. 5. Marinus Willett, Defender of the northern Frontier by Larry Lowenthal. 6. Pension Papers W6637.

****

James Leander Cathcart age 14

James Cathcart was born on 1 June, 1765 in Ireland, and he died on 6 October, 1843 in Washington D.C. He married Jane Bancker Woodside on 5 June, 1798 in Philadelphia. He received a yearly pension of $144.

"I entered into the Naval Service of the United States as a Midshipman on board the United States Frigate Confederacy, Captain Seth Harding in the month of October one thousand and seven hundred and Seventy nine; in the month of November of the same year I sailed in Said capacity on board said Frigate from the port of Philadelphia bound for Cadiz in Spain, having on board as passengers the Honorable John Jay, Minister Plenipotentiary of the United states to his Most Catholic Majesty, and William Carmichael Esquire his Secretary, also Mr. Gerard Minister from France to the United States, and several others whose names I do not remember."

John Jay served as the President of the Continental Congress from 1778 to 1779. On 27 September, 1779 he was appointed Minister to Spain with the mission to get financial aid, improve trade, and receive recognition of American Independence. He was given the status of plenipotentiary, which meant that he had full power of independent action on behalf of the American government.

William Carmichael was another important American diplomat, who earlier had been instrumental in recruiting the Marquis de Lafayette to join the American cause. He had been appointed as Secretary to the delegation to Spain headed by John Jay. Conrad Alexandre Gerard de Rayneval, the third dignitary that was on board the ship, was the first French diplomatic representative to the United States.

"Upon the voyage said frigate was dismasted in a gale of wind on the Banks of Newfoundland, and in consequence thereof put into Martinique under Jury masts, where she arrived about Christmas of the same year; the French Naval command of Martinique furnished said passengers with a French frigate to carry them to Europe which I believe was called the Aurora; I continued on board the Confederacy until she was captured and sent- __(cannot read next several words__) by two British Squadrons under the command of Admiral Arbuthnot and Sir James Gambier; I was sick with a fever when we landed as a prisoner in New York, and in that condition was put on board the Prison ship Good Hope from which I was sometimes afterwards removed to the "old Jersey"

Prison Ship where I was confined for several months. I continued a prisoner in New York until the month of March One thousand Seven hundred and Eighty two. I effected my escape with a certain young man named Benjamin Russell of Connecticut; I served the United States in the capacity of Midshipman as before stated, including the time I was detained as a prisoner in New York for the full term of two years and five months, and more."

After James left the service he joined the merchant fleet. While on board *The Maria Boston* on 25 July, 1785, he was captured by the Barbary priates. This ship was the first American vessel captured by these pirates. James spent the next eleven years as a slave in Algiers. During his captivity he became a Christian Clerk to the rulers. He became the mediator between the Algerian government and the United States Minister to Portugal. This led to the Treaty of Algiers of 1796 and brought him his freedom.

James returned to the United States, and because of his experiences and command of the Arabic and Turkish languages he was sent back as Consul General to Algiers, Tunis, and Tripoli. He later served in the diplomatic corps for the United States under three Presidents.

Sources: 1. Pension Rolls of 1835. 2. Pension Papers S12413. 3. The Compendium of American Genealogy, Vol. IV. 4. The Captives by James L. Cathcart and Jane Bancker Cathcart. 5. D.A.R. Lineage Book, Vol. 26.

****

Benjamin Chambers age 14

Benjamin Chambers was born on 4 January, 1764 in Chambersburg, Pennsylvania, and he died on 27 August, 1850 in Saline, Missouri. He married (1) Ruth McPerrin, the daughter of a minister, on 27 December, 1796. (2) Sarah Lawson Kemper, also the daughter of a minister, on 22 July, 1801. (3) Jane Woolridge on 20 November, 1837. Benjamin received a pension of $320 a year for his service.

"I entered the service of the United States in the year One thousand seven hundred and seventy eight as an ensign in the first Regiment of the Pennsylvania line on the continental establishment. Then commanded by my father, the late Colonel James Chambers. I continued in service as an officer until the close of the campaign of the year One thousand seven hundred and eighty, at the period last mentioned I resigned the commission of first Lieutenant in the regiment with the intention of obtaining an appointment in the regiment of Dragoons

commanded by the senior officers of the brigade. I never afterwards rejoined the service."

Benjamin probably belonged to Company A of the First Regiment. This company was formed from recruits of Franklin County where Benjamin was from, and was led by Captain James Chambers before he was promoted. Doctor James Thacher describes in his book, *Military Journal during the American Revolutionary War from 1775 to 1783*, the men in the regiment:

"They are remarkably stout and hardy men; many of them exceeding six feet in height. They are dressed in white frocks or rifle shirts and round hats. There men are remarkable for the accuracy of their aim; striking a mark with great certainty at two hundred yards distance. At a review, a company of them, while in a quick advance, fired their balls into objects of seven inches diameter at the distance of 250 yards . . . their shot have frequently proved fatal to British officers and soldiers who expose themselves to view at more than double the distance of common musket shot."

The majority of these men were of German descent, and the rest were Scots-Irish. They were also known as the Pennsylvania Rifle Regiment. Their weapon was the long rifle, which had greater range and accuracy than the muskets used by the British and the American army. The rifle had a range of 80 to 100 yards. In the hands of an expert, many in the regiment were just that, the range extended to 200-300 yards.

Benjamin Chambers was present at the Battle of Springfield, Connecticut Farms, and Bull's Ferry. The Battle of Bull's Ferry took place on 20 July, 1780. The 1st and 2nd Pennsylvania Regiments were ordered to destroy a British blockhouse at Bull's Ferry near New York City. The American forces began a bombardment of the blockhouse. After an hour with no results, Benjamin's Regiment became inpatient and charged the British position. The 2nd Regiment joined in the charge as the officers made attempts to stop the men from attacking. The Americans found the blockhouse impossible to capture so they had to retreat, which resulted in a British victory.

Sources: 1. Sons of the American Revolution Application. 2. Pennsylvania and New Jersey Church and Town Records 1708-1985. 3. Pension roll of 1835. 4. Pension Papers W10302. 5. Military Journal during the American Revolutionary War from 1775 to 1783 by James Thacher.

****

Edward Chambers age 12

Edward Chambers was born in Maryland in 1765. He enlisted in July of 1777 and served under Major Dean in the 3rd Maryland Regiment for three years. He was at the Battle of Camden and the Siege of Cornwallis in 1781. He also claimed to have served as George Washington's special guard.

This guard was authorized on 11 March, 1776 with the purpose to protect General Washington, the money, and official papers of the Continental Army. Washington had a set of requirements for the men of the guard: They should be sober, honest, and have good behavior. They should be from 5'8" to 5'10" tall, handsome, clean, and well made. Many years after the war was over it was not uncommon for older veterans to claim to have served in this guard.

Sources: 1. Pension Papers S34684. 2. Maryland Revolutionary War Records.

****

Isaac Chapman age 12

Isaac Chapman was born on 19 April, 1764 in Culpepper, Virginia, and he died on 29 May, 1836 in Giles County, Virginia. He married Elian Johnston in 1784 in Virginia. As a child he had two homes destroyed by Indians. The British recruited and armed the Indians to raid American settlements in the area. Isaac's pension request was rejected because his service against the Indians on the frontier was not considered military service even though he served under commissioned military officers.

"I enlisted March in 1776 me together with others repaired to Munseys fort in the County of Montgomery for the purposes of their protection against the incursion of the Indians at which place I remained until December following engaged in the protection of the defenceless women & children, and ranging the Country in pursuit of the Indians and guarding against their attack and warlike operations. I was then discharged. I was engaged nine months in the performance of this tour of duty The only officer attached to the fort was John Chapman Ensign in the Company Commanded by Thomas Burk Capt. and John Lucas Leutenant."

"My second tour of service commenced in the year 1777 in the month of April I again repaired to the above mentioned Fort performing

the duties specified in my foregoing tour of service – until the month of December following when I was discharged. I was engaged nine months in the performance of the duties of this tour. The only commanding officer at the Fort was John Chapman Ensign in Capt Burks Company."

"My third tour of service commenced in 1778. In the month of April I again repaired to the above mentioned Fort for the purpose aforesaid and whilst in the performance of said duties a company of volunteers under the Command of Capt. Brice Martin and Lieutenant John Swanson arrived & took command of the said fort. I remained at the said fort until the 1st of July following & was then discharged."

"I was there stationed three months. John Chapman acted as Ensign. My fourth tour of service was in 1779. In the month of April I repaired to Snidows Fort in the County aforesaid & performed the service __?__ in my first and second tour of service until the month of October following when I was discharged. I was engaged in the performance of this tour of duty Five months. The commanding officers were Christian Snidow Lieutenant & John Chapman Ensign."

"My fifth tour of service commenced in 1780. In the month of march I repaired to the last mentioned fort, at which place I performed the duties and services as aforesaid until the 13th day of June when I was discharged. I was engaged in the performance of this tour of duty three months. The commander ____?____ was Lieutenant Christian Snidow – Ensign John Chapman."

"My sixth tour of service commenced in July 1781. I volunteered & served under Captn George Pearis at Pearis's fort in the County aforesaid & there performed the services mentioned as aforesaid until the month of October following when I was discharged. I was engaged in the performance of this tour 3 months. My commanding officer was Capt'n. George Pearis."

Sources: 1. Tombstone 2. Sons of the American Revolution Application. 3. Pension Papers R1869.

****

George Champlin age 13

George Champlin was born on 24 December, 1765 in Westerly, Rhode Island, and he died on 15 March, 1848 in Lee, Massachusetts. At the age of thirteen George enlisted in the navy and also served on a privateer.

Sources: 1. D.A.R. Lineage Book, Vol. 109. 2. Tombstone. 3. Mayflower Births and Deaths, Vols. I & II.

****

James Chandler age 13

James Chandler was born on 29 November, 1761 in Andover, Massachusetts, and he died there on 1 December, 1835. He married Phebe Dane on 29 April, 1783. On 14 October, 1778 he was made a Fife Major in Colonel Titcomb's Regiment. James received a yearly pension of $88.

"About the month of July 1775 I enlisted as a fifer in the army of the revolution and was to serve to the end of December. I served in Captain Benjamin Ames' company in Col. James Frye's Regt. of Massachusetts troops till the time was out."

In 1775 James Chandler served in the 10th Massachusetts Militia commanded by Colonel James Frye of Andover. The regiment was disbanded at the end of 1775. It is stated in the D.A.R. Lineage Book that Chandler was a drummer and he was at the Battle of Bunker Hill. The 10th Massachusetts was at that battle, but James did not enlist until after the battle. James never mentioned in his pension papers that he played the drum.

"I then enlisted for one year & immediately entered January 1, 1776 in the company of Capt. Richard Shortridge in the Regt under Col. Enoch Poor, of the New Hampshire Line troops and served therein the time out; & then on the request of the officers, I enlisted & served for 6 weeks longer in the same company."

James served in 1776 in the 2nd New Hampshire, also known as the 8th Continental Regiment, under Colonel Enoch Poor. The regiment saw action at the Battle of Three Rivers fought on 8 June, 1776 and the Battle of Trenton fought on 26 December, 1776. At the Battle of Trenton the 8th Continental Regiment was part of Colonel Dudley Sargent's Brigade, who were assigned to take up position above the bridge at Trenton to catch men trying to ford the creek.

The enlistment of James Chandler was up at the end of December 1776. However, he was requested to serve for another 6 weeks. This additional term allowed James to participate in the American victory at the Battle of Princeton on 2 January, 1777.

"About June in the year 1780 I again enlisted as fifer for the term which I am very confident was 3 months."

Sources: 1. D.A.R. Lineage Book, Vol 48. 2. Sons of the American Revolution. 3. Tombstone. 4. Pension Papers 8891.

****

Martin Chandler age 13

Martin Chandler was born on 14 April, 1763 in Monmouth, New Jersey, and he died there on 9 November, 1835. He was married by Reverend Morgan to Meribah Chadwick on 30 October, 1787. Martin received $88 a year for his service.

"I enlisted for the term of Three years or during the Max in the Month of July One-thousand seven hundred and seventy seven in the state of New Jersey in the company commanded by Colonel Dayton in the line of the State of New Jersey on the New Jersey Continental establishment. I continued in the said corps about three years when I was transferred to a company commanded by Captain Ogden in the Regiment commanded by Colonel Ogden in the same line and on the same Establishment: I continued to serve in the said Corps about one year when apart of the same company was detached and placed under the command of Colonel Barbour and served under him about one year when the company was again placed under the command of Colonel Ogden until the expiration of the Max and on the fifth day of June 1783 I was honorably discharged."

"I was a Corporal in the service for three or four years before I was discharged and I was in the battle of Short Hills in the state of New Jersey, was in the company of General Sullivan against the Indians in Genesws, I was at the battle of Brandywine, at Germantown, Monmouth and under the command of LaFayette at the siege of Cornwallis and at the siege of one of the redoubts at Yorktown. I was wounded in the right ankle by a musket Ball at Elizabeth Town Point which was the only wound I received during my service."

Martin Chandler belonged to the 1st New Jersey Regiment. He was at the Battle of Short Hills, which took place in New Jersey on 26 June, 1777. The American troops under General Washington were outnumbered six to one. They were pushed back by the British, but they achieved their goal of delaying the British Army so that Washington could pull his forces back and avoid capture. The American flag, the stars and stripes, was adopted twelve days before the battle and may have flown for the first time at the battle. Some troops from both sides used poisoned bullets, musket balls dipped in fungus.

Martin was under the command of Lafayette when he and his unit attacked a redoubt at Yorktown. On 14 October two assault parties were formed to attack the remaining two redoubts protecting the forces of Cornwallis. Redoubt 9 was attacked by French troops and redoubt 10 would be attacked by the Americans which included Martin Chandler. The attack was led by Lt. Colonel Alexander Hamilton. The light infantry attacked under heavy fire, and once they breached the British line they engaged in heavy hand-to-hand fighting. Once the two redoubts were captured the forces of Cornwallis had no protection from American cannons, and they were forced to surrender.

Sources: 1. The Battle of the Short Hills by Robert A. Mayers. 2. "The Music of the Army..." An Abbreviated Study of the Ages of Musicians in the Continental Army, by John U. Rees. Originally published in The Brigade Dispatch Vol. XXIV, No. 4, autumn 1993. 3. New York Newspaper Extracts 1801-1890. 4. U.S. Pensioners 1818-1872. 5. Pension Papers W20853.

****

James K. Child age 14

Thomas Child age 13

James Child was born on 30 August, 1763 in Warren, Rhode Island, and he died on 22 March, 1837 in Haddam, Connecticut. He married three times, and his first wife was Prudence Brainerd who he married in April 1784.

His brother Thomas was born on 18 April, 1765 in Higganum, Connecticut, and he died on 2 May, 1856 in Chatham, Connecticut. He married Hannah Tyron on 19 January, 1786 in Chatham.

The two brothers went privateering during the Revolution and were taken prisoners and confined on board the old *Jersey* prison ship. They were sent on a cartel to Boston and there discharged. Both boys were sick and covered with vermin and left to walk and beg their way back to their home in Connecticut.

Thomas said that when he was passed over the side of the prison ship he heard a sentinel say, *"It would make but little difference whether that fellow went or not."* Years after the war James built gun-boats for the War of 1812.

Sources: 1. D.A.R. Magazine Vol. 17, July-Dec 1900. 2. Tombstone 3. North American Family Histories 1500-2000.

****

Salmon Child age 10

Salmon Child was born on 19 September, 1765 in Woodstock, Connecticut, and he died on 28 January, 1856 in Racine County, Wisconsin. He married Olive Rose on 7 January, 1787. He received a yearly pension of $63.33.

Early in the spring of 1776 ten year old Salmon enlisted as a waiter for his father, Captain Increase Child in Colonel DuBois' New York Regiment. In 1781 he enlisted as a private in Captain Holtham Dunham's Company of Colonel Marius Willett's New York Regiment. From August 1781 to April 1782 Salmon served as a waiter to Dr. Calvin Delano, a surgeon. Besides his duties as a waiter Salmon was able to go on several alarms against the British.

The Pension Bureau questioned Salmon's request for a pension based on his young age and serving as a waiter. Salmon replied back to them, *"I enlisted and subjected to the duties and obligations of a soldier and the employment. I was armed and equipped, paraded with the company at certain times, Mounted guard and drew the wages of a soldier."*

Sources: 1. Tombstone 2. Census of 1810, 1820, 1830, 1840, and 1850. 3. Genealogy of Child, Childs, & Childe Families of the Last & Present in the United States and the Canadas. 4. Sons of the American Revolution Application. 5. U.S. Pension Roll of 1835. 6. Pension Papers S21689.

****

Isom (Isham) Childers age 13

Isom Childers was born in 1766 in Warren County, North Carolina, and he died in 1841 in Lawrence County, Illinois. He married Patience Parker on 8 September, 1791 and they had 8 children. For his service he received $30 a year.

"I entered the service of the United States under the following officers and served as herein stated. I volunteered for the term of three months under Capt Blantain Col Sowel & Gen Sumner I marched from Warrenton in North Carolina to Waxhaw Creek where we were attacked by the enemy and returned to Charlotte in Maklenburg County where we there was a small skirmish. That part of this time I was with Gen Green. This was about the year 1779 but I cannot recollect certainly."

"I served another tour of three months as a volunteer under Capt Blantain, Col Sowel & Gen Sumner. I believe was in the year 1780 but I can't recollect the month. I was not with any regular officers. I still resided at the same place in Warren County North Carolina. In my marching I volunteered for another term of three months I was at Hillsboro and Salisbury in North Carolina and at the Wateree in South Carolina. I volunteered for another term of three months to assist Gen Washington in the siege of Cornwallis. I had marched till within about half a day's march from York when we heard the news of the surrender of Cornwallis."

Sources: 1. Register of Revolutionary Ancestors of the Indiana DAR. 2. Revolutionary Soldiers Buried in Illinois. 3. North Carolina Marriage Bonds 1741-1868. 4. Tombstone. 5. Sons of the American Revolution Application. 6. Census of 1830.

****

James Chisham age 13

James Chisham was born on 25 January, 1768 in Culpeper County, Virginia, and he died in September of 1838 in Battletown, Kentucky. He married Catherine Ranes in Virginia in 1789. He received a yearly pension of $23.33 for his service.

"In the year 1781 & early in the year, the month not recollected I served a militia tour of three months __?__ Capt Robt Pollard. James duval Leut & Charles Barns Ensign – time was taken __?__ in marching from point to Point. We had a small Battle with the British at Petersburg– James Slaughter was our Col. John Williams our Maj'r. Stuben & Mulenburg our Gen's. & at the close under Lafayette. after our return home a very short time I was called out to serve another tour of militia duty, I volunteered to serve the tour of Richard Runnells as his substitute under Capt Richard Webb of orange. Col Edwards & Maj'r. Welch regular officers commanded when we joined head quarter near Jamestown – at the Close of the 2 months I returned home."

The Battle of Petersburg, also called the Battle of Blandford, was fought on 25 April, 1781 shortly before the Battle of Yorktown. James Chisham refers to it as "a small battle", when actually it was a large battle involving over 3,500 men engaged for over three hours.

At this time in Virginia there were no regular continental army troops in the state, only Virginia militia. The Virginians were under the command of Baron von Steuben who had split his army into two corps. James was serving under General Peter Muhlenberg, and they were stationed on the south side of the James River. Peter Muhlenberg was a Lutheran minister who, when the British were threatening, stood in the pulpit saying, *"there is a time to pray and a time to fight, and that time has come now"*, while removing his preacher's robe to show his Continental Army colonel's uniform.

The Baron knew he could not win since he was outnumbered 2 to 1. His men, however, put up a spirited fight and the group James was with repelled several British attacks. Eventually, the Americans had to retreat and they did so in the greatest of order, despite the fact the British troops pressed hard on them.

Sources: 1. Virginia Marriage Records 1700-1850. 2. Historical Register of Virginians in the Revolution. 3. Pension Papers W8595. 4. April 2003 lecture by Robert P. Davis to the Sons of the American Revolution – Richmond Chapter.

****

Cornelius Chittenden age 14

Cornelius Chittenden was born on 6 April, 1766 in Killingworth, Connecticut, and he died on 24 December, 1858 in Westbrook, Connecticut. He married Rachel Porter on 29 December, 1781. They had 10 sons and seven daughters. He received a yearly pension of $80. Cornelius' father and three brothers also served in the Revolution.

"I enlisted in the Town of Killingworth of aforesaid, in November or December AD 1780 to serve in the army of the revolution. Three Years the company to which I belonged was commanded by Capt. Baldwin—the company was commanded toward the better part of the time by Capt Potter. That said company joined the Regiment at White Plains in the state of New York. The said Regiment was commanded by Col Swift. The brigade was commanded by Gen Persons. The American Army was then at White Plains. The said Regiment remained at White Plains most of the summer then went to Peekskill received __?__ __?__ he winter of 1781-

1782. The whole period of my service in that neighborhood at Stony Point and different places on the North river. I was in no battle serving the period of my said service. I was discharged from the service at West Point the 28th day of October 1783."

Cornelius enlisted in the 2nd Connecticut Regiment which was merged with the 9th Regiment in January 1781. It was re-organized and re-designated as the 3rd Connecticut Regiment.

Cornelius told his family that he was acquainted with George Washington, and on a review day had the honor of making Washington laugh while engaged in a conversation about his cousin. Cornelius and his wife were members of the Congregational Church until the church preached too strong on future punishment, so they left the church and became Methodist.

Cornelius and Rachel left the Methodist Church when it held *"to light of an opinion on the evil of slavery."* He helped to organize the First Wesleyan Methodist Church, which was very anti-slavery. Cornelius often said that the nation would suffer for the crime of slavery.

Sources: 1. Connecticut Revolutionary War Military Lists 1775-1783. 2. Early Connecticut Marriages. 3. Sons of the American Revolution Application. 4. Pension Papers S17880. 5. Year Book of the Society of Sons of the Revolution in the State if New York, 1899.

****

Daniel Christian age 13

Daniel Christian was born on 17 November, 1762 in Berks, Pennsylvania, and he died on 26 November, 1847 in Carroll, Illinois. He married Elizabeth Nikerk in 1785 in Berks. He received a yearly pension of $38.66.

"I served in the service of the United States in the month of September 1776 as a volunteer in Captain George Wills company at Reading Pennsylvania and marched with said company to the town of Amboy in New Jersey and I served in the said company two full months."

"I in December 1778 I entered Captain Kits Company which time he was stationed at Reading Pennsylvania, to guard the Continental stores and prisoners that a company commander by Captain Spoon, was to furnish a certain number of men for the continental army and that he __?__ the said company __/__ my __/__ __/__ on the first of June 1780 that the said company was attached to the 2nd brigade sixth regiment,

commanded by Col. Butler and in Major __?__ battalion and the commanding officer of the company in which I served after I joined the Continental army was Lieut Nott, I served in the said company as a private seven months—I marched from Reading to Philadelphia—from thence to Trenton New Jersey, from thence to Tappan where I joined the Regular Army and was placed under the command of the said Lieut Nott, about two months afterwards Genl Wayne with the first Brigade made an attack on a fortified block house belonging to the British on the North River and that some time he crossed the North River at Stony Point to attack New York then in possession of the enemy—but did not make the attempt and returned to the neighborhood of Morristown—from thence we marched to fort West Point after Genl Arnold had left said fort, where we remained about four weeks—from thence we returned to the vicinity of Morristown for winter quarters—I was discharged on the first of January 1781."

The Pennsylvania 6th Regiment took part in several small skirmishes after Daniel Christian joined it. They wintered in Morristown and on 1 January, 1781 they joined the munity of the Pennsylvania Regiments at Morristown. The men were unhappy over their extended service and receiving no pay. Many, including Daniel, were discharged.

Sources: 1. Tombstone 2. U.S. Pensioners 1818-1872. 3. Pension Papers S8201. 4. Lineage Book D.A.R. Vol. XLII, 1903.

****

Henri Christophe age 12 (African American)

Henri Christophe was born on 6 October, 1767 probably in Grenada, and he committed suicide on 18 October, 1820. He was brought as a slave to Saint Domingue, the former French colony now known as Haiti.

In 1779 Henri served with the French army as a drummer boy with a regiment described as one with people of color or colored people. His regiment fought at the Siege of Savannah, which was a joint Franco-American attempt to retake Savannah. It took place between 16 September and 18 October, 1779. The regiment had over 500 recruits from Saint Domingue. The battle was one of the bloodiest of the war and resulted in a British victory.

After the war Henri returned to the French colony of Saint Domingue, and as a slave he worked many different jobs with his pay going to his master. Starting with the slave uprising of 1791, which was the largest and most successful in the Western Hemisphere, he served as a soldier and quickly rose to become an officer. For five years he fought alongside Toussaint Louverture and finally defeated the French colonists. On 1 January, 1804 the colony declared its independence and was renamed Haiti. In June of 1802 Henri was elected president, and in 1811 he proclaimed himself King Henri I and became the first and only King of Haiti.

Sources: 1. African Americans at War: An Encyclopedia, Vol. 1 by Jonathan Sutherland. 2. Encyclopedia of slave Resistance and Rebellion, Vol. 1 edited by Junius P. Rodriguez.

****

Jonathan Cilley age 14

Jonathan Cilley was born on 18 March, 1762 in Nottingham, New Hampshire, and he died on 21 March, 1897 in Hamilton County, Ohio. He married Dorcus Butler, who was the daughter of a minister, on 3 July, 1786.

The statement of service was given by Dorcus Butler Cilley, the wife of Jonathan Cilley. She signed the statement with very poor handwriting.

"My husband Jonathan Cilley volunteered or was drafted, but to the best of my recollection the following is a correct statement of the history of the service, Joseph Cilley the father of the said Jonathan Cilley at the time of the breaking out of the Revolution resided in the Town of Nottingham in the County of Rockingham State of New Hampshire. He enlisted the service of the United States either as a Captain or Major, but was soon promoted to the office of Colonel. Young Jonathan Cilley afterwards my husband was left with his mother at home. He was a boy of 14 years of age (he was born the 8th of March 1762) at that time and ran away from his mother unknown to her and applied to one Captain Ford who was then enlisting men in this neighborhood. Captain Ford knew Jonathan and in consequence of his youth and believing that he wished to enlist against the consent of his parents would not receive him. Jonathan would not go home but followed Capt. Fords Company into the army where he met his father Colonel Joseph Cilley at the urgent request of young Jonathan, his father suffered him to remain and took him into his military family as a waiter. He was taken prisoner of the British and kept for some time when he was exchanged and rejoined his fathers Regiment (I think that he was taken prisoner at New York but of this fact I'm not certain) he was in the battle of Saratoga and in several skirmishes and

other engagements but the particulars I am unable to give. The said Jonathan, after remaining with his father Col. Joseph Cilley for some time (the length of time I cannot now state) he was promoted to the office of Ensign in same company belonging to his fathers Regiment but what particular company I cannot state. He served as Ensign for some time and then was promoted to the office of Lieutenant which station he filled until the close of the war. He was home at his mothers twice during the war on furlough and in the service from 1776 to the declaration of Peace."

At the start of the Revolution Colonel Joseph Cilley was appointed Major of the 2nd New Hampshire Regiment on 1 January, 1776. The unit was renamed the 1st New Hampshire Regiment. After the siege of Boston he was promoted to Lieutenant Colonel of the 1st New Hampshire Regiment. Jonathan joined the Regiment sometime in January of 1777, after his father was promoted.

The following is an account of Jonathan Cilley being a British prisoner. It is taken from a book of the New Hampshire 1st Regiment:

"When Col. Cilley marched from home he took with him his second son, Jonathan, who was probably less than fifteen years old. This was a very common at that time, and, no doubt, was often found very useful. When the sudden march from Ticonderoga took place this young man was taken prisoner; and, as he was a mere boy, the captor learning who he was, took him to Gen. Burgoyne, who ordered that he should be treated kindly, and provided with a pass to join his father. He also ordered that he might select from the captured baggage of the Americans, which was immense, any article of clothing he might wish. He therefore took the best looking coat he could find. It proved to belong to Maj. Hull (afterwards the celebrated Ge. Hull). He was also furnished with Burgoyne's proclamation to convey to his father. On reaching the regiment, he found it on parade, with his father in front. The Colonel seized one of the proclamations, and having read it, ordered them all to be torn in pieces, and said, "Thus will the British army be scattered."

The 1st Regiment was engaged in the Battle of Saratoga, Monmouth, Stony Point and Sullivan's campaign against the Iroquois and Tories in western New York. Jonathan was promoted to Ensign, and on 11 May, 1781 he was promoted to Lieutenant. After the war he received 200 acres of land in Ohio, which was next to the 300 acres his father received. Jonathan's wife also received a yearly pension of $320.

Sources: The History of the First New Hampshire in the War of the Revolution by Frederick Kidder, pages 95-96. 2. Sons of the American Revolution Application. 3. Lineage Book DAR Vol. 29 #28227. 4. The Constitution of the Society of Sons of the Revolution and the By-Laws and Articles Incorporation of the Ohio Society: Incorporated May 2, 1893. 5. Pension Papers W5246.

****

Burgess Clark age 14

Burgess Clark was born in 1763 in Goochland, Virginia, and he died on 22 October, 1850 in White County, Tennessee. He married Rhoda Morris on 14 August, 1799 in Richmond County, North Carolina. Rhoda received a widow's pension of $20 a year and a land bounty of 160 acres for the military service of Burgess.

"I entered the service of the United States under the following named officers and served as herein stated. I lived in the State of North Carolina, Chatham County. From the best estimate I can form, it was in the year 1777 that my Older brother, William Clark was drafted in the Company Commanded by Captain James Hearne, the name of the Lieutenant was Roger Griffith. The name of the Ensign I have forgotten. I was then only fourteen years of age, turned into his fifteenth year, and not subject to military duty: But in as much as my brother was drafted, and was compelled to go, I had a wish to go with him, and accordingly I became a substitute for Morgan Minter, who had been drafted in the same Company Commanded by the above named Officers. This tour was for three months. Captain Hearn marched his men to Charleston S. C. where I joined General Lincoln. I remained at Charleston until the expiration of my three months."

"My Second tour was also from Chatham County and likewise was three months – and I think it may have been three month, or perhaps more, after returning from the first Campaign, I Volunteered in the Company Commanded by Capt Joseph Johnson – who commanded a Company of drafted men. But the Captain being the half brother of mine I volunteered as above stated. I belonged to a Regiment Commanded by Col Collier, and I think the Major's name was Sharp. Captain Johnson's Company joined Gen Gates' Army – and marched to Campden. I was in the Battle which is called "Gates defeat" -- after Gates defeat, I with the balance of Capt Johnson's company, was stationed at Salisbury North Carolina, and there remained until my time expired. I was discharged at Salisbury, by Col Harper who had the Chief Command of the troops there Stationed."

"I beg leave to add to my Declaration that I served another tour against the Tories of three months in Chatham County this had escaped my recollection. I turned out as a volunteer this time under Capt <u>Alexander Clarke</u>. My Lieutenant's name not remembered – my Regiment was Commanded by Col Lutrell. I was in an engagement with the Tories on Cane Creek at Lindsey's Mill in Chatham County – here Colonel Luttrell was shot from his horse and killed – I got no discharge this time."

Burgess Clark was at the Battle of Camden fought on 16 August, 1780. The battle proved to be an overwhelming British victory. Burgess served in the 1st Brigade of the North Carolina militia under the command of Colonel John Collier. When the British attacked the Americans the North Carolina Militia was the only militia unit to hold its ground.

This author found the following story on the White County, Tennessee Web Site. It probably came from one of his grandchildren. I found it interesting that there is no mention of this account in the pension application of Burgess Clark.

"While serving in the Continental Army during the American Revolution, during one particular battle, Burgess suffered a serious head wound by a British sword which would end his fighting days. As there were no hospitals for treatment, injured soldiers were only administered basic first aid and then sent home. Often, a family member or neighbor assisted the injured man home and both men would be released from the army for the trip home. Such a neighbor agreed to help Burgess travel home, and the two departed on horseback."

"Only two days into the long trip home, Burgess' companion decided that he no longer wished to provide assistance to him, thinking the sorely wounded Burgess would die in the night. The neighbor decided that should Burgess awaken the next morning, he would just leave him. Burgess did awaken only to find the man staring down at him. Cursing at him, he said, "You have opened your old eyes for the last time. I'm going to leave you, so you're on your own now." And with that he left, taking the horse with him."

"On his own now and his head wounds needing attention, he was able to get to his feet and start walking for home. He had not walked far before coming upon a footpath leading off to a farmhouse in the distance. He could see smoke coming from the chimney and knew someone was there. Starting down the footpath, he came to the farmhouse. The people living there took him right in and tended his wounds, feeding and clothing him as needed. The man of the house, a continental army officer himself, was interested in the circumstances of Burgess' situation. After hearing what had happened, he sat right down and wrote a letter back to the army to tell them of this occurrence. Burgess stayed with the family for a few days, resting before he regained enough strength to continue on with his journey. Not having any form of transportation, Burgess was grateful for the kindness of these people, and even more so when they offered him an old mule to help him on his journey."

"Burgess had not gone far before he met a group of soldiers heading in the opposite direction. He was surprised to find that the man who deserted him was now shackled and the soldiers were taking him back to the army. As was tradition, such an offence was punishable by the placing of the offender in the "hottest" battle action. Burgess never heard from his neighbor again."

"Amos always remembered his grandfather's hair sticking out in all directions because Burgess could never get it to "part" correctly due to the scars of the head wounds he had suffered."

Sources: 1. White County Web site. 2. Census 1790, 1800, 1820, and 1830. 3. U.S. Pensioners 1818-1872. Pension Papers W2758.

****

John Clark age 13/14

John Clark was born on 12 August, 1765 in Lancaster County, Pennsylvania, and he died on 13 September, 1844 in Illinois. His wife's name was Mary.

"I entered the service of the United States as a volunteer I think it was in the year 1778 or 1779 which I cannot recollect but I am confident it was one of these years. That from this time tile 1782 I was frequently out in the public service as a volunteer to repel and guard against the incursions of the Wiandotts & Shawnese indians who frequently invaded that part of the country in which I lived which was then called Ohio county in the North Western part of Pennsylvania now Virginia ten miles West of the town of Washington in Pennsylvania. I was too young to be enrolled in any Company of Militia but when I went into actual service as a volunteer I mostly went with Captain Timothy Downings Company of Col. Williamsons Regiment. That the people of the Country who volunteered for service were distributed about in small parties who reconitered the Country to ascertain the movement of the Indians, to hunt their trails &

follow, & to give ___?___ to the inhabitants of their movements. This kind of service was frequent with me as a volunteer. I was in Teeters' fort on the waters of Buffaloe Creek in Ohio County then supposed to be in Pennsylvania, but since ascertained to be in Virginia for upward of six months during the years of 1778 & 1779. That the danger from the Indians became so threatening from the frequent massacre of the Indians, that the people of the Country found it necessary to take refuge in the forts and military stations of the country. That during this time I was under the command of Captain Samuel Teeters of the Riflemen. Me with my associates made frequent expeditions out from the fort into the adjacent Country. I think that I assisted to defend a military post formed by the Militia called Dadridges fort in said Ohio County during the years of 1779 & 1780. I was in this fort for several months I cannot recollect the exact time under the command of Captain Samuel Teeters. In the year 1781 I was with Captain Timothy Downing at a military post in the same county about twelve miles from the ohio river where we remained for several months & from which we often went out in scouting parties. That on the 26th day of May 1782 I think it was, that me & others with Captain Downing at their head rendezvoused on the Mingoe bottom about eighteen miles above the present scite of Wheeling in Virginia, on the north west side of the Ohio river, where we joined others amounting to about 489 rank & file, under the command of Col. Crawford. We marched across the present state of Ohio to the Sandusky Plains. That on the fifth day of June the Indian forces were about five hundred consisting principally of the Wyandotts and Shawnese & made their attack about two oClock P.M. Colonel Williamson was the second in Command and was very anxious to obtain Col. Crawford permission to charge the enemy on horseback; but it was denied him. We occupied a strip of timber on the west side of a small prairie ___?___ indians occupied the timber land on the East side of said Prairie about fifty yards from us the engagement with occasional cessations was kept up to the second day in the night; we were broken by the rush of the Indians upon us. It was supposed that the indians had discovered our preparation to retreat & as they were reinforced & much more numerous than we were, perhaps about three to our one, we broke & fled, Col. Crawford was taken prisoner & put to death by the Indians in a cruel manner. I retreated with Col. Williamson with about one hundred & fifty men who kept in a body; the next day about eleven O'Clock me, James Allen & Robert McBride of my neighborhood were in advance of the main body & passed through a piece of timber for a about a quarter of a mile. we had proceeded through the timber without suspecting danger but when the main body got into the timber we were attacked; but we kept up a regular & orderly retreat without much loss & were not pursued beyond the timber. During the skirmish Capt. Downing above named killed The half Moon a principle chief of the Shawnese. Me & my two assocates were prevented from joining the main body by the Indians between us. We continued our retreat upon ___?___ that we could not join our main body. In the course of the afternoon met with capt Hoagland who I think lived in the neighborhood of Redstone now Brownsville in Pennsylvania. The next day we four marched together till in the night on the trail of an Indian march; as we afterward learned. They had taken some of our __?__ horses & rode them which led us to suppose it to be ___?__ trail of our own party. Finding that in crossing a creek before dark that the stones were wet on the bank from the splashing of the water we concluded that we were within a short distance of them, & continued our pursuit for an hour after dark, when we discovered in the wood a few rods of us a fire. Captain Hoagland showed a determination to go to the fire. I requested & ___?__ not to go. I hailed them & enquired "who is there." The answer was, friend, with the indian pronounciation as I thought, & I so expressed himself to Captain Hoagland; & he proceeded toward their fire & observing no one near the fire, He hesitated in his advance, when some one from the Indian company in good English exclaimed, Captain Hoagland is that you, he answered yes & proceeded to the fire when he was instantly shot, and there was a general discharge of 60 or 100 guns in our direction but without any harm to either of the party we soon got together & abandoning our horses kept on our way toward home. on the seventh day after our retreat we reached the mingoe bottom on the Ohio the place where we started. this expedition occupied $80 under Col. Williamson with a body of seventy or eight men for a few days down the Ohio River in pursuit of a body of Indians who were said to have crossed the river below. I can safely say that the time I was in actual service during the time of the American Revolution was more than one year."*

During the Revolution Captain Samuel Teter served as commander of Doddridge Fort and Teter Fort. The defeat and death of Colonel Crawford, that John Clark records in his pension papers, is described in the section in this book under Francis Dunlavy age 14.

Colonel Williamson had captured a little less than 100 Indians in a raid in 1782. It was never clear if the captured Indians were a threat to the settlers. However, on 8 March, 1782, Colonel Williamson left the fate of the captured Indians in the hands of his men. The men were given the choice of taking the captives to Fort Pitt or putting them to death. The men voted to put them to death. *"They were then and there murdered in cold blood, with gun, and spear, and tomahawk, and scalping knife, and bludgeon and maul."* This became known as the Gnadenhutten Massacre. This is why the Indians took such revenge on Colonel Crawford.

John received $80.00 a year for his service. When he died his wife Mary filed for a widow's pension but it was rejected, because she did not have a record of their marriage and could not prove that it took place.

Sources: 1. Tombstone. 2. Census of 1830 & 1840. 3. U.S. Pension Roll of 1835. 4. Pension Papers W2003. 5. History of Shelby County, Ohio: With Illustrations and Biographical Sketches. 6. Notes on the Settlement and Indian Wars of the Western Parts of Virginia and Pennsylvania from 1763 to 1783, by Joseph Doddridge.

****

Christopher Clarke age 14

Christopher Clarke was born on 5 April, 1763 in Louisa County, Virginia, and he died on 1 February, 1851 in Fluvanna County, Virginia. He married Elizabeth Hope on 10 July, 1810. He received a yearly pension of $23.33.

"I entered the service of the State of Virginia, as a private in the Militia, during the Revolutionary War, as a substitute for my brother John Clarke, who was drafted in a company raised in Louisa county, for the purpose of guarding the British prisoners at the Albemarle Barracks the officers names I cannot now recollect, as they were all strangers to me at the time, and I have never seen any of them since, and he was then only fourteen or fifteen years old. I cannot say positively as to the year in which this service was rendered, but he believes it was in the year 1777 – possibly 1778. It was in the early part of the winter, and when I returned home there was snow upon the ground. Nor am I certain as to the length of the term, but believe it was for one month; or it may have been for three weeks, I am not positive which. I was marched to the Albemarle Barracks, where I remained the whole time I was in service, when I was discharged and returned home."

"In the Fall of the year 1780 I again entered the Service of the State of Virginia, as a private in the place of Alexander Toney, who was drafted in a company of Militia raised in Fluvanna County, commanded by Captain Leonard Thompson, Ensign Wm Bybee I believe there were no Lieutenants in the Company. I was marched to Richmond, where I __?__ a few days after the British had left that city from thence to Petersburg, and from thence to a place below Petersburg called Cabin Point where I

remained for nearly two months when I was marched back to Petersburg and discharged. After the Company arrived at Cabin Point, Captain Thompson resigned his Commission, in consequence of ill health, and returned home, and Ensign Bybee took command. I believe there was no officer in command at Cabin Point of a higher grade than Captain. Captain Henderson of the Albemarle Militia had the Chief command of the troops at Cabin Point."

"I returned home, and in the month of January 1781, I was drafted in a company of Virginia Militia as a private, in a company raised in Fluvanna County under the Command of Captain Samuel Richardson-- Lieutenants names not recollected, for a tour of two months; I was marched by Richmond to Williamsburg and from thence to York-town, and then to the Half House, between York and Hampton, where I remained about a month--was then marched to York, where I remained several weeks, from thence to Williamsburg where I remained until the end of three months from the time I was drafted, having been kept in service, by order of General Nelson, one month longer that the term for which he was drafted, when he was discharged."

"He returned home, and in July following, viz 1781 I again entered the Militia of the State, as a private, in the place of his Cousin William Clarke, who was drafted in a company raised in Louisa County commanded by Captain Wash, for a term of two months. I was marched to the Bowling Green, in Caroline County, Virginia, where my company joined a Regiment under the command of Colonel Taylor, and Major Campbell, first names not recollected. From Bowling Green I was marched to a place called Hubbards Old field, in Gloucester or King & Queen county, where I remained until the end of the term."

"A few weeks before the surrender of Lord Cornwallis Army at York town I was engaged whilst at Hubbards Old Field, frequently in scouting parties, intercepting the foraging parties of the enemy, who were then at York and Gloucester towns."

Sources: 1. Tombstone 2. U.S. Pensioners 1818-1872. 3. Sons of the American Revolution Application. 4. D.A.R. Lineage Book, Vol. 47. 5. Pension Papers W25426.

****

Nathaniel Clarke age 14

Nathaniel Clarke was born on 20 July, 1766 in Haverhill, Massachusetts, and he died on 19 March, 1846 in Plaistow, New

Hampshire. He married Abigail Woodman, and she received a yearly widow's pension of $88.

"I enlisted as a private soldier for three years in the Massachusetts line in the Continental Service and I served against the common enemy with fidelity till I was discharged the 23rd December 1783. I further depose that I was severely wounded in said service."

Nathaniel entered the service on 14 March, 1781 and marched to West Point in a company commanded by Captain Nehemiah Emerson of the 10th Massachusetts Regiment. Colonel Benjamin Tupper was the commanding officer during Nathaniel's three years of service. Nathaniel fought in a battle near Kingsbridge on 3 July, 1781. He was wounded in the knee by a musket ball and taken to the hospital. The ball was extracted by Dr. Eustis who became Secretary of War in 1809. When he was discharged on 23 December, 1783 he held the rank of Corporal.

Sources: 1. Massachusetts Society of the Sons of the American Revolution, 1901. 2. U.S. Pensioners 1818-1872. 3. Pension Papers S20687.

****

Peter Clayton age 14

Peter Clayton was born in 1764 in New York, and he died in 1838 in Duansburg, New York. He married Rachel Abby on 24 November, 1791 at her father's house in Duansburg. According to Rachael they were married by a Baptist Priest. Rachel had some education, because she could write her name. She received a widow's yearly pension of $80.

"I enlisted in the year 1777 in the 25th day of January under Captain John Stone of Paxton Lancaster County Major William North Lieutenant Colonel John Horby and Colonel Richard Humpton's Regiment being the tenth Pennsylvania Regiment and first Brigade commanded by General Anthony Wayne Pennsylvania Line for three years or during the war and I left the service soon after the Revolt of the Pennsylvania Line having served out my time."

Adam Hubley was the Lieutenant Colonel of the 10th Regiment during this time. Peter left the service sometime in January 1781, because the Pennsylvania Line Revolt, or munity, occurred on 1 January, 1781. The soldiers demanded better conditions and treatment. Many had been forced to stay after their enlistment time was up. On 12 January many of the men received their discharge papers, and Peter was probably one of them.

"I was in the Battles at Brandywine with General Wayne Germantown and White Marsh was taken prisoner at Germantown and obtained as a prisoner until after the Execution of Major Andre and then joined General Wayne at __?__ __?__ and was afterwards taken to Newark and was again restored to the army."

Peter was part of the Pennsylvania troops under the command of General Anthony Wayne at the Battle of Brandywine on 11 September, 1777. The Pennsylvania troops protected the American right flank of General Washington. They fought for nearly three hours until ordered to retreat. They were then ordered to harass the British rear in order to slow the advance of the British toward Pennsylvania.

Peter's description of his service may not be completely accurate. He claimed to be in the Battle of White Marsh. This battle was fought the first part of December 1777. Peter said that he was taken prisoner at the Battle of Germantown on 4 October, 1777. This means that he was a British prisoner when the Battle of White Marsh took place. He probably confused that battle with the Battle of Paoli.

The Battle of Paoli, which Peter was probably in, took place on 20 September, 1777. General Wayne and his Pennsylvania Regiments were left behind after Brandywine to harass the British rear. During the night of 20 September British forces engaged in a surprise attack on Wayne's camp. There were very few Americans killed, but there were reports of the British bayonetting Americans who tried to surrender. The engagement was later called the "Paoli Massacre" by the Americans.

The Americans had 53 killed and over 100 wounded in the battle. The reports of a massacre by the Americans were probably false, since there were so many wounded and 71 were taken prisoner. Many of the British troops lived in fear that the troops of General Wayne would try to seek revenge for the "massacre".

The third and last battle that Peter Clayton was in was another American defeat, the Battle of Germantown fought on 4 October, 1777. During the battle the Pennsylvania Line under General Wayne became disoriented in a fog, and as they pulled back ran into part of the American forces under General Green. The thick fog resulted in the two groups of

Americans firing on each other. Afterwards, the American army began to retreat and Peter was one of the 438 men captured.

After the battle a stray dog was found by some American troops. The dog was wearing an inscription on its collar indicating that he was the property of British General Howe, the man that had just defeated them. General Washington had the dog returned to Howe with a polite note. This is an indication of how respectable gentlemen, even in war, are supposed to act.

Peter was held captive until after the execution of British Major Andre on 2 October, 1780. This meant that he was a prisoner of war for three years. He was a soldier for less than a year before his capture. After he became free he rejoined the army and served until the middle of January 1781.

"According to the best of my recollection think I was a prisoner half of the time I was in the army,"

Sources: 1, U.S. Pensioners 1818-1872. 2. Census 1790 & 1800. 3. Pension Papers W20878. 4. Lineage Book D.A.R. Vol. LXI, 1907. 5. General Howe's Dog: George Washington, the Battle of Germantown, and the Dog who Crossed Enemy Lines by Caroline Tiger.

****

John Clearman age 12

John Clearman was born on 10 March, 1765 in New York, and he died on 9 March, 1857 in Morristown, New Jersey. He married Nancy Vandevear on 1 May, 1805. Because they married late they had only one child.

John's father was from France and acted as liaison officer between France and the Colonies during the Revolution. He was in France when the war began and was one of a hundred picked men that Lafayette brought with him to the colonies. Since John's father was a friend of George Washington, young John served as Washington's drummer boy. John later served as a private in Captain John Palhemus' Company of Colonel William Earl's 1st Regiment of New Jersey Troops. John received a grant of land in New York City for his service.

Sources: 1. Tombstone 2. Sons of the American Revolution Application, 3. U.S. Newspaper Extractions from the North East 1704-1930. 4. D.A.R. Lineage Book, Vol. 143.

****

Benjamin Clements age 14

Benjamin Clements was born in December of 1765 in Pittsylvania, Virginia, and he died in 1835 in Harrison County, Kentucky. He married (1) Sarah Bailey on 17 April, 1786 in Virginia and (2) Mildred Griffin on 13 September, 1831 in Stokes County, North Carolina. He received a pension of $100 a year for his service.

"I enlisted in the Army of the United States or Virginia State line and I am now ignorant which in the year 1779, under Captain Edmond Reed and served in Major John Nelson's Corps of Dragoons under the following named officers: Maj John Nelson, who was the highest in command: the Corps was composed of three Companies, I belonged to the first Company, of which Edmond Reed was Captain and a man by the name of Brunt or Brent was Lieutenant for a while, and after some time Brunt or Brent resigned and went away and was succeeded by a man by the name of Spencer: — ___?__ was first Captain of the second Company of said Corps, and left there and was succeeded by a man by the name of Armstrong--of the third Company of Nelson's Corps a man by the name of Armong was the Captain: I left the service in the year 1781 having served two years, the whole term of the term for which I enlisted; that I served under no other term of enlistment."

"I swear that when I entered the service I resided in Charlotte County in the State of Virginia – I was not actually engaged in any battle or battles – that shortly after I enlisted in Charlotte County Va. I was marched from there to old Williamsburg in Virginia, where I remained for some months, and from there was marched to Albemarle Barracks to guard Burgoyne's prisoners, where I remained until it was understood that Wallace's army was passing through the County, I with eleven others was sent to the South and placed along the road for the purpose of carrying expresses, I was thus engaged until shortly before Gates' defeat, at Camden in South Carolina, when I was sent back to the Albemarle Barracks; that before I returned to the Barracks I for a while composed one of the life guard of Decalb — that shortly after my return to the Barracks in Albemarle, we were informed of Gates' defeat, and that Wallace was proceeding with his army through the Country, whereupon we carried the prisoners whom we were guarding to Winchester in Virginia, where we remained about one week, when we returned to the Albemarle Barracks, and found that Tarlton and his Corps had been there and burnt the Barracks, we then pursued the enemy to Richmond a part of

which Town we had burnt – from there I was marched to Goode's Bridge — that I received a written discharge."

In his first tour of duty Benjamin served in Major John Nelson's State Cavalry Regiment of the Virginia Militia. This unit was raised in May 1779 and consisted of four troops. Benjamin was in the 1st Company commanded by Captain Edmond Reed.

Sources: 1. U.S. Revolutionary War Rolls 1775-1783. 2. Virginia Select Marriages 1785-1940. 3. Pension Papers W1230.

****

William Cleveland age 11

William Cleveland was born on 24 February, 1765 in Brooklyn, Connecticut, and he died on 3 December, 1834 in Greenfield, New York. He married Amy Tourtellote in 1791 in Massachusetts. He received a yearly pension of $80.

"I enlisted sometime in the month of April 1777 in the continental service for three years. Was then ordered to Hartford to have the small pox and sometime in June or July of the same year joined the army at the White Plains in the state of New York and was placed in a company commanded by Captain Wills Clift in the 3rd company Regiment command Colonel Willys and continued in service til the 10th day of April in the year 1780. I was in the Battle at Frogs Point"

William is found on the rolls of the 3rd Connecticut Continental Line under the command of Colonel Samuel Willys from 28 April, 1777 until 28 April, 1780. He said that he was at the Battle of Frog's Point. However, that battle was fought in 1776. William also said that he was stationed at White Plains in the summer of 1777. The 3rd Regiment under Colonel Willys was at White Plains, but it was in the summer of 1778. William was in the regiment from 1777 to 1780, but he may have been confused about the Battle of Frog's Point.

In Europe the practice of infecting people with a less-deadly form of small pox resulted in most of the British troops being immune to the disease. Most of the American troops were at risk of getting the disease, which could decimate the American army and put any hopes of victory in jeopardy. In 1777 General Washington ordered mandatory inoculation of all recruits who had not had small pox. This decision by Washington to inoculate the army was a stroke of brilliance. When William was inoculated with small pox he was required to stay in quarantine for 3 to 4 weeks.

Sources: 1. Record of Service of Connecticut Men in the War of the Revolution. 2. Sons of the American Revolution Application. 3. Tombstone 4. Pension Papers S12494. 5. Register of the Pennsylvania Society of the Sons of the Revolution, 1888-1898.

****

William Cliborne age 14

William Cliborne was born on 23 September, 1766 in Chesterfield, Virginia, and he died 12 March, 1845 in Halifax, Virginia. He married (1) Sarah Firth and after her death (2) Sarah Hile on 4 August, 1881 in Virginia. William and Sarah Hile were married by Parson Tucker. William was a courier for Marquis de Lafayette and he received a yearly pension of $40 for his service. Later in life he must have accumulated some wealth because in the 1820 census it showed he owned 44 slaves.

"I was a substitute for his father in the fourteenth year of his age I believe in the year 1780 and was commanded by Col Francis Goode & Capt David Patterson and marched to Dinwiddie Courthouse, and from thence to Petersburg, and there was discharged, after a tour of three months service."

"That a second time, I again, was a substitute for my father and rendezvoused, at Randolph's Mills near Petersburg, pursued Cornwallis and Tarlton under the Command of Demorques Delifate and Captain Creed Haskins retreated to Chesterfield Courthouse, and from thence crossing James River and towards the County of Culpepper, and round through Richmond to Bottom's bridges and was stationed there some time, and from there to Wiltown on James River and there was attached to Infantry under the command of Capt Scott and Col Robert Goode and was stationed at Sudberry's & Horner's, and was surprised by Tarlton and his Corse and was taken nearly all prisoners, the remnant with myself that was not taken, joined the army and seved until that tour of service elapsed."

"The third tour he served under Capt Branch in the Lower Part of Virginia three months more. That the fourth tour I was a substitute for Nicholas Robertson in the County of Chesterfield and marched under Capt George Markine from Chesterfield Courthouse, and from thence to Williamsburg, and from thence to Little York and after the surrender of Cornwallis was sent on under Gen'l Lawson to Winchester and served his

Last tour making in the whole of my service <u>twelve months</u> in the Revolutionary War."

Sources: 1. Sons of the American Revolution Application. 2. Virginia Marriages 1740-1850. 3. Census 1820. 4. U.S. Pensioners 1818-1872. 5. Pension Papers W10620.

****

Bartholomew Clute age 14

Bartholomew Clute was born on 30 December, 1764 in Schenectady, New York, and he died there on 15 December, 1840. He married Margarita Peek in December 1789. He received a yearly pension of $60.

"In the month of March or April in the year 1779 I entered in the Company of Artificers under the command of Captain John Clute and served in the said company for the full term of three months at Saratoga & other places in that vicinity. While there I found a large 12 Inch Brass Mortar which had been buried by the British at the surrender of Burgoyne & his army in the fall of the year 1777 for which piece of service General Schuyler allowed me a compensation."

Bartholomew served as an artificer, which was a person skilled at working on artillery devices in the field. He served under Captain Clute who was probably a relative. There were a total of 11 Clutes that served at this time in Schenectady.

"In the Summer of the year 1779 I volunteered with a detachment of Militia and Oneida Indians under Captain John B. Vrooman, and marched to Schoharie. In this expedition I assisted in capturing a party of runaway Tuscarora Indians."

"In the month of December in the year 1780 I was enrolled in the company of Militia commanded by Captain John Mynderse, while in said company of Captain Mynderse I was engaged in several expeditions; the principle of which were as follows."

"I went out as a scout with a party of about seventeen men under command of Lieut James Peek aforesaid. In the expedition I marched to Lake George and was in pursuit of a celebrated Spy named Joseph Bettis and his associates. I was also out as a scout or Indian spy on many other occasions, on one occasion I went to the interior of the town of Galaway after a tory named McGillcosay & captured him. In the last named I served with a party of Militia & Indians."

Joseph Bettis and his men gave information to the British and caused great concern in the area until he was caught and hung as a spy just before the end of the war.

"When Major Ross & Walter Butler made a descent on the Mohawk settlements in 1781 I was with the detachment of Militia which marched from Schenectady under Captain Thomas Brown Barker. On this occasion I marched as far west as Caughnawaga where I mounted guard for some time."

Sources: 1. A History of Schenectady During the Revolution by Willis Tracy Hanson. 2. U.S Pension Roll of 1835. 3. Pension Papers S12499.

****

William Coates age 14

William Coates was born on 15 December, 1760 in Caroline County, Virginia, and he died in October, 1844 in Summer County, Tennessee. He was married by Parson John Walker to Susannah Dismukes on 4 March, 1782. He enlisted in the army shortly before he turned 15 and served from 1775 to 1781. He received a pension of $8 a month.

"I enlisted for two years, and the next enlistment for three years and during the War, that first enlistment in the fall of the year 1775 in the State of Virginia in the company commanded by Captain Samuel Hawes in the 2nd Virginia Regiment commanded by Col. Spotswood in the line of the State of Virginia or the Continental establishment. I continued to serve both of my said terms faithfully and I was discharged after the battle of the Eutaw Springs, that he was in the Battles of Germantown, Brandywine, Monmouth, at the taking of Stony Point, and many other battles."

In a later statement he said he was at Valley Forge, and he fought at the Battle of Guilford Court House, Siege of Ninety-Six and Camden.

The 2nd Virginia Regiment was authorized by the Virginia Convention on 17 July, 1775. At the Battle of Brandywine, on 11 September, 1777 William Coates was in the 9th Company in the division commanded by Nathanael Green. During the battle they held off the British advance long enough for the rest of Washington's army to escape. William was also part of the American confusion at the Battle of Germantown fought on 4 October, 1777. His unit attacked the left side of the British line, and with the smoke from the cannons and muskets combined with the dense fog many of the men fired on other American units.

William also fought at the Battle of Hobkirk's Hill, sometimes called the Second Battle of Camden, fought on 25 April, 1781. This battle was witnessed by future president Andrew Jackson, who at the age of 14 was being held a prisoner of war by the British.

At the Battle of Stony Point William Coates was under the command of Colonel Christian Febiger. They were part of the group that attacked the fort from the south side. They were also engaged in heavy fighting because Colonel Febiger captured the British commander in person. Febiger later wrote to Virginia governor Thomas Jefferson,

"But as I had the honor to command all the troops from our State employed on that service I think it my duty, in justice to those brave men, to inform you that the front platoon of the forlorn hope consisted of 3/4 Virginians, and the front of the vanguard, of Virginians only, and the front of the column on the right of Posey's battalion composed of four companies of Virginians and two Pennsylvanians......the advance composed of 150 Volunteers, first entered the works. Seven of my men in the forlorn hope who entered first were either killed or wounded. I have the happiness to say that every officer and soldier behaved with a fortitude and bravery peculiar to men who are determined to be free, and overcame every danger and difficulty without confusion or delay, far surpassing any enterprise in which I have had an active part."

The final battle of the 2nd Virginia Regiment would be the Battle of Eutaw Springs fought on 8 September, 1781. The day began very hot with the Americans, short on rest and food advancing toward the springs. The Americans forced the British from their camp leaving their uneaten breakfast. The American troops stopped their advance, and they began eating the deserted breakfast and plundering the stores of food and liquor. They ignored the officer's commands to continue the fight. Soon the British regrouped and launched a counter attack and they forced the Americans out of the camp. The battle ended in a draw with both sides claiming a victory. The American commander Greene considered it a victory and later wrote, *"...principally indebeted for the victory we obtained to the free use of the bayonet made by the Virginians and Marylanders"*

Sources: 1. Virginia Land, Marriage, & Probate Records 1639-1850. 2. U.S. Pensioners 1818-1872. 3. A Guide to the Battles of the American Revolution by Theodore P. Savas and J. David Dameron. 4. Pension Papers W106751/2.

****

Ferris Cogswell age 14

Ferris Cogswell was born in 1767 in South Britain, Connecticut, and he died in 1836 in New York. He is on the payroll of Captain Richard Hurd's Company in the Regiment of the Militia commanded by Ira Allen. Ferris received pay for 17 days of service and 52 miles of travel for the alarm on 20 October, 1781.

Sources: 1. Sons of the American Revolution Application. 2. D.A.R. Lineage Book, Vol. 85.

****

John Cole age 12

John Cole was born on 18 December, 1764 in Connecticut, and he died on 13 January, 1854 in New York. He married Catherine Letts. She was a child when on 3 July, 1778 American settlers were massacred in the Wyoming Valley of Pennsylvania. The settlers were killed by Loyalists and their Iroquois allies. In the massacre, 360 men, women, and children were killed and many others escaped to the forest to later die of starvation. Catherine's father fled with her and two other children through the wilderness living off roots and berries. At one point he swam across a river with his three children clinging to his clothing.

John had joined the militia by 13 October, 1777 and saw his town burned on that date by the British at the Battle of Kingston. Kingston had become the first capital of New York in 1777 and the British marched on it in October. The residents knew the British were advancing and quickly moved the capital to Hurley. The British entered the town and began to burn the buildings and large amounts of wheat. John's mother stood on Hurley Mountain and watched the flames destroy her childhood home.

Sources: 1. Onondaga's Soldiers of the Revolution by the Onondaga Historical Society, 1895. 2. History of Bradford County by David Bradsby.

****

John Cole age 14

John Cole was born on 18 December, 1761 in Westchester County, New York, and he died on 13 January, 1854 in Onondaga County, New York. He was married to Pamila by Rev. Robert Campbell in September 1787 in Saratoga County, New York. He enlisted in September of 1776 about three months short of his 15th birthday. He received a yearly pension of $40.

"In the month of September 1776 I lived in the town of Stephentown, State of New York I then volunteered in the company commanded by Captain Weed and went to Stillwater where I was stationed for One Month *under Major Taylor who commanded a Battalion of New York Militia at that place."*

"In the month of September 1778 I volunteered with a single company under Captain Fisher at Stephentown aforesaid and went to Johnstown near the Mohawk River and was stationed there and at Stone Arabia at a Fort called Fort Pasigh or Paries [Fort Paris near Johnstown] *for* two months.*"*

"In the month of April 1779 I volunteered under Captain Sanford of the New York Militia & lived there at Ballstown, Saratoga County was stationed at Fort Plain in the early part of the summer I went with a part of the force at that place West Point on the Hudson as near as I can recollect was then attached to Col Dubois Regiment of Continental troops of the New York line was soon after that sent with a party to guard some prisoners about 30 or 40 (British & Cowboys) taken down the river went with them to Lancaster in Pennsylvania returned to New Burgh on the Hudson River and from thence went back to Fort plains was under Captain Dubois while at West Point."

Colonel Dubois was the commander of the 5th New York Regiment of Continental line. John Cole was assigned to guard some men called cowboys. During the early part of the revolution in the lower part of New York lawless bands of outlaws called "Cowboys" roamed the area. They supported the British side and would raid nearby settlers of their cattle and valuables.

"Soon after I returned to Fort Plain there was a battle at Stone Arabia and either this same day or the next was engaged with the troops from Fort Plain in another Battle near Col Clocks house saw Col Brown after he was killed and scalped by the British Indians and in that vicinity

until late in the fall or early in the winter recollect that much snow had fallen I went home."

The Battle of Stone Arabia, it also goes by several other names, was fought on 19 October, 1780. An army of Indians and Loyalists began to destroy homes and buildings in Stone Arabia. Members of Massachusetts and New York troops, including John Cole and led by Colonel Dubois, encountered the enemy on a farm owned by George Klock. After a small battle the enemy retreated.

Sources: 1. Onondaga's Soldiers of the Revolution by the Onondaga Historical Society, 1895. 2. Pension Papers W6926.

****

Henreitta Maria Cole teenager age unknown

Henreitta Cole was born on 13 March, 1763 in South Carolina, and she died on 17 February, 1854 in Pennsylvania. During the war she carried dispatches that contained important information.

Source: 1. D.A.R. Lineage Book, Vol. 39.

****

Daniel Coleman age 12

Daniel Coleman was born on 7 June, 1768 in Pittsylvania, Virginia, and he died there on 8 April, 1860. He married Anne Payne on 21 July, 1798 in Virginia.

He was an express courier under General Lafayette to deliver general orders. One set of orders he delivered sent troops to aid General Greene, who was retreating from General Cornwallis. After Daniel delivered the orders, the American troops under General Greene quickly moved, which allowed them to cross the Dan River safely. During this ride he rode nearly 50 miles and much of it on unmarked roads.

After the war Daniel held numerous offices of responsibility. He served as a Deputy Sheriff, General Assemblyman, Justice of the Peace, and Magistrate. He served as a Colonel with the 42nd Virginia Regiment in the War of 1812.

Sources: 1. D.A.R. Lineage Book, Vol. 37. 2. Tombstone 3. Daniel Coleman Chapter D.A.R. Georgetown, Texas. 4. Obituary written by General Benjamin Cabell.

****

Edward Coleman age 13

Edward Coleman was born in 1764. He stated in his pension application he was at the Battle of Germantown (4 October, 1777) and Valley Forge (winter 1777-1778), which would place his enlistment date no later than October 1777. This means that Edward enlisted at the age of 13, and since South Carolina did not arm slaves Edward probably served as a waiter. He claimed that he served for five years and six months and was discharged after the surrender of Cornwallis. This surrender took place in October of 1781, which means that Edward may have enlisted in 1776.

The first part of the pension application has several large ink spots making it impossible to read what is written. The spelling is also very poor.

"_____?_____
_I was in the Revolution against great Britain * _____?_____ all the Whole time In Capt'n. Sinclairs Company * that ___?___ Marion Inlisted him to join said Company as * the Day he Inlisted he Doth Not Say But he says the same Day I Inlisted I went In action In Munks Corner the British joined We fought a gainst Jeneral Lastly The Next at Pumpkin hill about 16 Miles Distance from the former The British gained The Next Camblin or Campden In South Carolina The British gained The Next at lower Charlott We gained The Next at orangeburgh in North Carolina We gained The Next at gilford Courthouse The British gained and there I got wounded with a Ball In my Knee and Doctor Hard Castle took Care of me six months after I got well the Next action at Blackstock we gained The Next at Catava River we gained the Next The Next at Blafford River and there I got wounded with a Bayonet In his side and Doctor Hardcastle took Care of me six months. Then when fit for servise the Next action at Little Jerman town We gained the Next he was In was at the Vally forge In pennsylvania (although we had many skirmages Not mention) the Next at Indian town we gained The Next at Little york and there we took Cornwallis and his army and some months after the taking of Cornwallis I got my Discharge."

"I then went to sea and has Ben in the East Indies and other places But Now has __?__ of and Lives in New york and is poor and has Not more then 25 Dollars worth of property In the world and hereing there Is a pension alloud for the old soldiers he wishes to have his as he knows he is Deserving of the same."

The following statement was a separate statement from the one above. The date for both statements is 19 June, 1829.

"I enlisted in the Company commanded by Captain Sinclair, in the regiment commanded by Colonel Mayhem or Maiham in the line of the State of South Carolina on the continental establishment, that although I cannot tell exactly the time when I entered said corp; yet that I am certain that I served in said corps for Five years and Six months; when after the capture of Cornwallis at Little York in the State of Virgina I was regularly discharged."

"The following are the reasons for not making earlier application for a pension are: that he the said Edward Coleman has been for a long time absent from the United States in the East Indies, and has earned a livelihood from following a seafaring life: and also from his ignorance of his rights, and privelges."

"The said Edward Coleman further declares that his occupation when he can get any employ is that sometimes of a Wood Sawyer, and sometimes that of a Labourer in a Store when he can obtain employment, at either of which he declares he cannot earn sufficient to subsist upon, owing to his advanced age, the many disabilities he labours under in consequence of the wounds received during his service in the Continental Army in the War of the Revolution. That his family consists of himself and his wife whose name is Rachael aged about Forty three years, who is very sickly and unable to labour as she is willing to do. That he has no personal property excepting clothing and bedding which are by no means equal to what is necessary."

The following statement is from Jacob Francis and is made on the same date as the others.

"On this Nineteenth day of June in the year of Our Lord One Thousand Eight Hundred and Twenty Nine Personally came and appeared before Richard Riker Recorder of said city; Jacob Francis a coloured man who made solemn oath that he is now about Sixty years of age, that during the War of the Revolution he was a servant in the French Army under the command of Rochambeau, that he was present at Little York in Virginia at the taking of Cornwallis, and although a Boy of Twelve or Thirteen years of Age he perfectly well remembers seeing Edward Coleman there, he belonged to the American Army, and was in the regiment belonging to the South Carolina line."

The following is a statement from Doctor Thomas Cook about the wounds Edward had from the war. The statement was made 20 June, 1829.

"Thomas Cook of the city of New York Doctor of Physic, being duly affirmed, doth depose and say that he has examined Edward Coleman a man of colour; that upon examination he found that said Coleman was wounded in the right knee apparently by a Ball; and that he appeared to be wounded in the Abdomen by a Bayonet. Affirmant is informed and verily believes it to be true that said wounds were received by said Coleman while in the Continental service in the War of the Revolution. and further affirmant saith not [signed] Thomas Cook M.D. One of the Affirmed to before me this 20th day of June 1829 Physicians of the N. York Hospital James Flanagan Justice of Peace President of the Med. Society of N. York"

This statement was made on 20 June, 1829 by Henry Forster, a friend of Edwards.

"Henry Forster of the City of New York, Assistant in the Ballast Office in said city now aged Sixty seven years; being duly sworn upon the Holy Evangelists deposeth and saith that he has been acquainted with Edward Coleman since the year One thousand Eight Hundred and Eleven; that during a part of the time he has been acquainted with said Coleman, he has occasionally went to sea as mate of a vessel, that said Edward Coleman was cook on board the ship Manchester in the London trade. Deponent saith that said Coleman was always during deponents acquaintance with him, a sober well behaved and industrious man; that said Coleman hath always been lame in the right knee ever since Deponents acquaintance with him, and said Deponent hath always understood and verily believes it to be true; that said lameness proceeded from and was occasioned by a Wound received by said Coleman while in the Continental Service during the War of the Revolution."

Edward's pension was rejected with no reason given. It is possible that Edward died soon after applying and had no chance to add additional proof of service.

Source: 1. Pension Papers R2160.

****

Robert Coleman age 14

Robert Coleman was born in 1766 in Virginia, and he died on 6 March, 1846 in Appomattox, Virginia. He married Elizabeth Burk around 1791. He received $20.00 a year for his service.

"I entered the service of the United States as a private soldier in the month of June or July in the year 1780 as a substitute for my father Samuel Coleman I marched from the county of Buckingham to the town of Petersburg under what officer I do not recollect, at Petersburg I was put under the command of Genl Buford my captain Was Graves of Culpepper I marched from Petersburg to Hillsborough in North Carolina, from thence I was marched into South Carolina under the command of Genl Stevens before I left the army I was under the command of Gen Green, I returned to North Carolina and was discharged just before the battle of Guilford."

He must have been a very successful farmer in Virginia. According to tax records he owned 765 acres of land in 1814. According to the census of 1820 he owned 17 slaves. He began selling his land off and by the 1840 census he owned only 12 slaves.

Sources: 1. Appomattox County Virginia Heritage. 2. Census of 1810, 1820, 1830, & 1840. 3. U.S. Pension Roll of 1835. 4. Pension papers S19255.

****

John Collinsworth age 13

John Collinsworth was born in 1763 in Culpeper County, Virginia, and he died 6 September, 1838 in St. Clair County, Illinois. He was married 3 June, 1790 to Mildred Laura Scarborough, and they had at least eight children.

John wrote in his pension application, *"In the year 1776 my brother Edmond Collinsworth went to muster in the County of Culpepper state of Virginia where there was a Lieutenant Wescot who was a recruiting officer enlisting soldiers for the term of two years in the continental volunteer companies The said Edmond enlisted and took the bounty. When he returned home and thought of what he had done he did not like it. I stated to my father that I would take his place and I did so. When the company was made up it was put under the command of Capt John Lee from Culpepper County Virginia."*

When he arrived in Alexandria on the Potomac, John and an another man joined the marine service for one year on board the sloop of war *Liberty* commanded by Captain Walter Brooks. In 1777 he volunteered for three years in the 1st Virginia State Regiment under the command of Colonel George Gibson. John, along with the 1st Virginia Militia, marched to Valley Forge during the winter of 1777-1778 to join with General George Washington.

The regiment was attached to the Brigade under General Peter Muhlenburg in the first part of June 1778. General Muhlenburg was an Anglican minister living in the Shenandoah Valley, when he felt the call to join the Revolution. The story is that he was reading the third chapter of Ecclesiastes to his congregation that begins, *"to everything there is a season."* When he got to the line, "a time for peace and a time for war," he took off his clerical robes to reveal his uniform.

"The army left Valley Forge and came up with the British army at Monmouth and on the 28th day of June General Lee commanding the van of American troops was ordered by the commander-in-chief to attack the retreating enemy Instead of obeying the order he conducted in an unworthy manner and greatly disconcerted the arrangements of the day."

General Lee disobeyed Washington's order to attack, instead he ordered a retreat after firing only one volley. When Washington was informed of Lee's behavior, he dressed Lee down publicly, had him arrested, and ordered his troops into the fight. The battle raged all day in heat over 100 degrees. It was said that heat stroke claimed more lives than musket fire. The battle ended in a draw.

"The battle was fougbt on 28th day of June 1778 and lasted all day. I was in the engagement all day At night the British left the field and moved on to sandy hook where they took shipping . From thence the army marched on through the Hersey and nothing more took place worthy of notice until the battle of Stony Point which was taken by the American army on the night of the 15th of July 1779. General Muhlenburg Brigade was ordered to draw near to the fort to cover a retreat if it should be necessary."

The Battle of Stony Point was a nighttime attack of highly trained selected troops commanded by General "Mad Anthony" Wayne. The daring attack defeated the British, which resulted in a huge moral victory for the Americans.

"As General Wayne had lost some of his men orders were given to fill up the Brigade I volunteered a few days after the battle of Stony Point and joined General Wayne and went on with said troops to Sandy Beach on the North river After we left Stony Point it was taken possession of by the British and in a short time after I was ordered to take three men and reconnoirter the fort which was fifteen miles off and to report any discovery I might make I accordingly reconnoirtered the fort but discovered nothing of importance and then returned to Sandy Beach after an absence of one day and night. I remained in General Waynes Brigade until I was discharged in the year 1780."

Washington did not intend to hold Stony Point. He abandoned it after taking the cannon and supplies. The British reoccupied it and, as James reported in his spying, nothing important was going on at the fort. The British abandoned it two months later.

James returned home after his discharge and in the early fall of 1781, just before the Battle of Kings Mountain 7 October, 1780, he volunteered with two drafted companies commanded by Captain Stephen Trigg and Captain George Pearis. They marched to join the fight at Kings Mountain, but after a couple of days march they learned that the battle was over.

"We had got within one or two days march when word was brought the battle was over. On the same night an express came that there was two hundred tories to cross the Adkin river the next morning and we marched on to meet them, We met and fought and conquered them 16 or 17 of the enemy were killed and wounded."

James is referring to the battle at Shallow Ford in North Carolina. A force of 600 Tories was attempting to cross the Yadkin River, and they were ambushed by 300 American militiamen. Captain George Pearis commanding a company of horsemen helped to defeat the Tories. Captain Pearis was one of four wounded Americans. After the battle James returned home. His last service was in September of 1782 against the Cherokee Indians, when the Americans destroyed thirteen towns and villages. He was awarded a pension of $80.00 a year for his service.

Sources: 1. Montgomery County, Virginia, The First Hundred Years by C.W. Crush and F. T. Ingelmire. 2. U.S. Revolutionary War Rolls. 3. Historical Register of Virginians in the Revolution. 4. Pension Papers S30965. 5. The Virginia Magazine of History and Biography Vol. 21 No. 4, Oct. 1913. 6. Colonial America and the American Revolution: The 25 Best Sites by Clint Johnson. 7. A Guide to the Battles of the American Revolution by Theodore P. Savas and J. David Dameron. 8. A History of Middle New River Settlements and Contiguous Territory by Davis Emmons Johnston.

****

John Conaway age 14

John Conaway was born on 16 October, 1762 in Virginia and he died on 25 October, 1841 in Marion County. He married Rachel Willison in 1780.

"That in the year 1776 as I now think I volunteered under captain Higgins on Big Cape Capon in what is now Hampshire county Virginia in a company of Virginia militia to go a Tour against the Indians on the north side of Ohio river. I was marched to what was then Beeson Town (now Union Town in Pensylvania. Thence to Pittsburg thence down the Ohio river to some point at or near Muskingum river. Thence out to the Indian Towns some distance from the Ohio river. I cannot now remember the waters it was on (but think it was Sciota) nor can I remember the name of the tribe of Indians but think it was the Shawnees I distinctly remember when the troops arrived the warriors were gone and The Virginia troops militia and others took the Squaws prisoners and cut down all their standing corn which grew in different places I think was in August. We were at many places in the Indian country and in the fall of that year we returned to Pittsburg with their squaws and Indian children probably in October. The troops started from home in March and returned at Christmas of the second year 1776 having been engaged and about on duty nine months."

"Then again in 1779 I was drafted to go a Tour on the western waters. started in June 1779 to perform a tour of six months in the Virginia Militia. I started under captain Wiggins a militia officer was marched to Pittsburg in Pa. There joined The command of General [Lachlan] McIntosh ascended the Ohio river to the mouth of Big Beaver creek there built a fort called fort McIntosh in honour of their General who was a Scotchman. continued there till about Christmas experienced great difficulties from Scarcity of rations. Here a serious difference arose between General McIntosh and Captn. Wiggins who resolved to hunt with his command for the relief of his and the other soldiers Genl. McIntosh thought it wholly inexpedient. refused the captain his assent put the captain in confinement The troops left the station about the month of December and returned home I was discharged at Christmas having been in service six months the term of his draft."

"I then removed to Pensylvania to what is now Bedford County and in the Spring of 1780 I was ordered out by Col George Woods as an Indian Spy under captain McCall. Spied in Bedford County Pa. from March 1780 till some time in December 1780 under captn McCall on the waters of Juniata some times on Reece Town branch, sometimes at and near a place afterwards called Franck Town. Captain McCall with a large portion of his company and a another captain with a company of Pensylvania Militia were slain in a battle with the Indians. I happened to be absent, sent to the settlement on duty at the time. I was not in the battle but I was one of the first on the ground to take up the slain and aid in burying them. There were but 16 of the two companies left but what were slain and those mostly absent on duty. I helped to bury the dead and pursued the Indians but the Indian forces augmented to about 600 and the troops had to retreat. I was discharged at Christmas. I was this season engaged as an Indian spie nine months."

"In 1781 I was drafted to go a tour of Three months in the Pensylvana militia. I was marched to a place on Juniata near where Bedford Courthouse now stands. I have forgotten the name of his capt I remember the sergents name was Beatty. In this campaign me and the troops built a Fort around the houses of Ashly and Woods and there acted as Indian spies. The residue of their Tour of three months to wit from March 1781 till June 1781."

"Then again in June 1781 I was raised out by Col. Woods as an Indian Spie under Segeant Beatty for three months. I spied mostly in Bedford County from June 1781 till October 1781 I was discharged."

"Then in March 1782 as well as I can recollect I was again raised out by Col. Woods as an Indian spie for three months in Bedford County under Captn. I cannot now remember the names of any officer except my brother Thomas Conaway who was the orderly sergeant. I spied from March 1782 till June and was discharged verbally."

"Then again in June 1782 I volunteered my services at the request of Col. Woods to act as an Indian spy for three months I was then ordered to ship from Bedford fort for Franks Town a distance of from 70 to 100 miles mostly a wilderness We spied up to Franks Town found it deserted. could get no provisions were compelled on their return to kill game for subsistence contrary to their general orders which was not to shoot except at Indians. I does not remember the names of captain or Leut. this Tour my second brother Thomas was sergeant again. I continued this tour from

June 1782 till October and was discharged this last tour was for three months I was verbally discharged by his colonel Geo. Woods."

"*I was very young when I started and the great lapse of time together with a decayed memory here conspired to errase from my recollection the scenes of my youth and many of the occurrences of the war. I remember such things only as made a strong impression at the time I remember amongst the slain of captains McCalls men a soldier named Dugan who was dreadfully mangled a stake drove through his body into the ground. The appearances in the weeds showed plainly that more than Dugan had met death there he was a brave and robust man we concluded that he had killed several Indians before he fell. we however found no dead Indians it was the Indians custom to conceal when they could their dead. being victors in this occasion they had done so."*

The pension application for John Conaway was rejected. This area of West Virginia had many fraudulent applications file by lawyers or agents seeking to make a quick dollar. Also many claims were rejected for those that served as Indians spies. If all or part of this claim is true we may never know.

Sources: 1. Tombstone 2. Marriages of the Northern Neck of Virginia 1649-1800. 3. Census 1830 & 1840. 4. West Virginians in the American Revolution. 5. Pension Papers R2244.

****

Moses Congleton age 13

Moses Congleton was born on 4 October, 1763 in Northampton County Pennsylvania, and he died 6 November, 1838 in Wellsburg West Virginia. He was married to Mary Grimes in the Presbyterian Church by the Reverend Francis Peppart on 18 May, 1788. After the war Moses was a wheelwright and he manufactured spinning wheels. He also served as the Sheriff of Wellsburg and was a Major in the War of 1812.

Mary received a widow's yearly pension of $88 and 160 acres for his service. When Mary first applied for the widow's pension she was rejected, because she was not a widow at the time of the passage of the pension act when she applied. Many letters supporting her were written to the pension bureau. One such letter was written on 3 December, 1839. Mary apparently had problems with two of her daughters after the death of Moses. The person wrote to an important friend, perhaps in Congress, asking for a personal favor.

In the letter he states that, *"...the husband left a reasonably good estate, but he also left two daughters, married to two fellows that have plundered from the poor widow all they could collect, and left her nearly destitute of the means of support. The daughters are certainly relatives of those of King Lear, for they have left the Mother lamenting the days she gave them birth. Immature children! For the father and mother toiled during life to support them, and they would now take the bed from under their widowed and aged mother."*

She did get help from people in high places. A bill was passed in both houses of Congress for money to be paid to, *"...Mary Congleton, widow of Moses Congleton, deceased, a soldier of the Revolution, the sum of one hundred and thirty-two dollars and sixty-six cents...".* This would be paid in addition to the yearly pension she would receive.

"In the year 1776, I, with the approbation of my father, being then a little more than thirteen years of age, volunteered my services, as a musician in the company commanded by Captain John Hays, in the battalion commanded by Major James Boyd, in Lieut. Col. John Liggets Regiment of Pennsylvania Militia. We marched from Northampton on the 2nd day of December 1776 to Philadelphia; thence to Trenton in New Jersey, and on the 2nd day of January 1777 was in the battle at that place, and on the night of that day was detailed in company with William Moffit, to repair the fires and keep them burning, with a view to deceive the enemy, whilst the American army withdrew towards Princetown. on the morning of the 3rd was taken by Col. Penrose to Crosswicks, where we joined Genl. Putnam's Brigade, from thence marched to Morristown, being Headquarters at which place we remained until the last of March 1777, when we were discharged; having served on this tour, as a Musician, four months."

"Another call for Militia was made by government, and on the first day of July 1777 I (with the approbation of his father) volunteered my service as a Musician in the company commanded by Captain John Shriver, Major James Boyd's Battalion and Colonel Stephen Ballet's Regiment of Northampton County Militia. We marched to Brandywine, near Wilmington, in the State of Delaware, being there unwell, and unfit for field duty, was, on the evening of the tenth of September 1777 detailed to aid in taking care of the Hospital; was thence marched to Philadelphia and thence to Bethleham, in Northampton county, where I remained until the expiration of my service, having served, as a musician, Three months,

and was discharged on or about the first day of October 1777 by Doct'r. Bond, chief Surgeon at the Hospital."

"On my return home (having but six miles to travel) on or about the first day of October 1777, another call having been made for militia, I found the troops nearly ready to march, and the commanding Officer of the company not being able to procure a Drummer, prevailed on my father, to permit me to accompany the troops, then about to march, when I volunteered my service, as a musician, in Captain George Cramer's company, the brave Major Boyds Battalion of Col. Traxeler's Regiment, Northampton county Militia, On the 5th day of October 1777 we marched, and joined the American camp, at White marsh, in Philadelphia County, where we remained on the lines to about the 5th day of January 1778, where we were discharged by Col. Traxellor, having served, on this tour, as a volunteer musician, three months."

"In the month of January 1778, another draft of Militia was made; Capt. James Lattimore was detailed to command the company, and being a relative of mine, and having no musician, he prevailed with my father to let me accompany him, as a Drummer, and I readily consented, have become much attached to a Soldier's life. On or about the first day of February 1778 we marched from northampton county to Quakertown, in Philadelphia county, and remained on the Enemys lines during the winter, with a view to prevent the enemy foraging, as well as to prevent the inhabitants from going to the enemy's camp to market. On or about the first day of May we were discharged by order of Genl. Patton there being no field officers taken from our part of the country; we were attached to a Regiment from Berks county, Penna. and the names of the field Officers Declarant cannot now recollect, they being strangers. In this tour of duty I served, as a volunteer Musician, Three months."

"When General Sullivan in the year 1779 marched against the Six Nations of Indians, a Class of Militia was called on to guard the public stores collected at Easttown, in Northampton County; and on the first day of June 1779 I volunteered his services as a Musician in Captain John Ralston's company of Northampton County Militia. The militia troops were under the direction of the Officers of the Regular Army, who were left to take care of the public stores, and by them I, and the company to which I belonged, were discharge, on or about the first day of September 1779. I, at present think, that Capt. Pittegrew, of the regular army, was in command, at that time and place."

" I served, in this last mentioned tour, as a volunteer musician Three months, and was discharged by capt. Pettigrew In the latter part of the Summer of the year 1779, when Brandt, one of leaders of the Indians and Tories made an attack on the Minnisinks settlement, a class of Northampton Militia was called to support that neighbourhood, when Captain Joseph Brown was detailed to command the company, and after obtaining permission from my father, I volunteered my services, as a Musician, on the first day of October 1779, we marched over the mountain into the neighbourhood of the settlement at the Minisinks; joined Colonel Jacob Stroud's Regiment of militia, and to which regiment the company to which Declarant belonged, was attached. Remained encamped at the Minisink settlement until the last day of December 1779 when I was discharged by Colo. Stroud; having served on this last mentioned tour of duty as a volunteer Musician, three months."

"About the last of June 1780 another call for militia from northampton County, was made to go to the state of New York, when Captain Jacob Hickman was detailed to command the company. By permission of my father I volunteered his services, as a Musician, and was marched from Northampton county on the 1st day of July 1780 to the state of New York; in which state, at Paramer's Mills, we joined Colo. John Vancamps regiment of Pennsylvania, Militia, and remained at the said mills the greater part of the time towards the latter part of it, was removed to New haven, in the State of Connecticut, at which place, the regiment and I was discharged, on or about the first day of October 1780 by Col. Vancamp. Having served, on this last mentioned tour of duty as a volunteer musician, Three months."

"In the Spring of the year 1781 the Indians became very troublesome on the frontiers of Northampton county, and government ordered out a company of Militia to guard the frontiers of that county, when on the first day of May 1781 I volunteered his services as a Musician under the command of Captain Philip Fleck, who was detailed to command the company of militia of northampton county. This company was attached to the Regiment of Militia commanded by Col. Nichols Karnes. In this last mentioned tour of militia duty I served as a volunteer musician three months, and was discharged by Colonel Nichols Kearns on the first day of august in the year 1781. Having served as above stated, Two years and one month as a Volunteer Musician, in the war of the Revolution, and for which he now claims a pension, I returned home, and the war having ceased in my neighbourhood, I never again entered the service, during that war."

This pension shows how important the drummer was to the American Army. On several different occasions the commanding officer asked the father of Moses to allow his son to serve.

After the Battle of Trenton, General Washington knew that he could not hold Trenton against British reinforcements. He took his men back across the Delaware River into Pennsylvania. On 2 January, 1777 The British forces arrived to face the American Army. After a few skirmishes British General Cornwallis believed he had the Americans trapped. That night Washington deployed 500 men, one was Moses, to keep the campfires going while the rest of his army marched to safety during the night. To keep their retreat secret they used no torches and had the wagon wheels muffled in heavy cloth.

Since the camp fires burned brightly all night the British were not aware that the American army had left. As the sun rose the next morning Cornwallis discovered the Americans had slipped away and were now safely in Princeton twelve mile away.

Sources: 1. U.S. Pensioners 1818-1872. 2. West Virginians in the American Revolution. 3. Pension Papers W4930.

****

John Cook age 14

John Cook was born on 25 December, 1761 in Handover, New Jersey, and he died on 24 October, 1837 in Will County, Illinois. He married Catherine on 17 September, 1792. She received his widow's pension of $80 a year.

"Some time in the summer of the year 1776 I entered as a volunteer into a company commanded by Captain David Bates of the New York militia and went with him to Long Island and was there under the command of Lord Stirling and was engaged in a battle in the neighbor of flat bush. After the defeat of the army at the place I returned with the company to New Jersey and remained with them in arms at Amboy and Elizabethtown for about two months when the company was discharged & I went home to my residence in Bloomfield."

John Cook fought at the Battle of Long Island on 27 August, 1776. The British victory gave them control of New York City.

"Afterwards I think late in the same year I entered the militia of the State of New Jersey as a substitute for Samuel Squires who was drafted

for the time of three months the company in which I enlisted was commanded by Obid or Obadiah Kitchell one Hathaway was Colonel and Winans the General who commanded. I cannot be positive to the time but it was at a time when General Washington with the army crossed and recrossed the Delaware river repeatedly and at one time took a good many prisoners. I served out the term of three months as the substitute for said Squire: I then returned to my residence."

"I again entered the militia of the State of New Jersey as a substitute for David Kamp who was drafted to serve in the company commanded by Captain David Bates, the same who commanded the company in which I volunteered to go to Long Island. I entered on this last mentioned term of service very soon after I returned as before stated. I immediately after such return the father of said Kamp applied to me as a substitute for his son David and I agreed to do so. I served as a substitute for three months and was stationed at greatest part of the time at Elizabethtown and Newark. One time I went over with about 70 or one Hundred volunteers to Staten Island under the command of Major Hayes and brought off a number of boats from that place. The militia with which I served at this time was commanded by General Williams."

"Afterwards in the summer season the Enemy crossed over from Staten Island to Elizabethtown Point and proceeded with the country and burned Springfield meeting house between that place and Elizabethtown. I was then sent out and served as a volunteer in the company commanded by Elizah Squires the Colonels name I do not recollect but the whole was under the command of General Heard. That time of my service at this time I do not now remember but according to my best recollection it was between two and three months. In June of 1781 I joined the troops under De la Fayette with a team consisting of four horses and a wagon was with them at the surrender of Lord Cornwallis I was under the immediate direction of Dr. Mott who was the commander of the wagons. I was taken sick while in the service and in consequence of my sickness lost two of horses."

On 6 June, 1780 about 5,000 British troops crossed from Staten Island to Elizabeth Point and took possession of Elizabethtown. On 23 June the British were reinforced and began to advance toward Springfield. John Cook's unit of militia set up a defensive line at Connecticut Farms outside of Springfield. The British quickly pushed the Americans out of Connecticut Farms. Later the Americans began to regroup with new reinforcements. The British decided to retreat and began to loot and burn

Connecticut Farms and Springfield on their way back to Elizabethtown Point.

Connecticut Farms was the home of the Reverend Caldwell, who preached in his church against the British rule. He was called "the Rebel High Priest" for his sermons for American liberty and his service as deputy quartermaster for the American army. His wife Hannah stayed home with their two young children. As the British advanced into Connecticut Farms, Hannah was shot dead through a window as she sat on the bed with her children. The neighbors were allowed to remove her body before the British looted and burned the house. Later the British said the Americans did it.

After burning and looting the homes in Springfield (except for four homes owned by supporters of the British) the British returned to Staten Island. This proved to be one of the final engagements of the Revolution in the north. The fighting would now be moved further south.

Sources: 1. Tombstone 2. U.S. Pension roll of 1835. 3. Pension Papers W22853. 4. Sons of the American Revolution Application.

****

John Cook age 14

John Cook was born on 9 December, 1761 in Hanover, Virginia, and he died in March of 1844 in Elbert, Georgia. He married Amy Nelson. John enlisted on 19 July, 1776 and received $40.00 a year for his service. After the Revolution he moved to Georgia, and according to the 1820 census he owned three slaves.

"The nineteenth day of July 1776, I entered the service of the United States as a volunteer under Captain John Leak, Lieutenant John Davis, Thomas Owens was our Major, Gen'l Rutherford commanded. I started from Guilford, North Carolina. We went through Salisbury and up to the head of Catawba near a fort called Cathey's fort, from that fort we Crossed the mountain and went down the Swamano River, thence to the Indian towns upon the Tennessee & its waters, and destroyed sixteen of their towns, I remained three months in that Tour, and returned home."

Griffith Rutherford was appointed Brigadier General of the Salisbury District in May of 1776. The Cherokee Indians, with the support of the British, began attacking American settlements and killed over thirty settlers. General Rutherford requested troops to deal with the Indians and

John Cook answered that call in July. The militia was made up of four regiments and during John's tour of three months they destroyed 36 Indian towns. When their job was finished, they returned home in October of 1776.

"*2nd Tour—I volunteered for three months, Richard Vernon was my Captain, Robert Vernon my Lieut and joined Genl Davidsons in the state of North Carolina _____unable to read a group of words_____ place, it was called Head quarters, not far distant from where Cornwallis and his army was stationed. I continued with Genl Davidson during this time. There was a little scrimmage in Charlotte, North Carolina. The army sometimes advanced and often retreated, being unable to come into contact with Cornwallis. Genl Davidson discharge us when the time of service had expired, on the other side of the Yadkin River, and I went home.*"

"*3rd Tour—In a short time after I returned home from the last tour, I volunteered under Captain Thomas Cook, a Mr. Oneal was Major, John Pacely was our Colonel. We marched down upon Deep River and dispersed a large body of Tories, said to be under the command of Col Fanning, I volunteered for three months, but did not stay all the time in service. The whole company was sent home until called for, but held ourselves in readiness (as ordered), when called upon.*"

"*4th Tour---I volunteered again about one month after _____?_____ tour was out under Captain Thomas Cook. Started from Guilford, NC, marched down Dan River to a place called the red House where the British had taken quarters Our Colonel was James Martin _____?_____ of Genl Greene. The British had dispersed from the red House. Genl Greene followed them, I continued with the army under his command during this service (three months).*"

The Red House John speaks of was probably near the Middle Hico Presbyterian Church in the Northeast corner of Caswell County and about six miles from the Dan River. A short distance from the church was an inn, or tavern painted red, and so it was known as "Red House." A detachment of British troops was encamped in the area after following General Greene, as he retreated across the Dan River.

"*5th Tour—I volunteered again (being unwilling to be drafted) for another Tour of three months under Capt Richard Vernon. We rendezvoused at Gilford Court House, NC, equipped and prepared for service—but was ordered to return to our homes and hold ourselves in readiness when called upon. We were not called upon in this Tour any further."*

Sources: 1. Rutherford's Expedition against the Indians, 1776, North Carolina Booklet 4, by Samuel A. Ashe. 2. Census of 1810, 1820, & 1840. 3. U.S. Pension Roll of 1835. 4. Pension Papers S16343.

****

Frederick Coons age 14

Frederick Coons was born in 1762 in Culpepper County, Virginia, and he died in 1831 in Fayette County. Kentucky. He married twice, (1) Ellen Anderson died in 1781 and they had five children (2) Mary Ann Matthews he married in 1788 and they had eight children. For his service he received $8.00 per month and 100 acres of land.

"I Frederick Coons enlisted in the year 1776 in the state of Virginia three years in the company commanded by Captain John Gallison of the Sixth Virginia Regiment and was discharged in 1779. I was in the battles of Brandy Wine, German Town Stony Point fort under Wayne and James Town."

The Battle of Brandywine was fought from sunrise to sunset on a hot and humid day on 11 September, 1777. During the battle Frederick Coons and his comrades of the 6th Virginia Regiment were under the command of Brigadier George Weedon. General Greene's troops formed to the left of the American line. During the day the American line began to weaken and collapse. General Greene sent General George Weedon's men to cover the road near the town of Dilworth. Their job was to hold off the British just long enough for the rest of the American Army to retreat.

By nightfall the entire American army was in retreat. It was estimated that 1,400 Americans were killed, captured, or wounded compared to nearly 600 British troops. Washington retreated into Pennsylvania and the British captured Philadelphia.

At the Battle of Germantown Frederick and the 6th Virginia were under the command of Major General Nathaniel Greene and Division commander Brigadier General George Weedon. The battle began at 5 a.m. on a foggy day on 4 October, 1777.

General Greene's troops, two-thirds of the army's strength, marched wide of the British line to attack the British right flank. The remainder of the American army would attack the center of the British line. Due to fog, bad roads, and getting lost due to taking the wrong road General Greene arrived at his appointed position late. General Greene's flank was attacked by the British and the 9th Virginia Regiment was cut off and had to surrender. The center of the British line repulsed the American troops and marched towards the troops of General Greene. The Americans fought well but they were still undertrained, outgeneraled, and the battle plans of Washington was too complex for amateurs. Once again they left the field in defeat.

Washington's army, including the 6th Virginia Regiment, marched toward Valley Forge to make winter quarters. There Washington camped not knowing if he would have an army to take the field in the spring.

There is a gap in the service record of Frederick Coons from the Battle of Germantown in October of 1777 to the Battle of Stony Point Fort in July of 1779. The 4th Virginia Regiment was at the Battle of Monmouth in 1778. Frederick makes no mention of Valley Forge, Monmouth, or any other activity in the year 1778. On 12 May, 1779 the 6th Virginia merged with and became the 2nd Virginia Regiment.

Frederick's last battle was at Stony Point Fort on 16 July, 1779. He and the 2nd Virginia Regiment were under the command of General Wayne. The 1,200 men along with Frederick, under the command of General Wayne, were considered the best soldiers in the Continental Army. Their mission was to attack and capture the fort during the night.

Security was so tight that on the way to the fort local dogs were killed to prevent them from barking and alerting the British. To prevent an accidental firing of a musket the men were ordered not to load their weapons and use only their bayonets. The only exception was the group of men that would create a diversion by attacking the center of the fort.

For encouragement General Washington said the first man to enter the fort would receive a bounty of $500.00, the second man $400.00, the third man $300.00, the fourth $200.00, and the fifth $100.00. Around midnight the Americans stormed and captured the fort. Most of the 750 British troops were killed, wounded, or captured. On the American side 15 were killed.

The bounty offered by General Washington was paid. Lt. Colonel Fleury was the first to enter the fort and he personally tore down the British flag. He was followed by Lt. Knox, then Sergeant Baker of the Virginia line, Sergeant Spencer, and Sergeant Donlop. Each of the Sergeants received multiple wounds.

During the attack the British soldiers with raised arms were not put to death as the British had done to the Americans in several battles. It was later said that King George III fought back tears when he heard of the "mercy" that had been shown to his troops.

Washington was so pleased with the victory that two days later he rode to the fort and shook hands with every man that was involved in the attack. A month later the Americans abandoned the fort.

Sources: 1. A Guide to the Battle of the American Revolution by Theodore P. Savas and J. David Dameron. 2. DAR # A025682. 3. Census of 1830. 4. U.S. Pensioners 1818-1872, 5. U.S. Revolutionary War Rolls 1775-1783. 6. Revolutionary War Pensions of Soldiers Who Settled in Fayette County, Kentucky. 7. Land Office Military Warrant # 1197. 8. Pension Papers S35844. 9. The Storming of Stony Point by Donald N. Moran, Sons of the American Revolution, Liberty Chapter. 10. The Enterprise in Contemplation: The Midnight Assault of Stony Point, by Don Loprieno.

****

Joel Copland age 14

Joel Copland was born on 28 June, 1766 in Chatham County, North Carolina, and he died on 3 July, 1836 in Saline County, Missouri. He married Rebecka Hutchison on 14 September, 1798 in Blount County, Tennessee. His pension application was rejected because he did not serve the required six months.

"*Sometime in the month of February or March in the year 1781, a Certain Major Roger Griffith, in the County aforesaid, collected a Company of volunteers, and marched them to Harrisburg in the State aforesaid and I was one of that Company the object of this movement was to Counteract the movements of the Tories of that section of Country, who were at that time very numerous. When we arrived at Harrisburg we there met Genl Butler with whom we Continued until we marched to Guilford Court House. I had been previously detailed to assist in collecting, and taking care of the stock and property of the Whigs of the neighborhood. So that I was not in the battle at Guilford Court house, which took place between General Green, and Lord Cornwallis. At and about one mile from Guilford Court house, Major R. Griffith gave me a furlough, and ordered me to return home and notify the Whigs of Chatham County, he was apprehensive the British might pass through that County and that they had better take measures to secure both their families and property in the event of their taking that direction. which they the British did having performed this service I was never more called into service by Major Griffith. The term of this tour of service was three months. Sometime in the month of June of the same year Colonel Dudley of the County of Hallifax raised about 250 man, mounted volunteers and among that number I was one. We marched with him through the Counties of Chatham, Rowan, Randolph and Guilford--in order to endeavor to hold the Tories in check. This term of service lasted about two or three months during which time we had considerable skirmishing with the Tories. After this, I returned to the County of Chatham, where I lived 10 or 12 years."*

Sources: 1. Census of 1790 and 1830. 2. Tombstone 3. Tennessee Marriages to 1825. 4. Pension Papers R2309.

****

Mayfield Crane age 13

Mayfield Crane was born in 1767 in North Carolina, and he died after 1842. He joined the South Carolina militia in 1779 as a substitute and served under Captain Thomas Brandon and Colonel William Farr. His tour of duty lasted about one year. Mayfield wrote in his pension papers,

"...had one Skirmish during this Tour in which our captain & forces were defeated & himself together with the rest of the men returned home, this battle took place on Briar Creek in Georgia & that it was a company which had detached itself from the main body—there was 3 or 4 killed & several wounded."

Mayfield volunteered again in the summer of 1779 and served in the 2nd Spartan Regiment of Militia under the command of Colonel Thomas Brandon. This tour lasted about one year. His final tour was served under General Sumter, Colonel Middleton, and Captain Philemon Waters.

Mayfield was present in the front line at the Battle of Eutaw Springs 3 March, 1779, *"...it was a warm contest & the Enemy kept the Ground from the Battle Colonel Middleton marched to what was called the four hole Bridge in South Carolina where we remained under Colonel Middleton until peace was concluded I received a discharge from Colonel Middleton after this campaign."*

After the war Mayfield moved to Pickens County, Alabama for sixteen years, and then he moved to Jefferson and then to Mississippi. He received $80.00 a year for his service.

Sources: 1. Records of Pickens County, Alabama Vol. 1 by Mrs. C.P. McGuire. 2. Alabama Pension Roll 1835. Pension paper for Mayfield Crane S30356.

****

Alexander Crawford age 14

Alexander Crawford was born on 12 February, 1765 in Oakham, Massachusetts, and he died there on 1 June, 1845. He married (1) Bethiah Willis on 25 June, 1788 and (2) Mary Henderson, his cousin, on 6 September, 1813. He was the youngest of the three generations of Crawfords that served in the American Revolution.

He enlisted on 3 October, 1779 and served until 10 November, 1779 in Captain William Henry's Company of guards at Castle and Governor's Island. When he enlisted he gave his age as eighteen years, so that he would be allowed to serve.

After the war Alexander became a gunsmith by trade. David Ames of the firm of Ames and Fobes, merchants in Oakham, was appointed by President Washington, who was the first superintendent of the Springfield armory. David took with him Alexander, who made the first gunlock and shared with Richard Beebe the honor of stocking the first gun made by the United States.

Source: 1. Soldiers of Oakham, Massachusetts, in the Revolutionary War by Henry Parks Wright. 2. Tombstone 3. Massachusetts Soldiers and Sailors in the American Revolution.

****

William Creemer age 14

William Creemer was born on 11 March, 1763 in Woodbridge, New Jersey, and he died on 5 April, 1828 North Haledon, New Jersey. After the death of his first wife he married Phoebe Johnson on 28 August, 1790 in New Jersey. He served as a fifer, and his widow received a yearly pension of $88.

"I entered the Service of the united States in the Revolutionary war in 1777 in the spring in the Jersey line First Regt. Commanded by Col. Mathias Ogden and John Holmes company. I served until the end of the war discharged in the year 1783."

William belonged to the 1st New Jersey Regiment under the command of Colonel Matthias Ogden, who served in that capacity from 1777 to 1783. William may have seen action at the Battles of Valcour Island, Brandywine, Germantown, Monmouth, Springfield, Short Hills, and Yorktown. He may have been on the Sullivan Expedition and spent the winter of 1777-1778 at Valley Forge. The regiment was disbanded on 3 November, 1783 at New Windsor, New York.

Sources: 1. Yearbook of Sons of the American Revolution of New York, 1909. 2. Pension Papers W17692. 3. Official Register of the Officers and Men of New Jersey in the Revolutionary War, 1872.

****

Ezekiel Croft age 14

Ezekiel Croft was born 10 January, 1762 in Duplin County, North Carolina, and he died after 1840. On 22 September, 1820 he received a certificate that said he was an Ordained Minister of the Gospel in the Baptist Church and was authorized to perform marriages. He served 6 months as a drummer, 6 months as a dragoon, and 13 months as a private in the militia. He received $86.66 a year for his service.

"On the 10th Nov 1778 or about that day, I entered the service of my country in the North Carolina militia of the continental troops. I engaged as a substitute for John White & commenced as a drummer was attached to Capt Enoch Davis' company of Colonel Frank Locke regiment under General Rutherford. I joined in Guilford County, North Carolina, was marched thro' Rowan County, Salisbury, Mecklenburg County & Charlotte into south Carolina, thro Camden & down Santee to Monks Corner, thence to the ten mile house, thence to the Savannah river at Parinsburg & up & down the left bank of the Savannah as the service required until the 9th of April 1779, when ZI received written discharge of my Capt herewith transmitted."

Colonel Francis Locke, the commanding officer for Ezekiel Croft, was appointed a colonel in the Frist Regiment of the Rowan militia. During Ezekiel's tour of duty the regiment spent 1778 keeping as eye on the Tories in the area, since there was little other activity in the south during this time.

"About the 13 May 1780, I enlisted as a substitute for Jacob McDaniel in Randolph county, N Carolina. I was mustered into Captain Robert McLains's company of drafted militia. I think Colonel Collier was the colonel & well know my company was attached to General Richard

Caswell's brigade. I was marched to Ramsey's Mill to Cross Creek, thence to the upper part of Randolph county, thence to Colston's old field near the Pedee in S Carolina, thence to a point below on that river where a junction was formed with General Rutherford, thence to Lynches Creek where they joined the division under major Genl Horatio Gates & Count De Kalb & thence with that division by Reasour's or Rougeley's mill & Clairmont to the old plain near Camden, whence they arrived on the 15th August."

"About two o'clock a.m. of the 16th, the skirmishing commenced between the pickets of Gate's army & the British under the Earl of Cornwallis. The Battle commenced so soon after the dawn that I had but little opportunity of observing the ground or the position of the different corps. I think the American artillery was placed near the center of General Gates forces & near to me and my company. I well remember that one of the causes of the retreat of the troops immediately next to me & my own company was the circumstances of Col Tarlton, as was said, having carried the artillery & turned it on the Americans. This was a three months tour, which had expired some three or four days prior to the Battle of Camden, but my company was retained until after that battle & its disasters prevented the giving of discharges."

Ezekiel was on the left flank of the American line positioned between the Delaware and Virginia militia during the Battle of Camden. In keeping with military tradition the British placed their best troops on their right flank facing the North Carolina troops. The British fired a volley and followed it with a bayonet charge. The militia's had no bayonets and began to panic and run. The panic soon spread to the North Carolina militia. General Gates, who was commanding far in the rear fled before the battle ended and kept riding away for several days. This defeat was the worst American loss in the entire war. The only good that came out of the battle was it showed that General Gates was an incompetent commander and was replaced by General Nathaniel Greene. Count de Kalb, a very able general, tried to rally his Maryland militia and was shot eleven times and later died from his wounds.

"About the 27th of August 1780 I, in the same county of Randolph, volunteered for a tour of six months under Captain John Hinds in Col John Sullivans regiment of horse. We were stationed at barracks in Chatham County, N.C. until December following, when was marched into S Carolina & at Cheraw hill, joined Genl Greene proceeded up the Yadkin

to the Trading Ford, & I remained under Genl Greene until my term expired."

"About the 30th March 1781, in Randolph County, I volunteered for three months under Captain Hinds & joined what was called the Randolph regiment now commanded by Colonel Thomas Dugan, Colonel Luttrell having been slain by the Tories. Their numbers & butcheries had multiplied since Gates' Defeat, & especially the monster David Fannon, at this period a colonel in the British service, was a dreadful scourge upon this colony. The Randolph regiment was mostly stationed at Bell's Mills on Deep river, whence it made various movements against the Tories. In one of these, in which Captain Hinds commanded in an attack upon the Tory Colonel some distance below the station on Deep River, I was desperately cut & mangled & left as dead on the ground, where some females of the Whigs found me & succeeded in preserving my life. I took the liberty to mention that the hands of Lucretia Stroud & Margaret Bane were employed in that kind office & have ever had my grateful recollection & blessings. I annexes the discharge of Captain Hinds in regard to the tour."

David Fanning was a former patriot who later became a Tory. He had numerous skirmishes with Whig militias, and on 5 July, 1781 he received a commission as a colonel in the Loyalist militia in Randolph and Chatham counties.

In early May of 1781 Fanning and eight men were camped at a friend's house on Deep River. Captain John Hinds of the Randolph militia and eleven men, one being Ezekiel Croft, learned where Fanning was and rode hard to capture him. As they reached the house where Fanning was they began to move in closer. Suddenly, Fanning and his men burst out of the house firing as they ran. They rushed pass the patriots killing one and severely wounding Ezekiel and fled into the woods. Captain Hinds and the remaining militia men took off after them and eventually captured two of Fanning's men. The captured Tories were promptly executed.

Ezekiel was severely wounded and left for dead. Fortunately, he was found by two Quaker women that lived in the Quaker settlement that was located on the Deep River. Lucretia Ogle Stroud and Margaret Bane had nursed wounded soldiers including British troops, and now they tended to Ezekiel and probably saved his life. Lucretia Ogle Stroud's brother Hercules Ogle was a patriot supporter. Lucretia is this author's 6th great aunt.

"In January or February 1782, I volunteered for six months in the same county of Randolph as a state ranger under Captain William Gray. Several such companies were raised to guard the civil authorities & their measures of military cooperation from the incessant assaults of the Tories. During this tour, I served under Colonel Dugan & and again was badly wounded. The chief affair that occurred was the defeat of Fanning by Colonel Dugan at Mrs. Spink's plantation, where I had the joy to see him overtaken & routed at a moment when he was engaged in hanging some Whigs he had captured."

"About the 1st of September 1782 I again volunteered for four months & served as a minute man or ranger for the state of North Carolina under Captain Hinds & York."

Sources: 1. U.S. General Land Office Records 1796-1907. 2. Census of 1830 & 1840. 3. Pension Papers S16739. 4. A Short History of the Ogle Family.

****

John Cronk age 13

John Cronk was born in 1765 in Greenburg, New York, and he died on 3 April, 1854 in Westchester County, New York. His claim for a pension was rejected because the service he performed was a type not provided for under the Pension Act.

"I was born the (now) Town of Greenburg, Westchester County New York in the Year 1764 I believe, I cannot tell the precise time as my father was taken and died a prisoner during the Revolutionary War and the family never after that lived at home. I resided during the Revolutionary War in the town of Sing Sing in the said County of Westchester. In the Spring of 1778 I volunteered as a private in a Company Commanded by Captain Arsor, John Oakly, Lieutenant, in Colonel Cortland regiment and proceeded to a place called Rumbout South East of Fishkill with cattle horses and sheep and pastured them during the season on the farms of Tories. In the beginning of the winter we moved the cattle etc. back to the North part of Westchester County and I was dismissed and returned home. Was engaged at this at the time seven or eight months."

"During the season I suffered severely for want of wholesome provisions particularly bread and salt, and the meat provided was often tainted and unfit for use. In the Spring of 1779 I volunteered again in the

Company aforesaid and was occupied as aforesaid in the safe keeping of horses and cattle and the property of the unprotected inhabitants & to prevent the British in New York from obtaining supplies and the Tories from stealing them and taking them to the British was employed the season all Summer."

Sources: 1. Tombstone 2. Pension Papers R2500.

****

William Cross age 14

Some sources have William's birth year as 1761 and others show it as 1762. This author believes 1762 is correct because William had a brother, Zachariah, who was born 25 March, 1761. Since they were not born twins it is more likely that William was born a year after his brother. William received $43.00 a year for his service.

"September 1776 I volunteered for a twelve mounts tour against the Cherokee Indians under Capt William hicks in the militia. I volunteered as a drummer we Rendezvoused at Edward Coxes on the north side of Holston River at the time last we lay there a few day then marched to Shoats ford on the south side of Holston River we took possession of Shoats fort and made that our head quarters during the whole tour we scouted through the country in quest of Indians we had no regular battle we had no officer higher than a Capt Gen'l Shelby ordered a number of Capts to fortify and keep possession a the forts along the Virginia line to keep the Indians from committing depredations in Virginia, as I was informed at that time, we served at this dime twelve months for which I claim pension. I served the whole time as a drummer."

"Again while living at the same place some time in August 1781 as near as I can recollect I was drafted for a three month tour against the British and tories under Capt Thomas Wallace in Col Isaac Shelbys Regiment of Militia we Rendezvoused on Indian Creek near the iron mountain at the last aforesaid we were there met by an express telling us that men were not wanted at that time we were then permitted to return home and held ourselves in readiness at a minits warning which we did and in about three weeks we were called upon again and we marched to the same ground under the same officers we lay there a few days there was a part of the company had horses and a part had none. Col Shelby gave gave press warrants to press horses to go to the High Hills of Santee I with a number of others were unable to press horses Col Shelby then ordered

me with the balance that had no horses to return to Ensign John Wallace and Sargent Abednago Hicks and guard the froonteers against the Indians which we did till the three months was out. I was Honorably but verbally discharged."

Sources: 1. 1830 Census. 2. U.S. Pensioners 1818-1872. 3. Baltimore County Families 1659-1759. 4. Pension Papers S3221.

****

Felix Curtis age 14

Felix Curtis was born on 9 December, 1762 in Waterbury, Connecticut. He enlisted about four months before his fifteenth birthday. According to his pension application he spent time in 1777 in the hospital with small pox. Felix received a monthly pension of $8.

"On the third day of August 1776 I enlisted at Hartford in the State of Connecticut under Captain Edward Bulkley shortly after my enlistment I proceeded to Peekskill in the state of New York. I was mustered in a Company commanded by Captain __?__ __?__ in a regiment Commanded by col. Samuel B. Webb in the continental line. I continued in said Company until the expiration of the Term of my enlistment, during the said term I was on duty at Peekskill and White Plains in the State of New York at Warrwick on Long Island and other places and was finally discharged at Kings ferry on the Hudson River in the State of New York. I was engaged in the expedition with General Sullivan on Rhode Island in the year 1778 and was in the battle of Springfield in the State of New Jersey in the year 1780."

Felix served in Colonel Samuel Webb's Additional Continental Regiment which later became the 9th Connecticut Regiment.

Sources: 1. Register of the District of Columbia Society of the American Revolution, 1896. 2. Pension Papers S43429.

****

Solomon Curtis age 13

Solomon Curtis was born in 1762 in Connecticut, and he died in November, 1826 in Canada. He married Hannah Taylor in 1780 in Massachusetts. Solomon's wife received a yearly pension of $80. After Hannah died her son filed for the pension to be passed to the heirs of Solomon and Hannah. Solomon made no service statement to the pension bureau, because he died before he could file, so the following information about Solomon's service is from his neighbors, children, and his brother.

Solomon first entered the army with his father, John Curtis on 8 May, 1775. They served in Captain Pettibone's 10th Company in the 4th Connecticut Regiment until 18 December, 1775. Solomon is found on the rolls of the 7th Company in the 4th Regiment under Colonel Benjamin Hinman. The 4th Regiment was raised on 27 April, 1775, and it was disbanded on 20 December, 1775. The Regiment saw action during the invasion of Canada.

Solomon and his father enlisted again in September 1778. During this enlistment John Curtis came down with yellow fever and died. When Solomon left the army, he took his mother, brothers, and sister and moved to Barrington, Massachusetts.

After he moved to Massachusetts, he enlisted from 15 May, 1778 to 7 February, 1779 in Captain Enoch Noble's Company under the command of Colonel Ezra Wood. On 19 July, 1779 he enlisted for one month and twenty-nine days in Captain Roswell Downing's Company of Colonel Powell's Regiment. He later enlisted on 25 October, 1779 for one month in Captain Adam Kasson's Company in Colonel Israel Chapin's Regiment.

In 1780 Solomon moved his family, including his bride Hannah, to Columbia County, New York. A friend of Solomon's wrote that he remembers after Solomon and Hannah married seeing *"Solomon bidding Hannah goodbye after the marriage and starting off with a pack on his back to join the army."* Hannah stayed with his mother and Solomon enlisted from 5 July, 1780 to 15 December, 1780 in Captain Pierce's Company in the 4th New York Regiment. Solomon was at West Point at the time of Benedict Arnold's treason, and he served as one of the guards at the execution of Major Andre.

After his enlistment was up he returned to his wife and family in New York. Later Solomon and Hannah moved to Massachusetts, and around 1791 they moved to Clarenceville, Canada. Solomon lived there until his death in 1826.

Sources: 1. D.A.R. Lineage Book, Vol. 37. 2. Pension Papers W23895. 3. The Record of Connecticut Men in the Military and Naval Service during the War of the Revolution by Henry Phelps Johnston.

****

Charles Cushing age 14

Charles Cushing was born on 23 May, 1764 in Rehoboth, Massachusetts, and he died on 27 December, 1841 in Seekonk, Massachusetts. He married Chloe Carpenter on 12 October, 1788. He received a yearly pension of $33.33 for his service.

"I was born Aug 23 1764 in Rehoboth Mass. And lived there when I entered the service in April 1778 for Eight Months as a private in Cap Jacob Fullers company and Col Joseph Jacobs regiment of Massachusetts Militia & served the whole time at Fall River & Liveton & was in Sullivan's expedition & in July & August 1779 I served as a substitute & private one month at Providence in Cap Joseph Franklins company of Massachusetts Militia & in February 1781 I served as a substitute & private one month at Newport in Cap John Whipples company of Rhode Island Militia."

Sources: 1. 500+ Revolutionary War Obituaries and Death Notices. By Mary Harrell-Sesniak. 2. Sons of the American Revolution Application. 3. Massachusetts Marriages 1633-1850. 4. U.S. Pensioners 1818-1872. 5. Pension Papers S21724.

****

Austin Dabney age 13 or 14 (African American)

Austin Dabney was born about 1765 in Wake County, North Carolina, and he died around 1830. He was a slave and belonged to Richard Aycock. They moved to Wilkes County, Georgia. When Richard was drafted into the militia, Richard sent Austin as his substitute. To avoid any problems because Austin was a slave, Richard claimed that Austin was born free.

Austin enlisted in August of 1778 and served in the Virginia militia under Captain Samuel Campbell. He first marched to Jarrett's Fort in Greenbrier, Virginia, and during this time he did service at Jarrett's Fort and at Benhive's Fort. About nine miles separated the two forts. Most of the time he served at these two forts was defending against Indian attacks.

After he was discharged Austin returned home and soon enlisted in the militia again. On this tour he was under the command of Captain Trigg, and he marched to Petersburg, Virginia and then to Cabin Point. At Cabin Point he was under the command of Colonel Meriwether and joined the army of General Muhlenberg. The army marched to Dismal Swamp and was engaged there in a skirmish with British troops. From there they marched to Gregory's Camp and then to Tan Yards where Austin was discharged. He served again under Captain Trigg totaling 12 months of service.

Austin obtained his freedom after the war and received a yearly pension of $60. For about ten years after the Revolution Austin was Captain of a company of militia in Bedford County, Virginia. He was banned from participating in the land lottery open to Revolutionary War veterans in 1819, but the legislature granted him acreage in Washington in 1821.

Georgia Governor Gilmer made the following observations of Austin Dabney:

"In the Beginning of the Revolutionary conflict, a man by the name of Aycock removed to Wilkes County, having in his possession a mulatto boy, who passed for and was treated as his slave. The boy had been called Austin, to which the Captain to whose company he was attached added Dabney."

"Dabney proved himself a good soldier. In many a skirmish with the British and Tories, he acted a conspicuous part. He was with Colonel Elijah Clarke in the battle at Kettle Creek, and was severely wounded by a rifle-ball passing through his thigh, by which he was made a cripple for life. He was unable to do further military duty, and was without means to procure due attention to his wound which threatened his life. In this suffering condition he was taken into the house of Mr. Harris, where he was kindly cared for until he recovered. He afterwards labored for Harris and his family more faithfully than any slave could have been made to do."

Giles Harris was a white soldier who lived in the area and cared for Austin in his home. The two men formed a close life-long bond. The Battle of Kettle Creek was fought on 14 February, 1779 between 300 to 400 Tories and around 500 militiamen. The Americans defeated the enemy and scattered the Tories.

One story that may or may not be true took place before the battle. Just before the battle Mary Hart's husband joined the rebel militia. Later two Tories forced their way into Mary's cabin and threatened to rape her if she did not fix them something to eat. When the two intruders were eating Mary grabbed a loaded musket that was hidden and pointed it toward the men. Because she was slightly crossed-eyed neither man was sure which one of them would be the target if she fired, so they did what she told them. She marched them with the musket pointed at their backs to the rebel camp and turned them in.

"At the close of the war, when prosperous times came, Austin Dabney acquired property. In the year 18__ he removed to Madison County, carrying with him his benefactor and family. Here he became noted for his great fondness for horses and the turf. He attended all the races in the neighboring counties, and betted to the extent of his means. His courteous behavior and good temper always secured him gentlemen backers. His means were aided by a pension which he received from the United States."

"In the distribution of the public lands by lottery among the people of Georgia the Legislature gave to Dabney a lot of land in the county of Walton. The Hon. Mr. Upson, then a representative from Oglethorpe, was the member who moved the passage of the law, giving him the lot of land."

"At the election for members of the Legislature the year after, the County of Madison was distracted by the animosity and strife of an Austin Dabney and an Anti-Austin Dabney party. Many of the people were highly incensed that a mulatto Negro should receive a gift of the land which belonged to the freemen of Georgia. Dabney soon after removed to the land given him by the state and carried with him the family of Harris, and continued to labor for them, and appropriated whatever he made for their support, except what was necessary for his coarse clothing and food. Upon his death, he left them all his property. The eldest son of his benefactor he sent to Franklin College, and afterwards supported him whilst he studied law with Mr. Upson, in Lexington. When Harris was undergoing his examination, Austin was standing outside of the bar, exhibiting great anxiety in his countenance; and when his young protégé was sworn in, he burst into a flood of tears. He understood his situation very well, and never was guilty of impertinence, He was one of the best chroniclers of the events of the Revolutionary War in Georgia."

"Judge Dooly thought much of him, for he had served under his father, Colonel Dooly. It was Dabney's custom to be at the public house at Madison, where the judge stopped during court, and he took much pains in seeing his horse well attended to. He frequently came into the room where the judges and lawyers were assembled on the evening before the *court, and seated himself upon a stool or some low place, where he would commence a parley with anyone who chose to talk with him."*

"He drew his pension in Savannah, where he went once a year for this purpose. On one occasion he went to savannah in company with his neighbor, Colonel Wyley Pope. They travelled together on the most familiar terms, until they arrived in the streets of the town. Then the Colonel observed to Austin that he was a man of sense, and knew that it was not suitable for him to be seen riding side by side with a colored man through the streets of Savannah; to which Austin replied that he understood that matter very well. Accordingly, when they came to the principle street, Austin checked his horse and fell behind. They had not gone very far before Colonel Pope passed by the house of General James Jackson, who was the governor of the state. Upon looking back, he saw the governor run out of the house, seize Austin's hand, shake it as if he had been his long absent brother, draw him off his horse, and carry him into his house, where they stayed whilst in town. Colonel Pope used to tell this anecdote with much glee, adding that he felt chagrined when he ascertained that whilst he passed his time at a tavern, unknown and uncared for, Austin was the honored guest of the Governor."

Sources: 1. Pension papers W3007 Record of Abstracts of Pension Papers Concerning Soldiers of the Revolutionary War, War of 1812 and Indian Wars who Settled in Wayne County, Kentucky. 2. Tombstone 3. Georgia's Landmarks, Memorials and Legends, Vol. II by Lucian Lamar Knight. 4. Revolutionary Pensioners. 5. African Americans in the Military by Catherine Reef. 6. Revolutionary War Amid Southern Chaos by George W. Hicks.

****

Asa Dains age 14

Asa Dains was born on 7 June, 1764 in Canterbury, Connecticut, and he died 4 May, 1842 in Meigs County, Ohio. He married Jane Kasson. He was 12 and the oldest when his father left for service in the Revolution. Asa served in the militia, the regular army, and as a privateer aboard the *Oliver Cromwell.*

"In the month of August A.D. 1778 being then a resident of the Town of Canterbury County of Windham State of Connecticut I enlisted for the term of one month in the company commanded by Captain Daniel Cady in the Regt. Commanded by Col. Chapman. I spent most of that time in Rhode Island in what was then called Genl. Sullivan's expedition until

driven off by the British. We were then stationed at Providence until the expiration of my time & was discharged. In the month of July AD 1779 I enlisted for the term of three months at the same town of Canterbury in the Company commanded by Capt Joseph Ransford in a Battalion commanded by Major Peters. I was stationed in New London during the time of my enlistment & was there discharged. In the month of Sept 1780 I enlisted on board of the Privateer Oliver Cromwell of New London & served on board of said privateer until the last of March or first of April."

The *Oliver Cromwell* was built in 1776 and at 80 feet was the largest full-rigged ship constructed in Connecticut. In June of 1779 it was captured by the British and renamed *Restoration*. Asa stated he enlisted on the ship in June of 1780, so he either got his dates confused or gave the wrong name for the ship.

"In (I believe) 1781 I served one month as a volunteer in the Company commanded by Capt Cargill at the time Arnold burned New London & massacred the men at Fort Griswold in Groton."

The massacre at Fort Griswold happened on 6 September, 1781 by British troops under the command of the American traitor Benedict Arnold. Much of New London was burned and American soldiers at Fort Griswold were reported to be massacred when they surrendered. One survivor, Stephen Hempstead said, *"After the massacre, they plundered us of everything we had, and left us literally naked."* The Americans also said that when the fort's commander gave up his sword in surrender he was immediately killed with it, and then the massacre started. The British version of the surrender makes no mention of a massacre.

"In Jan. 1782 I enlisted at the Town of Canterbury aforesaid for the term of two months in a Company commanded by Capt Clough in the Regt. Commanded by Col McClaren during the two months & I was there when discharged. In August next ensuing I enlisted at Canterbury for one year in the Company commanded by Capt Benjamin Durgee in the Regt commanded by Col McClaren I served during the term of my enlistment at New London & was there discharged on the 12th August 1783."

Asa Dains was probably serving in the 1st Connecticut Regiment, since it was made of men from the counties of Windham (where Asa was from) and Hartford, he served under Captain Benjamin Durgee which was his uncle.

After the war Asa and his family moved to Belpre, Ohio in 1798. They lived at a place called "The Farm", which was a frontier fortress until 1795 when the Indian threat was greatly reduced. For his role in bearing arms against the Indians he received 100 acres "up Duck Creek." His family was one of the first to settle in Meigs County, Ohio. Asa was a carpenter and millwright, and he built the first sawmill in the area. Asa received $50 a year for his service.

Sources: 1. A History of New London by Frances Manwaring Caulkins. 2. Tombstone 3. Sons of the American Revolution Application. 4. DAR # 36400. 5. Ohio Compiled Census 1790-1890. 6. Connecticut Town Birth Records, Pre 1870. 7. Official Roster of Soldiers of the American Revolution Buried in the State of Ohio. 8. Lineage Book, DAR. 9. U.S. Pensioners 1818-1872. 9. Pension Papers: W6960. 10. Excerpts from the Athens Messinger Newspaper, February 9, 1956 entitled "Early Meigs and Athens Residents Buried in Century Old Cemetery, by E.H. Harris.

****

Adam Dale age 14

Adam Dale was born on 14 July, 1768 in Worcester County, Maryland, and he died on 14 October, 1851 in Hazel Green, Alabama. He married Mary Hall on 24 February, 1790.

At the age of fourteen he enlisted in a company of boys raised at Snow Hill, Maryland to oppose General Cornwallis should the British army escape being bottled up at Yorktown. He later served in the Creek War under General Andrew Jackson. Adam raised and equipped a company of Tennessee Volunteers and made himself a Captain. The unit fought in the battles of Tallapoosa and Horse-shoe bend, Alabama.

His surviving children had his body removed from Alabama to Columbia, Tennessee after his wife's death. When they recovered the body from the grave they found it to be petrified.

Sources: 1. Lineage Book D.A.R. Vol. 53, 1905. 2. A Crane's Foot, Branches of the Gregg, Stuart, Robertson, Dobbs and Allied Families by E. Stuart Gregg, Jr. 3. History of DeKalb County, Tennessee 1915 by Will T. Hale.

****

Samuel Danforth age 14

Samuel Danforth was born c. 1762 in Massachusetts, and he died on 24 August, 1845 in Onondaga County, New York. He married Margaret

Mather Ball around 1818. He marched in a company commanded by Lieutenant John Dean on the alarm of 8 December, 1776, for the defense of Rhode Island. He was on the payroll for 3 days service. He enlisted again on 1 August, 1780 and served for nine days.

Sources: 1. Massachusetts Soldiers and Sailors in the Revolutionary War. 2. Revolutionary Soldiers Resident or Dying in Onondaga County, N.Y., prepared by Rev. W.M. Beauchamp for the Onondaga Historical Association, 1863.

****

John Darrow age 14

John Darrow was born on 9 December, 1763 in New Concord, New York, and he died on 4 July, 1854 in Middletown, Pennsylvania at the home of his son-in-law. He married Martha Herrick on 2 May, 1781 in Cherry Valley, New York. He received a yearly pension of $60. After the war John and his son-in-law had a salt well, from which they boiled brine and supplied salt to nearby settlers.

"In the month of May 1777 at the town of New Concord, in the county of Columbia and state of New York I entered the service of the United States as a waiter to my father George Darrow Adjutant of a Regiment of Volunteers commanded by Colonel McKinstry the regiment to which I belonged marched from New Concord to Bennington in Vermont—was stationed at that place about four weeks when the battle of Bennington was fought in which my father was engaged but I (being but a boy) remained during the engagement in the rear of the main army. The battle commenced in the afternoon—the Americans were forced to retreat before the enemy to a place called Bemis Heights—was stationed at Bemis Heights as near as I can recollect about five weeks. During which time the Battle of Bemis Heights was fought—during the engagement I, with other waiters were constantly employed in carrying water to the men engaged with the enemy. The Americans remained masters of the field—the British retreated the same night to Saratoga. The whole of the American forces pursued thence on the following morning to Saratoga themselves and preparing to make a hold defense—the American army immediately commenced throwing up entrenchment planting batteries and redoubts— and in the mean time reinforcements came in until the enemy were literally surrounded—Frequent Skirmishes took place between the two armies. The two armies lay at that place (as near as I can recollect) about a month when small actions took place between a part of the American Army commanded by General Arnold and the enemy and on the next day the

whole British army under Burgoyne surrendered prisoners of war. I went with my father to Albany to guard the prisoners who were taken to that place. After the arrival of the army at Albany and about the first of November me and my father were discharged and returned to New Concord having been in the service five months."

"At the town of New Concord in the county and state aforesaid I enlisted in a company commanded by Captain James Cannon for the time of nine months—Marched to Albany where I remained about three days— the company to which I belonged was there attached to a regiment under the command of Colonel Marinus Willet which regiment marched to Fort Plain on the Mohawk River, I remained with the regiment at Fort Plain until (as near as I can recollect) about the first of November—when a battle was fought between a party of British troops and the Americans in Johnstown, in which I was engaged, the enemy were repelled and driven from the field—and sometime in the month of December 1781 I was discharged by Col Willet at Fort Plain."

"In the latter part of March 1782, at the town of New Concord in the county and state aforesaid I enlisted as a volunteer in a company commanded by Captain Whelps for the term of nine months, went to Claverack—the company to which I belonged was attached to a Regiment of state troops under the command of Colonel Van Schaiek—I marched immediately to West Point on the North River was stationed at West Point according to the best of my recollections about four weeks that when the company to which I belonged was removed to a place called Smiths Clove (as near as I can recollect) about eight miles distance from West Point back from the river—I remained at that place in garrison, until the expiration of the term of my enlistment and was there discharged about the first of February 1783."

Sources: 1. The Bloodied Mohawk: The American Revolution in the Words of Fort Planks Defenders and Other Mohawk Valley Partisans by Kenneth D. Johnson. 2. Tombstone 3. U.S. Pension Roll of 1835. 4. Pension Papers W25511.

****

Catharine Martin Davidson age 10

Catharine Davidson was born on 16 May, 1768 in Northumberland, Pennsylvania, and she died c. 1816 in Pine Creek, New Jersey. She married Dr. James Davidson on 31 March, 1785.

After the Tory and Indian massacre in the Wyoming Valley on 3 July, 1778 the Americans fled to Fort Augusta near the home of Robert Martin. Catharine assisted her mother and younger sister in ministering to the wants of the fugitives. She took care of the sick and wounded who had crowded into their home and barn.

During the Great Runaway of 1779 she was again called upon to help in the relief of the many women and children who took refuge at Northumberland. This event was a mass evacuation of settlers from the frontier areas of north central Pennsylvania.

Sources: 1. Some Pennsylvania Women during the War of the Revolution edited by William Henry Egle. 2. Women Patriots of the American Revolution: a Biographical Dictionary by Charles E. Claghorn.

****

Ann Simpson Davis age 15

Ann Simpson Davis was born on 29 December, 1764 in Buckingham, Pennsylvania, and she died on 6 June, 1851 in Ohio. She married her childhood friend John Davis on 26 June, 1783. John enlisted at 16 and served in the army for more than five years.

Red-haired Ann was an excellent horsewoman, so it was not unusual for her Tory neighbors to see her riding around the country side. At the age of 15 she was handpicked by General Washington to carry messages to his generals while the army was in eastern Pennsylvania. Many times she carried messages smuggled in sacks of grain and vegetables, sometimes in bullets, and in her clothing. Many times she would deliver these messages at the various mills in and around the area. At times she would dress as an old woman, and more than once she had to swallow the messages when she was going to be searched.

Her service ended when General Washington left her area. Because she displayed uncommon bravery she received a letter of Commendation from Washington thanking her for her service.

Sources: 1. The Ann Simpson Davis Chapter, Daughters of the American Revolution. 2. Sons of the American Revolution Application. 3. Tombstone. 4. Women Patriots of the American Revolution: a Biographical Dictionary by Charles E. Claghorn.

****

David Davis age 14

David Davis was born in 1767 in Washington County, Maryland, and he died 7 January, 1837 in Monroe, Indiana. He married Esther Dobler on 2 April, 1796 in Virginia. He stated that he did not know what year he entered the service except it was the year Cornwallis surrendered, which would place the year at 1781. His pension claim was rejected pending further and more direct proof. Because he stated that he was drafted under the legal age of 16, they wanted to review his case. He probably died before anything was settled.

"By reason of old age and the consequent loss of memory I can not swear positively as to the date of the commencement of my services, but can state precisely the length of my service and the season of the year when commenced. I was drafted in the militia of the State of Virginia and entered the service of the United States in the War of the Revolution as a private Soldier in a Company of Foot of said Militia commanded by Captain James Newell, I can not state for how long precisely. At the time of the said draft the Officers conducting it stated that it would be for __?__ two & three months. I rendezvoused on the Frontier of Virginia. I think Colonel Lewis commanded the Frontiers at this time. I lived in the County of Wythe in said State of Virginia at the time of entering this service. I can not state the year in which he entered this service by its date, but I well recollects that it was the same year in which Lord Cornwallis was Captured at Yorktown Virginia. I well recollect also that I entered this service in the fall season of the year. I was with said company employed in scouting the Country in various directions within and about forty miles east from the fort hereinafter mentioned At the end of two months from the time of entering this service (a very heavy snow falling) the Officers dismissed me & comrades in the frontier country. I served in said tour faithfully and to the acceptance of his Officers fully and at least two months. All the services which are herin before or after stated were in the War of the Revolution in regularly embodied troops raised by authority."

"2d Tour I again entered the service, and enlisted as a private soldier in the State troops of the State of Virginia then living in Wythe County in said state in the service of the United States in the War of the Revolution in Company of Foot in the month of March in the year after that in which I served in my said first tour Said year in which this tour was made & served being the year after the year of the Capture of Lord Cornwallis by the French & Americans. I entered this service and enlisted for nine months in a Company of Foot commanded by Captain Robin

Crocket in the Regiment commanded by Col. Lewis, whose first name I have forgotten, or never knew it. Immediately after such enlistment I was mustered into the service and rendezvoused in what I thinks is now Tazwell County in the State of Virginia From this place of rendezvous I was marched in said Regiment and Company to the Frontiers of Virginia, crossing East River Wolf Creek & other streams and stationed at a place where a fort was partly built (one side being erected). Me and said troops completed said fort. The name of this place and fort I have forgotten although it appears to be on my tongues end. At this fort I was appointed first Corporal and continued to serve as such Corporal during the whole of my service under said enlistment which was nine months. I think said Fort was in what is now Wythe County Virginia. We had been stationed only a few days when the Shawnee Indians having stolen about 30 head of horses, I was ordered to take command of 28 men including myself and scout the neighbourhood which was done, but the Indians not being overtaken, after pursueing them some distance I returned with my command to said fort. Scouts were frequently marched out from said station in various directions. In this manner, in said fort and about it with fifteen days on a furlough to see my father I was employed untill about the end of my said engagement. I was employed constantly & laboriously when I was at the end of his time marched to Head Quarters in what I think is now Tazwell County Virginia and was there dismissed and received a written discharge James Taylor was the Lieutenant, and William Adams Ensign of said Company. During a short time of said nine months I acted as Sub Commissary weighing out rations &c. I served in said engagement at least nine months faithfully and to the satisfaction of my Officers."

Sources: 1. Virginia Marriages 1660-1800. 2. Pension Papers R2711.

****

Joseph Davis age 13

Joseph Davis was born on 24 October, 1767 in Dorchester County, Maryland. His pension application was rejected because it had no proof of service other than his oath. Also his real service amounted to just a couple of months.

"I was Born in the state Maryland, in Dorchester County in year of Our Lord 1767. In the Year 1780 my father being dead, my Mother removed to Virginia, in fauquire County. In the fall of that year there was a draught for 18 months, and it fell to the lot of William Pepper to go into that service and not being willing to leave home, he hired me to take his

place and I think that on the 17th day of February 1781 these men were called upon to rendesvous at Fauquier Court-house I then, and there appeared before Colonel H. Brook and was received by him in the place of Wm. Pepper; the same day took up the line of march for Fredericksburg under Capt G. Jennings, who took us to Fredericksburg, and delivered us to Colonel Tole a Continantal Officer, who was there waiting the arrival of those draughts. I was there enroll'd in Capt. John Willis's Company, but before the Ridgment was fill'd I was trafefered to Col. H. Lees Corps of light horse then in South Carolina whereas Lieutenant Skinner stoped at Fredericksburg from Philadelphia having in charge several of Lee's horses and three of his Dragoons having more horses than they could manage well, he applied to Col. Tole for assistance, myself and one more (James Bland) were sent with Lieut. Skinner with our own consents we went on as fast as we could pass'd Guilford Courthouse N.C. 15 days after the Battle at that place, proceeded to a place call'd Ninty-six, there we joined General Green's army which besieged the British Army under Lord Rowdon at that place. I then was placed in Col. Lee's Corps and attached to the second troop commanded by Capt. Rawdolph; The British were reenforced and and Gen. Green Raised the Siege. I continued in the army untill after the Battle at Utaw Springs 18 miles from Charleston S.C. I then was taken sick was not able to march with Corps, but followed when I recovered. Came up with them at Petersburg Virginia. This was in November 1781. Lord Cornwallis had then surredered his Army to Gen'l Washington, I then applied to Col. Lee to let me go home, to which he agreed; he then gave me a discharg and I got home about the middle of December in said year 1781 and thus my military career ended in the revlutionary war, in the 15 year of my age."

Source: 1. Pension Papers R2738.

****

Samuel Davis age 14

Samuel Davis was born on 15 January, 1762 in Litchfield, Connecticut, and he died on 31 May, 1849 in Dublin, Ohio. He married Elizabeth Smith on 21 August, 1793 in Kentucky. He received a yearly pension of $22.67.

"In entered the army of the United States in the year 1776 as a substitute for a man who had been drafted. I entered for six months and having served out my six months I returned home. I served in Col Smiths Regiment."

"In the year 1777 I went out with the Militia to Danbury in the state of Connecticut under Col Arnold. When we arrived at Danbury we found the town burnt and we pursued the British until ordered back. I was engaged in this service about one month this time."

"In the summer of 1778 I again substituted for a Drafted militia man for six months. I joined the army at Nelsons point, I think, under Captain Strong and Col Putnam commanded the Regiment. We were engaged building a fort, and I remained three days on fatigue (working on the fort) and then was detached in a Lieutenants guard to Litchfield to guard the military stores captured from Genl Burgoyne. I served my time and was discharged."

"In 1779 I went with the Militia to New Haven. The town was plundered and the enemy gone. I was then discharged. I then volunteered under Capt Wadsworth to guard West Haven and served there four months."

Danbury was burned and looted by the British on 26 April, 1777. On 5 July, 1799 2,600 British troops and loyalists landed in New Haven and raided the town.

"In 1779 me and those with me attacked some of the enemy who were landing an officer. The fire on both sides was kept up until the enemy were out of reach."

"In 1781, being an apprentice to one Samuel Abranther in Cheshire in said Connecticut he, Abanther, was drafted and sent me as his substitute. I joined the army at West Point under General Heath. Was sent from there to Stony Point. Remained there one night & went back to West Point in a sergeant's guard to protect boats and keep the ferry. I remained all summer and in the fall I was taken sick and was carried home in a wagon."

After the war Samuel moved to Kentucky and married. For several months in 1792 he served as an Indian spy and scout with several other men for the settlement in Mason County, Kentucky. In the War of 1812 he served as a Captain.

Sources: 1. U.S. Pension Roll of 1835. 2. Lineage Book D.A.R. Vol. 59, 1906. 3. Pension Papers S9380.

****

Paul Davison age 13

Paul Davison was born in 1765 in Ashford, Connecticut, and he died on 19 February, 1805 in Seneca, New York. He married Sally Gould in 1785. Paul served as a fifer from 2 June, 1778 to 28 February, 1783 in Nathaniel Webb's Company of the 4th Connecticut Regiment under the command of Colonel John Durkee. He later was appointed Fife Major in the Regiment. He received a yearly pension of $88.

Sources: 1. D.A.R. Lineage Book, Vol. 19. 2. Sons of the American Revolution Application. 3. Pension Papers S20962.

****

Solomon Day age 13

Solomon Day was born on 17 November, 1762 in Hartford County, Connecticut, and he died on 18 August, 1840 in Sandy Hill, New York. He enlisted in the militia in June of 1776 five months until his 14th birthday. He received a yearly pension of $87 for his service.

"In the month of June A.D. 1776 I enlisted in the Connecticut State troops for five weeks and entered the service under the command of Capt Burnham there was no other company officer and was marched to Seabrook about eighteen miles and was stationed on the sea shore in a house as a Guard next to Governor Griswold resident and object of the guard was to stop the smuggling of goods to Long Island and from Long Island at which time the Militia Troops Lay on said Island I remained there until the month of November when my term of enlistment expired and I received a written discharge. I served and performed by duty as a private soldier five months."

"In the month of November AD 1777 I volunteered and entered the service but do not recollect the names of my company officers. I belong and was under the command of Col Legget after was marched to New London and was stationed in a Fort called New London where I remained as a guard that ___?__ were in the Fort Continental Troops but I do not remember the names of the officers. On the first day of January AD 1777 when I was discharged by parole and I had served and done my duty six weeks as a private soldier."

"While in the town of Colchester aforesaid and in the month of June AD 1777 I enlisted in the Connecticut State Troops for six months under the command of Capt Brown and was attached to drive a team which

belonged to the United States and I was engaged in Transporting provisions and other supplies for the Army from Hartford to Fishkill ___? ___? And other places as I was directed and commanded by my officers. I preformed my duty as a private soldier six months and was discharged."

"In the month of June AD 1778 I enlisted in the State Troops line for six weeks under the command of Capt Northern and was again detached to drive one of the Continental teams and was engaged in transporting military stores and depositing them at Danbury—Fish Kill—Peeks Kill and at other places of deposit under the direction and orders of my officers and continued in the said service until in the month of December when I was discharged."

"In the month of April AD 1780 I enlisted in the State troops or Lives to fill up the Continental Army Continental line for one year. I was sent with several others to Peeks Kill where I joined Capt Gushom Mott Company of Artillery in Col Lambs Regiment of Artillery and was attached to Brig Gen Nixon's Brigade. I crossed the river and was marched to the English neighborhood that before I arrived there the British left and marched to New York I ___?___ at the British neighborhood once combined ___?___ ___?___ while there my Capt was taken sick and I was detached and sent with my Capt Mott to Morristown at the Hospital as nurse for Capt Mott and I remained there as ___?___ ___?___ until sometime late in the Fall and left him and I joined the company and army at New ___?___ New Jersey on the north river and was employed in building barracks for winter quarters and remained there until the month of January 1781 when Col Lamb informed his regiment that he would discharge all."

"I remember seeing Gen Washington, Gen Lafayette Gen Steuben and many other officers."

Sources: 1. U.S. Pension Roll of 1835. 2. Connecticut Town Births pre 1870. 3. Pension Papers S22721. 4. Year Book of the Sons of the Revolution in the State of New York 1899.

****

Charles Deake (Dake) age 14

Charles Deake was born on 26 March, 1763 in Hopkinton, Rhode Island, and he died 2 July, 1844 in Greenfield, New York. He married Abigail Waite Sherman on 13 October, 1789 in Rhode Island. Charles and his father are listed on the rolls of the New York Albany County Militia in Colonel John Blair's' Regiment and Colonel Van Woert's 16th Albany

Regiment. When British General John Burgoyne was defeated on 17 October, 1777 the 16th Albany Regiment stood down. After the war Charles and Abigail moved to Saratoga County and built a school in Daketown on the corner of his farm, and he taught school in the winter. He held several public offices during his life.

Sources: 1. Sons of the American Revolution Application. 2. New York in the Revolution as Colony and State, 2ed, 1898. 3. Real Daughters of the American Revolution by Margaret B. Harvey, 1912.

****

Adam Deets age 8 or 9

Adam Deets was born on 6 April c. 1768 in Virginia and he died on 9 August, 1834 in Ohio while away from home on business. He married (1) Rachel and (2) Mary Stiles in November, 1825.

In his pension application dated 24 April, 1818 he stated: *"I served as a Musician in the revolutionary war in Capt Kilpatricks company of the second Virginia line under Col Nevill for the term of six years, until the cessation of hostilities, I enlisted for during the war and received my discharge at Yorktown."*

In the pension statement on 5 June, 1820 he stated: *"I served in the Revolutionary war as follows, I enlisted in capt Kilpatrick Company Col Nevels Regiment Virginia State Line as a Musician about the second year of the war being then about 8 years old I enlisted for and served during the war. I was wounded and taken prisoner at Bluford defeat was afterwards exchanged and served out my time and was honorably discharged at Yorktown in Virginia."*

Colonel John Nevill commanded the 4th Virginia Regiment from 1778 to 1783. Adam was wounded and taken prisoner at the Battle of Waxhaws, also called Buford's Massacre on 29 May, 1780. There were 53 Americans taken prisoner and 151 were wounded. The dying and badly wounded were carried several miles where they were cared for by, among others, Mrs. Andrew Jackson and her two sons Robert and Andrew, the future president. At the end of the war Adam was a 13 year old veteran and he received a yearly pension of $96.

Sources: 1. Pension List of 1820 of Ohio. 2. Official Roster of the Soldiers of the American Revolution Buried in Ohio. 3. Pension Papers W598.

****

Gideon de Forest age 12

Gideon de Forest was born on 14 September, 1765 in Stratford, Connecticut, and he died on 9 December, 1840 in Otsego County, New York. He married Hannah Birdseye on 5 November, 1793 in New Haven County, Connecticut. He received a yearly pension of $80. Hannah asked for a widow's pension after Gideon died, but it was rejected. She could not supply adequate proof of marriage.

"I enlisted in the service of the United States on or about the first of March in the year 1778. I volunteered at Stratford in the state of Connecticut in Captain Birdseye's Militia Company for two months. Went to the Saw Pits at New York & was stationed at that place as a guard and was discharged."

Gideon served again for two months in August of 1778 under Captain Troops' Militia Company. After he was discharged, he enlisted again for two months in October under Captain Birdseye's Militia Company. This Captain might have been his future father-in-law. In the first of June of 1779 he enlisted as a substitute for Lyman Somers and was stationed in New Field. During these tours Gideon served as a guard in the area.

He had an interesting experience during his June enlistment, *"During this period of service I was stationed at a place called Wells Young as a sentinel with others not to let any boat or vessel pass without a permit from the governor. A sloop came down under command of Capt. Benjamin Brooks who on being hailed paid no attention until I fired a shot through his sail. He then came on shore & showed me his permit & then passed on his way & was soon taken by a British sloop supposed to have been by a previous understanding. The next time I saw the said Brooks he was in confinement in Stamford charged with this offence. Understood he was convicted & whipped 100 lashes."*

Gideon served a three month tour starting in December of 1779 under Captain Bothchford. In October of 1780 he volunteered for a two month tour, and he served as a guard around the Stratford area.

"On or about the first of March 1781 I enlisted in the Connecticut State troops for one year in Capt. Smith's Company Major Shipman's Battalion General Wittenberg's Brigade at Stratford. Went first to Stamford then to White Plains in the State of New York & was then attached to the left wing of the Army under General Washington.

Continued at that place until after General Washington left for Yorktown. Then was marched to Stamford. There we built a garrison & huts & went into winter quarters & on the first of March 1782 was discharged. I was in the battle of Frogs Point."

"In March of the year 1783 I enlisted for six months at Stratford in the Whale Boat service under Capt. Barlow and was in service about one month when on the news of peace I was discharged."

A whaleboat, not to be confused with a whaler, was an open rowboat usually about 30 feet long. The crew of 7 to 10 men would carry swords, clubs, or firearms to engage the enemy. By the end of the war, whale boat raids against the enemy were common around Long Island Sound.

Sources: 1. D.A.R. Lineage Book, Vol. 62. 2. Tombstone 3. Pension roll of 1835. 4. Pension Papers R2842.

****

Absalom Denny age 13

Absalom Denny was born on 4 March, 1762 in New York, and he died on 16 January, 1842 in Onondaga County, New York. He married Bethia Wetherhead in the fall of 1780.

"On the fourth of April 1776 I enlisted under Sergeant Rufus __?__ a recruiting officer for nine months and served as follows marched immediately through New York to a place opposite New York and lay in one ___ barn at or near Hoboken, then to the English neighborhood near Fort Lee, up till I was detached to Fort Washington. I served in Captain __?__ Smiths Company in Colonel __?__ Bradleys Regiment at Hoboken there lay three Regiments together."

"A short time before giving up Fort Washington sixteen men were detached from Captain Smiths Company to go to fort Washington among whom was me, James Weatherhead, John Chapman, Martin Eno, David Smith and John Randell, who joined the garrison as I understand commanded by Magaw, on the day of the surrender I saw the officer said to be the commander of the Fort who ordered out the men saying he was afraid of his life, ordered nothing to be done and no firing to taken place till he returned and then with his white handkerchief on his __?__ he went into a hollow and soon returned leading the whole British Army to where the Fort was surrendered. I with the rest of the garrison made prisoners.

I was then put in the Old Bridewell where I was kept prisoner about two months and was there paroled not to serve again during the war. I was then sent in a feeble state of health from starvation to the American Camp at Rye where I was __?__ __?__ as to have my father came and carried me home on the eighth of March 1777."

"In 1778 having recovered my health, notwithstanding my parole, went out in the service in an alarm and served about a week, but it was against the advice of my acquaintances."

When Fort Washington was surrendered on 16 November, 1776 the Hessians, in retribution for the high casualties they suffered while storming the fort, executed a number of the American riflemen. A total of 230 American officers and 2,607 American soldiers were taken prisoners. Only 800 were alive eighteen months later.

Sources: 1. Revolutionary Soldiers Resident or Dying in Onondaga County, N.Y., prepared by Rev. W.M. Beauchamp for the Onondaga Historical Association, 1863. 2. U.S. Pension Roll of 1835. 3. Pension Papers W20969.

****

John Denney age 13

John Denney was born on 24 August, 1766 in Amherst County, Virginia, and he died on 24 December, 1853 in Wayne County, Tennessee. He volunteered for the militia a few weeks before he turned 14.

"I volunteered in the army of the united States in the year 1780 as a private for thirty days under Col William Cabbel with about two hundred others to prevent the British from crossing James River in order to retake the british prisoners which were at the Barracks at or in Albemarle county Virginia, to the best of my recollection we volunteered about the last of July 1780 at Amherst court house in Virginia by the orders of said Col. And the next day we met at said court house of Amhurst and marched directly to Lynches ferry under our said Col. Cabbell on James River to oppose them & to prevent them crossing James River We ramained there & in the nighborhood watching for the british & in detachments and gathering all the water craft several miles up & down the River for the space of thirty days, & at the expiration of our tour we were informed by the Col. That he had been informd that the British had taken an alarm & gone back. He then marched us back to amherst court house & discharged us in writing."

"On the first day of July 1781 I believe, I was drafted under the orders of Col. William Cabbell of Amherst County Virginia as a private for four months to go to guard the British prisoners at the Barracks in Albemarle County, we rendezvoused at Amherst court house & marched under Capt. Samuel Cabbell (I think the son of Col. Wm. Cabbell) we were marched directly to said Barracks where I served the said tower of four months. and about the expiration of our said tower, orders came to Capt. Samuel Cabbel from the Col. to take the guard, by volunteer or otherwise & march & Guard the British Prisoners to the Pennsylvania line, & those of the company that were well volunteered to perform this tour of duty, & I did likewise volunteer for one month more as a private marched & Guarded the said British Prisoners to the Pennsylvania line & delived them to an officer & solders that met us on or at the Pennsylvania line, & our Captain Samuel Cabbell marched us back to Amhurst court house and there discharged us all in writing for five months as drafted and volunteer under his command."

He added the following note on the side of the first page of his statement, *"I think there was some inferior officers But our Col. Performed most of the command during the time. I do not now recollect them."* Officers in the militia were not always experienced soldiers, many times they were given command because they were wealthy or prominent people in the community.

Source: 1. Pension Papers R2875.

****

William Dickey age 13

William Dickey was born on 6 May, 1764 in Virginia, and he died on 28 June, 1832 in Macon County, Illinois. He married Mary Stephenson. William enlisted in 1777 and served as a gunner in the 1st Artillery Regiment of the Virginia Troops under Captain Waters and Colonel Carter.

Sources: 1. D.A.R. Lineage Book, Vol. 142. 2. Sons of the American Revolution Application.

****

Jeremiah Dixon age 14

Jeremiah Dixon was born on 15 June, 1764 in Pitt County, North Carolina, and he died on 26 July, 1835 in Andalusia, Alabama. On 10

August, 1785 he married Elizabeth Goff. After his death she received his pension of $40.00 a year. Jeremiah also received 274 acres for his service. This author found it interesting that on Jeremiah's tombstone it listed his children with their birth dates.

"I entered the service of the United States in the year one thousand seven hundred and seventy eight 1778 for six months in the State of North Carolina under Cap George falconer, Seth Stafford Lieutenant was in an engagement at Briar Creek (Georgia) with the British General Nash & Genl Bryan commanded served out my six months tour."

The Battle of Brier Creek occurred on 3 March, 1779, when an American force made up primarily of North Carolina militia was surprised and defeated by the British. As the British troops advanced they were given orders to fix bayonets and charge. Most of the militia did not have bayonets and broke ranks and fled into the swamp without firing a shot. Around 400 American troops were killed or captured.

"I volunteered a second time in the year 1781 for twelve months Called twelve months volunteers under Major Reding and Cap Thomas Armstrong in North Carolina. Marched and joined General green at the high hills of Santee in south Carolina was ____?____ in the 2nd regiment of North Carolina troops Col Archibald Little & Anthony Sharp Continental officers of the 2nd North Carolina which I was in was in the engagement with the British at the Eutaw Springs in the charge against the British at Dorchester—volunteered from the Grand Army and was then under the Command of Colonel Wm Washington & Col Lee as scouters served out my year and had a discharge."

Sources: 1. Census of 1790 & 1830. 2. Tombstone. 3. North Carolina & Tennessee Revolutionary War Land Warrants 1783-1843. Pension Papers S10565.

****

Benjamin Doak age 14

Benjamin Doak was born on 30 November, 1760 in Marblehead Massachusetts, and he died on 10 March, 1836 in Lynn, Massachusetts. He married Sarah Goodwin on 27 December, 1785. He received a yearly pension of $96.

He served in Captain Selman's 4th Company in Colonel John Glover's 21st Regiment from May to August, 1775. Benjamin's regiment was in the American siege of Boston in June, 1775. Most of the 21st

Regiment was composed of Marblehead mariners, who demonstrated a great degree of discipline and teamwork. Most of them were clad in sailor outfits of blue jackets and white caps.

Benjamin served in Captain Hooker's Company for seacoast defense in January and February 1776. From March 1776 to January 1777 he was a Quarter Gunner in Captain Pettyplace's Company of Marblehead Coast Guard Service. A Quarter Gunner would assist the gunner of the ship in keeping guns in proper order.

During his last tour of duty he received a bounty coat. This coat was promised to each man volunteering for eight months. It was regarded as quite a possession, so if you died before receiving the coat your family would be granted a sum of money in lieu of it.

Sources: 1. Genealogical & Personal Memories Relating to the Families of Boston & Eastern Massachusetts, Vol III, 1908, by William Richard Cutter. 2. Beside Old Hearthstones by Abram English Brown. 3. American Military Leaders from Colonial Times to the Present Vol. I A-L by John Fredriksen.

****

Richard Dodge age 13

Richard Dodge was born on 31 December, 1762 in New York City, and he died on 3 September, 1832 in New York. He married Sarah Irving, the sister of the writer Washington Irving, on 14 February, 1787 in New York City. He received a yearly pension of $80.

Richards's obituary from the Saratoga Sentinel Thursday, September 11, 1832: *"At Hudson, on the 2d inst., after a lingering illness Major General Richard Dodge, late of Johnstown, Montgomery County, merchant, in the 70th year of his age. Gen. Dodge was a soldier of the revolution. He entered the army at the early age of 13, under the care of his two brothers, Samuel and Henry, the one of whom was a captain and the other a lieutenant in the service. He was at the taking of Burgoyne and Cornwallis. During his after life, he took an active and very conspicuous part, and filled various public stations. Among others, he commanded the army and militia of Sacketts Harbor and the frontier, during the fall of 1811 and winter of 1813."*

Several sources report that Richard Dodge served in the 2nd New Hampshire Regiment during the revolution. However, he served with his brothers who served in New York Regiments. Also, Richard was from New York, and it would be hard to believe that the thirteen year old

Richard would travel to New Hampshire to enlist. In his pension application he states he was in the 2nd New York Regiment. After the war he became a surveyor living in Chaughnawaga, New York. During the War of 1812 he was a General and commanded the Mohawk Ranger Militia. For two years they were on duty along the frontier.

"I enlisted in the Continental Line of the Army of the Revolution for and during the war and continued in its service until its termination at which time I was a Musician in Captain Henry Dubois Company in the 2nd regiment of the New York Line."

"I was in the army at the battles preceding and at the capture of General Burgoyne in the year 1777. When I returned home in the spring of 1778 I enlisted at Fishs Kills in Captain Dubois Company in the 5th New York Regiment, Genl Clinton Brigade. I was at the capture of Lord Cornwallis and was discharged in the year 1783."

Richard served in the 2nd New York Regiment and was at Valley Forge and the Battles of Saratoga, Monmouth, and Yorktown. He was also on the Sullivan Expedition. His brother Samuel was a Lieutenant in the same Regiment. His other brother Henry was a Captain in the 4th New York Regiment. The 2nd Regiment was merged with the 5th Regiment on 1 January, 1781. With this merger all three brothers served together in the same Regiment.

Sources: 1. Sons of the American Revolution Application. 2. Saratoga Sentinel Obituary. 3. Tombstone 4. D.A.R. Lineage Book, Vol. 58.

****

Rachel Donelson 14

Rachel Donelson was born on 15 June, 1767 in Halifax County, Virginia, and she died on 22 December, 1828 in Nashville, Tennessee. In 1779 her father Colonel Donelson organized a group of flatboats to carry household goods, livestock, and 120 people to a new colony in the Cumberland River in Tennessee.

The trip took four months and nearly covered 1,000 miles until they reached Fort Nashborough on 24 April, 1780. They faced frozen rivers, starvation, Indian attacks, and rapids on the dangerous journey. Along the way 32 of the group died by drowning, illness, or Indian attacks. In 1781 the Indians attacked the fort. And Rachael assisted others in defending the fort. Young Rachel had on numerous occasions demonstrated her courage in facing the hardships of frontier life.

When she was around 18 she met and married Lewis Robards in 1785. However, Lewis constantly had irrational fits of jealous rage, and they separated numerous times. Because of physical abuse Rachael left him for good in 1790. She fled to Natchez, Mississippi to stay with friends. A friend of the family accompanied her serving as her protector on the journey. She assumed that her husband would file for divorce after she left him.

In 1791 Rachel married the man that protected her on her journey to Mississippi, 23 year old Andrew Jackson. Two years later the couple learned that Rachel's first husband never filed for the divorce. Later research showed that a friend of Lewis Robards had planted a fake article in the newspaper saying that the divorce had been granted. When divorce was really finalized in 1794 Andrew and Rachael were wed again in a small ceremony.

Jackson ran for president in 1828, and his opponents accused Rachael of being a bigamist and constantly attacked her character. Jackson won the election, but before he left for Washington, Rachel died from what may have been a heart attack. Jackson felt that the unjust attacks on her during the campaign was the true cause of her death.

Sources: 1. Women Patriots of the American Revolution: a Biographical Dictionary by Charles E. Claghorn. 2. More than Petticoats: Remarkable Tennessee Women by Susan Sawyer.

****

Thomas Donnell age 13

Thomas Donnell was born on 11 June, 1765 in Carlisle, Pennsylvania, and he died in December, 1833 in Fugit, Indiana. He married Nancy Barr on 16 June, 1789 in Pennsylvania. Thomas served as a Frontier Ranger in Westmoreland County, Pennsylvania between the years 1778 and 1783.

In 1764 governor Penn offered a reward of $150 for every male Indian prisoner over ten years old, and $134 for his scalp when killed. For every male or female under ten years of age he offered $130 when captured or $50 for the scalp when killed. By 1782 the offer was $100 for a dead Indian scalp or $150 if captured alive. The scalp hunting business reached its highest point in 1781 and 1782. The rangers scalped men, women, and children.

Sources: 1. D.A.R. Lineage Book, Vol. 48. 2. Sons of the American Revolution Application. 3. History of Westmoreland County, Vol. 1, chapter 11.

****

Betsy Dowdy age 16

Betsy Dowdy was born in 1759 in Currituck County, North Carolina. In the fall of 1775 Virginia's last Royal Governor, Lord Dunmore, was losing his control over the colony of Virginia. He soon gathered his army of Tories and captured Portsmouth, Virginia and then took over Norfolk. These two harbors were important to British control over the colonies. He then traveled south and captured the Great Bridge in North Carolina. During this march his army burned homes and slaughtered the livestock. At Great Bridge he built a stockade and installed two twelve-pound cannons. The patriots called his stockade the pig pen. These actions by Lord Dunmore had brought the war to North Carolina.

On the night of 10 December, 1775 a neighbor visited the Dowdy's home and told the family of the capture of the Great Bridge. He told them of the burning of homes and killing of the livestock. Killing the livestock especially alarmed Betsy, because she was fond of the wild horses that roamed the area. In this area were found Banker Ponies, which were descended from Arabian horses that were shipwrecked in the area several hundred years before. Over the years nature culled out the weak horses until Banker Ponies emerged as a tough breed.

The neighbor said that a group of militiamen were on the way to the Great Bridge to win it back. However, the neighbor expressed doubt that they would have enough men to be successful. He went on to say that General Skinner, fifty miles south, had a hundred soldiers, and if someone could take a message to him the General might get to the bridge in time to help the local militia.

Betsy went to bed but could not sleep. She worried that Dunmore's men would come to where she lived and kill the beloved Banker Ponies. She finally decided that she would ride the fifty miles and alert General Skinner and his men. She quickly got dressed and quietly left the house as her family slept. She mounted her pony Black Bess, and on the cold December night she headed south.

She and Black Bess swam across Currituck Sound, road through the Great Dismal Swamp, and then rode inland to the outskirts of Hertford where General Skinner and his men were camped. Cold and tired Betsy informed the General what had taken place at the Great Bridge. General Skinner called his men to arms and marched north. They arrived two days after the battle which the colonial militia had won. The General and his men were welcome reinforcements, because the additional men meant that Dunmore would not dare attack the Americans again.

The ride of Betsy Dowdy has been compared to the famous ride of Paul Revere, with both being a dangerous ride. However, Betsy's ride occurred in the freezing cold of winter and not in the spring when Revere road. Her ride covered 50 miles and his ride covered less than 20 miles. With sheer determination and physical strength, this 16 year old girl and her pony completed a remarkable feat.

Sources: 1. North Carolina Booklet, Vol 1, September 1, 1901, No. 5. 2. Women Patriots of the American Revolution: a Biographical Dictionary by Charles E. Claghorn. 3. Betsy Dowdy Chapter of the D.A.R. Elizabeth City, North Carolina.

****

Stephen Downing age 14

Stephen Downing was born on 20 February, 1762 in Windham County, Connecticut, and he died on 12 July, 1843 in Monroe County, Michigan. He married Susannah Helm on 16 August, 1784. Stephen also served with two of his sons in the War of 1812. He received a yearly pension of $70.

"In the year of our Lord one thousand seven hundred and seventy six I enlisted for six months in Canterbury & went to Groton in said county of Windham and was put under the command of Captain Latham in Fort Griswold the fort was under the command of the Militia in Groton. I remained at Fort Griswold six months and was discharged. The next year AD 1777 I enlisted again in Canterbury for six months and was stationed in New London I do not recollect the names of the officers in command, after the expiration of six months I was discharged and returned home again to my fathers home in Canterbury. In the AD 1778 I again enlisted in Canterbury in Captain Joseph Durkee company of state troops for nine months. The names of the Lieutenant was Timothy Adams, and was stationed at New London, & at New Haven, & at Stafford, & at Old Mills and was discharged about the middle of March the next year. At Old Mills said troops were sent to guard the frontier."

"In the year 1779 I was engaged on board the schooner Young Cromwell a privateer of New London under the command of Captain Wattles and on board of said schooner during the time took three prizes one loaded with salt, one with munitions, one British sloop with artillery men from New York bound for Charleston all taken into Hertford North Carolina I continued on board said Young Cromwell about nine months and was shipwrecked at Cape Fear Shoals North Carolina and returned by land. The next year AD 1780 I engaged again on board the Brig Marquis Layfette a privateer of New London under the command of Captain Hinman and continued six months on board and was discharged."

Sources: 1. Tombstone 2. Census of 1830. 3. Connecticut Town Birth Records, pre 1870. 4. Revolutionary War Rolls 1775-1783. 5. Michigan Military Records. 6. Sons of the American Revolution Application. 7. Pension Papers S29122.

****

Benjamin Drake age 13

Benjamin Drake was born on 18 April, 1766 in Peekskill, New York, and he died on 22 December, 1844 in North Monroeville, Ohio.

"I enter the service of the United States as a volunteer in the year AD 1779 in the fall of that year in the Militia of said state of New York in a company commanded by Captain Ebenezer Boyd in a Regiment commanded by Colonel Samuel Drake. David Ferris was a Lieutenant in my company, served a considerable time to guard cattle for the use of the army was stationed at Peekskill & neighborhood from Fall of the year 1779 to the next Fall and assisted __?__ cattle from Peekskill & that vicinity to the Army. My father lived about three miles from Peekskill and kept a great __?__ house for the American Army where has been seen General Washington."

Benjamin served in the 3rd Regiment of the Westchester New York Militia under Colonel Samuel Drake, who was probably his uncle. There were numerous Drake men in the regiment, which may have been cousins of Benjamin. Benjamin's father's name was Jeremiah. There was a Jeremiah Drake in the 3rd Regiment, and since his father was in the army they may have served together.

"In the Fall of the year 1780 I was enrolled in the Militia Guard on __?__. I then served in that county and vicinity until the peace."

> *"I was at Tarry Town when Major Andre was taken as a Spye by John Pauling, Isaac Van Wart & David Williams who were neighbors & was immediately & _?_ with them & they was his particular friends. I saw Daniel Strang an American of Westchester County a Spye hung at Peekskill. I also saw Edmund Palmer another American Spye hung on Gallows—who first joined the British & came out as a Spye. General McDougal then commanded at Peekskill when Fort Montgomery was taken which I think was in 1777. I was at Peekskill. I was there when Stony Point was taken by General Wayne, the time I saw General Washington was at my father's house, was at the time the American & French Army moved from Peekskill to the White plains—who marched from thence across the North river on their way to Yorktown in Virginia. My fathers name was Jeremiah Drake."*

The Peekskill "hanging tree" was a great white oak where British spy Daniel Strang was hanged in 1777. He was seen observing the American troops in the area, and when searched notes and sketches of the troops were discovered. He was convicted for spying and trying to raise a company of volunteers for the British army. The sentence was immediately carried out, and the 1,000 American troops encamped there were marched around the tree to witness his hanging. Daniel was then buried in a shallow grave at the foot of the tree.

Edmund Palmer, a Lieutenant in a Tory Regiment, was apprehended spying in the American camp. After his capture, Sir Henry Clinton, the commander of the British forces in New York City sent a messenger under the flag of truce to the American General Putman. The British General demanded the release of Edmund Palmer. General Putman sent the following reply back: *"Edmund Palmer, an officer in the enemy's service was taken as a spy, lurking within the American lines; be executed as a spy, and the flag is ordered to depart immediately."* It was signed Israel Putman. *"P.S. He has been accordingly executed."* Edmund also swung form the "hanging tree."

Sources: 1. The Picturesque Tourist; A Guide through the Northern and Eastern States and Canada, edited by O.L. Holley, 1844. 2. A Gazetteer of the State of New York, 1842. 3. Lineage Book National Society of the D.A.R., Vol. L, 1904. 4. Sons of the American Revolution Application. 5. Tombstone 6. U.S. Pension Roll 1835. 7. Pension Papers S2182.

****

Phoebe Reynolds Drake age 11

Phoebe Drake was born on 28 August, 1771 in Westchester County, New York, and she died on 21 November, 1853 in Dutchess County, New York. She married Jeremiah Drake.

Henry Reynolds, Phoebe's father, was a Quaker and an ardent defender of the cause of the colonies. He even took part as a soldier at the Battle of Stony Point. His outspoken support of the Patriots caused hatred among his Tory neighbors.

Late one night the Tories broke into the Reynold's home and beat Henry. His pregnant wife entered the room and seeing her bleeding husband on the floor went into convulsions. One of the younger children, Caleb, entered the room and was beaten unconscious. Phoebe, only 11 at the time, fought the men with such fury that it took two Tories to restrain her.

One of the intruders put a rope around Henry's neck and hung him in the living room of the house. Believing him to soon be dead they started to leave. Phoebe quickly cut her father down. The Tories threatened to kill her with a sword if she did not get away from her father. She was stabbed with the sword, and she promptly threw herself on her father to shield him. She was then beaten with a rope, pulled from her father, and thrown across the room.

Once again the Tories put the rope around Henry's neck and hung him. As they were leaving Phoebe again released him and threw herself on her father to protect him. Twice Phoebe was stabbed. The Tories took her father and threw him into a chest and closed the lid. Then they looted the house and left.

Phoebe, now covered with blood, attempted to remove her father from the chest. Her mother had recovered and helped her get Henry out of the chest and onto the bed. Both were relieved when Henry's groan indicated he was still alive.

While Phoebe administered aid to her father, her mother shouted, *"Oh, Phoebe! Phoebe! The house is on fire in three places! And I can't put it out, if it burns down over our heads."* The Tories had set fire to some flax and to two straw beds. Phoebe managed to put the fire out and tried to make her brother Caleb go to the neighbors for help. The poor injured boy was frozen with fear and would not budge. So, Phoebe left her home and started out to give the alarm to her neighbors. She warned her neighbors of the Tories, and a doctor was sent to the Reynold's farm. A group of armed settlers took out after the band of Tories.

Henry had over 30 wounds and fortunately none had hit a vital organ. One of his ears was nearly severed from his head, and one arm was so badly injured that he never regained use of it.

Sources: 1. Women Patriots of the American Revolution: a Biographical Dictionary by Charles E. Claghorn. 2. New York Times Article 7 December, 1879.

****

David Driskill age 14

David Driskill was born in 1763 in Grandville, North Carolina, and he died on 18 January, 1842 in Montgomery, Illinois. He married Agnes Green on 26 August, 1783 in North Carolina. She received a widow's pension of $80 a year.

"I enlisted in Orange County in the State of North Carolina in the month of October 1777 in the Company Commanded by Captain Benjamin Coleman of the 10th North Carolina Regiment commanded by Colonel Clark of the North Carolina Continental line and I continued to serve in the said Corps or in the service of the United States until the spring of 1780 when I was discharged at Wilmington in the State of North Carolina by Colonel Little or Lytle -- and that I was in the Battles of Stony Point and Monmouth and that I am in reduced circumstances and stands in need of the assistance of my country for support and has no other Evidence of said services than my own Declaration within my power."

David Driskill served under Colonel Thomas Clark, the commander of the 1st Regiment of the North Carolina Line. David was probably at Valley Forge, since the Battle of Monmouth, on 28 June, 1778 was fought after the American army broke camp at the winter quarters. During the Battle of Monmouth, David was among the troops at the right wing under the command of Nathanel Green.

At the Battle of Stony Point, on 16 July, 1779 David Driskill was in the 4th Regiment organized with six companies of Massachusetts troops and two of North Carolina. This regiment was commanded by Major William Hull of the 8th Massachusetts. The battle plan was to launch a surprise attack on the fort at midnight. All the regiments involved were to maintain silence before the attack. The men were not allowed to load their weapons, so that they would not be accidently discharged and alert the

British of the attack. The two companies of North Carolina were the exception to this order. They were to attack the center of the British defenses where the British expected the attack to come. Their attack with weapons firing was a diversionary tactic. While this was happening the other three regiments would perform a surprise attack on the north and south sides of the fort.

Sources: 1. Census 1830 and 1840. 2. North Carolina Marriage Index 1741-1868. 3. U.S. Pensioners 1818-1872.

****

William Drone age 14

William Drone was born in 1763, and he died on 24 February, 1824 in Fauquier, Virginia. He married Susanna Sheckells on 16 September, 1786 in Maryland. She received a widow's pension of $100 a year.

"I enlisted in January 1777 in the County of Loudon in the State of Virginia under Stephen Lewis a Cornet in a company of Cavalry commanded at that time by Captain John Rodolph of the Corps of Horse commanded by Col. Henry Lee of the state of Virginia, that I continued to serve in the said Corps in the service of the United States on continental establishment until the end of the Revolutionary War, when I was I discharged verbally from service in Charleston in the State of South Carolina, I was in the Battles at Guilford Ct House and Eutaw."

He later stated that he was *"....involved in the capture of several forts and numerous skirmishes."*

General Washington established mounted units in the Continental Army in the winter of 1776. In Janurary of 1777 he instructed that the new regiment was to have, besides a commander, one other field officer, a major, a regimental staff of an adjutant, a surgeon and a surgeon's mate, and 6 troops. Each troop would consist of a captain, lieutenant, a cornet (the lowest grade of a commissioned officer), a quartermaster, 2 sergeants, 2 corporals, a trumpeter, a farrier, person which has the skills of a blacksmith and veterinarian, and 34 privates.

William Drone served as a private under the command of Henry Lee III, also known as "Light-Horse Harry". Henry's son was Robert E. Lee the great Confederate General. In addition to taking part in the battles of Guilford Court House and Eutaw Springs, Lee and his men captured Forts Watson, Motte, Granby and Galphin.

Sources: 1. Maryland Marriages 1655-1850. 2. U.S. Pensioners 1848-1872. 3. Historical Register of Virginians in the Revolution. 4. Pension Papers W3785.

****

Marcus Duesler age 14

Marcus Duesler was born on 3 June, 1763 in Montgomery County, New York, and he died on 6 March, 1846 in Fulton County, New York. He received a pension of $40.77 a year for his service.

"*In May in the year 1778 I went as a substitute for a person whose name I do not now recollect. I served two or three weeks under the command of Captain Abraham Copeman- Lieutenant Joseph House- Ensign Jacob Snider and attached to Colonel Campbell Regiment. I knew Captain Jacob Deusendorft and Lieutenant George Countryman during this time. I stood guard & also went with the Regiment to Cherry Valley where I remained a few days & then returned home about the first of June 1778. I remained on duty keeping guard of Fort Plank until about the first of October 1778. When I was released from guard.*"

"*About the middle of July 1779 I went as a substitute for Leonard Kritan under the command of the same officers to Fort Stanwyx I was under the command of Quarter Master Sergeant Tucker who belonged as I understood to the Regular Army. I went as a guard to guard the provisions which was then being transported to the fort—after about four months I returned to fort Plank where I did duty in guarding the fort guarding laborers in the field until about the last of October in the same year.*"

"*In the Spring of the year 1780 I went again into the service as a volunteer to guard fort Plank under the same officers but particularly under the command of Lieutenant House. I remained there until about the middle of July of the same year when I was released from there and went to Fort Plain & to the North side of the Mohawk River opposite Fort Plain when I had an engagement with Sir William Johnson. At that engagement Colonel DuBois commanded the Regiment to which I belonged. After the Battle I again returned to Fort Plain when I done duty at different times & in different ways by guarding the Fort & the laborers until November following when I was released.*"

"In the month of March 1781 I enlisted for nine months in Colonel Willetts Regiment in Captain Gross' Company. In the year 1782 in the spring the particular month I cannot state I think it was May I volunteered my services as a militia man under the command of Colonel __?__ in Joseph House's Company Abraham Copeman my former Captain having been promoted to the office of Major. I acted as a Minute Man ready to go when called upon until about the middle of October. My duty was to watch the garrison at Fort Plane. I served at different times that season in all."

"In May 1783 I again volunteered to guard the Fort before mentioned I served as a Minute Man until the latter part of the summer of 1783 when I was discharged."

Sources: 1. New York Pensioners 1835. 2. Lineage Book National Society of the Daughters of the American Revolution, Vol. L, 1904. 3. Pension Papers S10589.

****

Nathaniel Dunham age 13

Nathaniel Dunham was born on 21 August, 1763 in Plymouth, Massachusetts, and he died on 20 August, 1830 in Onondaga County, New York. He enlisted on 8 July, 1777 and served in Captain Ezekiel Herrick's Company in the 1st Berkshire County Regiment commanded by Colonel John Ashley. The regiment was called up in July 1777 and was sent to Fort Edward for a month to reinforce the Northern Army. The regiment joined the gathering forces of General Gates, when he faced British General Burgoyne. When Burgoyne surrendered, the regiment was disbanded on 18 October, 1777.

Sources: 1. Dunham Genealogy. Deacon John Dunham of Plymouth, Massachusetts. 1589-1669, and His Descendants by Isaac Watson Dunham, 1907. 2. Massachusetts Soldiers and Sailors in the Revolutionary War. 3. Revolutionary Soldiers Resident or Dying in Onondaga County, N.Y., prepared by Rev. W.M. Beauchamp for the Onondaga Historical Association, 1863.

****

Francis Dunlavy age 14

Francis Dunlavy was born in the latter part of 1762 in Westchester, Virginia, and he died 6 November, 1839 in Lebanon, Ohio. Some sources put his birth year at 1761, however, in his pension statement he declares the date to be 1762. In 1792 he married a young widow, Mary Craig Carpenter.

"On or about the first day of October 1776 I volunteered as a private in the militia of the United States and in the company of Capt Isaac Cox, and David Steele Lieutenant & I encamped with said company on the second bank of Ohio river at a place then called Hollidys cove opposite a large Island in the now County of Brook Va. The company built a fort or chain of cabins called block-houses on said ground, & scouted or ranged up and down the River a certain distance every day, two at a time. This was one of a line of stations from Fort Pitt to Grave creek—saw not field officer but Col John Gibson, who passed and called at the stations along the River, as visiting or supervising them. Of Capt Coxes company were John Sappinton , Edward King & and some of the name Greathouse, who became notorious afterwards, as having been concerned in the murder of a number drunken Indians in the month of April 1774—remained there until the twentieth of December when I with the rest were discharged having served two months & one half and upwards."

The murder of the Indians that Francis talked about was called the Yellow Creek Massacre on 30 April, 1774 at yellow Creek on the upper Ohio River. Joshua Baker had a tavern in the area and had been warned not to sell liquor to the Indians. Chief Logan was camped nearby and he was a peaceful Indian that was not a troublemaker.

Daniel Greathouse was a cruel and bloodthirsty man who lived in the area and had a hatred for Indians. The Indian camp was too strong for Greathouse to attack, so he gathered 35 of his men and waited for a small part of the Indians to go to Baker's Tavern to drink. When the male and female Indians had become drunk at the tavern Greathouse and his men attacked them and tomahawked nine or ten of the Indians. Jacob Greathouse, brother of Daniel, killed a pregnant Indian, opened her belly and removed and scalped her unborn son.

Hearing the gunfire other members of the tribe got in their canoes and began to cross the river toward the tavern. Greathouse's men fired on them and killed several Indians. Daniel Greathouse took the scalps of the dead Indians and hung them from his belt. The next year Daniel died of the measles, and his brother Jacob died in an ambush in 1777.

"In the month of July 1777 I served the first half of a month for which time I had been drafted. Gen Hand had just arrived but brought no troops with him.—don't certainly recollect the names of any militia officers as I with other privates did duty in the Garrison under regular officers. Col John Gibson and some of the 13th Va regiment in the garrison, Capts Scott & David Steele, above named, well known about Pittsburg *during & many years both before & after the revolutionary war. Simon Girty a subaltern* [a person of lower status], *but at the time chiefly engaged in intercourse with the Indians many of whom were in and about that place and which I think was the reason that the Militia were called in at that time on or about the first of March 1778 I volunteered my services for one month rendevoused at Cox's station, waters of Peter creek Cols Isaac Cox & John Cannon attended to organize the men, after remaining about eight days, some negotiation took place in which it was agreed that the militia should give up their arms, and that certain recruits who were enlisting in the regular service, but who were not yet provided with arms, should take the place of the militia in stations of defence and that the latter should return to attend to their crops under this regulation were all were all (that is the militia) dismissed."*

"On or about the 15th of August following, I was drafted for one month rendezvoused at Pittsburg—put under the command of John Springer, Lieutenant, who was attached with his militia troops to Capt Ferrol lately from the Seaboard who had no troops of his own (but whose company of one years men shortly after arrival or were enlisted) but had a company of men detached from those of the 13th of Va. Capt Ferrol with his command marched or ranged the woods on the fronteer line to Wheeling, calling and visiting various stations, or places of resort for the surrounding inhabitants between Pittsburg & Wheeling, at the latter, relieved and took the place of a company of militia from Hamshire Va. under the command of Captain Daniel Cressap Brother to the celebrated Mike Cressap, remained in the Garrison at Wheeling some time, ranged or scouted the wood up and down the river and around the Garrison. Lieutenant Springer and his men returned to Pittsburg where at the close of the month we were discharged."

The celebrated Mike Cressap that Francis mentions is a militia leader who was going to lead a strike on Chief Logan's camp before the Yellow Creek Massacre took place. They decided to abandon the attack. When Chief Logan, on the other side of the river, heard the attack taking place and he assumed that it was being led by Mike Cressap.

Years later Chief Logan wrote: *"To Captain Cressap - What did you kill my people on Yellow Creek for. The white People killed my kin at Coneestoga a great while ago, & I thought nothing of that. But you killed my kin again on Yellow Creek, and took my cousin prisoner then I thought I must kill too; and I have been three time to war since but the Indian is not Angry only myself."*

"About the 5th October entered the company of Capt John Crow, as a substitute for Andrew Flood (subalterns not certainly recollected—rendevoused at mouth of Beaver G McIntosh commander in Chief, Col Stephenson (thinks Hugh) commanded the battalion or regiment that Capt Crow was in; Col Wm Crawford half brother to Stephen, the regiment or larger number of troops, also militia Col Evens with his troops was under Crawford Cols John Gibson of the 13 va. and Daniel Broadhead of the eighth Pennsylvania with their respective regiments or parts of them in the army Daniel Leet adjutant of the regular troops, but to which regiment attached don't recollect. Laughlin McIntosh son of the General, aid decamp or Brigade Major, great number of Militia from Hampshire, Berkely, Frederick, Rockingham, Augusta. 8 Botetourt Counties in Va. Cols John Morrow, Bowyer, Major Lockhart (of the staff) and others, Built a fort of much strength & capacity. On the 5th of November marched for the interior thro' the Indian country, as it was then called, crossed into the forks of Muskingum, some distance above the Moravian Towns, built Fort Lawrence not far from New Philadelphia—left Col Gibson & some regulars in the fort—returned to McIntosh, and was discharged about the 20th of December. On the 25th of August 1779 was drafted & redevoused at Fort Pitt—encamped three days in the Kings orchard on the banks of Alleghany River, fourth day in the afternoon marched up the river about 700 men, some light horse, & some Indians. Perhaps 60. Col Daniel Broadhead commanded part of his regiment along. Col. Gibson the next in command with part of 13 Va. Some independent companies, Col. Flannegan (I think Thomas commanded the militia I was in the company of Capt. Ellis. Joseph Beeler Jun. Lieutenant, Brigade Major Findley (not Samuel) & Major Varneer & Major Campbell of Steubnan ville (son of Andreg Monteur a Frenchman) a man of information and education, but a great savage. Marched up the Alleghany on the east side crossed Kistamenates at the mouth—crossed Crooked Creek and came to the Kittening where was a garrison. Lay some days at an old town on the River bottom some 12 miles above the kittening—marched up the river and crossed to the west side, some 15 miles below the mouth of French creek crossed the latter creek & moved on towards the Muncy Towns, met 30 or 40 Indian warriors defeated them, killing several & wounded some, who escaped, some fled up a steep hill to the west, some took to the river & escaped to an island, had none killed but 4 or 5 wounded on our side, thinks Jonathan Zane, a pilot or spy, was one of the latter, went into the Towns then abandoned lay there a nearly a week, cut up several hundred acres of corn growing along the river on each side, returned to Pittsburg all the way on the east side. John Ward, a youth, and perhaps an ensign, *but of what troops I don't recollect, had his thigh broken by his horse falling on a rock in a creek, ever since called slippery rock. Crossed the Alleghany opposite Pittsburg and was discharged about 29th September after serving inclusive about 35 days. Nota Bene Lieutenants John Hardin & Samuel Brady, first of the 13th Va. & the other 8th Pa. and who afterwards became famous in Indian warfare, were in the above expedition."*

The first of April 1782 Francis volunteered to march against hostile Indians for 10 days and then was released. On the 15th of May he volunteered again and served with about 500 troops mostly mounted on horseback. On about the 20th of May, 1782 they marched for the Indian Towns.

"......crossed the Muskingum below the Moravian town, then lately laid waste—up Kilbuck & Moheecan Forks—crossed over to Sandusky plain—met the Indians on the Western verge of the plains on the 4th of June P.M. had a battle—fought 'til dark with various success—had about 21 men killed & wounded—both parties lay on their arms all night within sight of each other. . Indians lay all round us next day, at long shot distance, some skirmishing, but no regular battle seem'd to increase considerably—appeared to be commanded by Simon Gerty above mentioned---I heard him speak often—knew his voice well—at the close of daylight on the 5th broke through the Indian lines, who appeared very much alarmed—we retreated all night without ever halting—stopped a few minutes in the morning to collect—had about 300 men when collected under Col. Davis Williamson about two O'clock the Indians on horseback overtook and attacked Capt Joseph Bean in particular was shot thro' the body but recovered—died some 12 years ago, Nelson County, Ky, where he had resided near thirty years. Major Harrison, Wm Crawford Jun. and some others killed or taken, continued the retreat—Indians pursued, and fired on us occasionally, but were repulsed when approaching near shot, a violent rain rendered fire arms nearly useless—encamped in the woods some miles east of the plains, Indians encamped about a mile off, we marched at daybreak, they fired on our rear at the moment of moving—killed or took some—did not pursue us, but betook themselves to the pursuit of straggling parties, who, from accident or design, had separated, among these were Col. Crawford John Slover & Dr. Knight &others, these three all taken—Crawford burnt—Dr. Knight & Slover made their escape, and returned home after some 20 days, I arrived at Mingo Bottom & crossed over about the 12th and was discharged the next day."

The battle that Francis describes is called the Sandusky expedition or Crawford's Defeat. In June of 1782 Crawford led 500 militiamen in order to destroy their towns along the Sandusky River in Ohio. The Indians and their allies the British were aware of the expedition. The militia was not well trained and lacked discipline. They wasted their rations, fired their musket at wild game even though ordered not to do so, and did not always shown up for guard duty.

After several days of marching they found an abandoned village and Crawford's officers held a council of war on 4 June. Some argued that the village was abandoned because the Indians knew they were coming and had organized their forces somewhere else. Others wanted to quit and return home. The council decided that they would finish their march that day and go no further. Scouts were sent ahead while the main body of troops had lunch. Soon a few members from the scouting party returned and alerted the troops that the Indians were coming.

A small skirmish began and the militia began driving the Indians back. By 4 in the afternoon more Indians joined the fight, and there was now a full scale battle going on. It was later reported that Francis Dunlevy had an engagement with an Indian of large proportions. The Indian had been seen creeping toward Francis in some brush, and as he got close the Indian threw his tomahawk at Francis. Luckily, he missed and the Indian made his mistake. The Indian was described as nearly seven feet tall and as frightfully ugly as he was large. Both sides broke off the attacks for the night. Dead men on both sides were scalped.

The next day on June 5th both sides kept their distance but fired back and forth. By the afternoon the militia noticed that the Indians had been reinforced by more Indians and about 100 British rangers. That night the militia council of war decided to begin their retreat. During the retreat Crawford and several other men were captured by the Indians.

The Indians had much hatred for the militia men, because of an earlier massacre of Indians by another group of militia men. The captive's faces were painted black which was a sign that they were going to be executed. Crawford was stripped and tortured for the next two hours. His ears were cut off, and according to reports, not less than seventy loads of powder were discharged on him. Then the Indian took turns applying burning pieces of wood to Crawford's bare body. Indian squaws would also place hot coals on his body. During this Crawford begged to be shot, but his pleas were met with laughter. As Crawford approached death the Indians scalped him.

One of the prisoners, a scout named John Slover, was stripped naked, and before he was tortured and burned he stole a pony and escaped. When the horse gave out he ran the rest of the way. He finally reached Fort Pitt on the 10th of July. After Francis reached safety he was discharged and returned home. He did not enlist again. I suspect that he had enough of the military life.

In 1790 Dunlavy graduated from Dickinson College in Carlisle, Pa. Two years later, after abandoning plans to become a minister in favor of education, Dunlavy moved to Columbia, near Cincinnati at the mouth of the Little Miami River and opened a school. In 1797 he moved to the Miami Valley in Ohio, opened a school, and became the first teacher in the area. After being elected to the Northwest Territorial Legislature in 1800 he left teaching.

In 1802 Francis Dunlavy was Hamilton County's top vote-getter for a seat at Ohio's constitutional convention and was one of the principle writers of the state constitution, where he lobbied unsuccessfully to grant suffrage to black men. His views on racial equality were unpopular and later cost him a career in politics.

In 1803 he was appointed President Judge for southwestern Ohio's Court of Common Pleas. He held this position for 14 years, despite that fact the he had never seriously studied law or been admitted to the bar. On horseback Dunlavy traveled his circuit throughout southwestern Ohio, undeterred by harsh weather conditions or flooded rivers. He missed only one court appearance during his tenure.

Sources: 1. Chronicles of Border Warfare by Alexander Withers. 2. Historical Register of Virginians in the Revolution. 3. Pension Paper S2526. 4. Documentary history of Dunmore's War, edited by Reuben Gold Thwaites and Louise Phelps Kellogg. 5. Ohio's Founding Fathers. 6. Year Book of the Ohio Society of the Sons of the American Revolution. 7. Brief History of the Military Career of Francis Dunlavy from the Warren County local History by Dallas Bogan. 8. An Historical Account of the Expedition against Sandusky under Col. William Crawford in 1782: with biographical sketches, personal reminiscences, and descriptions of interesting localities; including, also, details of the disastrous retreat, the barbarities of the savages, and the awful death of Crawford by torture.

****

Almon Dunston age 14

Almon Dunston was born in 1763, probably in Virginia, and he died 20 January, 1837. He married Alice Bristow on 17 December, 1814 in Virginia.

"I enlisted in the army of the United States in the year 1777 (the day and month I do not recollect) with Captain Philip Taliaferro of the second Virginia State Regiment of the State line commanded by Col. William Nelson. I served out the term of my enlistment as follows Vizt, under Col. Nelson about one year and the balance of the term being two years) I served under Col. [William] Brent, the Command of the said Regiment being transfered to him. that Capt. Taliaferro having resigned, Lieut. Machen Boswell was appointed Capt. of the Company under whom I served two years making three years the term for which I enlisted as aforesaid. I was a resident of the said County at the time of his enlistment I was engaged in the Battles of Powles Hook Monmouth Courthouse, and several skirmishes to the north. After I served out the said Term of three years, I again entered the Army as a substitute and served about eighteen months in that capacity to the south and until the end of the War, when I was honourably discharged."

Almon fought with the militia at the Battle of Paulus Hook on 29 August, 1779. The Americans were under the command of Major Light Horse Harry Lee, who had his horse troop and 400 infantrymen. He attacked the British in the middle of the night and captured 158 soldiers. Because the attack ended at dawn, the Americans had to retreat from the fort before the British could send reinforcements. Lee was going to burn the buildings, but did not because they contained sick British soldiers, women, and children.

American losses stood at 2 killed and 3 wounded, including Ezekiel Clark who had the end of his nose shot off. With this victory the British lost most of their control over New Jersey. A grateful Congress gave Major Lee $15,000 to be distributed among the soldiers engaged in the attack.

Sources: 1. Memorial of the Centennial Celebration of the Battle of Paulus Hook, August 19th 1879 with a History of the Early Settlement and Present Condition of Jersey City, New Jersey, edited by George H. Farriier. 2. U.S. Pension Roll of 1835. 3. Pension Papers W731.

****

William Dupuy age 14

William Dupuy was born on 17 October, 1766 in Edgefield, South Carolina, and he died on 11 September, 1851 in Hopkinsville, Kentucky. He received a yearly pension of $21.66.

"When 14 years old fond of adventure and much attached to Captain Solomon Newsom joined his company as a volunteer & from the partiality of his Captain was made a spy with one Samuel Moore. Rendezvoused at the Big Shoals of Ogeechee river in the summer or spring of 1780 or 1781 & then with 40 others took up the line of march. On the way were joined at the White Ponds General Irvin's brigade and proceeded to the Long Bluff on the Oconee river. Here I remained several months, (do not recollect exactly how long) during which time, I was daily engaged as an Indian spy with said Samuel Moore. I was then taken with Samuel Moore, James McCormick & 7 others as a bodyguard to attend General Irvin in his review of Fort Irvin, Fort Watley & two other forts the name of which I have forgot. After this service I was permitted to return home. Shortly after my return another alarm of Indians invasion threatening the country I went out with Lieutenant John Buckhalter marched under him to Booths island in the Oconee river. There remained some 8 or 9 weeks & was with Samuel Moore engaged as a spy. During this service I with Moore went as far out as the Creek called Shoulder bone."

"I was again discharged and returned home and afterwards joined a horse Company under Captain Nathan Fowler, and Major Ledbetter. Fowler was himself a spy went out in service & took me (Dupuy) and three others generally with him. In my excursions we explored the Indian country so far out as the Okmulgee, pursuing the upper Indian trading path that lead from the Oconee river. Was during this time engaged some 5 or 6 weeks. Twice or three times after this was called out by Buckhalter & served from 10 to 20 days do not exactly recollect. I would further state that during the two last years of the war I was considered at all times ready & willing to serve my country and is well satisfied his whole service exceeded the term of six months."

Years after the war was over he moved to Christian County, Kentucky and was a wealthy farmer. The 1850 Slave Census of the county reports that he owned 25 slaves. After his death in 1851, an article in the newspaper *The Kentucky Rifle* reported, *"He was one of the oldest citizens of this county, and was universally respected as one of the last of those noble patriots who fought over the cradle of the young republic."*

Sources: 1. U.S. Pensioners 1818-1872. 2. Christian & Trigg Counties, Kentucky History & Biography. 3. 1850 Slave Schedule Christian County, Kentucky. 4. Pension Papers S12821.

****

Fisk Durand age 10

Fisk Durand was born on 26 June, 1766 in Milford Connecticut, and he died on 18 April, 1841 in Westfield, New York. He married Mary "Poly" Ester Platt on 21 May, 1792. He enlisted with his older brother William. At the age of 13 Fisk had served his country for 30 months, and he was a veteran before many men had joined. Fisk received a yearly pension of $88.

"In June of the year 1776 when I was but 10 years old I enlisted for 7 or 8 months, with the consent of my father as a drummer under Capt. Hyne in the Continental State Troops and served out his time of 7 or 8 months. The garrison consisted of twenty men beside the Capt. & the gunner whose name was Joseph Davidson."

"At the expiration of my term of 7 or 8 months, which last mentioned term & served out in the same capacity as drummer in the same fort. Joseph Davidson the gunner during the first term was Capt. during the second term."

"In the year 1778 I again enlisted into the continental militia under Capt. Bradley Lieut. John Pruden and marched to Stamford where the company remained a month or more. The company was then ordered to join Col. Evan's at North__?__ which we did, and a few days after the regiment was marched to Horseneck. At this place I remained with my assignment till my term of enlistment had expired."

"About the first of September 1779 I again enlisted for 7 or 8 months under Capt. Peter Perritt Joseph Hull was Lieut. Was marched to Horseneck where my company joined the Regiment of Col. Mead. Henry Bull adjutant Joseph Whiting Sergeant Major. We spent the winter here at Horseneck and the spring of 1780 my term expired. Although young I was at each time regularly enlisted and bound to strict military duty."

Sources: 1. D.A.R. Lineage Book, Vol. 116. 2. Pension Application S12807. 3. New York Pensioners 1835. 4. Tombstone 5. Patterson Chapter, Westfield, Chautauqua County, New York, listing of Revolutionary War Soldiers.

****

William Eakin age 14

William Eakin was born on 8 October, 1765 in York, South Carolina, and he died on 11 July, 1840 in San Augustine, Texas. He married Elizabeth James on 5 February, 1793 in York, South Carolina. After the war he moved around and finally settled in Texas. In 1833-34 he arrived, by wagon train at the Old Stone Fort in Nacogdoches, Texas. He received a pension of $20 a year for his service.

"I entered the Service of the United States in York District South Carolina on 16 November 1780 as a volunteer and private Soldier in a Company of volunteers Commanded by Captain Joseph Hawe and Lieut Benjamin Rawan who were under the command of Col James Hathorn and was marched to Brandon's Mill upon Fairforest river in Union District South Carolina where I was kept for some time, I was then marched to Ninety Six where I was kept for six or seven weeks, and from there I was marched To the Fishdam ford on Broad river Fairfield District, where I remained some time, and from there to Wynsborough where I was Stationed upwards of two months -- and from that place I was marched to Lands-ford on the Catawba River, and from there to what was then called the old Nation ford where the volunteers under Col Hawthorn were Encamped for some time and from there I was marched to the mouth of Packolett River where it intersects Broad River, and from that to Biggenes ferry on the Catawba where I remained in service until the latter part of May or first of June 1781 -- when I was discharged."

Sources: 1. Census of 1800, 1810, 1820, & 1830. 2. Pension Roll of 1835. 3. Pension Papers W3530.

****

William Eddins age 14

William Eddins was born 7 December, 1764 in Lunenburg County, Virginia, and died 28 July, 1837 in Lincoln County, Tennessee. He married (1) Elizabeth Landrum who died in 1832. (2) Hannah Dedman on 19 October, 1833 in Alabama. He enlisted in the latter part of December 1778, which was just before his 15th birthday.

"In the latter part of the year 1778 I think in the latter part of December of that year when I was about fifteen years of age my father was drafted as a militia man in a company commanded by Capt. William freeman, from the County of Abaville in the State of South Carolina where we then resided. I entered the service of the United states as a substitute

in the place of my father at the age of about fifteen years & at the time above stated--the Company was raised for the purpose of guarding & protecting a little town called Ninety Six in said County, from the Tories, we went to Ninety Six & remained about three months there guarding the place under the command of Capt. Freeman, at the end of which time the company was discharged & we returned home."

"Shortly after my return home I think in the month of April 1779 I entered the service of the US as a volunteer in a company commanded by Captain John Calhoun—the company was raised for the purpose of opposing the common enemies of the country—British, Indians, & more particularly the tories who were then committing horrid depredations through the county—the company consisting perhaps of about a hundred men marched up to Michael Blanes plantation near Saluda River adjacent to swansys ferry where they stationed for six months, during which time they were constantly engaged scouting about through the country in pursuit of the Tories--nothing of note took place during this campaign, except that on one occation General Andrew Pickens came on with a company of men--we joined him and went down to Saluda old Town in pursuit of some noted Tories called Turners & drove them out of the Country--and that on another occasion under the same command of the same Captain, we went up Savannah river to Tugaloo & Keewee were in pursuit of the Cherokee Indians & Tories, & drove the Cherokees from the country—we returned home Gen Pickens--Col Robert Anderson, Major Samuel Taylor, were the commanding officers of this command, on another occasion my company joined Genl Pickens & we went with about eight hundred men down towards Charleston crossed the Cochran Swamp where we took a good many tories prisoners--From thence we marched across Bull Swamp & to the head of Edisto Swamp in pursuit of the Tories--& also down to the plantation of one Black a noted Tory who made his escape as we approached--we then returned to our encampment at Blames plantation where we remained occasionally scouting about through the country in pursuit of the tories until the six months expired--we were discharged & and I returned home I think about the first of October 1779."

"Immediately after my return home, I think in the month of October 1779--I joined a Company of Dragoons Commanded by Capt Robert Maxwell & Lieutenant William Mitchell--the company consisted of about three hundred men--I joined the Company in the County of Abbeville in the State of South Carolina until the end of the war with Great Britain--after the Company was formed we marched up to the Saluda river, & were stationed at the plantation of one Norris in Abbeville County, where we

remained occasionally reconnoitering the country until General Green came on with his army, before General Green arrived at our company of Dragoons had taken about thirty of the British soldiers that the British were then in Ninety Six--we continued scouting about through the country demolishing & destroying the house of the tories on Little river & Mudlick--we killed George Moore and shot Jo. Box two noted Tories. I guarded a noted Tory by the name of Robinson to the gullis [gallows] he was hanged. When General Green came home the company of Dragoons Genl Pickens whole army joined Genl greens army--we went on to besiege Ninety Six where the British army was forted in & under the command of Col Cruger--I was at the Siege of Ninety Six--Lord Raddon came out with a reinforcement to Col Cruger, & the American army then retreated & abandoned the siege--the Company of dragoons to which I belonged went on towards north Carolina with a view to join Genl Washington--until we heard of the defeat of Corn Wallis at Little York--after the abandonment of the Siege at Ninety Six our company were greatly scattered & dispersed through the Country, & were not in actual service for about four months after the Siege, but were not dismissed from service but having fled from the enemy, were engaged assisting the women & children on towards the north in different routes until we heard of Cornwallis's defeat at Little York when we all returned, which I think in the month of November 1781 to the best of my recollection."

The siege of Ninety-Six took place in western South Carolina from 22 May to 18 June, 1781. The siege centered upon an earthen fortification known as Star Fort in the village of Ninety-Six. American General Green was forced to end the siege when British reinforcements approached the fort. General Pickens's troops, including William Eddins, were ordered to protect the wagon train of supplies as the Americans retreated.

In July the British abandoned the fort and General Pickens was ordered to harass the retreating British troops under the command of Colonel Cruger. Since the British were leaving the backcountry of South Carolina, General Pickens was given the job of protecting the Tories from their Patriot neighbors who were seeking revenge against them.

"Immediately on our return we collected ourselves together, still under the command of Capt Maxwell & Lieutenant Mitchell rendezvoused at Benjamin Mitchell's plantation & continued reconnoitering & guarding the frontiers from the Indians & Tories, until February 1782--when General Pickens Regiment we all set out on a tour after the Cherokee

Indians & tories the Indians having joined the British--Genl Andrew Pickens, Col Robert Anderson, & Major Samuel Taylor were some of the field officers that were along, & commanded what was called the Long Cain Brigade--we marched up the savannah river & crossed at the Cherokee ford, from thence across the broad river in Georgia--thence up to & around curahee Mountain up to Chota town on Chota creek--where I & several others assisted in burying the bones of eleven of the American soldiers that had been murdered by the Indians who had been taken prisoner at the ford of long Cain with the baggage wagons by a company of Tories commanded by Capt Williams & by him given up to the Indians--we then marched up Chota creek & out at Chota gap, where Captain Maxwell & forty five of his chosen dragoons (I being one & in front of the charge) charged through a little town called Togajoy--the warriors firing fled--We encamped there about one week reconnoitering about, finding cribs of shelled corn & hollow trees of shelled corn from thence we marched to Quawasee town, at the three forks of Tennessee river, took the town & burnt it, whilst there me & twelve others were ordered to go & burned some Indians cabins in sight of the town on the opposite side of the river--when we were proceeding to do so & as we approached the cabins, we were fired upon by a body of Indians--two of the men (one by the name of George Patterson) were thrown from their horses they maintained their ground until about five hundred men came to their relief--We encamped that night on the spur of the mountain in sight of the town—there fell a very heavy snow that night--it was half thigh deep next morning--From thence we marched to the Horse Shoe town burning several villages on our way, we killed many Indians, & when we took Jack Doherty a half breed, prisoner, & killed a noted Tory by the name of Hal Crittenton--we encamped there for some time reconnoitered the country--From thence we marched to & took Ellejoy town, encamped there for some time & took many cattle--From thence we marched towards the State of Georgia, & while on the march & on the second morning of the march from this place Genl Pickens sent about three hundred of the soldiers back to bring up a fine mare that had tired down the evening before--I was one of the number ordered back—on our way back, we were attacked by a body of Indians--in this engagement I discovered an Indian endeavoring to get a shot at me--I charged upon him, the Indian broke and ran to a creek and jumped in, dove under the water, after he rose I shot him--wounded him, others of the soldiers came up a killed him--We then returned to the balance of the army & proceeded on our march to the state of Georgia & returned home about the last of April 1782, making a tour of about three months--This was a hard & fatiguing campaign--the Army lived on parched mill &

Indian cattle when we could get them--I remained home about twelve months, guarding the frontiers of the Country, occasionally under arms taking Tories."

General Pickens formed a troop of men to punish the Cherokees for raids against the settlers in the area. In fourteen days his troops burned thirteen towns and killed around forty Indians and captured many more. The troops used very little ammunition, because they charged the Indians with swords and bayonets.

William tells of being one of a dozen men selected to burn some Indian cabins. The men advanced and crossed a river and began to go up a hill where the cabins were. As they approached the cabins, the Indians fired upon them. Two of the troopers who were in the lead fell from their horses. The remainder of the men retreated and gathered together to resist the Indians until Pickens could rescue them.

The horses of the two fallen men ran back to the river, and the fallen men rose to a sitting position to face the Indians. William suggested to the Captain that the men should be rescued. The Captain thought it would be too risky but gave in due to the insistence of William. William caught the horses and led them to the two fallen men. He helped the wounded men mount and led them back to safety.

In April of 1783 William and the rest of the brigade marched to the lower part of the Cherokee Nation. They crossed the Chattahoochee River and 45 of the soldiers, William being one, destroyed Vans Town and Hotaran. According to Joseph McClaskey, in his pension application, they took many Indian prisoners and the Indians had many scalps.

In this area, *"....we encamped for some time & took several Tory prisoners, negroes & horses—two noted Tories named Sam Williams & Sam Tillett were tried condemned & Williams was hanged—after remaining here some time we marched to Selacoa town, where they found a basket full of white men's scalps--From thence to Pine log town & took it, stationed ourselves there for some time--about three hundred men (I was one of them) went from there & took old Coosa town on Coosa river, returned to PineTown to the balance of the army where an old Indian by the name of Tarapin came in to entreated for peace. We then ceased our hostilities against the Indians & returned home, I think about the 20th of October 1783 being out on this tour about five or six months, where we were discharged."*

After the fighting ended for William, he had very little money. His first crop of tobacco he made with the use of a horse. He overcame the hard times and soon began making a good living from his farming. In the early 1800's he began to preach the gospel as a Baptist preacher. William Eddins served a total of three years and nine months. For his service he received $80.00 a year, which his wife Hannah applied for after William's death in 1837.

There have been several stories told about William. These stories are taken from *The Huntsville Historical Review—From out of the Ashes—The Joel Eddins House* by J.P. Reeves, from vol. 32, #2, Summer--Fall 2007 and from a letter William sent to the Pension Bureau on 17 October, 1832.

Not long after William's first tour of service, he was taken prisoner with some other men one of which was his father. His horse was taken from him and given to one of the men guarding him. While moving the prisoners, the guard who had William's horse dismounted for a small drink of rum. William was allowed to stop with the guard, and as he took several drinks of rum the other guards and prisoners kept moving down the road. William noticed that his guard had placed his musket against a tree, so William grabbed it, mounted his own horse, and escaped.

William returned home to let his mother know that he had escaped. Before he retired to bed he hid the stolen musket in a hollow log. That night the Tories paid them a visit and were dragging William and his brother out of the house. William's mother told them to stop and soon the Tories left the family. William ran to the hollow log to retrieve the hidden gun and fired at the Tories, as they passed by a swamp near the house. Once he fired he took off and made his escape.

The Tories returned to the Eddin's home and stole everything of value. William's mother Elizabeth was attacked and wounded with a sword. Some sources reported that she was shot and killed. The Tories then torched the house and all surrounding buildings.

William's father Benjamin remained in a prison camp under the control of the Troy commander, Colonel John Cruger. The Colonel offered Benjamin his freedom and some money for his knowledge of the countryside. Benjamin refused and said that no amount of torture would get him to give any information. The Colonel felt moved by Benjamin's resolve and released him. Benjamin returned home and later served with his son, William, under General Pickens.

Sources: 1. Joseph McClaskey Pension Papers W1449. 2. "General Andrew Pickens", Clyde R. Ferguson Ph.D. dissertation, Duke University, 1960; facsimile print, Ann Arbor University microfilms, Inc. 2006. 3. Census of 1790, 1810, 1830, & 1840. 4. U.S. Revolutionary War Rolls 1775-1783. 5. U.S. Pension Roll of 1835. 6. Pension Papers S32230.

****

William Edgman age 14

William Edgman was born in Surry County, North Carolina in 1765, and he died in 1838 in Roane County, Tennessee. He married (1) Nancy Deatherage in 1784 and they had eight children before she died in 1815 (2) Nancy Bishop on 22 February, 1815. He received $43.33 a year for his service.

"I entered the service as well as recollected in the year 1779. I volunteered for three months the first time and was marched from Surry County to Wilmington, thee was out on scouting parties until the three months expired. I then went home where I remained but a short time when I was drafted for three months. I was marched near Wilmington where we had some skirmishes with the British and Tories. I continued in service about five months when I was discharged again by Capt joseph Cloud. My field officers in this last service were Maj. George Grimes & John Smith was the Colonel."

"I returned home again where I remained about two months when I was drafted again by the same Captain Cloud for the term of four months was marched through the lower parts of North Carolina & south on scouting parties served out the time when I was discharged by Capt Cloud. I returned home again where I remained for some time. Had an engagement above Wilmington with the tories the last time I was out."

Several sources indicate that William was at the Battle of King's Mountain fought on 7 October, 1780 in South Carolina near the border of North Carolina. He makes no mention of the battle, but this author suspects that he was there. The Captain he served under around this time was Captain Joseph Cloud who was at the battle. William also states that he was in the lower parts of North Carolina, and there is a William Edgman on the Battle of King's Mountain roll.

Sources: 1. Tennessee State Marriages 170-2002. 2. Census for 1830. 3. U.S. Pension Roll of 1835. 4. U.S. Pensioners 1818-1872. 5. Pension papers S1810.

****

Eliab Eggleston age 14

Eliab Eggleston was born on 23 March, 1762 in Stonington, Connecticut, and he died on 2 March, 1838 in Newbury, Ohio. He married his second wife Lucy Ingraham on 20 February, 1798.

"I enlisted in the capacity of a private in the service of the United States of America as a substitute in the month of April A.D. 1776 the perceived day of the month not recollected in the company under Capt Bartlett & Lieut Ellmore, at Spencertown, in the country of Albany now the county of Columbus and state of New York where I then resided and was ____?____ under the command of said officers through Klinckill, Kinderbrook, and Greenbush to Albany and was there _____ under the direction of Col James Weston, who at that time commanded a regiment of regular troops at Albany about one month when the company to which I belonged was detached from the regiment of Col Weston and attached to a regiment under the command of Col Willis and was marched to Stone Robby where I was taken sick with the measles and sent back to Albany the day preceding Willis defeat near Stone Robby. I remained in Albany in the hospital until sometime in August of the year last aforesaid when I was discharged and returned home, having been in service four months."

"In 1777 about the first of May I enlisted as a substitute and was marched to Greenbush where my company and the others called out at that time were formed into a regiment and placed under the command of Col Henry Livingston--I was then marched to the place now called Landingburgh where with my regiment I crossed the river into the Island between the two sprouts of the Mohawk river, on which Island were stationed several brigades--I remained there about two months when pursuant to orders, my regiment crossed the North Sprout of the Mohawk and was marched to Bemitts Heighttes, where my regiment was under the command of Gen Poor--the whole under the command of Gen Gates--I was then marched to Capt Woodworth's meadow where I lay near Gen Gates head quarters until the first battle commenced when his regiment and the regiment under the command of Col John McKinstry were sent to protect the garrison on "ploughed hill" where they lay until two battles were fought 'called among the soldiers Fridays battle and Tuesdays battle' and the British retreated to Saratoga, which was on the second day after the last battle was fought. I then in company with the Main army pursued the enemy to Schuylers Mills where I was engaged in the siege of Burgoyne's army until, as I think, the 17th of Oct when the enemy

surrendered--soon after we marched down to Rhinebeck and I was discharged."

The Battle of Bemis Heights began when British General John Burgoyne advanced south in New York from Canada in the fall of 1777. He fought with American troops on 19 September at Freeman's Farm in the First Battle of Saratoga. On 7 October the two armies again clashed. The next day the British began to retreat northward leaving their sick and injured behind and even their dead unburied. They sought safety in the wooded area and hills of Bemis Heights.

General Burgoyne was now trapped near Saratoga and was forced to surrender his army of 6,200 men on 17 October, 1777. This British defeat was a turning point of the war, because it won for the Americans foreign assistance which was necessary for their final victory.

"I was drafted at Nobletown in the county of Albany in the early part of April A.D. 1778 and was marched to the place on the North River, now called Hudson, where my company went on board boats and proceeded down the river to Coopers Strand and lay there about a week-- I was thence marched to Morristown in New Jersey and thence through Moravian town, Bethlehem, Eastown and Schuykill to Valley Forge to Pennsylvania where were Genl Pattersons Brigade and others--I was there attached to Col Cortlands regiment, and with the other recruits was inoculated for the small pox--Soon after my arrival at Valley Forge, all the troops who were able to bear arms were ordered to march to intercept the British who were on their way from Philadelphia to New York--I was declared by the surgeon unable to go, remained until about the first of August being confined with the small pox and yellow fever--I was then with other sick, carried to Yellow Springs and placed in the hospital and remained there and in that vinicity until October, when having recovered my health, I marched across Carrels ferry to Morristown in New Jersey, thence to Kings ferry and thence to White Plains where I joined the Company--I remained there about one month, when I was again taken sick and was sent to Albany where I remained until about the first of January A.D.1779 when I received a written discharge from Doct Smith of the hospital at said Albany."

During the Revolutionary War the threat of smallpox was a major concern for the army. Most British soldiers had already been exposed and were immune. Unfortunately, the Colonial troops were not. Medics would create a small wound in the healthy soldiers arm, and then they would rub some of the pus from the pox of an infected soldier into those wounds. This would give you a slight case of the pox and then you would be immune. This early method of inoculation had been learned from African slaves.

Since they had no way to control the dosage there was danger involved. If you received too large a dose you could die. Washington estimated that as many as two percent of inoculated soldiers could die. Without the inoculation more than one third of the soldiers could die, and another third would be too ill to fight if an outbreak occurred. This would in effect destroy his army. By the end of March 1778 all the soldiers at Valley Forge had been inoculated. It has been estimated that around one in fifty of inoculated soldiers died from the pox at Valley Forge.

The Yellow Springs Hospital, a military hospital and the first to be built in the country, was built about ten miles from Valley Forge. Hundreds of soldiers from the camp were cared for there. About 2,000 troops died at Valley Forge that winter.

"I again left Nobletown between the 20th and 30th of March 1779 and went to Soldier's Fortune, where I joined the company under the command of Capt Nathl. Dixon…which company belonged to the regiment under the command of Col Henry Jackson….and to the brigade of Genl Learned in April I was marched down to Peekskill where Genl Putman had the command of the forces assembled, among which I recollects Gen Patterson's brigade and the regiment of Col Bailey and of Col Michael Jackson--While there Lieut Smith a spy of the enemy was detected in camp, was tried and suffered punishment--Previous to his execution which was performed by bending down an oak sapling and fastening the culprit to it and suffering it to spring back by its won elasticity, I well recollect hearing Gen Putman declare in strong terms, that this enemy demanded Smith and that they should have him, but he would hang him first--After remaining a short time at Peekskill, my regiment was marched to Robinson's Farm on the North River and crossed to West Point, where was Gen Washington's head quarters at that time and where the Main army was assembled--I remained there until the latter part of June, when Gen Washington called for a number of volunteers from each regiment and went down under command of Capt Johnson and joined Gen Wayne at the English neighbor--There Capt Johnson's company was attached to a regiment under the command of Col Meigs--of the other officers I now recollect Col Febiger

Col Fleury, Col Butler and Major Murphy--I remained there until the afternoon of the 14th of July abd then was marched to Long Grove, a niche in the mountain—In the afternoon of the 15th about 4 o'clock the army under the command of Gen Wayne marched to Flemmings and lay there until about 12 oclock at night, when it crossed a bridge over a marsh and advanced upon Stony point--Immediately after crossing the bridge the picquette guard of the enemy fired upon Wayne's army--Gen Waynes army advanced in two columns, one led by Col Febiger and the other by Col Butler and immediately took the fort while a third column led by an officer unknown...advanced from a different direction and took two redoubts situate a short distance from the fort--In this battle I received a wound to the head from a bayonet the marks of which are still perceptible. Immediately after the capture of the Fort, its guns were turned upon the British shipping which lay in the River opposite the Fort--After the battle I remained a short time in Col Meigs regiment and then returned to West Point and again joined the regiment under Col Henry Jackson while there I was engaged in several scouting parties and remained until the first of January A.D. 1780."

The Battle of Stony Point occurred on 16 July, 1779. General Wayne led one column to attack the fort from the south. One column led by Major Hardy Murfree would attack the front of the fort so that the other two column could engaged in a surprise attack on the north and south sides of the fort. The column that would attack from the north consisted of the 2nd Regiment led by Colonel Butler and the 1st Regiment led by Colonel Christian Febiger. Eliab Eggleston was a member of the 2nd Regiment.

In the evening of the 15th Eliab and the rest of the troops were given a rum ration and their orders. Each man was given a white paper to pin to their hats to help them tell each other from the British in the darkness. The men approached the fort about 11:30 and prepared for the assault at midnight. The element of surprise was so important that the men were told that if anyone spoke, fired his weapon or took a step backward they would be executed on the spot. To inforce this order officers carried iron-tipped pikes ready to stick the first man who disobeyed the orders.

The American plan was successful and the fort was taken in less than an hour. The American losses were 15 killed and 83 wounded including a young Eliab with a head wound. The morning of the 16th the British guns in the fort were turned against British ships on the river. Firing was at long range and did little damage.

Eliab served a total of 27 months and received $80.00 a year for his service. His wife Lucy received his pension after his death in 1838.

Sources: 1. Census of 1810, 1820, and 1830. 2. Sons of the American Revolution Applications. 3. Tombstone. 4. The Official roster of the Soldiers of the American Revolution Buried in the State of Ohio. 5. National society of D.A.R. Lineage Book. 6. Pension Papers W2774. 7. The Storming of Stony Point on the Hudson by Henry Phelps Johnston. 8. Raccoon Brigade, Soldiers of the Revolution of Geauga County, Ohio by Jeannett Grosvenor.

****

Robert Ellis age 14

Robert Ellis was born on 1 May, 1766 in Massachusetts, and he died on 25 November, 1846 in Sidney, Maine. He married Mariam Longley in June 1790. She received a yearly widow's pension of $80.

"In July 1780 I enlisted as a private soldier in the service of the United States. During the war I was in the company commanded by Capt John Dimit and regiment commanded by Col George Ried of the second Regiment New Hampshire line. I served until June 3rd 1783. I was at the battle of Kingsbridge and under Col Reid against the Indians on the Mohawk river."

Sources: 1. U.S. Pensioners 1818-1872. 2. Maine Society sons of the American Revolution. 3. Pension Papers W23005.

****

Edward Evans age 14

Edward Evans was born on 9 May, 1767 in Amenia, New York, and he died after 1835. It was noted in his pension application that he was a Presbyterian Minister at one time. Edward received a yearly pension of $54.66.

"In A.D. 1782 in the month of April I enlisted for the term of nine months, & marched to the city of Albany, before joining any Regiment, I enlisted into a company commanded by Capt Jonathan Piercy, Josiah Richardson 1st Lieutenant , Lawrence Tempes 2nd Lieutenant & the Regiment was commanded by Col Marinus Willet, after a few weeks we were ordered to march from Albany to defend the frontier inhabitants from __?__ upon the Mohawk River and its vicinity, my first station, was at a place called Fort Hunter from thence I was ordered to a place called

Quarrystown where I was with a detachment under the command of Lieutenant Josiah Richardson, were stationed until sometime in October following, when we were ordered to rejoin the Regiment at Fort Plain for a short time orders were served for all to be inoculated for the small pox who had not previously had the disease, I was of the number who had previously had it. Sometime in January following the Regiment was joined by a Regiment from Rhode Island, & ordered on an expedition garrison & take the British garrison at Oswego which expedition failed by reason of treachery or ignorance of the pilot who was an Indian by the name of Capt John."

Colonel Marinus Willett, the commanding officer of the Tryon County Militia, was given the task of providing for the defense of the Mohawk Valley. In February 1783 he was sent with 500 troops out to capture the British fort at Oswego. As they approached the fort the Americans had several dogs with them killed, so that their barking would not alert the British. The fortifications of the fort proved to be too strong, so Willett ordered his men back to their base at Fort Plain.

Colonel Willett had not brought enough provisions, so on the way back the men dug up the dogs out of the snow and ate them. The Indians that acted as the American's guide became confused with the trail, and the men were taken through a swamp. This resulted in some Americans dying and others being victims of frostbite and being disabled.

"He led the troops into a swamp not sufficiently frozen to bear some __?__ and many so frozen that they lost some of their limbs, & some died, after this return to __?__ in the spring following, the regiment was ordered to Fort Herkimer & was on fatigue the most of the time until autumn in repairing roads, rebuilding Bridges, which had been destroyed by the enemy or our own people in their flight, to deter the progress of the former, & made good the retreat of the latter, the Regiment was ultimately, ordered to Fort Stanwix; to build a store & two Block Houses for the accommodations of the returning inhabitants their defense of the Indians & others who might assail them, & after accomplishing the object, were again ordered to Fort Herkimer & after some time had elapsed, were ordered to the city of Schenectady for winter quarters; when in the month of January 1784 I was verbally discharged from the service."

"At the time of my enlistment for the term of two years I had the pledge of being clothed & __?__, instantly; but the gun, bayonet, & cartridge box, only were provided. Not an article of clothing was furnished until the month of October following when each man drew a __?__ one

pair of small clothes one of shoes, & one pair of stockings, & many had neither hat or shirt to cover them. About the first of January after the first pledge was verified, when each man drew a full suit, but there were no further provisions, but I was discharged with my companions in arms in a destitute situation."

Sources: 1. The Bloodied Mohawk: The American Revolution in the Words of Fort Planks Defenders and Other Mohawk Valley Partisans by Kenneth D. Johnson. 2. Pension Papers S8437. 3. History of the Mohawk Valley: Gateway to the West 1614-1925, Vol. II, edited by Nelson Greene.

****

Joseph Evans age 14

Joseph Evans was born in 1760 in Virginia, and he died on 4 September, 1832 in Montgomery, Illinois. He married Elizabeth Earnest on 10 May, 1785 in Tennessee. He served in the 7th Virginia Regiment in a rifle battalion. He received a pension of $8 a month.

"I enlisted in the regular Service of the United States in the year 1774 in the State of Virginia in the company commanded by Captain Joseph Crocket of the Seventh Virginia regiment I continued in the said crops or in the service of the United States until the fall of the year 1779 when I was discharged from Service in the detachment commanded by Col. Thomas Butlar State of Pennsylvania & that my discharge is said to be lost at the burning of the war at W. City I was in the battles of Guins Island Bonbrook, Morristown, Monmouth, Brunswick, Edgefield and at the taking of Berguin and that he was with Col. Butler in all his Expeditions against [several Indian names are given, can't read] tribes of Indians."

The 7th Virginia Regiment was formed at Gloucester County Courthouse in the spring of 1776. It was commanded by Colonel William Dangerfield from February 1776 to August 1776, Colonel Crawford from August 1776 to March 1777, and Colonel Alexander McClanachan from March 1777 to May 1778. Colonel Thomas Butler served in a Pennsylvania Regiment.

Joseph stated that he was at Saratoga and the taking of General Burgoyne. No Virginia Regiments were present at that battle. The battle of Gwynn Island that started on 8 July, 1776 was a small battle involving the 3rd Virginia, which was a detachment of the 7th Virginia. Joseph stated that he was in this battle. The Virginia troops attacked Lord Dunmore,

Virginia's royal governor, at this island. It resulted in a small American victory.

At the Battle of Bound Brook on 13 April, 1777 Joseph was part of an outpost at bound Brook, New Jersey. The main continental Army was in winter quarters at Morristown. The outpost was surprised and defeated by a much larger force of British and Hessian troops. Later in the winter of 1777 Joseph would be at the winter quarters of Valley Forge. When he left Valley Forge, he was at the Battle of Monmouth in June of 1778.

Sources: 1. Census of 1810, 1820, & 1830. 2. Tennessee Marriages to 1825. 3. Pension Papers S35289.

****

Simeon Everly age 14

Simeon Everly was born on 15 October, 1763 in Cumberland County, Maryland, and he died on 16 March, 1843 in Monongalia County, West Virginia. He received a yearly pension of $30. He was dropped from the pension rolls in 1835, because there was a question if he really did do the service as stated.

"On the 10 day of June 1777 I volunteered in the Virginia Militia as a private and Indian Spy from Monongalia County when 14 years of age under Captain Joseph Neal, Lieutenant and Enigns names not recollected, Peter Popin Sergeant, for a tour of 3 months to defend the Northwestern frontiers of Virginia, I marched and spied through the Counties of Monongalia, Harrison, Lewis, Preston & Randolph in pursuit of the enemy that were nearly daily committing depredations on the western frontiers. We marched and spied constantly from what was called Martin's Fort, Stradler's Fort on Dunkard's Creek, Burress's Fort near Morgentown, Harrison's Fort, Coburn's Fort on Dunkard's Creek, Monongalia County, and Evans' Fort in the State of Pennsylvania, just across the Virginia line and through the before mentioned scope of country until the 10 of September following at which time I was discharged by Capt. Neels. That I was not in any battles or skirmishes during said tour, but recollect distinctly of the Indians coming on Dunkard's Creek, a branch of the West fork of the Monongalia river just before I volunteered to pursue them, and killed and drove off the most of the whites there settled, two men by the name of Wade and Robbins were killed. In this tour I saw Col. Martin who was our Commandant."

"On the 6 day of June 1779 I volunteered in the Virginia Militia as a private under Capt. Ferrell, Lieutenant's name not recollected,--Mauhon Ensign, and marched from Mongalia County, Virginia to Little Yok where we met Col. Clarke and was attached to his regiment, lay there a few days and from thence we marched to the mouth of Shirter that empties into the Ohio river, at which place some Indians lay in ambush, fired on us and killed three of Col. Clarke's men, from thence we marched to Wheeling Fort still lower down on the Ohio river, lay there several days making preparation to march on against the enemy; there saw Col. Morgan, Major Lowther, Capt. George Jackson and other officers, names not recollected. We there took water and descended the Ohio river to the mouth of Limestone just above the falls of the Ohio, we there took land and reconnoitered the country and forted where Louisville in Kentucky is now situate. I was there taken sick and lay there for about four weeks with the fever and ague. Col. Clarke and the most of the army went on. from there I marched to Harrod's station, on my way there I fell in with Col. Zach. Morgan, Capt. George Jackson, and other officers, but have forgotten their names. From there we retreated to Dick's river in Kentucky, lay there for some time and on the ___ day of December 1779 was discharged."

"That we then proceeded homeward, when we were within about 7 miles of Powell's station night overtook us, we kindled up a fire and lay down. about midnight we were aroused from our sleep by the firing of guns by the Indians. Several of our men were killed and wounded. disagreeable and cold as the weather was, those that could travel were bound to leave and seek shelter elsewhere. From there we marched on undisturbed and on the ___ day of April following I arrived home in Monongalia County. In this tour I volunteered for six months, but from the time I left home till my return was 9 months, making in all 9 months, provided the time I consumed in returning home is not reckoned, but if included makes 12 months."

The following statement was sent on 28 March, 1834, "Simeon Everly. draws $30. I the undersigned Simeon Everly at the requisition of the Secretary of War give the following narative of my age and Revolutionary Services to Wit – I was 71 yrs old the 18 of last October--Some time during the Revolutionary war my brother in Law William Martin was drafted--(it was then said for three months) I substituted in his place--there were 7 or 8 of us went down the Monongalia River to Elizabeth town 14 or 15 miles above Pittsburg there joined our Captain from Monongalia--Robert Ferrill--Gen'l. Clark was at that place with other soldiers. the whole army *under Gen'l. Clark went to the mouth of Shertee on the Ohio: remained there some time repairing the boats to descend the river, it eventually went down to Wheeling rested a while & then went on down to the mouth of the Kentucky River, and from there to the falls of Ohio and there encamped. I took sick & & went up into Kentucky--directly after I left Col. Morgan with his command in which I belonged was discharged--on the return of Morgans men I joined them. traveled with them a few days, & finally was compelled from indisposition to leave the men. remained sick in Kentucky some time--I joined Capt Ferrell at Elizabeth town some time in July-- Morgan & his men were discharged their time haveing expired some time late in the fall. I left the army about 3 weeks before Morgan was discharged--I was in service at least four months (4 months)--when quite young--I think April 1776 I done some neighbourhood service scouting-- never as an Indian Spy during the Revolutionary War."*

The grandson of Simeon Everly says of his grandfather, *"He was a slaveholder. But to those who desired freedom, it was granted at the age of 21 years. One day he gave an old slave a new suit of clothes and his freedom. The old slave was delighted at his owner's generosity, but after wandering around for a few days, he returned to forego the franchise granted and spent the remainder of days in the home of his former master."*

Sources: 1. History of Cloud County, Kansas by Holibaugh, Biography Section Simeon Oliver Everly. 2. U.S. Pension roll of 1835. 3. West Virginians in the American Revolution. 4. Pension Papers S8446.

****

Ebenezer Fain age 14

Ebenezer Fain was born on 27 August, 1762 in Chester County, Pennsylvania, and he died on 29 December, 1842 in Habersham County, Georgia. He married Mary Mercer on 6 June, 1781 in Jonesboro, Tennessee and they had 10 children. Ebenezer received a yearly pension of $40 for his service. His wife did not apply for a widow's pension, however, his son John did apply for his father's pension and it was rejected.

"I first entered the service of the United States under Captain James Montgomery in Washington County in the State of Virginia in June, One Thousand Seven Hundred and Seventy Six as a militiaman for the term of three months under the command of Col. William Christian when I was about fourteen years of age. I served during the said three months

at a place called Black's Fort and Montgomery's Station. During that time I was engaged in two battles with the Indians in one of which sixteen Indians were killed. Colonel Christian from Virginia marched in considerable force into the Cherokee Country while I was engaged in this service. I was discharged by Captain Montgomery and received pay two or three years afterwards at Abingdon in Virginia."

"I entered a Second term of duty under Captain William Trimble & Col Charles Robertson as a volunteer militia light horseman in Washington County, North Carolina, now Tennessee, the first of June One Thousand Seven Hundred and Eighty (1780). I marched to & remained at Gilbert Town for a week or two and then joined Col Charles McDowell's Regiment. Col Isaac Shelby and Col Elijah Clarke from Georgia were also there. I was marched with said troops to Edward Hampton's on the Pacolet River in South Carolina where a skirmish took place with the British. The Americans lost two men killed and took several prisoners among whom was a British Capt. Patterson. The detachment marched then to Broad River near the mouth of Buffalo Creek where while on sentry I shot a spy by the name of John Franklin and found an express from Lord Cornwallis to a Tory Captain Moore urging him to defend his fort and promising to reinforce him. We made a forced march to said Fort at a place called Thicketty in South Carolina and Captain Moore gave up the fort and surrendered himself and about 100 men as prisoners of war. We then set out to meet the promised reinforcements from the British Army and met them at a place called Musgrove's Mill. . Had an engagement with them and drove them back with considerable loss to them. They took shelter in the mill, barn and dwelling houses where we left them. Then we marched to Lawson's Fork near Wofford's Iron Works where we had an engagement with the British commanded by Major Dunlap. We were suddenly charged by the British in the night and after a short but severe struggle in which a number were severely wounded by the broadsword among the wounded was Col. Elijah Clarke of Georgia. were compelled to give way. The Americans after retreating a short distance again rallied and renewed the fight. The enemy was finally defeated. Their commander, Major Dunlap, was wounded and taken prisoner. After this I was placed under the command of Captain Cunningham and attached to Colonel Clarke's Regiment. Colonel Clarke marched for Georgia but hearing that Augusta & nearly all Georgia was in the hands of the British & Tories we marched back to Rutledge's Ford on the Saluda River. Colonel Clarke having heard that Major Ferguson with a strong detachment of British & Tories was marching up toward the mountains sent this declarant with an express to

Cols. Sevier & Shelby in Washington County, North Carolina, now Tennessee and I returned from them with one to Col. Clarke. And his time of service three months having expired, I returned home."

"In a very short time after I arrived at home at the solicitation of Col. Swain I entered the service again as the substitute of one Jacob Vance who was drafted & refused to serve. The legislature of North Carolina passed an Act that under such circumstances the drafted man should pay the substitute sixty dollars which the said Vance paid me after my return. This time I served three months having mustered in to service about the fifteenth of September of that said year in Washington County, North Carolina, now Tennessee, under Captain Christopher Taylor, John Sevier, Colonel. In this tour I served as a mounted man and marched thence to the Cowpens in South Carolina where we met Colonel Campbell of Virginia, Colonel Shelby, Colonel Cleveland and Colonel Williams. Thence we marched in pursuit of Maj. Ferguson and overtook him at Kings Mountain. I was engaged in that battle and received a wound in the leg. I accompanied the greater part of the Army to Rutherford, North Carolina & thence to Morganton as it is now called in Burke County, North Carolina and was in a short time thereafter discharged."

"I entered on a fourth tour of duty immediately after the close of the last under Captain Gibson in said County of Washington, North Carolina under Col. Sevier and as a volunteer light Horseman & marched to a place called the Big Island on the French Broad River in the Cherokee Nation near which an engagement with the Indians took place. They were defeated with a loss of fifteen or twenty killed. A few days afterwards we were joined by Col. Arthur Campbell of Virginia & from thence was marched to old Chota Town where we had a small skirmish and killed one Indian on the 24th of December of the same year. The next day Maj. Jesse Walton with a part of the force, this declarant among them, marched upon a town called Sitaco. Killed several Indians and took fifteen or twenty prisoners, mostly women and children & returned to headquarters at Chota. We then marched to Tellico towns (and were engaged in a skirmish). The Indians fled across the river and were pursued. We lost a Capt. Elliott killed. We then marched to big Hiwassee, took some prisoners and returned to Tellico. We then returned home. I was discharged at Jonesboro, now Tennessee in the last of February or first of March Seventeen Hundred and Eighty One having served upwards of two months."

"I was again called in to service & served as a light horseman in a Company of Rangers under Capt. Christopher Cunningham and under Cols. Sevier and Carter for the purpose of watching the Indians & Tories and guarding the Frontier. I was constantly marching & ranging through this country, principally through the Indian Country, and the frontiers of Washington County North Carolina, now Tennessee. I was in one skirmish with Indians. Me with some thirteen or fourteen others were attacked in a house. We defended ourselves from early morning til about mid-day and were relieved by Col. Sevier. The Indians had several killed. I entered this tour of duty on the first of April Seventeen Hundred and Eighty One and served six months having been discharged in October following. I received I think ten dollars a month for this service. I was actively engaged in the service of the United States during the Revolutionary War as herein before stated fifteen months and about one half."

In Ebenezer's second tour of duty he was in the Battle of Wofford's Iron Works fought in August of 1780. Here the Americans were attacked by a large detachment of British dragoons and mounted militia riflemen under the command of Major Dunlap. When the British attacked, the fighting raged hand-to-hand. After the battle both sides claimed victory.

Ebenezer was one of five brothers, along with their father, that served in the Revolution. All six were in the battle of Kings Mountain, and one brother was killed by Indians during the Revolution.

Sources: 1. Georgia Cherokee Land Lotter 1832. 2. Census of 1790, 1810, 1830, and 1840. 3. North Carolina and Tennessee Early Land Records 1753-1931. 4. Tombstone 5. Lineage Book DAR. 6. U.S. Pensioners 1818-1872. 7. Pension Papers R3421.

****

William Falls age 14

William Falls was born on 9 August, 1763 in Chester County, Pennsylvania, and he died on 1 February, 1837 in Iredell County, North Carolina. He married Mary Polly Simonton on 13 March, 1786. On his tombstone his name includes the title of Major. He was a private when the war ended, so this author assumes that he may have served in the local militia after the war. William enlisted in 1776 and served under his father Captain Gilbraith Falls. William received $64.46 for his service of 17 months.

"*I first served in Cherokee Campaign under Genl Rutherford, Col Locke in the company commanded by Captain Falls my Father and Lieutenant Neil--Was not old enough to be lible to draft but entered as a Volunteer, my Father went to Cathey's Fort on the Catawba River was there Six weeks, and I returned with the Wagons which could go no further through the Mountains.*"

"*My next tour was three a volunteer under Captain Falls and Lieutenant Sloan the Company was Stationed at Davidson's Fort on the Catawba River guarding the frontier Settlements from Indian invasion which was in the Spring of 1777 I think.*"

"*Was next out what was called Cross Creek Expedition about Fayetteville against Tories Gen Rutherford and Col Posley I think of Guilford commanded. Was a volunteer as before under my father Captain Falls during the Fall of 1777 or 78. Served six weeks and was then sent an express to Salisbury with letters.*"

"*Was next on a scouting tour of three months through Lincoln and rowan (now Iredell) on the Catawba River guarding the Fords on said River under Capt falls and Lieutenant Kerr. And was in frequent tours of some kinds afterwards a few days at a time dates not recollected.*"

"*Was next out on about the time of Ramsours Battle in June 1780, a week or so previous to it was in the Scout through Lincoln when it was perceived that the Tories was embodied I rode express to Genl Rutherford between Charlotte & Salisbury who immediately detached Capt Falls and lieutenant Byers with their company which I joined as a volunteer—marched to Lincoln by Sherrill's Ford on Catawba River to a Camp on Mountain creek—went to Ramsours under Col Locke and Major Rutherford was present in the Battle in which my Father Capt Falls was killed, I then came home being in service about twenty days.*"

The first real battle in which William was engaged in was a very bloody and personal battle. The Battle of Ramsour's Mill took place on 20 June, 1780 between Colonial and Tory militias. The Americans were outnumbered 3 to 1 and yet managed a victory. Both sides were short of ammunition, so there was much hand-to-hand fighting. It was particularly brutal, because it was fought between neighbors, near relations, and former friends.

William and his father were part of the Rowan County 1st Regiment mounted troops that led the attack. It was during this first attack that Captain Falls was killed. He was about one hundred and fifty yards east of the battle ground when he was shot in the chest and fell dead from his horse. While his body was on the ground, a Tory ran up to it and began to rob the body. As the Tory removed the Captain's watch, fourteen year old William saw what was happening and ran toward his father. William grabbed his father's sword and killed the Tory.

"In the fall of 1780 as well as I now recollect I again Volunteered for Three months, was selected with others to furnish the army with Beef Cattle under the direction of James Kerr purchasing agent Commissary. After this I was occationelly a guard on Catawba River under no regular command. On Cornwallis's appearance from south Carolina proclamation was made that all who would furnish themselves with a horse and serve for six weeks might claim service for three months on foot I joined a Company under Capt Byers with col Davidson, Col Dixon, Co McCall and Col Perkins—after Cornwallis crossed the Catawba in February 1781, we followed in after his army to the vicinity of Hillsboro North Carolina and joined Col Lee of the light horse near Hart's Mills Eight miles from Hillsboro. We Captured a Company of Tories and a British officer—Tarleton came out with 300 men from Hillsboro in pursuit of which Col Lee marched us and followed for five days. They came up with Piles a Tory Colonel who was said to have 350 men in his attachment. Piles under the belief that it was Tarleton's Horse made no preparation to resist and in consequence the greater part of his men (265 it was said) was killed. We maneuvered in the neighborhood a few days during which there was a skirmish with a party of British on Alamance--I shortly after joined General Green and maneuvered with him until my term expired."

The Battle of Haw River, also known as Piles Defeat, occurred on a cold day on 25 February, 1781 in North Carolina. Dr. John Pyle, the Tory commander, was riding along with his men when they came upon a column of mounted men. He mistakenly thought they were British troops under the command of Banastre Tarleton who he knew was in the area.

It was dusk, and the British and American mounted troops both wore green uniforms. Two of Pyle's scouts rode up to the mounted troops. One scout rode back to Pyle to tell him they had found Tarleton, while the other scout engaged the troop commander in conversation he believed to be the British commander. Soon the two opposing columns approached each other, and Pyle's column moved off the road in respect of what they thought were British dragoons.

The American troops under Colonel Lee rode passed with their swords drawn in salute. Meanwhile, the American foot soldiers had moved off the road and taken up positions in the woods. As Colonel Lee approached Pyle in the rear of the column they exchanged greetings, and they were shaking hands when someone began shouting and soon musket shots were fired. Once the fighting started the Americans were prepared, since they already had their swords drawn. Pyle was knocked from his horse and asked for mercy. Within 10 minutes the "battle" was over. The Tories had 90 men killed and 250 wounded. The American had one horse killed. This author is sure that the Americans that were there laughed about this "battle" for many years afterwards. This author doubts that too many of the surviving Tories would ever admit being there.

Sources: 1. The American Revolution in the Southern Colonies by David Lee Russell. 2. North Carolina Marriage Index, 1741-2004. 3. Tombstone. 4. U.S. Pension Roll of 1835. 5. U.S. Pensioners 1818-1872. 6. North Carolina Genealogy Webpage. 7. Pension Papers S6834. 8. A Guide to the Battles of the American Revolution by Theodore P. Savas & J. David Dameron.

****

Abijah Fairchild age 14

Abijah Fairchild was born on 2 October, 1763 in New Jersey, and he died on 8 April, 1843 in Wilkes County, Tennessee. He married Violate Gullet on 20 March, 1795 in Wilkes County, Tennessee. His pension claim was rejected because he did not serve for 6 months.

"I volunteered in the month of May 1777 and was called into service with the commission of Corpal under the command of Captain William Sloan (the inferior officer not recollected) and marched across the Blue Ridge down New River to Grayson County, Virginia as far as Coxes Settlement in pursuit of a band of Tories and Out Lyers, from which place we was returned to Wilkes where we remained in service Scouting and Guarding the Country for three months for which service he received no discharge as he now recollects of."

"In the month of May 1780 I volunteered and called into service under the command of Captain James Henderson, my inferior officer not now recollected and was marched to Crider's Fort in Burk County in pursuit of a band of Tories and out lyers who was commanded by a Tory Colo by the name of Roberts - we remained for some time scouting and

guarding the Country, when we marched back to Wilkes and remained in same guarding the Country for three months when we were dismissed."

"In the month of October 1779 I volunteered and was called into service under command of Captain Robert Cleveland and Richas Stonapher, I believe was our Lieutenant. We marched up the Yadkin River in pursuit of a band of Tories. I remained in service ten days when I was dismissed."

"In the latter part of the month of August I volunteered and was called into service under the Command of Col Benjamin Cleveland and Captain William Jackson and went on my march to Kings Mountain when I was taken lame in Burke County, when I was sent home on furlough. As soon as the battle was over at Kings Mountain and the Troops returned with the prisoners, I joined the troops at Wilkesboro under the same officers to guard the prisoners and marched to Old Richmond in Surry County and from that place to Salem where we remained for some time guarding the prisoners. When he returned home after having served two months."

"In the year 1781 I volunteered and was called into service under the Command of Captain Robert Cleveland and Richas Stone Scipher was our Lieutenant. We marched from Wilkes County down to the forks of the Yadkin in order to join Genl Green's army who was retreating from the British army, finding that the British was between us and Greene's army our Captain sent us home in the month of April. I am of the opinion that I was in service one month."

Sources: 1. North Carolina Marriage Index 1741-2004. 2. Census 1830. 3. Rejected or Suspended Applications for Revolutionary War Pensions Claims for North Carolina Residents 1850. 4. Pension Papers R3428.

****

Ezekiel Farmer age 14

Ezekiel Farmer was born in 1764 in Spartanburg, South Carolina, and he died in 1842 in Drake County, Ohio. His wife was named Florinda Jane Campbell.

"I entered the service of the United States as a volunteer in April of the year 1778 & served under Gen Green & Capt Blassinger for a term of seven months, all of which time I was with the 4th Regiment of Continentals—I started with the company from Farmins Creek which reinforced Genl Gates on the high hills of Santee after the battle of

Camden, thence after a skirmish, at Camden, I passed with the army, into North Carolina for safety, Charleston & Camden being then both in possession of the Enemy—I received my discharge there from Genl Green & returned home to South Carolina."

"I was drafted I think in January or February of the year 1779 for three months & again served under Capt Blasingame & Genl Green—I proceeded from Union County to Georgetown in South Carolina, thence to North Carolina, where my time expired."

"In April of the year 1780 I was again drafted for the term of three months & served under Genl Green, Capt Blassingsme & Maj Jolly; during which time I was engaged in no Battle, but laid most of the time near St. John's island watching the Enemy who were on the Island—my time having expired I received my discharge."

"I again volunteered in the summer of 1780 & served as a Ranger under Captains Avery, Young, & Watson in South Carolina for a term of eight months; in the fall of 1781 I was engaged with a scouting party under Capt John Putman, & Daniel Cromer, & Benjamin Watson for six or eight months--I served in all more than two years."

Sources: 1. Census of 1790, 1800, 1810, 1830, & 1840. 2. The Official Roster of Soldiers of the American Revolution Buried in the State of Ohio. 3. Roster of South Carolina Patriots in the American Revolution. 4. U.S. Pension Roll of 1835. 5. Pension Papers S16112.

****

Leonard Farrar age 14

Leonard Farrar was born on 4 April, 1764 in Goochland, Virginia, and he died on 30 April, 1836 in Franklin, Missouri. He was married to Mary Margaret Hamilton by the Reverend John Shateen around 1787 in South Carolina. He received a yearly pension of $40 and 116 acres in Missouri for his service.

"In the fall or first of the Winter of the Year seventeen hundred and seventy eight troops were raised in the County of Guilford in the state of North Carolina and one James Wilson an acquaintance of the family of this mine a citizen of Guilford County was drafted and I became his substitute then in my fourteenth or fifteenth year and joined a company commanded by Capt James Frost. Isam Hancock Lieutenant, Charles Dougherty first and Enoch Foster second Sergeant the regiment was commanded by Col. Hampton and Lt. Col. Hamright Genl. Lininton

commanded the brigade. I joined the troop in Guilford County and marched from thence by the way of Salisbury to Charleston, when at Charleston I had the small pox and was confined to the Hospital and hence knows but little of what was done on the part of the army. I received a discharge signed by his Col. Hampton Lt. Col. Hamright and Captain Frost which is lost. and I believe I received my discharge on the 24th day of March seventeen hundred and seventy nine for a Tour of three months. In the spring of the year seventeen hundred and eighty I believe I was drafted in Pitsylvania County Virginia and was attached to the Company of one Captain Burns or Burnet but was from the circumstances of my having a Rifle, removed with others who had Rifles into the Company of Captain Cowdan who was from Henry County in the State of Virginia and I marched by the way of Cobham & Petersburg in Virginia to a place called as I think the Maubin Hills where I joined the army commanded by Genl Lawson Col Tucker and Maj'r Holcomb. The Army marched from the Mauben Hills through the Country in different directions and to places the names of which are entirely forgotten; some time in the summer of the year seventeen hundred and eighty I received a discharge at the house of Capt. Cowdan in Henry County Virginia but does not recollect by whom it was signed. The discharge was for a Tour of three months service, and is lost. In the month of March in the year seventeen hundred and eighty one, one Mashack Stevens was drafted and he was the brother in law mine but when called on to go into the service he failed for some cause or other and on the day that the battle of Guilford was fought I then in the County of Pitsylvania in the state of Virginia hearing the report of the large guns at Guilford went to my Brother in law Mashack Stevens and proposed to substitute for him, and in the morning thereafter I went to Guilford Courthouse in the state of North Carolina (or near thereto) and reported myself as the substitute of said Stevens to Capt Joseph Morton who had previously raised a Company in Pitsylvania County and was by the said Capt mustered into service, on the day after, as this I recollect I was removed to another company the names of the officers of which are forgotten. but Genl Lee had the command of the troops. the army marched I was informed in pursuit of Cornwallis. after a considerable time (the precise time not recollected) I was sent in company with other soldiers to guard some Prisoners."

Sources: 1. Tombstone 2. Census 1790 & 1830. 3. U.S. General Land Office Records 1796-1907. 4. U.S. Pensioners 1818-1872. 5. Sons of the American Revolution. 6. Pension Papers S17406.

****

Pardon Field age 13

Pardon Field was born on 27 September, 1767 in Tolland, Connecticut, and he died on 5 January, 1832 in Nottawa, Michigan. He married Rachel Kent in 1787. He received a monthly pension of $8.

"Sometime toward the close of the year 1780 I enlisted as a private Soldier in the Fifth Connecticut Regiment in a company commanded by Captain Jonathan Little. I served from the time of my enlistment until sometime in the month of November, 1782 when I was discharged."

Pardon stated in his pension application that after the war he moved to Ohio in 1818. While there he built a small house on 25 acres of land rented for 23 cents a year from a local college.

Sources: 1. D.A.R. Lineage Book, Vol. 40. 2. Tombstone 3. U.S. Pensioners 1818-1872. 4. Pension Papers S43555.

****

Pardon Field age 14

Pardon Field was born on 13 April, 1761 in Rhode Island, and he died on 28 October, 1842 in Chester, Vermont. He married Elizabeth Williams on 5 January, 1782 His application for a pension was rejected because he did not serve six months.

"I entered the service of the United States as a Musician a fifer and served as herein stated enlisted in the town of Cranston State of Rhode Island in 1775 in the month of March or April under Capt. Frederick Williams and Col. Atwell for three months. Went to Lexington did not git there till the Battle was over continued at Lexington about six weeks and went back to Rhode Island and served out my time."

"I enlisted in 1776 on board a sloop the Providence under Sailing master Witfield Lieutenant Laten, Nathaniel Waterman and James Lockwood enlisted the same time that I did and went to the grand bank and had a battle with a British privateer but could not take her. Then we took a British Schooner loaded with coffee ___?___ and left her at Boston and I was discharged."

"I volunteered at the time the British landed on Newport Island under Col. Benjamin Arnold and Capt. Daniel Arnold _____cannot read several words___ went over to the Island about two hundred of us and hid

over __?__ in ambush around a certain Spring where the British came to get water. The next morning we arose and took them prisoner. In a few days the British undertook to drive us off Warnick neck with a 36 gun frigate but the tide was going out and she got on a reef of rock and there was considerable firing between us and night came on and the next tide she went off. There was one of our men wounded the enemy shot over our head."

Pardon is found on the rolls at Warnick Neck in the company commanded by Benjamin Arnold. Also, in the company is Nathan Waterman, which may be the same person he served with on the *Providence* in 1776.

"After they, the enemy, landed at Bristol and Burnt it we marched to Bristol but the enemy had left it before we got there. I staid at Bristol two weeks, then went to Biswell Mills and staid there a short time. General Sullivan understood that our company were oarsman he sent for us we joined his army and helped ferry the army over to Rhode Island about that time the French fleet came to Newport soon after we landed we had some skirmishes with their pickquit guards."

"We drove the enemy to the South of the Island and a British fleet have in sight the French fleet went out to meet them and was broken by a gale of wind and did not come to action. Then the British that was on the Island turned on our army and we had a battle. The British retreated. After the retreat our army went off the Inland. The British soon evacuated the Island and went to N.J. I went to the Island and was a fifer for another company and was discharged."

Pardon fought in the Battle of Rhode Island on 29 August, 1778. The French fleet sailed out to do battle with the British fleet, and a major storm broke out. The storm continued for two days scattering both fleets and causing much damage to the French flagship. The French fleet left the area to regroup. Without support of the French fleet, General Sullivan abandoned his plans to capture Newport and his army withdrew. Pardon was probably a member of the 2nd Rhode Island Regiment at this time.

Sources: 1. Tombstone 2. Sons of the American Revolution Application. 3. Pension Papers R3531. 4. Revolutionary Defenses in Rhode Island; an Historical Account of the Fortifications and Beacons Erected During the American Revolution, with Muster Rolls of the Companies Stationed along the Shores of Narragansett Bay by Edward Field, 1896.

****

Adam Jordan Files age 14

Adam Files was born on 10 March, 1764 in Augusta, Virginia, and he died on 11 August, 1840 in Polecat Springs, Alabama. He married Mary Baskin on 30 April, 1790, and they had 12 children. Adam enlisted in 1777 and served under Captain William Baskin his future brother-in-law.

"I was enrolled by my father in the winter of 1777 under Capt William Baskin in Abbeville district South Carolina and served a tour of six months. The Company was commanded by Capt Baskin. Lieutenant Files & 2nd Lieut Baskin a brother of the Captain. This Company was chiefly engaged in excursions against the Indians and for the purpose of protecting the frontier settlements in the part of ~~the Country South Carolina~~ from Savage depredations. During the whole of this service the Company was in no formal engagements nor under the command of any other officers than those above mentioned."

"The next service was performed under the same Captain under a draft for two or three months I was not exactly certain as to the time upon the frontiers against the Indians. This service was performed in the year 1778 in south Carolina."

"The third tour was performed under my father who was Lieutenant Files as a scouting party against the Indians. This service only continued about one month. The next service was performed after the capture of Charlestown by the British under Cap Files (who was promoted from 1st Lieutenant) and my company joined the army of Genl Morgan at Grindal shoals on Pacolet River South Carolina, the Militia being under the command of Genl Andrew Pickens. I was at the battle of the Cowpens under Genl Morgan. The right of the Army was commanded by Genl Pickens. The left by Col McCall and the Center by Genl Morgan. In this battle my father Captain files and my brother Jeremiah Files were severely wounded. The latter is now residing in the State of Alabama and is receiving a pension from the government in consequence of his wounds received in the above engagement in S Carolina. After the battle I was left at Genl McDowell's in north Carolina on the Catawba River to attend to the wounded and sick and remained there for some time until marched to the State of Virginia remained in Virginia a short time and returned back to South Carolina where in a skirmish Capt Files was taken prisoner and murdered by the Tories and Indians. I was present at this engagement when only five of the company made their escape. From this time to the close of the war I was frequently in service under Capt Baskin who

commanded the Company after the death of Capt Files in which served after peace was made with the Colonies and Great Britain."

At the Battle of Cowpens Adam and his brother were under the command of their father Captain Files in the 1st Spartan Regiment of South Carolina. The regiment was at the center of the American line. As they faced the British, General Morgan rode up and down the line telling them not to fire until the British got close. The militia fired their 2 or 3 shots and as ordered retreated. The British charged the retreating Americans and Tarleton, thinking the battle was won, ordered his dragoons to charge the fleeing Americans. The retreating Americans led the British into a trap.

It was at this time that Jeremiah, Adam's brother, was wounded. Jeremiah was severely cut by one of Tarleton's Dragoons on the head, left arm, and the right hand. After the battle he was taken to Gilbert in North Carolina and later taken to General McDowell's at the Quaker Meadows. He remained there for 16 days until he recovered from his wounds. He later enlisted several times and fought against the Indians, even though his arm was badly damaged. Jeremiah first enlisted in 1780 at the age of 15.

Captain John Files was captured during a skirmish with Tories and Indians in May of 1781. Adam was ordered by their father to leave him. Adam and four others in the company managed to escape. Captain Files was tortured and later murdered by the Tories and Indians. He had fought Indians for many years, and he probably had a deep hatred for them. When the Captain was 15 his parents were massacred by Indians.

"I served two tours in the Company of Capt Baskin commanded by Gen Pickens against the Cherokee Indians. The first tour was in the spring the second in the fall of the year after the evacuation of Charlestown by the British. The last service I performed was as guard at the treaty made by General Pickens and Colonel Hankins and others at General Pickens' plantation on Seneca River in Pendleton District S Carolina with the Cherokee Indians."

In all Adam Files had served nearly two years in the militia. For his service he received $60.00 a year.

Sources: 1. Jeremiah Files Pension Papers S13025. 2. Census of 1790, 1806, 1810, 1830, & 1840. 3. U.S. Pensioners 1818-1872. 4. Sons of the American Revolution Application. 5. Alabama Revolutionary War Soldiers. 6. Georgia's Landmarks, Memorials, & Legends. 7. South Carolina Marriage Index 1641-1965. 8. Pension papers S13026.

****

Paul Findley age 14

Paul Findley was born in January of 1762 in Newberry County, South Carolina, and he died on 12 July, 1843 in Laurens County, South Carolina. He married Mary Martin on 20 September, 1782 in Laurens County, South Carolina. He was a successful farmer, because according to the census of 1840 he owned 15 slaves. He received a yearly pension of $80.

"I entered the service of the United States at the age of fourteen years on the fifteenth day of August Seventeen hundred and Seventy six; I was an enlisted soldier or recruit and enrolled as such by one Sergeant Emmit for the particular service of a Corps of mounted horseman called to the best of my recollection by some one of the following names the Georgia Regulars or Provincials or Rangers, whose sole duty appeared to be the frontier protection of the Whigs against Indian depredations and Troy revolt in the State of Georgia I enlisted under the said Sergt. Emmit on the fifteenth day of August one thousand seven hundred & seventy six for the term or time of Eighteen months; that on the day of my enlistment I was a resident of and living in Craven District afterwards known as Ninety Six District and at present called Laurens District in the State of South Carolina; me with other recruits of like character were marched from the place by the said Sergt. Emmit to a place in the State of Georgia called Kettle creek, where I was placed under the command of one Capt. __ Mc Farlin who it appeared had rendezvoused my company at Kettle Creek for about the period of one month & from thence was marched __?__ said Capt. McFarlin's company by him to a place called Nails or Neal's fort on the frontier of Georgia where this company joined another but under Capt. I do not recollect; at which place about the number of three companies were embodied, collected, organized and from thence I was marched with the said troops under the command of Major __ Marberry either to a place called fort Barrington on the Altamaha River in the State of Georgia which place was designated their Head Quarters & from which place the troops alternately issued and moved in small squads & scouting parties up & down the said River & over the North & South bank through the country to check and intimidate the inroads of the Indians & other enemies of the Country for about the period of seven months ending in April or May 1777 seventeen hundred & seventy seven from fort Barrington the said troops were marched under the command of one Col. John Baker to East Florida near the sea coast and near the month of St. John's river & from thence was marched by change of course up to a place called Nassau Swamp where the said troops were defeated to the

number of about one hundred & twenty by a much greater and superior force of Indians & British who by stealth & address gained the superior advantage of enfilading the troops of Liberty between this impenetrable swamp & the enemies' lines in so embarrassed a situation as to terminate in their defeat and success to the Indian & British Victors. The remnant of the troops who individually escaped from this defeat subsequently met at Col. John Baker's plantation called Midway in the State of Georgia in a few days after their defeat at Nassau Swamp. From Col. Baker's plantation the troops were marched under his command to fort Barrington again where I remained with the troops about one month, when I was taken sick & removed to a hospital at a place called Darien about the month of June seventeen hundred & seventy seven. After my recovery I joined the said troops again at a place called fort Cochrane on the frontier of Georgia still under the command of Col. John Baker about the month of September in the year seventeen hundred & seventy seven. From fort Cochrane the said troops were marched in the month of January seventeen hundred & seventy eight to the City of Savannah by the said Col. John Baker, who with the troops remained in the city about one week; thence marched to Augusta in Georgia where I remained with the troops for four or five weeks, and to the end of the applicant's full term of enlistment for Eighteen months when I received an honorable written discharge."

The Battle of Thomas Creek occurred on 17 May, 1777. Private Paul Findley was part of 100 Georgia militia men under the command of Colonel John Baker. Baker's men were supposed to join with 400 Continental soldiers on the south bank of Thomas Creek. At dawn on the 17th the American militia was surprised by an attack of British troops. The outnumbered Americans scattered immediately, and some fled into Nassau Swamp while others mounted their horses and rode off. About 15 Americans were killed, and many of the captured troops were later killed by the Creek Indians that aided the British. The scattered Americans regrouped at the plantation owned by Colonel Baker.

"I forgot to mention in its proper place a battle the troops had with the Indians while stationed at fort Barrington which terminated in the defeat of the Indians with a loss on the part of the troops of five or six men & the loss on the part of the Indians not known to me. Also another battle fought by the troops against a Florida Scout of Tories or enemies on the banks of the Altamaha River about fifteen miles above Fort Barrington which battle terminated in favor of the Whig troops without loss, the enemy baggage was taken & they put to flight. My term of enlistment as aforesaid was fully served out by me viz., eighteen months and that with it ended his

service in the Georgia Campaign to wit February seventeen hundred & seventy eight."

"I entered the service of my country or of the United States as a drafted militia man for the term of three months under one Capt. William Richey who was attached to the Regiment Commanded by Col. Williams in Genl. Williamson's Brigade in the month of February Seventeen hundred & seventy nine, drafted in Craven County, Ninety Six District now Laurens District. I was then marched in this company to Savannah River with other troops opposite to Augusta on the Carolina bank, where the said troops remained vigilantly guarding & protecting their post from the advances of the British who were posted in Augusta & who evacuated Augusta in about a month after the arrival of the American troops on the bank of Savannah River as aforesaid. While I was stationed on the River with the American troops aforesaid, a number of Tory prisoners was brought in by Genl. Pickens & others to the number of about one hundred & fifty & were placed under the guard of Col. Williams' troops. From thence I with the American Troops were marched guarding the said prisoners to the town of Cambridge or Ninety Six where the prisoners were lodged in Jail and the Jail guarded for the remaining & full term of three months when I was verbally discharged."

"I entered the service either in the month of March or April seventeen hundred & eighty as a drafted militia man for the term of three months under Captain William Richey and a Lieut. John Carter who commanded the company in the absence of Capt. Richey who was not with the company in this tour of duty which Company with others were placed under the command of a Col. McCrary & marched from Craven County or Ninety six District now Laurens District where I was drafted to a place called Cupboard Creek in Georgia within a few miles of Augusta. From thence I was marched across Savannah River into Carolina and from the course towards Granby where the news of a large & superior force of British being near, which I believe induced the officers of the weak American force to dismiss us to effect escape from any enemy able for our destruction. I was out in this tour of duty at least two months when I was verbally dismissed or discharged as aforesaid."

"I entered the service again in June seventeen hundred & eighty one as a volunteer under the command of a Capt. William Harris in Ninety Six District now Laurens under whom I marched to the Cherokee nation by order form Col. Kilgore who commanded & conducted the expedition, in which the Indian's towns were burned, their corn destroyed, & several *of them killed after which the army returned to the settlements after an absence of about thirty days. I still continued in this company performing active & constant duty against an outlying handful of Tory robbers on the borders of South Carolina until the fall of the year 1782 month of September when peace was measurably restored to the Whigs & friends of Liberty in South Carolina. This ends the entire service of the applicant in the defense of his country the United States of America."*

Sources: 1. Census 1790, 1800, 1810, 1820, 1830, and 1840. 2. U.S. Pensioners 1818-1872. 3. Tombstone 4. Roster of South Carolina Patriots in American Revolution. 5. Pension Papers W9440.

****

William Flansburgh age 12 or 13

William Flansburgh was born 4 January, c. 1763 in Schenectady, New York, and he died after 1838. He received a yearly pension of $22.77. At the time of enlistment he was only 12 or 13. He was in the Battle of White Plains in 1776 and Monmouth in 1778.

In the spring of 1780 he enrolled under Captain Walter Vrooman in the New York Levies, and in the fall of the same year he was detailed with a company of about sixty men to destroy boats of the enemy lying on Onondaga Lake. While returning they were all taken prisoners, and Flansburgh was taken to London. He was later brought back to Canada, where he made his escape and reached Schenectady soon after the war was over.

Sources: 1. A History of Schenectady During the Revolution by Willis Tracy Hanson. 2. Pension Papers S21955.

****

Zephon Flower age 13

Zephon Flower was born on 30 November, 1765 in Hartford, Connecticut, and he died on 16 April, 1853 in Athens, Pennsylvania. He married Mary Patrick in Hartford on 28 March, 1785. He received a yearly pension of $100.

"I enlisted in 1779 for nine months and was discharged the first day of Jan, 1780 and on the 25th enlisted in the foot services for three years last afterwards into Col Elisha Sheldon's regiment of light Dragoons and

was to be returned from the 25th of Jan. 1780 and receive an honorable discharge dated I believe the 21st day of June 1783."

Zephon served as a private in Captain Davis Edgar's Company of Colonel Elisha Sheldon's Regiment, 2nd Regiment Light Dragoons of the Continental Line. On 28 April, 1781 he received a bounty of 50 pounds sterling, paid by the United States to the State of Connecticut, and granted to the town of New Hartford for expenses of recruiting in the Continental Army in 1781.

The regiment patrolled Southern Connecticut and New York and intercepted British supplies and protected colonists from Loyalists. This duty earned them the nickname "Watchdogs of the Highlands."

One researcher, Louise Welles Murry, wrote several accounts of Zephon's adventures while in the service. She wrote of his escape from capture by crawling through a port hole of a fort, just as a gunner was swinging the loaded cannon into place to fire. One story involved General Washington. Zephon was on guard duty one night when he was approached by General George Washington. Young Zephon halted the General and requested the countersign. Washington stopped, gave the countersign, they saluted, and as Washington left he tossed the boy a half dollar, saying, *"Good boy, good soldier."*

In 1801 Zephon was appointed a Major in the Militia Sheshequin, Pennsylvania. He was a noted surveyor, and he was appointed Deputy Surveyor of Bradford County. He laid out many of the early roads and helped to locate many obscure claims.

Sources: 1. A History of old Tioga Point and Early Athens, Pennsylvania, by Louise Welles Murray. 2. History of Bradford County, Pennsylvania. 3. Pension Papers S6856. 4. Sons of the American Revolution Application. 5. Historical Register of the Colorado Society of the Sons of the American Revolution, November 1, 1905 to February 1, 1912.

****

William Fones age 13

William Fones was born on 18 September, 1764 in North Kingston, Rhode Island, and he died on 22 April, 1839 in Wales, New York. He married Dorcas Sherman on 29 March, 1789 in New York, and they had 12 children. He received a yearly pension of $28.33.

"In the spring of 1778 at North Kingston in Rhode Island where I then resided I entered the service of the United States by joining a

Company of volunteer minute men under Capt. Peter Wright in a Regiment commanded by Col. Charles Dyer. The said company and I were a part of the shore Guard in said Town of North Kingston until the enemy left Rhode Island in the last part of the year 1779."

"I was always equipped & ready for actual Service at a minutes warning and constantly attended the regular parades of the company nearly every week and was very frequently engaged in Skirmishes but was in no battle during ___?__. The Skirmishes were when tories refugees made a landing & burnt house carrying off (if they could take them) prisoners & cattle. During the Service as aforesaid some of the enemy landed & burnt the house of John Allen & carried off cattle and at this time there was a Regiment of Blacks which I think belonged to the Continental establishment came from East Greenwich to North Kingston. This Regiment Col. Greene commanded and I think that Hagg was the name of the Major. At the same time Lieutenant of Artillery Oliva Corey came down to North Kingston & arrived about the same time or first before the Black Regiment. During the time aforesaid I was sometimes on Guard two or three nights with a week with almost every night during the time aforesaid was wither on Guard or at the Quarters of the Troops and the squad of the Company to which I belonged mostly Quartered at John Dyers the father of Ensign Dyer."

The 1st Rhode Island Regiment under the command of Colonel Christopher Greene became known as the "Black Regiment". In 1778 Rhode Island were facing a shortage of recruitments, so they decided to enlist slaves into the 1st Rhode Island Regiment. The Rhode Island Assembly voted in February of 1778 to enlist every "able-bodied negro, mulatto, or Indian man slave." The slaves had to be free and discharged from the service of their masters. An owner of a slave who enlisted would be paid fair market price for their slave.

The Regiment eventually totaled around 225 men with less than 140 African Americans. The Regiment fought in the Battle of Rhode Island in August 1778 and played a small roll. They had three men killed and 20 wounded or missing.

"Some part of the company was constantly on Guard Duty and the Company was frequently engaged in repelling the attack of small parties of the enemy who came & burnt buildings and I was in the service when the Enemy burned the Houses of Shirley Wescott & Daniel Hall."

"In March (I think) 1781 on the alarm that the enemy were going to land on Rhode or New Port Islands I again volunteered and entered under Capt. Pierce in Col. Charles Dyers Regiment. I think Dyer was not then with the Regiment but that Major Pates had the company. I entered the service at North Kingston aforesaid & crossed the Bay at Dikes New Town (now called Wickton and went on to New Port Island there about two weeks doing service guarding the Island. I recollect the Black Regiment and recollect seeing a Regiment of Ray Troops as they were called."

Sources: 1. U.S. Pensioners 1818-1872. 2. Pension Papers S25595. 3. D.A.R. Lineage Book, Vol. 107. 4. Deeds of Desperate Valor: The First Rhode Island Regiment by Gretchen A. Adams.

****

Asahel Foote age 14

Asahel Foote was born on 22 April, 1763 in Colchester, Connecticut, and he died on 8 March, 1841 in Lee, Massachusetts. He married Anna Abbott on 21 August, 1793 in Lee, Massachusetts. He received a yearly pension of $53.33.

"On the third day of July in the year 1777 I volunteered in the Company Commanded by Col. William Brown in the line of the State of Massachusetts. I enlisted in the town of Lee. We went immediately to Albany where we staid one week and where we were put into companies from Albany we marched to Schoharie for the purpose of guarding the town from the British and Indians and where we acted as scouts. In the town there were three forts. I was placed part of the time in one of them and part of the time in another."

"The Indians made no attacks upon the Forts, but our Scouting parties had frequent skirmishes with them. We were dismissed and commenced our return home on the 20 of November."

"I remained at home until July of the next summer when I was drafted in Capt. Marsh Company from Stockbridge, in Col. Browns Regiment. We marched to Albany from thence to Schoharie. After we had been at Schoharie some time the Indians came down upon it. I was then on guard and was first to give the alarm about the break of day. They had with them a howitzer and Four pounder for the purpose of throwing in upon our Fort shells and balls we had then but seventy men in the Fort. They commenced firing upon us for the purpose of burning our magazine.

They threw into the Fort about a dozen shells which set our Magazine on fire three times. Some of our men were not in mortality wounded. We had in the Fort some Rifle men from Virginia rangers who were not subject to the command of our officers. One of them shot down three different officers who had been sent by the enemy with a flag of truce as we suppose to discuss our surrender."

"The enemy reconvened till near night fell when they __?__ off and commenced their firing upon once of the other Forts from thence they went to then called Stone Robby to which place we followed them. They had arrived a short time before. On our way many cattle lay slaughtered hardly an animal to be seen living. Houses smoking in ruins and when we arrived at Stone Robby many of the inhibits was laying in __?__ yet unbounded. We were informed that the Indians had placed ten of the number in sight a short distance from the fort. Col. Brown had ordered his men to pursue them. They retired and led Col. Brown into an ambush made in a notch where they arose upon them and slaughtered almost all of them. Col. Brown fell the first fire and was deposited in his grave the day before we arrived."

Sir John Johnston with about 500 Indians, Tories, and British regulars attacked the Middle Fort at Schoharie, which according to Asahel Foote had only 70 defenders. Johnson sent out a parley flag to demand surrender. According to legend the flag bearer was fired upon by frontiersman Timothy Murphey. This happened three times and Johnson found the fortifications too strong and retreated from the fort.

Johnson and his men traveled across the Schoharie Valley and burnt everything in their path. They burned over one hundred buildings and took fifty prisoners. On 19 October, 1780 Colonel Brown and Sir John Johnson engaged in battle at Stone Arabia. Brown and his men took cover behind some trees and a fence, and Johnson and his men took cover about thirty yards away. At the start of the battle Colonel Brown was hit in the heart with a musket ball and fell off his horse and died. Colonel Brown died on his 36th birthday. The Indians scalped him and stripped his body.

The Indians began to outflank the Americans, and as the Americans retreated back to safety at Fort Paris many were killed in the retreat. In all over 45 of Colonel Brown's men were killed. The slain men were later taken back to Fort Paris and buried in a pit.

"I remained in this service until the last of Nov. and a few days over Four Months. I remained at home until the first of August 1781 when

a call was made upon the town of Lee to furnish a certain number of three years men. I was drafted and entered the company commanded by Captain Kellum in the Regiment in which Major Ashely of Stockbridge was Major. I went to Stockbridge to White Plains and then directly to West Point where I remained until the last of the next March when I was relieved by another person and returned home."

Sources: 1. D.A.R. Lineage Book, Vol. 39. 2. U.S. Pensioners of 1818-1872. 3. Pension Papers S13044. 4. Colonel John Brown: His Services in the Revolutionary War, Battle of Stone Arabia by Garret L. Roof. 5. Three Rivers Hudson-Mohawk-Schoharie; History from America's Most Famous Valleys by Klock's Churchyard Preservation Group.

****

James Forbes age 14

James Forbes was born in 1762 in Oakham, Massachusetts, and he died on 1 April, 1819 in Royalston, Massachusetts. He married Eleanor Brown on 12 September, 1782. When James died Eleanor was the administrator of his estate which contained $12.09. It was so small a sum that the Judge of Probate said: *"It would answer no valuable purpose if divided among the numerous creditors,"* so it was given to the widow to provide necessaries to support life.

In the summer of 1776 he enlisted for two months with Lieutenant Asa French, and he served at Dobbs Ferry, Tarrytown, and North Castle. He enlisted again on 5 May, 1777 for two months in Rhode Island in Captain Hodges's Company in the Regiment commanded by Colonel Whitney. This enlistment was important because of the critical situation of the Continental Army in New York. One-fifth of all able-bodied men under the age of 50 were called to serve for two months.

James re-enlisted on 2 July, 1777 in Captain Earll's Company in the Regiment commanded by Colonel Keyes. When he enlisted at West Point on 27 August, 1781 it was in the Continental Army in Captain Cutler's Company and Colonel Luke Drury's Regiment.

Source: 1. Soldiers of Oakham, Massachusetts, in the Revolutionary War by Henry Parks Wright.

****

Silas Force age 12

Silas Force was born on 1 January, 1766 in Prince Edward County, Virginia and he died c. 1859 in Henry, Kentucky. He married Sarah

Beasley in Virginia c. 1787. His application for a pension was rejected because he was underage and he did not join a military unit.

Soon after his birth his mother died leaving a husband and 13 children. In the winter of 1777 his father took the 7 younger children left Virginia and moved to the fort at Martin's Station in Kentucky. *"In March 1778 the Indians made an attack on the fort and young as I was being only 12 years of age or thereabouts at that time I volunteered and aided in the defence of it and the Indians were repelled."*

In June of 1778 his father died and a few days after his death the British and the Indians attacked the fort at Ruddle's Station a few miles away. Silas and the others at Martin's Station heard the guns from the battle and began to prepare for an attack on their fort. *"I again was mustered amongst the men for its defence and we dispatched two men for reinforcements one of whom was captured by the enemy and the other escaped."*

After one of the men dispatched from the fort had been captured the British officers demanded that the fort surrender. The commander of the fort realized that to fight was useless so and all that surrendered inside the fort became prisoners of war. *"All were taken by the British and Indians to Detroit where many of them including myself was kept until the summer of the year 1782. One of my sister died or was killed on the way to Detroit and his other sisters and my brother Hezekiah and myself were kept at Detroit and my brother John was sent to some other place."*

In the summer of 1782 the two warring sides agreed on an exchange of prisoners and Silas and the other prisoners were taken to Ticonderoga and exchanged. Silas and his brother John reached home about the 1st of September in 1782 after more than four years of captivity. Many of the people captured from the fort including his other sisters and brothers were dead.

Sources: 1. Rejection or Suspended Applications for Revolutionary War Pensions Claims of Kentucky Residents 1850. 2. Pension Papers R3650.

****

Augustus Ford age 9

Augustus Ford was born on 8 October, 1772 in Providence, Rhode Island, and he died on 4 August, 1855 in Sackets Harbor, New York. He married Demaris Rice in 1801, and she died in 1832. He then married Amy Stevens on 1 November, 1839. Augustus also served in the War of 1812.

At the age of nine Augustus shipped on board a privateer commanded by his mother's brother, who was sent out to the West Indies and brought back supplies for the Federal Army and furnished by the French. He served on the Continental frigate *Washington* and afterwards on several other privateers such as *Snakefish* and *Dolphin*. He served on the ship as a powder boy until the end of the war two years later.

In 1810 he received a commission with the rank of captain as a sailing master in the new American Navy. He first served on board the brig *Oneida*. Augustus sailed on board this ship during the War of 1812.

Sources: 1. Sons of the American Revolution Application. 2. Tombstone 3. Register of the District of Columbia Society of the American Revolution, 1896.

****

John Morrison Ford age 14

John Ford was born on 28 October, 1764 in Ireland, and he came to America as a young boy. His father soon died, and John went to sea at the age of nine or ten. Years later the sea captain died so John returned home. His pension was rejected for lack of proof of service.

"In April 1778 when I was 14 I volunteered or enlisted at Kingstown as a private for 18 months in a regiment under the command of Col Putman of the Massachusetts State Troops. This was at the time that Genl Sullivan in the year 1778 attempted to take Rhode Island from the possession of the British. I crossed at that time with my company and other troops over on the Island of Rhode Island and was in a very severe battle on the Island in August where I received three wounds. One on the calf of my leg, one in my side (both with the bayonet) and the other one on the lower right arm with the cutlass of a Hessian. After that battle the American troops retreated from the Island and I marched with my company to a station at Bristol where we remained for winter quarters."

The Battle of Rhode Island took place on Aquidneck Island on 29 August, 1778. This battle was notable because of the participation of the Rhode Island 1st Regiment. This regiment was composed of African Americans and Native Americans as well as European-American settlers. As the Hessians retreated from battle, they bayoneted the American wounded.

John Ford was fortunate that his bayonet wounds did not result in serious wounds. The British and Hessian bayonets were triangular in shape which made the wound it caused hard to repair. It would cause one side to stretch and break the wound open which could result in the person bleeding to death. Also, the bayonet was not sharp. It would have to be thrust into the enemy's body, which would tear and not cut the flesh. Today these kinds of bayonets are outlawed.

"In the next summer, the year 1780, I went to New London in Connecticut where in the forepart of that summer & volunteered as a private seaman or mariner to serve on board a privateer in the service of the United States a vessel of 16 guns called the "Cable Brig". I was engaged this tour only for a cruise. The vessel was commanded by Captain John Steel."

"After about 3 weeks after any engagement we sailed out from New London, and were only 3 or 4 days before we were taken prisoners by a British vessel called "The Revenge" a 50 gun ship. I was then taken as a prisoner of war to New York and confined as a prisoner on board the old "Jersey" prison ship. I was kept as a prisoner confined in that ship about 3 months where I suffered almost everything but death, and then I contrived to make my escape to Long Island and then went in disguise to the East part of Long Island to Lagharbour where I was assisted to go over to Saybrook in Connecticut and was not again in the service."

Source: 1. Pension Papers R3656.

****

James Forten age 14 (African American)

James Forten was born on 2 September, 1766 in Philadelphia, Pennsylvania, and he died on 15 March, 1842. He was born free and started working at the age of seven after the death of his father in a boating accident. He attended the African School run by the Quaker abolitionist Anthony Benezet. By age nine James left school to work full time to help provide for his family.

At the age of 14 James served on the privateer *Royal Louis*, commanded by Captain Stephen Decatur. Much of the time onboard he served as a powder boy. In 1781 his ship was captured by the British ship *Amphion* after a seven hour chase. James was concerned, because he knew that someone of his race would probably be sent to the West Indies and be a slave for the rest of his life.

Captain Bazely of the British ship had two sons on board and thought that James would make a fine companion for the boys. James and the captain's boys would often play marbles, which James soon excelled in. One of the boys bragged to his father how well James played the game. At the insistence of the Captain, James demonstrated his skill and impressed the Captain. James soon found that he was given greater freedom than a prisoner usually experienced.

When the British ship sailed into New York to take on supplies and drop her prisoners off the Captain made a surprising proposal to James. He wanted to take James to England with his sons, educate him and let him experience freedom and equality. James declined the offer saying, *"I signed up for the cause of liberty and I would not betray it."*

James was transferred to the infamous prison ship *Jersey*. Captain Bazely gave James a letter to deliver to the prison commander. It requested that James should not be forgotten on the list of exchanges. James was then removed to the prison ship and became prisoner 4102.

The conditions on the ship were very harsh. Thousands of men were crammed below deck where there was little light, no fresh air, little sanitation, and sparse food to eat. In addition the prisoners were treated brutally, and as many as eight prisoners a day died. A total of 11,000 men died on the *Jersey*. It is estimated that 8,000 men died from combat during the war.

When the British surrendered at Yorktown, negotiation for the release of prisoners took a long time. First to be released would be prisoners that served in the army or navy, and the privateers were last. Seven months after being placed on the *Jersey* James was finally released. He walked from New York to Trenton, New Jersey in his bare feet. When he returned home to Philadelphia it was obvious from his appearance that he had suffered a great deal.

Once he recovered he signed on a merchant ship and sailed to London. He worked for more than a year in a London shipyard. He returned to Philadelphia in 1786 and became an apprenticed sail-maker for Robert Bridges. He learned quickly and was promoted to foreman. Eventually, he owned the business and employed more than 40 workers.

On 10 November, 1803 James married Martha Beatte at the African Episcopal Church of Saint Thomas. She died the following year, and he never again mentioned her. He married again 10 December, 1805 to Charlotte Vandine.

By the 1820s James was one of the most influential black men in the country. Liberty for all people was important to him. He believed that this liberty should be gained without using violence. He spoke out against slavery and for equal rights for the rest of his life. He was one of the wealthiest Americans of his time, with holdings at over $100,000.

Sources; 1. Pirates and Privateers: The History of Maritime Piracy, Cindy Vallar, editor and reviewer. 2. The Colored Patriots of the American Revolution, with Sketches of Several Distinguished Colored Persons by William Cooper Nell.

****

Frederick Foscue age 14

Frederick Foscue was born on 18 November, 1766 in Craven County, North Carolina, and he died on 17 December, 1834 in Jones, North Carolina. He married Deve Simmons on 3 February, 1788 in Jones, North Carolina. According to the 1810 census he owned 14 slaves. He received a yearly pension of $20.

"In the January of 1780, I shipped at Newbern on board the Brig Industry, attached to Stanley's fleet. The Brig was armed, and belonged to Governor Nash in part. We were bound to St. Eustatins & arrived in the neighborhood of the Island & were attacked by the British corsairs in the night off St. Martin's. We beat them off after a pretty severe fight, & we arrived in the same night at St. Eustatius. We came to anchor in the midst of the British fleet, commanded by Admiral Rodney, supposing them to be Dutch. We were boarded by the ship's boats & taken after some fighting. We were made prisoners of war & sent to Antigua, & were kept in prison until the month of July & we then returned home being exchanged. After our return home hearing that the British were coming to Newbern, we were ordered out under the command of General Linnington, Colonel Avery & Captain Fredk Hargate. I was in Jones County when ordered out & we marched up in the neighborhood of Sander's Bridge where a party of our troops & the enemy had a skirmish. I was not in it. We followed the British towards Newbern, they having passed us, in order to keep down the tories. We continued under arms until the Spring after the British had evacuated Newbern, to keep down the tories, as they had done much damage & killed some of our best men. We were on this service upwards of six months. After we were disbanded I went again to Newbern & shipped on board the private armed Brig

Edward of 18 guns, commanded by Captain Goodhue. We cruised off Charleston & engaged a copper bottomed brig belonging to Glasgow, & captured her. The Brig was well armed & we had a considerable fight. Some short time after this we were pursued by two English frigates & we abandon our prize, there having elapsed but a few hours after the capture to the time of the pursuit, we had not time to remove the prisoners. We had no more fighting & after taking one or two small prizes we went in to port at Ocracoke & came to Newbern."

Sources: 1. 1820 Census. 2. U.S. Pensioners 1818-1872. 3. Sons of the American Revolution Application. 4. Pension Papers S2562.

****

William Fosdick age 13

William Fosdick was born on 27 April, 1762 in Massachusetts, and died in Angelica, New York in 1851. He responded at the age of thirteen to the first call for troops, after the battle of Lexington on 19 April, 1775. During this alarm he served for five days.

He enlisted on 12 May, 1775 as a fifer in the 9th Company of Connecticut troops, which was raised on the first call of the Legislature under Captain Jonathan Chester, in the Second Continental Regiment, commanded by General Spencer. William's regiment served at Bunker Hill. He also served at the siege of Boston.

Sources: 1. D.A.R. American Monthly Magazine, Vol X, 1897. 2. D.A.R. Lineage Book, Vol. 14. 3. Sons of the American Revolution Application.

****

Daniel Fox age 14

Daniel fox was born on 1 January, 1766 in Shenandoah County, Virginia, and he died 22 April, 1845 in Marshall, Kentucky. He married Elizabeth Foard in 1787 in Burke County, North Carolina. He received a yearly pension of $40 for his service.

"I volunteered in the County of Wilkes in the State of North Carolina in the year of our Lord one thousand seven hundred and Eighty as well as I at this distant date can recollect and in the fall season of that year but the precise month and day from the great lapse of time I cannot positively State; under the command of Captain Joel Lewis at Wilkes court house in said County & State, and marched from thence to Guilford court

house in Guilford county in the State of North Carolina, where I joined the 7th Regiment of said State then stiled and known as the Twelve months men, under the command of General Green; from thence I was marched under the command of General Greene to High Rock ford of Haw River in the State of North Carolina, where we remained a few days, and from thence was marched back again to Guilford court house; where I was Engaged in the Battle against the British army under the command of Lord Cornwallace, where the American army fled, and retreated into the Edge of Surry county in the State of North Carolina; and thence marched back to the Battleground to bury our dead Slain in the Battle, after this was accomplished, I was attached to Captain John Beaverly company and marched to Salisbury in Roane County in the State of North Carolina and was Stationed at that place to guard the Prisoners there; where I remained in that service Something like Eleven weeks; from thence I was marched to Randolph County in the State of North Carolina in pursuit of the Tory's, where I remained about Two months; I was then placed under the command of Captain Samuel Johnson, who was commanded by Major Hartgrove and marched from thence to the Borders of South Carolina in pursuit of the Torys, where we had a Small engagement with the Tories; which soon fled; and from thence we were marched into Chatham county in the State of North Carolina where we remained about seven weeks, in pursuit of another Band of Tories; whom we soon came up with and took about sixty of them and conveyed them to the Barracks at Salisbury; where I remained about two weeks and was placed under the command of Captain John Beaverly again who was commanded by Colonel Benjamin Cleaveland, and was thence marched in pursuit of the noted Tory Colonel Bryant with his Band, then we soon came up with and took about 25 of his band prisoners, whom we conveyed also to the Barracks at Salisbury where I remained about two months on guard duty; and generally remained on this duty at said Barracks, until I was finally discharged from the Service of the United States having served something over twelve months in all."

Sources: 1. North Carolina Marriage Index 1741-2004. 2. U.S. Pensioners 1818-1872. 3. Pension Papers W9443.

****

John Fox age 14

John Fox was born in Pennsylvania in 1767. His first request for a pension was rejected, because he provided little information about his enlistment or officers. His second statement provides great detail about his enlistment and captivity. His closing remarks have been included because they contain such passion.

"As near as I can recollect in the month of June 1780 me and a comrade named Michael Spatz [Michael was 16 years old at the time, he is in this section of the book] *were determined to Enlist to an Infantry Corps which at that time was Enlisting men for the Service of the United States in the Revolutionary War in Reading Berks County Penn. When on our way to a public House where they were Enlisting men for said Infantry Corps we met with a certain Officer who asked us boys which way we then answered him that we were going to Enlist to an Infantry Corps. He then said that his name was Seull that he was Enlisting men into the Service of the United States on the Continental Establishment as marines and that we should Enlist to him. That our case would be easier to enter with him and prevailed on us to comply* [He made have suggested to them that because of their young age they had a better chance of enlisting with him]. *We then agreed and we were brought before a Justice of the peace and for Berks County who administrated the usual oath and we received our bounty money."*

The Continental Marine's most important duty was to serve on a ship as a security force to protect the captain and his officers. During a naval battle the Marine sharpshooters were stationed on the ships' masts with the mission to shoot the enemy's officers, naval gunners, and helmsmen.

"The bounty money was in the Name of the United States for and during the war. We then remained in Reading and there was about seventy who belonged to us as marines. We marched to Wilmington where we entered on board a ship they called The Carolina."

"Unfortunately when on a certain day outside the Capes we were captured by the British Frigates. The British made us prisoners of war conveyed us to New York and confined us on board the Jersey Prison ship then lying on North River. A strong Hessian & British Guard was our doom in this Situation as Prisoners of War we remained at least Eleven months & treated by the Hessians & British with Savage brutality. Many many died of starvation others of the extreme cold and the treatment. On some days fourteen of the men died. Out of our seventy men only seven returned to their homes. Of the surviving I am one and Michael Spatz of Reading and Jacob Husher of Berks County are as far as I can learn the only ones who yet survive."

"I now humbly take to my country pure facts as they truly occurred and desire fair and impartial investigation of our Enlistment which we have solemnly swore to confiding in your Honorable bodies that the voice of pity may grant us Relief in the full decline of life being now far advanced in age poor and afflicted and further that our intentions were good when we did Enlist we entered for Liberty and equality."

The *Jersey* first began as a hospital ship, and around the summer of 1779 prisoners began being placed on board. Once it became a prison ship, the numbers of prisoners increased and the condition on board began a rapid decline. John van Dyke was a prisoner taken aboard toward the end of May 1780 and he said that the stench was so great he was afraid that it would kill him. He said that the rations for each man were so small it seemed impossible that a man could live on them. Van Dyke once returned from the galley with a piece of salt pork for his five messmates. It provided only one mouthful for each man for the entire day.

The British would encourage the prisoners to join the British navy as a way to be released from possible death on the *Jersey*. To encourage the prisoners one time, their rations were reduced to a single pint of water, eight ounces of condemned bread per day, and plus eight ounces of meat per week. Hundreds of men accepted the enlistment in the British navy rather than death on the *Jersey*. It was not unusual to hear, *"Five guineas bounty to any man that will enter his Majesty's service!"*

The dead prisoners were thrown overboard along with all waste products. It was not unusual to see human bones and skulls bleaching on the shore of Long Island. More than 11,000 men died on the sixteen prison ships from 1776 to 1783. This was nearly 3 times greater than the number of men who died in combat.

Sources: 1. Pension papers S2219. 2. American Prisoners of the Revolution by Danske Dandridge. 3. Forgotten Patriots, the Untold Story of American Prisoners During the Revolutionary War by Edwin G. Burrows.

****

Jeremiah Frazer age 12 or 13

Jeremiah Frazer was born on 20 January, 1763 in Scotch Plains, New Jersey, and he died on 16 August, 1847 in Oswego, New York. He received a monthly pension of $80. His pension was originally rejected, because his name appeared upon the return of the "Dead" of the New York Regiments. Further investigation revealed his name on a muster roll of

Van Schaick's Regiment listing him as *"enlisting in 1776 and was taken prisoner in 79."* Once the mistake was cleared up his pension was approved.

"I enlisted in the Continental Service in Capt Daniel Palmer's company in Col Holmes Regiment—I enlisted for Six months. I went from thence to Fort George on Lake George staid there about a month then went to St. John's in Canada by water, I was at the Siege of St. John's twenty-one days--we took St John's General Philip Schuyler commanded the expedition went from there to Montreal then to Quebec arrived there sometime in the winter of 1776. Stayed there till the Sixth day of May 1776 while I was at Montreal my six month service expired & I then and there Enlisted again under the same Captain into the same company for 6 months with my company retreated from Quebec to Albany. Arrived here sometime in May and was there two or three months then went to Johnstown remained there till about the first of September in that while and my second term of service expired."

Jeremiah's first enlistment was in the 4th Regiment of the New York Militia under the command of Colonel James Holmes. Jeremiah was present at the Siege of Fort St. John, which took place from 17 September to 3 November 1775. If Jeremiah was there it meant that he enlisted a year earlier than he reported. If he enlisted in 1775 it would make his enlistment at the age of 12. This author suspects that he enlisted in the 4th Regiment in 1775, and then reenlisted in the 1st Regiment under Colonel Van Schaick in 1776.

"I then enlisted again during the War in Capt John Grahams Company in the First Regiment of New York Levies commanded by Col Van Schaick. With the Regiment I went to Fort George continued there through the winter and till Gen Burgoyne came on the next season. We then evacuated Fort George and marched to Sandy Hill in Washington County, My Regiment was detached to go to fort Stanwix--remained there until last in the fall then returned to Schenacty into winter quarters where I remain until the first of April--was then ordered to Valley Forge in Pennsylvania--then joined the main American army under Gen Washington about the last of June the army marched in pursuit of the British Army that had left Philadelphia—the two armies met at Monmouth. I was in the battle."

Colonel Goose Van Schaick was given the 1st New York Regiment on 8 March, 1776. At the Battle of Monmouth his Regiment fought on the left wing of the army under the command of General William Alexander, Earl of Stirling.

"After the battle my Regiment went back to Fort Stanwix remained there till July following on the 28th of the same month 24 men under Lieutenant William Shudder was sent out and I with the 24 went to cut some hay—while out after hay the party were surprised and taken prisoner by a party of Indians commanded by a Frenchman—I was taken by the Indians to a place called Caughawaga in Lower Canada—I was kept till the first of December following the rest of the prisoners were delivered up in a few days—was taken from there to Montreal and delivered up to the British—was carried to Quebec and kept imprisoned till the close of the war. I was then released."

After Jeremiah was released, he went to a place below Quebec and lived there for four years. From there he moved to the Lake Champlain area and remained there for 3 years. Next, he moved to New Jersey and moved around the New Jersey and New York area until his death.

Sources: 1. The Bloodied Mohawk: The American Revolution in the Words of Fort Planks Defenders and Other Mohawk Valley Partisans by Kenneth D. Johnson. 2. New York Pensioners of 1835. 3. Pension Papers S13093.

****

James Frazier age 14

James Frazier was born on 10 April, 1767 in Culpeper County, Virginia, and died on 30 August, 1842 in Cedar Springs, South Carolina. He married Charity Wright Cotton in South Carolina. In the 1850 census Charity owned 20 slaves ages 6 months to 100.

"I entered the service as a volunteer Militia man, in Capt James Thomas' Company of Infantry on the 16th day of June 1781. John Ryan was regular Captain of the Company, but was then a prisoner the name of the _____? _____ officers I do not now recollect ---except Van Swearingen who was first Lieutenant--I do not know the battalion--but was under the command of Genl Pickens. I continued to serve in Edgefield District until the was marched up into Abbeville District to the Block house, & marched from there and immediately under the Command of Genl Pickens as a scouting party, or guard until I joined the Genl Green at Bacon's Bridge, near Charleston, was then drafted for one month and was discharged."

James served a total of 11 months and 12 days in the militia and received $38.00 a year for his service. The following obituary appeared in The Edgefield Advertiser newspaper:

"Died, at his residence, Cedar Springs, in Abbeville District, S.C., on August 30, 1842, James Frazier, in about the 78th year of his age. He was a native of Culpepper County, Virginia. During the revolutionary struggle, though too young to be called into the service of his country, (being about 16), yet his ardour led him to volunteer his services, and he entered the army under the command of General Greene, where he condoned eleven months, which was until peace was declared. He applied to Congress for a pension, and so clearly was his claim established that it was readily granted. In the year 1809, he became a member of the Baptist Church, at Bethany, Edgefield District, where his membership continued until the year before his death, at which time it was removed to a newly constituted church in the immediate vicinity of his residence."

His tombstone has the following inscription: *"He was one of those favored few, who at the call of his country ralleyed around the banner of liberty to breast the storm of Revolution and served 11 months and 20 days under General Green."*

I have included the will of James Frazier to show the wealth that he had accumulated. Less than 20% of farmers in the South owned slaves and the majority of them only had a couple. James was extremely wealthy because according to his will he owned at least 47 slaves. The will also shows how slaves were considered just property and how the slave families were broken up.

"I James Frazier of Cedar Springs of said State and District do make and ordain this my last will and testament, revoking all former wills by me made:"

Item 1st:

"It is my will that all my just and lawful debts be paid and I set apart and appropriate for that purpose the crop of cotton made this year on my plantation, and the following slaves sold to me by my son James F Frazier, to wit Beverly, Patty, Josephine, Elbert, Mary, Lucretia, Jerry, Emily, Russell, and Maria, or so many of them as may be necessary for the payment of my debts, and no more:"

Item 2nd:

"I give and bequeath to my beloved wife Charity in lieu and bar of her of her dower in my real estate for her sole use and benefit during her natural life the following negroes, viz; Anne, Isabel, Charles, Charlotte, Clara and her son Augustus, and Violet and her daughter Eliza, together with the future increase of said female slaves with full power to my said wife Charity to bequeath the aforesaid property, to whomever of my children by my marriage with her, or to her grand-children by such marriage she may think fit after her death; Charlotte above named and bequeath is the child of Rachael: Further I give and devise to my said wife Charity for her sole use and benefit during her natural life the one third part of my plantation in which I now live; this third part I intend to include the orchard with the use of the Cotton Gin and screw; also one third of the stock of all, Consisting of Horses, Cow, Hogs etc and one third of the plantation tools Consisting of wagons carts, ploughs etc: the stock and other things above enumerated to be divided and set apart to my said wife, by the valuation of three disinterested persons to be chosen by my Executers Also the choice of the third house hold and Kitchen furniture; which third of the house hold Kitchen furniture as well as shall have her third of the stock and plantation tools, she shall be at liberty to dispose of as she pleases. Further that she shall have the liberty of occupying and using during her life any part of my present dwelling house, or of living in any part of the present dwelling house, or of living in any other house on the plantation; or to have a convenient dwelling house and suitable Kitchen, and out-house, built in such part of the plantation as she may select, and fitted up for her residence, and the expense of the same to be paid by my executor:"

Item 3rd

"I further give and bequeath to my beloved wife as aforesaid during her natural life to be disposed by of by Will as she may make as aforesaid the following young negro slaves, Hiram, Caroline, and Julia Ellen children of Violet, and Henry and Washington Children of Clara; also the negro fellow Anthony; to be divided to my children or grandchildren as aforesaid"

Item 4th

"I give and bequeath to my grand-children Henry Walker, James A Walker, Sarah A Walker Joseph Walker and Allan B Walker, children of my deceased daughter Jane Walker, one negro girl named Priscilla with her future increase; and if any of my grand children named in this item of my will die, his or her interest to rest in the surviving children the sum of ten Dollars."

Item 5*th*

"I give and bequeath to my daughter Lucretia S. Davlin and son-in-law- Robert Davlin the following slaves to wit Frank, and her Children Lewis, John, Nancy, Elisa, Emily, Sam, and Oliver, with the future increases of the said female slaves, The same now being in the possession of my said son-in-law, I also give to my son-in-law R Davlin, Harriet and her children, Martha and Josephine."

Item 6*th*

"I give devise and bequeath to my son-in-law- Robert Davlin and my nephew John F Livingston during their joint lives and to the survivor, the plantation of which I now live containing seven hundred and eighty two acres more or less, subject however to the life estate of my wife aforesaid, also, the following slaves Hampton, Rachel, and children Willis, Lindsay, Tinsley, Flora and Sam, and the future increase of the said female also, Patrick a negro man, and should any of the negroes named in the first item of my will remain after the payment of my debts, I give and bequeath them to the said Robert and John F as aforesaid: To the said Robert and John F in trust for the use of the said John W Frazier my son during his natural life, free from the debts, Contracts, and obligations of my said son John W Frazier the said land and negroes and their increase to be discharged from the said trust, and divided according to the Act of assembly of this State for distribution between my daughter daughter-in-law Elizabeth L. and her children by the said John W Frazier then living and then the said Elizabeth die during the life time of said husband James W Frazier, then I hereby empower my son James F Frazier by will to depose of the land and negroes given in trust as aforesaid to such children as he may leave at the time of his death: and further that the said trustees with the consent of the said James W Frazier may change and substitute other Trustees, with the same power and duties of the said Robert Davlin and John Livingston, and may sell any or such part of the trust property aforesaid as may seem expedient or necessary to them, re-investing the proceeds arising from such sale Similar property or any way that may be deemed most expedient for the interest of the said James W Frazier, his wife and children."

Item 7*th*

"I also give and bequeath to the said Robert Davlin and John F Livingston in trust as aforesaid my stock of all kind, plantation tools implements of husbandry, House hold and Kitchen furniture, subject however to the provisions aforesaid to my beloved Wife Charity:"

Item 8th

"I charge my whole estate real and personal with the maintenance and support of my son Benjamin; charging as the readiest and proper way an annuity of seventy five dollars on the property given and bequeath to my wife Charity; the sum as an annuity on the trust property devised and bequeathed to Robert Davlin and John F Livingston: the said annuities so charged not to free my estate from the charge of the support of my said son Benjamin: I Commit the Care of the person of my son to his mother, and should he Robert Davlin and Lucretia Davlin."

Item 9th

"I give and bequeath to my grand-daughter Martha B Frazier one negro girl name Marion with her future increase to her and to such children she may leave living at the time of her death: and should my said grand-daughter die then to such person or persons as she may by will appoint: I also give to my said grand-daughter M B Frazier a horse worth one hundred Dollars, a saddle and bridle, to be chose out of my property by my executers—I also give and bequeath to her four sisters viz Mary, Rebecca, Charity, and Amanda the sum of Ten Dollars each."

Item 10th

"I give and bequeath to Robert Davlin and John F Livingston one negro girl named Sarah in trust and for the use of Edwin H Frazier the oldest son of Anne Conna, free from the debts,, Contracts, and obligations of the said Edwin H Frazier, with power to the said Trustees with the consent of the said Edwin H Frazier to dispose of the said negro woman Sarah and her increase by Will, and at the death of said Edwin H Frazier the trust to be discharged I also give the said Edwin H Frazier one horse saddle and bridal now in his possession:"

Item 11th

"Should there be any residue of my estate I give and devise the same to my grand-daughter Tallulah H Frazier."

"Lastly I appoint Thomas Thomson as my executor of this my last will and testament."

James and Charity had four children, and their daughter Jane died at age of 33 before the will was made in 1842. James appeared concerned about the care of his son Benjamin. Benjamin died after his father in 1842 at the age of 30. I suspect that he was impaired in some way, and he would have been unable to care for himself had he lived.

Sources: 1. *The Edgefield Advertiser,* 21 September 1842. 2. Tombstone. 3. U.S. Federal Census 1850—Slave Schedules. 4. Census 1810, 1820, and 1830. 5. U.S. Pension roll of 1835. 6. Pension Papers S21209. 7. Will

****

Sampson Freeman age 12

Sampson Freeman was born in 1765 in Ipswich, Massachusetts. He joined the navy at 12 and served as a waiter. He received a yearly pension of $48.

"In October 1777 I entered on board the United States Frigate Boston, Hector McNeil Esq. Commander at Newburyport Massachusetts for one year. I entered as a waiter to Lt. __?__ & as such sailed in the ship to Boston where we lay two or three months. That while at Boston I discovered that one McIntire, who was Captain of the stewards, was in the habit of stealing & carrying away from the ship, provisions & stores belonging to the officers."

The Captain of the Stewards was in charge of supplies and some equipment on the ship. He purchased and dispersed these supplies and because this position is one of an officer he would have his own room on the ship.

"This I made know to Capt. McNeil who examined particularly into the facts & circumstances of the case & upon finding that I had been uncommonly vigilant & afterwards to my duty & for this particular act was deserving of reward immediately displaced said McIntire from his situation of Capt. Of the stewards & appointed me in his room. That said McIntire immediately left the ship & I have never since heard of him."

"I continued to serve on board said ship during her cruise in my last named capacity until her return to Boston in 1778 when I was discharged. Having served at least nine months as Captain of the Stewards as aforesaid."

Sampson sailed on the *Boston* under Captain McNeill. The ship sailed out of Boston on 21 May, 1777 and cruised the North Atlantic with the USS *Handcock*. On 7 June they captured three prizes including the HMS *Fox,* which Sampson mentioned in one of his pension papers. The British captured the *Boston* when Charlestown fell and renamed her HMS *Charlestown*.

Source: 1. Pension Papers S17419.

****

Nathaniel Friend age 14

Nathaniel Friend was born on 16 December, 1764 in Wenham, Massachusetts, and he died on 20 February, 1848 in Beverly, Massachusetts. He married twice (1) Polly Butman on 18 April, 1788 and (2) Mary __?__ on 6 April, 1845. Nathaniel received a yearly pension of $80.

"I first enlisted as a volunteer for nine months in the company of foot commanded by Captain Speer in the sixth Massachusetts Regiment commanded by Colonel Nicholson. The town of Wenham raised six men of whom I was one. We went to West Point and there enlisted as aforesaid in Speer's Company and Nicolson's Regiment in which I served the whole term of the enlistment. I enlisted and joined said company in May 1780 and was discharged in the February following."

"In March 1781 after the expiration of my first term of service I volunteered again from the town of Danvers in said county and where I then lived and with others went to Boston and then to Newburg and then to West Point. Col. Israel Hutchinson of Danvers was muster master. On arriving at West Point I enlisted in Captain Haffield White's Company of foot in the fifth Massachusetts Regiment commanded by Colonel Rufus Putnam. Col Putnam was afterwards succeeded in the command by Colonel Newhale. I was discharged in January 1784. During this term from March 1781 till January 1784 I served in the army of the Revolution in New York, New Jersey, and Pennsylvania."

Sources: 1. D.A.R. Lineage Book, Vol. 41. 2. Pension Roll of 1835. 3. Pension Papers W697.

****

John Fulmer age 14

John Fulmer was born on 18 May, 1763 in Philadelphia, Pennsylvania, and he died there on 22 August, 1824. He married Anna Marie Krouskop. John was a boy of fourteen, and before the Battle of Brandywine he carried dispatches from General Washington to Lafayette. He later enlisted with the French troops.

Sources: 1. D.A.R. Lineage Book, Vol. 15. 2. Sons of the American Revolution Application.

****

Nathan Futrell age 7

Nathan Futrell was born 10 September, 1773 in Northampton County, North Carolina, and he died 31 August, 1829 in Trigg County, Kentucky. He is reputed to be the youngest drummer boy that served in the war. His service was probably short lived because of his age, and because he was a member of the militia. Little is known of his early life. He must have attended school In North Carolina, because he was quite literate. His father Thomas was recognized as a patriot in the revolution by giving aid to the North Carolina Army.

He married Charity Futrell about 1797 in Northampton County, North Carolina. Among her papers was a small yellow slip of paper with the following inscription: *"Jany. 3, 1829, My Consorte Nathan Futrell, served as a drummer player in the North Carolina Militia during the Revolution at the age of seven years.: Signed: Charity Futrell."*

Young boys were recruited to act as drummers. The drums played an important part in communicating on the battlefield. The various drum roles signaled different commands from the officers to the troops. At times the boys were treated as mascots by the adult soldiers. Sometimes the youngest boys received no pay but were given money by the officers. About 200 drummers served in the Revolution. The average age was around 20 with only a few below the age of 14.

They would sometimes have other duties during the day. They might serve or wait upon an officer, chop wood, or help the surgeon during sick call. At times they would march out with the fifes in front of the regiment and play a tune before the battle began.

Nathan and Charity moved to Christian Co, Kentucky in 1799 and settled on Donaldson Creek. They bought 2,000 acres of land on the waters of Ford Creek. Nathan was a farmer, surveyor, election officer, and he planted the first apple in Trigg Co. He erected one of the earliest primitive grist mills in Trigg County. He received an appointment as Justice of the Peace of Trigg County on 29 October, 1824.

Sources: 1. Echoes from The Past by Judy Maupin, a Column of Historical and Genealogical Anecdotes, Stories and Family Notes. Calloway County, Kentucky 2. CD185-Genealogies of Kentucky Families. 3. Vol III, Kentucky Land Grants Vol. 1 pg. 4. Kentucky historical marker. 5. The Beats of Battle: Images of Army Drummer Boys Endure by Elizabeth M. Collins, Soldiers The Official U.S. Army Magazine. 6. U.S. Civil War History & Genealogy-The Drummer Boys, genelogyforum.com.

****

Reuben Gage age 13

Reuben Gage was born on 24 August, 1765 in Yarmouth, Massachusetts, and he died on 2 February, 1849 in Delhi. Ohio. He was married to Mercy Ryder on 31 October, 1785. For his 6 months of service he received $20.00 a year pension.

"I enlisted in the month of July in the year Seventeen hundred and Eighty in the State of Massachusetts & recruiting officer took me to Springfield Connecticut Where the recruits assembled from thence marched me to join the army that was then stationed below West Point under the command of Gen. George Washington and while I was around Col. Lewar enrolled me in Ensign Deucer Company in the 16th Regiment which was commanded by Colonel Jackson the army was marched down toward New York until within about 20 miles and then was marched back to West Point in the month of October—and remained here until I was discharged. I was in the Army the same year Andre was hanged I saw him executed. I was discharged in the middle of January in the year 1781. I was about 14 years old when I enlisted I was five feet and one inch sufficiently high enough to pass muster."

The 16th Massachusetts Regiment was also called Henry Jackson's Additional Continental Regiment. It was raided 12 January, 1777 under Colonel Jackson. It was disbanded as part of a major reorganization of the army on 1 January, 1781. Major John Andre was hanged on 2 October, 1780 in Tappan, New York, which is located about 12 miles from New York City. Reuben's regiment must have been sent there for additional security.

The army had requirements for enlistments. The minimum height requirement was 5 feet 5 inches, you had to be 15 years or older, and you had to have an upper and a lower tooth meet so that you could bite off the top of a cartridge. Obviously, army recruiters looked the other way to fill recruitment quotas, since Reuben was 13 and only 5 foot and 1 inch tall.

Sources: 1. Census of 1840. 2. Tombstone. 3. Pension Papers S3387. 4. The Constitution of the Sons of the Revolution and By-Laws and Articles of Incorporation of the Ohio Society. 5. U.S. and International Marriage Records 1560-1900. 6. U.S. Pensioners 1818-1872. 7. Official Roster of Revolutionary War Soldiers Buried in Ohio.

****

Robert F. Gale age 12

Robert Gale was born in 1769 in Caroline County, Virginia, and he died on 21 December, 1847 in Shelby County, Kentucky. In 1801 he married Elizabeth Wood of Virginia who was nine years older.

He stated in his pension application, *"In the month of 1781 I came through the Wilderness from Orange County State of Virginia to Bryants Station in Kentucky that when I together with my fathers family came to said Station I found it in a state of warfare with the Indians. I arrived in Oct. 1781, I was placed on the muster roll that I immediately was called into actual service by the draft."*

Bryan Station (often misspelled Bryant's Station) was a fortified settlement in Lexington, Kentucky founded by two brothers around 1775. Shawnee Indians, allies of the British, lived in the area.

Robert stated, *"I was a private in Captain Robert Johnsons Company and served in said company guarding protecting and defending said fort, from Oct. 1781 until 1785 that Captain Robt Johnson's Company belonged Col. John Todds Regiment, who fell at the blue licks in august 1782. I was at said fort during all the time, except when I was out spying against Indians under the command of said Johnson."*

Robert refers to the Blue Licks campaign that was fought 19 August, 1782. It has been considered the last battle of the Revolutionary War, because it was fought ten months after the surrender of Cornwallis. About 182 Kentucky militia men led by Colonel John Todd fought about 50 British rangers and 300 Indians. The militia was ambushed and defeated. Robert wrote in his pension, *"I was not in the Blue Lick defeat because I was one of the guards at the Station left by special order at the time."*

In September of 1844 Robert moved to Platte County, Missouri because, *"he and his family are desirous of living together—a portion of them having already removed to the said state of Missouri, and the remainder intend to do so."* He moved back to Shelby County in March of 1853 and died 21 December, 1848. He left no widow. He was granted a pension of $60 a year.

Sources: 1. Revolutionary War Soldiers that Lived in Kentucky, Excerpt from "History of Kentucky" by Judge Lewis Collins, Vol. 1. 2. The Kentucky 1840 Census of Pensioners for Revolutionary or Military Services. 3. Abstracts of Pensions: Soldiers of the Revolution, 1812, and Indian Wars Who Settled the Blue Grass Region of Kentucky by Lucy Kate McGhee. 4. Pension application S31503. 5. 1840 Federal Census. 6. "We Are All Slaughtered Men": The Battle of Blue Licks by John M. Trowbridge found in Vol 42, No 2 Winter 2006 of Kentucky Ancestors.

****

Bedford Garris age 14

Bedford Garris was born in 1763 in Dobbs County, North Carolina, and he died in March of 1835 in Lancaster, South Carolina. He served a total of 4 years and in 1778 he served as a musician. He received a yearly pension of $80 and 640 acres for his service.

"I entered the Service of the United States under the following named officers and served as herein stated, I enlisted on the 4th of May 1777 in the 10th Regiment Commanded by Col Shepherd and served under Captain Heron for the Term of three years and in the year 1781 I enlisted Served a Tour of twelve months in the same Regiment and was discharged the 29th of January 1782 I Served the Tour of twelve months under Capt Armstrong I was at Battle of Monmouth and Siege of Charleston."

Sources 1. U.S. Pensioners 1818-1872. 2. Census of 1810 and 1830. 3. North Carolina and Tennessee Revolutionary War Bounty Land Grants. 4. Pension Papers S6876.

****

Jonathan Gates age 12

Jonathan Gates was born on 27 September, 1762 at Harvard, Massachusetts, and he died on 4 August, 1835 in Champion, New York. He married Zerviah Harris on 11 December, 1783 in Chesterfield, New Hampshire. Jonathan enlisted under his father in April, 1775 and he received a yearly pension of $46.66 for his service.

"I enlisted at Cambridge Massachusetts into Captain __?__ company & Jonathan gates Senior Lieutenant belonged to the Massachusetts line does not recollect the nd of Regiment, the regiment was commanded by Colonel Whitcomb & Whitney was Lieutenant Colonel marched from Cambridge to prospect Hill in Massachusetts—where I remained the Eight months of my enlistment & at expiration of said time I volunteered to stay with a majority of Colonel Whitcombs Regiment until new recruits come in and stayed there at my post for three months laying at prospect Hill making in eleven months service."

"Also in September 1777 or there abouts a short time before the taking of Burgoyne I enlisted at one of the Reinforcements under Captain Jonathan Gates Senior enlisted at Ashburnham County of Worcester Massachusetts—for one month Colonel Belloms was Colonel of the Regiment & we marched for the place where Burgoyne was taken near Bemis Heights."

"Also enlisted at Ashburnham County of Worcester State of Massachusetts in the year 1778 or 1779 for the three months & served in the state of Massachusetts Militia under Captain Jonathan Gates Senior marched from thence to Bound Brook in the state of New Jersey & remained stationed there the three months of enlistment Colonel Whitney was Colonel of the Regiment."

"Also in 1780 or 1781 I enlisted for six months at Ashburnham County & State aforesaid into Captain Fishs Company Regiment was commanded by Colonel Jackson marched from Ashburnham aforesaid to Providence Rhode Island & composed portion of the Continental line."

Sources: 1. Tombstone 2. Massachusetts Town & Vital Records 1620-1988. 3. Pension Papers W19492. 4. Worcester County, Massachusetts Memoirs, Vol. I.

****

Andrew Gault age 12

Andrew Gault was born in Ireland in 1764, and died on 8 January, 1832 in Mahoning County, Ohio. He married Eleanor Chesney on 22 April, 1788. He enlisted as a private on 18 September, 1776 perhaps in the New Hampshire Militia.

Sources: 1. Tombstone 2. The Official Roster of Revolutionary War Veterans Buried in the State of Ohio. 3. Immigrants to New England 1700-1775.

****

Emily Geiger age 16

Emily Geiger was born in 1765 in Lexington District, South Carolina, and she died in 1825. She married John Threwits.

In the summer of 1781 in South Carolina General Greene called for a volunteer messenger to carry a letter to General Sumter, but because the area was swarming with Tories no one volunteered. *"May I carry the letter,"* said Emily Geiger. *"They won't hurt a young girl. I am sure, and I know the way,"* she added. General Greene had no choice so he gave the letter to the young girl and also suggested she memorize it in case she was captured. Emily mounted her horse and off she rode sidesaddle.

On the second day of her ride she encountered three Tory scouts who stopped her and took her prisoner. She was taken to the Tory commander, Lord Rawdon, who in turn took her with her guards to a Tory home several miles away. In the home was Mrs. Buxton and her daughter, and both pretended to be Tory sympathizers because the area was thick with the cruel Tories.

Many years later in 1849 Mrs. Buxton's daughter recalled her meeting with Emily Geiger. *"I went with mother,"* she said, *"to see a woman prisoner. The door of the house was guarded by the younger scout, who was Peter Simons, son of a neighbor two miles away, and a right gallant young fellow he was. After the war he married my sister. I saw the young girl and I helped mother search her. We were amazed when we saw, instead of a brazen-faced, middle-aged woman, as we supposed a spy must be, a sweet young girl about my own age, looking as innocent as a pigeon. Our sympathies were with her, but mother performed her duty faithfully. We found nothing on her person that would afford a suspicion that she was a spy."*

They found no message, because when Emily was first brought into the house she was left alone by her guard for a few minutes. This was just enough time for her to tear up the General's letter and eat it piece by piece. Emily was thankful that before she had started the ride she memorized the letter in the event she was captured.

The scouts had no choice but to release the young girl. Mrs. Buxton gave Emily some refreshments and encouraged the young girl to stay on until morning. Emily politely refused saying that because the two armies were in the area, and she should ride on to her friend's house while it was still safe. Her guard Peter Simons, who was probably smitten with

Emily's beauty, offered to escort Emily to her friend's house. Again, she politely declined the invitation and rode off.

She later reached the camp of General Sumter and delivered the message almost word for word. Her ride had lasted three days and had taken her through swamps and forest. She took very little time to rest. General Sumter immediately marched his men to join with General Greene, and once they joined forces Lord Rowdon was compelled to retreat.

After Emily had returned to her home General Greene presented her with a pair of earrings and a breastpin. Years after the war ended, General Lafayette visited the United States and presented Emily with a silk shawl. A grand ball was given in Lafayette's honor in Charlestown and Emily was present, and they danced the first minuet together.

Many years after Emily's ride she visited the house in which she was searched. She thanked Mrs. Buxton for her kindness on that memorable day. Also, present was Mrs. Buxton's daughter who had married Emily's captor, Peter Simons. Emily and Peter compared stories of that long-ago day. Emily remarked that he was foolish to leave her unguarded for those few minutes giving her time to eat the message. Years later Peter Simons's son and Emily Geiger's daughter married.

Sources: 1. Women of the American Revolution by Elizabeth Ellet, 1848. 2. The Percy Anecdotes by Thomas Byerly and Joseph Clinton Robertson, Vol. 2, page 155, 1834. 3. Women Patriots of the American Revolution: a Biographical Dictionary by Charles E. Claghorn. 4. Five Hundred Plus Revolutionary War Obituaries and Death Notices by Mary Harrell-Sesniak.

****

John Geiger age 13

John Geiger was born in 1763 in Philadelphia, Pennsylvania, and he died on 17 July, 1839 in Northampton County, Philadelphia. He married Mary Seip and received a yearly pension of $26.64.

"In the month of August 1776 I voluntarily Joined a Company of Militia Commanded by Captain Michael Smith, Lieut. Thomas Armstrong in the capacity of a Drummer and marched from my residence in Rockhill Township Bucks County in said Commonwealth (which said Company belonged to the Battalion under the command of Col Arthur Erwin & Major William McHenry) through Princeton and New Brunswick to Perth Amboy in the State of New Jersey where we were stationed and remained

until the Two months for which the Militia was called out and were then discharged after a service of Two months."

"I came home and remained home until the ensuing Summer, when the Militia was again called out for the Defense of Philadelphia and other places, I at the request of Captain Emanus Gost who was in want of a Drummer voluntarily joined his company and marched from my place of residence aforesaid to the assistance of Washington under the command of Colonel McMaster & Major Correll who commanded the Battalion to which I was attached. Marched to Montgomery Square in the county of Montgomery and from there to a place called North Welch and from there to head quarters at Valley Forge where we arrived on the evening of the Third of October in the same year."

"We remained in and about Valley Forge until the Two months for which the company was called out and was then discharged. The enemy then had possession of Philadelphia. I came home and remained home for a short time when the Militia was again called out and I again voluntarily joined a company under the command of Captain Abraham Kaehlein in the capacity of Drummer and marched from the place of residence aforesaid to the lower end of Bucks County aforesaid to a place then and now called New Town where I joined other forces. I remained until the Two Months for which I had been called expired then was discharged."

"I was then called out to assist in taking prisoners from the Delaware River to the __?__ line, they were Prisoners taken from Genl Burgoyne."

Sources: 1. Pension Papers S22876. 2. North American Family Histories 1500-2000. 3. Register of the Pennsylvania Society of the Sons of the Revolution, 1888-1898.

****

Anthony Geohegan age 13

Anthony Geohegan was born on 6 June, 1764 in Maryland, and he died on 22 May, 1837 in Warren, Ohio. He married Ann Lilly on 21 December, 1792 in Kentucky. Anthony enlisted in March of 1778 just 3 months short of his 14th birthday. He served as a drummer in the 3rd Maryland Regiment commanded by Colonel Mordecai Gist and he was probably at the Battle of Monmouth in June of 1778. He received a pension of $80 a year for his service.

"In the spring of the year seventeen hundred and seventy eight. I enlisted in the service of the United States of American in a company commanded by Captain Benjamin Brooks in the third regiment of the Maryland line in which said company regiment & line I served until the close of the revolutionary war when I was honorably discharged."

Sources: 1. Kentucky Marriages 1802-1850. 2. Maryland Archives Vol XVIII. 3. U.S. Revolutionary Rolls 1775-1783. 4. Pension Papers W4964. 5. Sons of the American Revolution Application.

****

Joseph Gilbert age 12

Joseph Gilbert was born on 12 May, 1764 in Dutchess County, New York. His pension was rejected due to not enough evidence of service. He served under the command of his brother, Captain Elisha Gilbert.

"In the year 1776 I was called into the service of the United States by order of Captain Elisha Gilbert who then commanded a Company of Infantry of the Militia of the State of New York which Company belonged to a regiment commanded by Col Whiting and was stationed at or in the vicinity of New Lebanon. In the fall of 1776 a division of Munitions for said Regiment was appointed to the said Captain Gilberts Company and I who was then a member of the said Captain Gilberts Company was directed to take charge of said munitions by the said Captain Gilbert as a guard who did bring at the time surrounded by tories & Indians rendered it necessary that a ___?___ should be kept at the said Captain Gilberts house where said munitions were deposited for safety. During the deposit of the said munitions attempts were made to seize the same. I continued to guard until in the summer of 1777 I was called to take the place of William Foster who had been wounded and rendered unable for camp duty, the said Foster took my place as Guard as aforesaid when I went to near where Burgoyne was Stationed and joined the Company of the said Captain Gilbert where I served in said Company one month and was dismissed and returned home and assumed the duties as a guard as aforesaid and I further state that I served as a guard as aforesaid at the place aforesaid from the fall of 1776 until the spring of 1778 at all times unless called out to March on tours of duty."

"During said year the stores from Albany (munitions) were directed to be removed from Albany to Pittsfield East. I was directed to go

and assist in the removal of the same and did so and in which Service I Engaged Six days, my orders were received from Capt Gilbert aforesaid."

"The last of July or first of August as near as I can now recollect in the year 1778 I again Entered the service of the United States as a substitute for Stephen gray who was called out in the said Captain Gilberts Company. Lieutenant Gray was Lieutenant of said Company. The detachment marched to New Lebanon to Albany from there to Schenectady from thence up the Valley of the Mohawk to German Flats where the Regular army was that an engagement took place between the American Troops & the Tories & Indians in which Engagement I was. After the Enemy crossed the creek one of their officers who was called Col Brant was killed. The detachment in which I was in was ordered to pursue the enemy and I pursued them a march of four days when we were ordered to retreat back and after returning me together with the company was dismissed from duty."

"In the month of November 1778 about the first of the same a detachment was again ordered and under the command of Lieutenant Gray, I again went in said detachment as a Substitute for the said Stephen gray aforesaid. The company in which I marched proceeded to Albany when we were Joined by others and then marched to Albany where we were joined by others and then marched to a place called Cherry Valley we did not arrive at the place until after the Indians had consumed the buildings by fire after remaining then a short period we were then detached back and I was dismissed and returned home."

"During the year 1779 & part of the year 1780 I was on duty at short intervals. I was called to detect pursue and convey to persons such as were Suspected and caught in arms or otherwise against the government. My situation was such being a resident at the family of my brother Capt Elisha Gilbert aforesaid and the said Elisha having been engaged the most of his time on active duty or as a member of the general Committee. I was required with some few others serving in this immediate vicinity of the said Capt Gilbert to devote much of this time in the service of my country."

"I was again called out into Service of the United States as a Substitute for the said Stephen Grey aforesaid. Captain Bostwick commanded the detachment, we marched to Albany from there I went to Schenectady and from there marched to Old Schoharie where we Encamped and remained a short time when we were dismissed. And *returned home. The weather was cold the snow fell some inches whilst Encamped at Schoharie, think it was in November 1780."*

"In the year 1781 I was again called out as a Substitute for said Stephen Gray under the command of the said Captain Gilbert, this detachment included to Albany from there we proceeded up the Valley of the Mohawk to Fort Stanwix from there the detachment marched against a band of Indian & Tories at a place called Oriskany at which place I was in the engagement between the Americans and the Indians & Tories. In this tour I had a tedious campaign was destitute of food for three days with but little Exception. After remaining on duty two months and I was dismissed and returned home."

Sources: 1. The Bloodied Mohawk: The American Revolution in the Words of Fort Planks Defenders and Other Mohawk Valley Partisans by Kenneth D. Johnson. 2. Pension Papers R4009.

****

John Gill age 13 or 14

John Gill was born c. 1762 in Virginia, and he died on 29 November, 1842. He married Lettice Lee on 2 July, 1824. In one of Lettice's letters to the Pension Bureau she refers to John as serving as an orderly Sergeant. During the Civil War her pension was suspended. She had her pension restored after the war, when she made a proof of loyalty. She wrote a letter stating that she would support, protect, and defend the Constitution of the United Sates.

The pension agencies for the states that left the Union were suspended when the Civil War began. Congress passed an act on 4 February, 1862 for the payment of any pension to one who had taken up arms against the United States, in any manner encouraged the rebels, or manifested a sympathy with their cause was effectually prohibited. A person able to prove their continued loyalty in act and sympathy throughout the war could have their pension restored.

"I entered the Militia service of the United States in the Revolutionary War under the following named officer, and for the several following periods of time. 1st as a substitute for my father who was drafted in the Year 1776 for a period of Three Months, under Captn Robert Overall & Col. Churchill of 1st Virginia Regiment, and served out that time in the lower part of Virginia, about Williamsburg, York, Norfolk __?__ I was then very young for a soldier, say between 13 & 14 years of

age, and do not recollect the precise time of the year or month of entry or discharge. Spencer Anderson's certificate proves my being in service at that time and accompanies this declaration. 2d that I further served a period of 4 M'ths in 1781 under William Brent Captn in s' 1st Virginia Reg't. as a volunteer, in the capacity of Sergeant in s' Brent's company, that I entered on 1st January of s'. year and was discharged on the 1st of May – during this period of service I was in a battle with the enemy at Williamsburg, but rec'd no wound Charles B. Attwell who was ensign in the same company proves this tour of service, as well as my being sergeant in s' company – his Certificate accompanies this paper. 3d that he also served in the said year 1781 and as a volunteer and the term of about 4 Months under Captn Robert Warren & Col. Churchill in s' 1st Virginia Reg't turning out in a few days after I returned home from his second tour, and continuing in service till within about a Month of the surrender of Cornwallis at York. this term was also in the lower part of Virginia, as was all my service – I was not at York I do not recollect the precise date of entry on this last tour or exact period of discharge."

Sources: 1. U.S. Pensioners of 1818-1872. 2. Pension Papers W7520.

****

Asa Gillett age 13

Asa Gillett was born on 11 June, 1764 in Litchfield, Connecticut, and he died in 1838 in Clinton, Michigan. He married Naomi Hosford on 9 August, 1787 in Litchfield. He received a yearly pension of $96.

"I first enlisted in the army of the Revolution under Captain Taylor in Col Meads Regiment of Infantry in the latter part of the year 1777 and I enlisted in the town of county of Litchfield in the state of Massachusetts and I afterwards served under Captain Grant in the same Regiments. Afterwards enlisted into Col Sheldon's Regiment of Cavalry and was afterwards transferred from the cavalry (being unable to ride in consequence of wounds) to the infantry in Col Sheldon's Regiment and served in the Infantry until May '83 when I was discharged after serving five years, six months, and nineteen days."

"All the pay I received for my service was at the hands of Captain Stanton which was eighty dollars in one bill of Continental money and in sixteen dollars in Connecticut <u>shin plaster</u>. The eighty dollars mentioned before I dispersed of for a breakfast and one half of a gill of rum."

Once the war began gold and silver coins were scarce. Each state printed its own money to pay for the war, and because so much was printed and it was easy to copy, the paper money lost most of its value. When Asa was paid eighty dollars Continental money, the dollar was worth less than ¼ of a cent. It was just enough money to pay for breakfast and a bit of rum. Many people called the money "shin plasters," because they felt the only use it had was to bandage a sore leg.

"I was with Genl Anthony Wayne at the storming of Stony Point and was in the engagements previous to the surrender at Yorktown and sundry other engagements."

Asa was part of the American victory at Stony Point fought on 16 July, 1779. The attacking force was made up of four regiments. He was part of the 3rd Regiment which was made up of 8 companies of Massachusetts troops led by Colonel Jonathan Megis. General Anthony Wayne led the main attack force that consisted of the 1st and 3rd Regiments.

"I was severely wounded at Valentines Hill about eight miles north of White Plains. A detachment was ordered out to obstruct the passage of the enemy from New York into the country and while this said detachment was retreating I stopped to load my musket and while in the act of loading and partly facing the enemy I received a musket ball in my left leg on the inside just above the ankle joint which passed through the bone and splintered it badly. I was immediately taken off the field and carried to the heights where cannons were placed which opened upon the enemy with grape shot down their back. The surgeon of the Regiment Dr. Branson proposed immediate amputation but in my protesting he decided from amputation. I was not able to do military service from the time said wound was received which was in September 1779 until the month of May following."

Many of the Revolutionary War doctors believed that amputation was "the antibiotic of the day." They thought that if a body part was severely damaged by a musket ball, then the only way to stop the effect on the rest of the body was to amputate. There was no anesthesia or sterilization so it was a painful and deadly procedure. Officers would be given rum or brandy if available to dull the pain. Since Asa was an enlisted man he would have been given a wood stick to bite down on. Less than 35% of the patients survived.

Asa stated that after his discharge he returned home and at times was laid up for weeks due to the wound he received. Sometimes he required assistance just to get up. Much of the time he was unable to do any labor.

"I was again wounded in the thigh of the left leg on the last day of the battle of Yorktown by a musket ball passing through the thigh yet without injury to the bone. The surgeon stated that I bled so profusely that I would have bled to death had no appliance been at hand."

"I was again wounded by a grape shot grazing the top of my head which was received while boarding the enemy's vessel off Black Rock in Long Island Sound. The party succeeded in securing the vessel and bringing her safely in Black Rock Harbor. This happen March '83 just before I was discharged."

Sources: 1. Lineage Book D.A.R. Vol. 53, 1905. 2. Sons of the American Revolution Application. 3. U.S. Pension Roll of 1835. 4. Pension Papers S34898.

****

Robert Glascock age 14

Robert Glascock was born in 1765 in Virginia, and he died on 25 October, 1839 in Virginia. He married Nancy Ligon in Mecklenburg County, Virginia in 1834. She remarried twice after the death of Robert. He received a pension of $96 a year and 160 acres of land for his service as a fifer during the war. Nancy's widow's pension was suspended during the Civil War. She wrote a letter to the Pension Bureau declaring her oath of support to the United States. She stated that she had done spinning for other women during the war to get something to eat.

"I enlisted in the 15th Va. Reg't. commanded by Colo. Russel, in Chesterfield County Va, and marched to Valley forge in Harris' Company, ___?__ by Lieut Gibbs about the year 1777, and was afterwards consolidated with a __?__ the 7th Va Reg't., I continued to serve in said Corps, until about the year 1780 when I was discharged from service in Philadelphia, state of Pensylvania, by Colo. Frebecker; I was in the battles of Monmouth, Powlers Hook, Stony Point."

Robert joined the 15th Virginia at Valley Forge, and he was part of the 3rd Brigade under the command of Brigadier General William Woodford at the Battle of Monmouth on 28 June, 1778. At the Battle of Paulus Hook on 19 August, 1779 Robert was part of a 400 man infantry under the command of Major Light Horse Harry Lee. Major Lee launched a nighttime raid on a British fort in New Jersey. Robert was part of the

287

Virginia regiments commanded by Colonel Febiger at the Battle of Stony Point on 16 July, 1779.

Sources: 1. Census 1820. 2. U.S. Pensioners 1818-1872. 3. Virginia Marriages 1740-1850. 4. Pension Papers W11311.

****

Richard Goff age 13

Richard Goff was born on 9 September, 1763 in New London, Connecticut, and he died on 14 April, 1842 in New Berlin, New York. He married Polly Winchester on 28 August 1782 in Connecticut. He served 8 months in the army and one year and a half months as a privateer. On his first voyage he served as a cabin steward. For his service in the army he received a yearly pension of $29.65.

"On or about the first of May 1777 at Middletown on Connecticut River I enlisted and entered on board the ship Trumbull for one year in the United States Frigate Captain Dudley Salston, Lieu Malbury and White Gilbert Satstonsall Captain of Marines Adams purser. Went from there down the river to Lyme in Connecticut being the mouth of said River and there was employed in rigging the ship as She was a New Ship Great of the year but the ship could not go to sea on account of a Bar of Sand across the River until the next season. But before she went to sea I served the year out."

"In the year 1778 or 1779 enlisted as a Substitute in the Militia under Sergeant whose name I forgot to guard the Sea Shore between New London and Lyme in Connecticut and served about two months and was verbally discharged."

"Then went immediately into the United States Service as a Substitute and joined the army near West Point on the Hudson River State of New York in Capt Betts Company in Colonel Sherman's Regiment and in wither Pearsons or Huntingtons Brigade. Lay at West Point until late in the fall then Marched to Morristown in New Jersey and took up winter quarters. Lay there until about the middle of January when I was discharged about two hundred and forty miles from home. Snow very deep and no __?__ suffered very much both with hunger and cold because provisions could not be got to the army on account of the great depth of snow. Served about six months."

"The spring following in the month of May I enlisted on board the sloop Hawk under Captain Umsteadl at New London Connecticut and cruised between New York and the West Indies. Had a Battle with and took the ship Ginny from Liverpool Captain Smith bound for New York from where the British had passed on was __?__ by two copper bottom Frigates from New York but brought the ship into New London safe. Made a number of other voyages and in the fall I think in September was discharged and went home."

Sources: 1. D.A.R. Lineage Book, Vol. 13. 2. U.S. Pension Roll of 1835. 3. Pension Papers W24287.

****

Abraham Godwin age 13

Abraham Godwin was born on 16 July, 1763 in New York, and he died 5 October, 1835 in Paterson, New Jersey. He married Mary Munson on 9 May, 1783. He received a yearly pension of $108. He served as a fife Major.

David Godwin age 10

David Goodwin was born on 5 March, 1766 in New York, and he died on 31 January, 1852 in New York. He married Catherine Waldron on 18 March, 1791. He received 300 acres of land for his service. He served as a drummer.

Abraham and his brother David received permission from their mother to join the army in 1776. Their father Abraham was an officer in the army and was killed in February of 1777. Their older brother Captain Henry Godwin commanded a company in the 5th New York Regiment upstate at Fishkill, New York. The boys traveled north to serve under him; Abraham as a fifer and David as a drummer.

The 5th New York Regiment was authorized on 30 November, 1776 under the command of Colonel Lewis DuBois. The 5th was defeated with nearly two-thirds of the men killed or captured at the Battle of Fort Montgomery and Fort Clinton on 6 October, 1777. They would see more action in the Hudson Highlands and during the Sullivan Expedition. Both boys were probably at the defeat of Cornwallis.

After the war Abraham operated the family's hotel near the Great Falls of Paterson. Several years later he and Alexander Hamilton would meet there and discuss how to take advantage of the swift waters of the

Passaic and the falls. Abraham would be appointed a General in the New Jersey Militia in the war of 1812. In an interview in 1897 Abraham's grandson described him as a musician, painter, a poet, and an engraver.

In his pension application Abraham wrote, *"I enlisted in the continental Line of the army of the revolution for and during the war and continued in its service until its termination."*

His brother David applied for his land bounty of 300 acres and on 9 September, 1828 Abraham wrote to the pension bureau on his behalf, *"I take liberty of addressing you on a subject in which I feel considerably interested, it is the case of my brother David Godwin, who is as much entitled to a pension as I am only that he was not on the ground when the army was disbanded to received his discharge. He was very young and very small of his age and weakly withal, which made him receive many indulgencies from the officers of the Regiment, he became sick, and was suffered to go home on Furlough, some little time previous to the disbanding of the army and not minding in health, he was returned sick absent, and so remained. He was never discharged."*

"When he went to the land office to claim his Land Warrant they told him they could not find his name on any of the muster rolls. I am willing to take an oath that he enlisted at the same time as I did and for the same term. He did his duty as a musician for he was not old enough to be capable of doing any other kind of duty."

"My father being one of the proscribed rebels, it was impossible for us to remain at home with impunity and it was fortunate for us that we had a brother who was an officer in the army under whose protection we could throw ourselves on. I know not what might have been the consequences – that brother however is now, no more, his name was Henry. My brother David who is now living in the big city of New York has a large family to maintain in his old days."

Sources: 1. D.A.R. Lineage Book, Vol. 60. 2. Pension Papers S46359 for Abraham. 3. Pension Papers S17982 for David.

****

Thomas Gore age 14

Thomas Gore was born in 1763 in Wake, North Carolina, and he died in 1830 in Mississippi. He married Agnes Bledso on 18 September, 1786. He received a yearly pension of $48.

"I enlisted for the term of three years on the __ day of __ in the year of our Lord 1777 in the State of South Carolina in the company of cavalry commanded by Captain David Hopkins in the 3rd Regiment commanded by Col Wm Thompsom in the South Carolina line on the Continental establishment; I continued to serve in said corps for the term of three years when I was discharged in the State of South Carolina in the year 1780. I was in the battles of Sullivan's Island & of Sintellys."

In a letter to the Pension Bureau in March of 1818 he stated, *"I am a farmer but have no land, no family living with me and I depend on my friends for assistance."*

Sources: 1. North Carolina Marriage Index 1741-2004. 2. U.S. Pensioners 1818-1872. 3. Pension Papers S38746.

****

John Gorin age 14

John Gorin was born on 13 May, 1763 in Fairfax County, Virginia, and he died 5 August, 1837 in Glasgow County, Kentucky. He married Elizabeth Franklin c. 1786, and when she died in 1824 he married Elizabeth Turpin in 1825.

After the war John moved his family to Kentucky. During the War of 1812 he raised a group of Kentucky Volunteers and fought. He was a Major in the 10th Regiment (Barbours) Mounted Kentucky Volunteers.

"I entered the service of the United States under the following named officers, and served as herein stated. I was born & raised in the County of Fairfax, state of Virginia, near Alexandria, & in the year 1777 volunteered as a Soldier under Captain Thomas Pollard & Lieutenant William D. Neale in the Virginia Militia, & was attached to Cols Rumsey & Gilpins Regiment, & marched to Pennsylvania, & there was attached to Gen'l. Charles Scotts Brigade, under his excellency Gen'l George Washington, & was at the Battle of Germantown at which battle Genl Nash was killed _____ can't read a group of words _____ *and shortly afterwards I assisted in dislodging the Hessians at the Schuylkill Bridge near Philadelphia. I then prepared to go to the white Marsh but did not go. That he was then sent home for the winter. I do not recollect the exact period I served at this time, but think it was about 3 months. I obtained a Legal discharge but has now lost it. In this tour I acted as Sergeant."*

" Shortly after my return home the troops were called upon to guard Gen'l. Washingtons house. Dunmore was cruising in the Potomack River. I again volunteered and went with the troops, as a private."

"In 1781 I served as a Press Master in raising a troop of Horse & went to the place of Rendezvous I was then, after several __?__, from the beginning of said service, dismissed for the time being. In a short time the troops were again called for to join the Army in Virginia to put a stop to the British Army in that State, & I immediately joined Capt. Hugh Douglass's Company as an orderly Sergeant & served in that capacity, & was attached to Col Summers Regiment, and took up the line of march & joined the Army at the Maulin Hills below Richmond, and was there attached to Gen'l. Stevensons Brigade. Col Mereweather & Major John Hardiman took the command, being Regular officers, but having at the time no command until they took it as __?__. I marched to Williamsburgh thence moved on to Yorktown; was at the taking of Lord Cornwallis."

"I was then discharged; but afterwards, assisted Cornwallis's troops to Baltimore. I was on this tour 4 or 5 months, before the discharge was obtained; & some time after the discharge, cannot now recollect the exact time, I, after the surrender went home, but returned with waggons & met Cornwallis troops at Alexandria, from whence I assisted in conveying them & baggage to Baltimore."

Sources: 1. Sons of the American Revolution Application. 2. Tombstone 3. U.S. War of 1812 Service Records 1812-1815. 4. U.S. Pensioners 1818-1872. 5. Pension Papers W25643.

****

Hannah Gorton age 8

Hannah Gorton was born on 16 September, 1770 in Rhode Island, and she died on 6 May, 1863 in Providence, Rhode Island. Her father was a Lieutenant in the Rhode Island Militia. In the summer of 1779, at the age of 8, she carried water to the soldiers, fed them, changed their bandages, and washed their hands and faces. If caught aiding the rebels a person could be beaten, have their property taken, or killed. Years later Hannah married Jonathan Hill who became a Captain in the Rhode Island Militia.

Sources: 1. Census of 1850. 2. Women Patriots of the American Revolution: a Biographical Dictionary by Charles E. Claghorn.

****

Henry Gotham age 13/14

Henry Gotham was born in 1762 in Salem, Massachusetts, and he died 2 November, 1839 in Jefferson County, New York. He married (2) Betsy Wilson on 5 October, 1825. He enlisted in June of 1776 and received a pension of $8.00 a month.

In 1776 he served as a private in Captain Joseph Pettingill's Company, Colonel Wesson's Massachusetts Regiment and was discharged in February 1777.

He then enlisted as a private in Captain Dustin's Company, Colonel Mellan's Regiment and was discharged in February 1778. He was involved in several skirmishes.

Sources: 1. Pension Papers W1753. 2. Worcester County, Massachusetts Memoirs, Vol. I.

****

Daniel Granger age 13

Daniel Granger was born in Andover, Massachusetts on 2 March, 1762, and died in 1845 in Massachusetts. He married Polly Jordan on 8 April, 1792 and they had at least six children. He enlisted at the age of 13 as a drummer in the 2nd New Hampshire Regiment under the command of Colonel Enoch Poor.

Daniel describes his enlistment, *"...went down...to the Officers to offer my services...they questioned me a little and finally said that I might stay...if I thought that I could do the duty of a soldier."*

"Sometime in December I think of the year 1775 I enlisted in the company I think of Capt. Cliffs' about my recollection in Col. Enoch Poor's regiment as a substitute for my brother Jacob Granger who had engaged early in that year—and served about two & one half months til the march following at Winter Hill near Boston. I do not now remember any occurrence coming that period connected with any since particularly worthy of notice."

Daniel served part of the time as a drummer and part of the time as a soldier, for his older brother from December 1775 until 6 March, 1776. His brother had become ill from the cold winter, so Daniel's father sent Daniel to bring his brother home. His brother took the horse Daniel rode and went home, and Daniel joined the army.

One night on guard duty he was standing around a stump when some falling ice made a noise. Another sentry shouted out, fired a shot, and ran off. Daniel stood his guard with his musket ready until other men showed up. The next morning the officers questioned him about the event and were impressed with his bravery.

Daniel participated in the Siege of Boston, but before it ended on 16 March, 1776 his brother returned in good health, so Daniel returned home.

"In the year 1777 about the first of September I volunteered in the company of Capt Adam in the Regiment commanded by Col. Brickett. Immediately after my enlistment we marched to Battinkiled Where we were for some time stationed and thence to Stillwater. I was at Stillwater at the time Gen Burgoyne surrender the British troops under his command to Gen. Gates in the 17th of October. I was not however in any engagements of that time. I marched with our Regiment as a guard to the British troops to Cambridge. I was then discharged at the expiration of the four months for which I had enlisted."

The Battles of Saratoga took place on September 19 and on October 7, 1777 and they resulted in the defeat of the British General Burgoyne. This was the turning point of the war, for it was the catalyst that led France to recognize the independence of the United States and sign an alliance. Daniel did not participate in the battle, but he was able to watch and hear the fighting from his vantage point. Daniel's brother Jacob was wounded in the shoulder during the battle.

One day he visited some of the captured British troops. He made friends with a captured 14 year old soldier who was the son of a British officer. Daniel and the young boy talked for some time, and Daniel took pity on him but could not release him. Daniel later watched the surrender of General Burgoyne. Daniel wrote in his memoirs:

"I got as near to Gen' Gates' Markee as I could for the Crowd, and saw Gen' Burgoyne & Suit ride up, and dismount and go into Gen' Gates' Markee, and soon the Van of the Prisoners made their appearance, The Hesson Troops came first with their Baggage on Horses that were mere Skelletins, not able apparently to bear the wait of their own Carkeses. These Troops had some Women, who wore short Petty coats, bare footed, & bare Leged, with huge Packs on their backs, some carrying a child & leading an other or two, They were silent, civil, and looked quite subdued. The English Troops followed, and were cross and impudent

enough, they crossed the River that Night and encamped on a level Ground near the River, where they drew Rations and Cooked their suppers, they were very hungry, it was said that they had not drawn full Rations for several days, before the surrender, they had been cooped up in close quarters without Forrage for their Horses or Rations for the Troops."

After the battle Daniel extracted some musket balls from some of the trees on the battlefield as memorials of the battle. His regiment under the command of Colonel Brickett marched over 6,000 British prisoners back to Cambridge. It was a hard march, because the temperatures were cold and there were several inches of snow on the ground. Daniel wrote,

"I went into the British Camp that Eve', & because acquainted with several young Lads of about my Age, pleased with them, and they seemed to be pleased with me, & said that we were no longer Enemies. I traded with them. We had drawn Rations that Eve', some Whiskey & other articles which I sold to the Soldiers & got Silver Money, which was a rare article with us."

When the prisoners were taken back to Cambridge, sixteen year old Daniel's enlistment was up so he returned home to work on his father's farm.

"About the first of July 1778 I enlisted for four months under Capt Madison in Col. Wardsworth Regiment. We were stationed at Providence in that vicinity for sometime. I then went into Rhode Island & down we went to Newport where we remained until the British fleet render it no longer safe for us. In our retreat I was in the skirmishes with the British near Butt's hill. The night after this encounter our troops pitched their tents as they were about to make a stand. But as soon as it became dark silently decamped & passed over to the main land. We then marched to a place called Narragansett Pier where we were stationed at the time the expiration of the four months for which I enlisted I was discharged in November & returned home. I served during this campaign in this capacity of a drummer."

The skirmish Daniel wrote about was part of the Battle of Rhode Island fought on 29 August, 1778 near Newport. Butts Hill, where Daniel was located. This was about a half a mile northeast of the main battle area. Butts Hill was a fortified earthworks that served as a command post and a defensive position for the Americans. The Battle of Rhode Island was the only battle of the war in which an entirely segregated unit of African-American soldiers fought. The battle ended in a draw.

"In the year 1780 about the first of June as near as I can remember I enlisted for six months under Capt Sargent (Captain Paul Dudley Sargent) *& marched to a place called Claverack in the state of New York. When for some time with several others I was billeted upon the inhabitants. We were then ordered to West Point. Then I was stationed in fort Arnold the last of November or the first of December when the six months for which I enlisted having expired. I was discharged."*

Claverack was a Dutch settlement. For several days Daniel and several other men stayed with a Dutch family who provided them with food. Fort Arnold was named for Benedict Arnold until he betrayed the Americans, and then it was changed to Fort Clinton. The fort today has been taken in by the expansion of West Point.

"I was at West Point at the time of the discovery of Arnold's treason and of his escape. One of my messmates one _____ Wilson was in the detachment party of guards to whom Major Andre was surrender by those who had made him prisoner. I saw him when he first landed at West Point & again the next morning."

Daniel wrote that the troops were called out after the capture of Major Andre, because they expected the British might attack. He told of an encounter that terrified him, *"Once in the night I was called off with several others & required to go into the Magazine, to bring out cartridges, for the cannon & Lights were carried in & open, no lantons which was very hazardous. If a spark fell on the scattered powder, All must have been into Eternity in an Instant, I felt in more danger than I would have felt in Battle."*

Major John Andre after his capture was convicted as a spy and ordered to be hanged on 2 October, 1780. Daniel wrote of his execution,

"I saw Andre again the next Morning. I was permitted to go to the Window of the Room, where he was confined, Window being up. He was pacing the room, did not appear to notice me. And no doubt was contemplating his fate, which he very well understood. He left the Point that Day & was conducted down, near to headquarters, Where he was tried by a Court Marshal as a Spy, condemned as a Spy and hung as a Spy. I did not go down to see his executed. Altho some of my comrades did. It would not have been an agreeable sight to me, altho I knew that he was a Spy."

Daniel finished his military service in November of 1780 and returned home to the farm. Years later he taught school for several years New Hampshire and in Maine. In 1786 he settled in Saco, Maine and served as a collector of customs. In 1839 he moved for the last time to Eastport. He received a pension of $20.00 a year. His pension file is very extensive.

Sources: 1. Pension papers for Daniel Granger. 2. A Boy Soldier Under Washington: The Memoir of Daniel Granger, The Mississippi Valley Historical Review Vol. 16, No. 4 March, 1930. 3. Massachusetts Town and Vital Records, 1620-1988. 4. A Battlefield Atlas of the American Revolution by Craig L. Symonds, Cartography by William J. Clipson.

****

Paul Green age 14

Paul Green was born in 1763 in Georgia, and he died in Kentucky in 1837. He received a pension of $80 a year for his service.

"I enlisted in the army of the United States on the day of ____ 1777 at Annapolis in Capt. John Miles Company of the 6 Maryland Regiment Commanded by Colo. Otho Williams. I was some short time afterwards marched to Pennsylvania. I was in the Battle of Brandywine, also in the Battle at GermanTown, and afterwards went into winter quarters at Valley forge. I continued with my Regiment, but cannot distinctly recollect the different places I was marched to. I however recollect one fact well, that is the Regiment to which I was attached to being ordered to the South & being at Camden at Gates defeat where I was taken prisoner and detained nine months on Board a prison ship in the harbor near Charlestown. After an exchange took place me with others were sent back to Pennsylvania, I was stationed some time at Brandywine, then ordered back to Annapolis where I was honorably discharged, but that said discharge has been lost or mislaid."

British treatment of prisoners was very cruel during the war. They were confined to old ships where there was little room, food, and clothing. There were several prison ships at New York. Twenty-five hundred prisoners from Charleston were confined on one ship in Charleston harbor. In thirteen months one third of the number died from disease.

Sources: 1. Maryland Revolutionary War Records. 2. Kentucky Pension Rolls for 1835. 3. History of the United States by Frederick Hiram Clark. 4. Pension Papers S10767.

****

William Green age 11

William Green claimed to be born in 1765 in Craven County, North Carolina. He said he enlisted as a minute man for six months in 1780 or 1781. The battle he describes he was in was called the Battle of Moore's Creek, fought 27 February, 1776. This would make him around 11 years old. It's possible he is wrong about his birth date or he may have purposely given the incorrect dates for enlistment, which would indicate he was of the legal enlistment age. This would increase his chances of receiving a pension.

William said that he spent about 14 days training at New Bern and then they marched down to Moore's Creek. The militia consisted of about 800 men and they made fortifications on the east side of Moore's Bridge. William Green reported, *"according to expectation we met with a large band of Tories (about 800, including 600 Scots) under the command of McCloud (McLeod) who was killed in the action near our breast works."*

Just before dawn 80 of the Tories waving Scottish Claymore broadswords prematurely charged across the bridge. Scottish pipes were blaring and drums were beating, and the Scots yelled, *"King George and broadswords."* They were not aware that the patriots were waiting behind fortifications with their muskets aimed at them.

William Green stated, *"The Tories were nearly all Scotchmen. McCloud (McLeod) when he was first wounded he fell to his knees near the works and waved his sword. He was immediately shot dead. We took a good many prisoners."*

At least 30 of the Tories were killed and it was reported that McLeod had been struck by at least 20 musket balls. Only one patriot was killed, reported to be John Grady, in the rebel victory. Over the next few days the militia arrested about 850 Tories.

Once the battle had ended William said, *"We were then dismissed to go home and procure clean clothes, and be in readiness at a moments warning to march again."* That moment came very quickly. *"In about three or four days the Sergeants came around and notified us to rendezvous at one Stevenson's nine or ten miles from where I lived."*

Once the militia re-assembled they marched to an old fort outside of Wilmington. They stayed there repairing the fort and were released from duty about six months later. During the next year William served for very short periods of time. One time he volunteered under Captain Billy

George for three months, *"to sweep out and purge the County of all the filthy, thieving Tories who could be found. We went to work and in time did effectually cleanse the County of them."* William made no secret of how he felt about the hated Tories.

Sources: 1. The American Revolution in the Southern Colonies by David Lee Russell. 2. Pension Papers S34132. 3. A Guide to the Battles of the American Revolution by Theodore P. Savas and J. David Dameron.

****

Bartlee Greenwood age 14

Bartlee Greenwood was born on 18 July, 1764 in Charlotte, Virginia, and he died on 28 September, 1837 in Lincoln, Kentucky. He married Nancy Sublett on 13 October, 1785 in Virginia. The census reports that in 1830 he owned 3 slaves. Nancy received his yearly pension of $80.

"I enlisted as well as I recollects in the year 1777 for the term of the war at Hillsborough in the State of North Carolina in the company of Capt James Gunn in the regiment commanded by Colonel Anthony W White in the line of the State of Virginia on the Virginia continental establishment I continued to serve in the said corps for between four and five years, when I was dispatched to Petersburg in Virginia to guard some publick waggons, I was permitted by my officers to return to my Fathers in Charlotte County Virginia there to remain until called upon for service but was never afterwards called upon except to go to Richmond which I done and was permitted again to return to my Fathers which was in the year 1782 as well as I recollect."

Sources: 1. Census 1800, 1810, 1820, and 1830. 2. U.S. Pensioners 1818-1872. 3. Sons of the American Revolution Application. 4. Virginia Marriages 1785-1940. 5. Lincoln County Kentucky by Turner Publishing. 6. Pension Papers W3013.

****

William Guest age 14

William Guest was born on 30 December, 1762 in Frederick, Virginia and he died on 8 July, 1841 in Pickens County, South Carolina. He married Anna Allen on 23 July, 1779 in North Carolina. He received a yearly pension of $50 for his service.

Obituary from the South Carolina *Easley Messenger*: *"Another Revolutionary Patriot Gone; Departed this life on Thursday the 8th inst. At his residence in Pickens district near Fair Play, Capt. William Guest in* the 79th year of his age, leaving a disconsolate widow, sons, and daughters, together with a large circle of friends to mourn their irreparable loss. Few men have lived to this age and sustained a character so amiable as this worthy old citizen. He lived respected and died lamented by all who knew him. He served his time faithful in the revolutionary war, and resided for upwards of the last fifty years within two miles of the writer during which time his character has been the most charitable and virtuous."

"In June 1775 I enlisted in the Militia under Captain Elijah Isaacs for three months in Col Benjamin Clevelands Regiment, rendezvoused on the Yadkin River Wilkes County North Carolina where we remained in guarding the fort for the term of service, do not recollect the name of the Fort, was discharged at said Fort by the Captain. In March 1779 enlisted under Capt Moses Guest in a company of Mounted Infantry in the Regiment before mentioned and continued under said Captain until October 1781, rendezvoused at Wilkes Court House, was reviewed by Col Cleveland during this service we generally on scouting parties were marched to Watauga twice and near to Long Island on Holston, once after returning from said place went in pursuit Colonel Moore who commanded the Tories at Ramsours Mill from thence went in pursuit of Col Briant who commanded the Tories but hearing he had been defeated by Genl Sumter we returned to Wilkes in June, from June untill October we were employed in breaking up Tory camps in different parts of the Country, we were then marched under Col Cleveland to Kings Mountain defeated Col Ferguson, were marched as a guard in taking the Prisoners to Moravian Town, from this I was sent by order of Colonel Cleveland after Joseph Reid who was wounded at Kings Mountain and left at Doct Dobson's Burke County with orders to bring him to Wilkes and wait on him until he recovered from his wounds, about the Last of May joined the company again in Wilkes, was marched over the Mountains to Holston River E. Tennessee in pursuit of robbers and Tories which had fled from Moores defeat, returned back to Wilkes then was marched to the head of Catawba where we remained three or four weeks waiting for supplies when we were discharged in October 1781."

According to legend, Colonel Cleveland climbed up Rendezvous Mountain and blew his horn to summon some 200 Wilkes County militiamen and led them in the battle. In the fierce fighting, Cleveland's horse was shot from under him.

On 9 March, 1835 William Guest dictated the following additional declarations. It contains a little more detail than his first one.

"In June (as well as I recollect) 1777, I was then 15 years of Age Capt Isaacs of Wilkes County N.C. applied to me to volunteer to build & Guard a Fort on the head of the Yadkin near to Genl Lanore's House. I turned out volunteer for Three months and did go with the said Captain Isaacs & did help to build the Fort & guard it by order of Col Cleveland who commanded the Militia of Wilkes County. I was discharged at the End of Three months sometime in September and I was paid for these Three months service. That afterwards in March 1779 I turned out a volunteer in what was called the Minute Service a Corps ordered by the Legislature of North Carolina in 1778 to be raised on the Frontiers one company in Wilkes County of Mounted Infantry of which Company Moses Guest a brother of mine who was 12 years older was appointed Captain. And in the month of March 1779 we rendezvoused at Wilkesboro in said County and Had their horses & appraised, Inspected & mustered in the service. The service was against the Tories, Deserters, outliers and enemies of the United States, and we were ordered into the service & continued in it Continuously from the Month of March 1779 till June 1780 not less than Ten months; during all the time I followed no regular business except as a Soldier. It is true I was some days during that time permitted to visit my family and I was some days occasionally at home by leave of my Officers, but many times I has left home at night often late to join my Company. I do not at this late day now distinctly recollect all the incidents of the Tours & services of that period of 15 months but I do know that my wife made the crops during that period & did nearly all the work in the field. In June 1780 I volunteered or was yet considered & in the Minute Service and went under Capt Guest with Col Cleveland & all his effective force to Ramsours Mill against Col Moore who had 800 Tories stationed there but before Cleveland's Army arrived Genl Rutherford defeated Moore. I was then marched under Capt Guest – Major Micajah Lewis Col Benjamin Cleveland, to go to Hanging Rock against Tory Col Bryant, but before we arrived at Hanging Rock the Battle was fought. We then returned home or rather by Home & was marched into the lower part of Burke County and was there stationed on the Catawba River about two or three weeks – when Col Cleveland ordered Capt Moses Guest with his Company of mounted Infantry to cross the mountains & to Watauga in (what is) perhaps what is now Ashe County. We took some prisoners & returned to Wilkesboro, there joined Col Cleveland again & was ordered to keep the Tories under as much as possible as Ferguson was then

approaching the Mountains. In September or first of October having heard that Cols Campbell, Shelby & Sevier were coming over the Mountains, Col Cleveland collected all the men he could and joined Campbell on Mud Creek, head of the Catawba in Burke County and went on with them overtook Col Ferguson at Kings Mountain was in that Battle Early in the Engagement one of my messmates was wounded in the thigh who asked him if we gained the Battle not to leave him on the ground. After the Battle was over I went & found the wounded man & was directed by the Captain & Colonel to take him & the other wounded to Doct. Dobson's in Burke County. Afterwards was ordered to collect Beef & take to the Army at Wilkesboro which I did and went as one of the guard to Moravian Town – was then ordered by Col Cleveland to go back to Doct. Dobson's and take Reid the wounded man home & to nurse him till he got well which he did for Four months which was in June 1781. -- In June 1781 I was again a volunteer with Capt Guest Lieutenant Ferguson to go to the Long Island on Holston against the Tories and we took 4 or 5 prisoners & on the return took one deserter who was Hung – Was out not less than Three weeks this tour -- In August 1781 was called out as a volunteer & Col Heron who had the command appointed him Lieutenant but I got no commission -- that I recollects -- went with him to Cathey's Fort on the head of the Catawba rendezvoused there remained about Three weeks & a supply of ammunition could not be procured to go against the Indians & most of the men returned home. I was out not less than 4 weeks this time."

Sources: 1. Census 1840. 2. North Carolina Marriage Index 1741-2004. 3. U.S. Pensioners 1818-1872. 4. Pension Papers W21239.

****

Jacob Gundy age 13

Jacob Gundy was born on 13 October, 1765 in Lancaster, Pennsylvania and died in Vermilion County, Illinois on 24 September, 1845. He married Katherine Maurer (Maury) around 1784 and they had ten children. He entered the service on 25 April, 1779 nearly six months before his 14th birthday. *"I enlisted in the year AD 1779 as a waggoner or team driver with Sebastian Wolf as captain and Robert Patton as quarter master."*

He hauled provisions to the troops in New York and New Jersey for around twenty months and was discharged in December of 1781. He then enlisted in the militia again and served for about 80 days.

After the war he moved to Franklin County, Ohio and was the first to be elected Justice of the Peace in the area. He later moved to Vermilion County, Illinois.

Sources: 1. 1840 census. 2. Children and Youth in a New Nation edited by James Marten. 3. Pension Papers for Jacob Gundy S32284. 4. Revolutionary War Soldiers Buried in Illinois. 5. American Revolutionary Soldiers that Reside in Franklin County, Ohio by Ed Bristol.

****

Gabriel Gunn age 14

Gabriel Gunn was born on 24 February, 1767 in Orange County, North Carolina, and he died on 26 February, 1839 in Newton Georgia. He married Alsey Canup on 22 December, 1836. In 1820 he owned five slaves. He received a yearly pension of $38.40 for his service.

"I volunteered under Col Wm. Moore of Caswell County North Carolina and Josiah Cole as Captain, And continued in Service upwards of thirty days, and got a discharge the 12th March 1781. Secondly, I entered the service as a Substitute for Samuel Adams of Granville County North Carolina, for the term of three months in May 1781 under Col Wm. Gilland Stephen Merit, Captain, Thirdly, I entered the State legion October 11th, 1781 for the term of twelve months, in the place of Barnet Geter of Granville County and State aforesaid. And served until the 20th of May 1782, and then hired John Hix to serve the remainder of the tour and was bound for my faithful performance under Bennett Crafton Major and Samuel Jones as Captain."

In 1781 Gabriel joined the North Carolina State Legion under the command of Colonel Robert Smith. This unit was founded in August of 1781 by Brigadier General Rutherford. The regiment included both Infantry and Cavalry and it was styled similar to the regiment led by Lt. Colonel "Light Horse Harry" Lee of Virginia.

Sources: 1. Georgia Marriages to 1850. 2. Census 1800, 1820, and 1830. 3. U.S. Pensioners 1818-1872. 4. Pension Papers W7613.

****

John Peter Guyer age 11

John Guyer was born in March of 1765 in Franklin County, Pennsylvania and died on 24 May, 1854 in Franklin County, Pennsylvania. He married a woman named Elizabeth and they had eleven children.

John wrote in his pension application, *"I enlisted as a drummer for the term of twenty-one months, in the month of March in the year 1776 near Pittsburg in the company commanded by Captain Irwin in the regiment commanded by Colonel Miles in the line in the state of Pennsylvania."*

John's father Peter also enlisted in the 13th Pennsylvania State Rifle Regiment in Captain Irwin's Company under the command of Colonel Samuel Miles. The regiment was raised on 6 March, 1776 as a state militia regiment and later for service with the Continental Army.

Mary, the mother of John, accompanied them as a wash woman for the company. The family served for 21 months and were present at the battles of Fort Washington, Trenton, Princeton, Brandywine, and Germantown. At the Battle of Germantown Peter was wounded in the groin by a bayonet and shot in the leg. John was shot in the heel.

The Battle of Fort Washington was fought on 16 November, 1776 and was a British victory. At the Battle of Trenton, John and Peter Guyer crossed the Delaware River and helped to defeat the Hessians on 26 December, 1776. On 3 January, 1777 they helped Washington defeat the British at Princeton. The Battle at Brandywine was fought on 11 September, 1777 and was a British victory.

The Battle of Germantown was fought 4 October, 1777. The British victory ensured that Philadelphia would remain in the hands of General Howe for the winter. Unfortunately Washington's army would have to spend the harsh winter at Valley Forge. With John and Peter wounded and food and supplies scarce, it must have been a difficult march to Valley Forge. Due to Peter's two wounds, he was discharged and the family made the 140 mile trip back to their home.

John received a pension of $8.00 a month. His mother, not able to write, had someone write a letter in support of his getting a pension. She signed her name with an X.

Sources: 1. Federal Census of 1810, 1840, and 1850. 2. Book of American Revolutionary Soldiers, Archives 5th Ser. Vol 2. 3. Revolutionary War Rolls in Penn. 1775-1778. 4. Pension application for John Guyer S41567. 5. American Revolutionary Soldiers of Franklin County, Pennsylvania. 6. Sons of the American Revolution Membership Application. 7. Daughters of the American Revolution Magazine Vol. 46, Pennsylvania's patriotic Women during the Revolution.

****

John Gwin age 13

John Gwin was born in 1763 in Pennsylvania, and he died on 7 April, 1844 in Ohio. He married Mary Ammon at her father's house on 9 June, 1781. She received his pension of $8.00 a month. He enlisted as a drummer in 1776.

"I enlisted about 10 miles from Greensburgh in the State of Pennsylvania in the company commanded by Captain Cobe Sullivan which company was afterwards commanded by Captain Robert Vance in the thirteenth Virginia Regiment I think was afterwards called the ninth, I continued to serve in the said Corps in the service of the United States during the term of three years, or until about the twenty third day of December Seventeen hundred and seventy nine when I was discharged from service at Fort McIntosh in the State of Pennsylvania, I was in the battle of Brandywine, and served the whole of the above three years as a drummer, and on the Continental establishment."

The 13th Virginia Regiment was authorized on 16 September, 1776 and on 12 May, 1779 it was reorganized and became the 9th Virginia Regiment. At the Battle of Brandywine the regiment was under the command of Major General Nathanael Greene.

Source: 1. Pension Papers W7618.

****

Robert Hair age 14

Robert Hair was born on 9 May, 1763 in Brookfield, Massachusetts, and he died on 3 May, 1834 in Colrain, Massachusetts. He married Mary Keet around 1784.

He enlisted on 1 August, 1777 just weeks until his fifteenth birthday and he served in Captain Ralph Earll's Company in the Regiment commanded by Colonel Danforth Keyes for service in Rhode Island. At this time there was a threat to Rhode Island and 24 men from Oakham, Massachusetts answered the call and were expected to serve until 10 January, 1778. Robert answered the call, however, he deserted toward the end of October.

After Robert deserted, an advertisement appeared on 21 November, 1777 in the Massachusetts paper called the *Massachusetts Spy*. *"Deserted from my company in Col. Danforth Keyes regiment, Robert Hair, 5 ft high, belonging to Oakham in the County of Worcester. Whoever* *shall take up said deserter and confine him in some Goal in the state or return him to his regiment shall have $5.00 reward and all necessary charges paid by me. Ralph Earle, Capt."*

Robert returned to service because there was a receipt dated at Springfield on 9 November, 1782 which stated that Robert Hair had been accepted as a Continental Soldier for a term of three years from the town of Charlton.

The average desertion rate in the Continental Army was at 20 to 25 percent. In the latter years of the war the rate went down as the army became more professional. Punishments ranged to various number of lashes to death. The average penalty was 100 lashes.

Very few men deserted because of the fear of getting shot or killed. Cowards did not enlist in the first place. The soldier was serving with his friends and neighbors, and if he deserted how would he be able to face them back home? The deserter would also need to get family or friends to hide him from the people that would come looking for him.

So, what would cause the soldier to desert? Some did because they felt that military punishments in the camp were too harsh or unfair. Some officers would give up to 50 lashes for small and minor infractions. Most soldiers were farmers, so they might desert in the fall or spring because they were needed for planting at home. A failure to plant crops could lead to starvation for their families.

Since there was usually a signing bonus of one or more month's pay for enlisting, some men ran off to join another unit so that they could get the money. One dishonest man did this seven times and was hung for it.

Source: 1. Soldiers of Oakham, Massachusetts, in the Revolutionary War by Henry Parks Wright.

****

William Hallock age 13 or 14

William Hallock was born in 1764 in Stony Brook, New York, and he died on 11 April, 1817 in Derby, Connecticut. He married Ruth Hawkins on 7 October 1788. She was given a widow's pension of $20 a year based on one year of service. William served for five years.

The following pension statement was given by Ruth on 20 March, 1848.

"He entered the service at said Horseneck in the year 1777 as a private in a volunteer company of which Samuel Lockwood of the town of Greenwich was Captain. He served in said company during a period of five years or thereabouts, and while engaged therein, was taken prisoner by the British in a skirmish at said Horseneck and conveyed to the city of New York and confined in the Sugar House for a period of one year and two months, when his release was in some way effected."

The following statement was made by another prisoner by the name of Isaac Worden on 12 December, 1838, *"In prison he [William] slept in the company of Ebenezer Whilpley on a carpenters work bench turned bottom upward while in prison."*

Sources: 1. Year Book of the Connecticut Society of the Sons of the American Revolution for 1895 and 1896. 2. Pension Papers W25754.

****

Robert Hannah age 14

Robert Hannah was born on 1 April, 1761 in Charlotte, North Carolina, and he died 25 March, 1841 in Hale County, Alabama. He married (1) Mary Moore in 1783 and (2) Jane. According to the census he owned 9 slaves. Robert received a yearly pension of $186.66 for his service

"I entered the service of the United States as a volunteer in the year 1775 under Col. Neel against the Cherokee Indians and served in that tour about two months."

"I was then drafted in 1778 and marched again under the command of Col. Neel, Captain McAfee's Company to the State of Georgia on an expedition against the Cherokee Indians and Tories and served in that tour about three months. I was again drafted in 1779 and marched on to the Command of Col. Neel, Captain Sadler' Company on an expedition against the British to Orangeburg, Charleston and Stono and served about three months and dismissed shortly before the battle of Stono." In 1780 I was taken prisoner at home by the British, carried to Camden and lodged in Jail where I was kept eight weeks and then liberated by parole, but never was exchanged"

Robert was taken prisoner on 12 May, 1780, and he was later released from jail at the insistence of his father. When he was released on parole it meant that he promised not to take up arms again against the

British. It was not uncommon for soldiers on both sides to break parole and rejoin the war.

"I then volunteered and Joined Colonel Brattons Regiment and marched under the Command of Genl Sumter and fought at the battle of Fish dam Ford where the british were defeated and continued with Genl Sumter until the battle at Blackstock's and fought in said battle -- continued with Genl Sumter until the taking of Friday's Fort, then marched to Orangeburg under the command of Maj Wm Hanna and continued in the Army until the battle at the quarter-house where the British were again defeated. We then marched to Biggin Church and drove them in to Charleston and continued in the service until they evacuated Charleston. During the whole of his Service under the command of Genl Sumter in Colonel Bratton's Regiment, I served as a Lieutenant, by the appointment of Col Bratton which time was twelve months or more."

On 14 April, 1780 in Berkely County, South Carolina Robert Hanna and the rest of the regiment under the command of General Isaac Huger were involved with the Battle of Biggin Church. They were encamped in the area, and around three in the morning they were attacked by British troops and militia. The Americans managed to escape with little loss of life, however, they did lose large amounts of supplies and horses.

Robert was present at the Battle of Fishdam Ford on 9 November, 1780. General Sumter's men were warned of a possible British surprise attack. The officers had ordered the men to sleep with their weapons ready and to keep the fires burning. At one in the morning the British, under Colonel Twiggs, attacked the American pickets. Out of five shots fired by the pickets two of them hit Colonel Twiggs in the arm and leg.

General Sumter was in a deep sleep, and his orderly did not awaken him on the first alarm. The British party assigned to capture him were at his tent before the General could put on his coat. He ran out of his tent, leaped a fence, and escaped by the river bank. The British charged into camp, and they were blinded by the camp fires and paused. The American troops were ready and took careful aim and fired. After receiving heavy fire from the Americans the British began to fall back.

After the battle, a British surgeon was sent to the camp under a flag of truce to take care of the wounded troops left behind. He later reported that he had never seen so much injury done by so few troops in so short of time, since he had been in America.

The Battle of Blackstock's Farm was fought in South Carolina on 20 November, 1780. On the 18th hated British Lieutenant Colonel Banastre Tarleton and his Legion of Dragoons were bathing and watering their horses on the Broad River, when they were fired upon by some of General Sumter's militia. That night Tarleton put his men on flatboats and crossed the river in order to take the attack to the Americans. Tarleton had more than 800 British regulars under his command against the little larger number of militia. Tarleton had never been defeated so he probably was extremely confident about his chances, especially since he would be facing militia which had a history of running away in battle once shots were fired.

Sumter placed Colonel Henry Hampton and his South Carolina riflemen in the farm outbuildings. Other militiamen, including Robert Hanna, were placed behind fences and the surrounding woods. Later in the afternoon of the 20th Tarleton and his Dragoons engaged the militia in a frontal attack. Since he was so confident of success he did not wait for his infantry and artillery to catch up. The South Carolina militia did not run instead they held their ground and cut the charging dragoons to pieces. When the fighting ended the 270 dragoons had over 250 killed, wounded, or captured. After the battle it was reported that the road was blocked by dead and wounded British soldiers and horses. Not waiting for the British reinforcements to arrive the Americans slipped away during the night.

Tarleton had suffered his first defeat, and to make matters even worse it was at the hands of the militia. Although soundly defeated, Tarleton wrote in his battle report to Cornwallis that he had broken up and dispersed the Americans.

During the battle General Sumter was severely wounded, which turned out to be a stroke of luck for the Americans. With Sumter now out of action, General Washington gave the command to Nathanael Greene who was a superior strategist. Greene was now in command of the Southern Campaign, which in effect made him second-in-command of the entire Continental Army. With Greene now in command, the army enjoyed numerous victories in the south leading to the surrender of Cornwallis less than a year later.

Sources: 1. Census of 1790, 1810, 1820, and 1830. 2. Tombstone 3. Pension Roll of 1835. 4. Pension Papers S22290. 5. From Savannah to Yorktown: The American Revolution in the South by Henry Lumpkin.

****

William Hannaman age 14

William Hannaman was born on 14 November, 1763 in Cherry Valley, New York, and he died on 17 September, 1839 in Helt, Indiana. He married Mary Flesher on 11 October, 1788. William received a yearly pension of $20.

"I entered the service in the early part of the month of April 1778 when only turned of fourteen years old, as a volunteer for nine months, in Captain James Booth's Company of Virginia Militia. At the time I entered the service I was a resident of what was then called Augusta County in Virginia, now called Harrison County. I volunteered to keep Garrison at Nutter's Fort, on Elk Creek about a mile and a half above the town of Clarksburg in Virginia. This Fort was built for the purpose of protecting the Frontier against the Indians. I remained in the Fort and performed Garrison duty at Nutter's Fort until the fall or winter of the year 1778 until my term was expired. During this time I drew rations but received no other compensation. The Colonel of the Regiment to which Captain Booth's Company belonged was Colonel William Lowder. Colonel Lowder however never took command in actual service during the time of my service And in the Fort there was no other Captains or other superior officers in command except Captain Booth. Sometime in the year 1779 Captain Booth was killed by the Indians, while working in his cornfield. I who lived about three miles from where booth lived assisted in burying him."

Captain James Booth was killed on 16 June, 1778, while he and several soldiers were working in a cornfield near Coon's Fort. He was attacked by Indians and struck in the heart by an arrow. William Grundy was killed at the same time. Nathan Cochran, another soldier, was captured and held prisoner.

"I was also employed during the year 1781 in 1782 as an Indian Spy under the Orders of Colonel Lowder of Virginia. I served in the capacity of an Indian Spy during two seasons--about the Waters of the West fork of the Monongahela River in Virginia. My Tour of duty was to be out two days and to rest one day and night. I do not recollect how long I served as a spy--it was at least three months at a time in spring and summer of the years 1781 & 1782. I cannot state on oath to any particular length of time that I served as a Spy – but I served at different times, during the spring, summer and fall of the year '81 & '82, whenever I was called on--but is entirely unable to state the length of time. I served as a spy after

the end of the Revolution at different times & for these services I received $.83 a day."

On 11 November, 1833 William added this supplement to his pension request,

"I entered the service of the United States under the following named officers and served as herein stated. I entered the service early in the month of April in the year 1778 when about 14 years old as a volunteer for nine months in Captain James Booth's company of Virginia militia. At the time I entered the service I resided in the then County of Augusta, now Harrison County Virginia. I volunteered to keep Garrison at a Fort on Elk Creek called Nutter's Fort which stood about a mile and a half above Clarksburg in Virginia and was built for the protection of the frontiers against the Indians. I remained in this Fort and performed Garrison duty therein until my term of service was expired, which sometime in the fall or winter of the year 1778. During this time I received my Rations but had no other compensation. I never served with any Regular Soldiers, and is not acquainted with the names or rank of any of the Company or field officers of the Regulars. The Colonel of the Regiment to which Captain Booth's company belonged was Colonel William Lowder. Colonel Lowder never took command in actual service during my term of service, and in the Nutter's Fort there were no Captains or other superior officers in command excepting Captain Booth. Sometime in 1779 Captain Booth was killed by the Indians while at work on his farm. I assisted in burying him. I was also employed during the year 1781 and 1782 as an Indian Spy under the orders of Colonel Lowder of Virginia. I served as such for two seasons on the Waters of the West fork of the Monongahela River. My tour of duty was to be out two days and to rest one day and night. I do not recollect how long I served as a Spy, but it was at least three months during the spring and summer of each of the year 1781 and 1782. I cannot state precisely as to the length of time I served as a spy owing to my age and loss of memory excepting as follows. In the year 1781 I served not less than three months and in the year 1782 I served not less than three months. My service as a spy was as a volunteer. I also volunteered and served as an Indian Spy in the year 1782 or 1783 under Colonel George Jackson of Virginia. I cannot state precisely in which year but believes it to have been in the year 1783. Owing to my age and consequent loss of memory I cannot recollect the precise length that I served as a spy under Colonel Jackson except that it was not less than 3 months in one of the years 1782 or 1783."

Sources: 1. U.S. Pension Roll of 1835. 2. Roster of Soldiers & Patriots of the American Revolution Buried in Indiana. 3. Pension Papers S32299.

****

Abraham Haptonstall or Hapsonstall age 14

Abraham Haptonstall was born on 6 April 1761, in Orange County, New York, and he died on 22 October, 1847 in Knox County, Illinois. He married Rachel Margaret Price in 1784. He received a pension of $60 a year.

"I entered the service in the spring or the first part of the summer of 1775 volunteered in a company commanded by Captain Thomas Moffatt the Lieutenant's name was William Brady raised in Blooming grove Township Orange County State of New York for three months after the company was organized it was marched to a place on the east side of the North river called as I think Martneer's Rock and the company were there employed in building a small Fort situated a short distance above West Point, I served out my time and was honorably discharged."

"In the spring or first part of the Summer 1776 Phinehas Helms with whom I then lived was drafted to a tour of duty of three months in the county of Orange State of New York in the militia of that state I did that tour of duty for said Phinehas as a substitute under Captain Seth Martin Lieutenant William Bradley the company was marched to a notch in the Highlands called Stuts cove and were employed during the said notch or gap in the mountains on highlands in the state of New York to prevent the Tories from having any communication with the British Army and at the end of said three months I was discharged."

"Phinehas Helm was again called on to go by draft and I still living with him went for him as a substitute I think the draft was for six months with the scarcity of men required the men should be retained after their time expired. I was retained about three months as near as I can now recollect. I was in a company commanded by captain Thomas Moffet Lieutenant Samuel Strong was attached to a Regiment commanded by Colonel Nathaniel Woodhull and General James Clinton commanded this Brigade I think the draft was for six months but I was retained about nine months and after this service as aforesaid and I was discharged at Fort Montgomery."

"In the beginning of the summer of 1777 I was drafted in the Militia of the County of Orange State of were I resided for six months as

near as I can now remember, at first I marched on a tour to drive the Indians from the frontier. The tour was a very short one I was sent on to North River and stationed a short distance below Lings ferry for a few weeks two or three. I was ordered to West Point where I was stationed for a short time under the command of Captain Francis Smith. I was ordered to Fort Montgomery and was there again put under the command of Captain Francis Smith I was in the Battle of Fort Montgomery on the 6th of October 1777 when the British Army made its attack on the Fort and took it by storm after the battle I was taken sick with the measles and never again joined the army."

The Americans in Fort Montgomery were outnumbered 3 to 1, and they were bombarded throughout the day by British ships anchored in the Hudson River. Although the Americans lost the fort, they delayed the British long enough that the British were unable to aid General Burgoyne at Saratoga.

Sources: 1. Illinois Revolutionary War Veteran Burials 2. Pension Papers S32302.

****

Hezekiah Hardesty age 14

Hezekiah Hardesty was born on 2 September, 1763 in Talbot, Maryland, and he died in 1846 in Wabash, Illinois. He was married to Susannah Griffin on 20 March, 1784. He served in the 7th Battalion, 4th Company in the York County volunteers.

"I entered the service of the United states under Ensign Goodwin who was stationed at Atkinson's fort on the waters of the Monongahela in the state of Pennsylvania about the first of March 1778 as a substitute for John Hardesty and left the service about the first of April."

"I again entered the service of the United States under Captain Davis Owens regiment on command of Colonel McFarlan about the first of May 1778, I left the service about the first of May 1778, I left the service about the first of July after that I volunteered. I entered the service and marched to Jackson's Fort from there to the mouth of Grove creek there to the mouth of Fish creek then to the mouth of Fishing creek there up Fishing Creek and back to headquarters. Then to the head waters of Duncaid then across through the country to Fishing creek and up Fishing creek to the mouth of Grove creek & then to head quarters at Fort Jackson. I was acquainted no regular officers during this campaign."

"I again entered the service under Captain Ruble about the middle of October 1780 and left the same about the middle of November. After that I was a volunteer and marched to the mouth of Grove Creek on the Ohio River, thence to the mouth of Fish creek and then to the Ten Mile creek the place of my residence."

"I entered the service under Captain Cross General McIntosh about the first of September 1778 and left the said about the past of 1778. I was a substitute for Isaac Dcath as I now think. I marched to King Bottom on the Ohio river, then down the Ohio and crossed the same to little Beaver and back to Fort McIntosh."

"I again entered the service under General McIntosh about the first of April 1779 and left the same about the first of May. I was drafted from the place of my residence to fort McIntosh and then to Fort Lawrence."

"I again enter the service under Captain Joseph Bean & Colonel Crawford about the first of May 1782. I left the said about the first of June 1782 that I enlisted above, was a volunteer. I was in the battle of Crawford's defeat."

Hezekiah served a total of 10 months and received a yearly pension of $33.33. After the war he moved around a lot. He lived on Ten Mile Creek for two years after the war, and then he moved to Wheeling, Virginia. Two years later he moved to Columbus, Ohio one year later near Hamilton, Ohio, and then two years later to Bourbon County, Kentucky. Seven years later he moved to White Water, Ohio, and after five years he moved for the last time to Illinois to live with a son.

Sources: 1. Census of 1820 & 1840. 2. U.S. Pensioners 1818-1872. 3. Revolutionary War Soldiers Buried in Illinois. 4. Pension Papers S32296.

****

Thomas Hardy age 14

Thomas Hardy was born on 22 February, 1766 in Lunenburg, Virginia, and he died on 27 August, 1847 in Claiborne, Tennessee. He married Martha Cocke on 30 April, 1788 in Virginia. He received a yearly pension of $20 for his service.

"In the fall of the year 1781 I entered the Militia Service of the United States, as a substitute for John Hardy – under Captain William Ragsdale & Lieutenant Sterling Niblet, the name of the Ensign who

commanded in said Company I cannot recollect, I think that it was Overstreet Wyat. My field Officers when I entered the service were Colonel David Stokes and Major Anthony Street. I was enrolled at Lunenburg Courthouse – and marched from said County to Petersburg and from thence to James' River to a place called hog Island and during this tour of duty which was for three months I was engaged in marching to different points upon the North east side of James' River watching the movements of the British forces, and engaged in rearing & strengthening fortifications, but was engaged in no battle – and at the expiration of said three months service, I was honorably discharged."

"Afterwards in the year 1781 in the month of July the day of the month I cannot recollect in the County of Lunenburg in the State of Virginia I again entered the militia Service of the United States as a substitute for William Benford for three months under Captain Joseph Night, the name of the Lieutenant who commanded in said Company I cannot recollect, the Ensign who commanded in said Company was Baxter Petit Pool, the field officer commanding the Company when I entered it was Major John Overstreet, Colonel Lindsay commanded the Regiment afterwards. I was marched from Lunenburg Courthouse in the State of Virginia to Prince Edward Courthouse in the same State, from thence, down James River to point of fork or Pointy fork, from this I was marched in various directions as there was a demand until I was marched to Gloucester, and __?__ down to the __?__ of little York, where I remained until the surrender of Cornwallis in the month of October 1781. After the Surrender of Cornwallis I was marched to Richmond as one of the guard over the refugees – where I was honorably discharged in the month of October 1781."

Sources: 1. U.S. Pension Roll of 1835. 2. Pension Papers W361.

****

Jehiel Harmon age 14

Jehiel Harmon was born on 5 October, 1762 in Suffield, Connecticut, and he died on 3 March, 1845 in Winnebago County, Illinois. He married Betsey West on 5 May, 1801 in Suffield, Connecticut. He first enlisted to take the place of an older brother who was ill and had to leave the service. He received a pension of $38.12 a year for his service.

"In May 1777 I went under a draft from the militia to the State of New York. Benjamin Allen was Captain I served this tour three and a half

months. The next year 1778 I think in August I was drafted from the Militia I went to New London Ct. Returned to Honington Connt, where we were discharged we ___?__ But two or three days at New London there sailed to Hampton where we guarded the Point."

"In 1780 the first of August I think I was again drafted from the militia and ordered to New York to fill vacancies in the companies of the regular army. We were occupied in cowboys and guarding against them and the enemy. Lieut McDowel was the adjutant who deserted & was subsequently executed at Hartford before I was discharged."

Jehiel stated that in New York he guarded against the cowboys. Lieutenant Colonel James DeLancey was a leader of a band of New York Loyalists. Before the war James wanted to remain neutral. One day in 1776 a group of American patriots visited his home and stole one of his best horses and two sets of harnesses. This event caused him to give his support to the British. He and his men would raid homes taking supplies, and killing anyone that resisted. His men were referred to as "DeLancey's Cowboys" because they were horsemen and they would steal cows in order to supply the British troops stationed in Manhattan.

Sources: 1. Illinois Society DAR. 2. Tombstone 3. U.S. Pension Roll of 1835. 4. Pension Papers W25759.

****

Joseph Harper age 14

Joseph Harper was born on 18 August, 1762 in Oakham, Massachusetts, and he died in May of 1820 in Ohio. He married Abigail Bacon on 13 December, 1781. He enlisted in the army nearly three weeks before his 15th birthday. His older brother Robert also served at various times.

He served in Rhode Island as a private in Captain Earll's Company in the Regiment commanded by Colonel Keyes's from 1 August, 1777 until 4 January, 1778. He was part of a 1,500 man army organized because of the threat to Rhode Island.

From 30 March to 2 July, 1778 he was in Captain Thomas Whipple's Company of guards at Rutland. He was sent with several men that were either too young or too old for regular duty. On 2 August, 1778 he enlisted in Captain Gilbert's Company in the Regiment commanded by Colonel Josiah Whitney for a term of one month in Rhode Island. This enlistment was due to the alarm of a possible attack on Rhode Island. Joseph was part of 554 men called out to join General Sullivan. When Joseph enlisted in the Continental Army for six months on 7 July, 1780, he was listed as 5 feet 8 inches tall and with a dark complexion.

Source: 1. Soldiers of Oakham, Massachusetts, in the Revolutionary War by Henry Parks Wright.

****

John Harrington age 13

John Harrington was born on 8 February, 1764 in Poughkeepsie, New York, and he died 9 November, 1841 in Ohio. He stated in his pension application that he enlisted the year that Fort Anne was taken, which would place his enlistment after 8 July, 1777.

John served for less than six months under McGee's Company with Colonel Henry Livingston's 3rd Regiment of New York Levies. Lieutenant Colonel Henry Brockholst Livingston led the 3rd Regiment from 1775 to 1777.

The pension application for John Harrington was rejected, because he served less than 6 months. The rejection letter indicated that the affidavit, from Hannah Landon, attesting to his additional service time was rejected because, "....*no woman being considered as a competent witness as to military service.*"

Sources: U.S. Headstone Applications for Military Veterans. 2. Pension Papers R4640.

****

Ebenezer Hart age 14

Ebenezer Hart was born on 21 November, 1762 in Lynnfield, Massachusetts and he died on 26 March, 1840 in Lynn, Massachusetts. He married Polly on 25 October, 1792. He enlisted on 15 February, 1777 and served until 1783. According to a letter from the War Department in was a Sargent. He received a yearly pension of $80.

"*In the beginning of the year 1777 I enlisted as a private in Capt. Ebenezer Winship's Company in Col. Rufus Putnam's 5th Mass'tts Regim't. in Gen. Nixon's Brigade to serve during the War, and did serve six years and till the 12th June A.D. 1783 when I was discharged at Newburg by Col. Cobb and Maj. Burnham.*"

The Battle of Saratoga, 19 September to 7 October, 1777 was the only battle Ebenezer Hart participated in. He was a part of the 5th Massachusetts on the American right wing under the command of General John Nixon.

Sources: 1. Massachusetts Town birth Records 1620-1850. 2. Sons of the American Revolution Applications. 3. Tombstone 4. Pension Papers W14852.

****

Henry Hart age14

Henry Hart was born on 22 December, 1763 in Edgecombe County, North Carolina, and he died on 21 July, 1840 in Greene County, Alabama. He married Martha Smith on 17 October, 1827. Martha was refused a widow's pension, because she could not prove they were married and had no proof of Henry's service in South Carolina.

Henry entered the service in the month of May 1778 in the State of South Carolina. He served under Colonel James Screven, and he was stationed at the Savannah River until his enlistment was up in July of 1778. A few days after he was home the militia called him out again.

"I joined the Continental soldiers of the under the command of General Lincoln Colonel Scirvin and Major Sheppard of their part, I also joined there the French Army under the command of Count d'Estaing, in a few days we were put in action, to wit, the Town of Savannah was then in possession of the British, us with the Army's was placed with the French Army in their entrenchments as they were then throwing up their breastworks to storm the Town, in one night and kept up a regular firing and bombarding all night there was both French and Americans killed & wounded. They the French and Americans continued to keep up the siege for three weeks but I after the first night's action, was always kept at Picket guard and was not in the engagement and states that this battle."

The British deserted the town, and Henry was discharged about the middle of September. He was called out again about two weeks later and joined in scouting parties annoying the Tories. Toward the end of winter he was discharged, and he returned home. Later, in the spring he was called out again, and this time he joined a horse troop.

"...on the 7th of August of that year we went lower down in the district and on the same day we overtook two Tories and one of them was killed, we kept the other until the night after being camped, we were fired on by

a company of Tories and all killed but 15, my Captain was not killed but acted the coward & we left him being just 30 in number, 15 was left, me with a few others returned home and we were so few in number we were occasionally under Captain Vince, during the fall of 1779, and when without a Captain scouted about the best we could, not being able to collect any more men, we were likewise frequently taken under the command of Captain Joshua Inman from Augusta Georgia as my services required ___? ___ we were able after a while to collect a few more men and chose a Captain of our own making who was not a commissioned officer, name not recollected, and kept up a small scouting party for that year in 1780 and until the British evacuated Charleston, and I finally after all operations of Revolution was ceased went home which was, I believe, in November 1782."

Sources: 1. U.S. Pension Roll of 1835. 2. Census of 1830 and 1840. 3. Alabama Revolutionary War Soldiers. 4. Virginia Marriages 1740-1850. Pension Papers R4699.

****

Lowden Harwell age 13

Lowden Harwell was born on 13 May, 1765 in Brunswick County, Virginia, and he died in 1838 in Marlboro, South Carolina. He married Mary Hodge. He stated in his pension application that he joined the army at the age of 13. His pension application was rejected, because he could not prove his service under Colonel Washington. Without that proof he did not serve enough time to qualify for a pension.

"I entered the service as a volunteer under Capt Jacob Duck, in a light horse company raised by Col Philip Allston & before Col P. Allston had completed his Regiment we were attacked at Colonel Allston's own house by the Tories commanded by Col Fanning in which engagement the Americans were defeated."

One night Colonel Fanning had stayed at the home of another Tory and friend, Kenneth Black. The next morning Fanning left and Kenneth Black accompanied him a few miles serving as a guide. On the way back home Black saw Colonel Alston and his men, so he tried to escape from them. Colonel Alston's men caught him and, while begging for his life, they smashed Black's head with their rifle butts. The next day Colonel Fanning was at Black's home when the dead man's wife informed Fanning what had happened to her husband. Colonel Fanning wanted vengeance so he gathered his men to attack Colonel Alston at his home.

Early Sunday morning on 29 July, 1781 Fanning captured two guards outside the Alston home. Two other guards woke up and sounded the alarm warning Lowden Harwell and the rest of the men who were asleep on the porch. The Patriots barricaded themselves inside the house and Colonel Alston protected his children by standing them up on a small table inside the brick fireplace.

The Tories were under heavy fire and attempts to charge the house resulted in several men receiving wounds. The men pulled an oxcart from the barn, filled it with hay, and then set it on fire. The plan was to roll it next to the house and burn it down.

Colonel Alston knew that his time was up and decided to surrender. His wife, Temperance, asked that her husband allow her to conduct the surrender. They both felt if the Colonel was to walk outside he would be shot. She carried a white flag outside, and when Fanning saw it he asked her to meet him half way. Temperance faced Fanning and said that they would surrender as long as no one was harmed, otherwise they would continue to fight. Fanning agreed and he kept his word to her and no one was harmed. The Patriots surrendered and were immediately paroled. Colonel Alston sent Lowden and the rest of the men home and told them to rest until the next time they were needed.

"I remained with Capt Duck in Col Allstons Regiment about three months, then volunteered in Maj Cages Company Genl Butler commanding: I then returned to Chatham Court House N. Ca. & entered Col Washington's Troop, under Capt Wm. Gouldson as a substitute in place of Charles Newton a regular soldier, during the time I was in Col Washington's Troop & soon after I entered the Troop, we attacked the Tories in N. Ca. (at what place I do not now recollect) commanded by Col McDugald in which engagement the Tories were defeated & nearly all killed, then we marched to Fayetteville N. Ca. from thence to Newbern where we remained a short time from thence we marched to Petersburg Virginia where we were stationed about a month, from thence Col Washington marched his Troop near the confluence of the Roanoke & Maherrin rivers, then I obtained a furlough to go home for a short time, but I did not remain home a half hour, but immediately joined Maj Cages company Genl Butler commanding officer: & soon after that the Americans under Col Mayburn attacked the Tories commanded by Cols McNeill & Fanning at Lindleys Mill on cane Creek near Haw river, in said engagement the Tories were defeated and a great many killed, then we pursued the same company of Tories towards Wilmington N. Ca. met with

the British & Tories at a place called the Brown Marsh near Wilmington the British & Tories attacked the Americans in the night, but were defeated with some loss, we then pursued them down to Wilmington but on our arrival in Wilmington we found that the British & Tories had embarked on the British Ships & sailed off, we (the Americans) then took the American prisoners, whom the British had left in Wilmington & carried them to Hillsboro N. Ca, I then went back to Colonel Washington's Troop, remained a short time & the term for which I had substituted as a regular Soldier expired, then received a discharge from Colonel Washington."

The Battle of Lindley's Mill occurred on 13 September, 1781. The Tories under the command of Colonel David Fanning captured North Carolina Governor Thomas Burke and 13 high-ranking officials on 12 September. Lowden Harwell was one of 300 men under General Butler who set an ambush at Lindley's Mill the next day.

When the Tories approached the Patriots, they sprung their trap. The battle raged for four hours until the Patriots, outnumbered 2 to 1, were forced to retreat due to mounting casualties. During the battle, Tory leader Colonel McNeill and Patriot Colonel Nall met in single combat. They each fired at the same instant and killed each other. This battle closed the war in North Carolina. One month later General Cornwallis would surrender his army ending the war.

"In the year 1778 Three months as a volunteer private under Captain Jacob Duck. In the year 1778 three months as a private in a company of mounted militia men commanded by Major Cage – raised for the pursuing the British & Tories in N. Ca. where ever their presence might be necessary. From this time to the year 1783 I served as a substitute in Colonel Washington's Troops. I believe that Washington's Troops belonged to the United States Army. If they did – I cannot prove my service by two witnesses as required. All those persons who could be of any Service to me as witnesses are either dead or live at such distances from me that I cannot avail myself of their testimony."

Sources: 1. Revolutionary Incidents and Sketches of Character: Chiefly in the "Old North State" by Eli Washington Caruthers. 2. U.S. and International Marriage Records 1560-1900. 3. Pension Papers R4718.

****

Stephen Haskell age 14

Stephen Haskell was born on 11 April, 1763 in Essex, Massachusetts, and he died on 21 February, 1847 in Dudley, Massachusetts. He married Rachel Larned on 15 May, 1785.

"I enlisted in the army of the United States as early as the year 1777 or 178 [it was later determined that he enlisted on 11 June, 1777] *with Alpheus Bowers of Thompson in the County of Windham and State of Connecticut and served as follows under the following officers. In the month of June I enlisted in the town of Woodstock in Said County and State into the company commanded by Captain John Kies of Ashford and Colonel Eleys Regiment of the County of Windham and State of Connecticut for six months. After joining the company we marched to Fort Griswold and remained there in actual service two months and were then sent on an Expedition to Newport Rhode Island and on being remanded to New London we were ordered to New York where our Colonel Eli was taken prisoner on the Sound during the winter. This being was the close of my first six months service."*

Colonel Ely was a well-known physician who raised a regiment of regular troops. He was captured by the British on 9 December, 1777, while with his Regiment on a ship crossing the sound from Connecticut to Long Island. His Regiment, along with other Continental forces were going to attack the British.

"I did not enlist again until 1779 under Captain Webb of Windham County State of Connecticut for six months more served as follows. From the said town of Woodstock I joined my company and marched to New London and began actual service there and in a short time were ordered to head quarters at Robersons plains below West Point and in the month of September 1779 we marched to New Jersey being in actual service all the time and went into winter quarters at Morristown when we were dismissed."

Stephen enlisted one last time in 1780 for one year. He was in Colonel Rand's Regiment, and he served in Long Island and West Point. Toward the end of his service he served in Virginia.

Sources: 1. The Ely Ancestry by Beach and Ely, 1902. 2. Sons of the American Revolution Application. 3. Pension Papers S29859.

****

Herman Hatch age 13

Herman Hatch was born on 14 June, 1766 in Tolland, Connecticut, and he died on 14 September, 1842 in Newark, New Jersey. He received a yearly pension of $80.

"In the month of December in A.D. year 1780. I enlisted into the service of the United States for three years at the town of Willington in the State of Connecticut. Sometime in the month of April 1781 I joined the American army at Connecticut. On the Hudson River in the state of New York in the company commanded by Captain Walker in the third Regiment of the Connecticut Line commanded by Colonel Samuel Webb. I continued to serve until sometime in the month of Oct 1783."

Sources: 1. D.A.R. Lineage Book, Vol. 20. 2. Sons of the American Revolution Application. 3. Pension Papers S34393.

****

Jeremiah Hatch age 14

Jeremiah Hatch was born on 25 September, 1766 in Oblong, New York, and he died on 23 May, 1851 in Iowa. He married Elizabeth Haight on 23 November, 1789. He enlisted on 10 April, 1781, which was five months until his 15th birthday. He received a yearly pension of $88.

His father Nathaniel was in the army, and he died of smallpox on 3 July, 1776. Jeremiah, who had six brothers and sisters, was bound out to a miller for five years. One day his master, who did not treat Jeremiah very kindly, sent him to the mill with a sack of grain. On the way to the mill Jeremiah met an army recruiting officer. The man convinced Jeremiah to leave the mean man he was bound to and join the army.

Jeremiah was too young to enlist so he lied about his age, saying he was 17. He also gave the name of a different town as his place of residence. The recruiter probably knew he was too young and encouraged him to give the false information. He enlisted, and it was reported that he stood 5 feet tall with dark complexion and eyes. He listed his occupation as a laborer and his place of residence as Topsfield. He became a fifer in the Company commanded by Captain Tisdale and in the 3rd Massachusetts Regiment commanded by Colonel Greaton.

"I was a Musician in Captain Tisdale or Woodbridge's Company and the third regiment of the Massachusetts Line."

After the war Jeremiah was given the title of Captain and placed in command of a militia company in his hometown. Jeremiah was a Mormon, and in 1846 when the Mormons in the area began to migrate west, Jeremiah and his family decided to go with them. Before the family could leave they were robbed and forced out of their home. They escaped in an open wagon and eventually made it to Nebraska. Jeremiah's wife died there on 17 December, 1847, and Jeremiah died there in May of 1852. The remainder of his family reached Utah in 1852.

Sources: 1. Willing Hands, a Biography of Lorenzo Hill Hatch 1826-1910 by Jo Ann R. Hatch. 2. Sons of the American Revolution Application. 3. Pension Papers S18007.

****

Jacob Hauser age 12

Jacob Hauser was born on 1 August, 1765 in Brussels, Germany. His pension was rejected, because he needed a more detailed account of his service.

"In the month of September or October in the year 1777 at Herkimer in the State of New York I was enrolled in the Militia, into the company of Captain Frederick Getman belonging to the regiment of Col Peter Bellinger—Frederick Bellinger was Lieut Colo in said regiment. I was call out into service & was stationed at Fort Herkimer in the state aforesaid, when I was taken prisoner by the Indians. This was in the month of July or August in the year 1778. I was taken to Niagara & then to Canada. I was with the Indians four years & nine months & then ran away. My father killed by the Indians at Herkimer aforesaid, in 1779 in July, & scalped. My brother was taken prisoner at the same time. The Indians took my fathers scalp to Canada, with my brother & then exhibited to me the scalp of my father & told me I would see my father again—They put the scalp upon the top of a staff & held it up at me. I was tomahawked by the Indians thrice times. The scars are now visible on my head. This was at Cayuga Lake. I then ran the gauntlet, as it was called, thrice times."

Many Native American historians say that scalping was not a New England tribal practice before contact with Europeans. It became a retaliatory act against the colonists. The colonies had offered scalp bounty as early as 1688. Massachusetts Bay Colony offered up to $60 for a Native American scalp. In Salem redeemed scalps hung along the walls of the town courthouse until 1785.

Scalping was a painful experience but did not always cause death. Nicholas Bovie was shot, tomahawked, and scalped by the Indians at Fort Stanwix in 1777. He recovered enough to return to duty and earned the nickname "Scalped Nick."

Many times Indian tribes had their male captives run the gauntlet. A large number of Squaws and Indian boys would line up in two rows and the captive was forced to run between them. The distance they had to run would vary with the size of the tribe. As the captive ran the Indians would beat him with sticks, clubs, or anything handy. Sometimes the captive would be killed before he reached the end.

"The men of my camp were out __?__, & __?__ from the main part and filled with __?__. I ran away from the Indians in the month of December 1784 with a young lady from Virginia who had been with the Indians about two years by the name of Betsey Jones—Her sister had married a British officer by the name of David Service who resided at Niagara. We took a horse, a saddle, a bridle from the Indians. The young lady rode behind me upon the horse. I left the lady at her sisters Mrs. Service. I was retaken by the Indians & taken to Johnstown. I got the Indians drunk with liquor which I purchased with the money I received for the horse which I took from the Indians & had sold. I was retaken again & taken to the two mile creek—I again got the Indians drunk & made my escape."

"I crossed the Niagara River & went into the country until Spring—In the spring I happen to come in Contact with the Indian Chief whose prisoner I had been & was then delivered up as a prisoner of war to Colo Aaron Hayat—I remained at Niagara about one year & was a waiter for Samuel Shut—Colo Hayat gave me a pass & I came home to Herkimer by the way of Lake Ontario & Oswego. I was gone from home six years & nine months."

Sources: 1. The Bloodied Mohawk: The American Revolution in the Words of Fort Planks Defenders and Other Mohawk Valley Partisans by Kenneth D. Johnson. 2. Pension Papers R4754. 3. Captured by the Indians: 15 Firsthand Accounts, 1750-1870 by Frederick Drimmer

****

Andrew Hauver age 11

Andrew Hauver was born on 24 December, 1764 in Palatine, New York, and he died on 6 July, 1848 Chenango, New York. He married

Catherine Pulver on 8 April, 1787 in New York. His pension was rejected, because the pension office said that guard duty on the banks of the Hudson was not military duty and even if it was so, he was too young to serve. Andrew enlisted on 1 April, 1776 at the age of 11. A letter protesting the decision was written by a friend. However, the decision stood.

"I first entered the service as a Volunteer in the Militia in the year 1776. The company was divided into classes one of which class was constantly on duty and I was out as a "Guard" as often as two nights in each week for a period of three years with the exception of one month in the fall of 1178, when I volunteered as a substitute for John Moule in a company commanded by Lieutenant Jeremiah Miller, in Colonel Hendrick Van Rensselaer's Regiment, General Robert Van Rensselaer in the expedition up the Mohawk Valley. This expedition was commenced in September 1778 and I did duty as a private in said company for one month."

Sources: 1. Census 1820, 1830, & 1840. 2. Sons of the American Revolution Application. 3. Tombstone 4. Pension Papers R4755. 5. The Bloodied Mohawk: The American Revolution in the Words of Fort Planks Defenders and Other Mohawk Valley Partisans by Kenneth D. Johnson.

****

Christopher Hawkins age 13

Christopher Hawkins was born on 8 June, 1764 in North Providence, Rhode Island. He died on 25 February, 1837 in Newport, New York. He died of dropsical consumption while sitting in his chair. He married Dorcas Whipple and they had 7 children.

Christopher came from a large and poor family. At the age of 12 he was an indentured apprentice to the farmer Aaron Mason. In May 1777 he ran away from the farm and signed up on an American privateer schooner called the *Eagle*. He was made the cabin boy by the ship's commander, Captain Potter. The *Eagle* was a small schooner with 12 small carriage guns looking for British ships sailing between New York and England. She sailed all the way to the English coast, and since she did not see any ships to capture she headed back home. Nearing New York the *Eagle* encountered a storm and nearly sunk. She was then overtaken by a 20 gun British ship called the *Sphynx* and was captured.

After taken prisoner, Christopher was taken to New York and placed on board the prison ship the *Asia* that was anchored in the East

River. After three weeks Christopher was taken off the prison ship, and he was placed on board the 28 gun ship the *Maidstone*. For the next 18 months he served as a waiter for various British officers.

Christopher began to earn the trust of the officers and, when he and another boy were sent ashore in New York with a message, Christopher found the opportunity to escape and he took it. By November 1778 he had made his way back home to Providence. He remained in the service of Obadiah Olney of Smithfield for the next 2 or 3 years, until the urge to go to sea overcame him.

He went to Providence where he joined a 16 gun privateer brig commanded by Captain Whipple. On the fifth day at sea the vessel was captured, and Christopher again found himself a prisoner of the British. Again, he was taken to New York and this time placed aboard the infamous prison ship *Jersey*.

"My allowance of food was limited, and what I had was of the worst description, and utterly unfit for a human being. My drink was blackish water taken from the sides of the ship, where all the filth and refuse was thrown. Biscuits, eaten by weevils, through and through; bread sour, and often covered with mold; meet, discolored and petrified by age, and through which myriads of maggots leaped about in play; these constituted my daily fare."

In October 1781 Hawkins and a shipmate, William Waterman, devised a plan to escape. In the lower decks where there were no guards, there were gun ports secured by iron bars. The two boys got an old axe and a crow-bar, and during a heavy thunderstorm they worked the bars loose from one of the port-holes. The boys were let down the side of the ship with the aid of another prisoner using a rope. When the two boys reached the water they parted company and swam away.

"I kept along close to the side of the ship until I gained the stern, and then left the ship. This was all done very slowly, sinking my body as deep in the water as possible, without stopping my course, until I was at such a distance from her that my motions in the water would not create attention from those on board. After gaining a suitable distance from the ship, I hailed Waterman three times. He did not answer me. I have never seen him since he left the Old Jersey to this day."

After three hours of swimming Christopher reached land, cold, and nearly exhausted. After hiding out for several days, he received help from a family of farmers. They provided him with food and clothes. A day or two later he left the family and was arrested at Oyster Bay by a band of refugees. They decided to take him back to the prison ship in New York. Fortunately, Hawkins was able to escape from them, and he finally made his way back home.

Sources: 1. The Life and Adventures of Christopher Hawkins; a Prisoner on board the "Old Jersey" Prison Ship during the War of the Revolution, by Christopher Hawkins. 2. Tombstone. 3. In Pursuit of Liberty Coming of Age in the American Revolution by Emmy E. Werner. 4. U.S. Pensioners 1818-1872.

****

Samuel Hawkins age 14

Samuel Hawkins was born on 4 June, 1762 in New Haven, Connecticut, and he died on 7 July, 1840 in New Haven. He married Hannah French on 2 December, 1782 in New Haven. He received a yearly pension of $44.10 for his service.

"I enlisted I think in October 1776 under Capt Daniel Holbrook for 6 months into a Company of Continental State Troops. Radford Whiting was Lieutenant of said Company & the Ensign was from the town of Milford but his name is not remembered. In this tour I served at Stamford New Field & Milford acting as guard & a Regiment having been assembled at New Haven we were then discharged."

"In September 1777 I was drafted for one month duty & was sent to a place called Oyster River between Milford and New Haven where I was joined by about 30 under the command of Lieutenant Radford Whiting with whom I served out said time. Previous to this the same year as I believe in June & July I was detached to serve as a guard over Continental Stores deposited at a place in Derby ever since called Park Hallow & over a number of prisoners confined in the town house in said Derby taken by Reuben Tucker & others. I was in this service about two months."

"At the alarm of the British landing at New Haven in July 1779 I turned out to oppose them acting under Capt Daniel Halbrook & meeting the British on the hill below New Haven fought them tile they entend & left the town & then proceeded to Fairfield where I again met the enemy. I remember that there Richard Mansfield was wounded in the neck near to me. I was this engaged about one week."

Samuel was among over 1,000 militia men who opposed the British when they landed at New Haven in July of 1779. British Major General Tryon and 2,600 troops were brought to New Haven by the British fleet. The troops began to destroy public stores, ships in the harbor, and seizing the town's armaments. The gathering militia, intense heat, and the abundance of seized liquor the British troops were consuming forced General Tyron to leave.

British General Garth sent a dispatch to General Henry Clinton that read: *"Dear Sir--We have had a little difficulty with the rebels in coming hither, but I hop the loss is not much. The troops are greatly fatigued through heat....the enemy are following us with cannon and heavier than what we have."*

"I was called up in the night on alarm & marched to the Rasatonie River about a mile & then to Strafford I remember one night seeing a boat from which all in it fled to the woods & escaped which having brought to Derby was sold for the public benefit."

Sources: 1. 6th Report of the National Society of the DAR Oct. 11, 1902. 2. Connecticut Town Birth Records pre 1870. 3. U.S. Pensioners 1818-1872. 4. Pension Papers W13387. 5. The British Invasion of New Haven, Connecticut: Together with Some Account of Their Landing and Burning of the Towns of Fairfield and Norwalk July 1779 by Charles Hervey Townsend.

****

William Hawkins age 14

William Hawkins was born on 30 June, 1764 in Rockbridge County, Virginia, and he died after 1839. He married a woman named Elizabeth. He received a yearly pension of $20 for his service.

"I was born on the 30th day of June in the year 1764 in the County of Rockbridge State of Virginia -- my first tour of duty was in the capacity of a pack-horse man for the Army under the command of Genl McIntosh who in the fall of 1778 marched against the North-western Indians -- my then extreme youth prevents me recollecting the precise day or even month upon which that tour of Duty was performed."

"In the fall of 1780 Col George Skillern at the town of Fincastle Botetourt County Virginia called for volunteers I Volunteered under Capt James Robinson and under his command marched through the Country watered by the rivers Dan and Smith crossing both to old Hosier town

North Carolina where Major Campbell met and took the Command of the Company in which I was – marched through Salem to the Yadkin River, crossed it to Salisbury from there to Fifers in the State of North Carolina. Joined the Army under General Morgan at or near a place called Ran Sower's Mill from thence marched to Salisbury North Carolina – from thence to Guilford Courthouse in February 1781 was discharged the written evidence of which is lost."

"I returned to Botetourt -- in August 1781 became a substitute for one Robert Harvey in a Company commanded by one Capt John Galaway rendezvoused at Burrill's mill 2 ½ miles below Williamsburg Va Joined a Regiment of riflemen commanded by Col Samuel Lewis marched to Yorktown Va there joined the Army under Genl Washington there continued and participated in the siege and capture of Lord Cornwallis after the consummation of which as one of the Guards went with the English prisoners 100 miles towards Winchester but before reaching that place received from Major Patrick Lockhart a written discharge which I have since lost."

Sources: 1. U.S. Pension Roll of 1835. 2. Pension Papers S6960.

****

Benjamin Hayward age 14

Benjamin Hayward was born on 3 April, 1767 in Bridgewater, Massachusetts, and he died on 26 November, 1795 in Stockton, New York. He married Hannah Way on 23 July, 1787 in New York. She received a widow's yearly pension of $88.

Benjamin enlisted on 24 April, 1781 and served as a fifer in Patterson's Brigade of the 1st Massachusetts Line. In his pension application his wife mentions that he served with Robert Shurtleff. This was the name used by Deborah Sampson when she disguised herself as a man and served in the army for a year and a half. She was the only female soldier that received a pension.

Sources: 1. Sons of the American Revolution Application. 2. Pension Papers W19649. 3. D.A.R. Lineage Book, Vol 33, 1900.

****

James Head age 13

James Head was born in December of 1767 in Grandville County, North Carolina, and died 27 October, 1851 in South Carolina. His father also served with him in the war. In the 1820 census he owned twenty-one slaves, and in the 1830 census the number of slaves was reduced to seven.

He first entered the service in 1780, *"I entered at an early age in October 1780 in Spartanburg District the place my father moved from North Carolina. I served under Lt. Miles of Capt Ford's company in Col. Roebucks regiment. Went with Lt. Miles to the frontier on Green River and served continued for three months to keep check in the Indians."*

James became ill with smallpox and returned home the first part of 1781. Once recovered he joined his old regiment and went on scouting parties into North Carolina. After his enlistment was up in the summer of 1781, he served several three month tours in 1781 and 1782.

His pension claim was rejected, because two men that testified to his service were sent letters to be certified and they never responded back. Being underage did not help his case, because the pension administration said he would not have been called out. He also was not listed on the payrolls. It is possible that his father was given his pay and there was no need to list James on the rolls.

Sources: 1. Pension papers R4814. 2. Census of 1820 and 1830. 3. Obituary from the Edgefield Advertiser 11 March, 1852.

****

James W. Head age 13

James Head was born in July 1766 in Massachusetts, and died after 1855. According to his brother John's affidavit to support his brother's claim for a pension, the Purser of the frigate *Queen of France* Samuel Wall *"frequently visited my father's family and urged my parents to let brother James go the cruise with them and promised of they would consent he should have an office when they got to sea."*

"I enlisted at Boston as midshipman of twenty guns commanded by Captain Rathburn in Oct. AD 1779 and sailed in November of that year and cruised on the coast of Bermuda and went into Charlestown South Carolina in December and lay there in company with the ship Providence commanded Whipple, ship Boston Captain Tucker & ship Ranger all U.S.

vessels and all surrendered to the British in May 1780. After the close of the war I removed to Warren where I now live."

James wrote a further account of his service in 1855. *"I was on board the American armed ship Queen of France commanded by Captain Rathburn—Enlisted in Boston—sailed shortly after in company with other armed vessels for Charleston South Carolina, where we arrived Commodore Whipple commanded the fleet, at Charlestown we were landed to man the Forts. The troops were under command of Genl Lincoln. I was present and engaged in the siege of Charleston and captured with the American Army—returned to Providence in a cartel and discharged in June 1780."*

James's brother, John, gave more information of the siege in his affidavit, *"The Queen of France there sunk to prevent the British fleet coming up the channel. The officers and crew were placed in the fort under the command of command of General Lincoln. The fort was taken by the British after a sever bombardment."* John went on to state that James was deaf in one ear when he returned home and was not deaf when he joined the navy.

More than 5,000 Americans troops were captured at Charleston, including General Benjamin Lincoln and Commodore Abraham Whipple. James Head was captured and returned home in a cartel (prisoner exchange) a few weeks after his capture. James received a yearly pension of $45.66. His rate or capacity on the vessel's payroll was listed as "Boy". His pension was granted at the rate of "Seaman".

Source: 1. Pension Papers S19326.

****

William Heath age 14

William Heath was born on 1 September, 1674 in Hampstead, New Hampshire, and he died on 6 September, 1840 in Mount Desert, Maine. He received a yearly pension of $80 and 100 acres of land for his service. He served for four years in the New Hampshire line. For some reason his claim was placed in a rejection jacket and never taken out. His statement in the application was extremely brief, and he furnished no proof and yet his application was accepted.

"In the month of June 1779 I enlisted in the Revolutionary War for four years During the War In David McGregore's company Col Scammell Regiment."

William served in the 3rd New Hampshire Regiment under Colonel Alexander Scammell and may have been present for the Battle of Newtown on 29 August, 1779. This regiment was the third of three regiments raised by the state of New Hampshire.

Sources: 1. Pension Papers R4831. 2. Lineage Book D.A.R. Vol. XXX, 1899. 3. U.S. Pensioners 1818-1872.

****

Hallam Hempstead age 14

Hallam Hempstead was born on 1 June, 1763 in New London, Connecticut, and died on 25 July, 1833 in Portsmouth, Ohio. He enlisted in May 1777 just before his 15th birthday. His brother Daniel, who was 7 years older, died on the prison ship *Jersey* in 1781. His other older brother Samuel was lame from a wound suffered in battle. Hallam enlisted in the 1st Company of the 3rd Regiment of the Connecticut Militia.

Sources: 1. Tombstone 2. Headstone Applications. 3. D.A.R. Lineage Book, Vol. 125.

****

Frederick Hesser age 13

Frederick Hesser was born on 6 July 1763 in Philadelphia County, Pennsylvania, and he died in 1851 in Schuylkill County, Pennsylvania. He received a yearly pension of $33.13.

"I entered the service in the month of September 1776 at the Trap [Trappe] *in the county of Philadelphia (now Montgomery) under the command of Captain Andrew Redheffer Lieutenants Schlaughter and Dull Ensign Peacock Major in the Regiment commanded by Colonel John Moore Lieutenant Colonel George Smith Major Solomon Bush. I enlisted into the service in said company as a drummer and marched from the Trap to Amboy in the State of New Jersey from thence I marched with the regiment about eighteen miles to Staten Island where there was a slight skirmish with the Hessians. I returned with the regiment to Amboy from thence I marched with my company to Elizabeth Town thence to Newark after sometime I marched to Fort Lee where I remained until Fort Lee was evacuated by the American troops* [19 November, 1776]. *I was not*

engaged in any battle during this time. The term for which I enlisted was three months but in consequence of my becoming sick was permitted to return home two or three weeks before the expiration of that term."

"I again entered the service as a drummer in the spring following as a substitute. I marched from the Trap to Bristol from thence after some I marched with my regiment to Coryells Ferry then crossed the Delaware into New Jersey then to Prince Town New Brunswick crossed the bridges over the Raritan River past Amboy to Woodbridge then to Quibbletown. The regiment there lay within about two miles of the place where the battle was fought between the American Army under the command of General Sterling and the British and we could distinctly hear the firing. From thence I marched with my regiment to join the American Army then encamped at Middlebrook Mountain where I remained until my Regiment was discharged."

"I again entered into the service as a substitute in the capacity of a drummer with Regiment commanded by Colonel John Moore. I marched to Philadelphia and from thence to Fort Mifflin and thence to Wilmington thence to Newport from thence to Brandywine Creek. I was present at and engaged in the battle at Brandywine."

At the Battle of Brandywine fought on 11 September, 1777 Frederick Hesser was part of the Pennsylvania Militia under the command of Major General John Armstrong. The militia was ordered to hold the far left side of the American line. They also had the additional task of guarding the army's supplies. When the Americans were defeated and began to retreat, General Armstrong's men began to move the supplies after dark.

"From thence I accompanied the army in their retreat to Chester from thence I marched to Philadelphia from there I was dispatched together with a company of Fifty men to Flag Island for the purpose of opening the banks and cutting ditches through to let the water overflow the Island. I joined the Militia under General Potter again at Warrick Furnace in Chester County. I remember that Major Solomon Bush received a wound in the thigh in a skirmish with the Hessians at the White Horse. From Warrick Furnace I marched with the Brigade to Metechim from thence to Germantown. The Brigade was not engaged in the Battle of Germantown but I well remember hearing firing. After the battle I marched to Trap where I received my discharge."

The Battle of Whitehorse Tavern, also called the Battle of the Clouds, was fought on 16 September, 1776 five days after the Battle of Brandywine. When British commander William Howe was informed that the American army was less than 10 miles from his camp, he decided to attack and defeat Washington once and for all.

As the two armies prepared to fight a heavy rainfall began. The rain was so fast and furious, and within minutes the ground which was already saturated became a lake of mud. This made movement of the men almost impossible. The rain and high winds ruined gunpowder and paper cartridges. The British decided to make a bayonet charge and even that was impossible. Washington who was not prepared for battle made a quick retreat, and thanks to the heavy rain his army was saved. Because of the hard rain and wind the event was nicknamed "The Battle of the Clouds." A total of 20 men were killed and 18 wounded.

"I again entered the service about a month afterwards in the militia as a Substitute and served for two months. The Regiment lay at White Marsh. During this time nothing particular occurred. I was frequently sent with scouting parties."

Sources: 1. Pension Roll of 1835. 2. Lineage Book National Society of the D.A.R. Vol. 27, 1898. 3. Pension Papers S22292.

****

Simeon Hewitt age 14

Simeon Hewitt was born on 21 June, 1765 in New London, Connecticut, and he died on 10 there July, 1843. He married Mahala on 18 January, 1787. Simeon was eager to enlist as his father's substitute and because his father was a neighbor of one of the officers he agreed.

"I enlisted or was taken as a substitute for my father Simeon I lived with there of Stonington in County with whom I lived and who was drafted from the militia to serve a tour of duty in the militia of two months at New London in said County Capt Christopher Brown commanded the company & Strawford Billings was Lieutenant both of Stonington the latter was next neighbor to my father & it was agreeable to accept me as a substitute for my father althou I was not then sixteen years of age. My father marched to New London, & the next day I reprised thither by his direction & the officers agreed to take me on trial, with an agreement on the part of my father to return if I did not serve the purpose. On trial they were satisfied with my services I performed the whole tour of duty for two

months and was discharged at the end of that time. I cannot recollect the day of my joining the company I know it was in the year 1779 & that it was in the month of October that I repaired to New London in the service & that it was in the month of December 1779 when I was discharged."

"In the month of February AD 1781 I enlisted into a company commanded by Capt Charles Miles who then lived in Preston in said county for the term of one year to commence on the first of March AD 1781. I was mustered at Stonington by Sergeant William Ellis & soon after I think in the month of April 1781 marched with a part of said company to New Haven then we again mustered & marched from that place to Stamford, Horseneck & White Plain & were at several places in that vicinity until we went into winter quarter at Stamford in said state. During this time several skirmishes occurred in one of which Capt Miles was taken prisoner at __?__ & several men were killed. (viz) John Benjamin & Benjamin Goff about thirty privates taken prisoner & several wounded."

"I continued to serve at the period for which I was enlisted & was honorably discharged at Stamford in the month of March of 1782."

"In the summer following (viz) the summer of 1782 the precise time not being recollected, but it was during the season of haying, upon some alarm from Rhode Island on one Sabbath day the militia was called for by Capt John Swain of Stonington & he proposed to raise a volunteer corps & I remember well that he promised a Silver Dollar to the soldier who should first volunteer, which was taken by Tibe Baldwin. We were promised that if we would then volunteer it should serve for the next two months tour in the militia that being the period for which Militia were then drafted. I volunteered & marched to Rhode Island & joined a company by Capt Joshua Whitford but the alarm having subsided we returned having actually served only fourteen or fifteen days."

"In the autumn of that year I served two months in the militia at Fort Griswold in Groton near New London commencing as I believe in the month of October or November as a substitute for one Gilbert Holmes of Stonington who was drafted from the militia for two months tour of two months & was discharged."

Sources: 1. U.S. Pension Roll of 1835. 2. Census of 1800, 1810, and 1830. 3. Tombstone 4. U.S. Pensioners 1818-1872 Connecticut Men in the Revolutionary War. 5. Pension Papers W25766.

****

Jabez Hicks age 12

Jabez Hicks was born on 28 January, 1763 in Dighton, Massachusetts, and he died on 9 April, 1827 in Bristol, New York. He married Anna Francis on 1 January, 1787. He enlisted as a private in Captain Joseph Willmark's Company, Colonel John Hathaway's Regiment. After the war he held various offices and was a deacon in the Baptist Church.

Sources: 1. History of Ontario County, New York, 1893. 2. Lineage Book National Society of the D.A.R., Vol. L, 1904.

****

Henry Hill age 8

Henry Hill was born on 22 December, 1768 in Schenectady, New York, and he died on 16 September, 1828 in Amsterdam, New York. He married Eleanor Patterson on 18 August, 1789. Henry received a yearly pension of $88.

The reason that Henry and his brother Nicholas (also in this book) joined the army at the young age of 8 and 10 occurred in 1774. Their father Henry, a fearless patriot, made a remark in the presence of British military officers, which was construed by them as disrespectful to their King. For that remark Henry was overpowered and unmercifully whipped in the presence of his wife and his two sons.

The indignities and insults heaped upon their father angered the two boys, and they were determined to avenge his treatment the first chance they got. In the winter of 1776-1777 they joined Captain Aaron Austin's Company of the 2nd Regiment as drummer boys. They were in active service until the end of the war. The boys were not regularly mustered in for the first couple of years because of their young age.

Henry served in the 1st New York Regiment which was organized in New York City in 1775. He participated at the Battles of Saratoga, Monmouth, and he witnessed the ceremony of the surrender of Cornwallis at Yorktown. Henry was engaged in active Indian service under Major Peter Ganzvoort at Fort Stanwix, and under Colonel Van Schaick, and General John Sullivan in the famous Sullivan Expedition. In 1779 he would officially enlist in the regiment. He was discharged in 1783.

"I enlisted at Albany in the state of New York in the year 1779 in the company of Captain Douglas Blucker Colonel Van Schaicks Regiment

called the 1ˢᵗ Regiment as a drummer for during the war. I continued in said company and regiment until the close of the war."

Sources: 1. U.S. Pension Roll of 1835. 2. Tombstone 3. Sons of the American Revolution Application. 4. Pension Papers W23279. 5. Heroes of the American Revolution and Their Descendants: Battle of Long Island by Henry Whittemore, pages entitled Hill and Allied Families.

****

Nicholas Hill age 10

Nicholas Hill was born on 22 December, 1766 in Schenectady, New York, and he died due to a fall on 14 June, 1856 in Florida, New York. He married four times, (1) Anna Newkirk, (2) Catherine Rowe, (3) Sarah Mosher, and (4) Sarah Hegeman. He had children by all of his wives. Nicholas received a yearly pension of $120.

The reason that Nicholas and his brother Henry (also in this book) joined the army at the young age of 10 and 8 occurred in 1774. Their father Henry, a fearless patriot, made a remark in the presence of British military officers, which was construed by them as disrespectful to their King. For that remark Henry was overpowered and unmercifully whipped in the presence of his wife and his two sons.

The indignities and insults heaped upon their father angered the two boys, and they were determined to avenge his treatment the first chance they got. In the winter of 1776-1777 they joined Captain Aaron Austin's Company of the 2ⁿᵈ Regiment as drummer boys. They were in active service until the end of the war. Nicholas later served as a Sergeant in the Company of Captain Hicks in the 1ˢᵗ New York Regiment. The boys were not regularly mustered in for the first couple of years because of their young age.

"I enlisted in the Continental Line of the army of the Revolution for and during the war until its determination. I was a sergeant in Captain Benjamin's Company of the first Regiment of the New York Line."

"On this Eleventh day of July A.D. one thousand eight hundred and fifty five, personally appeared before me, a Justice of the Peace-- within and for the County and State aforesaid, Nicholas Hill--aged Eighty nine--years, a resident of Florida, Montgomery County in the State of New York, who being duly sworn according to law, declares that he is the identical Nicholas Hill, who was a Drummer in the Company, commanded by Captain Aaron Austin - in the First New York regiment of Infantry ,

commanded by Lieutenant Colonel Cornelius Van Dike in the War with Great Britain, Known as the Revolutionary War-- that he enlisted at Albany N.Y. on or about the fifteenth day of December A.D. Seventeen hundred & seventy six for the term of during the War and continued in actual service in said War for the term of five years and was honorably discharged at Newburgh N.Y. on the eighth - day of June - A.D. Seventeen hundred and eighty three."

Nicholas served in the 1st New York Regiment, which was organized in New York City in 1775. He participated at the Battles of Saratoga, Monmouth, and witnessed the ceremony of the surrender of Cornwallis at Yorktown. Nicholas was engaged in active Indian service under Major Peter Ganzevoort at Fort Stanwix and Colonel Van Schaick and General John Sullivan in the famous Sullivan Expedition.

The first important service he performed soon after he enlisted, Colonel Ganzevoort sent him with a message to headquarters at Albany of a possible Indian attack on Fort Stanwix in the winter of 1777. Nicholas was sent with a young man named Snook, who met with an accident and had to drop out about half-way through the journey. Nicholas discovered that he was being pursued by Indians, so he ran all night through the snow and delivered his message the next day. He later described his thoughts as he approached Albany that morning, *"the smoke from the forts and houses stood up through the still morning air like a forest of ghostly white tree tops."*

Nicholas was at Valley Forge during the winter of 1777-78. The next year he spent the winter at Morristown. This was known as the "Hard Winter" because of the harsh conditions. On 3 January, 1780 a heavy snowstorm hit the camp. When tents blew off, soldiers were *"buried like sheep under the snow...almost smothered in the storm."* The weather made it impossible to get supplies to the men. Many men had no coats, shirts, or shoes and were on the verge of starvation. *"For a Fortnight past the Troops both Officers and Men, have been almost perishing for want,"* George Washington wrote in a letter to civilian officials dated January 8.

Nicholas told stores about the suffering of the troops during that cold winter. He said on one occasion the army was near starvation, and rations of a gill of whiskey for each man was distributed. A big Irishman named Valentine kindly offered to share with him his own ration, and gave Nicholas about a teaspoon of the whiskey. Because Nicholas was in an exhausted condition the small amount of spirits overpowered him, and he laid down apparently lifeless. The Irishman took him on his back and carried him for miles until they reached a place that could provide proper treatment for Nicholas.

The hardships of Nicholas and his brother Henry caught the eye of General Baron Von Steuben. The General was aware that the boys' parents had died soon after they entered the army and offered to adopt the two boys. Nicholas declined the offer.

After the war his sister Martha and brother Henry were all that remained of the family, of which he was the eldest surviving. In 1803 he became a Methodist clergyman and settled on a farm in Florida, New York. He was described as a man of deep piety and as a preacher he was simple, earnest, yet fearless to proclaiming the truth as he believed it.

Sources: 1. U.S. Pension Roll of 1835. 2. Tombstone 3. Sons of the American Revolution Application. 4. Pension Papers W11284. 5. Heroes of the American Revolution and Their Descendants: Battle of Long Island by Henry Whittemore, pages entitled Hill and Allied Families. 6. D.A.R. Lineage Book, Vol. 142. 7. The University Magazine, Vol. VIII, #1 New York January 1893.

****

Joseph Hillard age 14

Joseph Hillard was born in May of 1762 probably in Virginia. When he enlisted he received a bounty which he gave part of it to his father for when he returned home.

"I enlisted in the year 1776 in the County of Charles City in the State of Virginia in the company commanded by Captain Rose of the Sixth Virginia Regiment on Continental establishment. I continued to serve in the said Corps until I was transferred to the Fourth Regiment in which I served except during the time I was a prisoner, until after the siege of York when I was discharged from service in Richmond in the State of Virginia. I was in the battles of Monmouth was at the taking of Stony Point was in the American Army at Charleston when I was taken prisoner; and I am in reduced circumstances and stand in need of the assistance of my country for support,"

"In the year 1780 I enlisted in the Army of the revolution against the common enemy of my country for the term of "during the war," and served in the company commanded by Captain John Stokes and in the Regiment No. Six under command of Colonel Neville of the Virginia line, and continued in the service aforesaid until the close of the war in 1783,

when I was regularly discharged from the said sixth Regiment, commanded by Colonel Neville."

Brigadier General Lachlan McIntosh later wrote the following to the Pension Bureau, *"This Certifies that Joseph Hilliard a Soldier Enlisted during the War in Captain Stokes's Company and 2nd Virginia Regiment, commanded by Colonel John Neville was made a prisoner with his Colonel by the British at the capture of Charles town. That in the summer of the year 1780 I had him taken out of the prison Ship to wait upon me at Haddrell's Point, and continued in that Capacity ever since until this Day, and in all that time found him to be a Sober honest young man. I further Certify that the said Joseph Hilliard received no part of his pay, by my order or direction, or to buy knowledge since lived with me. Given under my hand at Savannah in Georgia this 19th Day of May 1783."*

Joseph Hillard was one of 5,000 Americans troops captured at Charleston on 12 May, 1780. This surrender was the largest of an American force until 1862 when Union forces surrender at Harper's Ferry. This defeat in 1780 left no American Army in the South, the area was open for the British to take.

Source: 1. Pension Papers S38033.

****

Gaius Hitchcock age 14

Gaius Hitchcock was born on 30 April, 1764 in Springfield, Massachusetts, and he died on 12 August, 1843 in Waitsfield, Vermont. His father had him enlist at a young age because *"it might prevent him from being drafted and be more exposed to danger and hardship."*

"In the spring of 1778 being then very young I believe about the 1st day of April 1778 I entered for one and a half months as a waiter to Captain Bryant then stationed at Springfield Ms. I served out my full term of enlistment and was discharged. Was employed when not waiting upon Captain Bryant in preparing cartridges & ammunition & in carrying them from place where aforesaid to the armory."

The Springfield armory located in Springfield, Massachusetts was the main center for the storage of munitions during the American Revolution. The site was selected by General Washington in 1777, because it was at the intersection of three rivers and four major roads. It was north of a waterfall which protected it from ships. During the war they manufactured cartridges, gun carriages, stored muskets, cannons, and other weapons.

"In 1779 I enlisted for two months under Captain Bryant as a waiter & was employed at the arsenal at Springfield, part of the time in preparing ammunition and as a sentinel. Discharge on the 16th day of May."

Gaius would serve several more short terms preparing ammunition and guard Duty. On two terms he marched into the countryside and took part in scouting parties. He served a total of 8 and 1/2 months from 1778 until 1781.

Sources: 1. U.S. Pension Roll of 1835. 2. D.A.R. Lineage Book, Vol. 43. 3. Pension Papers S19339.

****

Culpeper Hoadley age 13

Culpeper Hoadley was born on 10 September, 1764 in Waterbury, Connecticut, and he died on 21 May, 1857 in New Haven County, Connecticut. He married Molly Lewis on 5 February, 1786 in Connecticut, and they died six months apart. He served as a drummer and received a yearly pension of $33.66.

"About the middle of April 1778 I enlisted for one year into a company commanded by Captain Jesse Curtis in the Continental State Troops in a Regt. Commanded by Col. Thadus Cook (though whole Regt. Was not called out at a time) and were stationed on the sea shore when I served the full term of one year."

"While I was at Nantucket I was in a small battle my company and a company of refugees who lost their captain in the skirmish and three men lost on our side."

Sources: 1. Tombstone 2. Sons of the American Revolution Application. 3. Pension Papers S17492. 4. Yearbook of the Connecticut Society of the Sons of the American Revolution.

****

Nathaniel Hodges age 14

Nathaniel Hodges was born in 1762 in Norton, Massachusetts, and he died in 1843 in Duxbury, Massachusetts. Seth Sprague of Duxbury was appointed guardian of Nathaniel Hodges, because Nathaniel was judged to be an insane person.

"July 1 1776 I enlisted for six months into a company raised by authority of the State of Massachusetts commanded by William Watson Andrew Sampson was Lieutenant. I was stationed at the Gurnet at the entrance of Plymouth Harbor at which place I served until the last of December 1776."

"I went in the expedition to Penobscot & served three months in the expedition. I was wounded in the head by a musket ball & two buck shot which may have contributed to my present Idiotic condition. I have been for so many years Idiotic & insane that I cannot give any distinct amount of the term."

The Penobscot Expedition was a 4,000 man naval expedition of the Revolutionary War. It consisted of 19 warships, 24 transport ships, and more than 1,000 militiamen. The purpose of the expedition was to capture a 750 man British garrison on the Penobscot Peninsula in Maine. It ended as a great British victory, and it was the worst U.S. naval defeat until Pearl Harbor in December of 1941. The Americans lost numerous ships and over 470 men, while the British lost only 13 men.

Nathaniel said that he received a head wound from a musket ball and buck shot. Both sides used the Buck and Ball load in their muzzle-loading muskets. The load would consist of a .50 or .70 caliber musket ball that was combined with three to six buckshot pellets. It was usually used in close contact fighting.

Sources: 1. U.S. Pensioners 1818-1872. 2. Lineage Book National Society of the D.A.R. Vol. 35, 1901. 3. Pension Papers S29913.

****

Prosser Hogan age 13

Prosser Hogan was born in 1764, and he died 3 November, 1831 in Monroe, Indiana. He married Mary Whooley in 1786. In his pension application he reported,

"...a little before the battle of Germantown I believes was in 1777 I enlisted as a regular Soldier & received the bounty in the County of Guilford North Carolina in the American Continental Army in the revolutionary war with Great Britain in the company of Captain Anthony

Sharp in the 9th Regiment commanded by Colonel Clark and in the North Carolina line for three years."

The 9th North Carolina Regiment was organized in the spring and summer of 1777 and the Battle of Germantown was 4 October, 1777. This would indicate that Prosser may have joined sometime in September and participated in the Battle of Germantown. The 9th North Carolina spent the winter at Valley Forge in 1777-1778, and it was disbanded during this time because of lack of manpower. On 15 May, 1778 the remains of the 9th North Carolina were placed in the North Carolina Line led by Colonel Thomas Clark, who was in the 1st North Carolina and placed under the command of Major General Lafayette.

"Before the end of the war I was taken prisoner at Charlestown South Carolina and deserted from the British at that place."

The Regiment arrived at Charleston in March of 1780, and Colonel Clark and his 287 men were captured and became prisoners after the fall of Charlestown on 12 May, 1780. There is no record of how long Prosser remained a prisoner. He was granted a pension of $8.00 a month.

Sources: 1. A Guide to the Battles of the American Revolution by Theodore P. Savas and J. David Dameron. 2. Pension papers for Prosser Hogan. 3. Roster of the Continental Line from North Carolina. 4. Kentucky Marriages 1802-1850.

****

Veline Hoisington age 14

Veline Hoisington was born in 1762 in Farmington, Connecticut, and he died on 6 September, 1846 in Somerset, Michigan. He married Hannah Green in 1790 in Woodstock, Vermont. He received a yearly pension of $80 for his service.

"In the year 1776 in the month of February I enlisted in the company of Captain Benjamin Wait in the Town of Woodstock Vermont Regiment commanded by Major Hoisington my father and I was waiter to my father. This Major Hoisington commanded three companies of volunteer Rangers to Guard the frontiers of Vermont about the Sources of the Connecticut River. This was the corps I belonged to. I first marched up the Connecticut River to a place called the great Ox, bow was employed in building a Stockade fort where I staid and made the place the head quarters from whence the business was to scout on the Canada line to prevent the depradations of the Indians and Tories staid in this place until

the first of January 1777 when all were discharged until further orders Returned to WoodStock aforesaid this campaign was ten months and an half--received no written discharge the 28th of Jany 1777."

Joab Hoisington, Veline's father, was commissioned a Colonel of the "Upper Regiment" in Vermont, which he mainly organized at his own expense. He died of small pox in camp at Newbury, Vermont in 1776.

After the death of his father, Veline joined with Seth Warner one of the leaders of the Green Mountain Boys. This group had disbanded before 1777, when Vermont declared its independence from Great Britain. The Vermont Republic was a republic for 14 years and in 1791 was admitted to the United States as the 14th state. Veline Hoisington joined the remnants of the Green Mountain Boys which are now called the Green Mountain Continental Rangers.

"Major Hoisington my father died and I was turned into the Ranks and in the first of May following I was marched to Rutland from thence to Castleton in Vermont and from thence to Mount Independence opposite Ticonderoga here I staid untill Berguoine drove them away we retreated to Hubbardtown we were now attached to Col. Warners Regiment from the time of Major Hoisington death until we carried to Mount Independece Since we were under the Command of the oldest Captain of the Regiment or Battalion whose name was Benjamin Wait from Hubbardtown we were marched to Castleton from thence to Manchester from thence to Paulet from thence to Bennington where I was engaged in that memorable battle was one that charged the Hessions on the Hill who had made themselves a slight Brestwork of Rails-- which was earned with great Slaughter after the battle we followed down to Stillwater did not cross the river untill Berguoin surrendered but was stationed on the east side to prevent him from crossing the River. after the Surrender of Burguoin I was passed over the River on to the battle ground from thence I was marched to Fort Edward from thence to Fort Ann from thence to White Hall from thence to Diamond Island in lake George near its outlet from thence to Ticonderoga which was just left by the British troops here we were discharged the first of December after a hard Campaign of eight months had no written discharge. returned to Woodstock and staid untill the first of May1778 where we were marched to Albany State of New York to recieve our clothing here we staid until the month of September following when we were discharged by General Stark had a written discharge signed by the aforesaid General Stark which discharge is lost then he returned home to

Woodstock and arrived on the 20th of September 1778 this campain lasted four months and twenty days in the Year 1780."

The Battle of Bennington took place on 16 August, 1777 in Walloomsac, New York about 10 miles from Bennington, Vermont. The Americans were led by General John Stark and reinforced by the men, which included Veline under Colonel Seth Warner. The Hessians had constructed a small redoubt at the crest of the hill.

On the sunny morning of the 16th the Americans had surrounded the Hessians. The American commander Stark faced the Hessians, drew his sword and said, *"My men, there are your enemies the red-coats and the tories. We must conquer them,--or tonight Millie Stark will be a widow."* With that announcement the battle had begun. Stark's men were able to get closer to the Hessians without alarming them. The Germans who spoke no English had been told that soldiers with pieces of white paper in their hats were allies, and they should not be fired upon. Stark had also heard this and had many of the men wear bits of white paper in their hats.

British reinforcements arrived toward the end of the battle, and they were driven away by Colonel Warner and his boys from Vermont. In General Starks report to General Gates, several days later, he wrote, *"Colonel Warner's superior skill in the action was of extraordinary service to me; I would be glad if he and his men could be recommended to Congress."* Veline Hoisington is considered a hero at the age of 15.

This small battle reduced British General Burgoyne's army in size by almost 1,000 men. This played a role in his defeat by the Americans at the Battle of Saratoga in a few weeks.

"In the first of April I enlisted into Captain Issac Safford's Company of Rangers commanded by Ebenezer Allen Major Comandant of a battalion of Rangers consisting of three companies to guard the frontier. Marched to Pitsford Vermont north of Rutland on OtterCreek. here we built a Picket fort and called it Fort Vengeance. Immediately after this fort was finished Capt Safford's Company to which I belonged was sent to White River on the East Side of the Green Mountain where I was employed in building another fort in the Town of Bethel where I staid until the first of January 1781. When I was discharged had a written discharged signed by Capt. Isaac Saford which discharge is lost. This campaign lasted eight months."

"In March 1781 I enlisted for one month as a private under the command of Beriah Green a Lieutenant to block the motions of the Indians on the frontiers. Went to the fort at Bethel and staid out this month and was discharged. had a written discharge which is lost."

"Sometime in the 1st of April same year I was hired in captain John Benjamin's Company to Guard the lines, this was in consequence of a draft in that part of the State of Vermonth that Each of the farmers should hire a man for nine months to Guard the lines from the depradations of the Indians and tories. I was hired by three farmers. I was stationed at the fort at Bethel aforesaid where I was employed in scouting parties through the whole term of nine months which ended some time in February 1782. When I was discharged."

"I then returned to Woodstock and sometime in the month of Feby 1782 I went to Boston Massachusetts and Entered myself on board the Dean Frigate, a privateer as a marine in a company commanded by Captain Delaware. The ship was Commanded by Captain Samuel Nicholson. Sailed the tenth day of March to the South to intercept the British Vessels bound from and to the West India Islands in this cruise we took seven prizes. The last prize captured was an Eighteen Gun frigate I think the Captains name was Thomson took a large number of prisoners do not know how many. Returned to Boston the tenth day of June same year. This trip was three months. I cannot prove all my services because my messmates and fellow soldiers are mostly dead."

In February of 1782 Captain Nicholson was ordered to sea to cruise off the West Indies. He was ordered to exchange prisoners and send rum and salt prizes to Charleston, South Carolina. During the cruise captured the *Mary* going to Barbados with a cargo worth five thousand sterling. In then captured the American Brig *Elizabeth* going to Saint Thomas with tobacco and stores, *HMS Jackal*, and two British privateers named *Swallow* and *Regulator*. He returned to port with a damaged ship full of sick crewmen and prisoners. Veline Hoisington, at the age of 20, was now ready to leave the life of the army and the sea behind him and return home to Vermont.

Sources: 1. Captain Samuel Nicholson A Monograph by J. Philip London. 2. A Memorial and Biographical Record of Iowa. 3. Sons of the American Revolution Application. 4. U.S. Pensioner Roll of 1835. 5. Massachusetts Soldiers and Sailors in the War of the Revolution Vol 8. 6. Vermont Men in the Revolutionary War. 7. The Battle of Bennington: Soldiers &

Civilians by Michael P. Gabriel. 8. The History of the Battle of Bennington Vermont by Frank Warrell Coburn.

****

Jonathan Holcomb age 12

Jonathan Holcomb was born on 19 June, 1762 in Sheffield, Massachusetts, and he died on 1 October, 1847 in Mason, Ohio. He married Hannah Everest on 11 April, 1786. He received a pension of $66 a year for his service.

"I enlisted in a minute company on the 25 of April 1775 under Capt John Fellows Lieut Daniel Borders and Ensign Michael Holcolm all of Sheffield Co Berkshire state of Massachusetts (when I began to blow the fife)." During this time Jonathan marched around the Springfield area until he was discharged the last of December. He enlisted again in May of 1776 and was discharged after two months.

"I Enlisted with Lieut Hubbell for three years my father considered me to young for that service but agree I might serve as a post by which I did for eighteen months. In 1778 April Enlisted under Capt Denning and Lieut Toomis for nine months."

During this tour he was stationed in Albany and for a while stood guard at General Washington's door with orders that no one should pass. One day a Dutch girl with produce tried to pass and he pushed her back. The General came out and saw the girl and purchased some strawberries from her. Later Jonathan served on a duty to cover the bones of the wounded dead from General Burgoyne's captured army. In July or August of 1778 Jonathan became ill and was discharged and sent home.

"In the year 1779 in July I Enlisted as a fifer for a tour of eight months to guard public stores at Bennington Vermont." By now most of the fighting had shifted to the south. After the war Jonathan graduated from Yale College and became a doctor. He practiced medicine in New Jersey, Pennsylvania and in 1814 he moved his family to Warren County, Ohio.

Sources: 1. Annual Obituary Notices of Eminent Persons who have died in the United States for 1858 by Hon. Nathan Crosby, 1859. 2. Massachusetts Town and Vital Records 1620-1988. 3. Tombstone 4. Pension Papers W1609.

****

John Holland age 13

John Holland was born in 1765 at Prince George County, Virginia, and he died on 3 August, 1842 in Sumterville, Alabama. He married Jane on 31 August, 1786 in South Carolina. He received a yearly pension of $80 and 150 acres of land for his service. It was reported in the 1840 census that he owned 16 slaves.

"I enlisted in the Army of the United States in the year 1778....I belonged to a company commanded by Captain John Bowie."

Captain John Bowie commanded the 5th South Carolina Regiment which was merged into the 1st South Carolina Regiment in 1780. John Holland served as a drummer and may have been at the Siege of Savannah from 16 September to 18 October, 1779.

Sources: 1. Census 1840. 2. Alabama Revolutionary War Soldiers. 3. U.S. General Land Office Records 1796-1907. 4. U.S. Pension Roll of 1835. 5. Pension Papers R5139.

****

Thomas Hollaway age 13

Thomas Hollaway was born in 1763, and he died after 1835. He enlisted in the Virginia militia in 1777 and received a pension of $31.66 per year.

"I enlisted in the militia of Virginia in the 1776 under the Command of Captain Willis Wilson and Marched to Smithfield at which time I served at least six weeks. In 1777 my next tour was on James River at a place called Edwards under Command of Captain Wilson and served six weeks. In 1778 I Marched to Swans Point under the Command of Lieutenant Berriman and served six weeks. In 1779 I marched again under command of Jacob Faulcan and went to a place called the Burnt Mills and served about six weeks. In 1781 I again marched to Broad Water Bridge under command of Captain William Hart and joined the main Army and marched up the river to Petersburg and was at the battle of Petersburg..."

The Battle of Petersburg took place on 25 April, 1781. Over 2,000 British troops defeated nearly 1,000 American troops commanded by Major General Baron von Steuben. The militia fought a hard battle and made a disciplined retreat.

"...and marched to Richmond and served the same length of time--the same year I was again marched to a place called Babs and was

under the command of Colonel Willis Wells and served six weeks also the same year I marched under the Command of Major Boyce over the Siege of little York and served about the same time."

Sources: 1. Pension Papers S5562. 2. U.S. Pension Roll of 1835. 3. Revolutionary War Rolls 1775-1783

****

Justus Holly age 13

Justus Holly was born on 3 February, 1763 in Sharon, Connecticut, and he died on 29 April, 1849 in Dorset, Vermont. He married Elizabeth Field on 9 September, 1790. He is described in the book *The Story of Dorset* on page 74.

"...the Justus who played the fife so persuasively at the Battle of Bennington....before his marriage he made his home in Bennington, but the road to Dorset was so familiar to him that, one occasion, eager to see his bride elect, he walked it in half a day."

Justus was a fifer in Captain Robinson's Company at the Battle of Bennington fought on 16 August, 1777. Before the battle he asked his captain to let him take a gun, but because of his youth he was told that his fife would have a more powerful effect. At least one American fifer was killed in the battle.

Sources: 1. Massachusetts Society of the Sons of the American Revolution, 1920. 2. Sons of the American Revolution Application. 3. Tombstone 4. The Story of Dorset by Zephine Humphrey and Elizabeth Sykes Lee, 1971.

****

James Holmes age 11

James Holmes was born in South Carolina in 1768. He entered the army at the age of 11 in 1779 probably serving as a waiter. *"I enlisted with my father when a small boy just barely able to bear arms. I marched to Greenville to Seneca a fort on Savannah River. At which place I staid and not far from it for the term of one year and then was furloughed and I returned home to see my mother and to get some better health and staid some weeks and then returned to the war. I was again furloughed and went again home and returned agreeable to furlough and some time after I was taken sick and my father hired a man to serve in my place and fort Seneca was surrendered and before I recovered the War ended."*

James served under Captain Benjamin Tutt who was in the 5th Provincial Regiment which later became part of the South Carolina line. This unit was an independent unit that guarded the frontier against Indians and Tories. James applied for a pension which was rejected. He did not have proof of service to get a pension because he did not spend enough time with a regular army unit, although he did claim to have received his bounty of 200 acres.

Source: 1. Pension Papers R5171.

****

Increase Hooker age 11

Increase Hooker was born on 2 November, 1765 in Woodbury, Connecticut, and he died on 16 November, 1849 in Onondaga County, New York. He was with Ethan Allen and the Green Mountain Boys, and he was at the Battle at Bennington fought on 16 August, 1777. New Hampshire and Massachusetts militiamen, along with members of the Green Mountain Boys, defeated a large British force. This victory played a key role into bringing France into the war on the American side.

Sources: 1. Sons of the American Revolution Application. 2. Gazetteer & Business Directory of Cortland County, New York for 1869. 3. Connecticut Town Birth Records pre-1810. 4. Revolutionary Soldiers Resident or Dying in Onondaga County, N.Y., prepared by Rev. W.M. Beauchamp for the Onondaga Historical Association, 1863.

****

Charles Hooks age 13

Charles Hooks was born on 20 February, 1768 in Bertie, North Carolina, and he died on 18 October, 1843 in Montgomery, Alabama. He married three times: (1) Betsey Williams in 1789, (2) Kitty Dickson 1795, who probably died in childbirth, and (3) Anne Hunter in 1796. The Census of 1840 showed that he was a man of wealth because he owned 15 slaves.

His older sister Mary Hooks married Lieutenant Ezekiel Slocumb, who commanded a troop of Light Horse to watch the enemy and punish the Tories. In April of 1781, just after the battle of Guilford Court House, the British Colonel Tarleton made his headquarters at the Slocumb home in Wayne County. Charles Hooks was away with his brother-in-law Lieutenant Slocumb in hot pursuit of some Tory marauders. As they returned home, they were not aware that several hundred British troops were stationed at Slocumb's home.

While the British were there gun fire could be heard in the distance, which alarmed the British. Charles and Lieutenant Slocumb had been engaged with some Tories and were nearly home, when a faithful slave warned them in time that the British were on the farm. Quickly the two patriots turned around, and with one bound they jumped a fence amid a volley of musket balls from the British guards.

After the war Charles served in the legislature from Duplin County in the early 1800's, and he served as a member of Congress in 1816-1817 and again in 1819-1825.

Sources: 1. Revolutionary Soldiers Buried in Alabama by Annie R. Mell. 2. Census of 1840. 3. Sons of the American Revolution Application. 4. Tombstone 5. D.A.R. Lineage Book, Vol. 29.

****

Absalom Hooper age 12

Absalom Hooper was born in 1765 in Broad River, South Carolina and he died 9 December, 1845 in Jackson County, North Carolina. By the time he was 18 he had served for 7 years, shot twice, captured twice, and been in several battles. He married Sarah Salers and the home of his uncle in September 1788 in Elbert County, Georgia. He received a yearly pension of $80. Sarah received Absalom's pension after his death plus a bounty of 160 acres of land.

"I enlisted in the army of the United States in the year 1776, with Captain Richard Dogged and Served in the South Carolina regiment under the following named officers Colonel William Henderson Commandant, Major __ Brown, Captain Richard Doggett & Lieutenant Jesse Baker I enlisted during the war and was discharged by Captain Jesse Baker (who was promoted after the death of Capt Doggett who was killed in the Battle of Stono) near Columbia South Carolina as believe in the year 1783."

At the Battle of Stono Ferry fought on 20 June 1779 Absalom was in the 6th South Carolina Regiment under the command of Lieutenant Colonel William Henderson. He was in the company led by Captain William Doggett who was killed in the battle. Also killed in this battle was Hugh Jackson, the brother of future president Andrew Jackson. During the battle Absalom's unit was on the left wing and made first contact with the enemy.

" I was born and lived at the time of my enlistment on the main Broad River, South Carolina near the mouth of Green River, But owing to my entering the Service at between twelve & thirteen years of age I do not recollect the name of the County or district, I ran away from my mother who was a widow and an adherent of the Tories and enlisted in the city of Charleston, South Carolina and received a Bounty of thirty dollars in Continental money & was to receive five Dollars per month pay & a bounty of Six hundred &forty acres of land at the end of the war I never received my pay or land & has never parted with my right by contract or otherwise, I was in Sullivan's Island under the command of Genl Howe & in the engagement when it was attacked by the British forces under the command of Sir Henry Clinton, from Charleston I was marched under the command of Genl Howe in to Florida against the British post on little St. Mary's which was evacuated by then on the approach of the American forces after which the army returned to Charleston about the time the British took Savannah. Genl. Lincoln took the command, I was marched under him to Purysburg in South Carolina above Savannah & after Nashes defeat I was marched up to August Ga. & crossed the river into Georgia about that time the enemy Crossed Savannah River at Jubley's ferry & marched in the direction for Charleston and the war moved down the river & crossed it at a place called the three Sisters & pursued them when the Americans arrived at Bacon's bridge on the Edislac River they found that they had fortified and Built Stono fort I was in the attack on that fort under the said Col Henderson in the regiment called the new infantry, from that place the British retired into Beaufort Island & the American forced marched to Seldon Bull's opposite to the Island where they remained some time from thence the American army marched by way of Purysburg, Jubley's ferry & to the Siege of Savannah at the time it was besieged by the French Genl d'Estaing & the American forces, in that Siege I was wounded in the right arm by a musket, that after that battle the americans returned to Charleston where we remained until the town was besieged by Sir Henry Clinton & Lord Cornwallace when I was again wounded by a musket that in the left thigh and taken prisoner & kept Confined in the Hospital for five months at close prisoner as soon as I felt sufficiently recovered and an opportunity offered I escaped leaving my company prisoners of War with the British in Charleston and fled to the frontier of Georgia to an uncle & was there taken by the Tories and confined five days and released after being tried by a Tory Court Martial. Shortly after which he heard of Col Clark of Georgia Militia & his regiment being on its march to Augusta, that regiment I joined and was enrolled in Captain Daniel Runnold's Company and marched with it to that place where they *took Brown and Greysons forts and their Garrisons, from that place I was marched with Clarke's regiment to freeman's Station on the frontier of Georgia, after remaining there a short time I together with said regiment was marched to Big Briar Creek to dislodge a party of Tories, after performing that Service the Regiment returned to Freeman's Station not long after said Regiment moved into South Carolina and joined the troops under the Command of Genl Pickens and under his command they united forces of Pickens and Clarke attacked a party of the enemy composed of British & tories Lying on Little River, South Carolina who were commanded as I now think by Lord Rawdon where there was a skirmish between the advance parties of the two armies & the British retreated to Ninety Six, Clarke's Regiment in which I was returned to Freemans Station not long after me with said Regiment was marched to the last siege of Savannah where Genl Wayne Commanded, after the enemy left that coast I was marched back in Clarke's regiment to Freeman's Station & shortly after I in said regiment went on expedition against the cherokee Indians and after their being defeated in a Battle at the Long Swamp on the Highlowa River in said Nation the Regiment again returned to Freeman's Station, not long after which Peace was declared & I was discharged as before stated. My not joining my regiment after my escape was owing to its being removed to the East after being exchanged from Charleston."*

Sources: 1. Census 1820, 1830, and 1840. 2. U.S. Pensioners 1818-1872. 3. Tombstone 4. Pension Papers W7813.

****

Nicholas Horne age 14

Nicholas Horne was born on 25 November, 1762 in Goochland County, Virginia and he died on 23 February, 1835 in Knoxville, Tennessee. He married Rebecca Badget c. 1782 at Surry, North Carolina. According to the census he owned 8 slaves in 1810. He received a yearly pension of $34.33.

"Sometime about the 1st of July 1776, being then but 13 or 14 but large of my age, I enrolled myself together with three of my brothers, as a volunteer into a company of cavalry commanded by Capt William Shepherd, with my brother JOHN HORN as Lieutenant; I rendezvoused at one Myers in said county of Surry and my company was attached to a regiment under Colonel Joseph Williams; I marched with my said regiment into Virginia and crossed New River came on to the Holston River which I crossed not far from the Long Island, from there I came on

to Buckingham's Island in French Broad, sometime before I reached this last Island when and where I cannot now recollect, my regiment joined the main army under the command of Genl Christie, from Buckingham's Island, I crossed to the south side of French Broad and marched on to the Tennessee river, which I crossed not far from the mouth of Telico River, the army then marched up and down the river and about through the Cherokee Nation, destroying the crops and burning the house of the Indians, in this service a part of the army were employed for several weeks after which many of the Indian Chiefs met Genl Christie, near the Tennessee River and held a treaty there after which the army marched home pretty nearly along the same scout and I was discharged. I think I served in this campaign nearly six months; I recollect it was but a short time before Christmas when I was discharged."

"Sometime in the summer of 1780 I think in July I enrolled himself in Surry County (N. C.) as a volunteer into a company of cavalry under my former Captain William Shepherd and under him marched and joined the main army under Genl Rutherford after continuing with the main army three or four weeks, and marching with them toward Campden, when I with my company was detached from the main army and marched under the command of Col. afterwards Genl. Davisson, to dispense a company of tories who were collected at the mouth of Rocky river, after killing some and dispensing the rest of the tories, I and the detachment with me joined the main army, I think in this skirmish Genl. Davisson was wounded in the hip; after disposing of the spoils which had been taken in this scout, by public sale, I with my company left the main army and returned home, I think I was six weeks in this service; sometime after this last campaign I was out against the tories in the county of Surry (N.C.) under my same Captain Shepherd, as a volunteer, for a term of 3 weeks I was in the army of the United States as a volunteer private, eight months for which I claim a pension."

Sources: 1. Census of 1790, 1810, and 1830. 2. U.S. Pension Roll of 1835. 3. Pension Papers S4395.

****

John Hudson age 12

John Hudson was born in Westchester, New York on 12 June, 1768, and he died in Cincinnati, Ohio on 23 July, 1847. He enlisted in the First New York Regiment two months before his thirteenth birthday.

The following narrative is from Charles Cist's Cincinnati Miscellany, 1846: Cist's Advertiser a Weekly Sheet Vol. III Cincinnati, January 28, 1846. Narrative of John Hudson a Revolutionary soldier and now a resident in Cincinnati. Recorded in his own words:

"I was born in Westchester, New York, on the 12th June, 1768, and am now, of course, nearly seventy-eight years of age. In April, 1781, there was a levy raised for the defense of the state from domestic enemies, to enable the regular troops of the New York line to march to such points as might be required. In this levy I enlisted, in what was then called King's district, Albany County, and is now Canaan, in Columbia County, marched to Saratoga, where having been drilled one week as a soldier, I enlisted in the Continental service, in which I remained to the end of the War of Independence, mounting guard repeatedly over the very graves of those who fell in our battles with Burgoyne. I remained at Saratoga until the middle of July, 1781, when Col. Van Schoyek's regiment, to which I belonged, was directed to join the combined armies at Dobbs' ferry on the Hudson River, under the command of Gen. Washington and Count Rochambeau. On the march I carried a British grenadier's musket, as much longer and heavier than the old-fashioned Continentals, as these would outweigh and out reach with their bayonets, the modern article made at Springfield or Harper's ferry. On this musket I carried a bayonet, which never left it only when it was taken off to be cleaned and polished, for it had no scabbard. Besides this weight I bore a cartouch box, with forty rounds ball cartridge, and knapsack with twenty rounds more, and my clothes, blanket and four days provisions. After reaching the grand army, we started up the east side of the Hudson river to Verplank's Point, and crossed over to Stony Point, memorable as the spot were Gen. Wayne retaliated on the British troops—the surprise and massacre of Paoli. I helped to draw cannon up into that very fort, which it became necessary to fortify when we were about to leave for Virginia. We carried on our march boats so large that it took a wagon and eight horses to draw them, and two inch plank in quantities, by the same conveyance. These were to enable us to form flotillas to cross our troops upon the water courses which lay on our route. In this way, after passing the Hudson we crossed the Delaware at Trenton, N.J., and marched by the way of Brandywine creek to the head of Elk River, now Elkton, but then nothing but an old frame warehouse there. Here we lay three days, and during this period I received the only pay I ever drew for my services during the war, being six French crowns, which were a part of what Robert Morris borrowed on his own credit from the French commander, to supply the most urgent

necessities of the soldiers. My comrades received the same amount. Those three days were spent in getting our heavy munitions from the Delaware across the Elk River. Here the cannon, etc., were sent by water to Baltimore, and thence by the Chesapeake Bay into Virginia. The army marched—crossing the Susquehanna at Havre de Grace, on their way—to Baltimore, where they encamped at Howard's hill, where six hundred head of cattle were slaughtered and salted for our use. Thence we sailed to the mouth of James River, encountering an equinoctial storm or remarkable fury, which lasted eight days, checking our progress that entire period, sweeping our decks fore and aft, and drenching us all to the skin. To crown our troubles we had nothing to eat but coarse barley bread, baked for the horses, which had become mouldy and wormy, but we were fain to use it, as an alternative to starvation. On the 25th Sept. we reached our place of debarkation, 40 miles up the James River, six miles from Williamsburg, the then seat of government of Virginia. The object of our expedition was to capture the English army under Lord Cornwallis, which lay entrenched at Yorktown on the York River, southeast of the point we had struck, which enabled us to gain the rear of his position. The Marquis de la Fayette we found stationed at Williamsburg, expecting our arrival and support."

Vol.111, Feb. 4, 1846 #2

"I neglected to state, in its proper place, a remarkable circumstance which occurred while I was at Saratoga, which may as well be brought in here as at a later stage of this narrative. When I reached Saratoga, the levy of which I formed a part, was stationed in a hovel made of slab, which was opposite Schuyler's saw-mill. Here we lay on the bare ground, having not even a bundle of straw to put under us. Some few nights after we took possession of these lodgings, and in the course of a pitch dark night, our acting adjutant roused us up, and demanded of the officer in command, a detachment of a sergeant, corporal, and twelve privates for immediate service. Of these twelve I was made one, and in the course of a few minutes we were all ready, and followed the adjutant to Gen. Schuyler's residence. We were there taken into a bedroom where there were two men prisoners, who were pinioned by the arms. The adjutant, giving them in charge to the sergeant in command with strict exhortations to watch them carefully, departed with the guard whose place we were about to take. The next morning about nine o'clock, Capt Austin, in whose company I afterwards enlisted, came marching down with his command and five drums and fifes, a black silk handkerchief on each *drum, and all the drums snared. A Negro accompanied the party as hangman, who on entering the room fastened ropes around the men's necks, who were then taken out and marched off. I was at this time a boy of thirteen years of age, fresh from the peaceable employments of a country life, and the awe and horror with which these preparations inspired me may be readily conjectured. Our own party remained behind in the bedroom, waiting further orders. Gen. Schuyler was at this period commander-in-chief of the northern frontier, and absent at the time from home, and I was informed that Mrs. Schuyler, with some feeling of jealousy that her husband's authority should be infringed, sent a note to the commander of the garrison, inquiring of him how he expected to account to the General, his superior officer, for the lives of men about to be executed without a trial, or even an examination. I understood that this had the effect of taking the prisoners down from the tree to which they were already fastened. They were then brought back to the bedroom with the same solemnity as they had been taken away, and a boat being prepared at the Hudson river, not more than a quarter of a mile distance, they were put in charge of a guard of regulars and sent down to Albany. One of these men was Solomon Meeker, a private in Capt. Austin's company, and the other was a British deserter named John Higginbottom, who it was judged was a reality a spy, and had been tampering with Meeker to lead him to desert, if not for worse purposes. Meeker, I believe, never was put to trial, for we took him out of Albany jail on our march to the Chesapeake. As to Higginbottom, many years after the period of which I am now speaking, and long after the war was at a close, I became acquainted with him, recognizing him as soon as I saw him, and reminding him of these things. He acknowledged himself to be the man, and stated that he dad got clear at Albany by representing himself as a deserter, which led them at last to let him off. He confessed to me that had had been, however, a spy, and as such had came to Saratoga, and that he had entered that for at daylight, and in a few hours would have been off and discovered enough to the British forces to bring on a body of Indians and tories from Canada sufficient to have destroyed every human being about the place. We see by this, on how narrow pivot very important events turn, and the necessity of prompt and vigorous action in time of danger. Let me now resume the narrative of our Virginia campaign, and first let me state the cause of my enlistment in the regular service."*

"The levies mounted guard with the regular troops, and one morning just after being relieved at the usual hour, I had gone into our quarters and was sitting on the ground with my gun between my knees, when it went off accidentally and apparently without cause, the ball passing out of the hovel, but injuring no one. However, it was an offence punishable with one hundred lashes, and the corporal of the quarter guard immediately came in with a file of men and took me to the guard house. Here a conversation took place between the sergeant major and quarter-master sergeant, and one of them remarked with an oath, that it was a shame to give a boy like this an hundred lashes for what was notoriously an accident. This was said, purposely loud enough for me to hear. Then turning to me he added... "come my lad, the best way for you to get out of this, will be to enlist—come along with us". I jumped up immediately, and had my name entered on the muster roll of the company, which was that of Captain Austin, and now I was fairly entered for the campaign."

"We landed, as I have already stated, on the 25th September, 1781, and here we drew provisions, and made the first meal for eight days in any degree of comfort. As evening approached, we took up our line of march for Williamsburg, which we reached some time that night and a very dark one it was. As soon as we arrived I was put in the commissary's guard. Williamsburg was six miles from our landing place and twelve from Yorktown, our destined theatre of employment. Every six men, on their march had a tent and tent poles, and camp kettle, and in addition to the heavy load I have already stated I was carrying, that tent was thrown over my shoulders in my regular turn of carrying it. At that time I was advanced in my fourteenth year, only from the 12th of June to the 25th of September. We found Lafayette with the Americans troops, landed by Admiral De Barras, a few days before, to reinforce his detachment. As I was up all night in the service assigned me, I had ample opportunity of noticing the bustle of marching and preparing to march, which kept others as well as myself awake the whole night. As the morning dawned I saw nothing but small parties which were following the army; probably piquet guards, whose duty not being over till daylight, had delayed them, and who were now pushing on to overtake the main body of the army. The exposure of that night made me very unwell and I rode part of the day on the commissary's wagon. In the course of that afternoon we caught up with the army, when I was relieved from this post and rejoined my own company."

Vol. III iii, Feb. 11, 1846 #3

"On reaching my company I heard discharges on cannon fired in quick succession, and the sound of their balls sticking some object. Inquiring what was doing, of my associates, I was told, that they had raised a redoubt the morning of their arrival and that the balls were from the enemy, who were striking a large oak tree in front of the redoubt. On that very day, as I afterwards learnt, Col. A. Scammel, who was out with a reconnoitering party was taken prisoner by Tarleton's light horse and inhumanly murdered after his capture. I was told also, that the night before, the Marquis de la Fayette, with a party of Frenchmen who had been landed from the fleet had stormed two batteries of two twelve pounders to each battery, putting every man to the sword—literally—as the very privates among the French wore that weapon. These events all took place n the 26th September, 1781, and I refer particularly to this date to remove an impression erroneously but extensively prevalent, that the important events of this siege were crowded all into one night at a later date."

"Our army was composed of three divisions, and throughout the siege of Yorktown, which had now commenced, each division was twenty-four hours in the works and forty-eight in the camp. One of these divisions was under command of Brig. Gen. James Clinton, and to this was attached the New York line. I belonged to the oldest company of the oldest regiment of these troops, which of course was the head of the column. We left the camp a short time before sundown, and marching along a road, came to a high mound of earth, and wheeling short round to the right, we reached within a few feet of the end of a cause way, made of pitch-pine logs recently put down, perhaps fifteen or twenty rods long. This crossed a marsh, otherwise impossible. Yorktown was virtually an island, the river passing at an elbow, two sides of it—and an extensive deep marsh faced the other side."

"We marched over the causeway to the batteries which I have already stated were stormed by Lafayette. I saw two embrasures to each battery, which proved that there had been the same number of cannon. These, with the dead, had been all removed, and the batteries being thirty feet apart, we marched between the two. Everything that I could see there was covered with blood."

"We passed these batteries a short distance, the night approaching, when we were halted, every man directed to sit down, and neither to talk nor leave his place. As I had been sick through that day, and had, like the rest, my knapsack on my back, I laid my cartouch box under my head, and with my musket in my arms, soon fell asleep. During my repose a sudden and violent rain came on, falling in torrents, which failed, however, to wake me, such had been my fatigue. In the course of the night—I cannot tell at what time—the noncommissioned officers came along the ranks, and without saying a word, woke us all and got us to our feet. I rose up with the rain dripping from my clothes. We were directed to shift our arms to the right shoulder, and each man to put his right hand on the shoulder of his file leader, marching in two ranks, the right in front. The road being clear of all obstructions, our progress was uninterrupted, although nothing was visible—no man being able even to see his comrade. We finally halted, and every man had a spade put into his hands. Shortly afterwards—the rain still pouring down—a party of men, with gabions, came along. I will describe them, for the better comprehension of my narrative. Sticks are cut about five feet in length, of the thickness of a man's wrist; one end is sharpened and set in the ground, in a circle of perhaps three feet diameter. Flexible brush, about the size a hoop-pole, with such branches as adhere to them, are interlaced as in making a basket, working upwards from the bottom. The gabion this made is thrown on its side, a long pole run through it, and passed on the shoulders of as many men an can get beneath it. These were placed, when brought to the ground for use, in such position as the engineer judged proper, the stakes being, as before, pressed into the earth. We were then directed, and as at first, merely by signs, to commence three feet inside of where they had been placed, and shovel up earth sufficient to fill the gabions. The ground was of sand, which being thoroughly wet by the rain, was very easy digging. We shoveled until we filled these gabions, and finished by throwing up a bank in front, when the work was completed. The gabions being side and side the earth formed a solid line of breast works, through which a cannon ball could not pass. From what I afterwards saw of the efficacy of this description of defense in repelling cannon balls, there is no doubt that it is a better protection than a stone wall six feet thick, and has this advantage, that it can be made in a few hours. Not a single cannon ball penetrated this defense during the whole siege."

"It ceased raining just as the day was about to dawn, when we observed that our artillery had thrown up a battery a few rods from our right and on the bank of the river; and had raised a lofty flag staff with the star spangled banner streaming to the wind upon it. This was called Matchem's battery, being erected under the direction of a captain of that name, who retained it as his command during the siege. I wish it distinctly understood, that we were so near the British lines with these defenses that there never were any other works erected in our front, in the whole progress of the campaign. After it was fully daylight, the British had the hardihood to come out with a six pounder, immediately in front of the battery I had assisted to construct, and so near to us that a horseman could have shot any one of these artillerists with his pistol. There they stood firing their piece rapidly for half an hour, battering at the fortification without any apparent effect. After they found that we treated them with silent contempt, for we took no notice of them, they desisted and returned to their own lines. Our allies, the French, who occupied our left, were doubtless busy, what in what way I had no means of knowing."

"I am very confident that there was no firing on our part upon the enemy for eight days; while they were keeping up a constant cannonade, night and day, during that period. General Washington and Count Rochambeau used to ride to the rear of the works, side by side, each equipped with a spy glass, of which they made frequent use. This was repeated every day while we were raising other works, assisting the French, and strengthening batteries. On the ninth day—the 4th or 5th of October—the generals, as usual, came down, attended with their retinue, and General Washington, not seeing Captain Matchem, inquired where he was. He was shown where the Captain lay asleep upon a plank, in the open air. The General chide him gently for thus exposing himself, asking him why he did not go into his marquee. He answered spiritedly that he would never enter his marquee till he had stopped that bull dog from barking—alluding to a twelve pounder in the wall of the town, which had been playing night and day on his battery, annoying him greatly. Washington then directed him to open his battery immediately, the Generals riding back as customary. There was now a general shout among the soldiers, that we should now see some fun. In my simplicity, I asked "what fun?" Up to this time I had never seen a cannon fired. "Don't you see those matchets burning" they replied. I looked and saw them on staffs, four of five feet long, at the side of the guns."

Vol.III, Cincinnati, Feb. 25, 1846 #4

"Captain Matchem accordingly fired his field piece, which was a twelve pounder. The ball, however, had been directed too low, and struck the bottom of the embrasure. He then corrected his aim and threw the second shot, which struck the mouth of his enemy's cannon, in rather an oblique direction, commencing a breach about eighteen inches from the muzzle of the piece, and tore off its side for that distance. This I had the curiosity and opportunity to ascertain exactly, after the surrender of the place. The fire thus opened from the battery, served as a signal to the French on the left, who commenced firing from their whole train of artillery. I was informed by competent persons at the time, that the combined forces were prepared to fire as much as sixty shot, or shells, at a volley, in less time than once every minute, and frequently did so. Inside the walls of Yorktown, and visible above these walls, were several frame buildings, which soon were battered to pieces under the allied fire, the shattered fragments flying in all directions, and killing and wounding by their fall, without doubt, numbers of the British troops."

"South of the town, and at the left wing of the French forces, the ground rose up into land of considerable height, where the enemy had several out posts, one of which, and the largest, annoyed the French excessively, destroying the lives of numbers in their lines. In consequence of this the commanders-in-chief decided to carry them at the point of the bayonet, which was accomplished by the French grenadiers, who bore in this service the hand grenades, from which that species of troops drive their title, and which they only employ when about to storm an entrenchment. These grenades are bombs in miniature. They are about the size of a mock orange, and being carried to the ground in the haversacks of the grenadiers are hurled in showers into the works, as their assailants advance. On the same night the Marquis de la Fayette, with the American troops stormed the walls of the town in front of Matchem's battery. The Marquis and his party obtained possession of the British guns, which were immediately turned upon their own defenses, and kept in the hands of the storming force until daylight enabled the enemy to concentre their troops and drive the assailants off. The ordinary narrative of the siege of Yorktown condenses the whole history of it into this bloody and eventful night, as though that period embraced every event of importance in that campaign: but this is not the fact, for from the opening of our works by the first fire from the battery of Capt. Matchem, on the 4th or 5th October, there was an incessant cannonading kept up on both sides, which lasted until the evening of the 19th October, when the surrender took place."

"Such was the vivacity of both attack and defense of Yorktown, that between the flashes from the guns and from the fuses of the shells, it was rendered light enough for us to attend to all necessary work during *any portion of night, through the whole period of fifteen days which I have alluded to."*

"One night during the siege a major of the 43d regiment, sallied our on the besiegers with his command of several hundreds, and actually captured one of the French batteries, spiking their guns. By this time the whole line had taken the alarm, and he met with so warm a reception, that he was glad to regain the town, with such of his troops as he was not obliged to leave behind in dead and wounded upon the field."

"After this, and as a consequence of this incident, we had a piquet guard placed in advance of our batteries, and just under the muzzle of the enemy's guns. I was myself one of that guards one night. We had double centinels placed all along under the line of the British works, who were stationed each with one knee to the ground and the gun cocked lying on the other, our hail being to give three smart taps on our cartouch boxes. Our instructions were to fire instantly when the same signal was not repeated."

"Those taps resembled greatly the flapping of the wings of the turkey buzzard, which abounded from the number of the unburied dead lying in the neighbourhood, and would have been ascribed by the enemy to these birds, if the din of the cannon had permitted the signal, during any interval of their discharges, to be heard and noticed."

"During the siege there had been remarked conspicuously a large house, built of white marble which Capt. Matchem had spared, knowing it to be the property of Gen Hugh Nelson, whose estate lay in the neighbourhood. The General, on his arrival, which took place a few days after, inquired why he did not fire on that building. Matchem accordingly gave the reason. Never mind my property, replied the Gen.; rap away at it. Matchem then fired one ball, which made its way through the house. Where the ball entered, it made a small breach, but where it came out if forced a very large opening. After the surrender, I learned that there were a number of the British officers had made it their quarters, but they abandoned it as soon as this shot was fired, fearing more would follow. But this was the first and the last, as I distinctly recollect."

"Lord Cornwallis, finding that he had no prospect of obtaining relief from Sir Henry Clinton determined finally to surrender, which he did on the evening of the 19th October. On the 20th, we marched into

Yorktown, and relieved the British guard there. On the 21st, the enemy's troops marched out and laid down their arms. On the 22nd, they were marched off with a heavy escort, for Lancaster, Pennsylvania. On the 23rd, as I was informed, the Marquis de la Fayette embarked for France, to carry tidings of the welcome event which was then generally supposed the close of the revolutionary struggle."

"Our army staid at Yorktown until cold weather set in, for the purpose of leveling the works. We found hundreds of shells which had not exploded, from the circumstance of the fuse falling undermost in which case they do not go off. These we gathered up in wagons, and put them on board vessels to take to Gen. Greene, who was still carrying on the war in South Carolina. There was a party of French prisoners who had gathered up a four house wagon load of these shells. By some _____ not easily explained, an explosion took place, which tore the wagon to fragments; killed the horses, and twelve of the Frenchmen employed in the service. I saw these twelve men neatly laid out in a marquee all in a row with white linen burial clothes. This would not have been done for them, or any one else, during the progress of the siege."

John Hudson later moved to Cincinnati, Ohio and received $8.00 per month for his service.

Sources: 1. 1840 Census. 2. Abstract of Graves of Revolutionary Patriots. 3. Connecticut Hale Cemetery Inscriptions and Newspaper Notices, 1629-1934. 4. The Official Roster of the Soldiers of the American Revolution Buried in Ohio. 5. U.S. Pensioners 1818-1872. 6. Tombstone of John Hudson. 7. Pension Papers S41665. 8. In Pursuit of Liberty by Emmy E. Werner.

****

Samuel Hudson age 12

Samuel Hudson was born in South Carolina in 1765, and died after 1830. In his pension application he swore, *"I enlisted for the term of 4 years in the year 1776 in the State of South Carolina in the company commanded by Captain Uriah Gooding in the Regiment commanded by Colonel Henderson in the line of the State of South Carolina…".*

Lieutenant Colonel William Henderson commanded the 3rd South Carolina Ranger Regiment and Captain Uriah Goodwin commanded the 3rd Company. This regiment was raised on 6 June, 1775 at Ninety-Six Court House. Young Samuel Hudson would have seen his first action at the First Battle of Savannah on 29 December, 1778. The British troops overwhelmed a small American army. He was also present on 20 June, 1779 at the Battle of Stono Ferry when a larger American force failed to defeat the rear guard of the retreating British army. At the Siege of Savannah on 16 September, 1779 he was in one of the bloodiest defeats in the war when over 900 American were killed, wounded, or taken prisoner.

Samuel states in his pension, *"...I continued to serve in the said Corps until about the year 1780 when I was taken prisoner & was therefore never regularly discharged from the service..."* He was taken prisoner on 12 May, 1780 when the army surrendered to the British at the Battle of Charleston. The British captured 5,700 American Soldiers and 1,000 sailors at Charleston. The men captured faced a horrible fate because over 45% of American prisoners of war died in captivity. The officers were soon paroled.

Samuel would have been around 16 at the time of his capture. He was probably taken to St. Augustine, Florida since that is where large groups of militia were sent. The regular Continental forces were placed in prisons in and around the city, such as the old barracks where the College of Charleston is today. A few troops and most of the sailors were placed aboard the dreaded prison ships.

Samuel was granted a pension of $8.00 a month in 1830.

Sources: 1. Nothing But Blood and slaughter, Vol 2 by Patrick O'Kelly. 2. Continental Army Payroll Records, 1779, Book 89. 3. Pension Application S34931. 4. Roster of South Carolina Patriots in the American Revolution. 5. A Guide to the Battles of the American Revolution by Theodore P. Savas and J. David Dameron.

****

Benjamin Hughes age 14

Benjamin Hughes was born on 7 October, 1763 in Hanover County, Virginia, and he died on 24 June, 1838 in Smith County, Tennessee. He married Susannah Tucker on 7 November, 1807 and she received a yearly widow's pension of $90. Benjamin and Susannah moved to Tennessee to be near her father. He was at the Battle of Brandywine fought in September 1777 which would make him 14 when he enlisted, probably in the early spring.

"I first entered the service as a volunteer for the term of six months in a Company of Dragoons raised and commanded by a Capt Elisha White

of the County of Hanover and State of Virginia and did serve accordingly as a private in said Company for the said term of six months, and was honorably discharged at in the said period, but obtain no written discharge. The said tour of duty was performed in the State of Virginia at Smithfield (and the surrounding Country.) The said Company of Dragoons was attached to and armed force commanded by General Vance."

"Within a few days after I was discharged from said service, I engaged to serve, and did serve as a substitute for a man named Drury Hodges in the regular army, for eighteen months. This last enlistment was made at Smithfield in the State of Virginia. The Company in which I served as a substitute was commanded by Capt Samuel Hubbard. A few days after this last engagement I marched with the Company to which I belonged to the State of Maryland, & from thence to Pennsylvania where I was engaged in the battle of Brandywine, after which the Company returned to Maryland where I continued to serve until his term of enlistment 18 months expired."

"About three days after my return from this service, I again enlisted in the County of Hanover as a volunteer in a dragoon Company raised and commanded by Capt William Tinsley of the said County of Hanover, for the term of six months, which term I of accordingly served in & about Williamsburg in the State of Virginia, and during said period was engaged in two battles one at Malvern Hills & the other at Charles City Court House. The armed force to which I at this time was attached was commanded by Colonels Monroe, Mercer, Seawell, & Winston."

"That after this to wit in the month of May in the year 1781 I served another tour of duty of three months as a private in the militia of Virginia (being drafted as such), in a Company Commanded by Capt Thomas Richardson. This term of service was performed at Richmond, and up and down James River in the State of Virginia. Upon this occasion the militia rendezvoused at New Castle in the County of Hanover and from thence marched to York, & Hampton, where I was regularly discharged in writing"

"That after this tower, on the same day October the year 1781 I with my Company, on that of which I was a member, commanded by Captain William Anderson, who and other Companies then at Gloucester were commanded by Colonel Monroe, were impressed or detached to guard some British Prisoners taken on the Gloucester side, at the time

when on the other side Lord Cornwallis with his command were captured, from thence to the Town of Winchester in Virginia, in the performance of which tour of duty I was engaged 21 days, when I was dismissed by Captain Anderson by the Colonel Monroe's orders sometime about the last of October 1781."

Sources: 1. U.S. Pension Roll of 1835. 2. Census of 1810, 1820, and 1830. 3. Some Tennessee Heroes of the Revolution. 4. Kentucky Marriages 1802-1850. 5. Pension Papers S3079.

****

James Hull age 12

James Hull was born on 17 December, 1763 in Wallingford, Connecticut, and he died after 1820.

"I enlisted for the term of <u>one year</u> in the last of 1775 or the beginning of 1776, in the State of Massachusetts in the company commanded by Captain Edward Seagrave in the Regt. Commanded by Col joseph Reed in the line of the State of Massachusetts on the Contential Establishment. I continued to serve about six months when by reason of sickness in the family I hired a man to take my place."

"In the spring of 1778 I enlisted for the term of <u>nine months</u> in the state of Massachusetts in the Company commanded by Captain Sargeant in the Regt commanded by Col Stephens. I continued to serve in the same corps until that period expired. I served other periods of less than 9 months, making in all about <u>2 years.</u>"

James was very poor in his later years. In his application he stated that he had no property other than what he was wearing. He was unable to work and except for the son he lived with, had no other family.

Sources: 1. Revolutionary War Period: Bible, Family & Marriage Records. 2. Pension Papers S33325.

****

John Hullderman age 14

John Hullderman was born on 2 August, 1768 in Frederick County, Maryland, and he died after 1853 probably in Virginia. He enlisted 1 March, 1783 five months before his 15th birthday. He stated in his pension application that he when he enlisted he spent, *"in hard money twenty dollars to clothe and equip myself."* His pension was rejected because his service was after the war was over in 1781.

"I volunteered as a soldier under Captain Jacob Coon who was stationed at Martinsburg Virginia in the year 1783 and first day of March of that year. I continued as a volunteer until the close of the revolutionary war, I found my own military equipment & and I always held myself in readiness to go into the field of battle when called upon, I followed no lucrative or civil employment while in the service, I was in no engagement while in the service, during my time of service I was called upon but once to march against the enemy who lay at the frontier and that these orders were given on one evening to march the next morning -- these orders were countermanded on the next morning by the receipt of an express; stating that peace was made. The time that I was stationed at Martinsburg in close quartering was eighteen months; the exact time I was in the service I cannot distinctly recollect, but that I can recollect that I was in service (though not in any close quartering as the first eighteen months) till the end of the war."

Source: 1. Pension Papers R5365.

****

Abijah Hunt age 14

Abijah Hunt was born on 17 March, 1762 in Newton, New Jersey, and he died on 10 April, 1852 in Belvidere, New Jersey. He received a yearly pension of $100. His four brothers also served, and his brother Davis is found in the spy section of this book.

"I was born in the town Newton, County of Sussex & State of New Jersey on the 17th March 1762. That in the year 1776 I enlisted as a volunteer in Capt. Brittain's Company & Col. Spencer's Regt in the Service of the United States & marched from Chatham to a place called Connecticut farms, to the number of about 250 men, and had a skirmish at that place with a foraging party of the enemy, in which the Americans beat them & made prisoners of about 80 Hessians and a small number of British horse; that upon the British evacuating Elizabethtown, the Americans took possession of it; and I having been stationed there with the Regt continued to do duty there until my enlistment had Expired, and then was discharged and returned home; that a brother of mine who had also enlisted into the same Company was likewise in the aforesaid

Skirmish; and immediately thereafter, enlisted in Col. Spencer's, or the 5th Jersey, Regt for 3 years during the war. In the winter of 1776/7, when General Washington was with the Army at Valley Forge, I volunteered and served in the place of my said Brother (who was sick) for 3 months; and upon his recovery, was relieved by him, after the Expiration thereof."

"In the fall of 1779, I in company with my Brother James Hunt shipped on board the Luzerne Letter of Marque, at Philadelphia, Carrying 18 Guns, commanded by Capt. Thomas Bell; that sometime in the ensuing Spring, the Luzerne, being then on her homeward bound voyage from France, was captured by an English Frigate of 32 Guns; I with the rest of the Crew of the Luzerne, was landed at Limerick in Ireland, and after being there about 3 weeks were sent to the Cove of Cork, and there put on board of the Lenox an English 74 gun Ship, and there remained a prisoner, until I landed at Plymouth in England, and was then Confined in the Mill prison for alleged piracy and high treason, there to remain until the King should be pleased to order them for trial; I was thus Confined for one year lacking 15 days; when after the capture of Lord Cornwallis and his Army, I with the other American prisoners were suffered to be exchanged, and sailed in a Cartill, and arrived at Philadelphia after an absence of one year and 9 months."

"Soon, or within a few weeks thereafter, I shipped himself on board the Frigate South Carolina of 40 guns & 783 men Commanded by Capt. John Joiner as a midshipman of the first Class Capable of Navigating a vessel of the first Class into any port, and lay at the port of Philadelphia, and in the River, about 2 months and then put to sea on a cruise, and after being out about 20 hours, the South Carolina was captured by a 56 gun Ship and 2 British frigates, and sent into the port of New York, -- where the prisoners were put on board the Prison Ship and there confined, until paroled, and continued on parole until peace was declared. My pay on board the South Carolina was $30 as he understood per month; and that the length of his Service on board her and Prisoner was 15 months and upwards."

Joshua Mersereau was a shipmate of Abijah Hunt and wrote a letter in support of Abjiah's pension. In the letter it was written that the father of Abijah brought Abijah with him to Philadelphia, and he introduced him to Commodore Gillon and recommended his son as a suitable person to be a midshipman on board the *South Carolina*.

After they were captured by the British the prisoners hatched a plot to take over the ship from their captors, and they enlisted Abijah to sail the ship for them. The plot was discovered, and the prisoners were ordered below to the wardroom. The prisoners were taken to New York and then placed on board the prison ship *Scorpion*.

Sources: 1. Tombstone 2. Pension Roll of 1835. 3. Pension Papers S23271.

****

Davis Hunt age 14

Davis Hunt was born on 10 October, 1763 in Newton New Jersey, and he died on 3 April, 1839. His wife Jerusha received a yearly widow's pension of $40. His other three brothers also served in the war. His brother Abijah is found in this book. Davis also served in the War of 1812 in Captain George W. Chapman's Independent Veteran Corps of Artillery, New York City Brigade.

"In the month of June 1778 I entered the service of the United States to serve for the war either as a volunteer or as enlisted I cannot specify which but I think my name was enrolled among the regular soldiers—as an assistant and waiter for Major John Johnson a Quarter Master in the Jersey line & continued to serve said Major Johnson for a year & received the pay of year to wit one hundred dollars besides a ginnea and five shillings. I was serving that time stationed at Trenton, my duty was to attend to deliver orders during Major Johnsons absence from Trenton to the Brigade wagons for the army and instruct the drivers where to carry their loads for delivery. I also took care of said Johnsons horses and carried orders for him around the country about the furnishing provisions etc. Near the expiration of that year when riding to Morristown with Major Johnsons orders I narrowly escaped a scouting party of the enemy near Maiden head and received a severe wound in my head & also on my knee. I became thereby incapacitated from further service and obtained from Major Johnson written permission to return home to be cured of my wounds."

"In the fall of 1779 I volunteered in the said service under my brother Robert Hunt a Captain of volunteer dragoons raised near Elizabeth Town for partisans service & from that time and during the years & in 1780 & 1781 I was employed by my said brother & in 1780 by General Dayton as a spy in the enemys lines & as an express rider for the purpose of gaining & carrying intelligence of the enemys movements to Genl Dayton & sometimes to Genl Washingtons head quarters. In the summer of 1780 while the enemy occupied Elizabeth Town I was sent into

the town by my said brother as a spy to get information of their strengths & intentions with instructions to give the earliest intelligence of their movements & report whether it would be ___?__ my brothers squadron (which then lay in ambush a short distance from said town) to make an attack on them or not. I was the first to give information of the enemys intention to leave Elizabeth Town & take up a position at Springfield, & was sent the same morning by my said brother to carry the report to Major Cragg at Rahway & to several other posts in the neighborhood. When the enemy moved to Springfield I was directed to raise the country sound & actually killed my horse in performing said service. After the battle of Springfield I was employed by General Dayton as a spy in the enemys lines to find out their actual condition & intentions & was engaged until the British finally evacuated Elizabeth Town in the fall of 1780 a period of nine months. I was during this time & frequently after employed as an express rider by Genl Dayton & by my said brother Capt Hunt to carry dispatches to the main army under Genl Washington & various other directions & while in such service I was on more than one occasion wounded & was once badly frozen that I nearly perished."

"I well remember the first interview between Genl Washington & Gates after the capture of Burgoyne near Elizabeth Town where Gen Gates at the head of 1500 men came from the North to join Washington. Among the continental & militia regiments I knew many of the officers as Gen Dayton, Cols Spencer, Ogden and Stockton, Major Cragg & many others to whom I carried dispatches."

Sources: 1. Pension Papers W25803.

****

Richard Hurst age 14

Richard Hurst was born on 3 March, 1762 in Gloucester County, Virginia, and he died on 20 February, 1838 in Virginia. He received a yearly pension of $53.66 for his service.

"I was commanded by Capt Richard Billups, Colo. Sir John Peyton, Major Throgmorton and Major Boswell were the field-officers, I took my father's place about 1777 before I had reached fifteen, about 1778 I entered in my own stead and continued off and on until the siege at York. I stayed at home scarcely any in the time, I was down on York River when Lord Corn Wallice surrendered and saw the British flag lowered and the American hoisted in the Fort; I left the service shortly after about 1781

October; I was in one engagement on the British lines in York County an officer from New York whose name I do not recollect commanded me at the time, I was in another engagement at Frank Thornton's place near Glou. Town when Houlder Hudgins and Major Wicks commanded, this last engagement was about the last of September 1781 during the time Cornwallice was at York. I resided in Kingston Parish Gloucester County when I entered the service and I resided there ever since my discharge until this period."

"I went out as a militia man and volunteered repeatedly while in service once to go to Williamsburg and at other times two other places. I marched through a part of King & Queen County, through New Kent, to Williamsburg and to Burwell's ferry, this was at the time Arnold came down James River, at Williamsburg I was under General Nelson, Major Nelson and Captain Armistead of the Continental line, at another time under Lieutenant Digges of the same line."

"For one month I served in Williamsburg in the year 1776 under Henry Forest Capt, called out by order of Col Peyton, For three months I served at Gwynn's Island under the same officers 1777 called out by like order; For two months I served in a barge belonging to the United States commanded by Capt Nicholas Lawrence in 1778; For one month I served in another barge belonging to the United States commanded by Capt John Rogers these barges were in active service all the time plying the creeks and bay. For two months I was stationed at Gloucester Court House with the G. Militia called into service by the Colonel. I was under Capt R. Billups. For three months I served in a tour to James River at the time Arnold went up the River. I volunteered under Captain Tabb and Houlder Hudgins in 1780 we were placed under General Lee after we got to Williamsburg in 1781 For __ months and three days I was stationed with the G. Militia at Hubbard's Old fields under Capt Houlder Hudgins on the same tours I was stationed for three months and __ days at Seawell's Old field near the enemy's line. For one month during the same year I served another tour down the York River. I belong to the Regiment of militia for the County of Gloucester the number I do not recollect."

Sources: 1. U.S. Pension roll of 1835. 2. Pension Papers S9593.

****

John Hutt age 14

John Hutt was born on 5 September, 1763 in Westmoreland, Virginia, and he died on 25 August, 1833 in Chillicothe, Ohio. He married Elizabeth Crockwell on 3 March, 1799. John received a yearly pension of $80 and 100 acres of land.

"I enlisted in the army of the United States in the year 1778 with Capt. John Mazarett for the term of three years and served in the Virginia State line of artillery as a common soldier. My father's record of the birth of his children in his family Bible states I was born the 5th day of Sept 1763 Northern Neck of Virginia, Westmoreland County. Before I was 15 years of age being well grown in height above 5 feet 10 inches tolerably proportioned to my height and age I enlisted as above stated, a Lieut. Turnbull, I think his first name was Stephen, perhaps the 2nd Lieut was named Kemp belonged to the same company. Turnbull was married to a lady near Hampton, where British barbarity worse than savage cruelty was inflicted on a widow of that name in the late war. Here I was stationed for about 18 or 20 months more or less I cannot be special as to time; about this time, the continental congress called upon the State of Virginia to form and embody a Southern army, they (Virginia) having more state troops than was necessary for her internal defense, converted the surplus demanded for the requisition hence a part was taken from the three divisions of the regiment stationed at Norfolk and Portsmouth, Hampton and the memorable York Town Va. Here I believe the regiment was organized and I am strongly impressed that Capt. Christopher Roan took the command of the company to which I belonged and ever after commanded till discharged, thus prepared we marched to Williamsburg and joined a regiment of infantry commanded by Col. Porterfield (poor fellow I saw him wounded on the morning of Gates' defeat (as I was informed)."

At this time John Hutt was a member of the Virginia State Garrison. The unit was authorized in June of 1778 under the command of Lieutenant Charles Porterfield. The purpose of the unit was to garrison the harbor fortifications of the state. Colonel Porterfield was wounded at the Battle of Camden on 16 August, 1780, and he died on 10 January, 1781.

"Thus the line of march commenced to the South, we crossed James River at old James Town, thence Roanoke at Taylor's Ferry, thence into North Carolina (here I weighed 164 Pounds) thence to Hillsborough thence to memorable Guilford Court House thence to Salisbury, thence to a place called Piper's Fifer's where we encamped all night, early on the

next morning leaving this place we marched thro a heavy rain till about on down 12 miles, encamped on a beautiful green, the army had just retired to their tents when on a sudden a secret and hasty alarm was given of Buford's defeat; we were in a few minutes on the retreat and by sun up the next morning a part of the army was at the place they had left but the morning before, then back again to Guilford Court house where we tarried about 8 days."

The Battle of Waxhaws, also called Budford's Massacre, occurred on 29 May, 1780. Over 300 Americans were killed, wounded, or captured at this defeat in South Carolina.

"Col. Porterfield then took a circulatory rout to Hillsborough where we joined a division of the Maryland and Delaware troops commanded by Genl Smallwood and Guess, Gest or Gist, I remember not which; Buford with the remains of his regiment on the right and the artillery in front of Buford, I am not certain but I believe Col Harrison commanded the Part of Artillery which now became more formidable than before. About the same time I suppose Genl Gates took the command in chief and the army marched to where he was met near Camden by Cornwallace the British commander and totally defeated. I was on the reserve at (Rudgeleys) Mills about 5 miles in the rear with some of the baggage & a part of this shattered and scattered army was collected at Hillsborough where I first saw Genl Green (the warrior or fighting General). Genl Greene marching into South Carolina leaving a small detachment behind at Hillsborough myself being one of the number, whether orders were previously given or received afterwards I am unable to determine, however with hasty and speedy marches this detachment arrived and joined the main army on their retreat across the Pee Dee or Yadkin Rivers into Virginia the very day on which they crossed one of the said rivers here another detachment was then formed and added to this one together with all the heavy baggage commanded by Col Buford, returned on the same route, we again crossed the Roanoke at Taylor's Ferry, it was reported that Genl Greene with the main army also crossed the Dan into Virginia on the same day, here Capt Roan was separated from the detachment with a number of Artillery whose term of service had and were expiring and marched to the now city of Richmond, where I was with other discharged in 1781 at what time I do not recollect."

"I then returned to a comfortable home with my Mother. I had been home but a few days before I had the honor of being enrolled amongst the Bulwark of Civil Liberty (Militia). Times continued perilous,

Cornwallis entered Virginia with his army. Something must be done. Militia must turn out by drafts, this I could not brook, I turned out a volunteer horseman tolerably equipped at my own expense, in 2 or 3 weeks this draft was discharged but another followed close upon its heels, I again volunteered in the foot service called light Infantry, and forsooth, I was made orderly Sergeant. You well recollect Cornwallis surrendered at York Town Va. I was on the Gloucester Side, Col. Nelson commanded the regiment at the time. I never was in any battle but marching, Stationary or retreating--until now when I heard a few whistling bullets but was not engaged in the act of fighting being on the right wing, the enemy when attacked, retreated. The foregoing is a brief view of my service in the revolutionary war."

John Hutt was in the Virginia militia under the command of General Thomas Nelson. John belonged to the regiment under General Weedon, which was placed across from Yorktown at Gloucester Point facing 700 British troops under the command of Colonel Banastre Tarleton. The British troops tried to evacuate the area on 16 October, but bad weather and the American bombardment made it impossible. The next day British General Cornwallis surrendered his army.

Private William Dye claimed to have witness the surrender of the British. He said he saw an officer come out to General Washington and stick his sword into the ground. Washington took the sword, looked at it, and then handed it back to the officer again.

"I was well acquainted with Col Henry Lee who commanded the partisan Legion of horse to the South, his son Henry went to school to a brother of mine, we lived in the same county (Westmoreland), his Seat was called Stratford. After Buford's defeat Doctor Seldom the surgeon of our regiment was sent by Flagg to take charge of the wounded, accomplishing his object returned to our Camp on the Yadkin river. I heard my name called, it was called by Selden to show me a wounded man he brought away with him as a waiter. If you had been there you might have counted one wound for each State then confederated, 13 in number all above his shoulders about 3 inches long. Here we had plenty of green corn to eat, substantially so, until we could make fires, officers and soldiers all upon a level as to diet."

"Another tale and a part I know to be a fact that a cannon was fired at a late hour of one night while Porterfield commanded and was encamped on a dense settlement of Tories. It was said to alarm and awe them, a report next morning spread abroad that one of Col Porterfield's regiment had stolen a shirt and trousers and for safe keeping had put them in the gun that was fired. The wide spreading sheet of flaming light spread over the encampment and the loss of the soldier's shirt and trousers was the cause of much sport and laughter amongst the soldiers in camp. Since writing the foregoing I have been examining the life of Washington Vol. 4 printed by Wayne, Philadelphia and find page 170 Col Harrison did comment on the Artillery to the South, same page I find Porterfield within one day's march of Buford when defeated by Tarlton, next page for green corn, also page 178 I find Genl Gist and page 172 Rugeley's Mill or Clermont trusting and believing the foregoing will be all sufficient to establish satisfactory of any being a Soldier in the revolutionary army."*

William Hutt, a younger brother of John, wrote this account of John's return home from the war.

"I perfectly recollect the day he returned from the Army, home to the house of our mother, I being then a boy at school – he passed the school-house where I was, and the Teacher, myself and the scholars generally went out to see him and congratulate him on his safe return. I also well remember that during the same year that he returned from the Army as above stated, he went to the siege of York town Virginia, was at the surrender of Lord Cornwallis and the Army under his command."

On 13 November, 1801 John Hutt and his family moved to Chillicothe, Ohio. At this time John was a licensed preacher of the Methodist Church, and he later became one of the first associate justices in Ross County. In April of 1802 John and his wife Elizabeth started a school for girls, which was one of the first in Ohio. The Hutt School taught young ladies proper skills and Mrs. Hutt taught morals. In the early 1800's John was a hotel keeper and merchant.

John came from a background of owning slaves. Tax records show that his mother in 1787 owned 16 slaves. His brother owned slaves and John may have owned them before he came to Ohio. In Ohio John became very outspoken against the owning of slaves.

Sources: 1. Tombstone 2. Virginia Marriages 1740-1850. 3. Census 1820. 4. DAR #42362. 5. Official Roster of the Soldiers of the American Revolution buried in the State of Ohio. 6. Pension Papers S17507. 7. Pension Papers of William Dye R8719. 8. Waverly News and Chillicothe Gazette 1894, Pioneer History. 9. Memoirs of the Lower Ohio Valley: Personal and Genealogical, Volume 2. 10. State Centennial History of the County of Ross.

****

Irvine Hyde age 14

Irvine Hyde was born on 23 February, 1762 in Mecklenburg County, Virginia, and he died on 10 January, 1838 in Tennessee. He received a pension of $80 a year. His wife Mary applied for his pension after he died, and it was rejected.

"About the year 1776 I having been the number 2 (according to the regulation the men were numbered from 1 to 10 and served in turn) was called as a militia soldier while living in said County for the term of three months my Captain was by the name of Richard Whitton, were marched to Petersburg and was there discharged, he does not remember how long he was in this tour of duty but believes about six weeks."

"Some six months after this I was ordered out on a tour of duty in the service of the United States for 3 months to guard the fairies over the Roan Oake River to prevent the British from landing in this expedition I was in active service a good part of the said 3 months and was liable the whole time to obey orders at a moment's warning."

"Next after and about the year 1781 was called out as a militia soldier together with about 300 others for the term of six months to go to the siege of Little York said Army rendezvoused at H. Delaney's Tavern Elijah Graves was our Captain James Hunt our Lieutenant and Lewis Burrell our Colonel. From thence I marched with said army to hog Island on James River and from thence to Williamsburg remained there one day until orders were received from General Washington at what point we should join him, the Army was ordered to __?__ back and go up the River and cross above the fork that they might be out of all danger of the enemy accordingly I marched with said Army across above said fork of York River and down the Gloshar side to head quarters. On the arrival of this army there was selected out of it for special service one hundred fifty Grenadiers of which I was chosen one and fifty well built men for light infantry. I was put under one Stephen Mabury as Captain Commander of said Grenadiers and marched down near to the picket guard of the British and there remained on duty every day for about 3 or 4 months until he was discharged having nearly completed the six months."

"I was called out to duty and for which whole time I was liable to serve if ordered by his officers. I remained under the command of said Maberry until an order was issued to attempt one night to scale the walls of Glosher in the attempt of which affiant's Capt Maberry was the foremost with me and the rest of the grenadiers except one company of Grenadiers *of the regular troops which went before being first fire upon by the Sentinel then by the cannon of the Fort Just as the whole army had reached the place assigned to it French troops and all being about 10,000 strong and when I had reached so near the wall that night that he put his hand on it the Army was ordered to __?__ every moment we expect the word to be given to scale the walls which no doubt would have been bloody work at least it was so thought by all, my Captain Maberry having undergone so much fear during the firing of the cannon, and the guard and during that awful moment of suspense when we expected every moment the command to mount the walls that next morning he resigned his commission and returned home. I was put under a regular officer after this and served under him until the siege was raised and Lord Cornwallis surrendered &, I cannot now recollect the name of this last officer under whom he served."*

"I remember to have seen Col Talton on the day of the surrender riding a fine imported Stallion called black and all Black, Affiant knew this horse well for he had once belonged to one Sir Peyton Skipwith of Virginia. After the British had surrendered and stacked their arms I was ordered with others to collect the arms that had been left laying about after this we were ordered to headquarters to our respective companies there obtained our certificates, I have lost mine and were verbally discharged."

Days after the surrender of Cornwallis the townspeople of Yorktown sought to take items that the British had taken from them. Lieutenant Colonel Banastre Tarleton was publicly humiliated, when a man, named Mr. Day, threatened the Colonel with a wooden stick demanding the return of the horse he was riding. The Colonel gave up the animal without a fuss, which delighted the crowd of onlookers.

Sources: 1. U.S. Pension Roll of 1835. 2. Pension Papers R5464. 3. Let the Drums Roll: veterans and Patriots of the Revolutionary War Who Settled in Maury County, Tennessee by Marise Parrish Lightfoot. 4. The Guns of Independence: The Siege of Yorktown, 1781 by Jerome A. Green.

****

Andrew Jackson age 14

Andrew Jackson's father died shortly before Andrew was born on 15 March, 1767 in Waxhaws, which was on the border of North and South Carolina. Andrew always claimed South Carolina as his birth state. Andrew's mother hoped he would become a Presbyterian minister, but she saw that there was little chance for that to happen. Young Andrew enjoyed playing pranks, cursing, and fighting, which was hardly the proper background for becoming a minister.

When Andrew was 13 his brother Hugh got his mother's permission to join the American army. At the Battle of Stono fought on 20 June, 1779 Hugh was ill and told not to engage in the battle, however, he joined in the battle. He died after the battle from heat exhaustion and fatigue.

In 1781 he was 14 when he first took part in the revolution. *"I was never regularly enlisted, being only fourteen when the war practically ended. Whenever I took the field it was with Colonel Davie, who never put me in the ranks, but used me as a mounted orderly or messenger for which I was well fitted, being a good rider and knowing all the roads in that region. The only weapons I had were a pistol that Colonel Davie gave me and a small fowling-piece that my Uncle Crawford lent me."*

"I was in one skirmish, that of Sands House, and there they caught me, along with my brother Robert and my cousin Tom Crawford."

Andrew and Robert were now prisoners of the hated British dragoons. During their captivity one of the officers approached Andrew and ordered the young boy to clean off his boots. Andrew, who was noted for his temper replied, *"Sir, I am a prisoner of war and claim to be treated as such."*

The officer became enraged that a young boy, and a despicable rebel besides that, would address him in such a manner. The officer drew his saber and swung it at Andrew who ducked and at the same time raised his left hand to block the blow. The saber cut Andrew's head and gashed his fingers. Andrew would carry the scars from this encounter for the rest of his life. As an adult he would sometimes run his fingers over the scar on his head as a reminder for his hatred for the British. The officer then shipped Andrew and Robert off to a prison at Camden, South Carolina.

British prisons were noted for their harsh conditions and treatment. Their prisons had no bedding, medicine, and little food. Soon both boys contracted the dreaded small pox. Their mother was determined to get the boys released to save them. Some accounts suggest that she arranged a prisoner exchange of British soldiers for her boys and several other Americans. Another account reports that an exchange was taking place at the time, and she persuaded the British to include her two sons in the exchange. Whatever happened she managed the release of her boys and faced a long journey home with only two horses to carry the three of them.

Poor Robert was so sick that he could not sit upright and had to be lashed to the horse. She rode the other horse, and Andrew walked along side with bare feet. Just before they reached home there was a hard rain that soaked the weary travelers. Two days later Robert died, and Andrew was down with the pox and a fever. When Andrew finally recovered he said, *"When it left me, I was a skeleton, not quite six feet long and a little over six inches thick! It took me all the rest of that year (1781) to recover my strength and get flesh enough to hide my bones."* By the time he recovered Cornwallis had surrendered and the war was almost over in the south.

Andrew's mother went to Charleston Harbor to care for her cousins who were among the sick and wounded Americans in British prison ships. While there she caught cholera and died. When the war had finally ended in September of 1783, Andrew had lost his father, mother, and both brothers during the war. He blamed the British for his loses. Andrew probably never imagined that he would grow up to become the 7th President of the United States.

Sources: 1. Best little Stories from the American Revolution by C. Brian Kelly. 2. A History of Andrew Jackson by Augustus C. Buell, 1904. 3. Life of Andrew Jackson by Marquis James, 1938. 4. Young Andrew Jackson in the Carolinas: A Revolutionary Boy by Jennifer Hunksicker.

****

Matthew Jackson age 14

Matthew Jackson was born on 16 January, 1763 in Massachusetts, and he died on 14 July, 1823 in Cincinnati, Ohio. He married Jane Campbell in New York on 4 October, 1792. She received his pension of $80.00 a year after his death.

"In the month of March in the year seventeen hundred & seventy seven I enlisted as a private joining for three years..." Matthew enlisted for three years as a fifer and served under Captain Caleb Keen's Company which was commanded by Colonel William Shephard in the 4th Massachusetts Regiment. Matthew spent the winter of 1777-78 at Valley Forge and was present at the Battle of Monmouth on 28 June, 1778.

During this battle Matthew and the 4th Massachusetts was part of the 2nd Massachusetts Brigade under the command of Brigadier General

John Glover, who was under command of Major General Lord Stirling. Lord Stirling's troops were on the left flank of the American forces. During the battle they repulsed a British attack of the 42nd (Black Watch) Regiment. The Americans claimed a victory on that hot summer day.

The 4th Massachusetts also participated in the Battle of Rhode Island on 29 August, 1778. One important event happened at this battle. The 1st Rhode Island, under Colonel Christopher Greene, was composed of African Americans, Native Americans, as well as European-American settlers. Most of the African Americans were former slaves and the General Assembly of Rhode Island compensated their former owners for the loss of these men's services

On 7 October, 1778 Matthew was with the 4th Massachusetts, when it was led by Major General Benedict Arnold against British General Burgoyne at Saratoga. The battle took place in a wooded area south of Saratoga called Bemis Heights. This American victory was a turning point in the American Revolution. When the King of France was informed of this victory, he was willing to enter the war on the side of the Americans.

The original song to the tune of Yankee Doodle was first sung by British officers to make fun of the colonial people. At the beginning of the Revolution the colonists changed up the words to the tune and sang it to mock the British. On October 17 Burgoyne surrendered his sword to General Gates, who promptly returned it. The 6,000 men British army marched out to surrender their arms, while the American musicians played "Yankee Doodle" which highly insulted the British. Fifteen year old fifer Matthew Jackson was playing "Yankee Doodle" that day.

Matthew was discharged on 30 March, 1780 at Middle Highlands opposite West Point. He enlisted again as a fifer in April 1782 in Captain Timothy Allen's Company of Colonel Samuel B. Webb's 1st Connecticut Regiment. In June of 1783 he was transferred to Captain Elisha Hopkins Company of light infantry commanded by Lieutenant Colonel William Hull. He served there as a fifer until 4 January, 1784, when he was discharged.

When former soldiers like Matthew applied for a pension, they not only had to prove service but they were required to make an accounting of their individual financial worth to show that they were in need of the pension. Many soldiers included their possessions and their worth. To show an example I have Matthew's list of possessions. He did not mention any other income, land or debts. He listed his wife and the ages of all his children. He stated 8 of them were capable of supporting themselves (they were over 20 years of age) and 3 were not capable.

From 4 September, 1820:

2 cow's supposed to be each worth $18.00.........$36.00

3 Swine & pigs worth............................$25.00

1—2 horse wagon..............................$40.00

1 set of Harness, considerably worn...............$15.00

1 plow..$15.00

Household furniture (exclusive of wearing

Apparel and necessary bedding) consisting

of 1 Table, 3 chairs, a few knives & forks, Tea

cups & saucers and plates etc. suppose

to be worth..................................$10.00

                total $135.00

Sources: 1. Saratoga: Turning Point of America's Revolutionary War, by Richard M. Ketchum. 2. The Battle of Rhode Island, by Charles Warren Lippitt. 3. Sons of the American Revolution Application. 4. Massachusetts Soldiers and Sailors in the Revolutionary War, Vol. 8. 5. Pension Application W10142.

****

Enoch Jenkins age 14

Enoch Jenkins was born on 16 August, 1763 in Malden, Massachusetts, and he died on 5 January, 1846 in Java, New York. He married Hannah Day. Enoch received a yearly pension of $96.

"I enlisted for the term of three years on the 20 Day of May 1777 in the State of Massachusetts in the company commanded by Capt. Ephraim Cleveland in the Regiment Commanded by Col. Michael Jackson in the line of Massachusetts. I continued in said corps until 1780 then enlisted during the war in the light Infantry commanded by Capt. John Bumbam and continued to serve in said Company until the 12th of June 1783."

Enoch belonged to the 8th Massachusetts Regiment that was raised on 23 April, 1775. Colonel Michael Jackson was given command of the Regiment in 1 January, 1777. Enoch and the 8th Regiment were commanded by General Gates at the Battle of Saratoga fought on 19 September and on 7 October, 1777.

According to the *Memoirs of General Lafayette*, *"General Baron Von Steuben while reviewing our regiment noticed in the ranks a very spruce young lad. The boy was handsomely formed, standing erect, with the air of a soldier, his gun and equipment in perfect order. The Baron, struck with his military appearance, patted under his chin to elevate his head still more erect, viewed him with a smile, and said, "How long have you been a soldier? You are one pretty soldier in miniature, how old are you?" "Seventeen, sir." "Have you got a wife?" Then calling to the colonel, he said, "Col. Jackson, this is one fine soldier in miniature."*

Sources: 1. Vermont Pensioners 1835. 2. Tombstone 3. D.A.R. Lineage Book, Vol. 15. 4. Pension Papers S39776. 5. Memoirs of Gen Lafayette, 1825.

****

John Jenks age 12

John Jenks was born in 1768 in Providence, Rhode Island, and he died 19 October, 1843 in Wyoming, Pennsylvania. He married Penelope Webb in 1795.

His father John Jenks was an officer of a unit of minutemen at the beginning of the revolution and fought at Lexington. He was wounded and placed in a meeting house in Roxbury and died soon afterwards leaving a wife and three children.

After his father's death, John about 8 years old was apprenticed to Samuel Whipple a distance relative of Ashford, Connecticut. When John turned 12, he couldn't wait to get away from his guardian who he apparently did not like. He ran away, and as he stated in his pension application, *"I first enlisted at Ashford, Connecticut but mustered out being then 12 years old."*

Mr. Whipple was drafted and *"managed the affair as to get me enlisted and mustered among the same recruits from whom a short time before I had been mustered out!"* So on 15 April, 1780 12 year old John Seymour Jenks became a drummer in Captain Selah Benton's 7th Company of the 5th Regiment Regular Continental Line under the command of Col. Sherman. Records record that he received a bounty of 30 pounds.

"I was transferred to Captain Walkers 2nd Company of the 3rd Regiment commanded by Samuel B. Webb. I was discharge at West Point in 1783." He was discharged the 20th of August.

John would have been present at the Battle of Springfield, New Jersey which was fought 23 June, 1780. The British were hoping to attack Washington's Army at Morristown, New Jersey. One thousand five hundred Continentals with an undetermined number of militia defeated six thousand British troops. The British were unable to advance and were forced to withdraw. This was one of the final major battles of the war in the north. The Americans suffered 62 casualties and the British had over 250.

After his discharge, he returned to his old master to finish out his service to him. He found that he was free, so he returned to Providence, Rhode Island to help support his widowed mother. He soon left and followed a seafaring life from 1783 until 1794. After his marriage to Penelope they moved to Orange County, New York.

In 1818 he applied for a pension and had no trouble proving his service because all the men in the company remembered the *"Little Blue Drummer Boy"* named Jenks. He wrote in his application, *"my occupation is that of a common school teacher or laborer as occasion may require— I am infirm by a rupture which I received in the army. I am not able to do more than one-third of the labor of an able bodied man. My wife is afflicted with asthma."* He showed that he owed over $700 to friends that had helped to support him. He was given a pension of $8.00 a month, and in 1821 he received a bounty land grant of 100 acres in Pennsylvania.

Sources: 1. Pension application S39775. 2. Lists and Returns of Connecticut Men in the Revolution, 1775-1783 by Connecticut historical Society. 3. The Record of Connecticut Men in the Military and Naval Service during the Revolution by Henry Johnston. 4. The Oxford Handbook of the American Revolution. 5. Children and Youth in a New Nation by James Marten. 6. Sons of the American Revolution Application.

****

Nicholas Johnston age 14

Nicholas Johnston was born on 24 February, 1764 in Dumfries, Scotland, and he died on 24 December, 1821 in Hamilton County, Ohio. At about the age of 13 he was conscripted into the British Army. In 1778 he deserted and floated down the Hudson River in the winter to join the American Army. After the war he moved to Cincinnati in 1789, when it was still called Losantiville.

Sources: 1. Tombstone 2. The Official Roster of the Soldiers of the American Revolution Buried in the State of Ohio.

****

Epaphras Jones age 13

Epaphras Jones was born on 19 February, 1764 in Hartford, Connecticut, and he died 15 February, 1847 in New Albany, Indiana. He married (1) Mary "Polly" Read on 8 June, 1788 in Massachusetts and (2) Mary Ann Silliman on 25 January, 1822 one year after the death of Polly. He served with his brother Richard 9also in this book). Epaphras received a yearly pension of $80 for his service.

"I enlisted in the Army of the United States in May 1777 with (not recollected) and served in the (not recollected) Regiment of the Continental line under the following named offices Samuel B Webb, Col Williams, Levington, Lt Col Ebenezer Nutington, Maj Tho Wanter, Capt of Grenadiers Robert Walker, Capt of Infantry James Watson (may be Jr.) Williams—Wells—Wright—part of the Captains of Battalion, Cols Charles Hopkins, subaltern officers Flower, Sargt--Major West surgeon—I left the service May 1780 having served three years. I enlisted in the town of Hartford County of Hartford and State of Connecticut was at the Battle of Rhode Island (but not in it) was one of the band of musicians attached to the Regt do not recollect what particular company."

A subaltern officer is the term used to describe commissioned officers below the rank of captain. The Continental Army did not have enough money to buy uniforms for the men so they needed a way for soldiers to be able to tell who commissioned officers were. Field officers could have red or pink colored cockades (a knot of ribbons) in their hats, the captains had yellow or buff, and the subalterns had green.

"Service of the Regiment were 1777 at the north River--Peekskill—Fishkill—New Windsor to Kingston I returned and halted at West Point the winter of 1777 and 1778 where we built Fort Webb. In the year 1778 moved to Rhode Island were at providence—Bristol—Warren-- ? Ferry—winter of 1778-1779 in barracks at Norton Massachusetts after the British evacuated the inland of Rhode Island we took possession of Newport Rhode Island crossed from thence to Greenwich continued our

march through Connecticut by way of Hartford to ___?___ point on the North River crossed to Stony Point thence to Hackensack New Jersey proceeded on our march to Morristown New Jersey where we intended until January then halted through the winter of 1779 and 1780 received a discharge May 1780."

Sources: 1. Massachusetts Marriage 1633-1850. 2. Indiana Marriage Index 1800-1941. 3. Census 1820, 1830, & 1840. 4. U.S. Revolutionary War Rolls 1775-1783. 5. Pension Papers S16889.

****

Horatio Jones age 13

Horatio Jones was born on 19 November, 1763 in Chester County, Pennsylvania, and he died on 18 August, 1836 in Geneseo, New York. He was married to Sarah Whitmore in 1784 in Schenectady, New York by the Rev. Samuel Kirkland. After Sally's death, Horatio married Elizabeth Starr in 1793 in Groveland, New York. Young Horatio worked in his father's gunsmith shop and became a skilled marksman. He was very good at riding, wrestling, and running.

"I entered the service of the United States in character of a Musician being a fifer in the autumn of the year 1776. I volunteered into the company of Rifle men commended by Captain James Parker in the Regiment commanded by Col. John Piper and I resided at the time of my so entering the said service at a place called then Old Fort Littleton in Bedford County and State of Pennsylvania. I joined the company in that neighborhood. We were immediately marched to Philadelphia and from thence after a short space to Trenton and finally to Princeton in New Jersey where we were quartered in the college at Princeton where I remained till in the winter when being attacked by the small pox. I was removed to a Pox hospital some two miles from the college where I remained long confined with that disease. I was quartered at the college General Putman who was at that time in command at that place had his quarters a short distance perhaps half a mile from the college and I used very frequently to see General Putman and his aid whose names I believe was Humphrey. I have often been present when scouting parties received their orders or __?__ from General Putman. I remained till spring or early summer when the Regiment was discharged and I returned home barely recovered from the effects of the small pox."

"After I returned from this expedition it was previous to the expedition of Col Brodhead engaged in those several tours of duty in the

service of the United States in each of which I volunteered on one of these occasions I went as one of a company to guard the Public Stores where were sent from Philadelphia to Pittsburgh and on another of these occasions I was employed in guarding the Tories who had been imprisoned in Bedford Jail in both of these engagements I was employed six months."

"In the Spring of the year 1778 I entered said service again as a volunteer near the Borough of Bedford in the state of Pennsylvania under Captain John More commanding a company of rangers or spies as they were called. Soon after entering the said company we were marched to a Block House on the Frankstown Branch of the Juniata River in the state of Pennsylvania. The company was stationed to keep the Indians back from the frontier settlements. We were frequently engaged in scouting parties and remained in the service during this engagement nine months."

"In the summer of the year 1779 enlisted under Capt Irwin but Captain Irwin did not accompany the company in the service. John Jemison first Lieutenant and Henry Armstrong Second Lieutenant was in command. I immediately marched to Pittsburgh in Philadelphia where the Regiment assembled and was under the command of Col Broadhead. We remained at Pittsburgh several weeks from thence we marched up the Allegany River and at the Brokenstraw narrows on the Allegany River a skirmish was had with the Indians which several Indians were killed from thence we marched to the towns of Seneca and Delaware's on the head waters of the Allegany River and destroyed their house grain cattle etc. From thence the Regiment returned to Pittsburgh but the company to which I belonged stopped at Old Fort Katanion where we remained under Lieutenant Jamison as a frontier guard till the winter when we descended the river to Pittsburg from thence we were marched to a place called Hannoks Town where we remained till spring. I returned home having performed the tour of duty."

"Either in the early part of the summer of 1780 or 1781 and in which year I am unable to recollect being at my Fathers house where I then resided where I then received information that a small party of Indians had within a few miles attacked and killed two men and carried off one woman captive. Captain John Boyd of the United States Army was there at Bedford in the recruiting and immediately upon receiving this information called for volunteers to join the twelve recruits there under him to go in pursuit of the Indians. Twenty persons of which I was one immediately volunteered to go under the said Captain Boyd."

"We immediately commenced the pursuit and during the next day arrived at the Block House on the Frankston branch of the Juniata where I had previously been quartered. We remained till early the next morning when we continued the pursuit and about four miles from the said Bloch House met with a Body of 83 Indians under the __?__ if several of their chiefs who immediately commenced a vigorous attack and after killing eight whites and taking seven prisoners and dispensing the residual of the company immediately removed with me who with Captain Boyd and five others were prisoners over the Allegany Mountains to Cananda on the head waters of the Genesce River in the state of New York."

"After many perils and severe trails I was adopted into the Indian nation. Captain Boyd was delivered over to the British and I was detained till after the peace and in fact I remained a prisoner with the Indians till after the Treaty of Fort Stanwix and was not given up by them with the other prisoners in pursuance of that Treaty. I remained until the year 1785 before I got clear of the Indians."

Captain Boyd led his men, including Horatio, in pursuit of the Indians that had raided the settlement. One morning the unit was trapped by the Indians in an ambush. Horatio tried to run to safety but was captured. A man called Jack Berry, half-white and half-Indian, told Horatio that he did not need to be afraid and that he would make a good Indian boy. A Seneca woman had asked Berry to find a captive to replace her son that had been killed in battle.

Horatio saw several of the American captives tortured and killed as the party made their way to the Indian village. He gained the respect of the Seneca, because Horatio showed no sign of hunger, fatigue, or anger. Once when one of the Indians killed a deer, Horatio and several other young Indians were sent to retrieve the animal. A foot race to the fallen animal began between Horatio and the fasted Indian runner named Sharp Shins. The Indian earned the name as a runner from the British at Fort Niagara. They said he ran so fast that his shins cut the air. Horatio beat Sharp Shins to the deer, and as a result he won further respect from the Indians and the hatred of Sharp Shins. Horatio now was treated a little more leniently than the other prisoners.

When the group finally reached the Indian camp at Caneadea, the captives were forced to run the gauntlet. Many Indian tribes had this ceremony for the amusement of the tribe and for the captives to atone for their people's wrongs to the Indians. Each prisoner would have to run a certain distance from the starting point to the council house. The route was between two lines of old men, squaws, and young boys armed with various weapons to strike the captives as they ran by.

Horatio was able to run the gauntlet with minimal injury thanks to what Jack Berry whispered to him. Berry told Horatio the trick was to follow very close behind the next to last runner and stay near one line of attackers. By staying near the line it would prevent the attackers to have ample time or room to hit him. The trick was successful for Horatio. However, the man in front of him was beaten so badly that his head was nearly sliced off. Besides Horatio, Captain Boyd survived the gauntlet and was later turned over to the British.

That night at council Horatio was accepted into the Indian tribe. Jack Berry told the council that he was asked to bring a young boy back to replace the son that one of the women had lost. The woman was the sister of the Chief of the tribe, Chief Shongo. Horatio was welcomed into the tribe and was given the name Hoc-sa-go-Wah, which meant "handsome boy." His adoptive Indian mother thought he was the most handsome young man she had ever seen. In time Horatio would gain great influence over the Indians. They grew to respect his honesty, bravery, and strength.

Horatio realized that with nearly 200 miles of wilderness from home and without a compass or trail, that escape was not very possible. He accepted his situation, learned their language, and entered into the life as a tribe member. He became fluent in the language of the Seneca and served as an interpreter. He took on the job of questioning white captives, trying to please his Indian family and saving the captives from harm.

Major Van Campen was captured by the Seneca Indians and taken back to the village for interrogation by Horatio. The Major had earlier earned a reputation as an Indian killer. In April of 1782 the Major was captured and held by a small group of Indians, and he was able to escape when he got free and killed his captives. If his new captives learned of what he had done, they would quickly put him to death.

When the Indians and their captive arrived at the village, he was questioned by Horatio who knew who the Major was. The Indians asked Horatio if he knew the prisoner's name. Horatio answered truthfully, "I have never seen him before." Horatio knew of the Major, but this was the first time he had ever seen him. He kept the Major's secret and the Indians later turned the Major over to the British. Horatio had saved the Major's life.

Horatio became famous throughout the region. A British officer, Captain Powell, offered to buy at any price Horatio's freedom from the Seneca. The Indian chief refused saying that the boy was sent by the Great Spirit as a special gift for the good of the tribe. He ended by saying, *"A Seneca will not sell his own blood."* Horatio was later appointed a chief with the new name of Ta-ya-da-o-who-koh meaning "lying across," symbolizing his bonding of whites with Indians.

In one of the other captive's tribe was a young white woman named Sarah Whitmore. She confided in Horatio of her concerns about an Indian she did not like wanting to marry her. Horatio solved the problem by asking her to marry him. They were married by a missionary in 1784 after being freed by the Treaty of Stanwix.

The Treaty of Fort Stanwix was finalized on 22 October, 1784 between the United States and the nations of the Iroquois League. Land was exchanged and prisoners were to be returned. In 1797 The Treaty of Big Tree was signed between the Seneca Nation and the United States. Horatio, who had gained his freedom, was one of two interpreters present. The Indians gave up their rights to nearly all of their traditional homeland in the State of New York.

In 1785 Horatio became a fur trader, and he built a log cabin for his family on Seneca Lake. One evening a young man came to his door. He had just started a career as a trapper and was now lost. He purchased the entire stock of Horatio's furs and hired him to collect pelts exclusively for him and to deliver them to New York City. This partnership between Horatio Jones and John Jacob Astor continued for many years.

In 1780 Horatio was appointed by George Washington as an agent and interpreter for the six nations. For the next 40 years he served in this capacity, while helping to negotiate treaties and keeping the peace between the Indians and the whites. He was also the favorite interpreter for the great Indian orator Red Jacket. Since Red Jacket liked to drink to the excess at times, Horatio was also called upon to sober him when it was time to give a speech.

When Sarah died in 1792 he married 17 year old Elizabeth Starr in 1793. They were given a 3,000 acre farm by the Indians. The Indians feared the area was haunted by a headless ghost, but they thought Horatio's powers would be able to counteract its evil.

In his later years he became a prosperous farmer and kept contact with many of his old friends. At one dinner, given in his honor, several Indian chiefs were invited including his old rival Sharp Shins. The two old men smoked a peace pipe to put an end to their rivalry.

When a former soldier files for a pension he is required to have people write to attest to his having served. Two of the letters written on behalf of Horatio Jones were a little different from the usual letters written.

Written in January of 1834 by Major Moses Van Campen:

"I & a detachment of rifleman were attacked by Indians on 16 April, 1782. All the Americans were killed except me and nine of my men. We were taken prisoners & taken to the Indian village. I was separated from my men and taken to a camp of warriors. I was soon surrounded by a large number of savages and understood a prisoner was sent for to examine me. I found the prisoner was Horatio Jones who had been taken prisoner in Capt. John Boyd's company of Riflemen in April or May of 1781. He had learned to speak their language and the said Jones was the interpreter."

"The said Jones knew that I had been a prisoner before with the Indians and had killed the party, which the said Jones kept as a secret from the Indians and was the means of saving my life."

The next letter was written on 27 January, 1834 and signed with the mark of four of the Indians that held Horatio captive:

"We were of the party of Seneka Indians that took Horatio Jones on the waters of the Juanita in the state of Pennsylvania and fighting under Captain John Boyd in the Revolutionary War. We also certify that he was kept a prisoner among the Indians about four years." Signed with their x mark.   Sunfish   Big Snow   Blue Eyes   Col Pollard

Sworn and given to the Justice of the Peace, D.H. Bissell"

The pension office did not give Horatio credit for the 4 years he spent in captivity, because they said that there was no proof that he was in the military service under Captain Boyd. He was considered a civilian volunteer. He was awarded a yearly pension of $80 for his earlier service.

Sources: 1. History of Livingston County, New York 1678-1881, by Doty Smith, 1876. 2. Sketches of Border Adventures in the Life of Major Moses Van Campen by John Hubbard, 1842. 3. The Divided Ground-Indians, Settlers, & Northern Borderland of the American Revolution by Alan Taylor. 4. Ghosts & Hauntings of the Finger Lakes by Patti Unvericht.

5. Lineage Book D.A.R. Vol. 39, 1906. 6. U.S. Pension Roll of 1835. 7. Sons of the American Revolution Application. 8. Tombstone. 9. Pension Papers S23728.

****

Reuben Jones age 13

Reuben Jones was born on 5 October, 1766 in Craven County, South Carolina, and he died on 1 February, 1836 in Tuscaloosa, Alabama. He married Rebecca Golden in 1788 in Wilkes, Georgia. His pension was rejected, because he did not serve as a soldier for six months. Since he was a wealthy man he died not needing his pension.

According to his will he had at least 8 slaves that he left to his heirs. He apparently cared about his slaves, because he had a very unusual request in his will:

"It is my will and desire that my Negroes may be taken good care of & that none of them be hired out at Public Auction, notwithstanding they may be hired by minors, but to be hired out as private sales particularly Negro women & children."

Slaves sold at private auctions usually went for a better price and to a better "class" of buyer. The slaves that did not sell would then be taken to public auctions. Buyers there might be more likely to abuse their slaves.

"I was born in the year 1766 on the Hills of Santee Craven County South Carolina 20 miles from Cainbden on the Charleston Road -- at which place I continued to reside until the war, & at about the close of this 13th year in the fall of the year 1779 I volunteered under a press Master whose name was James McCormack acting as was understood in behalf of the United States troops & army, and authorized so to do by General Richardson. I did not engage in any particular period of service, but served that Fall and winter something more than four months. This service consisted of driving livestock to Moncks Corner; at which place it was butchered & thence carried by water to Charleston -- for this Service I received no pay. The next fall (1780) and after Gates defeat I joined Marion under Captain Nettles, for an unlimited service, & was with him through the fall of '80 and winter of '81 and the whole about two or three months; I was while thus engaged in the Battle or skirmish of Rights Bluff on Santee River, it is sometimes called Scoto Lake & sometimes Fort Watson. After this I returned home, & in the spring of '81 I engaged as a Waggoner under General Greene and served as such till fall. He was not far off when the Battle Eutaw Springs occurred, & was there with others

guarded by Captain Nettles. In the fall of 1781 I was engaged as an Express by James McCormick who acted under the authority of General Greene, while acting as an express I performed a great deal of dangerous service, when not immediately acting I staid at the house of said McCormick who was my uncle I marriage -- & I am an Orphan. I was afterwards employed to carry a Flag to Charleston to procure the release of an orphan child that was there which was near the close of the war & nearly completes my service, which altogether of amounts to about the time of 22 months."

Most of the service performed by Reuben consisted of driving wagons or carrying messages. This was not considered military service by the Pension Bureau. When he said he carried the flag to Charleston, he meant that he went there under a flag of truce. The Battle of Wright's Bluff occurred on 24 February, 1781. American General Sumter unsuccessfully tried to take a British fort at Wright's Bluff.

Sources: 1. Carry Me Back: The Domestic Slave Trade in American Life by Steven Deyle. 2. Will of Reuben Jones. 3. Sons of the American Revolution Application. 4. Pension Papers R5738.

****

Richard Jones age 14

Richard Jones was born on 8 June, 1766 in Guilford County, North Carolina, and he died on 14 August, 1857 in Tennessee. He married Mary Agnes Buchanan on 29 December, 1785.

"I entered the service of the United States under Captain Besheres in the State of North Carolina in the year 1780 where I was at that time resided and marched to the State of South Carolina where we had an engagement with the Tories and a parcel of British officers at a place called Colson's on the Pede River -- Gen Davidson was the commanding officer, and during the engagement received a wound which caused me to remain at that place for some length of time. From this place I was marched through different portions of South Carolina, and went to the Cheraws, which had been ____? __ __? __ fire some short time before the Army reached -- and pursued the enemy to Cambden. The Army was now under the command of General Gates. I was not in the battle that was fought at Camden having been left behind with the sick during this __?__ I believe that I was some part of the time under the command of Gen Sumpter."

I was honorably discharged from the service near Springfield in New Jersey."

It should be noted that Colonel Webb commanded the 9th Connecticut Regiment which was generally used to defend Connecticut, southern New York, and northern New Jersey.

The following is a letter in Richard's pension application from his brother Epaphras who was a musician in the same regiment and 3 years older. He shares quite a tale from a newspaper. He also gives a glimpse about what life was like during the harsh winter of 1779-80. He tells how his brother Richard met Mrs. Washington at a party in camp.

"He was put under the particular care of Capt Watson by his father of mine. He was considered to be a good fifer as was in the Regt tho "at that tender age"" In the year Seventeen hundred and Seventy Seven Col Webb took him with him on an expedition to Long Island with whom he was taken prisoner and taken to Newport Rhode Island I belonged to a band of Musicians in the same Regt. Which ___?__ did not accompany the expedition but were ordered to Hartford Connecticut when on our arrival we found our Col Webb who had been Paroled & my brother Richard was brought home by him to my father. Richard stated that he was taken on board Admiral Kipplers Ship when an officer asked him if he knew him? He replied, yes sir, it is Gen Phillips. The Gen took him into the cabin gave him a glass of wine and told him when he wanted anything to come to him--Gen Phillips had seen my brother at my fathers house."

"Soon after Col Webbs liberation a publication came out in Providence Rhode Island paper stating that 'A boy taken prisoner with Col Webb on board Admiral Kipplers ship was asked by an officer who he was? Repl'd he was one of King Handcocks Men, How came you one of King Handcocks men? [maybe a reference to John Handcock, President of the Continental Congress] *I enlisted to fight for him. Can you flog one of King Georges Men? Yes, if he is not bigger than me. The officers set up the Boatswains Boy as King George and the boy with Col Webb as King Handcock--they fought--King Handcock flogged King George and they gave him his liberty.'"*

"The services of our Regt were principally by the Hudson River Rhode Island and the hard winter of 1779-80 at the heights of Morristown New Jersey at the ___?__ place the sufferings of the army were great. A hard winter no shelter but thin tents to the middle of Jan--but a single blanket to a man--snowing ___?___ very little provisions, sometimes

Richard was in the Battle of Colson's Mill fought on 21 July, 1780. It was fought between American militia and Loyalist militia. The American commander, General Davidson, and his men were trying to surround the enemy at a farm house they were gathering at. A short battle developed resulting in the Americans killing several men and taking some prisoners. The rest of the Loyalists escaped into the countryside. General Davidson was one of two Americans wounded. The General was the only person in uniform, so he made a very inviting target.

"From this place I returned home, where I received orders to march to New Providence on a term of duty of 2 months and 14 days under the command of Captain Besheres and General Davidson as the commanding officer. After this term of service expired I returned home, and remained for some time when I volunteered under Colonel James Martin who raised a company of horsemen to suppress the Tories and British foraging parties in the County of Guilford. James Martin the officer under whom I first volunteered was wounded at a place called Alimance in a skirmish with the British when his Brother Samuel Martin took the command of the Company. I served in all between 8 and 9 months."

Sources: 1. Census of 1820 & 1830. 2. U.S. Pensions Roll of 1835. 3. Pension Papers W26799.

****

Richard Lord Jones age 10

Richard Jones was born on 15 March, 1767 in Connecticut, and he died on 23 July, 1852 in New Albany, Indiana. He married Elizabeth Clark on 3 July, 1806 in the Presbyterian Church by the Rev. Romine. On Richard's original tombstone it reads *"A musician in the Army of the Revolution."* The newer government issued stone reads *"Ten Year Old Fifer."* Richard served with his brother Epaphras, who is found in the 13 year old section in this book. He received a monthly pension of $8. Richard was a manufacturing merchant and lost his business and wealth due to the War of 1812.

"I enlisted as a fifer for the term of three years on the 20th day of June 1777 in the state of Connecticut in the company commanded by Capt James Watson the first year & the remaining past of the term of this service by Capt Samuel Williams, in the Regiment commanded Col Sam B. Webb in the line of the state of Connecticut in the Continental Establishment. I continued to serve in the Said Corps until the 20th day of June 1780 when

none--clothing nearly worn out. The officers of the Regt on a review by Gen Washington & his staff cut up their shirts & furnished each soldier with sufficient cloth to show a small white collar over his stock but hold not a shirt to their backs, the troops appreciated in such fine order--that Gen Washington was highly pleased Gen Layfette letter to Gov Reed 1780 stated the distress of the Army."

"At a dinner given by the field officers of our Regt in the Spring of 1780 to Generals Washington—Green--Layfette at which was Mrs. Washington & Mrs Green our band was before the hut for their amusement My brother was called in & introduced by Col Webb to the Ladies—he sang them a song--was presented with a glass of wine and Mrs. Washington presented him with a three dollar Continental bill which I presume he has to this day. I was discharge the service May Seventeen hundred & Eighty One and Richard Jones was discharged in June of Said year."

Sources: 1. Tombstone 2. New York Marriage Newspaper Extracts 1801-1880. 3. U.S. Newspaper Extractions from the Northeast 1704-1930. 4. Pension Papers W765. 5. Year Book of the Sons of the Revolution in the State of New York 1899.

****

Simeon Justice age 12

Simeon Justice was born on 4 June, 1765 in Pittsylvania, Virginia, and he died on 15 January, 1854 in Perry, Kentucky. He married Dalpha Johnson on 6 October, 1834 in Kentucky. Simeon enlisted with his 17 year old brother John and their father. The Census of 1840 records that Simeon owned 5 slaves. He received a yearly pension of $88.

Some members of the Justice ancestors claim that in the painting *Spirit of '76* the drummer is Simeon and the fifer is his brother John. The artist, Archibalt Williard, painted the scene for the Centennial Exposition of 1876. The figure in the middle was his own father, a gray-haired Baptist minister. The fifer was Hugh Mosher, who had been a fifer in the Civil War. The model for the drummer was Henry K. Devereux, the son of General Devereux.

"I was born in Pittsylvania County Virginia on the 4th day of June 1765, my age was recorded in the family Bible, which my father left at his death & which I suppose my mother has also left as she is likewise dead and died in South Carolina a few years ago. From Virginia I went with my father to Rutherford County North Carolina & and a short time removed

to Ninety Six district in South Carolina in which district at Fort Rutledge, me,, my father John Justice and my brother John Justice, on the first day of June 1777 enlisted or volunteered under Captain Benjamin Tutt -- who paid each of us $30 in Cash as bounty money -- our enlistment was for three years, which I served out, the greater part of the time at Fort Rutledge, but about four months, to wit from February to May 1780, me with a few others were sent from Fort Rutledge to Augusta in Georgia. It was early in June 1780 before I returned to Fort Rutledge & my time had expired but as times were very squally it was thought imprudent to discharge the men at the Fort. In a few weeks after I returned to Fort Rutledge, that place was taken by the British and me with all of Captain Tutt's Company who were then in the Fort were taken prisoners and on the 2nd day of July I was suffered to go at large on parole -- his parole is here shown -- And on the said 2nd of July, on the back of my parole, Captain Benjamin Tutt gave me my discharge. I served about one year of my time as a private and the remainder as the drummer to the Company."

Sources: 1. The Mentor, Vol. 9, Number 6, July 1, 1925. 2. Kentucky Pension roll of 1835. 3. Roster of South Carolina Patriots in the American Revolution. 4. Census 1840. 5. Pension Papers W7946.

****

Jared Kelley age 14

Jared Kelley was born on 7 April, 1764 in New Jersey, and he died on 3 September, 1822 in Springfield, New Jersey. His wife Mary received a widow's pension of $50 a year.

"I enlisted at Springfield in the county of Essex and state aforesaid in Captain Elinkinson Little's Company in the first Regiment of the New Jersey line commanded by Col. Matthias Ogden sone time in the spring of the year seventeen hundred and seventy-eight. I continued in said Regiment about six months during which time I was engaged in the Battle of Short Hills in the county of Essex aforesaid and was discharged at Mendham in Morris County."

Jared was in the Battle of Short Hills, which took place on 26 June, 1777. British General Howe had moved his army into the area in hopes of luring General Washington into a fight. Although there were several small skirmishes, the battle consisted mainly of each army moving men around either trying to engage in a fight or avoid one.

"I enlisted in said service in the month of January or February in the year seventeen hundred and eighty one at Springfield aforesaid in Capt Robert Neal's Company in the ___ Regiment of the Jersey line commanded by Col Samuels Sealy and continued in said Regiment one full year when I was honorably discharged at Second River in Essex county aforesaid."

Sources: 1. New Jersey Pensioners 1835. 2. Tombstone 3. U.S. Pension Roll of 1835. 4. Pension Papers W114.

****

David Kennedy age 12

David Kennedy was born in 1768 in Burke County, North Carolina, and he died on 21 September, 1850 in Garrard County, Kentucky. He married his second wife Jane Cox on 20 July, 1794 in Kentucky. He received a pension of $80 for his 4 or 5 years of service.

"I enlisted as a Spy in the spring of the year 1780 in the then District of Kentucky, at Kennedy's Station under Captain Andrew Kennedy, I served faithfully as an Indian Spy from that period until after long after the peace of 1783, the Indian War not having terminated. I believe it was about the 15th May 1780 when I first enlisted, and I was in active service constantly in spying and Hunting and was off and on for four or five years sent out with his company on what was called the wilderness trace to protect the newcomers against Indian depredations and hostilities. The service I performed was of the severest and hardest kind, finding my own arms, my own provisions, and my own clothing if clothing it could be called and always surrounded with danger. The movements of my company were as understood principally under the control of General Benjamin Logan, who was himself often with us, and often told us when and where to go. I have never received a cent for all my services. I have no written evidence of my service but I can establish facts which I hope will be satisfactory."

Sources: 1. U. S. Pensioners 1818-1872. 2. Pension Papers W7973.

****

John Kennelly age 8

John Kennelly was born on 21 December, 1768 in Fulton County, New York, and he died on 21 August, 1828 in Montgomery County, New York. His father John Kennelly Sr. was taken prisoner by a band of Indians in 1775. At the end of his third day of captivity he escaped and returned home to his family. He immediately took his family to an American fort for safety.

John Sr. then took his son John Jr., who was eight years old, and they both enlisted in February or March 1777 in the army. John Jr. was assigned as a drummer under Captains John O'Hara and Richard Lloyd in Colonel Moses Hazen's Regiment that was called "Congress' Own Regiment." John Kennelly Jr. served from 1777 until he was discharged on 13 June, 1783. John Jr. was at the Battle of White Plains and Yorktown. He saved his discharge papers that were signed by George Washington. John received a monthly pension of $8.

"I enlisted Sometime in the month of February or March in the year One thousand Seven hundred and Seventy Seven as a Drummer for and During the War and continued to perform that Duty until the time of my Discharge."

Sources: 1. Our County and its People: A Descriptive and Biographical Record of Saratoga County, New York. 2. New York Pensioners 1827-1870. 3. Pension Papers S42778. 4. The Bloodied Mohawk: The American Revolution in the Words of Fort Planks Defenders and Other Mohawk Valley Partisans by Kenneth D. Johnson.

****

Rodham Kenner age 14

Rodham Kenner was born on 3 August, 1763 in Fauquier County, Virginia, and he died on 24 August, 1842 in Logan County, Kentucky. He married (1) Eleanor Wroe on 29 December, 1790 and she died in 1799. He married (2) Elizabeth Haddox on 11 November, 1800. He received a yearly pension of $144 and 100 acres of land for his service. He was a farmer that owned 5 slaves.

"I enlisted as a Seaman on board the RoGally Page at Fredericksburg Virginia in August 1777 commanded by Captain James Markham [this was Rodham's uncle] *the names of the Lieutenants on board of said Galley were Richard and Henry Lightburn, from Fredericksburg. We sailed to the capes and were stationed in the Chesapeake Bay; after remaining on board the above named Galley I was transferred or turned over to the Ship Draggon Mounting sixteen Carriage Guns, which was commanded also by said Captain James Markham, the names of the Lieutenants were William Parker and Thomas Chandler, the name of the Surgeon was Swoap I had been on board the said Galley twelve or fifteen months before I was transferred as above stated, but the*

precise time I cannot recollect. I recollect also the name of the Sailing Master was Smith who killed a sailor on board with a hand spike by the name of Boswell when we were in the Act of anchoring in James River at a point not far from James town after cruising for some months in the Bay the Government bought a Brigg which had been sunk by reason of damage done by the ice in James River, the crew of the Draggon was employed in raising this Brigg, after she was repaired and fitted for sea, She was called the Jefferson in honor of Thomas Jefferson who was then Governor of Virginia, and was Captain Markham and a crew of the Draggon which he had before commanded were turned to the said Brig Jefferson there not being a sufficient number of us to man the Ship Draggon, We cruised for upwards of twelve months in the Bay and off the Coast in said Brigg during which time we took seven prizes the most of them small craft from New York which was about that time in possession of the British, at or about the close of the Cruise the whole of our little fleet which was in this part of the Bay was driven up James River a much Superior British force, and into the Chickahominy River to what was called the Ship Yard: whilst our little fleet composed of the following Vessels to wit the Ship Draggon, the Brigg Jefferson and the Thetis a 36 gun Ship a Short time previous had been launched at said Ship Yard, and several Galleys, lay at said Ship Yard an express reached us from Colonel Travis who lived near James town informing us that a British Ship aground off that place. One of the Roe Gallies which lay at the Shipyard was immediately fitted up and manned & placed under the command of our said Lieutenant Chandler and sent down to attack the British Ship, I was one of the Crew of this Galley, we sailed down and about the time we were within about two miles of her, we also ran aground, about sunset in the evening, the next morning about daylight we got off and soon discovered the British ship was also afloat and her boats towing her out into the Channel there being a Calm. We immediately made an attack upon her, the firing continued from both sides for about two hours, at about the expiration of this time two of our Row boats were discovered coming down to our relief well manned with musketeers; our Commander immediately ordered us to bear down up the British Ship, but we soon discovered two British Ships sailing up, which compelled us to abandon the idea of taking her. We again sailed up to the Ship Yard in the Chickahominy River, not long after this I left the naval service having served about three years and eight months."

"A Short time after I left the Navy say two or three months, I volunteered in a Company of Militia in my native County Fauquier in the State of Virginia under the command of Captain John Ball, Joseph Nelson *was Lieutenant in said Company and Thomas Nelson was Ensign. We rendezvoused at the Mobbin Hills, after we were organized our Company was placed in a Regiment Commanded by Colonel Elias Edmunds. We marched to the neighborhood of Williamsburg where Cornwallis then lay. After some time I was drawn to Yorktown I continued in the service until about the 1st of October 1781 at which time my tour of three months expired and being sick was taken home."*

Sources: 1. Census of 1820, 1830, & 1840. 2. U.S. Pension Roll of 1835. 3. Pension Papers S1228.

****

John Kercheval age 14

John Kercheval was born on 12 September, 1762 in Spotsylvania County, Virginia, and he died on 1 October, 1839 in Orangeburg, Kentucky. He married Jane Berry on 23 January, 1785. He received a yearly pension of $40, and she received a yearly widow's pension of $80. The Census of 1830 stated that he owned 9 slaves.

"I entered the service of the United States in the month of December 1776 in a Company of Volunteers raised by Captain Charles M Thurston, Philip Bush 1st Lieutenant Edward Smith 2nd Lieutenant and John Gilkison Ensign I marched with said Company about the 21st of said month and I distinctly recollect we arrived at Frederick Town on Christmas day about 12 o'clock 1776, we crossed Potomac at Harpers Ferry, we proceeded on the Road from Frederick Town by McAlister's Town, York Town & crossed the Susquehanna River on the Ice at Anderson's ferry staid all night in the Lancaster, passed thro the city of Philadelphia and halted at a Village called Frankfort a few miles beyond the City then on by Bristol, crossed the delaware River to Trenton, Prince Town and arrived at Morris Town about the 10th January then the headquarters of Genl Washington and in three or four days marched to Baskins Ridge where we were Stationed under the command of Genl Lord Sterling there was also at that place a Company of Light Horse commanded by Capt Caul of Bland's Reg of Virginia Cavalry and a Company of Rifle men belong to the Regiment commanded by Colonel & Lt. Colo. McCoy and Wilson called the Catannian Regiment of rifle men and towards the latter part of February Capt Thurston's Company of volunteers, Capt Cauls troop of Horse and the Rifle men marched to a small village called Quibble Town in the direction to Brunswick where a part of the British Army was Stationed and the next morning our Party was

joined by a Regiment of Maryland militia commanded by Colonel Beatty from or near Frederick Town we marched until about 1 o'clock when we met a detachment of British Infantry and Horse men, a sharp action ensued in which Captain Thurston was wounded and six of his Company was killed and wounded together with several of the rifle men and militia, the battle continued until Capt Caul discovered a much larger number of the British approaching and having dismounted some of his Horse men and mounting the wounded we retreated and returned back to Quibble Town from which we had marched that morning, the next day we returned to Lord Stirling's Quarters and was discharged in May following having been about six months."

"I intended to Join the Regiment under Thurston whenever he was able to take the field, the Colonel however did not return until the summer and was not then entirely recovered of his wound, he states that I went to see him and informed him that when ever he was able to take the field I would join as a volunteer, the Regiment ___?__ ___?___ by and understanding that General Burgoyne was proceeding towards New York from Canada and it being the opinion of Gentlemen in our Country that I would endeavor to make my way to New York to join the British Army there and being willing to join his Country men I started about the first of August 1777 and entered a Volunteer in the Company of Captain Thomas Berry of the 8th Virginia Regiment. The field Officers at that time was Bowman & Clark and the Brigade General Scott __?__ in Captain Berry's Company Baldwin and Eastin and the following named Persons, were some of the soldiers whose names I think must be enrolled in Captain Berry's Company now in the War Office if they were returned and preserved there, Charles Jones, Vernon Dunn, Isaac Dunn, Solomon Redman, John Robinson, __?__ Redman, William Orr, Thomas Hampton, ___?__ Mitchan, Michael Dean, and others I think I could name on Reflection, the Reason of my joining Captain Berry's Company in preference to any other was that Captain Berry was a near neighbor to his Father in Frederick County Virginia, when he raised his company. I continued to serve with the 8th Regiment until the latter part of the year 1778 in which year my Father sold his property at a __?__ of Twelve months and requested that I should return Home for the purpose of going with him to the Kentucky Country in the fall 1779 and the Indians being so Troublesome and the reduced value of the Money he __?__ for the property he sold compelled him to relinquish his previous determination of moving."

John joined the 8th Virginia Regiment in August of 1777. The Regiment at the start of 1777 had joined George Washington's main army as part of the 4th Brigade under the command of Brigadier General Charles Scott. At the Battles of Brandywine on 11 September, 1777 and Germantown on 4 October, 1777 John saw plenty of action on the American left wing. He then spent the winter at Valley Forge and trained under Baron von Stebun.

After Valley Forge, John was at the Battle of Monmouth on 28 June, 1778. The 4th Virginia was in the division placed under the command of Major General Charles Lee. Lee first turned the command of the advanced force down, because he had doubts about Washington's battle plan. When the division was increased by 5,000 men the command was given to Marquis de Layfayette. Lee changed his mind and requested the command back.

During the battle Lee overestimated the number of British troops he was facing, so he ordered a retreat after firing only one volley. Washington was advancing with the main force, when he encountered the retreating Americans. Washington asked who ordered this retreat and was told it was General Lee. *"Damn him,"* was the reply. He rode off and found General Lee and dressed him down publically and relieved him of command. In July Lee was court-martialed and relieved of his command for one year.

"Early in the spring of the year 1780 I was determined to go and join the Southern Army to which many of his old acquaintances in the Army had gone and proceeded as far as Albemarle Barracks in the spring of 1780 and at the Barracks met with Colonel Wood with whom he was acquainted. Wood requested to take charge of a __?__ of British Prisoners, then to be sent to Winchester Virginia which were ordered to be delivered to Col Kennady, the Commanding Officer at that place I remained there with the prisoners until a Guard could be collected to take charge of them that after I was relieved of the charge I again intended to go to the South but the fall of Charles Town and the deranged state of the Army in consequence thereof induced me to decline preceding for some time and before I could make it convenient again, Virginia was likely to be the site of War."

"I therefore remained at his Father's until Arnold landed in Virginia and I went to Richmond in Virginia and proceeded to join

General Baron Steuben not far from Peters burg, the next day after his defeat at that place and on General Lafayette's arrival in Virginia I went and entered a volunteer in Col. Stewart's Regiment of Regulars and was shortly afterwards appointed an assistant in the Quarter Masters Department by Maj John Prior in June was ordered to Williamsburg Virginia to make arrangements for the accommodation of the American Prisoners then about to return from Charles Town South Carolina & then returned to the Army and continued to execute such orders in the Quarter Masters ___?___ as I received and marched with the Army to the Siege of York Town, remained there until the surrender of Lord Cornwallis."

"About 12 or 14 days after the commencement of the siege an enterprise was undertaken the object of which was to take by storm to British Redoubts one to be taken by a detachment of the American Line and the other by a detachment of the French. I applied to the officer appointed to command the Americans for permission to accompany them and was refused I then applied to Maj Lamotte a French gentleman and then an officer in the division of General Lafayette with whom I had become well acquainted during the time I served with Col Stewart's Regiment to procure permission for me to go with the french detachment and Maj Lamotte went with him to the French officer, introduced him and obtained his ___?___ for him to accompany the command which he did, the parties marched in the night with silence moved each to the place of attack and almost at the same moment carried the places by storm. The French officer and Major Lamotte both gave a certificate highly complementary and recommended me in strong terms as worthy of a Commission in the regular service of the Virginia line. I delivered the Certificate to General Thomas Nelson who was then with the Army in command of the Virginia militia and I think was afterwards elected Governor of Virginia to succeed Mr. Jefferson, and was promised by General Nelson the first vacancy that required to be filled in the Virginia line I marched with the British prisoners to Winchester then returned to my Father's in the neighborhood and it being the General Opinion that the war would soon end."

At the Battle of Yorktown John volunteered to join the men assigned to take the British redoubts #9 and #10. This was going to be a very dangerous undertaking, so why would John want to risk his life when the war was nearly over. The author believes that John was looking for a way to earn a commission as an officer in the army by engaging in something daring. The Americans were going to assault redoubt #10 and the French #9. John stated in his pension application that the American commander, which was Alexander Hamilton, refused his offer. As a favor

John was permitted to join the French attack on redoubt #10. Both attacks were successful.

In 1782 John Kercheval entered into the Sheriff's business under his father. He entered with the understanding that if the commission as an officer in the army, was offered John could quit and immediately join the army. His father sent John to Kentucky to supervise some land claims. John remained in Kentucky until the end of the year and returned to Virginia. His dream of an army commission never materialized.

In 1798 he moved with his family, his mother, and his younger brother, James, to Mason County, Kentucky. Some of the journey was by flatboat down the Ohio River. They landed near the mouth of Limestone Creek and moved about seven miles inland. There they cleared the land and built a log cabin on the high ground. In 1812 John raised a company to fight in the War of 1812, and he called two of his sons from Virginia to serve.

Sources: 1. Census 1830. 2. Sons of the American Revolution Application. 3. U.S. Pensioners 1818-1872. 4. Pension Papers W3023. 5. Something About the Kercheval Family by Buerdon Groves Parry and Lee Kerchval Carr included in the book Genealogies of Kentucky Families, Vol 1 A-M.

****

Nicholas Kern age 11

Nicholas Kern was born on 2 December, 1764 in Egypt, Pennsylvania, and he died there on 6 November, 1819. He married Catherine Sauger on 4 August, 1789.

In August of 1776 Nicholas was sent by his father to take a load of wheat from Egypt to Philadelphia, which was a distance of about 60 miles. On the return trip Nicholas was ordered to haul wounded patriots from the Battle of Long Island (22 August, 1776) to Amboy, New Jersey, which was a distance of about 75 miles. Once at Amboy he was sent with another load of wounded men back to Philadelphia. He was gone a total of four weeks, and during this time his father did not know of his whereabouts.

Sources: 1. Sons of the American Revolution Application. 2. D.A.R. Lineage Book, Vol. 54.

****

James Kidd age 14

James Kidd was born on 22 April, 1766 in Grandville County, North Carolina. He married Lucy Jopling on 29 December, 1790. He received a yearly pension of $20.

"*I substituted for Isaac Bryant who was a Stewart for Colonel Nicholas of Albemarle County in said State, and entered the service under Colonel __ Richardson of the Militia, Major __ Woods, Captain James Woods, Lieutenant Horsley Goodman, Ensign Woods, all of the Militia, in the month of March 1781 at which time I was not fifteen years old by about a month. I resided when I entered the service in the County of Albemarle and State aforesaid, and rendezvoused at Sneeds Tavern below Charlottesville in said County, there was three companies rendezvoused at that place, the other Companies were commanded by Capt Miller & Capt Taliaferro, the Companies were then marched by the way of the three notched road to Richmond and was sometime on the march, to & fro, before we arrived at Richmond, where we drawed arms and joined the Army under General Nelson and was some time under General Lawson the forces then marched to Bottoms bridge, the British Army was then on the South side of James River marching to and fro, making feints, as I was informed to deceive our forces, the forces were constantly moving, at one time we marched to Newkent Courthouse, and then on the road towards Williamsburg, the British then made a feint, and it was said they were returning to Richmond, the forces were then divided some came up the Meadows Bridge, to keep in hearing of the British, and some took the road towards Richmond & some were left below Newkent Courthouse as a guard, at this time I was taken sick and remained sick north of the road, that leads from Newkent Courthouse to Williamsburg. How long I was sick I do not recollect but it was several weeks, after I had partly recovered Lieutenant Horsley Goodman & Sergeant Clarke called for me and I went with them to four Miles Creek below Richmond where I joined the Army again under the same Officers, about this time my tour of service of three months was about expiring, and Captain Nailor beat up for volunteers to join a Company to go down near to James town, I was the first who stepped out as a volunteer, the Company was formed and marched down by the Meadows Bridge, by the right hand road near the James River, near to James Town where the Company remained some time as a guard, until the news came, that the British forces were crossing the River at James Town part of them did cross, it was then that orders that the whole forces should unite, but General Waine brought on the action first General Lafayette laid with his forces on the opposite side of a Morass, as a reserve – the battle with Wayne was of short duration, the British embarked and went to York; at this time the news came that the British forces who remained on the South of James River were returning towards Richmond, when the Company under Capt Nailor in which I was, with several other companies were ordered back to Richmond to guard it; and the Companies marched as far back as the Malvern Hills, at this place I was again taken very sick, and I was sent by Sergeant Dudley & Moore to Richmond to get a hospital & medical aid."*

James is probably referring to The Battle of Green Spring, where the Americans were defeated on 6 July, 1781. General Anthony Wayne was ambushed by British forces under Cornwallis. This was the last major land battle before the Siege of Yorktown in October of 1781.

"I was recd by the Doctor and in a very few days it was reported that and insurrection of the Negroes was about to break out at Richmond to be aided by the British. I was then put into a Baggage Wagon, and went with several single Wagons, & guards to each, and was finally left at Col Boswell's tavern in Louisa, at that place the wagon in which I was, by some means got on fire, and before they could get me out I was very badly burnt on my shoulders & back, at that time unable to help myself and I staid there until my friends heard from me and they sent for me and I got home sometime in the early part of October having remained in the service a little upwards of six months. I remained disabled to work for fifteen months after I got home and is now a cripple from the burn & disease."

In 1833 James made the following statement, *"...when I volunteered under Captain Nailor I heard no inquiry made about my age, they wanted volunteers and I was in the service I presumed I was considered a good volunteer. I never knew anyone refused to be received who was able to raise a musket. Soldiers were wanted and so far as I know all were received who were willing to enter the service when the relations made no objections."*

Source: 1. Pension Papers S18481.

****

James H. Kidd age 14

James Kidd was born in 1764 in Mecklenburg County, Virginia, and hedied in 1840 in Oglethorpe, Georgia. He entered the army in 1779, and I assume that he was 14 at the time and did not turn 15 until after January. He received a yearly pension of $36.

"I was drafted in the militia of Virginia and entered the Service of the United States in the month of January in the year 1779 as a private in the company commanded by Capt Reuben Vaughn & served in the regiment commanded by Col. Lewellen Burwell the General under whom I first served was Gen Francis Mason whom I joined at Granville Court house North Carolina I was then marched by the way of Hillsborough, Salisbury, & Charlotte in North Carolina & Camden in South Carolina & joined General Lincoln at Bacons Bridge near Charleston S.C. was in a Skirmish near the place and afterwards in the battle of Stono I was then marched back to Virginia & discharged by Capt. Vaughn in the month of July."

At the Battle of Stono Ferry on 20 June, 1779 James was part of the Virginia Militia that was held in reserve. The battle was a British victory.

"From my desire to go in the army I reported myself old enough to be put on the Militia roll which was done and I was in a few days after drafted for the above service and entered the army at about fifteen years of age."

"In the year 1780 I was again drafted as a private for a three months tour of Duty in the Virginia Militia & marched under the command of Captain John Kendrick from Mecklenburg to Williamsburg in Virginia & was then ordered back how long I served this term I do not know ___?___ but I know not less than two months."

"Again in the year seventeen hundred & eighty one I Volunteered in the County of Mecklenburg in of Virginia & served a three months tour of duty commencing in January & ending in April in the company commanded by Captain John Brown whose company was attached to the regiment commanded by Col. Robert Muntford & Major Tucker. The regiment joined the command of General Lawson at Skipwiths ferry on the roanoak river after which he with Gen Lawsons command joined Gen. Greene at haw river in North Carolina, I was at the battle of Guilford & afterwards at Ramsey's Mill on the deep river & was then detached as Guard or part of guard and sent with prisoners to Albemarle court house in Virginia & was then marched back to Mecklenburg & discharged by Capt Brown. After my discharge, the company was to draw some salt at which time we were required to present their discharges, in order to show our right to draw I presented my discharge & never received it back and it was lost to me."

At the Battle of Guilford Court House fought on 15 March, 1781, James and his Virginia militia under the command of General Lawson was in the second line protecting the left flank. They were under heavy fire until they broke in the afternoon of the battle. Although, it was a British victory, Cornwallis lost 25% of his force. Another victory such as this, and he would lose the war. The older brother of James was in the Battle of Guilford Court House and in the same company (see next person, William Kidd).

James was present for the Battle of Ramsey's Mill fought on 19 March, 1781. After the battle at Guilford Court House, Cornwallis retreated with his army and stopped at Ramsey's Mill. Here he would tend to the wounded and gather provisions from the local people. During this time the Patriot army pursued and harassed them.

Source: 1. U.S. Pension Roll of 1835. 2. Pension Papers S16436.

****

William Kidd age 14

William Kidd was born on 16 December, 1763 in Mecklenburg County, Virginia, and he died on 8 March, 1845 in Oglethorpe, Georgia. He married Judith Carter on 8 August, 1781 in Mecklenburg, Virginia. After the war he was apparently a wealthy farmer, and according to the Census of 1830 he owned 10 slaves.

"*I was born in Mecklinburg county in Virginia on the 16th December 1763, according to the account handed down to me by his parents, there being no record of my age as far as I know. I lived in Mecklinburg when I entered the militia service in the revolutionary war, & lived there until I moved to Georgia in 1799, & settled in Oglethorpe county where I have lived ever since & where I now live. When I was near fifteen years old--to wit in the summer of 1778-- being well grown of my age I was employed as a substitute in the place of one William Perry for a tour of five months military service in the Revolutionary war against Great Britain. I was received as a substitute & performed the whole tour under the command of General Lewis & Captain Anderson. I marched first to Portsmouth & then to Turkey Point not far from Baltimore & my only duty during the expedition was simply marching & guarding. I had no battle & not so much as a skirmish---when the time expired I was discharged at Portsmouth.*"

"In the year 1780, I performed another tour of military service in the militia of Virginia, of five months duration, as a substitute for my father James Kidd, who had been drafted for that length of time. I left home this trip I think in the month of May. During this tour I marched to Hillsborough in North Carolina under the command of Captain Benjamin Ferrel my regiment (the number of which I do not now recollect) was commanded by colonel Lukes or Lucas From Hillsborough I marched to the Gum swamp near Camden South Carolina, when under General Gates I was defeated by Cornwallis & Tarlton. During this engagement I was severely wounded by a cut on the left shoulder which I received from the sword of the enemy. My post in this battle was among the regulars on the right wing of the army--the evening before the battle the following plan was formed, which was executed the next day. Four men were selected out of the company of each militia captain so as to correspond with the number of regulars, & these select militia men & regulars were placed alternately along in the right wing of the army & of this number I was one. I fought in the Brigade commanded by General Stephens Being defeated I retreated to Charlotte & thence to Hillsborough. I was carried home, where I received a permit to remain until I had sufficiently recovered."

The Battle of Camden, also called The Battle of Gum Swamp, was fought on 16 August, 1780. When the British troops began the battle just after dawn, they fired a volley into the militia regiments facing them and then did a bayonet charge. The majority of the militia units broke and ran into the woods. This was not unusual behavior for most militia units. When American General Andrew Pickens complained to General Green about the conduct of the militia, he said they were, *"among the worst of men,"* he had ever commanded. General Green replied he was, *"sorry that Militia desert you, but it is the practice of all Militia."* This was also known to the British, and it would later be used to help defeat them at The Battle of Cowpens.

William stated that before the battle some militia men were spaced in between regular army troops. I suspect that this might have been done in hope that the militia men would stand and fight with the regulars and not run. So perhaps William was part of one of these groups.

William also stated that he received a severe sword wound in the shoulder. During the battle, Tarleton's Legion of Dragoons was there and did mount a cavalry charge. They would charge into the troops swinging their swords at the fleeing troops. This may have been how William was wounded.

"My time expired before I got well enough to march & I never received a discharge from this campaign. In 1781, I volunteered for seven weeks, under the command at first of Captain Swepston & after a little while I joined a corps of rifle men under the command of Captain Brown--I do not recollect the precise date of the beginning or end of this short tour; but I know that I was in the Battle of Guilford during its continuance--my principle officer here was General Greene--I belonged to General Lawson's Brigade and Colonel Munford's Regiment--my situation in this Battle was in the right wing of the army. I was discharged from this tour near Deep River in N. Carolina, but has lost my discharge."

At the Battle of Guilford Court House William was in the same regiment as his brother James (previous person), and I would suspect they were close together. I can image how relieved they were, when they saw that they both survived the battle without injury.

Sources: 1. Census 1820, 1830, and 1840. 2. Virginia Marriages 1660-1800. 3. U.S. Pensions Roll of 1835. 4. Pension Papers S31796.

****

James Kincaid age 13

James Kincaid was born 10 March, 1763 in Albemarle County, Virginia, and he died on 8 July, 1841 in Platte County, Missouri. He married Sarah Wilson on 4 February, 1784. His brother Captain Joseph Kincaid was killed at the Battle of Blue Licks, which was one of the last battles of the Revolutionary War. In 1774 their father John Kincaid joined a militia force raised by Daniel Boone to fight against Indians.

"I entered the service of the United States under the following named officers and served as herein stated. The first Service I ___?__ was as a volunteer scout ____?____ under the command of Capt John Duncan. At this time my Father lived in a settlement called Castle Wood on Clinch River about 25 miles north of Abingdon of Virginia a __?__ __?__ Powell's valley had been settled but the settlers were driven off by the Indians a good many of them could not bring their plunder with them, but hid it. John Duncan was ordered out with a Company of Militia with orders to Guard the people who had left their property returned them to collect it together and bring it into the settlement. he was one of Duncan's company at this time Capt Joseph Martin was stationed at the rye Cove fort on Clinch River in order to Guard the frontiers of Va (for it was a frontier fort) I kept Two Spies who were Brothers (towit) John and James Bunch — When we got into the Valley we met with those Spies. they then went with us down to what was called Martin's Station in said Valley but we found no one there – they all had fled. One of the settlers that was with us who had fled from the Valley by the name of Daviss (called Capt. Daviss) before the people fled he lived at Owens Station Ten miles below Martins. We took up at Martin's Station Some time after Daviss petitioned Duncan for a few men to go down to Owen's with him to collect his plunder five men was granted him one of whom was James Bunch and collected the plunder accordingly as I understood and returning back to Camp the Indians waylaid the path and fired upon them and wounded Bunch killed a by the name of Boman at the place and wounded another by the name of Jamison. as Bunch __?__ __?__ with him a piece but he never got in. three of the party got in that night two of whom were Bunch and Daviss. The next day Duncan went down with all his force except a few he left to guard the wounded. I was one that went down. Went to the place and there found Boman dead. Daviss took us to a spot where he said an Indian stood whom he shot at. We went to the place and found a good deal of Blood. We then took their trail and followed them but not a great way as it appeared they had scattered – We returned back and burid the Dead thence to Camp this circumstance Broke up the expedition Bunch grew very sick and we had to take him to his Company at the Rye Cove. We were then all dismissed and returned home. as well as he can recollect this took place in 1776. I do not recollect the particular month but it was in warm weather. I was not more than four or five weeks out according to my recollection at this time."

"The next expedition I went was to Kentucky under the command of Col. John Boman of Bedford County Va – as well as I recollect Henry Poullin from said Cty as I also understood was one of his Captains. — Boman as I understood was ordered out by the State of Virginia to reinforce the Stations in Ky. as they came on through the neighbourhood of Abingdon a man by the name of Wm Bush met with Capt Paullin and was told as he understood by him if he would raise a leftenant's quota which was called 24 men he said Bush should have the command of the Second Leftenant in his Paullins Company at that time said Bush resided in our neighbourhood in Castle Wood on Clinch River Va. he then did recruit his 24 men Two of whom were my Brother Joseph and myself. by the leave of our Father we enlisted I do not recollect at present for how long and marched with Bush and overtook Boman and his Batalion or Regiment at the ford of the Cumberland River and joined the Company of Capt Paullin and from thence marched to Boonsborough and got there about the 14 day of Aug't 1777 at this time I understood there were but

Two other Stations in the County Logan and Harrod. I remained there 16 or 20 days aiding the people to gather in their corn which they had been prevented the year before from geting in to fort. the Indians being troublesom. Col. Calloway who lived with his family in the fort at that time had been into Virginia and as I understood had expected to have returned with Boman but failed to get up with him. When he returned home to the fort he informed us that on the trail that he had traveled on he found a man killed by the Indians as he supposed and that the Indians had Broke in upon the settlements of Castlewood and had killed seven or eight families. Upon this information my Brother and myself and others became uneasy with regard to our friends in Castlewood and petitioned Col Boman for a discharge in order that we might go to their relief – he granted the discharge – observing at the same time that he had the authority to take men from the frontiers. We returned home and on our way home we fell in with the Clinch Spiys who corroberated the statements of Calloway stated several families had been killed and the Ballance were all in forts. We found it so when we got into the settlements. We were about 46 or 50 days out."

"The next expedition was to Illinois under the command of Col. John Montgomery from Virginia it was understood that George Rogers Clark had been sent by the State of Virginia to take possession of the British Garrisons that were in the Illinois County. It was further understood by me that said Clark was to carry an expedition against Detroyet. And in order to enable him the more to do so the State of Virginia sent to his aid Col John Montgomery with about one hundred and thirty men. to recruit those men Thomas Quirk and others were employed. Both when my Brother Joseph Kincaid and myself __?__ __?__ one year. This was early in the year 1779 and __?__ __?__ at the Long Island of Holston At which place they were met by Col. Evan Shelby __?__ __?__ and forty Militias. We __?__ __?__ From thence Shelby and his Militia returned. Montgomery and his force went on to __?__?__ Clark. But previous to ___?__ at the __?__ aforesaid __?__ of Quarter Master Sargent under the Quarter Master ___?___ I stayed there a few weeks Thence we went to __?__ some by water and some by land. there we met three small companys of Malitia from Ky. Col. Clark __?__ that he __?__ men enough to carry his expedition ____?____ Finding on my return that my Father did not want me to return to service after my ___?____ was out I hired a man by the name Joshua Prewit as a Substitute and went in my place."

"The next summer 1780 I went another expedition under the command of the said Col Clark. On this expedition I was ___?___ under Capt. John Brown. Our principle officers Beside Clark and Logan were Daniel Brown Hugh__?__ and John Logan. This expedition was in the spring 1782. We were out on that expedition about five or six weeks. The next ___?___ was Scott and Wilkerson's against the Wabash Indians. As well as I now recollect it was 1791. We were thirty three days on that expedition."

The following is a statement made a year after the previous statement. It contains a little more information about his service.

"In the year 1780 early in the month of July I volunteered to go an expedition as a private soldier against the Shawnee Indians as stated in my former declaration herein refered to under the Command of Col. James Harrod. We marched from Harrods station to the Falls of Ohio. there we joined Genl. Clark and I remained in service I think I can safely say eight weeks. after this Expedition I was appointment Ensign in the Malitia in the Company of Capt Joseph Kincaid and belonged to Col James Harrods Regiment and that by the order of said Col James Harrod I was placed at Macafee's Station and had under my command Twenty four men and remained in service one month as aforesaid guarding said fort. This was in the summer 1781. In the year 1782 early in the Summer I did serve a Term of one month more at guarding of public property at the mouth of Shawnee Run still acting as ensign this was also by the command of Col. James Harrod. In this year 1782 after the service rendered at the mouth of Shawnee Run I was In the Celebrated Battle of the Blue licks as stated in my Declaration aforesaid. We heard of the attack made by the Indians on Briants Station about thirty four miles from the same on the south side of Kentucky River at Harrods Station my Brother Joseph Kincaid was Capt then of a company John Irven was his leftenant & this Deponant was his Ensign an express came to his Brother informing him of the attack afs'd. this was on the 17th of August. that evening we raised fifteen men we started about sun down and marched all night and about day break we got to Lexington Fort. thence to Briants Station got there about 7 o'clock the next morning started from Briants Station about 10 oclock with about 180 men – overtook the Indians on the 19th. Give them Battle and got defeated there as I stated before my Brother Joseph was killed I was 9 days in service at that time."

The Battle of Blue Licks was fought on 18 August, 1782. A group of about 50 Loyalists and 300 Indians raided into Kentucky and began to leave after two days. A force of Kentucky militiamen began to pursue them. As the Kentuckians got close one of the leaders, Daniel Boone a very skilled woodsman, suspected a trap and wanted to wait for reinforcements. Another leader, Hugh McGary, wanted to prove he was no coward and wanted to attack at once. He mounted his horse and yelled out, *"Them that ain't cowards, follow me."* As the men began to attack Boone replied, *"We are all slaughtered men."*

As Boone had feared they rode into a trap. Many Indians were concealed in the bushy ravine and almost surrounded the Kentucky militiamen. They tried to retreat back down the hill and had to fight hand-to-hand with the Indians behind them. Boone grabbed a horse and told his 23 year old son, Israel to get on it. As soon as Israel mounted the horse, he fell to the ground and was shot dead with a bullet wound to the neck. Daniel then grabbed the horse and retreated. He later retrieved his son's body and brought it back to the fort.

Many of the mounted men escaped, while most of the men on foot were slaughtered. Of the 180 Kentucky militiamen 72 were killed, including Captain Joseph Kincaid. Years later whenever Daniel Boone spoke of the defeat, he would be overcome with grief and openly cry.

"The next service I rendered was against the Shawnee Indians under the Command of Gen'l. Clark & Benjamin Logan as stated in my former Declaration refferance being herein made thereto for particulars – I acted as Leftenant in that expedition under Capt John Irven I was in service on this expedition I think at least five weeks — Some time after the expedition last spoken of I was appointed Capt of a malitia Company and Commissioned by the State of Virginia in the County of Mercer in the District of Ky. and in the year 1787 I was ordered by Col Gabriel Madison Commandant of the Cty aforesaid to take the command of a company to go against the Cherokee Indians under the command of Col. Benjamin Logan It was expected that aid would have been furnished from Logan to Cumberland settlement. We went to the place of Rendesvous But Logan did not receive the expected aid and the expedition fell through I was in. I was out about 7 days. About this time the Indians was quite troublesome __?__ coming into the settlement frequently and stealing horses & killing people and I was ordered out frequently for the purpose of ranging the County as Capt aforesaid I cannot now recollect the numbers of days I was in this kind of service but no hesitation in saying I was at least fifteen days."

"The next expedition I went was Scott & Wilkersons expedition as stated in my Declaration herein refered to. In that expedition I was a private I was in service thirty three days."

Sources: 1. Lincoln County, Kentucky Marriages 1780-1851. 2. Pension roll of 1835. 3. The Encyclopedia of Northern Kentucky edited by Paul A. Tenkotte, James C. Claypool. 4. The Pictorial Field-Book of the Revolution Vol I by Benson John Lossing. 5. Pension Papers S16907.

****

Samuel Kincaid age 11

Samuel Kincaid was born in Ireland on 9 November, 1763 and died on 9 December, 1865 in Ripley, Indiana. He came to America with his father Thomas, who was a victim of the dreaded "Press gang." In Ireland many young men were kidnapped, bound and gagged aboard British troop ships and brought to American to fight in the army. Once here many of the Irish were quick to desert and eager to join with the Americans to fight against the British. They were very welcome by the American army because most of the Irish were very familiar with muskets and cannons.

To avoid arrest by the British most of the Irish that deserted would change their names because a reward was offer for their capture. If they were captured in battle they would probably be executed on the spot. According to one account, Irish born John Carroll refused to change his name saying, *"No I'll keep my own name. They'll be welcome to hang what's left of me when they get me."* Some of the Irish deserters fought under their real names at the Battle of Bunker Hill. Thomas Kincaid did not change his name when he and his 11 year old son Samuel joined the American cause. Thomas was made a Sergeant and Samuel became a drummer.

The Battle of Bunker Hill was fought on 17 June, 1775 nearly five months before Samuel Kincaid would reach his 12th birthday. The British force was able to capture the ground but at a very high cost in manpower. Their casualty rate was 42% which was high even by their standards. The British were surprised at how well the untrained Americans fought. British General Thomas Gage remarked, *"These Rebels are not the despicable rabble too many of us have supposed."*

Samuel married Merium Stewart in New York in 1794. They moved from New York to Pennsylvania, from there to Ohio, then to Kentucky and finally settled in Illinois.

Sources; 1. Revolutionary Soldiers Buried in Illinois, Crawford County. 2. Census 1840 & 1850. 3. Tombstone 4. History of Crawford and Clark Counties, Illinois, edited by William Henry Perrin. 4. Rebels in Arms: The Irishmen of Bunker Hill, June 2004 edition of the Boston Irish Reporter, by Peter F. Stevens.

****

Lemuel King age 11

Lemuel King was born on 29 September, 1765 in Bolton, Connecticut, and he died on 17 November, 1827 in Connecticut. He married Jane Brownson on 16 December, 1790 in Connecticut. He enlisted as a drummer in February of 1777 at the age of 11.

"I entered the Continental Army in the service of the United States of America in the ninth Massachusetts Bay Regiment in the Company commanded by Captain Martin Dix in the month of February of year of our Lord Seventeen hundred & Seventy Seven in which company I served three years until the fifteenth day of February Seventeen hundred Eighty when I was regularly & honorably discharged the said Regiment was commanded by Colonel James Wesson."

The 9th Regiment participated at the Siege of Fort Stanwix, Battle of Saratoga, Valley Forge, and Battle of Monmouth. The Regiment was referred to as the "George Washington Regiment." Colonel James Wesson was the commanding officer from November 1776 to January 1781.

During the evening of 22 March, 1780, about 400 British and Hessian troops crossed the Hudson River from New York. Their mission was to attack the American troops at Paramus. As they passed through Hackensack at about 3 in the morning, they burned the courthouse, jail, and two houses.

A small company of 20 to 30 militia had retired for the night in various places around town. Once aroused by the enemy, most escaped and ran for the woods. Some made in to Paramus and alerted the American troops encamped there. Lemuel was wounded during the brief encounter and taken prisoner. Because of his age, he was later released. One resident of Hackensack gave an eyewitness account of the British raid.

"One half of the enemy marched quietly through. When the rear, consisting mostly of Hessians, arrived, they broke open the doors and windows, robbed and plundered, and took prisoners a few peaceable inhabitants, among whom was Mr. Archibald Campbell. This gentleman, who had been for several weeks confined to his bed with the rheumatism, they forced into the street and compelled to follow them. Often in their rear, they threatened to shoot him if he did not hasten his pace. In the subsequent confusion he escaped and hid in the cellar of a house opposite the New Bridge. He lived until 1798 and never experienced a return of the rheumatism."

Years after the war Lemuel became a successful businessman His company furnished various foods to the army during the War of 1812, he owned a stage route in Massachusetts which carried the government mail. He later lived at the King's Inn, a popular establishment in the state.

In 1824 General Lafayette visited the United States and on 3 September he visited the King's Inn. Lemuel King was personally known to Lafayette and this was the reason he visited the Inn. Hezekiah King, the son of Lemuel, left this record of the visit:

"Forty years after the day, General Lafayette and the few remaining Revolutionary soldiers met in the parlor, assembled here by their old comrade Lemuel King."

Sources: 1. Historical Collections of the State of New Jersey by John Warner and Henry Howe. 2. U.S. Pensioners 1818-1872. 3. Connecticut Deaths & Burial Index 1650-1934. 4. Year Book of the Sons of the Revolution in the State of New York 1899. 5. Sons of the American Revolution Application. 6. Cascades and Courage: The History of the Town of Vernon & the City of Rockville, Connecticut.

****

Lemuel King age 14

Lemuel King was born on 20 September, 1765 in Bolton, Connecticut, and he died on 17 November, 1827 in Connecticut. He was married to Jane Brownson on 16 December, 1790 by Pastor Ebenezer Kellogg. Lemuel's pension was increased to $96 a year due to his one year service and the extent of his wounds.

Lemuel made no statement of service to the pension board. This author gathered facts of his service from the letters submitted to the pension board from his wife and people that knew him. The pension board wrote that he served for 12 months which would put his enlistment sometime early in 1779, which would make his age 14 or even possibly 13.

Lemuel was at the raid on Horse neck 10 December, 1780 and received 7 severe cuts from the saber. John McGregory served with Lemuel that day, and in his letter to the pension board he said, *"We served at Horse neck or Stamford, we were kept near the line of the town between Horse neck & Stamford. Our employment was to stand guard & go out upon patrols to guard this part of the country from the cowboys & tories. While I was here I saw Lemuel King who was dreadfully wounded & then lay languishing with his wounds & in this condition Doctor Hamilton an __?__ Surgeon of Somers in Connecticut was sent down to see and assist King."*

On 17 March, 1783 Doctor Asa Hamilton wrote to the pension board describing the wounds of Lemuel. *"This may certify that Lemuel King was a patient of mine by reason of wounds he received by the enemy at Horse neck in December 1780. Three wounds by cutlasses on the head one around his shoulder, whereby the shoulder blade was laid bare, also one wound on the upper side of the arm and one on the lower arm bone it being laid bare, also one in the knee by which the knee pan was separated from the adjacent parts by means where he yet remains a cripple."*

On 10 October, 1838 Roswell Smith sent the following statement to the pension board, *"My brother David Smith was with him [Lemuel] in the same company in one campaign viz. in Capt Oziah Bissels company, at Horse neck when they were attacked by the Tory light horse, or refugees, they were attacked in the night and King received seven wounds to the bone and was left for dead he was crippled after that all his days. He was a very large Man, and enlisted when he was less than sixteen years of age, and a real soldier the officers confiding in his courage strength & address soon made him a corporal & used to send him after deserters. All this I have heard by Brother of said Lemuel King tell repeatedly."*

Note: This author used as a source the application from the Sons of the American Revolution. The information used in ½ of the application is correct. However, the information on Lemuel after he is out of the service is not correct. That information is about another Lemuel King that enlisted in the army at the age of 11. He is also found in this book.

Sources: 1. Sons of the American Revolution Application. 2. Pension Papers W26179. 3. U.S. Pension Roll of 1835. 4. Lineage Book National Society D.A.R. Vol. 27, 1898.

****

Thomas King age 14

Thomas King was born in 1764 in Haverstraw, New York, and he died in 1864 at Adams Basin, New York. He enlisted at the age of 14 as a teamster at the time Washington crossed the Hudson River into New Jersey. He was at the Battle of Trenton.

Source: 1. D.A.R. Lineage Book, Vol. 51.

****

David Kinsley 13

David Kinsley was born on 22 April, 1764 in Charlemont, Massachusetts, and he died on 27 September, 1828 in Fletcher, Vermont. He married Lucy Montague on 29 November, 1787. He was given a yearly pension of $53.26.

David enlisted in 1777 under Captain William Hutchens, Captain Samuel Robinson, and Colonel Fletcher. He fought at the Battle of Bennington on 16 August, 1777.

Sources: 1. Vermont Men in the Revolutionary War. 2. D.A.R. Lineage Book, Vol. 70.

****

William Kirkland age 14

William Kirkland was born in 1762 in Kershaw County, South Carolina and he died on 4 October, 1838 in Autauga County, Alabama. He married Elizabeth Perry before 1790. He received a yearly pension of 72.33 and 80 and ½ acres for his service.

"I entered the service of the United States while engaged in the war of the Revolution sometime in the year A.D. 1776, as a substitute for Thomas Hill in Kershaw District in the State of South Carolina -- served under Captain John Graves, Maj Lyon, Col Robert Goodwin and Gen Williamson -- crossed the Savannah River at Augusta and march through the State of Georgia, and met Gen __?__ with the regular troops, who came around by water, at the mouth of the St. Mary's River -- I served in this tour 4 months."

"After the expedition to Florida was concluded, I was drafted in Kershaw District South Carolina and served under Captain Joseph

Kershaw -- marched to the quarter House near Charleston, and thence to Puranburg on the Savannah, while the British troops lay at Savannah -- In this tour I served 2 months."

"I was a 2nd time drafted in Kershaw District South Carolina and served under Captain Starks and Col Thomas Taylor and marched to Orangeburg, in this Tour I served 2 months."

"I then served under the command of Capt Stark three weeks at McCord's Ferry."

"My last service was under the command of Gen Thomas Sumpter 12 months, while the British troops occupied Charleston S C and their Head Quarters were at Camden."

Sources: 1. Alabama Revolutionary War Soldiers. 2. U.S. General Land Office Records 1796-1907. 3. Pension Papers S32361.

****

Benjamin Kitchen age 13

Benjamin Kitchen was born in 1763 in Southampton, Virginia, and he died on 22 April, 1849 in Louisiana. He left Virginia at an early age and moved to North Carolina. Benjamin received a pension of $48.00 a year for his service. He was married first to Helen Mason Daniels and later married Laviva who applied for benefits after Benjamin died. His son received 160 acres of land for his father's service in the war.

He joined the North Carolina militia around the last of January of 1776 at the age of 13. He served in the 3rd Regiment Continental Line under Colonel William Alston. A few weeks later Benjamin fought in the victory of the Battle of Moore's Creek Bridge.

"...in five or six days before the action of Moore's Creek against the Tories, my Regiment joined the Regiment of Colonel Richard Caswell and I was in that engagement under said Caswell's command—and after taking the Tories the Regiment to which I was attached guarded them to the town of Halifax in North Carolina where I was appointed and did the duty of 1st Sergeant during the imprisonment of the Tories at that place, in a few weeks I was discharged."

In May of 1776 Benjamin again volunteered and served under Captain William Brinkley in the 1st North Carolina Company of the militia commanded by Colonel William Alston. The company marched to Charleston and joined the army commanded by General Charles Lee.

"I was with him at the bridge of Boots opposite to Sullivan's Island on the Charleston side at the time of the battle [Battle of Sullivan's Island] *with the five British ships on the 28th day of June of 1776 and saw one of the British ships explode, directly after the engagement the Regiment to which I belonged marched directly to Savannah, after our arrival there, say about 10 days which we were allowed to dress skins to make leggings to march through the palmetto swamp to Hosoboy Island our companies were detached from the Regiment to which I belonged and I among them, to break up the British hospitals there, when we arrived there the British had abandoned the Hospitals and I returned immediately to Savannah where I was discharged in the summer month I cannot recollect."*

The Battle of Sullivan's Island was fought on 28 June, 1776 and resulted in an American victory. Benjamin was part of the militia forces outside of the fort that helped to build a bridge of boats that would provide a means of retreat for the fort's garrison. It was not successful because there were not enough boats to bridge the one mile from the island the fort was on to the mainland.

"Early in the month of November 1776 I became the substitute for a man, who was drafted from a remote part of the County Nash North Carolina and a stranger to me I think was named Josiah Sessions to serve for a period of months in a company commanded by Captain William Lewis in a regiment commanded by Colonel Hogan."

Benjamin was appointed a sergeant, and the company was consolidated with the 5th North Carolina Militia under the command of Captain John Baker. They marched to Trenton shortly after Washington defeated the Hessians on 25 December, 1776. Lieutenant Burns left the company, and Benjamin was appointed to take his place temporarily. The regiment left for West Point, and Benjamin was ordered to stay behind and take care of the sick men. Once they were cleared to travel he was to march them to headquarters. In about six weeks they were able to march, so Benjamin took them to West Point. The regiment then left West Point and went back to Philadelphia to spend the winter.

During the Revolutionary War the threat of smallpox was a major concern for the army. Most British soldiers had already been exposed and were immune. Unfortunately, the Colonial troops were not. Medics would create a small wound in the healthy soldier's arm and then they would rub some of the pus from the pox of an infected soldier into that wound. This would give him a slight case of the pox, and then he would be immune. This early method of inoculation had been learned from African slaves.

Since they had no way to control the dosage, there was danger involved. If you received too large a dose you could die. Washington estimated that as many as two percent of inoculated soldiers could die. Without the inoculation more than one third of the soldiers could die, and another third would be too ill to fight if an outbreak occurred.

"...we were ordered back to Philadelphia to the barracks to spend the remained of the winter it being ascertained that that situation did not agree with the Southern troops, when the troops were inoculated with the smallpox and a large number of them died. In the latter part of April or May we were marched to the head of Elk by land and then took water to Norfolk in Virginia and from thence to Halifax in North Carolina and there discharged the nine months having expired."

In November of 1777 Nash County, North Carolina was given a quota to provide soldiers for an eighteen month enlistment, so once again Benjamin enlisted and was placed in command of the recruits. The soldiers were marched to Charleston and joined General Benjamin Lincoln.

"After we had been at Charleston a month or two the siege of Charleston commenced by water and afterwards by land I was confined several months by the siege and experienced great want of provisions Just before the surrender of Charlestown I think three days, General Lincoln gave orders for all the officers to appear at headquarters, when we met, the General told us that from extreme suffering of his soldiers, and the murmurings of the citizens he would be obliged to surrender in a few days and observed that all the militia and state troops that chose to risk their escape by the night had permission to do so, and I with my company together with three or 400 others crossed the River in the night and effected our escape and with difficulty escaped the vigilance of the Tories and returned home after having served seven or eight months."

Around the first of July in 1780 Colonel Thomas Hunter in Nash County raised a company of horse soldiers to patrol the area. The Colonel, *"was informed the Tories were doing a great deal of mischief after the fall of Charleston."* Benjamin was appointed a Captain of the 250 man company. They rode around the lower part of North Carolina and then into South Carolina.

"General Richard Caswell was on his way with a large body of militia too and we bent our course to him, and Joined him near the Fish dam Ford on Broad River in North Carolina and about four or five days before the battle near Camden we effected a Junction with the troops of General Gates and on the 16th of August 1780 we fought the unfortunate battle of Camden and I was slightly wounded by a splinter caused by a cannon ball."

"After the defeat near Camden we were ordered to rally at hanging rock, several weeks this the volunteer troop of horse to which I was attached, together with the troops commanded by Captain Joseph Scott Cray was ordered out by General Caswell to reconnoiter the country and try and fall in with one Colonel Bryan who was said commanded a large body of seven or 800 Tories, we took some seven or eight of them who were stragglers returned home and were disbanded after having been on duty about three months."

During the Battle of Camden the British opened the battle when the right flank fired a volley into the militia regiments. The British then charged the militia with their Bayonets which the militia did not have. The militia panicked and ran. The panic soon spread to the North Carolina militia where Benjamin was. Soon the whole American left wing broke and fled.

Benjamin served again in the militia as a captain when Cornwallis passed through on his way to Yorktown. He served until after the British surrender at Yorktown. After the war Benjamin moved to Georgia and then to Mississippi. In January of 1816 he moved to Rapides Parish in Louisiana. In the Louisiana 1820 Federal Census it recorded Benjamin as having 21 slaves.

Sources: 1. Pension Papers S3197. 2. Widow's Application W47613. 3. The Catchings & Holiday Families and Various Related Families by Mary Clendinen Torrey. 4. Census of 1820. 5. Sons of the American Revolution Application. 6. U.S. Pensioners 1818-1872. 7.

DAR Ancestor # A065768. 8. A Guide to the Battles of the American Revolution by Theodore P. Savas and J. David Dameron.

****

Jeremiah Klumph or Clump age 11

Jeremiah Klumph was born 23 March, 1769 in Otsego County, New York and he died on 26 October, 1855 in Wayne County, Michigan. He married Amanda Norton in 1797 in New York.

"I enlisted the serving of the United States in the Revolutionary War and served as follows: In January, 1781, I volunteered enlisted at Albany under Col Hewes, during the War, to serve as a express rider and was then engaged as an express under Col Hewes until near the last of January aforesaid when I was sent by Col Hewes to Claverack Landing with a letter to Major Wolf until June 1782 and all that time engaged as an express & in carrying & conveying letters to Albany, Saratoga, Schenectady, Great Barrington and to Gen Washington. I was at Pukskill as express when Cornwallis was taken. In July 1782 I was sent by Major Wolf to Albany and there remained under the command of Major Quackinboss as an express and in driving a train till the close of the war in 1783 when I was discharged by Major Quackinboss at Albany."

His request for a pension was rejected as stated in this letter sent to him: *"There appears to have been but one Corps of Express Riders in the Revolutionary Army. And the declarant did not belong to it. The alleged service as an Express Rider, as well as that of a Teamster is not provided for under the Act of 7 June 1832. The case is, therefore rejected. He served but according to law his service is not recognized."* What was not mentioned in the letter is that if he was captured while an express rider he would have hanged as a spy.

Sources: 1. Pension Papers R6007. 2. Sons of the American Revolution Application. 3. Michigan, a Centennial of the State and its People.

****

James Knapp age 13

James Knapp was born on 31 January, 1764 in Dutchess County, New York, and he died on 15 July, 1831 in Yates County, New York. He married Lucy Griswold Ball on 6 March, 1785 in New York. He received a yearly pension of $96. James also received the badge of merit for his six years of service. His father also was a soldier, and he died in October of 1777 in one of the Sugar House Prisons in New York.

"I enlisted the first day of February 1777 in Dutchess County, in the State of New York during the war in the company commanded by Captain Benjamin Pelton in Colonel Van Cortlandt's Regiment in the New York Line and I continued to serve in said corps until the eighth day of June 1783 at which time I received my honorable discharge."

James served as a drummer in the 2nd company of the 2nd Regiment of the New York Line commanded by Colonel Philip Cortlandt. James was present at the Battles of Saratoga, Monmouth, and Yorktown. He also participated in the Sullivan Expedition. The Regiment was furloughed on 2 June, 1793 at Newburgh, New York.

Several years after the war James had a friend, David Ceashey, sent to get his land warrant from the bureau in Washington. Afterwards, David told James that there had been a fire in the War Department, and the land warrant could not be recovered. Later, James learned that this was not the case so he wrote to the bureau asking if David did get the warrant, and if he did not James wanted to know what he could do to secure it. This author found no reply from the bureau in his pension papers.

Sources: 1. New York in the Revolution as a State, 2nd Edition, 1898. 2. D.A.R. Lineage Book, Vol. 9. 3. Pension Papers S42800.

****

Richard Knight age 9

Richard Knight was born in 1767 at Long Island, New York, and he died on 28 December, 1849 in Liverpool, Pennsylvania. Two of his three wives were (1) Sarah Berry and (2) Sarah Boyer who he married in 1798.

Richard was taken along by his father when he enlisted in the army as a private and he enlisted his son as a drummer. On 1 September, 1776 they joined Captain John Betty's Company in the 5th Pennsylvania Regiment under the command of Colonel Robert Magaw. During the Battle of Fort Washington many members of the 6th Regiment, including Colonel Robert Magaw, were captured. The remaining men in the 6th Regiment were put into the 5th Pennsylvania Regiment under the command of Lt. Colonel Josiah Harmer. Richard Knight was attached to the company of Captain Walter Finney, and Richard's name appears on the roll through 17 January, 1780.

Richard fought at the Battle of Brandywine on 11 September, 1777. More troops fought at this battle than any other battle in the American Revolution. The battle was also the longest single-day battle during the war, and with continuous fighting for 11 hours. Richard also fought at the Battles of Germantown and Monmouth, and in 1779 he took part in the Sullivan Expedition. Richard later served in the War of 1812 as a Captain in Kennedy's 1st Regiment in Pennsylvania.

Sources: 1. Sons of the American Revolution Application. 2. D.A.R.

****

Peter Koons age 11

Peter Koons was born on 30 June, 1765 in Canajoharie, New York, and he died on 14 February, 1837 in Catskill, New York. His wife Lydia died one year after he did. He received a yearly pension of $20. His pension was later suspended because he was too young.

"I entered the Levies of the United States as a Volunteer in the month of March 1777. I was enlisted in a Company commanded by Capt Van Everen, General Herkimer was the commander. I served for the term of one year and Eight months as one of a scouting party, Fighting Indians & Tories we were required by Genl Herkimer to be in constant readiness I went from Canajoharie to the town of Dover in the county of Dutchess in the fall of the year 1780, first of October, where I joined Capt Valentine Wheeler's company of Militia, where I did duty for the term of nine months. I them enlisted in Capt __?__ Company of Militia called four monthly men, where I did duty for the term of four months from the first of July to the first day of November which was the year 1781. I marched from Dover to Fishkill where we joined Col Wrizenbelts Regiment. Marched from thence to West Point and from thence to Crump Pond. Our __?__ name was Welch, Lieut Ounderson and Burgess Finch. The Regiment was in the month of August ordered to March for Albany from thence the Regiment was ordered to Saratoga, I with a part of my company were detained at Albany to guard the city and the prisoners."

Sources: 1. The Bloodied Mohawk: The American Revolution in the Words of Fort Planks Defenders and Other Mohawk Valley Partisans by Kenneth D. Johnson. 2. Pension Papers R2266.

****

George Kuhns age 13

George Kuhns was born on 28 November, 1762 in Lancaster, Pennsylvania, and he died there on 18 January, 1835. He married Susanna Hubert on 23 July, 1786 in Lancaster. She applied for and received a widow's yearly pension of $80.

George enlisted in July of 1776 in Colonel James Cunningham's Regiment in the Company commanded by Captain Graff. George was a member of the1st Regiment Flying Camp Battalion of Lancaster County, which was a home guard. They acted like a police force guarding barracks, government buildings, and etc.

At the Battle of Long Island on 27 August, 1776 George's unit was assigned to the brigade under American General William Alexander (Lord Sterling). They were stationed on the right side of the American line and were surrounded and took heavy losses. General Alexander was captured. George may also have been at the Battles of Trenton and Princeton. In 1777 he served for four months in Captain Crawford's Company.

After the war George was one of the veteran escorts, when the Marquis de Lafayette was on his visit to the United States in 1824-25. Lafayette passed near Lancaster County on 31 January, 1825.

Sources: 1. Register of the Pennsylvania Society of the Sons of the Revolution, 1888-1898. 2. Sons of the American Revolution Application. 3. U.S. Pensioners 1818-1872.

****

Elijah Lacey age 14

Elijah Lacey was born on 14 October, 1764 in Hanover, Virginia, and he died on 25 April, 1846 in Hall, Indiana. He married Frankey Holland on 26 October, 1787 in Virginia. He received a yearly pension of $38.33.

"I entered the service of the United States (or Colonies) in Goochland County in the state of Virginia, in the year 1778 in the fall of that year, as a volunteer, under the command of Captain Parrish for a tour of three months, which I fully served, And at the close of the tour I was verbally discharged as was also the remainder of the company to which I belonged; the day on which I entered the service I cannot recollect nor the month, but I know it was in autumn. There was only one Company called out of Goochland County, at the time I entered the service, and it was

attached (as well as he recollects) or placed under the command of Major (or Col) Taylor of the regular Army. The whole as well in the Cavalry belonging to the body of troops then stationed at the <u>Albemarle barracks,</u> were under the command of Colonel Bland (of the Cavalry). There were at that time a body of prisoners of Hessians I believe under the guard of bland & Taylor. I served the whole of the tour at that place, and was generally kept on duty guarding the said prisoners, with the exception of a few days that I was with some others detailed to guard the cavalry horses near Charlottesville, while they were in pasture. I recollect Captain Timberlake of the regulars, also lieutenant White of the regulars: my own lieutenant was Rutherford, and my brother, Matthew Lacy was ensign."

"The Second tour was commenced in the summer of 1780. It was for three months: I was a volunteer, and as such performed said Tour: I entered the service for this tour under Captain Gideon Hatcher of Goochland county, and was marched down as low as Cabin Point where the troops were stationed some time. I was under or attached to the command of Major McGill, and also I recollect a French field officer, whose name was pronounced de Cloma--the adjutant, was named Kennedy; -- My lieutenant on this campaign as well as the former was David Rutherford --my Ensign was a cousin of mine named Ellit Lacy--It was apprehended that the enemy would commit some depredations on the South side of James River, below Petersburg -- and they (the Corps to which I belonged) were engaged frequently in marching up and down the River, in order to protect that section of the Country from the ravages of a part of the British army. I cannot state the day on which I entered the service on this tour--I know only that it was in the summer season, and I think my time expired at the beginning of autumn."

"In the fall of the year 1780 I again turned out a volunteer and entered the service under Captain Tom Royster (I was still residing in Goochland) -- I went with Royster to Richmond, from Richmond I was marched to the Maubin Hills or Meadow bridges, opposite old James Town: here I was stationed a short time under a Colonel Woodson but sometime after, I was placed under the command of Colonel Gregory Smith of the light infantry at Williamsburg -- In this Corps I underwent much fatigue and when I had been in the service on this tour about two months I was so afflicted with the Rheumatism, that I was compelled to accept a discharge, and by slow and painful traveling to return home."

"I remember I again entered the service as a volunteer from Goochland County under Captain Miller and lieutenant Britt and joined a *body of troops under Colonel William Fleming, and shortly after I was under Colonel Taylor, and Major Campbell. We crossed York River at West Point in to Gloucester County, where we were occupied in guarding that section until after the capture of Lord Cornwallis – I entered the service in the month of August – and I left it (having been discharged verbally, together with the company to which I belonged) sometime in October, as well as I now recollect I believe I was out on this tour about two months."*

Sources: 1. Tombstone 2. U.S. Pensioners 1818-1872. 3. Historical Register of Virginians in the Revolution. 4. Pension Papers W10189.

****

Andrew Lackey age 13

Andrew Lackey was born on 25 October, 1763 in Lancaster County, Pennsylvania, and he died on 26 September, 1841 in Estill County, Kentucky. He married Elizabeth c. 1783 in Virginia. Andrew enlisted in March of 1777 just 7 months until his 14th birthday. He had made captain by the time he was 18. He owned 1 slave at the time of his death. He received a yearly pension of $30 for his service.

"I entered the service of the United States in March 1777 as a substitute for Job Fletcher, under Capt. Robert Cravens. I rendezvoused at Staunton, Virginia, and was marched through the country in company with several companies of militia, and I think joined some continental troops whilst out, but was then not quite fifteen years old, and did not become acquainted with the names of many officers, nor did I pay much attention to the geography of the country; these circumstances when in correlation with the great lapse of time renders it out of my power to name any other offers or any further circumstances concerning this tour. I only recollect that I served three months and was then discharged."

"About the last of May or first of June 1778 I again entered the service of the United States as a substitute for a man by the name of Crocket, his christian name I do not now recollect. But I rendezvoused again at Stanton, Virginia, under Capt. Long, and was marched from Stanton through the country to Richmond, Virginia, or near that, where I was united with the main army, and there remained in readiness for active operations with the British army till my term of service expired, when I was discharged. I served three months during this tour."

"*I again entered the service of the United States in July 1779, as a volunteer, in a Company of Rangers, under Capt. Ralph Stewart and Lieut. Westfall. I rendezvoused at this time at Westfall's Station, Moningahalie county, Virginia I was marched into the mountains in search of the Indians, and after scouring the country for some time, in search of them, would return back to the Station, get a fresh supply of provisions and start again, and continued on in this way, returning occasionally for provisions, till I was discharged. I served six months this tour before I was discharged.*"

"*I again entered the service of the United States in May 1781 as Lieut. in a volunteer militia company, commanded by Capt. Joseph Friend, Maj. William Lauder Col. Morgan and Gen. George Rogers Clark. I rendezvoused at the New Store not far from the old Red Stone Fort. Here Capt Friend was compelled to return home and I was commissioned Captain of the Company. I recollect Col. Morgan handed me my Commission, which I think was signed by Gen. G. R. Clark. We went from the point of rendezvous to Pittsburg with thirteen boat loads of Flour together with some Powder. I had charge of two of the boats and delivered them up at Pittsburg. From Pittsburg we went by water in boats to Wheeling, Va. where we remained a few days to recruit more men, and from Wheeling to the Falls of the Ohio, (now Louisville, Ky.) where I was stationed, and there remained till his term of service expired, when I was discharged. I served three months during this tour as Captain. I was born in Lancaster county, Pennsylvania. My father moved from this to Augusta county, Virginia, and from this to Moningahalia county, Va. where I resided at each time of his entering the service.*"

"*I was one of the men that assisted in guarding the families and corn fields, whilst they were cultivated, during this period and when at the stations, occasionally assisting in the cultivation of the crops. I also stood guard of nights as well as days whenever it fell to my lot to do so. Capt. Robert Cravens was out twice with his company assisting us to keep off the Indians, whilst the whites could raise corn and other provisions for subsistence. Capt. Long also served one or two tours, one I know, with my company in the same manner and for the same purposes.*"

Andrew later made a supplementary statement explaining how he came to hear about the pension he was eligible for.

"*The reason I did not apply sooner for a pension is this – I live in a retired part of the county, do not take nor never did take any newspaper except three numbers many years since, I never saw the act of Congress granting pensions, above referred to, and did not know any thing about its provisions, but heard it said that it was necessary for a soldier in the Revolution to prove his services before I could obtain a pension, and not knowing of any person then living, that could establish my services by, I made up my mind that it was unnecessary for me to apply or trouble my mind about it and therefore never attempted it, or thought any thing more about it till the Rev. John H. Brown was on a fishing excursion and came to my house to stay all night, and asked me whether or not he was a soldier in the revolutionary army and being answered in the affirmative, he enquired of him whether or not I was drawing a pension, and having answered this in the negative, and gave him the reasons above assigned, Mr. Brown went on to explain to me the law of Congress, and after hearing his explination of it I concluded that I would apply, and thereupon procured a friend to draw up my declaration for me. This I did as soon as I could after my conversation with Mr. Brown."*

Sources: 1. U.S. Pensioners 1818-1872. 2. Census 1820 and 1840. 3. Pension Papers S30533.

****

Lewis Land age 14

Lewis Land was born in 1762 in Virginia, and he died on 28 July, 1854 in Greenville, South Carolina. He married (1) Eleanor who died in 1805, (2) Elizabeth Ray who died in 1842, and (3) Obedience West and Lewis were married by Isaac Lemmons on 27 August, 1842. Obedience received his yearly pension of $80, and she also received a bounty 160 acres of land for the service of her husband.

"In the month of January in the year 1776 I enlisted under Captain Walter Vowellsin the first Regiment of Virginia State Troops, commanded by __?__, Lieutenant Colonel Bruntand Colonel George Gibson, in Orange County in the State of Virginia for the term of three years --marched to Williamsburg Virginia where Captain Vowells took the small pox, returned home and died; in Captain Lee succeeded him in the command, which marched to Alexandria where the Regiment had the small pox--after its recovery, marched and joined the main Army at the White Marsh Camps. Captain Lee was then promoted to the rank and command of Major and Captain William Haufler succeeded to the command, and marched thence to Winter Quarters at the Valley Forge on the Schuylkill River; I was in active service for three years and in the year 1779 was engaged in the taking of the Stony Point Fort on the 15th of July by

General Wayne's Army; and in August following he was in the battle of Monmouth In the year 1779 I was discharged by Colonel George Gibson at Fredericktown in the State of Maryland having completed my 3 years Service."

Lewis was confused about the dates of the two battles he was in. The Battle of Monmouth was fought on 28 June, 1778 after his regiment had left Valley Forge. At the Battle of Monmouth Lewis was a member of the 1st Virginia Regiment under the command of Major General Nathanael Greene. At the Battle of Stony Point, fought on 16 July, 1779, he was in the 1st Regiment under the command of Colonel Christian Febiger. Lewis was discharged in 1779 and had he remained with 1st Virginia he would have been taken prisoner at Charleston in 1780.

Sources: 1. U.S. Pensioners 1818-1872. 2. Pension Papers W26200.

****

Dicey Langston age 15

Dicey Langston was born on 14 May, 1766 in Laurens County, South Carolina, and she died on 23 May, 1837 in Greenville County, South Carolina. She married Thomas Springfield on 9 January, 1783.

By the time Dicey was 15 she was as good a shot and horsewoman as anyone in the county. During the war her brothers and a small group of patriots made a camp several miles from the Langston farm. The area was a hotbed of Tory activity, and persons that supported the patriots had to be careful. Since many of the neighbors and some of the relatives of Dicey were loyal to the Tories it was easy for her to gather information on Tory activity when she went for visits.

The Tories began to wonder why so much information about their movements were getting to the rebels. The Tories began to suspect that Solomon Langston was involved with spying and perhaps his daughter as well. One time they paid Solomon a visit, and they threatened him and said that if Dicey was involved in spying they would hold him accountable for her actions. Solomon knew that she had been giving information to her brother's camp and demanded that she stop. She agreed but after a brief period of time she continued with her spying.

In 1781 she heard that a ruthless gang of Tories called the Bloody Scouts and led by the infamous Bloody Bill Cunningham, was in the area. The gang had burned homes and massacred rebels and their supporters during the past year. Dicey learned that the gang was planning to raid a village known as Little Eden, which was also near her brother's camp. She knew that she had to warn her brother.

She decided that the safest way to travel was by foot and at night. She left late one night and stayed off the roads keeping to the fields and woods. She came upon a creek that had become swollen by the spring rains. As she crossed the creek she lost her footing and the swift cold water carried her downstream trying to pull her under. She finally pulled herself up on the river bank and laid there to regain her strength. She was exhausted and cold, but she knew that she had to continue to her brother's camp.

She finally made it to her brother's camp and warned them of the imminent attack. The men had just returned from an expedition and, like Dicey, were also cold and tired. She built a fire and made them hoecakes to eat. The men took the food and left to warn the people in the area of the Tory attack. When the Bloody Scouts arrived the next morning, they found the camp deserted and the people in the area had vanished. Dicey's act of courage had saved many lives.

After Dicey gave the soldiers food she returned home, and she once again went through fields, woods, and crossing cold streams. Dicey made it back home in time to dry off and prepare breakfast for her father. As Solomon ate she did not mention what had transpired during the night. The Bloody Scouts were angry that their mission had failed and, although they could not prove it, they suspected that Solomon Langston was behind it.

Later, they paid a visit to the Langston home with the intent of killing Solomon and looting the house. When the Tories arrived at the Langston home they entered and pointed a gun at Solomon. Before they could fire, Dicey quickly jumped between her father and the man pointing the pistol. She told them that they would have to kill her first. One of the Tories was so impressed with the young girl's courage, that he stopped the man from discharging his pistol and made the men leave.

This would not be the last time that Dicey would stand up to the threats of the Tories. On one occasion she was returning from meeting some rebel friends in the Spartanburg area, when she was stopped by a group of Tories. They demanded to know where she had been and the names of the people, or she would die in her tracks. Dicey replied, *"Shoot me if you dare! I will not tell you."* She then removed a handkerchief that covered her neck and the top of her chest, as if to offer a place to be shot. The man was about to fire when another man stopped him and saved Dicey's life.

On another occasion she was home alone when several Tories began banging on her door demanding entrance. She answered back in a stern voice that they should leave at once. The men began talking among themselves trying to decide what to do. Finally, they gave up and left.

Her brother James, a rebel leader, had left a rifle in her care and told her to keep it until he sent for it. One day a group of men showed up at the Langston home asking for the rifle. She retrieved the rifle, and as she entered back into the room where the men were she remembered that her brother said that if anyone came to claim the rifle they should give a countersign to prove that they were patriots. Dicey did not recognize these men and feared they might be Tories, so she asked for the countersign. One of the men told her it was a little late to be making conditions since the rifle and her were clearly in their possession. Dicey cocked the rifle and pointed it at the man and said, "If the gun is in your possession, take charge of here!" The man could tell by her look and the tone of her voice that she meant business. He quickly gave the countersign, and they all had a good laugh. One of the men remarked to Dicey that she was certainly worthy to be called the sister of James Langston.

Sources: 1. Women Patriots of the American Revolution: a Biographical Dictionary by Charles E. Claghorn. 2. The Women of the American Revolution by Elizabeth F. Ellet, 3rd edition, 1849. 3. Women in the American Revolution by Paul Engle.

****

Presley Larkins age 13

Presley Larkins was born on 14 March, 1763 in Shenandoah County, Virginia, and he died after 4 November, 1851 in Kentucky. In the war he served in the same company as his father Anthony. Presley served in the army or state militia off and on until he was nearly fifty years old.

Presley's pension application statement was not easy to follow. He tended to jump around and combine his war service with service after the war. The following is his first statement from 1835.

"I enlisted in the Army of the United States in Virginia, as fifer, in the year 1777, with a Lieutenant I think by the name of Lyles, in my 12th or 13th year and served in the same company with my father, Anthony Larkins, who was also a regular. I do not now recollect the Regiment, or

the officers. I served as fifer during the war, and think I was discharged in the year 1782 or 1783. I think I enlisted during the War, and served until the War expired and the Army was disbanded. I lived near Stover town in Virginia, was in several Indian skirmishes – two at Paxson's Glades – one at Fort Chisel – both on New River in Virginia. I was also in several Indian skirmishes at Watauga and on Holson River in the same State, in which I remained during the service. I do not know, but supposes my name will be found on the Virginia roll."

"I also enlisted ___?___ ___?___ the age of about 28 years in Tennessee under Captain Jacob Tipton for six months, and before my term had expired, I enlisted for three years being then at Fort Washington – now Cincinnati, under Lieutenant Pasters, belonging to the company of Captain Joseph Munford in the first Regiment of light infantry. I still remained in Captain Tipton's Company until my term of six months expired, while in said Company I was in the engagement in which General St. Clair was defeated, commonly called St. Clair's defeat. I then joined Munford's Company, who being killed in the last mentioned battle, Lieutenant Pastors took command. I had my leg broke in __?__ to build a Fort Jefferson, from whence I was carried to Cincinnati on horseback – being unable to walk – thence to Vincennes where I recovered. I remained at Vincennes until Wayne's Treaty, when I was by Captain Pastors, recommend to the proper officer for a discharge."

"I enlisted in first Regiment of light infantry at New Port in Kentucky between 1810 and 1811, at the age of 47 or 48 years, under Lieutenant Brison – from whose Company, I was transferred to that of Captain S.__?__ where I served my full term – being five years. I was in two skirmishes on the Mississippi River with the British and Indians. During my stay at New Port I had my hip mashed by a box of guns falling on me. I was Honorable discharged by General Smith at St. Louis in 1815."

The next statement was given 19 March, 1836 from a friend that served with Presley, Peter Stout.

"I became acquainted with said Larkins as early as the year 1777 as I believe – When I first became acquainted with him, he the said Larkins was a Fifer in the American Army about that time at Staunton in the State of Virginia, – I continued to know said Larkins from that time (1777) to the close of the war, 4 or 5 years – From my intimacy with said Larkins I have no hesitation in saying that he the said Larkins continued in the American service from the time I first knew him until the action at the defeated Camps (or it was then called, now Crab Orchard in Kentucky) which was as near as I can recollect about the close of the war – I was in the American service as a minute man and was during the whole revolutionary war either in active service or on furlough – I well remember that said Larkins was very young when I first knew him. That the soldiers would frequently make fun of him the said Larkins on account of his extreme youthfulness. They nicknamed him from that circumstance "Larkin Wisdom."

The following are amended declarations from Presley. The first is from 9 December, 1843 and the second is from 18 December, 1843. Presley amended his declaration, because on 26 February, 1836 he had received a letter from the Pension Office rejecting his application. Presley began sending them more information.

"Floyd County Kentucky December the 9th 1843 The deposition of Robert McBride taken before Lindsey Layne a Justice of the Peace in and for the County of Floyd and State of Kentucky he deposeth and saith that he was well acquainted with Presley Larkins who now lives in the County of Johnson and State of Kentucky who is an applicant for a pension as a revolutionary soldier he states that his first acquaintance with him was in the State of Virginia he states that his first acquaintance with him was in the year 1777 or 1778 that he was then an enlisted soldier a Fifer and war his uniform dress as a musician he was then engaged in the recruiting service, I seen his Captain he was a dark complected man and a Frenchman his name I don't now recollect as it was a singular name this was at a place called Paxton's Glades I then seen him in service as a recruiting Fifer at Chissels mines and at that place the company that he belonged to was sent for to join the main Army and Presley Larkins was left for I recollect that he had the smallpox and was blind with the disease he then afterwards got well and I then seen him at Tolbert's fort on the Watauga River still in the service as a Fifer I seen him on his return from Kings Mountain battle he was all the time I speak of a Fifer and in the enlisted Service amongst the regular troops and from the time I seen him at Paxton's Glades until the last time I seen him at Tolbert's Fort was upwards of three years during all the aforementioned time he was in the Regular service as a musician, a Fifer. I afterward served with him in Wayne's Army and we were both at St. Clair's defeat now Indiana during the last mentioned campaign Presley Larkin got his leg broke at Fort Jefferson in repairing the fort a log fell on him and mashed his ankle and broke his leg and made him a fenel [?] cripple he then was under Captain Pasters and Colonel Hamtomack he states when he first seen Presley

Larkins at Paxton's glades, he was very young to be in the service he looked to be a boy about 15 years of age or probably not more than 14."

"Amended Declaration of Presley Larkins who is an applicant for a pension as a revolutionary Soldier he declares that while he was in the service as an enlisted Soldier in General Sinkler Army under Captain Thomas Pasters and Colonel Hamtomack that in the year of 1792 that he was wounded in his leg and ankle in the raising a knew addition to Fort Jefferson now Indiana he declares that a log fell of the building on him and mashed his ankle and broke his leg and has made him a cripple so that his leg has furrished [?] and is the time a cripple and much smaller than the other he further states that he has Become almost helpless not able to work but very little he lives alone in a small house by himself and has become a County Charge to the County of Johnson and he therefore asked of government to aid him under the laws of Congress granting pensions to invalid and crippled Soldiers."

The following statement was made by 91 year old Presley on 4 November, 1851.

"Presley Larkins a resident of the County of Johnson and State of Kentucky aged 91 years who being duly sworn according to law doth on his oath make the following declaration in order to obtain the benefit of the provision of Congress or made by the act of Congress passed. That he was a recruiting fife major in the Company commanded by Lieutenant Lyles in a recruiting party in the war of the revolution, that he enlisted at Staunton Virginia in the fall of 1778 as near as he can recollect, he states he enlisted during the war and started from Stanton Virginia in a recruiting party between Stanton & Lexington says they drew their clothes at Lexington, he says they went down as far as Millerstown to the reviewing of recruits, there they were sent back to New River Virginia for more recruits and he was taken with smallpox on the road & left blind at a place where the recruits were stationed near what was called Paxton's Glades where he remained for about one month when his Mother came after him and carried him to East Tennessee on Watauga River where he remained until he entirely recovered. When he recovered Colonel Tipton sent after him to carry Expresses to Fort Chisel. After which time he was kept by the Colonel as express Carrier until the close of the Revolution. Sometimes for Colonel Sevier Some time Colonel Campbell & at other times under Colonel Tipton & was discharged from under the command of Captain Caldwell shortly after peace was made. He makes this

declaration for the purpose of obtaining the amount of pension that may be found due him."

The following is part of the rejection letter Presley received from the pension office on 26 February, 1836. It explains why his pension application was rejected.

"He alleges to have enlisted in Virginia at the age of 12 or 13. The supplicant named does not appear on the rolls of service in the office. It is doubtful whether he would have been enlisted at so early an age as thirteen, and the alleged service was not such in war performed by the regular troops of Virginia. His alleged service was on the frontier of Virginia, exposed to the hostile incursions of the Indians. It is very doubtful that he performed such services during the Revolutionary War as to entitle him to a pension under the act of 7 June 1832."

Source: Pension Papers R6168.

****

William Latham age 10

William Latham was born in 18 August, 1771, and he died at sea c. 1792 near Indonesia. His father, Captain William Latham, was with the 8th Connecticut Militia Regiment stationed at Fort Griswold. His son, William, was taken to Fort Griswold and his father said. *"He might be serviceable in bringing ammunition from the magazine,"* so William Jr. was spoken of as a "powder monkey."

The fort was captured on 6 September, 1781, by the British led by the American traitor Benedict Arnold. Captain Latham was wounded in the thigh and taken with the other prisoners to New York. His son William was placed under guard with the other prisoners.

As the town of New London was being looted and burned by the British the wife of Captain Latham and her daughter Mary made their way to the fort to look for her husband and son. She first went to Ebenezer Avery's house which was being used by a hospital. At the door, the sentry held out his rifle to prevent them from entering. Unafraid Mrs. Latham put his rifle aside and went into the house. Once inside she saw wounded friends and neighbors but did not find her family. She kept looking all night and in the morning she went to the headquarters' of Arnold and asked about her son.

She found young William sitting with the other prisoners paralyzed with terror and in great distress. It was the 7th of September and the boy had no food since the night of the 5th. He was fatigued from the heat and the fear of all he had seen in the battle. He had a piece of bread in his hand but had not eaten it for fear that the British had poisoned it.

Mrs. Latham knew Arnold well since he was a native of Norwich. She said to him, *"Benedict Arnold, I come for my child. Not to ask him but demand him of you." "Take him,"* replied Arnold. *"Take him, and don't you bring him up a damned rebel." "I shall take him,"* she said, *"and teach him to despise the name of a traitor."*

All members of the Latham family survived the war. William, now around 20 years old took to the sea. On one voyage to the West India Islands, he went ashore to shop for gifts for the family. A British man-of-war was in the harbor and a press gang seized him and took him aboard the ship. He was forced to perform hard labor aboard the ship for months.

News of what had happen reached William's family in New London. Letters for William's release from the American government and his family were dispatched to the British government. The British government ignored their requests and finally William's brother-in-law went to England to plead William's case in person. Money was left in England for his passage home should he be released. His ship returned to England and he was released and he returned home in the late 1790's. William's brothers and sisters were all grown and married. William became restless and aimless and once again he went to sea. This time he was never heard from again.

Sources: 1. Genealogical Notes of the Williams and Gallup Families by Charles F. Williams, 1897, pages 92-93. 2. Connecticut Town Birth Records, pre 1870. 3. The Connecticut Magazine, Vol. 9 William Farrand Felch, George Atwell, H. Phelps Arms, and Francis Treelyan Miller, 1905.

****

Samuel Lee age 13

Samuel Lee was born on 8 March, 1767 in Barre, Massachusetts, and he died there on 17 October, 1839. He married Mary Mixter on 14 March, 1805. He enlisted two months before his fourteenth birthday. He was older looking for his young age and was 5'10" tall. He received a yearly pension of $80.

"*I enlisted in the year 1781 and to the best of my recollection in the month of Jan and served in the ninth Regiment of the Massachusetts Line under the following field officers Col Henry Jackson, Lieut Col David Cobb, Major Prescott In a company previously commanded by Capt Hunt but during my service Capt Watson. In the Regiment I served until 1782. Then the ninth Regiment being broken up I was transferred into the 3rd Mass. Regiment previously commanded by Col Grenton but during my service by Col Millin in the company commanded by Capt Pritchard and in this Regiment I served till Oct 28 1783.*"

"*Soon after I entered the Service I was detached into a light infantry Regiment called a flying Regiment commanded by Col Scammell and marched to the enemies lines where I was actively engaged in the service __?__ duties appropriate for the peculiar service. On the 3 of July I was engaged in the battle near Kingsbridge—After performing the duties of a Soldier in a flying Regt. Till August I marched to Virginia and was engaged in active duty through the Siege of Yorktown, was engaged in storming the enemies Fort under the command of Col Hamilton. After the siege and surrender of Yorktown I returned to the northern Army and rejoined the ninth Regiment.*"

The "flying camp" was a mobile strategic reserved of troops that were formed by General Washington. Colonel William Scammell was placed in command of Scammell Light Infantry Regiment that Samuel Lee served in.

Samuel Lee was part of a regiment commanded by Colonel Alexander Hamilton that attacked the British redoubt No. 10 at Yorktown on 14 October, 1781. The Americans attacked with bayonets, and their muskets unloaded so that an accidental shot would not alert the British. In less than 10 minutes and with few causalities they were victorious.

After the war Samuel attended school and taught school for several years. When the town organized a militia after the war, he joined and over the years he rose in the ranks. In 1808 he was appointed the rank of Brigadier General, which then was a post of honor.

Sources: 1. Sons of the American Revolution Application. 2. Massachusetts Society of Sons of the American Revolution, 1899. 3. Pension Papers W8039.

****

Jeannette Leman age 12

Jeannette Leman was born in 1768 in Ireland, and she died on 8 October, 1856 in South Carolina. She married William Walker. She carried secret dispatches to General Thomas Sumter in South Carolina. On one occasion she passed through a camp of Tories with a dispatch concealed in the heel of her stocking, which she had purposely knit a double heel.

Sources: 1. Tombstone 2. D.A.R. Lineage Book, Vol. 47.

****

James Lemmon age 12

James Lemmon was born in April of 1763 in Hagerstown, Maryland, and he died on July 4, 1857 in Dallas County, Texas. He married (1) Sarah Carr who died in 1813 and (2) Amy Rawlins in 1818. He had a total of 14 children.

He served as a messenger boy because it was safer for boys to carry messages than men. He carried messages from the camp of George Washington to that of his father, Captain Robert Lemmon. He lived in Washington's camp in Valley Forge and affectionately called Washington "Uncle George." James entered the Continental Army as a private serving with the 4th Virginia as a private until the end of the war.

James lived in Kentucky until the death of his first wife. After he married Sarah Carr they moved to Illinois. In the early 1840's one of his sons, his brother, and several friends moved to Texas. They liked Texas so much that James' son, Robert, walked back to Illinois to bring the rest of the family. James Lemmon is one of the few Revolutionary War soldiers buried in Texas.

Sources: 1. Sons of the American Revolution Application. 2. Archives of Maryland Vol XVI. 3. Article from the Dallas Morning News 1948.

****

Joshua Lester age 14

Joshua Lester was born in 1763 in Connecticut, and he died on 29 August, 1846 in New London, Connecticut. He enlisted on 1 June, 1777 in a company commanded by Captain John Johnson and afterwards by Captain Andrew Griswold. The company was not attached to any regiment, but it was employed in guarding the coast between the

Connecticut and Niantic Rivers. The duty was sometimes performed on land and sometimes on water.

Sources: 1. Revolutionary Soldiers Resident or Dying in Onondaga County, N.Y., prepared by Rev. W.M. Beauchamp for the Onondaga Historical Association, 1863. 2. Sons of the American Revolution Application. 3. Hale Collection of Cemetery Inscriptions & Newspaper Notices 1629-1934.

****

Jeremiah Levering age 12

Jeremiah Levering was born in Philadelphia in 1766 to Jacob and Elizabeth Levering. Very little is known about him. There is a court record that reads: *"The Board taking into consideration the case of Jeremiah Levering a child of fourteen or fifteen years of age, who has been enlisted as a soldier in Col. Proctor's regiment, but not taught to beat the drum or blow the fife, and being of small stature and weakly habits. Resolved, That is the opinion of this Board he should be discharged, and that Col. Proctor be directed to discharge him accordingly."*

Jeremiah apparently join the army at the age of 12 in 1778 because the above document is dated April 7, 1781. Colonel Proctor commanded the 4th Continental Artillery Regiment. During the time that Jeremiah served the regiment saw action at the Battle of Monmouth in 1778, during the Sullivan Expedition against the Iroquois Indians in 1779, and the Battle of Bull's Ferry in 1780.

Since Jeremiah was considered too young and was discharged he received no pension, even though he served for three years. The Philadelphia Directory for 1798 has him recorded as a laborer living on Budd Street. Jeremiah was living in 1807.

Sources: 1. Col. Thomas Proctor by Donna Bluemink. 2. Lee Depreciation List Vol. 1, page 129. 3. Levering Family, History and Genealogy. 4. Colonial Records, Vol. 12, page 686.

****

Timothy Lewis age 14

Timothy Lewis was born on 24 May, 1764 in Ashfield, Massachusetts, and he died on 31 May, 1858 in Boone County, Illinois. He received a yearly pension of $46.66 for his service.

"*In the months of April 1779 a few days before I was fifteen years of age ...all who were able to bear arms in that town were classed, my father whose name was also Timothy Lewis belonged to a class which was drawn to post with the Massachusetts Militia for six months, as I believe my father at this time sent me to take his place. I went to <u>Hatfield in Massachusetts</u> where I was enrolled in Captain Densmores company of Militia: whose Lieutenants name was Flemmings from that place I marched to New London, Cont. where I joined the Regiment Commanded by Col. Dickerson, as I believe. At this time I was kept upon guard also I remained at that place in the above service until late in the fall of that year--and at least six months and I believe no more.*"

"*I then returned home and remained until April or May of the year 1780, when my father was again drawn in his class and I went in his stead under Captain Isaac Newton of the town of Colebain Mass. The company was formed at Worthington Mass, from that place I marched to a place called Kinderhook in the State of New York where we joined Col. Maxwells Regiment from that place we marched immediately to West Point where General Benedict Arnold was in command: at that place I was again upon fatigue a part of the time repairing fort __?__ during that summer while I was there the heavy guns and ammunition taken with General Burgoyne were brought to West Point, I helped to unload them from the Vessels which brought them: I was a part of the time on guard and some times chopping wood and getting timber: I remained there until the weather became very cold, and as much as <u>Eight Months</u>, when the six months had expired for which my father had been drawn--did not discharge me and I was kept <u>there two or three months</u> longer as I believe, I then returned home.*"

"*Among other occurrences of the Revolution I remember the following to have taken place while I was actually in the service, on the 22nd day of September 1780 I saw Major Andre who had been captured as a spy on the previous and distinctly recollect the circumstances of his (Andre) being sent off to Head Quarters for trial.*"

"*I also recollect that on the day previous to Andre's capture General B. Arnold Inspected the Troops at West Point and I among the rest, and also the circumstances of General Arnold leaving his quarters in the evening, of that day, and going on board the Vulture: then lying in the River below West Point in waiting for Andre and Arnold.*"

Benedict Arnold was at the breakfast table, when he received a note about the capture of his ally Major Andre. He read it and showing no emotion excused himself, left the table, and went upstairs to talk with his wife Peggy. He told her he needed to escape down river, and that he would provide for her. He went back downstairs and had an aid bring him his horse. He needed to leave at once, because General Washington would soon be there and have him placed under arrest. Arnold mounted his horse and rode off down the Hudson to a waiting British ship. After riding nearly two hours he reached the British ship *The Vulture*. From the ship he wrote a letter to Washington requesting that his wife be given safe passage to her family in Philadelphia. Washington being a gentleman honored the request.

"At that time and for some time afterwards, Famine and Death stared the Troops in the face from the scarcity of Provisions, the want of Clothing and the disease consequence upon the sufferings, and I among many others was so much enfeebled, and diseased from the above causes, that I could not go home after I was discharged until my father came for that purpose and carried me home."

Sources: 1. History of West Point by Edward Boynton. 2. Tombstone 3. Massachusetts Town & Vital Records 1620-1988. 3. New York Pensioners 1835. 4. Pension Papers S13732.

****

William Liddell age 14

William Liddell was born on 10 March, 1702 in Annapolis, Maryland, and he died on 23 August, 1836 in Gwinnett, Georgia. He married Ruth Keith on 3 February, 1784. He received a pension of $50 a year for his service. He became a wealthy farmer owning 13 slaves in 1830.

"I entered the service of the United States in the year 1776 under Captain William Baskins Lieutenant James Baskins -- in what was then Ninety Six District in the State of South Carolina – I was in Service in the fort at Bull Town in said district about one month & was sick one month at the same place -- That Some time in the year 1778 as I believe -- I volunteered under Captain James McCall -- Subordinate officers not recollected. Were ordered on an expedition to Saint Augustine in Florida -- attached to Major Pickens' Brigade or Division of General Williamson's Army – We went as far as St. Mary's river in Florida -- after crossing said River General Howe took the Command -- and by his orders were discharged and returned home -- that said term of service continued three months or more."

"Sometime in the year 1779 I again volunteered under Captain Andrew Miller -- subordinate officers not recollected -- and went on an expedition commanded by General Williamson against the Cherokee indians -- into the Cherokee nation -- to big Sumach Town on Hywassee River -- thence to Coosawattie thence to Eastanmollie -- thence to a town called Pine Log on High Tower River -- and soon after returned home having never been in any battle – I believe I was engaged in said last Term of service two months or more."

"In the year 1780 I again volunteered under Captain William Baskins attached to Colonel Pickens' Division and marched to the State of Georgia to a Station opposite Beech island -- was Stationed at said place until news arrived of the surrender of Charleston--I then went with the Army to Congaree to a place called Friday's Ferry on said river -- after lying at said Ferry a few days -- we returned home but was not discharged until sometime after returning home was ordered out to a place called Cowhead -- where Colonel Pickens Surrendered his command to and took British protection for himself and his Division – I was engaged in said Service about two months."

"I again volunteered in the same year 1780 -- under Captain James McCall and marched through the Indian lands to North Carolina and joined Colonel McDowell's Division of North Carolina Militia -- remained under the command of Colonel McDowell for some Considerable time -- then joined Colonel Elijah Clarke -- who commanded a division of the Georgia Militia -- and who had also come with his division into North Carolina -- & under his command continued under his (Colonel Clarke's) command -- scouting about after the Tories near the line between North and South Carolina -- and occasionally in either State -- until about the first of August 1780"

"I went then to Charlotte in Mecklenburg County North Carolina -- still under the command of Colonel Clarke -- intending to Join General Gates -- On reaching Charlotte was informed of the defeat of General Gates near Camden and then joined Major Davy's horse company and went under his command in the South Carolina and reconnoitering the British for some time near Camden in the neighborhood of the Battle ground where Gates was defeated -- returned to Charlotte -- From Charlotte I went under the command of Colonel Clarke & Captain McCall aforesaid -- on the frontiers of the Indian territories & State of South Carolina -- and at length arrived at home in Ninety Six district South Carolina aforesaid sometime in September."

"I next went under the officers aforesaid -- To wit -- Colonel Clarke & Captain McCall to North Carolina -- to a settlement called ___?__ Heard of Ferguson's defeat at King's mountain -- went to Burke County in said State (NC) after scouting about some time in Burke County aforesaid we returned to South Carolina and took & burnt a Fort from the Tories somewhere on the waters of Broad River -- name of the Fort not recollected -- after scouting for some time in the neighborhood -- we fell in with a company of Tories at Lawson's fork of Broad River -- and had a severe skirmish -- at which a few men were lost on each side and our officers taken prisoners by -- our party – I left my party about the first of December – I was engaged in said last mentioned service about five months or more."

"I then volunteered sometime about the first of August 1781 under Captain Moses Liddell of Colonel Pickens' Regiment or Division to march against the British at Eutaw Springs--I was chosen a spy to watch the movements of the Hostile Indians on the frontiers of South Carolina -- I was employed in such service about one month."

"I volunteered again in 1782 -- under Captain Baskins aforesaid -- attached to (then) General Pickens' Division of the State Militia -- and proceeded under General Pickens -- two Beaver dam Creek in the State of Georgia -- where we met with Colonel Clarke -- and in company with him and his Division -- march into the Cherokee nation -- to a Town called Long Swamp which we destroyed with fire from thence to Pine log -- from thence to Coosawatty -- which we also destroyed -- thence to Eastan allia which we found had been already destroyed by Colonel Savage -- from thence I returned home and was discharged finally."

Sources: 1. U.S. Pensioners 1818-1872. 2. Census 1830. 3. Pension Papers W3835.

****

John Light age 14

John Light was born on 4 March, 1766 in Halifax County, Virginia, and he died after 1834 in Tennessee. He received a yearly pension of $20.

"I was born in Halifax County in the State of Virginia in the year 1766--on the fourth day of the month I cannot remember, not having any record of my age in his possession; there was one & I believe it is in the possession of my brother. From Halifax County, I moved into what is now Washington County Tennessee then a part of North Carolina. Here I was

living when I entered the service of the United States as a Volunteer under Captain Benjamin Clark & Lieutenant John Wheeler & Shelby was our Colonel. Our company on this side the Mountain rendezvoused at a place called Dunging's Mill, from this Mill we were marched on toward King's Mountain, crossing in our march the Yellow Mountain. On our march we were joined by Col. Cleveland's Regiment, after which time, there was a Council of the Officers, for the purpose of adopting some energetic measures to defeat General Furgason, who was at that time marching before us collecting all the Tories in the Country around his standard. That the determination of the Council was to pursue him with all possible speed and engage him before he would have time to augment his forces by the call he had made on the Tories. The Command was given to Col. Campbell and on we marched night & day. One or two days before the battle of King's Mountain, as well as I recollect, we came to a place where the British & Tories had camped the over night & had left in great Hurry leaving behind them their provisions, from this place the mounted men were ordered to hasten in the pursuit leaving the foot companies to follow on, I belonged to a foot company & of course was not in the battle, but in my march following the mounted men, I met them a short distance from King's Mountain, returning with the prisoners they had taken in the engagement. The prisoners were then put into the custody of foot Companies who had been following on, we hung some of the Tories who had been most active & troublesome during the Contest with the British, & the rest they marched as far as Holt's Mill where we guarded them sometime. I entered this term of service about the first of September as well as I now remember & it lasted at least three months."

"*In the year 1781 the month I do not remember but think it was the winter of the year I again entered the service as a volunteer under the same Captain & Lieutenant Smith & Colonel Clark for the purpose of entering the Cherokee Nation & weaken them by burning their Towns & killing such as might oppose; that from Washington County we marched into the Indian nation to an Indian Town on the Tennessee river called Chota, at this Town we remained a day or two during which time we killed several Indians who were lurking & spying about the Town, we then left this place after burning the town and marched on through several other Indian towns which I cannot now name having forgotten, & also burnt & killed the Indians we found about them, during this expedition Captain Elliot was killed while in the pursuit of some Indians. After burning the Indian Towns through which we passed we would range the Country in search of Indians & horses which had been taken from the settlers; we found many horses. I was discharged from the service by his Captain who signed my discharge, but I have likewise lost this discharge, not taking any care of it. This term of service lasted three months."*

Sources: 1. U.S. Pensioners 1818-1872. 2. Census 1830 & 1840. 3. Pension Papers S4549.

****

Francis Lighthall age 12

Francis Lighthall was born on 17 January, 1765 in Palatine, New York, and he died there on 28 May, 1836. He married Sarah Fye who received a yearly widow's pension of $80. They were married in New York on 26 February, 1786.

"I volunteered into the service as a Militia Man in the forepart of September 1777 at Schenectady and marched men under Colo. Warner to join the army there at Stillwater in Saratoga County and state aforesaid, where I was joined to the army under General Gates, and was kept on duty and in service about two months and a half. I was not in the Battle against Burgoyne's army but we were kept in reserves and in readiness to be called in if necessity required. At the time I so volunteered in Schenectady, I resided in the County of Herkimer but was at Schenectady aforesaid and there volunteered at the solicitation of two of my Brothers William and John Lighthall whose names may be found I Believe in the pension list for revolutionary service."

His brother John Lighthall served off and on from 1776 until 1783. Their other brother William enlisted in 1776 and was *"highly distinguished for his bravery in the Battle of Bennington."* William was taken prisoner and taken to Canada until exchanged in 1782. A third brother of John, Lancaster, was born in 1761 and he enlisted at the age of fifteen in 1777.

"In the month of January 1778 I was called upon by Colo Bellinger and the war committee at Herkimer and sent by them with a package of papers to Gen. Washington on account of Gen Washingtons business as for some other causes I think about two weeks, when I received from Gen Washington a package of papers for the committee and then I returned to Herkimer aforesaid, the snow was drifts, roads badly broke and the going bad and I was employed in that duty in service about two months and a half."

"About the first of April following I was called into service in a company commanded by Capt Frederick Bell in Colo Bellingers Regiment was stationed at Fort Herkimer there kept on duty & out in scouting parties until about the middle of July when I with a small party commanded was captured--I was transferee to another party of Indians & was then taken to Niagara where I was hired out by them to a white man from whom I escaped & came towards home but was pursued by the Indians, caught, taken back, tried & commend to be killed, but was saved by Colo John Butler with whom I was well acquainted, on the Mohawk River before I went to Canada, who bought my life, kept me as a servant a while & then put me into the British service where I was kept in Canada until the Spring of 1781. I was taken to Oswego there put to work fortifying that place."

Colonel John Butler was a loyalist who led a militia unit known as Butler's Rangers. The Rangers engaged in skirmishes in the norther frontier.

"Soon afterwards I, with some other persons in the like situation embraced the first opportunity, escaped from them & I with great joy soon found myself among my friends & countrymen, where I arrived about the first of July."

"In July 1781 & soon after I returned as aforesaid I entered the service under Capt Starring in Colo Bellingers regiment was called to Fort Herkimer there kept on duty & out in scouting parties, as circumstances required and called out South in a party to Youngs Lake was to kept on duty toward winter where the savage and troy hostilities of the season in a __?__ ceased, the precise time I was on duty after I returned as aforesaid, I cannot state, think I did four months actual duty in the service of my country."

"About the first of May 1782 I was again called into service by Capt Starring was stationed at Fort Herkimer I was then kept on duty out in parties to guard the inhabitants & in scouting parties as circumstances required, I was used to kept on duty until the month of November, I did, as I believe full five months actual duty."

After the war New York Governor George Clinton appointed Francis Lighthall as a gunner in Captain Peter C. Fox's Company of "Uniform" Artillery and Francis served many years until his age would not permit military duty.

Sources: 1. U.S. Pensioners 1818-1872. 2. Tombstone 3. The History of Montgomery County and Fulton Counties, New York. 4. Pension Papers W20470. 5. Lineage Book National Society of the D.A.R. Vol. L, 1904. 6. A History of Schenectady during the Revolution.

****

Isaac Linton age 14

Isaac Linton was born in October 1764 in Frederick County, Maryland, and he died in 1835 in Brooke, West Virginia. He married Susanna Richards on 4 February, 1793 in Frederick County, Maryland. He received a yearly pension of $50.

"In the year 1777 or 1778 I cant certainly say which, but I was then 14 yrs old I volunteered in Frederick county for 6 months. Marched from there under Capt. Ralph Hillery to Baltimore, where we remained for about two weeks, and was then ordered back to Frederick Town after being at that place for about three weeks repairing the barracks our company was discharged. was in active service not less than four weeks. one Col. Beatty came to us whilst at Balt. said our services was not required and that we might go home."

"In November or December in same year, our company although discharged as before stated was called on to go to the Potomac River, at Nolens Ferry to __?__ at that place and guard to Frederick barracks, the British Prisoners. we went accordingly and continued in service at the Barracks in Frederick Town until we fully six months in actual service, including the time we were in service in Baltimore and at Frederick as before stated. before being discharged as before stated there was about seven full Companies at Fredericktown guarding the british Prissoners. they were under the command of either Col. Johnson or Col. Beatty I cant say which. I was not a Musician but private soldier."

"The same company commanded by same officers was called on again in the following December for three months. we went to the Barrack at same place and remained in service there for the Three months. I think Col. Beatty commanded on this occasion. In august 1779 I was drafted for three months and served at same place. done same duty under Capt. John Burket. I think about a year after the last preseding term. perhaps not more than nine months."

"I was drafted again for 3 mo. served at same place and done same duty. under Capt. Chaplin. Beatty was comadant at the Barracks

when __?__ *the last mentioned tours was done. I repeat that I was drafted in the two last mentioned tours. I proved my services by Thomas Bucy of Ohio. in the last mentioned service I was engaged in the capture of some tories in the mountains – they were Hung. Capt McLuny wrote my Declaration – to whom I made the same statement in substance now made. July 9, 1835."*

Sources; 1. Maryland Marriages 1655-1850. 2. Maryland Revolutionary War Records. 3. West Virginians in the American Revolution. 4. U.S. Pensioners 1818-1872. 5. Pension Papers S5690.

****

George Livesay age 14

George Livesay was born in 1674 in fort Bedford, Virginia, and he died on 19 May, 1837 in Kylesford, Tennessee. He married Nancy Anderson before 1794 and they had 11 children. He received a year pension of $23.33, his wife's widow's pension was rejected for lack of proper proof of marriage. His pension file is under the last name spelled Levisey.

"I entered the service of the United States as a volunteer sometime in June 1778 in Henry County State of Virginia under Col. Arthur, and Captain Hill, and was marched against the tories in the Counties of Bedford and Henry and continued two months in in Service and was discharged sometime in August 1778 having served fully two months."

"I again entered the said service of the united states, by being drafted in the month of March in the year 1781 in the county of Henry aforesaid and served in Captain Renfroe's company in the regiment commanded by Col. Lyon, of the militia, and after rendezvousing at Henry old Court House I was marched with his regiment into North Carolina on the waters of Dan River, with the intention of joining General Green but his regiment was halted at the cross roads, on the waters of Dan River, in order to prevent Col. Tarlton from laying waste and attacking the settlements on that river, a report having reached Col. Lyon that Col Tarleton was approaching that quarter, and after remaining about three months in said service I with the balance of my company, was discharged sometime in the month of June 1781 and returned home."

"Again I entered the said service as a volunteer in the county of Franklin in the State of Virginia under Captain Thomas Hale & Ensign Thomas Hill in the Regiment of militia commanded by Col. Richardson

about the middle of July 1781 and was marched from Pittsylvania Court House (where the company rendezvoused) to within about fifteen miles below Richmond and after remaining there sometime the Marquis Layfayette took command of the army there where his head quarters, was, and after crossing the river, the army moved on past Richmond and crossed chickahominy Swamp and from thence to Pomonky River, which was crossed and a few days after this I was with my company permitted to return home having served two months the time I volunteered, which was about the middle of September as well as I now recollect when I was dischared, in the year 1781."

Sources: 1. Sons of the American Revolution Application. 2. Historical Register of Virginians in the Revolution. 3. Pension Papers R6304.

****

Henry Livingston age 14

Henry Livingston was born on 1 March, 1764 in Virginia, and he died on 22 May, 1834 in Overton, Tennessee. He married Susannah Carmack on 21 March, 1793. His pension was rejected, because the service he provided was driving pack-horses and was it was not considered military service. Henry applied for a Revolutionary War pension based on his service as a pack-horse driver during 1778, while transporting provisions from Virginia to Fort McIntosh on the Ohio River. The pack train of fifty-two horses was cared for by nine men and the captain, who was Henry's brother Peter Livingston. Susannah's widow's application was submitted in 1852 when she was age seventy-five, and it was rejected for the same reason.

"As I now recollects in August 1778 I was hired as a substitute by Samuuel Livingston my brother who had been drafted. I then lived on the North fork of Holstin Washington County, Virginia. I then with nine men and their Captain Peter Livingston another brother, took charge of some pack horses in the neighbourhood of Abindon Virginia. We remained there about fifteen days. From that place we marched on with the pack horses to Botetourt County Virginia. From that place we went on to Staunton there we received flour, and packed our horses, fifty two in number. From that place we went with our horses & packs to fort McIntosh on the Ohio river from that place we went to the big Turcaraway. There were about three hundred soldiers and a great increase of pack horses and at that place we joined the army which was waiting for provisions. The gen'l. in Command was called McIntosh. we marched on until we got within about

thirty miles of the Delaware nation of Indians. There the army was met by some of the Indians who raised a flag for peace, and after marching about ten miles farther peace was made. We remained at this place about one month with the pack horses. We then left the army and was sent to fort Pitt, and from that place we marched with our horses to Fort McIntosh, and at that place was discharged, being about six hundred miles from home. I was out on this campaign until the 29 day of March ensuing. I became acquainted with Col. McIntosh son of Genl. McIntosh. I was very young at that time but I was capable of driving and attending to horses. "

The following is an account of an Indian raid by Chief Benge on the farm of Henry and Peter Livingston in Virginia in the spring of 1794. I have included this account of the raid to give the reader a better understanding of the danger of frontier life in the 1700's.

Henry Livingston and his brother had settled on the North Holston near the present town of Mendota. The two men owned nearly 2,000 acres and relied on farm work done by relatives, neighbors, and slaves.

At the time of the Indian attack Henry and his wife, Susanna, were living with Peter and his wife Elizabeth. Susanna and Henry had been married a little over a year. Also, in the home was the mother of the two boys, who at the time of the Indian attack was tomahawked and died four days later.

Chief Benge was mainly interested in capturing Negro slaves to take north and sell. The presence of slaves on the Livingston farm tempted him to risk the attack.

"April 6, 1794 "About 10 o'clock in the morning, as I was sitting in my house, the fierceness of the dog's barking alarmed me. I looked out and saw seven Indians approaching the house (Henry and Peter Livingston's Farm on the Holston River), armed and painted in a frightful manner. No person was then within, but a child of ten years old (her daughter Susannah Livingston), and another of two (her son Nathan Francis Livingston), and my sucking infant (Henrietta). My husband and his brother Henry had just before walked out to a barn at some distance in the field. My sister-in-law, Susanna, was with the remaining children in an out-house. Old Mrs. Livingston was in the garden."

"I immediately shut and fastened the door; they (the Indians) came furiously up, and tried to burst it open, demanding of me several times to open the door, which I refused. They then fired two guns; one ball

pierced through the door, but did me no damage. I then thought of my husband's rifle, took it down but it being double triggered, I was at a loss; at length I fired through the door, but it not being well aimed I did no execution; however the Indians retired from that place and soon after that an old adjoining house was on fire, and I and my children suffering much from the smoke. I opened the door and an Indian immediately advanced and took me prisoner, together with the two children."

"I then discovered that they had my remaining children in their possession, my sister Sukey, a wench with her young child, a negro man of Edward Callihan's and a negro boy of our own about eight years old. They were fearful of going into the house I left, to plunder, supposing that it had been a man that shot at them, and was yet within. So our whole clothing and household furniture were consumed in the flames, which I was then pleased to see, rather than that it should be of use to the savages."

"We were all hurried a short distance, where the Indians were very busy, dividing and putting up in packs for each to carry his part of the booty taken. I observed them careless about the children, and most of the Indians being some distance off in front, I called with a low voice to my eldest daughter, gave her my youngest child, and told them all to run towards neighbor John Russell's. They, with reluctance, left me, sometimes halting, sometimes looking back. I beckoned them to go, although I inwardly felt pangs not to be expressed on account of our doleful separation. The two Indians in the rear either did not notice this scene, or they were willing the children might run back. That evening the Indians crossed Clinch Mountain and went as far as Cooper creek, distant about eight miles."

"April 7th, set out early in the morning, crossed Clinch river at McLean's fish dam about twelve o'clock, then steered northwardly towards the head of Stoney creek. There the Indians camped carelessly, had no back spy nor kept sentries out. This day's journey was about twenty miles."

"April 8th. Continued in camp until the sun was more than an hour high; then set out slowly and traveled five or six miles and camped near the foot of Powell's mountain. This day Benge, the Indian chief, became more pleasant, and spoke freely to the prisoners. He told them he was about to carry them to the Cherokee towns. That in his route in the wilderness was his brother with two other Indians hunting, so that he might have provision when he returned. That at his camp were several white prisoners taken from Kentucky, with horses and saddles to carry them to the towns. He made enquiry for several persons on Holston, particularly old General Shelby, and said he would pay him a visit during the ensuing summer, and take away all his negroes. He frequently enquired who had negroes, and threatened he would have them all off the North Holston. He said all the Chickamooga towns were for war, and would soon be very troublesome to the white folks. This day two of the party were sent by Benge ahead to hunt."

"April 9th. After traveling about five miles, which was over Powell's mountain, and near the foot of the Stone mountain, a party of thirteen men under command of Lieutenant Vincent Hobbs, of the militia of Lee county, met the enemy in front, attacked and killed Benge the first fire, I being at that time some distance off in the rear. The Indian who was my guard at first halted on hearing the firing. He then ordered me to run, which I performed slowly. He attempted to strike me in the head with the tomahawk, which I defended as well as I could with my arm. By this time two of our people came in view, which encouraged me to struggle all I could. The Indian making an effort at this instant pushed me backward and I fell over a log, at the same time aiming a violent blow at my head, which in part spent its force on me and laid me for dead. The first thing I afterwards remembered was my good friends around me, giving me all the assistance in their power for my relief. They told me I was senseless for about an hour."

Certified this 15th day of April, 1794. A. Campbell

"An account of the raid, in Elizabeth (Head) Livingston's own words (from interview by Colonel Arthur Campbell, who led the militia that caught and killed Captain Benge)"

Shortly after the Indians were killed, Henry Livingston together with Peter, arrived on the scene very relieved that their wives had been saved. Susanna, Henry's wife, had been in the group immediately led by Chief Benge. Once Elizabeth was recovered enough for travel they all started back home.

Sources: 1. Tombstone 2. Census 1820 and 1830. 3. Pension papers R6394. 4. Annals of Southwest Virginia by L.P. Summers.

****

Drury Logan age 14

Drury Logan was born in 1762 in Halifax County, Virginia, and he died in 1859 in Rutherford County, North Carolina. He married Sarah Moore on 27 February, 1783. He received a pension of $80 a year. Drury had at least 5 slaves on his farm in 1800. Login is the spelling of his last name in his pension file.

"In the year 1776 then 14 years of age I became a General Volunteer this Section of the Country was overrun by the Tories and Indians and every person that was a friend to Independence and able to bear arms had to do so for his own safety I was stationed on the lines to guard the frontiers against the Indians and Tories I was sometimes at Russells Station sometimes at Waddletons Station part of time I was under Capt Harden sometimes under Captain Abraham Kirkendol we had no Regular Officers I scarcely ever went home and when I did it was only for a few days I am not certain of the year but shortly before the Surrender of Charleston I was ordered on to Charleston under Capt Robert Alexander Soon after our Arrival at that place it was surrendered to the British forces we all got Paroled and returned home prisoners of war I was taken several times by the Tories and taken to the principle officers but they always Released me the Tories had me confined at the Battle of Kings Mountain after that battle I was released from my parole and immediately was ordered on to the lines I was part of the time under Capt James Gray and sometimes Capt Vansant we was kept in a moving position did not lay any length of time at any one place there was a call then for men to go a southern Tour. I enlisted for 10 months under Capt Levy Johnston we belonged to his regiment commanded by Col John Thomas on our march we stormed and took Fridays fort It was a short distance from where Columbia now stands we on that ground joined the main army under General Sumter. We marched down the river to Buck head where we was stationed for some time from there I was at the Battle at Nelsons Ferry I was in the Battle at Goose Creek and at the scrimmage at the Governers Gate I was the bearer of dispatches from Genl Sumter to General Green when he raised the Siege of Ninety Six at the time that Lord Rawdon was marching on his forces for the relief of the fort on my return I got to the Juniper Springs I met some of the troops retreating from that place we joined the main army under General Sumter at Shiers ferry we was at that place for some time and returned home soon after our return I was a volunteer to go to Cross Creek under Capt Whitesides Col Robert Porter had the command we was only marched to Catabaw [Catawba] and from that place we was ordered back to the lines after peace was made."

The Battle of Goose Creek fought on 15 July, 1781 was not much of a battle. American General Sumter sent troops to the various approaches to Charlestown in hopes of disrupting the British communications and outposts. Drury was among a unit that seized Goose Creek Bridge with very little opposition.

At the end of his service declaration Drury is asked several questions. He gave an interesting explanation for his answer

Question} How were you called into service were you drafted did you volunteer or were you a substitute and if a substitute for whom Answer} *"My Father and family was living on the frontier I had been fond of a rifle from the time I was able to lod one I volunteered myself as one of the guard on the lines where I was contained for a considerable time there was a call for volunteers to go to Charleston I volunteered myself under Capt Robert Alexander I think this was in the year 1778 we was taken at Charleston and paroled as prisoners of war and returned home I was released immediately after the Battle at Kings Mountain where the Tories had me in custody I was immediately a volunteer for the lines soon after I enlisted for ten months under Levy Johnston I was in Continental Service from 1776 to the end of the war only when I was a prisoner and then I spent fully half of my time on the lines the Tories caught me with my rifle was the reason they took me prisoner and I expected if they had gained the day at Kings Mountain they would have hung me but providence carried it otherways."*

Sources: 1. North Carolina Marriage Index 1741-2004. 2. Census 1800. 3. Pension Papers W5464.

****

Richard Lord age 14

Richard Lord was born on 14 January, 1765 in Lyme, Connecticut, and he died on 6 September, 1843 in Sharon, Michigan. He married Deborah Jewett his second cousin in 1790. He enlisted on 12 December, 1779 in the 2nd Connecticut Regiment under the command of Colonel Zebulon Butler.

Sources; 1. Connecticut Revolutionary War Lists 1775-83. 2. Revolutionary Soldiers Resident or Dying in Onondaga County, N.Y., prepared by Rev. W.M. Beauchamp for the Onondaga Historical Association, 1863.

****

Mark Love age 13

Mark Love was born in 1763 in Ireland, and he died on 30 November, 1831 at Mount Vernon, Virginia. He married (1) Sarah Orr in 1782 and (2) Elizabeth Prator on 26 September, 1819. In his pension application he said he enlisted in 1776 or 1777. He must have enlisted in 1776 because the Battle of Sullivan's Island, which he stated he was in was fought on 28 June, 1776. He received a yearly pension of $96.

"I enlisted at 96 District, near White Hall South Carolina, in the company commanded by Captain Perumhuff of the Regiment commanded by Colonel Wm Thompson -- We were Mounted Rangers, Enlisted for eighteen months -- at the place aforesaid on the __ day of __ 1776 or 7 and I continued to serve in said Corps or in the Service of the United States in the Continental Army against the Common Enemy until the expiration of his said term of 18 months – I was discharged Honorably from the Service at the ten mile House near Charleston South Carolina by Captain Worley of Colonel Thompson's Regiment – I was in the Battles of Sullivan's Island -- in Fort Moultrie, when it was attacked -- Fort McIntosh where I was taken Prisoner -- at Guilford -- Eutaw Springs -- the Hanging Rock, & Rocky Mount under General Sumter -- but at some of these places & battles I was only a volunteer."

Mark served in the 3rd Regiment of South Carolina Rangers assigned to the 1st Carolina Brigade. At the Battle of Sullivan's Island the British tried to land troops from their ships. Mark Love's Regiment, under the command of Colonel William Thompson, directed heavy fire toward the British and kept the enemy from landing.

The Battle of Fort McIntosh fought in February of 1777 was where Mark Love was taken prisoner. Captain Richard Winn of the 3rd Regiment of Carolina Horse with Mark as a member, arrived at the fort with 40 men to aid in the defense of the frontier. This unit, along with 20 Continental troops from Georgia, began to rebuild the stockade.

A group of Tories made a surprise assault on the fort. Fighting continued all day of 17 February, and the Tories were waiting for British reinforcements. When the reinforcements arrived, a message was sent to the fort to surrender. Powder was running low and they were surrounded, so Captain Winn agreed to surrender as long as the British would guarantee their safety. Winn had heard of prisoners being killed by the Indians that had joined the British. The British gave their word that the

Americans would be safe and the Americans, along with Mark Love, arrived safely at Fort Barrington two days later.

Sources: 1. Kentucky Marriages 1802-1850. 2. Census 1790, 1820, and 1830. 3. Revolutionary Soldiers in Kentucky. 4. History of Georgia by Hugh McCall. 5. Pension Papers S36045.

****

Christopher Loving age 14

Christopher Loving was born on 30 December, 1763 in James City, Virginia, and he died on 27 September, 1830 in Floyd, Virginia. He married Judith Seay on 20 November, 1792 in Virginia. In 1820 he owned 3 slaves. He received a pension of $8 a month.

"I enlisted in the year 1777 when I was but 14 years of age, and the State of South Carolina in a Company commanded by Captain Linticomb on Continental establishment for three years in the 6th Regiment of South Carolina troops on Continental establishment commanded by Colonel Thomas Sumpter & Lt Col Henderson in the Army commanded by General Multree afterwards by General Lincoln, that I was at the battle of Savanna and the Siege of Charleston in South Carolina where I was at the close of the siege taken prisoner by the British and detained as a prisoner for nine weeks when I made his escape from the City of Charleston and afterwards joined Colonel Lacy & Lt Col McGriff as a volunteer my enlistment being expired as well as I now recollects. That I was with them at King's Mountain and there had a battle, after which I joined General Thomas Sumter and was in a skirmish at Black Stock's on Tyger River, that I then joined Captain Montgomery's Company of Mounted riflemen under the Command of Genl Morgan & was at the Battle of Cowpens, that I then joined a volunteer Company under the command of Captain Jacob Barnett in a Regiment commanded by Colonel Henry Hampton and under the command of Genl Sumter and was at the battle of the Eutaw Springs under the Command of General Green that I during my said services was very badly wounded and had my right hand nearly cut off by a broad sword and my left arm very much wounded in several places so as to render them but of minor service to me."

When Christopher Loving enlisted, he was a member of the 6th South Carolina Regiment. This regiment was merged into the 2nd South Carolina in February of 1780, just before the capture of Charleston when Christopher was taken prisoner.

When the Americans were taken prisoner their muskets were brought to the powder magazine inside the city. The Hessian officer in charge told his men that some of the muskets might still be loaded. Some of his men paid no attention to his warning and put loaded muskets in with the powder. One of the muskets fired and ignited 180 barrels of powder. It has been estimated that when it happened it caused hundreds of other muskets to go off. Nearly 200 hundred people were killed including 30 British soldiers.

Christopher fought at the Battle of King's Mountain on 7 October, 1780 under Colonel Edward Lacey. Some historians believe that Colonel Lacey and his men were given the honor of the first assault on the enemy, which took place on the north side of the mountain. At the skirmish at Blackstock on 20 November, 1780 Christopher was a member of the Turkey Creek Regiment of Militia and again under the command of Colonel Lacey.

At the Battle of Eutaw Springs on 8 September, 1781 Christopher was a member of Hampton's Regiment of Light Dragoons that formed in July of 1780. This militia unit was under the command of Lt. Colonel Henry Hampton.

Sources: 1. Census 1810, 1820, and 1830. 2. U.S. Pensioners 1818-1872. 3. Fluvanna County Marriage Bonds 1777-1801. 4. Roster of South Carolina Patriots in the American Revolution. 5. Pension Papers S38153.

****

Sybil Ludington age 16

Sybil Ludington was born on 5 April, 1761 in Fredericksburg, New York, and she died on 26 February, 1839 in Patterson, New York. She married Edmond Ogden in 1784.

Sybil's father Henry Ludington was a patriot, and in 1776 he was appointed a Colonel in the 7th Dutchess County Militia. The area his regiment guarded was important, because it was the most direct route the British would take to and from Connecticut and the coast on Long Island Sound. The regiment also prevented Tories from obtaining supplies for the British.

Since Henry was a wanted man, Sybil felt obligated to guard and protect him from any dangers that threatened him. One night Ichabod Prosser, a hated Tory, and his men surrounded the Ludington house in hopes of capturing or killing Samuel. Sybil enlisted the help of her oldest sister to fool the Tories.

The two girls were guarding the house with their weapons ready to fire. When the Tories were spotted the girls sounded the alarm. Immediately, candles were lit in every room and the girls, along with several other family members, began marching back and forth in front of the widows. It appeared to the Tories hiding outside that the house was heavily guarded, so they marched on to the next town.

A message was sent to Colonel Ludington at his home on 26 April, 1777. The message warned that the British were a few miles away in Danbury, Connecticut. They had uncovered American military stores and then began burning and looting the town. Unfortunately Colonel Ludington's 400 militia men were on furlough and were scattered around the county. It would take a rider all night to alert the men to the British threat.

Sybil told her father she would make the ride, and over the objections of her father she began to prepare for the ride. Around 9 at night she began the 40 mile ride that would take her to the towns of Carmel, Mahopac, Kent Cliffs, and Farmers Mills. Before she left her father gave a large thick stick to bang on the doors of the home to wake the sleeping men. He warned her to be on the lookout for Tory outlaws that roamed the area.

Off she rode to alert the countryside. Each home she came to she would bang on the door with the stick until a candle inside was lit. Then she would yell, *"The British are burning Danbury! Muster at Ludington's Mill."* This same scene was created all night until she returned home the next morning. Once during the night she even had to fight off an outlaw.

By the time she got back to the mill yard it was swarming with militiamen, and later the militia caught up with the retreating British and beat them back. The British boarded their ships and sailed away. They never attempted a similar raid.

Sources: 1. Sybil Ludington The Call to Arms by V.T. Dacquino. 2. Danbury's Burning: The Story of Sybil Ludington's Ride by Anne Grant.

****

Jacob Lusk age 12

Jacob Lusk was born in 1766 in Claversack, New York, and he died in 1839 in Michigan. He married Elizabeth Phillips on 27 May, 1787 in Claversack, New York. He received a yearly pension of $80. He also served with his brother Michael, who enlisted at the age of 11 and his brother William who enlisted at the age of 14.

"I volunteered for one month under the command of Capt Burger Claugh, Went from Claverack then Albany County now Columbia County State of New York Marched to Canajoharie about three miles north of the Mohawk River to a little fort called fort plank At that place Col. Gordon Commanded, I was at the fort when the Indians destroyed Cherry Valley. I served out the tour I volunteered in the fall of 1778 for the __?__ month."

"In the following Spring of 1779 the Militia of the County of Albany and perhaps that of all the State were divided in Classes of twelve each (or there abouts) Each of these Classes had to furnish a man for the term of Nine Months, And that one of these Classes did hire me. I was mustered at Col. Peter Van Ness's then sent without a commissioned officer, to fort Plank above named where I was put under the command of Col Lieutenant Col Weissenfels who then Commanded the fourth New York Regiment Called Livingstons Regiment I was sent to Stone Robbia [Arabia] *under the command of Captain Norton. About the first of June the company marched up to Stone Robbie* [Arabia] *and marched to Bowman's Creek there the whole Regiment encamped and commenced carrying boats and provisions across from the Mohawk River to Otsego Lake, the head of the Susquehanna River. About the first of July 1779 the camp was broken up at Bowmans Creek and march over the country to foot of Otsego Lane. Here Brigadier General Clinton took the command of all the forces. In this place was built a dam across the outlet of the lake about the last of July. Let out the water embarked in the boats and descended the Susquehanna to Tioga Point. On our way down the River we met a detachment sent by Gen Sullivan to know if we were coming. We stayed a few days at Tioga Point. Then commenced our march northwesterly to Seneca Lake."*

Jacob Lusk is listed on the roll of the 4th Regiment of the New York line under the command of Lt. Colonel Federick Weissenfels. The 4th Regiment that Jacob Lusk belonged to joined up with the troops under General Clinton. General Washington ordered General James Clinton to assemble a fourth brigade at Schenectady and moved up the Mohawk River Valley to Cansjoharie and then to Otsego Lake as a staging point.

They later joined up with three brigades under the command of General Sullivan.

"We marched up the Chemung River but we had not proceeded more than 10 miles before we came where the Indians and Tories had made a stand. They had made a brest work of logs from the River nearly to the mountains but it was soon forced and the Enemy driven off. Numbers of them were killed. I do not remember of any of our men killed. I was not in the Battle being a little more than Twelve Years of age was in the rear to Guard the pack horses. We encamped that night, and the next, on the ground. The Enemy left. General Sullivan informed us that we had only provisions enough to last us to travel but 80 miles further and that to accomplish the objects of the expedition we should go 160 miles and made a proposition to go on half allowance and those of the army who felt disposed to pursue the enemy on the condition of having but half rations were requested to give their cheer. The air was sent with the unanimous shout. The next day we marched for the Seneca Lake in a northerly direction and after somedays I saw the Lake at the outlet opposite were Geneva now stands. We continued our march forded the outlet of the Lake and encamped in a place Called then Canadergo Castle. An Indian Settlement Now Called Old Castle, we found a large orchard of apple trees and plenty of green corn. While at Old Castle I took lame and was ordered back to the Camp at Tioga Point."

"With then two hundred others these Americans under General Sullivan returned from the expedition then embarked and descended the Susquehanna River to a place then called Wyoming to which is now called Wilksbury, Pennsylvania and from thence to Easton, Pennsylvania where they crossed the Delaware River into New Jersey. The Army then proceeded through Moravene Town a small village on their march towards Morristown. At Pumpton plains Sullivan's Army was inspected by General George Washington before proceeding to Basking Ridge about three miles from Morristown, where we arrived about the first of December and commenced building Huts for winter quarters. About the last days of December I was discharged and returned home."

"In the year 1780 was again hired by a class as before. Mustered as before and went to Albany and thence was sent to Johnstown North of the Mohawk River and here put into the company of Captain Vroman. We here relieved a Company of Regular troops. We belonged to Col Harpers Regiment. We were ordered to Schenectady to guard boats that were transporting flour to fort Stanwix and then I returned to Johnstown. In the latter part of the season we were ordered to Herkimer whence were embodied under Major Benschoten, Col Harper was not with us and I was then marched for Fort Stanwix we fell in with a body of Indians, defeated them and proceeded without further trouble to Fort Stanwix. Relieved a Regiment of Regulars a Company of Artillery belonging to the Regular troops combined with us. Here we staid about two months and were relieved by a Regiment of Regular troops and while I was in this General Van Rensselaer fought a Battle on the Mohawk River. Sent an expedition to Major Van Benschoten to head the Enemy off at Oneida Lake, a detachment of Sixty or Seventy men were defeated and were all killed and taken except two. We then marched slowly to Schenectady, and were then discharged about the first of December."

"In the year 1781 in the Spring of that Year was again hired by a class sent to Albany from thence to Johnstown. I was under the command of Captain Cannon Regiment commanded by Col Willet New York State Troops. Here but a short time marched to fort Plain on the South side of the Mohawk River. Here Col Willet command in person and that sometime in the month of June I think a body of Indians were discovered at a place called Turlock, Col Willet called all the men he could and marched for the Enemy and I was one who marched with Col Willet."

"Started from Fort Plain about dusk expecting to reach the Indian Camp before day; but did not arrive until five in the morning & the Col. Divided us into three divisions one was to show themselves to the Enemy and retreat So as to bring the Enemy between the two other divisions, one of which was Commanded by Col Willett and the other by Major Kean or Mc Kean, a severe Combat ensued Major McKean received his death wound near my side and I received a wound in my third finger of my right hand and that there was from twenty five to forty killed and Wounded but the Enemy were defeated. We found two white children Massacred and recovered Some cattle then Returned to fort Plain from thence we marched to Herkimer at this place the Indians had killed Capt Ellsworth and Some others just before we arrived at that place staid at the last mentioned place nearly through the Summer and at fort Dayton. I then marched to fort Plain from there in Cap. Cannons Company to Ballstown and built a fort."

"I enlisted in the Company of Capt Cannon Regiment of Col Willet for the term of three years at the end of the aforesaid Eight months. The men that had enlisted were called levies and Received furlough until Spring 1781. First December I was mustered at Albany by a man named Lansing I think, and Received from him a Certificate for five hundred acres *of Bounty Lands, Marched to Schoharie lay a short time at the lower fort and then marched to the upper fort and staid there through the Summer in the fall marched to fort Plain from thence to Johnstown Continued there till the beginning of Winter then marched to fort plain where I was inoculated for the Small pox and I was next marched to Herkimer. Staid there until the first of February 1783 a Rhode Island Regiment Joined Us here. A detachment was ordered to March to Reduce Oswego a fort on lake Ontario Col Willets Regiment all went across Oneida Lake in Sleighs then left them. Were misled by our Pilot and were Obliged to return to Herkimer much frozen And Starved and that I remained at Herkimer until Spring when an officer arrived from the East with news of peace and I staid at Herkimer and other places near through the Summer. Was at fort Plain when General Washington Came then went as one of a Guard with the General to fort Stanwix and returned with him to fort Plain. Herkimer Late in the fall the Regiment marched to Schenectady and there Staid until the first of January 1784 when we were discharged."*

Sources: 1. The Bloodied Mohawk: The American Revolution in the Words of Fort Planks Defenders and Other Mohawk Valley Partisans by Kenneth D. Johnson. 2. New York in the Revolution as Colony and State, 2nd edition, 1898. 3. Pension Papers S29302.

****

Michael Lusk age 11

Michael Lusk was born on 22 July, 1770 in Claversack, New York, and he died on 4 July, 1839 in New York. He married Elizabeth Groat on 20 October, 1789. He enlisted on 1 May, 1782 and received a yearly pension of $30. His brother Jacob, who enlisted at the age of 12, served with him in the 4th Regiment New York Levies. His brother William who enlisted at fourteen (he probably enlisted younger) also served with him.

"In the year 1782 I did enlist for nine months under the command of Captain Nathaniel Henry in the town of Kinderhook then Albany County now Columbia County, the lieutenant name was Vandeparrack, Ensign Mathus Tratton, Col Willet Regiment of the New York State Troops. I was then marched to Albany from thence to Schenectady from thence I soon went to fort hunter at the mouth of Schahame Creek from thence I went to Johnstown north of the Mohawk River there I was stationed at that place as a guard under the command of Lieutenant Johnson. From thence I marched to Chautauqua thence to fort plain where I staid and served out my nine months which expired of the first of January 1783. I staid until the

middle of January on account of my having had the small pox and entirely recovered at the time I received my discharge."

Sources: 1.The Bloodied Mohawk: The American Revolution in the Words of Fort Planks Defenders and Other Mohawk Valley Partisans by Kenneth D. Johnson. 2. New York in the Revolution as Colony and State, 2nd edition, 1898. 3. Pension Papers W20542.

****

William Lusk age 14

William Lusk was born on 24 November, 1765 in Claversack New York, and he died on 28 March, 1829 in New York. He served with his brothers Jacob, who enlisted at 12, and his brother Michael, who enlisted at 11. All three boys served in the Levies of the 4th New York Regiment. William is found on the Regiment's roll in 1779. He probably enlisted younger than the age of 14. The Levies were drafts from different militia regiments, which could be called upon to serve outside of the state.

Sources: 1. The Bloodied Mohawk: The American Revolution in the Words of Fort Planks Defenders and Other Mohawk Valley Partisans by Kenneth D. Johnson. 2. New York in the Revolution as Colony and State, 2nd edition, 1898. 3. Pension Papers W20542.

****

Elisha Lyman age 13

Elisha Lyman was born on 27 June, 1765 in Lebanon, Connecticut, and he died on 23 February, 1849 in Groton, Connecticut. His second wife was Abigail Bloyd, and they were married by the Reverend Achley on 1 October, 1835 in New London, Connecticut.

"In the year 1779 in the month of May I was drafted into the company commanded by Captain Elias Blip of said Lebanon to go to New London and Groton, I was not quite fourteen years of age but was large and stout for my age. It was very inconvenient for my father to leave home I purposed to Captain Blip to take me as a substitute which said Captain agreed to do and I according joined the company in the month of May. Marched to New London and thence crossed to Croton when said company was stationed on the hill where the monument now stands near the Fort. I was in the service for the time of <u>three months</u> when I was discharged in the month of August."

"Shortly after I returned home another draft of men was made to supply the places of those whose tern had expired at New London and Groton and Josiah Rockmill with others was drafted for three months to

go to New London or Groton to serve, I having become __?__ with military life engaged with said Rockmill to go as a substitute for him and in the month of September again entered the service at said Groton and served for the full term of <u>three months</u> and was discharged in the month of December."

"In the month of February in the year 1780 a call was made by Gen Washington for men to fill the ranks of the Continental army & early in the spring of that year a draft of militia was made for that purpose. David Trumbull of said Lebanon (a son of the then Governor of Connecticut and a brother of the late Governor) among others was drafted for <u>nine months service</u> either to go himself or furnish a substitute. I immediately afterwards said David Trumbull applied for me to be his substitute and made a contract to that affect. In the month of April 1780 I with seven other individuals left Lebanon to join the Continental Army then at Nelson's point opposite __?__ Point in the state of New York. I joined the army on the 1st of May and belonged to the Company commanded by Capt Richard Douglass of New London. Capt Douglass company belonged to the Regiment of Colonel Starr of Danbury con. the Regiment belonged to Gen Jedediah Huntingtons Brigade in the course of a few weeks the army crossed the Hudson at Kings ferry and moved into New Jersey. The army moved from place to place during the season but no remarkable events took place except the capture trial condemnation & execution of Major Andre and the expectation of a battle when the enemy ran up to Tappan, the army then marched to attack us but the enemy __?__ off before our arrival. When Major Andre was executed at Orangestown I was in the inside column which formed the hollow square around the gallows. I served the full term of nine months without interruption and was discharged."

General Jedediah Huntington was appointed one of the members of the board at the trial of Major Andre. Major Andre was executed on 2 October, 1780 in the Dutch village of Tappan, (Orangetown). He was executed near the center of the camp of the American Army. There was an exterior guard of five hundred Infantry that surrounded the area. There was also an inner guard, Elisha was part of this, under the command of a Captain. None were allowed within this inner square except the officers on duty and the Assistants of the Provost Marshal

"In the month of April 1781 Isaiah Loomis of said Lebanon received directions from the proper authorities to enlist teamsters for the Continental Army. In the month of April 1781 at the said Lebanon I *enlisted as a teamster into the army for the term of eight months under said Loomis. Immediately after my enlistment I with the others enlisted for that purpose left Lebanon under the command of the conduction said Isiah Loomis. Marched to Hartford thence to Dobsons ferry on the Hudson when we joined the army and were attached to Genl Huntington's Brigade. I continued to serve without interruption the full term of* eight months *during which time I performed team work for the army from place to place and on one occasion I came to Connecticut for provisions for the army which I obtained & carried back. Cornwallis was taken at Yorktown in October I was discharged."*

Sources: 1. The New England Magazine Vol. 6, 1834. 2. Tombstone 3. U.S. Pensioners 1818-1872. 4. Pension Papers W8267.

****

Elijah Lynch age 14

Elijah Lynch was born in 1765 in Campbell, Virginia, and he died 20 December, 1839 in Rockingham County, Tennessee.

"I enlisted in the Army of the United States in the year 1778 with Captain James Curtly and served in the __ Regiment of the Guards in the line and served under the following officers for the first year in the company of Captain James Curtly at the end of which time __ Porter was appointed Captain of the same company in which I continued during the whole term of his service – Colonel Francis Taylor, Major John Roberts were the officers of the Regiment at the time of Elisting I resided in the County of Culpeper & State of Virginia and enlisted at the Court House of said County and marched to the Barracks in Albemarle County Virginia where I remained as one of the Guard of the prisoners of that Station until for three years at the end of which time I marched to Winchester Virginia where he remained four months when he was regularly discharged in the year 1781 after having served three years & four months & that his discharge was unfortunate as to have destroyed by fire."

Elijah Lynch belonged to the Virginia Regiment of Guards under the command of Colonel Francis Taylor. The guard was created to guard over the captured army of British General John Burgoyne in 1777 kept at Albemarle Barracks from January 1779 until February 1781.

Sources: 1. U.S. Pensioners 1818-1872. Pension Application of Francis Taylor R19418. 3. Pension Papers W5032.

****

Eliezer McA (MacKee, McCay) age 13

Eliezer McA was born in 1766 in Charleston, South Carolina, and he died in Missouri after 1846. In his pension application he stated, *"at the age of about or in my 13th year I entered the Army of the United States, at Charlestown South Carolina. I think in the month of January or Fegruary, in the year 1779."*

He served as a bugler in a company of rangers under Captain McA. He was in the battle at Camden, where most of his company were killed. He then transferred to a company commanded by Captain Robert Maxwell, and he served as a drummer for a year. After the Battle of Eutaw Springs, he went into the hospital to recover from his wounds. When he recovered from his wounds, *"I was retained by the Surgeon of the hospital Dr. William Russell to be a nurse until the close of the war."*

"I served as a Musician as aforesaid from the early part of 1779 to the battle of the Eutaw Springs, and from my recovery at the Hospital to the end of the War, I was a nurse in the Hospital. The most of my first term of service under Capt. William McA was spent against the Indians and Tories in the upper part of Ninety Six District, that when not in active service Capt. McA's Company was Stationed at Senaka, Occasionally at Cheowee Station was thence marched to the Battle at Camden where as aforesaid by Capt. in the greater part of his Company was Killed, was then marched back to Seneca Station, from thence I was sent as Drummer with Captains Hannah and Nicholson of North Carolina to raise troops to meet Col. Ferguson at King's Mountain, but did not arrive there until after the Battle, thence, returned to Pickens Fort in Ninety Six district, thence to the best of my recollection our Regiment marched to Join General Morgan and fought at the Battle of the Cow Pens, thence returned to our former Station in Ninety Six District, thence I think to the 2nd Battle at Camden, thence to our old station, shortly after our return, I was sent with Col. Clark to recruit, when we occasionally fell in with a British Major I think Dunlap who commanded a small party of English and a large party of Tories, surprised and defeated them. Killing their commander and many of his men I think we then crossed the Savannah River and fought the Battle of Kettle Creek, thence returned to the Siege of Ninety Six, thence General Greene retired across the Saluda River to Reedy River and after recruiting a short time took up the line of march for Eutaw Springs, there being a supernumerary number of Musicians this Affiant then fell into the Ranks and fought the Battle in the Company commanded by Capt. Wilson, Col. Anderson formerly Col. Pickens Regiment, Col. Pickens having been

promoted, Col. Anderson took the command, was injured and sent to the Hospital as before stated."

"I was in several Skirmishing fights or battles with the Indians The following incident took place during my services which I thinks worthy to relate a scouting party came in contact with a large party of Indians and were beaten by the Indians and forced to fly -- On the retreat I came up with Patrick Calhoun father of Honorable John C. Calhoun, the said Calhoun was unable to keep up with the Main body of the party, that said Patrick Calhoun requested me to remain with him. Calhoun and myself were soon separated a short distance and overtaken by the pursuing Indians, the pursuers taking advantage of our separation, one of them attacked Mr. Calhoun and prostrated him on the ground, and while in the act of dispatching him Calhoun, I fired on the Indian and saved the life of Mr. Calhoun, the other Indian in the meantime, for there were 2 who seemed to have devoted themselves to the destruction of me and Mr. Calhoun, had advanced on me, his gun being empty, and in turn Mr. Calhoun came to my rescue and saved me. I think this incident still fresh in the memory of the Calhoun family."

Sources: 1. Roster of South Carolina Patriots in the American Revolution. 2. Pension Papers R6578.

****

John McAlister age 14

John McAlister was born on 12 February, 1765 in Argyle Shire, Scotland, and he died on 24 December, 1848 in Richmond County, North Carolina. John came to this country in 1775. His 4th wife was Sarah Diggs and they married on 12 July, 1819. He received a yearly pension of $60. After his death the widow's pension was raised to $80 a year. Sarah's widow's pension was suspended during the Civil War. Once the war ended she swore an oath of loyalty, and the pension was restored. In 1870 her pension was increased to $96 a year.

"I entered the Service of the United States under Captain Moses Chambers, as a volunteer the first of October 1779 and Served <u>three months</u> in the Service of keeping guard at Haleys ferry on the Pedee River--the British being as was said in the Adjoining State viz -- South Carolina, that the 1st of January 1780 I volunteered his Services under Captain William Wall in the light horse of Richmond County as a minute Man ready at all times when called into Service and was in two engagements against the Tories at Betty's Bridge on Drowning Creek when Col Thomas

Wade Col David Love Col Thomas Crawford and others commanded which first engagement was in the month of August and the last of September 1781 I was __?__ skirmishes during the time of my service and in the __?__ February 1781 I was appointed Sergeant in Captain William Wall's Company that in the month of December 1781 he ___?___ with some Tories taken by Colonel Crawford and Captain William Wall as prisoners to the __?_ of Salisbury in Rowan County in this ___?___ officer of the Guard, and delivered them safe, but one that made his escape – in the year of 1781 I was sent to Salisbury for ammunition I had to go to Genl Rutherford's fifteen miles N. W. of Salisbury before I could get any for Colonel Thomas Crawford and Captain Wall's company, I served two years and three months in the Service of the United States two years of which time I served in the capacity of first Sergeant in Captain Wall's company of Horse they being always called out to serve the neighboring Counties of Moore & Robeson, formerly Bladen, where the enemies of the Country or of the American cause resorted to and lived in, that the before mentioned, Wade, Love, Crawford and Edward Williams were the different Colonels I served under, I believe I had a Sergeants or Cornet's Commission but has lost it by reason that I never expected to have any use or call for it, that after the British left this State the Tories were not troublesome and the Whigs slackened in searching for them, and we were not called out, and my discharge, if he had one, it is lost as well as my commission and that at the last Battle at Beattys Bridge I was the only Scotchmen who was in the American Army of perhaps 400 men that I well was known to be a Whig by many men in Anson & Montgomery and now Richmond Counties that are now deceased and gone to their long home."

  John McAlister was in both Battles at Bettis's Bridge. The first was fought on 4 August, 1781 between the Anson County Militia led by Colonel Thomas Wade and a Loyalist force commanded by Colonel Hector McNeil and Colonel Duncan Ray. The patriots engaged the Loyalist force in the evening and by midnight had defeated them.

  The two forces met again on 1 September, 1781, but this time the Loyalists were reinforced by the famous and hated Loyalist, Colonel David Fanning. As Fanning began to position his troops, someone accidently fired his musket and the battle began early. After ninety minutes of fighting the Patriots line broke, and they began retreating. Fanning's men pursued the Patriots for seven miles taking many prisoners. This victory encouraged Colonel Fanning to attack Hillsborough 12 days later, the temporary state capital of North Carolina.

Sources: 1. Pension roll of 1835. 2. Pension Papers W1887. 3. Battles and Engagements of the American Revolution in North Carolina by Robinson P. Blackwell.

****

Hugh McBrayer age 13

Hugh McBrayer was born in Virginia in 1768, and he died in Kentucky after 1835. A note in his pension file stated that the application was rejected because he was 13 years of age, underage, and had not enlisted in the army at the time of his capture. Hugh never married. The name Hugh McBrayer is found on the pay roll of a company of mounted volunteers in Kentucky 13 June to 16 October, 1794.

"My father moved to Kentucky in the year of 1779 in Company with the McAfees and settled at their station about seven miles below Harrodsburg in the spring of 1781 me and my brother had crossed the river for the purpose of hobbling the horses so that they could be found next morning, it was in the dusk of Evening 16 Indians suddenly came upon us, Seized me—my brother made his escape across the river into the fort, the Indians carried me forthwith without stopping to Detroit and delivered him into the hands of the British who paid the indians for the service out of the English store—they had been employed by the British to war on us. There was a store called the Kings store at Detroit kept by the Indian Agent called Piero Banbee, Capt. Bird commanded at Detroit he had about 100 prisoners Captured principally at the Blue Licks defeat and at Bryant's and Riddle's stations. I remained a prisoner with others at Detroit until the summer of 1783, we were then shipped to the falls of Niagara, from thence to Montreal in lower Canada, from thence we were sent across to Ticondaroga, and at the mouth of Wood Creek delivered and received by the regular officers of the Revolutionary army, then in command, we were thus delivered up as prisoners of War upon peace being made, we were then marched near the place where Burgoyne had surrendered and were there discharged, and I then returned home to Kentucky, by the way of Botetourt County Va where my father had moved from and from there went in company with Robt McMillan, his family and my father's family who were moving to Kentucky."

Sources: Pension Papers R6588. 2. American Militia in the Frontier Wars 1790-1796.

****

James McCaw age 13

James McCaw was born in Antrim County, Ireland in 1762, and he died on 5 March, 1840 in Chester County, South Carolina. He married (1) Martha Morton who died before 1789, and (2) Sarah McWilliams. James immigrated with his parents William and Ann to South Carolina with a group of Scotch Presbyterians around 1771.

He enlisted as a volunteer in Colonel Lacey's Regiment in captain Dixon's Company and he served in the Snow Campaign in 1775. This campaign was one of the first major military operations of the war. It took place in November and December in the Appalachian Mountains. The Americans marched against the Loyalists' recruiting centers in South Carolina. The colonists were successful taking prisoners and supplies. Because of the heavy snow they marched back home, and most of the men including James went home.

James volunteered again under the same commanders in 1776 and served for three months. He stated in his pension papers, *"...marched to Charleston was in hearing of the Battle of fort Moultrie."* This battle was called the Battle of Sullivan's Island and was an American victory. His third tour was under the same command, *"...volunteered again under my former officers in the year 1779 marched to Charleston at the time the British drove General Moultrie on the 28th of June served three months and was dismissed."*

He volunteered a fourth and fifth time under the same officers. The fourth time he marched to Orangeburg and was dismissed after three months. The fifth time he marched to Black Swamp and served for three months. It's important to remember that the militia would be called to serve, if the enemy was marching toward the area or even if this was a rumored threat. Sometimes it was just a rumor so after a period of time the men when home.

James served with the 6th South Carolina Regiment a sixth time and this tour was filled with fighting. *"After the fall of Charleston in the year 1780 volunteered in Captain Pagan's Company Colonel Lacey Regiment under General Sumter was at the Skirmish at Williamson's Plantation where Captain Huck was killed was at the Battle of Rocky-Mount, Battle of Hanging-rock and at the skirmish at Fish dam Ford on Broad River Served six months when dismissed."*

The Skirmish at Williamson's Plantation, where eighteen year old James McCaw fought, was a small but great victory for the Americans. The victory gave the South Carolina back country a boost. The frontier militia, a band of farmers, had defeated the feared British soldiers. After the skirmish many local men wanted to join the militia. The victory might not have been possible without the help of a young girl and a slave.

In June of 1780 the British officer who commanded a British Provincial Regiment ordered Captain Christian Huck to take a command of men to the area and find the rebel leaders in order to persuade other locals to join the British side. He marched into one district, gathered all the men together, with most being old, and proclaimed, *"even if the rebels were as thick as trees, and Jesus Christ would come down and lead them, he would still defeat them."*

After making his boast, Captain Huck confiscated all the men's horses. The theft and the tirade did not make many friends with the local people. He was given the nickname, *"the swearing captain."*

On 11 July, 1780 Captain Huck, with his four hundred British cavalry, arrived at the home of colonial Colonel William Bratton and asked his wife where her husband was. She replied that the Colonel was with the American Colonel Sumter. Captain Huck told her that if her husband would join him, he would gain a commission. The Colonel's wife replied, *"I desire that he should remain in Colonel Sumter's command even if he lost his life."* One of the British soldiers attempted to kill her for those remarks but was stopped. Captain Huck left, however not before he arrested three old men on trumped up charges.

Around this time a neighbor's younger sister, Mary McClure, and a slave named Watt provided the militia commander with some valuable intelligence on the movements of Captain Huck. The militiamen arrived in the vicinity that night and prepared to attack Captain Huck. The next day they attacked the British from three sides and completely destroyed the British regiment. The braggart, Captain Huck, was killed.

Less than a month later James participated in the Battle of Hanging Rock. The 6th Regiment led by Colonel Thomas Sumter was sent on a campaign to harass or destroy a British outpost in South Carolina. They met at Hanging Rock on 6 August, 1780 and fought a three hour battle without pause on a very hot day. They were unable to completely destroy the British, because they lacked enough ammunition and many men began to pass out from the excessive heat. The British lost 192 men and the Americans loss was only 12. Perhaps James was among a group of American troops that came across a storage of British rum. They paused in the fighting to help themselves to the rum, and they became so drunk they could not rejoin the battle and had to return to their camp.

On 9 November, 1780 James was at the Battle of Fishdam Ford. His regiment had been wary to the possibility of a surprise attack by the British, which was something they liked to do. Around one in the morning of November 9th the British attacked and were repelled by the alert Americans. This battle occurred near the home of James in Chester County. Soon after the battle his enlistment was up and James McCaw walked home.

In the year 1781 James answered the call again for two months and served under newly promoted General Sumter. *"I volunteered in 1781 under Captain Fair and Colonel Pickens Regiment marched to Georgia had two Skirmishes with the Indians and made some prisoners then fought with the British at Governor Wright's Plantation in Georgia Colonel Twiggs commanded for two months."*

James probably left the army around the siege of Yorktown in the fall of 1781. He later married and lived in Chester County, South Carolina for the rest of his life. The 1830 census reports that he had one slave. He was granted a pension of $80.00 a year for his service.

Sources: 1. Christian Huck quote from memoirs of Col. William and Maj. Joseph McLunkin. 2. Publications of the Southern History Association Vol. 1 by Colyer Meriwether. 3. Census of 1820, 1830, and 1840. 4. Pension Papers of James McCaw S18117. 5. A Guide to the Battles of the American Revolution by Savas and Dameron. 6. U.S. the Pension Roll of 1835.

****

Samuel McClung Age 14

Samuel McClung was born on 5 March, 1763 in Baltimore, Maryland, and he died in 1850 at Hanover, Pennsylvania. His pension was probably rejected because he had not enlisted in the regular army or militia.

"I entered the service of the United States in the year 1777 on the last week in June or first week in July under the following circumstances and under the following named officers and served as hereinafter stated. I lived at the time I entered the service in Baltimore County, Maryland and

was generally occupied in driving my father's team of horses and waggons from that place to Baltimore and other places. About the first of July 1777 I hauled a load of sugar and salt for Edward Murry to Baltimore which load I delivered to the Consynee at Fell point in Baltimore. Soon after I discharged my load myself and team . . . pressed into the Service of the United States by Thomas Foard a forage Master in the Service by whom I was attached to the division Commander by col. Darby Lun which consisted of five Companies under the following named Captains: Edward Oldham, Joshua Rutledge, Joshua Miles, John C. Owens and William Harvey, which several companies do officered marched in about 2 weeks from Baltimore to join the Regular Army under Washington, on the Brandywine. We marched directly towards Philadelphia, myself and three other teamsters who were also pressed into the Service in Baltimore hauling all the artillery, stores and camp equipages. We did not form a junction with the Main Army until the 5th day of October following at Germantown in Penn. which was the day after the Memorable battle at that place. When we arrived at Germantown the day after the battle, I with my team, was immediately engaged in hauling the wounded to the neighboring houses and barns which were converted into Hospitals for the time being. I think I was detained with my team at and about Germantown for about two months from which place about the first of December we were marched by Gen. Washington across the Delaware River into the State of Jersey to a place which I think was called Prospect Hill where the militia were discharged and the regulars went into winter quarters. Myself and John Deal were detained in the Service of the Regulars and were dispatched with our teams about the middle of December under the Command of forage Master William Guinn of the Regulars, with a platoon of soldiers as a guard to each waggon, to the North River for two heavy Cannon, each of which made a good load for a team. I think we brought these cannon from Saratoga in New York. On account of the great distance to be travelled, the extreme severity of the weather and the interruptions of the enemy, we did not get back with these Cannon until Spring. I think we were engaged about four months in this excursion. When we arrived with the Cannon where the main army were encamped they were mounted on a floating battery in the Delaware river. We remained with the Army at the place engaged in various services until Some time in the Summer of 1778 when it was ordered to march to the South and myself and Deal compelled to accompany it From New Jersey where we marched to Philadelphia from thence to the Susquehana river thence direct to Baltimore thence to the Patapico where Elliott mills now stands thence (I think) to Georgetown on the Potomac thence across Virginia toward the

Carolinas. I was taken with my waggon into North Carolina. We Scarcely ever knew where we were going, it was our business to just follow the Army, Sometimes we would travel one day in one direction and the next in a different direction so that we rarely knew our destination and gave ourselves but little uneasiness on that point. The army had been separated into various divisions before we reached the Carolinas. Soon after the detachment to which I was joined reached Carolina, it being encamped, was attacked in the night and driven off by the enemy with the loss of nearly all its baggage. As soon as the Camp was attacked, myself and Deal hitched up our teams and started off in the night to Save our teams from being destroyed or carried off. We remained in the neighborhood until we learned the fate our detachment and then started for home in Baltimore Co., Maryland which place we reached about the first of November being about one month after the rout of the Americans in Carolina."

"When we arrived in Baltimore on our return we unloaded the little that remained in our waggon at the magazine at Falls Point and then went directly home, having been out in the Service full sixteen months. During all this time we were engaged continually either in hauling in provisions from the Country under the forage Master or hauling the baggage for the army. When on march . . . I was born in Baltimore County, State of Maryland in St. James parish, on the 5th day of March 1763."

"The reason why I have not produced a Clergyman to Certify for me is simply that the Rev. Elisha McCurdy who I am picked to attend for me has not come to Court. He lives 2 1/2 miles from the County town and perhaps found it inconvenient to attend. I know no person living who has a personal knowledge of my Service. I have no documentary evidence to prove my Service. I never received any compensation for all the Services I rendered the United States except one Shirt and one pair of Shoes which were given me by forage Master Guinn. I drew my rations regularly on the other Soldiers and God know sometimes they were poor enough."

Sources: 1. Census 1820 and 1840. 2. Maryland Revolutionary War Records. 3. Pension Papers R6626.

****

John McCord age 13

John McCord was born on 25 November, 1763 in Albemarle, Virginia and he died on 2 November, 1842 in Albertville, South Carolina. He married (1) Margaret Stuart and (2) Betty Short. His pension was rejected because he did not serve for 6 months.

"I entered the service of the United States as a volunteer at the early age of 13 years in the summer of the year 1776, I enrolled by name in a militia company commanded by one Capt. Joseph Pickens who was under the command of Col. Pickens (afterwards General) and I performed military duty in the company of said Capt. Joseph Pickens for 2 weeks or more in Capt. Pickens. I was both young & of slender frame, & weak habit of body, I would ascense me from the service & part of the soldiers duty and confine me to such duty less oppressive to me and equally serviceable to the their Company on condition that I would give up to a more ablebodied soldier my rifle, power born, & shot bag to which I agreed Capt. Pickens then employed me in various light duties for the benefit of the company, such as shelling corn, carrying it to mill, returning with it in meal, procuring other provisions, assisting in driving & bringing in beeves to the soldiers, superintending the provision stores, attending on prisoners & on the sick when necessary, going messages &c &c. That subsequently in the winter after the battle of the Eutaw in this State this I volunteered under a Capt. Liddell and performed under him a tour of duty of at least 2 weeks service, And that after this last duty, I enlisted in a corps placed under the command of a Lieut. Matthew Finley by General Pickens, who authorized & caused this court to be raised for the express purpose of guarding the public property and stores of the militia located at a place called General Pickens Block house in Abbeville District, at which place I performed Military or guard duty for the full period of 3 months over the public stores aforesaid, and under the said Matthew Finley who acted as Lieut. of the corps guards. And in a short time after the expiration of my term of 3 months enlistment in this guard Corps, General Pickens caused a guard to be raised & drafted from the militia for the protection of the said public property and I was drafted for the period of 2 months which term of time I faithfully served & for field under one Lieut. Turk who commanded this drafted guard Corps over the public stores & property at the said General Pickens Block-house. I was called upon by General Pickens to constitute one of his body guard from Abbeville District or Ninety Six to a place called Tolls Station on Saluda River I volunteered my services, & did act as his bodyguard with others; fully 10 days, which ended my service for the United States, and which in the aggregate I

compute as fully 6 months and 10 days service I performed for the United States during the Revolutionary war."

Sources: 1. Pension Papers R6646. 2. Sons of the American Revolution Application. 3. U.S. Headstone Application for Military Veterans.

****

Hugh McDonald age 14

Hugh McDonald was born in 1762 in Scotland, and he died on 24 September, 1828 in Somerset, Kentucky. The McDonalds came from Scotland to North Carolina around 1774. Hugh married Rebecca Rogers on 22 September, 1778 in Fairfield County, South Carolina. In addition to his yearly pension, he received a land bounty of 640 acres.

"On or about the 10th of June 1776, in the town of Cross Creek (now Fayetteville) in the State of North Carolina, I the said Hugh McDonald enlisted in the company commanded by Capt. Arthur Council, of the 6th Regiment of the North Carolina line, on the Continental establishment in the war of the revolution, during the war; I continued to serve in the service of the United States, in said company & in others to which I was transferred, until the end of the said war, when, being a prisoner & sent in a cartel from Charleston to Philadelphia, was set at liberty at the latter place, (peace being then proclaimed) & was permitted to go home; I was in the battles of Brandywine, Germantown, Monmouth, Stono & Gates defeat, where I was taken prisoner & so continued till peace; and that I am in reduced circumstances & stands in need of the assistance of his country for support."

Hugh served in Captain Arthur Council's Company in the 6th North Carolina Regiment under the command of Colonel Gideon Lamb. The 6th Regiment was organized during the spring and summer of 1776 at Halifax, North Carolina. At the Battle of Brandywine Hugh was part of the main army under the command of Brigadier General Francis Nash.

At the Battle of Germantown on 4 October, 1777 Hugh was under the command of Major General William Alexander, also called Lord Stirling. Lord Stirling's troops were held in reserve behind General Sullivan. The North Carolina Regiments helped to cover the retreat of the American Army after they were defeated.

Because they were so far from home, the North Carolina troops were the poorest supplied of all the units. Their rate of desertion, however, was 10% and the lowest in the entire army which averaged 18%. Because their manpower had shrunk, the 6th North Carolina Regiment merged with the 1St North Carolina Regiment under the command of Colonel Thomas Clark.

In June they left Valley Forge and engaged the British at the Battle of Monmouth. The North Carolina Regiments were on the right wing under the command of Major General Nathanael Greene. British General Cornwallis personally led a heavy attack against Greene's troops. The British attack failed due to the American cannon fire and the accurate volleys from the Continental troops.

The next battle that Hugh McDonald was in was the Battle of Stono Ferry on 20 June, 1779. In this defeat the Americans advanced in two wings. Hugh was advancing through thick woods under the command of General Jethro Sumner. The Americans began to withdraw when the British were reinforced.

The Battle of Camden on 16 August, 1780 was when Hugh was captured. General Gates placed the untried North Carolina militia on his left flank. Another North Carolina militia group was placed in the center next to a Delaware Regiment. When the battle began, most of the militia broke and ran without firing a shot. The North Carolina Regiment in the center next to Delaware stayed and put up a fight. I believe that Hugh may have been part of this group of North Carolina men, since this unit was trained and Hugh had been in numerous battles. Over 1,000 Americans were captured including Hugh McDonald.

After the death of her husband Rebecca McDonald filed for a widow's pension. She received a yearly pension of $90. She told a remarkable story of love and devotion that had to be included in this section.

"I am the widow of Hugh McDonald who was a private soldier both in the regular Service and Militia during the Revolution. I declare that my Hugh McDonald enlisted as a private Soldier in Chester District in the State of South Carolina for the term of 15 months and faithfully served out his 15 months in a Company Commanded by Capt. Brown whose Company belonged to Colonel Sumter's Regiment. This enlistment must have taken place in Seventeen seventy Five or Six, it being previous to my marriage. I was married to my husband the aforesaid Hugh McDonald on the 22nd day of September Seventeen hundred Seventy Eight in Fairfield District in the State of South Carolina by a Magistrate by the

name of Walker Little upwards of one year after our marriage my husband Hugh McDonald volunteered in the Service of his country and served as a Dragoon or light horseman in a Company commanded by Captain McClure in Sumter's Regiment and the said Hugh McDonald marched with said company down towards Camden and had a Skirmish and the Company was on the retreat when the said Hugh McDonald and part of the Company was taken by the British and made prisoners of war and sent down to Camden and put in jail where they lay for a about 6 weeks with the smallpox and then the said Hugh McDonald with some other prisoners were taken by the British down to Charlestown and put on board the prison ships, the prisoners being attacked with the fever they were sent on shore to the barracks where I visited my husband and waited on him during his sickness and when he recovered which was in a few weeks the said Hugh was again sent back to the prison ships and I accompanied him to the said ships and there continued with my husband until he was sent round to Old Jamestown in the State of Virginia where she and her husband were landed and there her husband was exchanged, I & my husband were then 500 miles from home and my husband not yet entirely recovered from his Ship fever nor did he recover for several months thereafter, the exchange took place in the month of August and the I and my husband did not get home until the 10th of May following. In the fall of the year 1778 and shortly after my marriage my husband the said Hugh McDonald went out as a volunteer on foot with Capt. Nixon Company and was out for several weeks. The said Hugh McDonald when taken prisoner lost his horse and all his equipage which he never was paid for."

In February of 1776 Hugh's father, a Tory, took him along with him to the Battle of Moore's Creek. Both were taken prisoner by the patriot militia, and they were both set free to return home. That June Hugh and his father were working in their field, when they heard patriot horsemen approaching. Hugh's father hid, and the patriot officers ordered Hugh to guide them through the settlement. Hugh refused and claimed that if he did his father would kill him. The patriots forced him to go with them and later released him. Once released, Hugh who was fearful of his father, refused to go home. He decided to join the patriot army and sought out an officer that he knew and trusted.

Hugh McDonald wrote in the form of a journal his experiences in the American Revolution. The following are excerpts from his journal, which are found in the North Carolina University Magazine of December 1853. This excerpt tells how he came to join the American army.

"*Notwithstanding this scouring,*" at Moore's Creek, "*and the just contempt of our fellow citizens, we remained in heart as still tories as ever. This expedition took place in the month of February, 1776, from which we returned and began to repair our fences for a crop the ensuing summer. About the first of June, a report was circulated that a company of lighthorse were coming into the settlement; and, as a guilty conscience needs no accuser, every one thought they were after him. The report was that Col. Alston had sent out four or five men to cite us all to muster at Henry Eagle's, on Bear Creek, upon which our poor deluded people took refuge in the swamps. On a certain day, when we were ploughing in the field, news came to my father that the light horse were in the settlement and a request that he would conceal himself. He went to the house of his brother-in-law to give him notice, and ordered me to take the horse out of the plough, turn him loose, and follow him as fast as I could. I went to the horse, but never having ploughed any in my life, I was trying how I could plough, when five men on horseback appeared at the fence, one of whom, Dan'l Buie, knew me and asked me what I was doing here. I answered that my father lived here; and he said he was not aware of that. 'Come,' he says, you must go with us to pilot us through the settlement; for we have a boy here with us who has come far enough. He is six miles from home and is tired enough.—' His name was Thomas Graham, and he lived near the head of McLennon's creek. I told Mr. Buie that I dare not go, for, if I did, my father would kill me. He then alighted from his horse, and walked into the field, ungeared the horse and took him outside the fence.*"

"*He then put up the fence again; and, leading me by the hand, put me on behind one of the company, whose name was Gaster, and discharged the other boy. We then went to Daniel Shaw's, thence to John Morrison's (shoemaker), thence to Alexander McLeod's, father of merchant John McLeod, who died in Fayetteville, thence to Alexander Shaw's, (blacksmith), thence to old Hugh McSwan's, who gave half a crown for a small gourd when we landed in America. Here I was ordered to go home, but I refused, and went with them to the muster at Eagle's. Next day Col. Phillip Alston appeared at the muster, when these men told him that they had taken a boy to pilot them a little way through the settlement and that they could not get clear of him. The Colonel personally insisted on my going back to my father; but I told them I would not; for I had told them the consequence of my going with them before they took me. Seeing he could not prevail with me, he got a man by the name of Daniel McQueen, a noted bard, to take me home to my father, but I told him that I was determined to hang to them. Col. Alston then took me with him and treated me kindly. Mrs. Alston desired me to go to school with her children until she could send my father word to come after me, and she would make peace between us; but her friendly offers were also rejected."*

"On the following Tuesday I went with the same company of horsemen to Fayetteville, where I met a gentleman by the name of Dan'l. Porterfield, a Lieutenant in Capt. Authur Council's company, who asked me if I did not wish to enlist. I told him, not with him; but I wanted to see a Mr. Hilton who, I understood, was in the army, and wherever he was I wished to be. He told me that he and Hilton were of one company, and if Hilton did not tell me so, he would take back the money and let me go with Hilton. I then took the money and was received into the service of the U. S. June 10th, 1776, and in the fourteenth year of my age."

The following excerpt shows not all people supported the rebel cause. It also demonstrates that the Tory feelings were just as strong as the feelings of the patriots.

"We stopped two days at Williamsburg and rested. We then marched on and crossed the James river at the town of Richmond, where there were fishers; and having gotten leave there also to draw the siene, every man took as many fish as he wanted. While passing through the town a shoemaker stood in his door and cried, "Hurrah for King George," of which no one took any notice; but after halting in a wood, a little distance beyond, where we cooked and ate our fish, the shoemaker came to us and began again to hurrah for King George. When the General and his aids mounted and started, he still followed them, hurrahing for King George. Upon which the General ordered him to be taken back to the river and ducked. We brought a long rope, which we tied about the middle, round his middle, and sesawed him backwards and forwards until we had him nearly drowned, but every time he got his head above water he would cry for King George. The General having then ordered him to be tarred and feathered, a feather bed was taken from his own house, where were his wife and four likely daughters crying and beseeching their father to hold his tongue, but still he would not. We tore the bed open and knocked the top out of a tar barrel, into which we plunged him headlong. He was then drawn out by the heels and rolled in the feathers until he was a sight but still he would hurra for King George. The General now ordered him to be drummed out of the West end of town, and told him expressly that if he plagued him any more in that way he would have him shot. So we saw no more of the shoemaker."

Not all the dangers faced by Hugh McDonald were in battle. During the Revolutionary War, 8,000 died from wounds inflicted in battle and 17,000 died from disease.

"We then marched on until we came to the Potomac river; but, early in the morning, we were halted and all the doctors called upon to inoculate the men with the small pox, which took them until two o'clock. We then crossed the river at Georgetown, about 8 miles above Alexandria, near the place where Washington city now stands. There we got houses and stayed until we were well of the smallpox. I having had the pox before, attended on the officers of my company until they got well, but what is very strange, in the whole Brigade, there was not one man lost by pox, except one by the name of Griffin, who, after he had got able to go about, I thought he was well, imprudently went to swim in the Potomac, and next morning was found dead. About the last of June we left Georgetown for Philadelphia. About twelve miles from Baltimore, I was taken sick and helpless in the road, Lieutenant Dudley, Sergeant Dudley and some others stayed to bury me, when it was thought that I would die but, seeing that I was not dying nor coming to my senses they took me on their back, turn about, until they came up with a wagon. The doctors saw me, but would not venture to give me anything, as they did not understand my complaint. I lay so until about midnight, when our sutler, who had been gone four days after a load of whiskey, came into camp. Lieutenant Hadley got some spirit, about a spoonful, down my throat which he thought helped me. He then gave me about a wine glassful, and in about fifteen or twenty minutes I came to my speech. Finding that the whiskey helped me, he gave it to me until daylight, at which time my complaint was discovered to be measles. I was then put into a wagon and carefully nursed by Lieut. Hadley, until I got well."

"Going on our march, about two miles above Susquehanna river, I saw an old woman with her son and daughter about twelve years old, and on hearing her speak to them in my mother tongue, I asked her how she came here. She thanked her Maker, that she had met with one who could talk with her, and told me that her son had been transported for a frivolous crime, committed in his own country, that he had been sentenced to be sold for seven years servitude in the State of Maryland, and that having no other son, and not willing to have a separation from him for ever, she had followed him here with her little daughter. I told him if he would enlist with us, he would finish his servitude at once. He said, if he thought so, he would do it. I told him that no man dare take him out of the

service and I would ensure him. Upon which I gave him two dollars and told him he should have the rest of his bounty. Before night the old woman said she would go also, and when I urged her not to do it, she was determined, and going for her baggage, she returned to camp that night."

Sources: 1. North Carolina and Tennessee Revolutionary War Land Warrants. 2. Pension Papers S41837 & W8438. 3. U.S. Pensioners 1818-1872. 4. Roster of Know Soldiers of the 6th Regiment North Caroline Line. 5. Becoming Men of Some Consequence: Youth and Military Service in the Revolutionary War by John A. Ruddiman. 6. Memoir by Hugh McDonald (extract) North Carolina University Magazine, December 1853, Vol. 11, pages 828-837.

****

Samuel McGaughy age 14

Samuel McGaughy was born on 15 July, 1763 in York County, Pennsylvania, and he died on 5 January, 1841 in Lawrence County, Alabama. He married Jane McLaughlin on 24 February, 1784 in Tennessee. He joined the army in place of his father just a few months shy of his 15th birthday. He was promoted to the rank of Captain by the time he was 18. Samuel received a yearly pension of $233.32, and upon his death his wife received a widow's yearly pension of $133.33.

"I was born in the York County, State of Pennsylvania on the 15th day of July 1763 according to the information given made by my parents and the record in their family Bible. At nine years of age my father moved to Holstein River near Washington County Virginia. I was living in a Fort when the Revolutionary war began. In the spring of 1778, the Indians made war & my father was called on and I substituted in his place and served one month as a guard under Captain John Shelby on Clinch River."

"In August of the same year I served in the same capacity at the same place one month under Captain James Montgomery, both these on foot. In the first of March 1779, I volunteered and enrolled myself as such under Captain James Montgomery to go against the Chicka Maggy Indians, they at war with the whites. Six hundred troops were raised commanded by Colonel Evan Shelby Senior. We were joined by three hundred regular troops commanded by Col Montgomery of Virginia. We proceeded down Tennessee River in Boats to their towns near the Suck. We landed, destroyed three towns, killed some of their men & took a number of their women and children prisoners. Col Montgomery marched to join Genl Clarke at Illinois and Col Shelby returned home. I got home about the middle of May. I performed this service on foot."

The Chickamauga Indians, with assistance from the British, had been harassing the patriot settlers in Virginia. Virginia governor Patrick Henry ordered Colonel Evan Shelby and his 700 volunteers to march against the Chickamauga towns. They destroyed 11 towns, twenty thousand bushels of corn, but only killed six Indian warriors. The majority of the warriors were gone at the time.

"In the fall of 1779, the Settlements in Kentucky being __?__ much harassed by the Indians, I again took the field and as a volunteer under Captain John McKee of Rockbridge County State of Virginia, as a Mounted Rifleman, became one of his Spies and served in that capacity Seven months and was discharged."

"In the Summer of 1780 as well as I can recollect I again volunteered under Captain Andrew Cowan to go against the British and Tories in South Carolina, as a Mounted Rifleman. Colonel Isaac Shelby commanded this expedition. We marched to South Carolina and there joined General Charles McDowell, chief in command. I was in several skirmishes, two hard battles, one on the Tigre River and the other on North Pacolet River. We were successful in both. I was one of those who Stormed on its fort and took one hundred Tories and one British officer prisoner. The British officer was sent to train and discipline the Tories. I was discharged after a tour of four months."

Samuel may be describing the attack on Fort Thicketty on 26 July, 1780. Colonel Shelby and his army of 600 troops, including Samuel, captured the Tory garrison without firing a shot. At sunrise on the 26th Colonel Shelby sent a demand to surrender to the fort's commander Captain Moore. The Captain replied he would defend the fort to the last man. Colonel Shelby formed his men within view of the fort and again demanded that the Loyalists surrender. When Captain Moore saw that he was outnumbered six to one, he quickly changed his mind.

"In the fall of 1780 as well as I can now recollect, the British and Tories under Ferguson drove General McDowell over the mountains to the western waters. Almost every man was called on to meet them, Colonel Shelby from Sullivan County, Colonel Sevier from Washington County, North Carolina and Colonel Campbell from Washington County, Virginia each had the head of Mounted Rifle regiments. I was attached to the company commanded by Captain John Pemberton in the Regiment of Col. Shelby. Col. Campbell was appointed to take the chief command of our forces and we went in pursuit of the enemy who had retreated to Kings mountain where he made a stand. We attacked them, killed Ferguson, their commander, and killed and took nearly the whole Army. In this campaign I served as a volunteer Mounted Rifleman, six weeks."

Samuel fought in the Battle of Kings Mountain on 7 October, 1780. His commander, Colonel Shelby, charged the enemy, and it was reported he yelled, *"Shout like hell and fight like devils."* The men obeyed his orders and repelled several British bayonet attacks. When some of the Tories began to surrender, many of the patriots gave no quarter until their officers regained control over their men. The patriots were seeking revenge for alleged killings of surrendering militiamen at the Battle of Waxhaws.

"Some short time after the above campaign, I volunteered as a private under Captain Andrew Cowan and went a tour in the Mounted Rifle service against the Cherokee Indians. Colonel Russell of Sullivan County commanded a Regiment to which we were attached. We joined Colonel Arthur Campbell of Virginia who took the chief command. We proceeded to their towns on the Tennessee and French Broad Rivers, destroyed them and killed many of their warriors. They sued for peace and we returned home in February or March 1781. I was detained in this service four months as well as I can now remember."

"In the month of April 1781, Thomas Wallace and myself raised by voluntary enlistment a large company of Mounted Infantry for four months service. Wallace was elected Captain and I was chosen Lieutenant. Isaac Shelby commanded the Regiment as first Colonel and Isaac Bledsoe as Lieutenant Colonel. As soon as our forces could be organized and in the same month, we marched to the seat of war in South Carolina and joined Genl Green who was then in command there. We were sent in advance of General Greene to General Marion. We continued with Marion our time out. Col. Shelby and Captain Wallace being called home on some account, Colonel Bledsoe took the command of the Regiment and I was appointed Captain in place of Wallace. General Marion made an animated appeal to our patriotism and requested that we would remain with him longer. I as Captain beat up for volunteers and obtained sufficient number to constitute a company and we agreed to continue in service two months longer, believing that time would close the war. At the end of the said two months service, we were discharged. I will further state that when Colonel Shelby went home, many of the man went with him, and by that means the number of regiments was reduced and my company was attached to Col. Sevier's Regiment from whom I received a commission as Captain and I believe the enclosed defaced paper to be the

same, which I have found among my old papers since I made my former declaration."

"In this last tour of two months service, we pursued the British & Tories. General Greene commanded us, and at the Eutaw Springs, we fought the most bloody battle I was in during the war. We gained a complete victory over the enemy. As well as I remember this was in the month of September in 1781. In this battle Col Washington commanded our light horse & General Marion the troops of militia I was in. This tour of service, including the six months in actual service in the field and the time necessary marching to and from the seat of war, was eight months."

At the Battle of Eutaw Springs on 8 September, 1781 Samuel was in the militia under the command of General Francis Marion. His unit was in the center of the American line of battle, and behind them were the regular continental troops. Marion's militiamen held their ground. However, when the North Carolina militia broke and ran, the regular continental troops were brought in to take their place. Samuel McGaugly stood his ground and fired seventeen rounds less than a hundred yards from the British lines. One of the men, Benjamin Thomson, later said it was the *"most severely fought battle"* he had ever taken part in.

The battle inflicted high causalities on both sides. It was one of the bloodiest and most hotly contested close-quarter battles of the entire war. At the end of the day both sides claimed victory. In one month the British would surrender at Yorkown.

Sources: 1. Tombstone 2. Pension Papers W9981. 3. The Road to Guilford Court House: The American Revolution in the Carolinas by John Buchanan.

****

Isaac McKinzie age 14

Isaac McKinzie was born c. 1764 in Virginia, and he died after 1850. He married Jean Johnston on 1 February, 1789. He received a yearly pension of $25.

"I volunteered in the County of Montgomery and State of Virginia for Three months under Captain John Davis and entered the Service on the first of September 1777--William Preston was Colonel--I was Stationed at Muncey's Fort on Walker's Creek a Branch of New River I served there three months as a volunteer and was Discharged by Captain Davis--And in the latter part of August 1780 I was again called into

Service by the County Commander I joined the Army at the Lead Mines on New River the last Week in August 1780 under Captain John Lucas Major Joseph Cloyd, Colonel Walter Crockett, I was stationed at the Lead Mines two weeks was then Marched to Surry Court house in North Carolina then to Adkin where we lay one week at little above the Shallow ford thence we were marched towards King's Mountain sixteen miles and met the prisoners taken at the Battle of King's Mountain __?__ was then turned and guarded the prisoners to the Moravian Towns and Stayed one week as a guard thence I was marched to Montgomery County and State of Virginia and Discharged by Captain Lucas I was under Captain Lucas in the service for two and one half months. I again entered the Service the first week in January 1781 under Captain James Binns– Colonel William Preston--Major Joseph Cloyd and was marched to Harbords Ferry on New River where we was stationed one week, thence was marched to Surry Court House in North Carolina thence to the Moravian Towns, thence to Guilford Court house where We was stationed about Ten days and attached to the Army of General Pickens and remained until the last of February 1781 and was with our officers dismissed from the command of General Pickens and was marched to Montgomery County Virginia and after been in Service my last Tour for two months was discharged."

Isaac mentions Moravian towns in North Carolina. The Moravians were German-speaking Protestants that came to North Carolina from Pennsylvania. They founded the towns of Bethabara, Bethania, and Salem in the middle of the 1700's.

Sources: 1. U.S. Pensioners 1818-1872. 2. Virginia Marriages 1660-1800. 3. Pension Papers S30571.

****

James McMeans age 13

James McMeans was born on 29 January, 1767 in Pennsylvania, and he died after 1836 in Missouri. His pension was rejected because he did not prove he served the required six months.

The following pension statement was given on 24 March, 1835, *"In the year 1780 I joined the Troops of General George Rogers Clark at Louisville in the now State of Kentucky in Captain Pickett's Company and went from thence to the Iron Banks and assisted in building a Fort and remained there about six months, went from thence to New Orleans, and from thence to the Island of Cuba, then enlisted on board of the Count De Grasse Ship in the Service of the United States commanded by Captain*

Griffin; and after cruising about five weeks in the Gulf of Mexico and about the West India Islands, said ship was surrounded by an English fleet and was driven on shore and blown up by order of the Captain somewhere on the coast of Cuba. I then went to Havana and entered on board of a ship bound to Calais in France & was captured by the English and carried prisoner to New York and was kept a prisoner until peace was declared. I only received $8 bounty at the time I entered on board the Count De Grasse ship which is all he ever received from the United States."

The additional statement was given on 6 November, 1825, *"I entered as such private and volunteer into the Company commanded by <u>Captain James Piggott</u>, in which said Company formed a part of the Regiment under the command of <u>Colonel George Rogers Clark</u>, in the Virginia line. I entered into the said service at the Falls of the Ohio under the said Captain Piggott, and served therein from time to time and under various officers for between two and three years, sometimes in the capacity of such volunteer, at others, acting as an Indian Spy, and again in the militia service. That according to the best of my recollection, I served ten months under the said Captain Piggott. I was also six months under the command of Major J. Harlin, who was slain in the "Battle of the Blue Licks". I do not remember the names of the other officers under whom I served, or the length of time. I was also in the Battle under the command of General Wayne, when he defeated the Indians on the Western frontier, under the command of Captain Henry Lindsey two months and eight days. While under the command of Captain Piggott, at the Iron Banks on the Mississippi River, the Fort was attacked by a party of Indians, who were headed by a British officer by the name of Colbert: I was in many other skirmishes, and received a wound in his right arm, which has ever since considerably disabled him."*

Source: 1. Pension Papers R6793.

****

Nicholas Madeira age 13 or 14

Nicholas Madeira was born on 26 December, 1763 in Berks County, Pennsylvania, and he died on 7 September, 1835 in Morgantown, West Virginia. His three brothers, Michael, Casper, and Christian served in the army. His pension was rejected, because he did not provide service proof. Several people sent letters confirming his service but they were relatives.

Note: the person that wrote the following original document had beautiful neat handwriting. This was one of the easiest documents to read.

"I entered the service of the United States, at the age of about fifteen years, in the year 1777 as a musician (drummer) at Reading Pennsylvania, under a captain whose name I cannot recollect in a regement of Pennsylvania militia, under the command of Col ____ and Major Linley--we marched to Chester, where we joined the main army. Gen'l. ____ Wayne commanding the Pennsylvania line."

Nicholas was born on 26 December, 1763. He states that he entered the army in 1777 before the Battle of Brandywine on 11 September, 1777. This would make him 14 at the time of enlistment and not 15. His brother Michael stated in a proof of service statement dated 27 May, 1833, *"I testify with confidence that Nicholas entered the service in 1776."* This would make Nicholas 13 when he enlisted. Whichever date is chosen he is still underage.

"Gen'l. Washington was at Chester I believe when we arrived there--from Chester we marched to Brandywine, in which battle I was in from that battle, we marched back to Chester, from thence I marched with the army towards Germantown, on the road to which I was discharged, having served out two months, the term of my engagement, in the militia of Pennsylvania."

"I again entered the service of the United States, for seven months, as a substitute for ____ in a company of militia commanded by Capt Kennedy, attached to the seventh Pennsylvania regiment, commanded by Major or Col Chambers being called seven-months men, at Reading in the year 1780--that from Reading we marched to Philadelphia, and I with others were sworn in, before Nicholson mayor of that city – from Philadelphia to Trenton we went in a sloop – from Trenton we marched to the neighbourhood of Morristown and joined the regiment – Gen'l. Wayne was commander of the first Division, and Gen'l. St. Clair the second of the troops then there – we immediately marched towards the North river, and crossed the river I beleive at a ferry called King's ferry, when we soon met the enemy, and had to retreat across the ferry – we then went down the river to Stoney point, where we remained eight or ten days during which time Gen'l. Arnold, deserted to the enemy, going on board of a ship at Stoney point on his way from West Point to New York – whilst at Stoney point the Commissary refused to furnish us flour, for five or six days fearing the flour was poisoned, as treason had appeared in the camp during which the troops lived on meat and apples – from Stoney point the

Pennsylvania and Deleware troops under Gan'l Wayne, marched to Bargain point, where we remained over a saturday night, and slept with our knapsacks on, expecting an engagement--from Bargain point we went directly to Morristown and built our huts for winter quarters--I think it must have been toward spring, that the Pennsylvania line revolted in consequence of some misunderstanding about those who enlisted for three years and during the war--that I recollect he was on Gen'l. Wayne's guard the night of the revolt--that the Pennsylvania line moved off to Trenton, where they were met by the Board of War (as they were called) and a number of the enlisted troops discharged, and those that had enlisted for during the war returned to duty--that at Trenton, I was discharged, after having served the said seven months, which discharge he has long since lost."

Nicholas Maderia is listed on the roll of the 7th Pennsylvania in Captain Samuel Kennedy's Company of Seven Months Men.

Early in 1781 many of the men in the Pennsylvania line began to munity. Pennsylvania was one of the stingiest states in paying its soldiers. Many of these men signed up for three years and received a $20.00 bounty, while other states were paying hundreds of dollars. At this time New Jersey even paid a bounty of $1,000.

So for three years these men had put their lives on the line, suffered hardships, and harsh discipline. It was bad enough they had no money, but it meant their families back home were not getting any money. These men signed up for three years, and now their officers told them they could not leave at the end of their enlistment and must stay until the end of the war. So, many did the only thing they could do, which was to rise up in protest.

The British offered them a full pardon and their back pay, if they would join them. Very few took advantage of the offer. General Wayne listened to the men's complaints, and a Board of Sergeants was set up to speak for them. The crisis began to end when a discharge process began. Over half of the Pennsylvania was discharged and many of them later reenlisted and were given a bonus.

"I again entered the service of the United States, in the spring of 1781, by enlisted with Capt. Fasick at Reading Pennsylvania for one year, to join the French Artillery--from Reading Capt. Fasick, with sixteen or eighteen enlisted men, marched to Morristown, where we joined the French troops consisting of three regiments, besides the horse and one

German regiment all under the command of Rochambeau,--from Morristown, we marched by Trenton, Philadelphia, Baltimore, Alexandria, Fredericksburg, Williamsburgh and Yorktown, where we was at the time of Gen'l Cornwallis's surrender being engaged in the whole siege--that the French troops were ordered to remain in Virginia during the winter, and I with them wintered at Williamsburgh--in the spring of 1782, I march with the French troops to the North, and about the latter part of summer I was discharged at a place called Crompen in the state of New York after having served sixteen or seventeen months, although I had enlisted but for one year."

"I believe it was in the summer of the year 1778 or 1779 I marched as a drummer, to a company of militia, commanded as well as I can recollect by Capt. Miller from Reading in an expedition against the Indians & Tories near Menasinon the Deleware river, Major John Cunies or Konies, was along, a small man with a hump-back, also adjutant Lighthizer, that they marched through Alenstown Bethlehem Eastown and thence to the village of Menasing--we had no engagement with the indians or tories, after remaining two months at that village we returned to Reading, and was discharged by a general discharge."

Sources: 1.The Pennsylvania Line Mutiny, its Origins, and Patriotism by Charles S. Yordy III. 2. West Virginia in the Revolution. 3. Sons of the American Revolution Application. 4. Pennsylvania in the War of the Revolution Battalions and Lines. 5. Pension Papers R21708.

****

James Magee age 13

James Magee was born on 6 December, 1762 in Sussex County, Virginia, and he died on 7 September, 1850 in Jefferson, Tennessee. He enlisted in the army four months before his 14th birthday.

"In the summer of 1776 my brother Willie MaGee was drafted in Sussex County in the state of Virginia, under Capt. Jesse Williamson for a one month tour. My mother being a widow, and Willie being the oldest son, I went as a substitute for the said Willie."

The company gathered at the Sussex Court House and then marched to Portsmouth on the James River. *"From thence we marched to Portsmouth and Norfolk was then lying in ashes on the opposite side of the River....while I was there, there was no engagement between the enemy & the US troops but there was frequent cannonading between the American* batteries and the Roebuck and Kingfisher, two ships of enemy, which played up and down the James River." His enlistment expired, and he was marched back to Sussex County.

"That in April 1777 as well as I can recollect, my brother Drury MaGee was drafted in the same County of Sussex & State of Virginia, under the command of Capt. ____Smith, for a one month tour. My family being in a delicate state of health I agreed to serve the tour for him." During this tour James marched the same route back to Portsmouth and watched more cannon fire between the Americans and the same two British ships. After six weeks James was marched back home.

"About the first of March 1778, one John Izzard, having served the term of two years for which he had enlisted, enlisted for another term of three years in the 15th Virginia Regiment under the command of Col. David Mason—the said Izzard's father, having died, he applied to me to serve in his stead until he could settle the business of his father's estate—I consented to do so, and proceeded from said County of Sussex, where I still lived and said Izzards to Williamsburg—at which place Izzard presented me to Col. Mason as his substitute, and I was excepted as such—the 15th regiment was then lying there waiting for clothing to march to the north to join Genl Washington—I was immediately placed in the shop of one Nickerson, a tailor, where me and four others (that being all in the Regiment that could sew) remained until the Regiment was equipped, which was some time in August."

When the regiment's marching orders were given they got about 20 miles, when they were joined by John Izzard so James returned home. He said that he could not recall any of the officers' names because he was never paraded with the men due to the fact that he spent his whole time in the tailor shop sewing.

In the fall of 1779 James got married perhaps to Margaret Calaway. He may have remarried after her death to Agnes Johnson in 1791. He and his new wife moved to Caswell County, North Carolina. In 1780 James was drafted for a three month tour with the Caswell County Regiment of Militia under Colonel William Moore. James was discharged at Guilford Courthouse, North Carolina when his tour expired.

In June of 1781 James was again drafted, and he was marched to Camden, South Carolina to join with General Nathanael Green. When the Americans arrived at High Hills they found that the British had left and were camped at Eutaw Springs.

"We encamped but a few days on the Hills, till Col. Washington had spied out their situation, of which he informed the board of war—the next night, as well I recollects the 20th August, we were marched about 10 o'clock at night—On our march down the next morning, we met and fired upon a rooting party of the enemy, who were coming out to get potatoes, which was the commencement of the battle."

James would find himself and the rest of the North Carolina militia in the front line facing the British at the Battle of Eutaw Springs on 8 September, 1781. *"General Greene formed his auxiliary and the regulars in the rear until he brought the enemy within the ambush there formed—Colonel Malmedy having discovered the enemy lying close to the ground, directed the men upon the word "halt" to fire at the ground, which was done with such success, that Malmedy did not retreat but continued to keep up the fight until Genl Greene rode up. Greene in turning his horse to ride back to his artillery had his horse shot from under him whereupon he dismounted Col. Williams and marched his regulars & artillery to the battle ground, where the twelve months men and the militia opened upon the right and left, and Green marched through in front of the battle--Col Malmedy commanded the right wing of the twelve months men & militia & Col. Washington was on the right wing with his troop of horse--Col. Farmer commanded the left wing of the militia & twelve months men & run--as he turned to run, his horse was shot—Col. Lea with his troop of horse was on the left wing—Col Washington with his troop of horse, charged the Queens regt. The 71st called the "Buffs"--as he returned his horse was bayoneted & he taken prisoner as he was informed. The British were driven beyond their baggage, when our men commenced rummaging their tents, drinking rum &c &c which the enemy discovering, came back upon us & drove us back into the woods, where we formed again. We charged them a second time & drove them off of the ground. In the evening the enemy sent a flag stating that Greene might keep the ground if he would bury the dead. Greene returned for answer, that his honor was great enough to bury the dead & the ground he would keep anyhow. The next day we dug trenches just below the brick house in which we buried the dead. We were then ordered to march to Salisbury with the prisoners, where we were to be discharged.—the prisoners were left at Salisbury and we marched to Guilford Court House where we were discharged by Majors Humphries & Parrish as we had left our Col. under arrest."*

The battle ended in somewhat of a stalemate. The British won a tactical victory, but since they did not stop General Greene from his operations they had to leave most of their conquests in the south. This was the last major battle of the war in the Carolinas. Colonel William Washington was severely wounded and captured. He spent the rest of the war as a prisoner of war in Charleston, South Carolina. James Magee said that his Colonel was under arrest after the battle. This author could not find any proof of this, however, some officers were not very pleased with the performance of the North Carolina Regiment in the battle.

James received a pension of $53.33 a year for his service. This author found no record that his wife filed for widow's benefits after his death in 1850.

Sources: 1. Calendar and Record of the Revolutionary War in the South: 1780-1781 by William Thomas Sherman. 2. Census of 1830 and 1840. 3. Pension Papers S1555. 4. A Guide to the Battles of the American Revolution by Savas and Dameron.

****

James March age 11

James March was born on 9 February, 1769 in Scarborough, Maine, and he died on 29 March, 1823 in Gorham, Maine. He served as a fifer in Captain Jedidiah Goodwin's Company at the age of eleven years. In 1781 he served as a private in Captain John Reed's Company in Samuel McCobb's Regiment.

Sources: 1. New England Historical & Genealogical Register 1847-2011. 2. D.A.R. Lineage Book, Vol. 48.

****

Nathaniel Martin age 13

Nathaniel Martin was born on 31 August, 1762 in Piscataway, New Jersey, and he died on 17 June, 1854 in Wantage, New Jersey. He married a woman name Elsy on 10 February, 1777. Most researchers show that he had a different wife, but according to his pension application Elsy was the only one. She was 19 and Nathaniel was 15 when they got married. Elsy received a yearly widow's pension of $60.

His statement of service was given by his wife in 1837. She gives a very detailed account of his service which is unusual. Most wives recall little of the service.

"On the first of April 1776 the said Nathaniel was drafted under Capt. Potter and marched from near Woodbridge to Amboy and then stationed the month out. Sometime in the early part of June 1776 Nathaniel enlisted under Capt. __?__ for 6 months."

In 1777 Nathaniel served a few weeks in January. *"The enemy then had possession of New Brunswick—in the month of February me and Nathaniel were married."* In March, April, and June of 1777 Nathaniel is called out for short tours lasting less than a month each. Elsy states that her husband was engaged in the Battle of Monmouth in June of 1778. He also serves short tours in February and July of 1779. Nathaniel's brother Gersham was drafted in the summer of 1779, so Nathaniel took care of the harvest on his brother's farm.

Nathaniel served short tours again in January, April, and May of 1780. He fought in the battles of Connecticut Farms on 7 June, 1780 and Springfield on 23 June, 1780. He also served several tours of duty for a month in 1781 and 1782.

Sources: 1. U.S. Pensioners of 1835. 2. Sons of the American Revolution Application. 3. Tombstone 4. D.A.R. Lineage Book, Vol. 85. 5. Pension Papers W7393.

****

Daniel Martling age 11

Daniel Martling was born on 4 October, 1763 in Tappan, New York, and he died in 1834 in New York. His pension application was rejected because they could not find his name of any North Carolina rolls or some of the officers named.

"I was born at Tappan in the State of New York on the 4th day of October, 1763: I have no record of my age, except my own entry in my family Bible. In the month of June, 1775, while at Powle's Hook, I was taken prisoner by the British and retained under suspicion of being a spy. As such a prisoner, I remained with British Army: -- was taken to Brooklyn, & thence was taken on shipboard, with a force, under command of Col. Campbell, to Savannah (Georgia). After arriving at Savannah General Provost had command of the forces: With my Army, I remained a prisoner till after Charleston was taken by the British; and was then transferred, a prisoner, to the Army of Lord Rawdon and remained with him till June 1781; and then, having been detained a prisoner for 5 years, and having made one ineffectual attempt to escape, I escaped, near the River Enoree in South Carolina; and immediately fell in with Major Lee's

troop of horse, I volunteered with them; and pursued the British, from whom I had escaped, to near Eutaw Springs, but was not personally present in the battle there fought. After this, encamped, in company with Lee's Troop, with General Greene's Army, at the High Hills of Santee (South Carolina): In this service I remained 2 months; and then obtained a pass from General Greene, for one Isaac Lent, and myself to come on to State of New York: under this pass we came into North Carolina, near Hillsboro, where the State was raising a Regiment, to suppress and take Tories, and guard the deliberations of their assembly. I & Lent both enlisted in this Regiment, under Col. Moore and Major Crafton in Capt. Jones's company; here I served, till about the last of May, and was then discharged, having served in this Regiment nine months: I had a written discharge signed by Major Crafton, but has since lost it. I then came home to Tappan."

Source: Pension Papers transcribed by Will Graves R6983.

****

Isaac Mason age 14

Isaac Mason was born on 4 April, 1767 in Somerset County, New Jersey, and he died on 30 January, 1856 in Davis, Iowa. He married (1) Anna Clark who died in 1846 and (2) Margaret White on 30 September, 1847. He received a yearly pension of $55.63. Isaac also served in the War of 1812 as a private in Captain Hull's Company.

"I entered the service of the United States in the year that Cornwallis surrendered as a volunteer together with my father and two brothers. Our house and property had been burnt by the Indians & Tories sometime previously, I enrolled himself in Captain Putnam's Company of New York Militia. Wm Wallace was Lieutenant and on the 1st May entered the service, at Johnstown, in the garrison or stone fort, being the County Jail fitted up for that purpose. Major Little was called the garrison Major, and resided in the fort. Col. Vader who resided near Johnstown also commanded, there was also a Major Scouten. Col. Willett had the chief command, he commanded the forces from Fort Stanwix to Schenectady. We performed constant duty on guard and on Scouts. On the 22d day of October which date I marked on a tree & saw many years after. The whole force of the Country was called out under Col. Willett to oppose Major Ross and Captain Butler and a party of British and Indians, there were somewhere about 400, men of all descriptions under Col. Willett, we left garrison in search of the enemy, leaving Eleven old men to take care of

the Fort, we missed the enemy, who took a road by Tripes Hill and surprised the town and garrison, and attacked it, but were repulsed with the cannon, the force under Col. Willett, came up. The British and Indians formed in a field. Willet advanced to about 8 rods of them under fire, and then fired, charged and broke their lines, they retreated, formed again, broke our line and took our cannon, Lieutenant Wallace commanded, the youngest of us, among whom I was, we formed in the line, the cannon was retook, the British retreated and were pursued about 8 miles. We took about 40 prisoners, Lieut Wallace commanded 49 person, most of whom were under 16 yrs of age, several of whom were killed."

"I was constantly on duty not less than six months, after which and during the winter we kept garrison by turns. I served a week after intervals of two weeks during the winter making one third of the time. About the first of April I began to garrison duty constantly in the year and continued till 1st of November under the same officers. We were after our scouts and once me and several others found a family scalped by Indians whom we believed. During the summer a small party of British rangers and Indians attacked the picket guard of the fort and killed some of them. I was called out, but they were drive off by some of our men who were garrisoned in the meeting house arriving the winter I was in the garrison on duty and was discharged in May."

William Wallace was serving in this same Company and regiment, and this is probably the same company that Isaac and Jeremiah Jr. were serving in as they were under 16 years of age. Their brother-in-law William Scarborough, who was in Putnam's Company with John Mason, was killed in the Battle of Johnstown. William Wallace was an officer and signed affidavits in both Isaac and Jeremiah's pensions, and stated that he saw them engage in said battle and gave them orders. Isaac's description of the battle is close to Col. Willett's description of the battle.

Sources: 1. Tombstone 2. Sons of the American Revolution Application. 3. U.S. Pension Roll of 1835. 4. The Bloodied Mohawk: The American Revolution in the Words of Fort Planks Defenders and Other Mohawk Valley Partisans by Kenneth D. Johnson.

****

Jeremiah Mason age 14

Jeremiah Mason was born on 1 May, 1766 in Somerset County, New Jersey. He enlisted in May 1780 at the age of 14. He served in the same regiment as his brother Isaac, who enlisted at the age of 14 in 1781. Jeremiah's pension was rejected because, *"He was only 14 years old in*

1780 when he enlisted. No boy at that age could perform military duty in the ranks & the regulations respecting enlistments forbid the exception of each. Your claim is therefore rejected." A later letter in his pension application said he did not prove that he served for six months.

"I entered in the service in the year 1780 as near as I recollect in the month of May the day I cannot state. I was listed in Captain __?__ company. The other officers of the company do not recollect. During the time I served there were several field officers who had command of the regiment in which I was to wit, Colonel Willet, Colonel Livingston, some previous to my enrollment and some Subsequent. I resided in Johnstown during the whole time of the war and previous to my being enlisted was called out frequently in case of emergency and was out __?__ there during the whole time of the war until I was enlisted in the Military in 1780."

"My parents resided in the town of Johnston and in the village, and my father and brothers was also in the army. I was at the battle fought by Colonel Willet at Johnstown. I was one who helped bury the dead after the battle. I was in the Regiment that lay at Johnstown from the spring in Month of May 1780 until that fighting. Major Ross was the British officer who commanded at Johnstown the British side. I still remained as a soldier after said battle until the war ended and I cannot tell how long it was after the battle I remained in the service but recollecting to the best of my knowledge I think I was in the service after I was enrolled about two years. Sometime in the year 1781 or 1782 that news came of peace being had between Britain and our people, but they continued us in the service on account of the Indians & Tories frequently returning and attacking the inhabitants. I volunteered when I was enrolled. I continued under Captain in whose company I was enrolled until the following winter 1781."

William Wallace was serving in this same company and regiment, and this is probably the same company that Isaac and Jeremiah Jr. were serving in as they were under 16 years of age. Their brother-in-law William Scarborough, who was in Putnam's Company with John Mason, was killed in the Battle of Johnstown. William Wallace, an officer, signed affidavits in both Isaac and Jeremiah's pensions and stated that he saw them engage in said battle and that he gave them orders. Isaac's description of the battle is close to Col. Willett's description of the battle.

John Mason, the oldest brother, is listed on the Company Muster Roll for Capt. Garret Putnam's company in Col. Willett's Regt. John was wounded in the left side at the Battle of Johnstown (Pension No. W18479 N.Y.).

The Battle of Johnstown occurred on 25 October, 1781. Around noon the British, under Major Ross and the Americans under Colonel Marinus Willett, met in several small skirmishes in and around Johnstown. The captain of the Tory Militia, Walter Butler, was killed in the American victory.

During one of the battles Joseph Wagner, one of the American militiamen, shot a British officer as the Americans retreated. After the battle, Wagner went back to the battlefield and found the wounded officer. Wagner told him, *"My dear sir, I am the man who shot you in the afternoon, but I have a fellow feeling for you. Permit me and I will take you to our camp, where you shall receive kind treatment and good care. "The officer replied, "I would rather die on this spot, than leave it with a damed rebel!"*. Wagner granted the man his request and left him to die.

Sources: 1. The Bloodied Mohawk: The American Revolution in the Words of Fort Planks Defenders and Other Mohawk Valley Partisans by Kenneth D. Johnson. 2. Pension Papers R6996. 3. History of Schoharie County and Border Wars of New York, Vol. 2, by Jeptha R. Simms.

****

Peter Mason age 14

Peter Mason was born on 22 August, 1764 in Lancaster County, Virginia, and he died c.1843 in Jay County, Indiana. He married Polly Sagathy on 12 September, 1805. He received a yearly pension of $40.

He enlisted in the army at the age of 14 on 24 October, 1778 and continued until sometime after the surrender of Cornwallis at Yorktown. After he was discharged he went to sea for about seven years.

Sources: 1. Virginia Marriages 1740-1850. 2. U.S. Pensioners 1818-1872. 3. Roster of Soldiers and Patriots of the American Revolution Buries in Indiana. 4. Pension Papers S32394.

****

John Massey age 13

John Massey was born 30 May, 1765 in Hanover County, Virginia and he died c. 1834 in Tennessee. He married Sarah McDaniel on 19 October, 1781 in Amherst County, Virginia. He enlisted a few months before his 14th birthday.

"I entered the service, as a substitute in the place of Thomas Hammonds who had been drafted for Eighteen months in the Company of Captain Kilpatrick, at a place then called "Cumberland Old Courthouse – barricks" in Virginia – but in what County I have no recollection, as I was then very young, not exceeding, I believe fourteen years of age; was wholly illiterate, and has so remained ever since. Captain Kilpatrick's Company was attached to a Regiment of Militia Commanded by Colonel Feebecker. I believe, that this was in the month of February or March 1779. From the place where I entered the service, I marched with the Troops to Manchester Virginia, for the purpose of guarding the magazine, which was then at that place. I was very sick nearly all the time I remained at Manchester, and in consequence of my extreme indisposition, can only recollect, in general terms, the object for which the men were stationed at Manchester. The eighteen months for which I engaged as a substitute, expired without me having to be stationed any where except at the "Old Barracks" above mentioned and at Manchester: At or near the time of the expiration of the period for which I substituted, I enlisted at Manchester, in the United States army, as I believe. After my enlistment, I was sent to "Winchester Barracks" to guard some prisoners who were called "Burgoyne's men," or "Burgoyne's hessians." I cannot recollect to what Regiment I belonged after my enlistment. It was but a short time before the surrender of Lord Cornwallis as well as I can remember. I was again the victim of disease at Winchester, and obtained a furlough, and left there; and returned to Amherst County Virginia where I afterwards resided. And before my furlough expired, the war terminated, and the news of the surrender of Lord Cornwallis reached me, just as I was about to return to join the army."

John Massey served under Colonel Hans Christian Febiger who commanded the 2nd Virginia Regiment. Ripley's Believe it or Not wrote that Colonel Febiger is known as the only soldier who took part in every important battle of the Revolution from Bunker Hill to Yorktown.

Sources: 1. Ripley's Believe it or Not! February 20, 1942. 2. Sons of the American Revolution Application. 3. Census of 1820 and 1830. 4. Pension Papers S1918.

****

Peter Matthews age 12 or 13

Peter Matthews was born in July of 1763 in Montgomery County, Pennsylvania, and he died 30 November, 1840 in Crawford County,

Missouri. He married (1) Margaret Coffman and after her death he married (2) Rebecca Pidcock on 16 March, 1828.

In his pension application Peter said that Colonel Bird of the Pennsylvania militia was at the house of his father in the summer of 1776. There was no fifer attached to the Colonel's regiment so the Colonel persuaded Peter's father to let him take his son as the fifer. His father agreed so Peter, who just turned 13, was in the militia. His adventure was just beginning.

"In July or August 1776 I volunteered as a Fifer under Captain Hagger & Colonel Bird of the Pennsylvania militia I rendezvoused at my residence. I marched then to Philadelphia where I remained a few days and then marched through Trenton in New Jersey thence thru in Princeton Burnswick Elizabeth town and Newark to Paulus Hook where I was stationed until my term expired. I again volunteered for a tour of six months of Capt. Redheffer of German Town Pennsylvania of the Pennsylvania militia and was in a Regiment commanded by Colonel Smith. I aided in capturing some English and Hessian Soldiers on Staten Island this enterprise was headed by Col Smith who was wounded in one of his arms. From Staten Island I was marched to __?__ and from thence to the neighborhood of Fort Lee and was stationed there when Gen Washington reached that post from White Plains with the main army at that point about one month after I volunteered under Capt Redheffer me and the picket Guard with which I served was surprised by a party of Enemy Light Horse and I was wounded in my left leg sand taken prisoner."

Peter served three months in his first tour and was captured one month after starting his second tour. He enlisted in July or August which would mean he was captured around the Fort Lee area probably in November of 1776. The Battle of Fort Lee took place on 20 November, 1776 and forced the retreat of General Washington. In the rapid retreat the American troops left behind valuable tools, equipment, weapons, and food. The future of the revolution looked very dark. During this retreat Thomas Paine composed, in his pamphlet *The American Crisis*, the famous opening lines, *"These are the times that try men's souls: The summer soldier and the sunshine patriot will, in crisis, shrink from the service of his country; but he that stands it now, deserves the love and thanks of man and woman."*

"I was conveyed to the city of New York where the Enemy at that time was under Gen Sir William Howe. After remaining at New York a short time I was placed on board of a British prison ship and transported

to Halifax and from thence to Liverpool in England where being quartered in the house of one James Brindle and detained until the Spring of 1781 when I was permitted to embark on board a British Merchantman bound to the West Indies and when out to sea eight or ten days the Merchantman was captured by American Privateers commanded by Captain Duhaddaway and taken into Boston where I was released and returned home have served my county faithfully."

Peter later writes in his pension application, *"I think that when I was taken to Liverpool as a prisoner of war that Mr. Brindle was compensated for my board and clothing by the British or Americans.*

Peter was away from home almost five years as a soldier and a prisoner of war. He received $8.00 a month for his service. Included in his file is a paper called Statement Showing Service of Peter Matthews and lists his time of service. Included on it is a handwritten note, *"It is doubtful that the applicant is entitled to a pension for more than six months. He was taken into the service at an early age of 12 years. No allowance can be made for the time that he was in England as he was not confined as a prisoner which there, in all probability accounted of his youth but was being with a private individual in Liverpool for whom no doubt performed services for his support."*

This poor twelve year old is wounded, captured, and transported to a strange land against his will for four years and a government official acts like the lad was on holiday abroad.

After the death of Peter in 1840 his wife Rebecca files for a widow's pension. She sent a letter dated June of 1855, to the Pension Bureau reminding them of Peter's service. Due to her advanced years she gave a strange narrative about his service. She wrote that Peter enlisted in 1776, and fought in the Battle of Bunker Hill (fought in 1775) was wounded and taken prisoner, sent to China then to Halifax and there made his escape to an American ship.

She did receive a widow's pension of $33.33 a year. After her death one of her daughters petitioned the Pension Bureau for back money she believed her mother should have received. The correspondence goes on until the early 1860's.

Sources: 1. Revolutionary War New Jersey, The Online Field Guide to New Jersey's Revolutionary War Historical Sites. 2. Tombstone. 3. Pension Papers W5334.

****

William Matthews age 14

William Matthews was born on 10 April, 1763 in Mecklenburg County, Virginia, and he died on 18 July, 1855 in Jackson County, Georgia. He received a yearly pension of $66.66. He was a slave owner.

"I enlisted in Lincoln County North Carolina at the age of 14 years under Capt. James Pettigrew, John Long first Lieut., -- attached to the Battalion of Col. Samuel Jack -- I enlisted for 2 years especially for service in the State of Georgia -- I was marched from North Carolina to Georgia, Wilkes County -- was stationed on Little River for some time as a guard for the frontiers against the Indians & Tories -- During my stay at Little River station I was in no skirmishes with the Indians or Tories -- After remaining some time at the above mentioned Station, the regiment was Placed under Governor Houston, & marched to Florida in order to suppress the British & Indians & Tories in that quarter who were in the habit of making incursions upon the settlements of Georgia -- this expedition is Commonly Known by the name of the "Florida Expedition" -- The Troops remained below the Florida line about one month -- the Division to which I was attached never had any fighting or skirmishing. -- There were was some skirmishing amongst some detached parties of Cavalry but I never was in any of it -- I think I was gone 4 months on the Florida Expedition or thereabouts -- Immediately after my return from Florida & after serving but one of the 2 years for which I enlisted I was discharged."

"I enlisted in the year 1777 and was discharged in 1778 -- I afterwards, in 1779 volunteered my services in the same County of Lincoln North Carolina as a substitute in Capt. Clark's company & Col. Charles McDowell's regiment for three months -- the regiment joined Genl Lincoln's Army below Augusta on the South Carolina side of the river, and marched for Charleston, -- met the British at Stono & fought the battle of that name -- I was not in the battle, but was stationed 3 or 4 miles below Stono to prevent intercourse between the Army & shipping of the British. My term of service was out shortly after the battle & I was discharged -- but received no written discharge."

"In the December following this discharge, I volunteered as a substitute in Capt. Mooney's Company & Col. Hamright's regiment in the County of Lincoln North Carolina for 3 months, was marched immediately to Charleston to defend the city -- was in no action skirmish or encounter during the tour, & was discharged in the Spring but a few days before the British forces enclosed the City."

"Again about the latter part of the year 1780 or first of 1781 I again substituted for 3 months & joined General Greene's Army near Camden after Gates Defeat -- after remaining 2 months with him, General Green discharged us in consequence of his inability to furnish of us with arms -- I received no written discharge -- I volunteered several times to scout for the Tories in Lincoln County North Carolina but performed no regular tour of service."

I found a mystery associated with William Matthews. The above declaration in his own words is about his service. Below is an obituary of William Matthews from the *Edgefield Advertiser* dated 2 January, 1856. Everything about it is correct except the information about his service. This raises the questions: did they print the wrong service record or did William or his family give the wrong information to the paper?

"Died at his residence in Jackson County, Georgia, on July 18,1855, William Matthews, in the 92nd year of his age. He was born in Lunenburg County, Virginia, April 10, 1763. While he was quite young, his father removed to what is now Lincoln County, N.C. In 1778, at the age of fifteen, he entered the regular army under Genetal Lincoln, and was enrolled in the artillery. he was in the action of Stony Ferry; and was subsequently detached from General Lincoln's army, to General Howe in Florida. He was in the unfortunate assault upon the British in Savannah. When Charleston fell into the hands of the enemy, he was present, but made his escape in the darkness of night, to avoid falling as a prisoner of war into the hands of the British. When Gates took command of the Southern Army, Mr. Matthews was one of that army, but missed being at the disastrous battle of Camden, by his having been previously dispatched with others under Colonel Thomas Polk, to intercept some Tories, who had assembled in the neighborhood of Ramsour's Mills. He was in action under General Green, all the time he had the command of the Southern Army, and when during Greene's celebrated retreat, General Davidson was slain upon the hands of the Yadkin, Mr. Matthews helped to bear of the death body of that hero. At the storming of Ninety-Six, he was one of the bodyguards of General Kosciusko, while engaged in planning the attack. Mr. Matthews took part in the battle of Eutaw Springs, and subsequently, accompanied the army in his triumphant march into Charleston. After the disbanding of the army, Mr. Matthews accompanied some young men - with whom he had formed an intimacy in the army - to their homes in Mecklenburg County, N.C., in the neighborhood of Steel Creek Church, where he first became acquainted with Presbyterians. About a year afterwards, he returned to his father in Edgefield, S.C., to

which place the old gentleman had removed during the War. After marrying and living in that State about ten years, he removed and settled in Franklin County, Georgia - in that part which now forms Jackson County, on a tract of land granted to him as bounty for Revolutionary services. Soon after his settlement in Georgia, he united with the Presbyterian Church, at Bethesda, on Sandy Creek and was chosen one of the ruling elders. He, as Representative, served is county in the Legislature 17 times as a Senator."

The Edgefield Advertiser, January 2, 1856

Sources: 1. Pension Roll of 1835. 2. The Georgia Frontier: Revolutionary War Families to the mid-1800'3 by Jeannette Holland Austin. 3. Pension Papers S31842.

****

Jacob Mattlock (Matlack) age 14

Jacob Mattlock was born on 19 December, 1762 in Waterford, New Jersey, and he died on 2 February, 1857 in Philadelphia, Pennsylvania. He married Sibylla Ellis on 28 December, 1782 in Philadelphia. He received a yearly pension of $56.66. Like many other veterans his discharge papers were destroyed in a house fire.

"In the month of August 1777 I entered as a volunteer in a company commanded by Capt John stokes in Col Ellis Regiment of New Jersey Militia, the Company paraded at Haddonfield, where we were quartered. We remained alet [alert] one month and were discharged. The British army was then in Philadelphia and we frequently went down to Coopers Ferry and stood guard there."

"I next entered as a volunteer in a Company Commanded by apt John Stokes in Col Joseph Ellis Regiment this was early in the month of October 1777 we remained out three months and during this period we were at Haddonfield Woodbury Red Bank and other places within a few miles of Philadelphia. We were at Red Bank, but not in the Battle in the month of November 1777 we had a skirmish with the enemy, near Gloucester, in which a Lieut. Lucus belonging to one of the ____?___ Companies was killed. In the later period of this service perhaps in the month of December an English Brig. Got caught in the Ice in the River Delaware a little below Philadelphia,, the Ice became hard enough to bear, and we went out on the Ice and took her, we stript her of whatever was valuable about her such as her sails Rigging & made prisoners of the men and took the whole to Haddonfield the Brig was not armed and had

nothing in her, that I remember but some Barrels of Beef which we took out and then left her as the Ice was beginning to move."

"I next entered as a volunteer in a Company Commanded by Capt John Hider, this was in the month of March 1777. We lay most of the time at Haddonfield and remained in service one month and were discharged Cols Ellis & Williams commanded the Regiment during this service."

"I next entered the six months service in a Company Commanded by Capt John Davis in Gen Heards Brigade this was in the month of July 1779 we paraded at Haddonfield and Marched to Morristown where we waited till the other troops from Fort Jersey arrived we then marched to Princeton & New Brunswick to Elizabeth Town where we remained five or six weeks, we then went back to Elizabeth Town where we remained until discharged. During this period had a skirmish with the Refugees at Amboy, they had crossed the River from Staten Island and had taken a number of Cattle we succeeded in retaking some of the Cattle and driving the Refugees off, during this service also, one of our sergeants lost an arm in a skirmish one night, with the Refugees."

Between fifteen and twenty percent of Americans in the colonies kept their allegiance to the British Crown. Many times these Loyalists were dealt with harshly by the Patriots. Loyalty oaths were sometimes imposed by the people suspected of expressing sympathy to the British cause. Some had their lands and homes taken away, which forced them to become refugees in the area. Sometimes, they had to steal food and other supplies in order to survive.

"I next entered the six months service in a company Commanded by Captain Jehu Wood in this war in the latter part of June or first part of July 1780—We paraded at Haddonfield and marched from there through Morristown Mount Holly Allentown to Monmouth where we halted, and staid about two or three days, we were then adverted to Middletown to Relieve some troops that were there whose term of service had expired. We remained at Middletown until we were discharged which was a few days after New Years in 1781, during this time we had a slight skirmish with refugees and one of our corporals got shot through the thick part of the thigh, after we went to Middletown we were Commanded by col John Holmes who lived in the neighborhood during this tour, there was a County Court held at Monmouth Court House at which Court five men were condemned to be hung—four refugees and one young man for a Rape. Whilst the Court was in session there was a guard Continually kept around the Court House and __?__day and night, the Guard was *composed of men from Middletown, I was one of them, after Court a number of us were sent to Elizabethtown point with prisoners of War, where they were exchanged for some of our own men that had been prisoners of War in New York. The whole time that I served during the war was little more than seventeen months."*

Sources: 1. Sons of the American Revolution Application. 2. Pennsylvania Marriage Records 1700-1821. 3. U.S. Pensioners 1818-1872. Pension Papers S2756. 4. The Revolutionary War by Charles Patrick Neimeyer.

****

James Maxwell age 11

James Maxwell was born on 2 September, 1764 in Monson, Massachusetts, and he died on 18 January, 1848 in Unadilla, New York. He married Cloe Burt on 18 April, 1790 in Massachusetts.

James ran away at the age of 11 and joined the army as a drummer. He served with the troops of General Arnold during the Battle of Quebec fought on 31 December, 1775. The Americans failed to take Quebec City, so they dug entrenchments outside of the city and sat out the winter. When British reinforcements began to arrive, the Americans began to retreat in May. On 18 June, 1776 General Arnold and his troops were the last to leave Canada.

Lack of food and smallpox made the retreat very difficult on the men. It was reported that James suffered greatly from lack of food at this time. The group of men that he was with killed and ate two dogs that had been following them.

Sources: 1. Lineage Book D.A.R. Vol. 53, 1905. 2. Sons of the American Revolution Application. 3. Massachusetts Town and Vital Records 1620-1988.

****

Alexander Meek age 14

Alexander Meek was born on 14 December, 1764 in Cumberland County, Maryland, and he died on 8 September, 1857 in Panola County, Mississippi. He married Elizabeth Keys on 25 September, 1791 in Virginia. He had four brothers and two uncles that served in the Revolution. He received a yearly pension of $21.22.

"I was born in Cumberland County Maryland on the 14th December 1764 according to a record of my age now in my possession.

Sometime in the month of July 1779, living then in Washington County Virginia & having enrolled my name on the muster roll, although not quite fifteen years of age, I was drafted and entered the service of the United States for a tour of three months in the Regiment commanded by Colonel Archer Campbell. I was placed in the command of Major William Edmiston with about four hundred men on scouting parties & sent against the Tories in Wythe County & about the Iron Mountain who were ravaging the country and murdering the people in that quarter. The company to which I was attached was commanded by a Sergeant John Robertson – but the Tories disappeared upon our approach, so that we had no action with them & we returned home."

"About the first of September 1780, we were again drafted for a three months tour under Colonel Campbell & Major Edmiston, my company being commanded by Captain James Dysart & 1st Lieutenant Samuel Meek who was my brother – the No. of the Regiment I now forget. We rendezvoused at Abingdon Virginia and was marched to the Watauga River in what is now East Tennessee where we joined the North Carolina troops under Col Shelby. We then marched on through North Carolina over the Yellow mountain crossing ___?___ about 8 or 9 miles from King's Mountain in the southern boundary of North Carolina. I was in the battle at King's Mountain, where our troops were under the command of Colonel (or as I think he then was General) William Campbell at this battle I think we took about a thousand prisoners, British & Tories who were commanded by an officer by the name of Ferguson. In this battle our forces were commanded by Col Campbell, Col Cleveland, Col Bluford, Col Shelby--after our victory we started toward Richmond with our prisoners, their baggage wagons __?__ when after traveling three or four days we understood that Lord Cornwallis was following us to retake our prisoners (though our information was not correct) a council or court martial was held, in which it was determined to burn their baggage wagons (which was accordingly done) and to hang about thirty of the Tories, but we hung only nine. I myself holding the cow hides to cut the strings to hang them with – we then continued our march night & day for four or five days, when we were met by the regular troops (but I cannot recollect by whom they were commanded) we were then dismissed."

"About the first of December of the same year I volunteered in the same Regiment & still commanded by Colonel Archer Campbell & one Major Christian the company to which I belonged commanded by Captain Robert Kyle. We were then ordered against the Cherokee Indians & marched to the Tellico Towns on the Tennessee River between French

Broad & Tennessee rivers we joined the North Carolina forces who were then put under the command of Colonel Campbell. We took some prisoners & then eighty of us (40 being Virginians & 40 Carolinians) were left to guard them, while the balance of the Army went to the Hiwassee to destroyed the Indian towns there: when they returned, we destroyed the Tellico Towns, burning houses, corn and everything we could find. We then marched back, we were dismissed and went home about the last of January."

Alexander Meeks was full of vinegar as an old man. At his grandson's wedding Alexander must have made the day memorable for more than one reason. He was described by one of the relatives as, *"A ridiculous figure in a black velvet coat, with knee britches, sild stockings, and silver-buckled shoes wearing a dusty wig and ill fitted false teeth carved of wood, he played his violin and carried on like an Irishman. From the attention given him, you would have thought him the center of attention instead of the bride."*

He outlived his wife by several years. At the last reunion of Revolutionary Veterans in North Mississippi, only 3 vets attended, and two were carried to the reunion. Old man Meeks walked in and spent the afternoon dancing.

Charlotte, the daughter of Alexander, took care of him after the death of his wife in 1841. Alexander died at his son's house after falling and breaking a hip while playing with his grandchildren. He left most of his possessions to Charlotte.

"Know all men by these present that I, Alexander Meek of Marshall County, State of Mississippi. In consideration of the natural love and affection which I have and bear toward my daughter Charlotte Meek of same County and state, and the affectionate care she has given me in my old age, and for the sum of one dollar by her to be paid, and by these I do bargain and sell to my daughter one negro slave (woman) named Harriet, about 17 years of age, and her infant child named Adeline and their increase, also one good horse, saddle and bridle, one cow and calf and half of all my household and kitchen furniture..."

Sources: 1. Guy Meek of Anne Arundel County, Maryland: Descendants, Intermarriages and Neighbors, Vol 2. (1600-2004 by Melton P. Meek, page 405. 2. Census 1830 & 1840. 3. Sons of the American Revolution Application. 4. DAR Patriot Index. 5. U.S. Pension Roll of 1835. 6. Tombstone 7. Will of Alexander Meek.

****

Basil Meek age 12

Basil Meek was born on 7 March, 1763 in Virginia, and he died on 12 January, 1844 in Indiana. He married a woman by the name of Eleanor Roberts. He served in Captain Hugh Stevenson's Company from August 1775 to October of the same year.

Sources: 1. Revolutionary War Soldiers Buried in Illinois. 2. Index Roll of Honor, DAR. 3. Sons of the American Revolution Application. 4. Tombstone.

****

Caleb Meeker age 7

Caleb Meeker was born in 1769 in Springfield, New Jersey, and he there died on 4 April, 1817. He married Susan Skinner, who was 4 years older, in June of 1785. Caleb served with his father Captain Joseph Meeker in the 5th Company of the 1st Establishment of the 1st Regiment of New Jersey. Caleb enlisted on 2 January, 1776 and served as a fifer for one year. He later served in various tours in the New Jersey Militia as a fifer.

Caleb died before he could apply for a pension and give his service information. His wife Susan provided the information and received a widow's yearly pension of $44. She gave an interesting account of living in Springfield, when the British burned the town in June of 1780. She was fifteen at the time, and her future husband Caleb was in the militia at the battle.

"My father was Jonathan Skinner who lived in Springfield in the war. That village seemed to be the seat of war. Two battles were fought on that ground with the enemy & I believe my husband was personally engaged in both. The church & town were burnt by the enemy in the last engagement. My father's house & furniture were all consumed & the whole family were turned out into the street without shelter, without food, & with no clothing except the suit we then wore. The cornfields & harvest fields were all laid waste & destroyed."

She wrote in the pension application the date of her marriage, and the dates of the birth of her children were in the family Bible. Unfortunately, the Bible was burnt by her oldest son, *"who was subject to insanity. It occurred on a visit home while the insanity was upon him in or about the year 1832. He threw the Bible into the fire and burnt it to ashes."*

Various friends that served with Caleb wrote letters to the pension bureau in support of his service. Robert Pearson a friend of the family said that Caleb served in his father's company in the Canadian Expedition.

Robert Young wrote to the pension bureau and stated that he served numerous times with Caleb in the militia. He stated, *"I recollect him at a battle at Acquackanonk Bridge in which Genl Winds commanded the Militia in the early part of the fall 78 or 79."* Because of defeats General Washington began retreating across New Jersey. The army crossed Acquackanonk Bridge and destroyed it on 21 November, 1776.

Robert also wrote that he and Caleb went, *"in an Expedition against the Indians in the summer season upon the Minisink & Delaware, Meeker was out under Capt. Horton & Genl winds. I remember Meeker also at the battle of Connecticut farms & Springfield in May & June 1780 when Mrs. Caldwell was killed & Springfield burnt."*

British soldiers shot Mrs. Caldwell in her home and then searched her body. They carried her outside and proceeded to burn her house down. This murder was probably committed, because she was the wife of Reverend James Caldwell who was an ardent supporter of the patriots.

During the Battle of Springfield some of the American marksmen were running low on wadding for their muskets. Reverend Caldwell rode to his church and grabbed a load of hymn books published by English clergyman Isaac Watts. Caldwell returned to the soldiers and began tearing pages out of the books and gave them to the men to use for wadding. As he did this he was yelling, *"Give 'em Watts, boys."*

His act did not turn the battle in favor of the Americans, but the heroic act of the "Fighting Chaplain" was passed on until Washington Irving recorded it in his biography of George Washington.

> *"Who's that riding in on horse-back*
> *Parson Caldwell, boys; Hooray!*
> *Red-Coats call him "Fighting Chaplain,*
> *How they hate him! Well they may!"*

Sources: 1. Sons of the American Revolution Application. 2. D.A.R. Lineage Book, Vol. 19. 3. Pension Papers W7443. 4. Revolutionary Women in the War for American Independence by Elizabeth Fries Ellet and Lincoln Diamant. 5. The American View February 27, 1014. 6. The Life of George Washington by Washington Irving.

****

Obed Meeker age 14

Obed Meeker was born on 5 November, 1763 in Elizabeth, New Jersey, and he died there on 7 November, 1834. He married Elizabeth Crane on 13 March, 1824. He received a yearly pension of $40.

"In the year 1778 in the spring I think it was April I enlisted in the New Jersey State Troops under the command of Cols Leely and Ely, Capt. John Schudder. I served a year in this enlistment. The first part of this service we laid in the town of Elizabeth for the purpose of filling up the company, and after it was filled up we marched to Tappan at Dobbs Ferry on the Hudson River, and encamped in the woods a short distance from the Fort which was then erected. I remained there with the company about three months and then returned to Connecticut farms in the then township of Elizabeth in the County of Essex and State of New Jersey--and encamped there and continued thus encamped until the weather became to cool to stay in camp, we removed to Rahway and there remained until the expiration of the years service and only one dollar pay for my services."

Source: 1. Pension Papers W5370.

****

Asa Merrill age 13 or14

Asa Merrill was born in 1764 in Massachusetts, and he died on 7 October, 1840 in New York. He married Sarah who died in the same year as her husband.

"I served in the Revolutionary War as follows for three years from May 1777 to May 1780. I enlisted to serve for the three years, in the town of Townsend of Middlesex State of Massachusetts in Captain Hugh Maxwells company in the Regiment of Massachusetts troops commanded by Colonel Bailley and served in the said Corps the whole term and was regularly discharged."

Asa was a member of the 2nd Massachusetts Regiment Volunteer Infantry under the command of Colonel John Bailey and Major Hugh Maxwell. Asa and the regiment participated in the Battles of Trenton, Princeton, Saratoga, and Monmouth, and they spent the winter of 1777-1778 at Valley Forge.

At the Battle of Trenton, on 26 December, 1776 Asa was part of Colonel John Glover's Brigade, who took up position on the far side of the bridge, over the Assunpink River, that would prevent the enemy's escape across the bridge. Some books indicate the Hessians were drunk that night after celebrating Christmas. One of the Americans at the battle had supervised the captured Hessians after the battle, and said he was sure that no liquor was consumed that night. The Germans were tired and caught by surprise but were not drunk that night.

Asa was part of General Learned's Brigade at the Battle of Saratoga in the fall of 1777. This brigade was not very effective during the battle after they got lost in the woods. Toward the end of the battle they were engaged in light contact.

Asa Merrill listed his assets and debts in his pension application. Under debt was $20 for a church pew. It was common practice in the 1700's for churches to rent or auction off pews in order to raise money. Pews in the front might sell for 5 or 6 times what the pews in the back sold for. Free seats, which carried a social stigma, were in the very back or in the upstairs gallery. Families that owned or rented their pews would add personal items to them such as cushions, footrests, armrests, and any other items for comfort.

In his assets he included 30 books, which were described as mainly school books valued at $12. This was common for homes in New England to provide books for their children's schooling. More of the people in New England could read and write than the people in the southern colonies.

Sources: 1. Onondaga's Soldiers of the Revolution by the Onondaga Historical Society, 1895. 2. Tombstone 3. Census 1820, 1830, & 1840. U.S. Pensioners 1818-1872. 4. Historical Register of Officers of the Continental Army during the War of the Revolution April 1775-Dec. 1783. 5. Pension Papers S43025.

****

Charles Merriman age 14

Charles Merriman was born on 29 August, 1762 in Wallingford, Connecticut, and he died on 26 August, 1829 in Watertown, Connecticut. He married Anna Punderson on 16 May, 1784 in Watertown, Connecticut.

He enlisted as a drum major on 1 July, 1777 two months before his 15th birthday. He served in the company of Captain Joseph Mansfield in the 6th Regiment of the Connecticut Continental Line under Colonel William Douglas. In 1781-1782 he was Drum Major in the 4th Regiment Connecticut Line under Col. Zebulon Butler.

Sources: 1. Connecticut Men in the War of the Revolution. 2. Sons of the American Revolution Application. 3. Year Book of the Sons of the Revolution in the State of New York 1899. 4. Connecticut Deaths and Burials Index 1650-1934. 5. Connecticut Town Marriage Records pre 1870. 6. Tombstone 7. U.S. Revolutionary War Rolls 1775-1783.

****

Jacob Micheller age 14

Jacob Micheller was born in 1764, and he died in April of 1844 in Ohio. He married Mary on 3 March, 1842. He received a yearly pension of $60.00.

"I entered the service of the United States as a volunteer in the month of August 1778, and served for one month *in Col. Caleb Fifer's Regiment of the North Carolina Line, and served under the following named officers to wit General Rutherford, Col. Fifer, Major White -- Capt. Rice (or Reese) (lieutenants name forgotten) and Ensign Russell. I left the service in the month of September 1778 after serving faithfully for one month."*

"I then afterwards in the month of July 1779 entered the service a second time as a volunteer in Col. Fifer's Regiment of the North Carolina Militia and served for two years and four months *under the command of General Rutherford, Col. Caleb Fifer, Major James White and Capt __?__ . I left the service the 2nd time in the month of November 1781 after serving faithfully for* 2 years & 4 months *which added to the first tour of one month makes* two years and five months *for which I claim a pension. I resided at the time of his entering the service in Machlenberg County North Carolina. I entered the service as a volunteer. During my first tour for one month I marched from Mecklenburg County to Charlotte, from thence, to the twelve mile Creek, from thence to Buffalo Creek, and Pedee to Little River, from thence back to Mecklenburg County where I was discharged. During my second tour of service I marched from Mecklenburg County to Camden S. Carolina from thence back to Mecklenburg County from thence to __?__ Farms in Montgomery County -- where he was verbally discharged."*

"In the month of September 1781, as I was returning from States Borough to Charlotte I was attacked and robbed by a Tory (as he supposes) of $600 in specie which I had of my own money and was taking it to my residence in Mecklenburg County, the villain assaulted me with a drawn sword and gave me a severe wound on the head which so disabled him that I was insensible to what transpired afterwards for a considerable

time. He had obtained permission of his officers to go home for a few days."

Sources: 1. Pension Roll of 1835. 2. Pension Papers W25706.

****

John Middleton age 13

John Middleton was born in Lancaster County, Pennsylvania on 24 April, 1764, and he died in Highland County, Ohio on 31 January, 1857. He married a woman named Eleanor on 28 March, 1797. She received his widow's pension of $40.00 a year.

John first enlisted the Virginia Militia in September 1777 and served for three months under Captain Thomas Buck. The militia was sent to Fort Pitt commanded by Colonel John Gibson to defend the fort against British and Indian attack.

In July John was drafted to serve for three months under Captain Darby Downey. In March of 1778 he was drafted for another three months under Captain Jacob Pennywit. During this time, *"...we remained at Richmond several weeks & that whilst there was sent out with 40 others as a scouting party—we took 7 British prisoners in the neighborhood of Richmond."*

John was drafted for one year in the militia regiment commanded by Colonel John Brown. *"After I was drafted I detected and took prisoners two American deserters—I put them in prison at Woodstock. These prisoners were soon released from jail by a man named Henry Aleshiter."*

In 1780 John served his final tour of three months when he was drafted at Woodstock and served again under Captain Jacob Pennywit. For his service he received $40.00 per year for his one year service in the Virginia militia.

Sources: 1. U.S. Pension Roll of 1835. 2. Pension Papers S2847.

****

Valentine Miller age 13

Valentine Miller was born on 27 December, 1762 in Loudon County, Virginia, and he died on 29 November, 1843 in Mad River, Ohio. His pension was rejection because he need 2 witnesses for proof of service.

"Some time in the month of December 1776 I enlisted as a Revolutionary Soldier under Captain William George for the term of three years in the County of Loudon where I was born I enlisted about ten months before General Burgoyne was defeated and his Army taken by the Americans I lacked about one month of being fourteen years old when I enlisted, but being unusually large strong and healthy & of my age I was received and fully served the said Term of three years in said War and received my discharge in the State of Pennsylvania signed by General Casey. I had received my said discharge and had returned home – I was drafted for six months as a militia man, and was in service as such at little York in Virginia, at the time Cornwallis surrendered. That shortly after that surrender, I with others of the militia were discharged & having served the full six months. I was never wounded whilst in said war. And has never received my bounty in land or any pension and is on no Pension list. During the term of my enlistment I was at Mud Island fort, eight miles from Philadelphia which was commanded by Col Samuel Smith in the place was attacked by the British and was eventually taken – that at that place my Capt (George) was wounded, taken prisoner and he understood died, that my company were all killed or taken prisoner except eight with myself and we were afterwards attached to other companies, I was also at the taking of General Burgoyne and his Army in October 1777. The Officers under whom I principally served during my enlistment as far as I can recollect their names were General Casey, Col Samuel Smith, Col Clappen, Cap William George, Lieutenant Stairs, Ensign D. Harens. I was in no general or principal engagement during said war except at Mud Island, the taking of General Burgoyne and the Siege of little York when Cornwallis was taken in October 1781."

The Siege of Mud Island Fort or Siege of Fort Mifflin took place from 26 September to 16 November, 1777. British land batteries and a British naval squadron bombarded the fort. The Americans finally evacuated the fort on the night of the 16th at a great loss of life. The British took possession of the fort and were appalled at the damage and the blood and body parts strew about the inside of the fort. Joseph Plumb Martin, a 17 year old Connecticut soldier who was there wrote years later, *"Our men were cut up like cornstalks…the whole area of the fort was as completely plowed as a field…If ever destruction was complete, it was here."*

Sources: 1. Pension Papers R7227. 2. Census 1810, 1830, and 1840. 3. Yankee Doodle Boy: A Young Soldier's Adventure in the American Revolution, Told by Himself by Joseph Plumb Martin.

****

George Mills age 14

George Mills was born on 17 January, 1765 in Berks County, Pennsylvania, and he died on 1 December, 1858 in Chemung County, New York. He married Jenny Murphy.

George served as a private at the age of 14 in Captain Caleb Pierce's Company in the Chester County Militia of Pennsylvania. He served for six months. Three months for his father and three months for himself. There is a record from the Pennsylvania State Archives that shows him serving in the 6th Battalion in the Ashtown Company under Colonel Thomas Poor dated on 7 June, 1779.

After the war George was the first merchant in the village of Havana and kept the first tavern there. In 1797 Louis Phillippe, later the King of France, was a guest of George at his hotel.

Sources: 1. Tombstone 2. D.A.R. Lineage Book, Vol. 109.

****

Benjamin Mitchell age 13

Benjamin Mitchell was born on 8 December, 1762 in Cumberland County, Maine, and he died there on 28 March, 1841. He married Sarah Fogg on 12 May, 1785 in Maine. He received a yearly pension of $28.58. He served in the army as a substitute for his uncle Robert, and he served as a marine in the Navy.

"I entered the service of the United states in January 1776 at Cape Elizabeth for nine months in a company commanded by Captain Morton in col. Mitchell's Regiment and served until October. Afterwards in 1781 I served on board the Sloop Defence, a state vessel, commanded by James Nevins and served for two months."

Sources: 1. D.A.R. Lineage Book, Vol. 32. 2. Pension Papers S18982.

****

Alexander Montgomery age 14

Alexander Montgomery was born on 10 December, 1761 in Massachusetts, and he died in 1840. He received a yearly pension of $66.67.

"In December 1775 I volunteered at Cambridge, Massachusetts to take the place of Timothy Brown in Col. James M Varnums Regiment of Massachusetts troops, and in Capt James Varnums company served as a private in that company at Cambridge for the term of five months. I enlisted as a substitute the first of December 1775 and served in the company till the last of April 1776."

"In December 1776 I enlisted at said Andover as a substitute for John Marston who was drafted, I enlisted the service as a private soldier under Capt Nathaniel Marshes company in Col Pickerings Regiment of Militia and marched from said Andover 3m about December 15, 1776; through Danbury Conn, Tarrytown, Kings bridge Fishkill to the Jersies where I served the time for which I enlisted out, which was for three months and was discharged at Bound Brook about the first of April 1777, about 400 miles from home."

"About the first of June 1778 I enlisted as a private soldier in the army of the revolution for the term of nine months and on or about June 18, 1778 I passed muster at Fishkill N.Y. by a Continental Officer and was immediately sent to Fort Putnam on West Point and there set to work where I continued 5 or 6 weeks then was ordered into Capt Benjamin Farnums company in Col Tupper's Regiment, in Gen Patterson's Brigade where under the command of said Tupper and Lieut Stephen Abbot, I served till the full term of enlistment had expired was discharged at West Point in the latter part of March 1779 between two and three hundred miles from home."

"About June 1oth 1780 I enlisted for the three months and marched as a private soldier in the militia in the company of John Abbot in Col Wades regiment from said Andover to Gloveneck N.Y. then to Fishkill where I remained till the expiration of my time of enlistment and was dismissed at New Windsor after having served three months, 230 miles from home."

Many times a recruit was discharged miles from home. This would mean a long walk sometimes over rough terrain and in poor weather conditions. Depending on these conditions and health, he might be able to cover 100 miles in about 4 days. The soldier might be given provisions, if available before he left, and maybe he would even be given service credit for the time he traveled. While on the road he would also be at the mercy of the enemy or robbers.

Sources: 1. U.S. Pension Roll of 1835. 2. Pension Papers S13985. 3. Massachusetts Society of the Sons of the American Revolution, 1893.

****

John Montgomery age 13

John Montgomery was born on 5 August, 1762 probably in North Carolina, and he died on 26 January, 1845 in Peoria County, Illinois. He married (1) his first cousin Susanna Porter on his birthday 5 August, 1785. After she died in 1802 he married (2) Elizabeth Harris. He enlisted in June of 1777 just 2 months before his 14th birthday.

"I enlisted in the Army of the United States in the year 1777 by Thomas Quirk who was a recruiting Officer under Nathan Reed (Captain), and I was placed under Captain John Snoddy until I would be called upon by said Reed ___?___ ___?___ in the Continental service (said Snoddy was Captain at Moore's Fort in the then Washington County State of Virginia). When I marched into the Continental service I served in the 7th Regiment of the Virginia line under the following named Officers; to wit, – ___?___ his first name not recollected, and instead of marching into said service, under Reed, I marched and served under Captain James Dasey or Dezzard (the precise sound of the name not recollected); my Major was David Ward; my Colonel was William Campbell when I enlisted as aforesaid enlisted for five years, and I think I enlisted sometime in the month of June of said year and was discharged at the expiration of said five years, and served out one term of enlistment ending sometime in the year 1782. When I ___?___ ___?___ in said Moores fort Washington County State of Virginia; I marched from said Fort the spring after I enlisted about 25 miles to Abbington in the County of Washington State of Virginia where I remained under Captain Dasey until I marched to the Guilford battle in which I was engaged (but a few days before that engagement I was engaged in the skirmish at Whitsells Mills after said Guilford battle I was sent back to said Moores Fort and placed under Captain Snoddy where I remained until I was discharged as above mentioned."

After the war John returned home to his parent's farm in Virginia. John was recommended as a Lieutenant in the County Militia on 22 August, 1797. In 1802 he was certified for a Captain of the 2nd Battalion 72nd Regiment.

He moved with his wife and children to Floyd County, Kentucky, about 1821. At the end of three years, about 1824, he took his family in wagons and carefully avoiding the Indians arrived safely in Franklin County, Indiana, where he remained for seven years. In 1826 the children from his first marriage were grown and were no longer living with him. Living with him was his wife Susanna and their two daughters, Sarah and Susanna ages 14 and 11. In 1835 John and his wife moved to Peoria County, Illinois with their daughter Sarah and her family.

John Montgomery's obituary taken from a column titled "Peoria's Past" written by Bill Adams in the *Peoria Journal Star*:

"John Montgomery, a veteran of the Revolutionary War, died in Peoria yesterday at the age of 80. He was buried in Princeville Cemetery, and on his gravestone was inscribed simply: "A veteran of the Revolution". Born in Virginia, Montgomery moved to North Carolina with his family when the colonies started fighting for their independence. He was only a lad in his teens when his father took him down to the Continental Army headquarters and saw him enlist to fight the Redcoats. He served until the close of the war. Then he came west and settled in Peoria County. He was much in demand as a fiddler for neighborhood dances and usually carried the flag at the head of patriotic parades."

Sources: 1. Census 1830 & 1840. 2. Tombstone 3. Pension Roll of 1835. 4. Soldiers of the American Revolution buried in Illinois. 5. Pension Papers S33124.

****

Lemuel Moody age 10

Lemuel Moody was born on 30 June, 1767 in Portland, Maine, and he died there on 11 August, 1846. He married Emma Crosby on 4 January, 1797 in Maine. Around 1777 Lemuel joined the navy and served as a waterboy and waiter.

Over the years he rose in the ranks and became a merchant mariner and captain of the schooner *Betsy*. In 1799 he was returning from South America with a cargo of coffee, molasses, and cotton, when he was captured by a French privateer on April 20th. Captain Moody and his men were imprisoned on the island of Guadeloupe and they were released in July.

In 1807 Portland Monument selected Lemuel to staff the Observatory. He became active on the Portland waterfront and was in the business of shipping. By 1825 he became the sole owner of the Portland Observatory.

Sources: 1. Fishermen's Voice, Vol. 13, No. 5 – May 2008. 2. D.A.R. Lineage Book, Vol. 17.

****

Behethland Moore age 15

Behethland Moore was born on 24 December, 1764 in Faugwier County, Virginia, and she died on 2 December, 1853 at the home of her son in Edgefield, South Carolina

Behethland had several encounters with the enemy soldiers at a young age. One time a small band of Tories was ransacking the Moore house and commanded a servant to bring them the horses in the barn. Behethland commanded the young servant not to obey the Tory order. The soldier grew angry and threatened to beat the servant if he did not obey the order. Again, Behethland told the boy to stay where he was. The Tory then raised his fist to strike the boy and Behethland quickly got between the boy and the Tory and refused to move. The soldier lowered his fist and walked away.

On another occasion in 1780 a small skirmish took place near her home between Colonel Washington's cavalry and the Tory militia led by Lord Rawdon. After the fighting ended several of the Tory militiamen entered Behethland's home in search of plunder. The only people inside the house were Behethland, two younger brothers, her mother, and a friend Fanny Smith. Luckily, the family had been warned in advance that the Tories were in the area so they hid their most valuable possessions.

A soldier searching upstairs found two barrels of apples, which he began to roll down the stairs to another soldier below. Behethland and her brother had spent the whole morning picking the apples and were not happy that their work would go to waste. The young teenager grew angry, and showing no fear she ordered the men to stop at once because the apples belonged to her. A Tory officer standing nearby was impressed with the young girl's courage and ordered the men to stop.

The officer told his men that they would have all the fruit they could eat in the morning, when they were at the rebel Wallace's camp. After the Tories had left Behethland told her mother that she must get to the camp of Captain Wallace and warn them that the Tories were going to attack. The rebel camp was across the Saluda River a few miles upstream from the Moore home.

As the sun began to go down over the horizon, the 15 year old Behethland, a younger brother, and their friend Fanny got a canoe and began to paddle to the rebel camp. As they paddled each kept an eye toward shore hoping they would not spot any Tories. They paddled for miles, their bodies ached with pain, and their hands became raw from the constant paddling. Finally, they saw the flickering light from several campfires and they knew they had reached their destination.

The trio delivered their message of warning to Captain Wallace and turned to leave. The Captain asked them to stay and eat and rest. Behethland refused and told the Captain they needed to return home. The three children returned back to the Moore house just before daybreak and they were totally exhausted from their all night journey. The next day when the Tories reached the American camp they found it deserted.

Around noon the day Behethland returned home, a young rebel officer rode up to the Moore house and asked to speak to the girl that carried the message that saved the rebel soldiers. Word had spread through the ranks of her daring adventure, and he was sent to hear her story. The young Captain Butler was quite surprised when a beautiful girl introduced herself as the person he sought. Behethland was herself drawn to the handsome young officer in uniform, and she was eager to spend time with him telling her story.

For the next several years the young Captain found every excuse possible to visit the Moore farm to talk with Behethland. In 1784 Behethland and Captain William Butler were married. William later served in Congress for thirteen years, and during the war of 1812 he was made a Major General in command of the South Carolina forces at Camden.

Sources: 1. Women in American History by John A. Logan, 1912. 2. Women Patriots of the American Revolution: a Biographical Dictionary by Charles E. Claghorn. 3. The Romance of the Revolution: Being True Stories of Adventure, romantic Incidents, Hairbreadth Escapes, and Heroic Exploits of the Days of '76.

****

Robert Moore age 14

Robert Moore was born on 8 April, 1763 in Kitter, Maine, and he died on 5 February, 1852. He enlisted on the ship *Ranger* commanded by

John Paul Jones on its first voyage on 1 November, 1777. His name is found on the rolls of the sailors. Robert later enlisted in the army for a year. He also enlisted in August 1776 on the continental frigate *Raleigh* and put his height as five feet three inches tall. He never returned on board the ship. His pension was rejected until more information could be gathered.

The *Ranger* sailed for France with a crew of 140 men on 1 November, 1777, carrying dispatches telling of Burgoyne's surrender. Before they reached France two British prizes were captured. The ship arrived at Nantes, France on 2 December.

"I enlisted as a soldier in the service of the United States in the summer of 1779 and in the company commanded by Captain Ebenezer Deering for the term of one year."

Sources: 1. John Paul Founder of the American Navy-A History by Augustus C. Buell (ship roll on page 340). 2. D.A.R. Lineage Book, Vol. 41. 3. Pension Papers R7353.

****

Daniel Morris age 14

Daniel Morris was born on 24 December, 1764 in Currituck County, North Carolina, and he died 29 October, 1855 in Hart County, Kentucky. He married (1) Abbie Murden who died in 1810 (2) Nancy Key he married on 17 October, 1822 in Grayson County, Kentucky by Martin Letterback, a minister of the Gospel. Daniel received a yearly pension of $26.66 and a land bounty of 160 acres for his service.

"I was drafted to serve a tour in the militia in Halifax County North Carolina in the month of July 1779 where I then resided and I entered the service of the United States in the American Revolution under Captain John Williams the Lieutenant was Preston Brooks in the Regiment commanded by Colonel Robert Powers, we rendezvoused at the town of Halifax in said County, from thence marched to Chatham Court house in North Carolina, the whole of Colonel Powers Regiment marched to that place. From thence marched down to south Carolina, in pursuit of some tories & British forces in said State which the said Col Powers had received orders to endeavor to subdue. We were engaged in marching through the country, in pursuit of the scouts of the enemy, but about the time we entered South Carolina the American Army & British, had an engagement & after that time the British scouting parties and Tories, kept, pretty much with the main army -- we marched on a place called Fairs

honary in South Carolina not very far from Augustain Georgia where we were stationed a short time, & from thence we marched to Cross Creek, which was not a very great distance from New Bern; from Cross Creek myself and the balance of said troops then with us at that place was discharged; In this tour he served 4 months, according to the best of his recollection."

"I was drafted for 3 months this tour, but in consequence of some Tories British and a few Indians having embodied themselves near Cross Creek; our Colonel detained us a month longer, in order to disperse & subdue this force we marched to said Creek, but they had disappeared."

"I again entered the service in the same State and County in the year 1781 the 1st of February under Captain Samuel Crowell Lieutenant Henry Bradford, Ensign Edley Morris under Colonel Reed, who was a Continental officer sent to take command of us, in this service I entered as a volunteer in the militia the Regiment rendezvoused at Halifax in said County, from thence we marched to Hillsboro North Carolina, from thence we marched to the Reedy fork of Little Buffalo Creek, where we had a smart engagement with the British, in which we lost about seven men killed, and several wounded, in which action each party retreated; how many of the enemy we killed we never ascertained; from this place we marched to Guilford Courthouse, in which engagement I was together with the whole of Colonel Reed's Regiment. The __?__ of which engagement, is well known from the history of the Country; from Guilford Courthouse we pursued the British to deep River, and remained there eight days, but having lost our artillery at Guilford we did not think it safe to attack the enemy without artillery. The enemy by making a temporary bridge of Ramsour's rails & taken from his farm, crossed the River, when we had them pressed in the fork thereof. From Ramsour's Mills on said River we marched to Camden in South Carolina, and was in the siege of Camden and remained there a few days, near which Lord Rawdon was encamped with his forces, but he gave us the slip & put out when we were preparing for and expecting an engagement with him & his forces. General Green was our commander in chief, from this place we were marched to pee dee River at Haley's ferry where Colonel John Webb, by orders of the General discharged us, not thinking it safe to discharge us in small companies at a distance from home."

Sources: 1. Census 1810, 1820, 1830, 1840, & 1850. 2. U.S. Pensioners 1818-1872. 3. Pension Papers W12494.

****

David Hamilton Morris age 10

David Morris was born on 11 July, 1769 in Hanover, New Jersey, and died on 3 April, 1843 in Miami, Ohio. He married Eva Ann Sailor (Saylor) in 1803. He was a revolutionary war soldier and Indian fighter. In order to enlist at 10 he obtained the permission of his widowed mother with the understanding from Captain James Christie that David would serve as his waiter and the Captain would look out for him.

"I enlisted in the army of the United States in the later part of the year 1779 or the beginning of 1780. I cannot state with accuracy the precise date but well recollected it was in severe cold weather, and was about new year, whether shortly before or shortly after I can not say. I can however state that I was in service in what was called the cold winter of 1780, I enlisted at Morristown heights in the state of New Jersey in the company commanded by Captain James Christie in the third Pennsylvania Regiment under Col. Thomas Craig."

"I enlisted for the term of three years or during the war the regiment to which I belong was attached to what was called the Flying Camp under the command of Genl Wayne. I served in New Jersey & New York in the year 1780. The occupation of the Flying Camp was to watch the motions of the enemy & to regulate its movement accordingly. I continue in that regiment attached to the Flying Camp until the revolt of the Pennsylvania line in the early part of 17___ when my Captain was ordered to Carlisle in Pennsylvania on the recruiting service I accompanied him."

During the winter of 1780-1781 conditions for the army were terrible leading to a small revolt. Pennsylvania was one of the stingiest states in paying their soldiers. Many were not paid during their entire three year enlistment. At the start of 1781 the problem reached a crisis. Soldiers from different regiments armed themselves and prepared to leave camp without permission. A few shots were fired and one officer was killed. The soldiers promised not to defect to the British but wanted action taken on their problems. Over half the men in the Pennsylvania line left the army only to later reenlist.

The "Flying Camps" were special battalions of Pennsylvania Line troops recruited to serve long periods of enlistments to protect the frontier against the Indians. Carlisle served as a munitions depot for the Americans during the war.

"...after arriving at Carlisle when I was for some time engaged in learning to be a drummer..." Daniel helped his Captain with recruitment at Carlisle. By the summer of 1783 the war was winding down with peace talks going on in Europe. There were still British troops stationed in America and small battles continued with the Tories.

"Whilst the treat was pending in Europe Capt Christie went to Philad to visit his wife and did not return. But when Orders were given for Discharging the troops he wrote to me to come to Phil. Where I would receive my discharge. Which I arranged to do. And had got 42 miles on the way when I engaged with the company of the Pa. Militia then on their way to Wyomming to quell the Yankee insurrection I proceeded to locust ridge with a horse load of provisions there the Advanced Guard lay. In the morning following the yankies commenced a brisk fire upon us in which I received a dangerous wound."

David wrote that the skirmish was between some people from New England and some from Pennsylvania and that he accidently got involved in the skirmish. A musket ball passed through his body and he was also slightly wounded in his right hand. After the skirmish a surgeon took care of David until he was able to travel. He left there and when to his mother's home to fully recover. He felt it was not worth going on to Philadelphia to get his discharge papers. He later got his discharge from Captain Christy in New York.

In 1786 David went to Philadelphia to the war office where he received a certificate for $40.00 and he later received a certificate for 200 acres of land for his services. Later he enlisted in Captain Joseph Ashton's company of Infantry to fight Indians.

In 1790 he enlisted in General Josiah Harmar's army. In October of that year they engaged the Indians and were defeated by a confederation of tribes led by Chief Little Turtle. One hundred and twenty militia men were killed. In the summer of 1792 David was discharged and returned to his home in New Jersey after serving nearly five years.

David's pension application was approved and he was to receive $80 a year for his service. Later that year he received a letter rejecting his claim for a pension. Letters from David and the government went back and forth. In the end his claim was rejected and the reason sent to him in writing,

"This claim rises upon an alleged service in the ranks as a common soldier in a marching regiment between the age of 11 & 13 years. As in was contrary to the regulations of the service to enlist one of his age, and as he could not have <u>discharged</u> the <u>duties of a soldier</u> at that period of life, he can have no claim to a gratuity found under the rendition of a soldiers service. This claim is therefore disallowed this paper placed on file."

Sources: 1. History of Miami County, Ohio by Witt Beers & Co. 2. Pension Papers for David Morris. 3. 1820 and 1840 Census. 4. Sons of the American Revolution Membership Application S9038.

****

<u>David Morris</u> age 14

David Morris was born on 24 August, 1762 in New Haven, Connecticut, and he died on 21 May, 1833 in Connecticut. He married a woman named Dinah. Thaddeus Ford stated in a in a letter in support of David's service that they served together sometime during April and June of 1777. This would mean that David enlisted a few months, probably in June, before he turned 15. David received a yearly pension of $39.34.

"In the summer of 1777, I entered the service of the United States as a substitute in Capt Samuel Peak's Company and went to Burwell's Farm in Milford near the Sea Shore. Our business was to keep guard, we had no skirmishes only one company was stationed there, and the names of the other officers I do not remember. I remained in the service a little more than three months when we were discharged."

"In the year of 1778 or 1779 I cannot certainly tell which, I was drafted about the 1st of June to go to Horse Neck. I was attached to Capt Smith's Company I believe in Col Wills Regt. I do not remember the names of the other officers by the Comp or Regt. Col Mead's was stationed at Horse Neck near us. We were employed daily in keeping guard, and in scouting parties. While we were there word came that two refuges had come up to a small house and that they were under arms. A detachment of me was immediately sent out, who went down and took them and brought them into camp, where they were tried and sentenced to receive thirty nine lashes. I saw the punishment inflicted, and immediately was detached as one of the guards to conduct them to the jail of Windham County. I was unwell at the time and when I arrived at Milford with the guard and prisoners I was unable to proceed further, and my brother went in my place. This was 3 or 4 days before my term of service expired."

"In the winter of 1780 I was a member of a sergeant's guard consisting of twelve men, and stationed at Burwell's Farm near the sea shore in Milford County. I remained there in the service of the United States three months and I think some longer. The guard was commanded by Sergeant Solomon Baldwin. I do not remember whether I enlisted or was drafted into this service. We were discharged in the month of March."

David enlisted again in March of 1782 for 4 months and marched to Horse Neck. During this period of time they were on guard and did some scouting. During this tour, *"We attacked the enemy at one time at Horse Neck and had action there which lasted for an hour or two, When the tide rising we were obliged to retreat, to being cut off."*

Sources: 1. U.S. Pensioners of 1818-1872. 2. Pension Papers S44542.

****

Joseph Kirk Munson age 14

Joseph Munson was born in 1765 in New Haven, Connecticut, and he died there on December 2, 1842. He married Lucinda Sears. He enlisted in the alarm of New Haven on 4 July, 1779 as a drummer in Captain Joseph Birdseye's Company and Colonel Samuel Whiting's Regiment of the Continental Militia.

Joseph answered the alarm on 4 July, 1779 that a force of British troops were going to land at New Haven. The next day several thousand British troops invaded and began destroying public stores, ships in the harbor, and seizing the town's weapons. There were even reports of the British soldiers slashing necklaces off women's necks. The local militia gathered and put up a fight but were not strong enough to repel the attack. Later, as the militia grew in size the British withdrew.

Sources: 1. Sons of the American Revolution Application. 2. Year Book of the Sons of the Revolution in the State of New York 1899. 3. D.A.R Lineage Book Vol LVI, 1906. 4. The British Invasion of New Haven, Connecticut.

****

Samuel Myers age 13

Samuel Myers was born on 20 July, 1765 in Harlem, New York, and he died on 30 January, 1859 in New York. He married Rebecca Waldron. Samuel served as an express rider for about 18 months. His father served as a blacksmith for the army. Samuel received a yearly pension of $90 for his service. Years later the government recognized the importance of the express rider and the dangers they faced, so they gave an express rider the pension of a Captain which increased Samuels's pension to $300 a year.

Express riders were under the quartermaster department, and the horses that Samuel rode were owned by the army. One of the men that served with Samuel said of him, *"he was considered smart on a horse."*

"I entered the service of the United States in the summer of 1778 under the command of Colonel Udney Hay at the quartermaster Department in the town of Fishkill, Genl Washington's headquarters and Rode as an express for some time until Col. Hugh's took command of said department and continued riding as an Express under said Hughes direction until said Department was broken up or removed, while I was under Hay and Hugh at Fishkill."

"I rode to many different places some of which are the following— to Danbury Connecticut with express to Major Stair, to Col. Wadsworth Granville to Judge Ward Fredericksburg to Major Campbell quartermaster at Peekskill, Nicholas Quackenbush quarter master at Albany, Genl Washington at West Point, Genl Green at New Windsor Genl McDougal at Peekskill Timothy Pickering at New Burghs quarter master, Genl Major Hill Hartford, Col Morehouse, at Dover."

"Continually on the move during my said term to George Clintons at Poughkeepsie governor of the State. I rode with Genl Lafayette from Fishkill to that Stormy at Hopewell a distance of about eight miles as a guide in the night time, also as a guide for Count Rochambeau from Col. Morehouse in Dover to Genl. Washington's headquarters at New Windsor—all the above named officers were personally know to me."

Count de Rochambeau was a French nobleman who had a major role in the Revolutionary War. He served as commander-in-chief of the French Expeditionary Force that helped fight the British in the colonies.

"After the said department Broke up I went into the commissary's store in Fishkill and served as an assistant scales man and in driving Cattle from Fishkill to Peekskill & West Point for about four months under Comfort and Joshua Sands, Army contractors."

Sources: 1. D.A.R. Lineage Book, Vol. 33. 2. Pension Papers S23331.

****

Reuben Nail age 14

Reuben Nail was born in 1761 in Amherst County, Virginia, and he died in April, 1847 in Tattnall, Georgia. He received a yearly pension of $40.

"I enlisted as a volunteer under Captain John Pullum in the spring of 1775 in the County of Wilkes in the State of Georgia and was first stationed at Petersburg on the Savannah River for the space of two months at the expiration of which we marched up Broad River about twenty five miles from thence and built the Garrisons called Nailes fort, and was stationed under Captain Joseph Nail where we had frequent skirmishes with the Indians, and remained there under the orders of Colonel John Dooley until the Capture of Charleston by the British when we were compelled to leave Fort Nail and we fled to South Carolina and joined Colonel Elijah Clarke at ninety six district of said State and after a period of two months we joined General Morgan at Grindal Shoals on Pacolet River, we then marched to the Cowpens where we had an engagement with Colonel Talton and defeated him and his army. We then were ordered by General Morgan to march as a guard over some prisoners to Island Ford on the Catawba River in the State of North Carolina we were then ordered down to Batey's Ford on the same River and put under the command of Major James Jackson at which place we engaged Lord Cornwallis for the space of teo hours when we were defeated -- we fled and attempted to join General Morgan but were prevented by the British and we succeeded in joining Col. Clarke and marched back to South Carolina where we had an engagement at Mapers Mill with Major Dunlap and succeeded in killing him and defeating his Army. We then marched with the prisoners back to North Carolina to the County of Rutherford we staid there four or five days and then marched back to Georgia and rendezvoused at Rightsborough in the County of Richmond (now Columbia County) and marched to Augusta and joined Colonel Clarke again, where we had several skirmishes with the British, Indians and Tories after Augusta was taken from the British we marched against the Cherokee Indians under Col. Clarke and had an engagement with them at the long swamp Town on the High Souer River where we defeated them after which we made a Treaty with them and returned home and received a verbal discharge by Colonel Clarke."

At the Battle of Cowpens, 17 January, 1781, Reuben was a member of one of the companies of Georgia militiamen under the command of Major Cunningham. They were placed in the 1st line facing the British and order to fire three volleys and then fall back and run to the place where the horses were being kept. This would bring the advancing British into a trap. The plan worked and led to the defeat of the British forces.

Sources: 1. Tombstone 2. Census 1830 & 1840. 3. U.S. Pensioners 1818-1872. 4. Pension Papers S31877.

****

Jason Newton age 14

Jason Newton was born on 7 January, 1762 in Lanesboro, Massachusetts, and he died in June of 1842 in Ira, Vermont. He married for a second time to Susannah on 30 August, 1796. He received a yearly pension of $86.88.

"In 1776 my uncle was drafted, to an alarm, and I took his place as a substitute and was attached to Capt. Low's Company, in Col. Simonds Regiment of Militia. We marched thru Bennington to Castleton where we remained a few weeks according to my recollection. I served over a month in this town."

"In 1778, in May, I enlisted into the army to fill a vacancy, & we marched to Fishkill and after passing muster went to White Plains, & was in Capt. Cleveland's Company I think, but I do not recollect the Col., in Learned's Brigade for a short time, and was soon after attached to Col. Morgan's Corps of Rifle Men, and was out with him through the summer & fall until we went into winter quarters at Poughkeepsie. I was discharged at West Point 1779, having served nine months."

"In May 1779 I again enlisted at Lanesboro, Mass into Maj. Cogswell's Company, Col. Vose's Reg't of the Massachusetts & served in said Regt as an orderly Corporal until March 1780, & was discharged at the Highland, State of N. York, below Fishkill, by Col. Vose."

"In 1781 I volunteered to substitute in Capt. Sam'l Clark in Col. Willett's Reg't. I was under Maj. Rowly's command. I served four months in said company as a Sergeant. We performed duty as scouts on the Mohawk River, & built a blockhouse at Fort Plain near. I further served about six weeks as a substitute for Sam'l Newton whilst he went home, in Capt. Miller's Company, in Col. Vose's Reg't, & a short time before I went on duty on the Mohawk River as above stated. I was at the Battle of Johnstown."

535

"The first time I saw Gen'l Washington he was walking on the walls of the Fort at Peekskill, dressed in a long blue __?__ with other officers in full dress. I asked "What plow jogger that was, with our officers". I was replied to with an oath, "Don't call him a plow jogger, it is Gen'l Washington."

The Battle of Johnstown was an American victory on 25 October, 1781. Colonel Willett and his patriot militiamen chased a raiding party of British soldiers, Tories, and Mohawk warriors. The Colonel caught the raiders at Johnstown just after noon. It was one of the last battles of the Revolutionary War.

Sources: 1. Tombstone 2. D.A.R. Lineage Book, Vol. 41. 3. Pension Papers W1985.

****

Moses Newton age 14

Moses Newton was born on 14 August, 1776, and he died in 1826 in Jefferson County, Georgia. He married Elizabeth Hudspeth c. 1793. He enlisted at 14 to serve with his older brother John. He was present for the attack on Savannah, taken prisoner at Charlestown, and was confined in the city but managed to escape. His brother died on a prison ship in Charleston harbor. His brother and one other soldier have a monument erected to them in Savannah.

According to the story John Newton and William Jasper led a group of soldiers and rescued a number of American prisoners from the British. The event did happen, but there was no mention of John Newton's role in it until years later. John was mentioned in the book *The Life of General Francis Marion* written by M. L. "Parson" Weems. General Peter Horry who took part in the campaigned gave the information of the rescue to Parson Weems. He, however, did not mention that John Newtown had a role. In fact, the General said that Newton was a thief and a villain and accused Parson Weems of exaggeration and fabrication. Weems did have a history of stretching the truth a bit. He was the one that wrote the story of George Washington and the Cherry Tree.

Sources: 1. D.A.R. Lineage Book, Vol. 36. 2. South Carolinians in the Revolution. 3. The Piedmont Chronicles by Marshall McCart.

****

Jonathan Nickerson age 14

Jonathan Nickerson was born in 1762 in Ridgefield, Connecticut, and he died on 21 December, 1840 in Cairo, New York. He married Philena Noble. He received a yearly pension of $112.

"In February or March 1776 I entered the service by enlistment in the Quarter Master's department in the town of Danbury, county of Fairfield, state of Connecticut as an artificer [artificers were skilled artisans and mechanics who kept military equipment in good working order, this could include carpenters, blacksmiths, sadlers, and etc.] *for the term of one year under Captain Clark, who kept the office of the department at that time. Maj Ezra Starr was assistant quarter master general. I worked the first part of the time building barracks and workshops, the latter part of the time at building wagons and carriages, ironing them, and at other smiths work. I was informed that the department was under the Continental establishment, and as there were large stores deposited in this town, there was a commissary and paymaster who acted in the department and gave me my rations and pay. The commissary's name I believe was Edwards, and the paymaster Everett. I quartered in the barracks and served out the full period of my enlistment."*

"I further say that in April 1777 I was informed that a British force had landed and was proceeding towards Danbury. I volunteered and proceeded to said Danbury, where I found the British in possession of the said and the stores. The stores were burnt by the British, consisting, as was said, of 1,800 bbls of beef and pork, 100 hhds of rim, 1,790 tents. I pursued the enemy under Genl Wooster to Ridgefield, where he (Genl W.) was wounded. We pursued them to their ships, when I returned."

British troops began a destruction of Danbury on 21 April, 1777. American Generals Wooster, Silliman, and Arnold led a force of 500 men in a surprise attack on the British as they began to withdraw. During the attack General Wooster was hit by a musket ball and later died from his injuries.

"In the month of Feb or March 1780 or 1781, then living in the town of Ridgefield, Fairfield County, state of Connecticut, a detachments of the militia was called out to proceed to the lines then kept at or near Horseneck, state of Connecticut. I volunteered my services with others, as was said, for thirty days. I was marched to Horseneck and there joined a company commanded by Capt. Richard Shute, name of lieutenant, Frisby, at first commanded by Col John Mead, afterwards by Col Canfield. After

being there a short time, I enlisted to serve nine months. A Sergeant Little had orders to recruit, whit whom I enlisted. Served in the same company & under the same officers."

"After I had served under my enlistment for two or three months my regiment was ordered on a scout by order as was said of General Waterbury. Marched to or near White Plains and made a halt as was supposed for the night. After calling out the guard there were ordered two scouts to be taken, consisting of one Sergeant, one corporal, and twelve privates each, and the say was, "Who will volunteer?" Sergeant Little, me and several others belonging to the same company volunteered. The Sergeant being unacquainted with the scout, he was directed to proceed. A pilot was procured for his party. This party of Sergeant Littles of which I was one, left the Regiment and proceeded down towards the British lines for several miles till very late at night. Made no discoveries. Put up at a house where the people had fled and left empty, between the lines, & refreshed themselves & staid till near day light. Then proceeded on towards the British lines kept, as they were informed at Frogs Neck."

"They proceeded down to within two or three miles of the British encampment when we discovered a number of horses in a meadow near a house-went to the house found two armed men watching the horses-disarmed & examined them-said they & five others turned out the horses to feed-did not know where the saddles & bridles were. Caught the eight horses & took the two men prisoners & commenced returning to the Regiment."

"Had gone about four miles on the return when we discovered a drove of cattle, 44 head, driven towards the British lines-held a council and concluded to attack them. Rushed upon them dismounted, & turned the horses loose into the drove. Several shots fired-& one of their men fell. The rest ran. None hurt on the American side & in the bustle-the two prisoners escaped. The man wounded had his thigh shot through and bone fractured-left him & requested a family nearby to take care of him. In the skirmish, the cattle and horses ran into a grove nearby-collected them together & proceeded on. Sent forward to find the regiment-found they had moved where we did not know."

"A little distance below and east of White Plain we were overtaken by a party of British horse 70 or 80 in number said to belong to Colonel Delanceys corps. The horse came upon the path full speed and were in the midst of the cattle and horses before the party could move through the drove calling out "Surrender you damned rebels surrender" Several of the party were struck down when I presented my musket to surrender instead of receiving it I was struck down to the ground my skull fractured and cut through the bone for four inches or more and while lying on the ground was rode over and struck four strokes in the head and several in the body with a cutlass. No one of the party escaped except the pilot (named Honam) to carry the news to camp one of the party after the British left was alive & was brought in by the inhabitants to the house where I was."

"After I had been stripped of my neckcloth and silver shoe buckles and my pockets searched by the British, they discovered that I was not dead for I had lain perfectly still before plunder. The captain then asked me to what troops I belonged and how many there were of the party which I told him. Capt said one had escaped and asked me if I could ride with them to the British lines. I answered I could not tell as I did not know how bad my wounds were. I was then put on the with them perhaps half or three quarters of a mile when I grew faint with the loss of blood and clung down by the horses mane in the road and told them I could go no further with them. Someone asked "shall we kill him?" The captain said "no let him alone he will die soon himself.""

"I asked capt to tell the people in the next house to come and bring me in. Said he would & presumed he did for in about half an hour a number of the inhabitants living between the lines came and carried me into the house of one Joseph Hart in a blanket-they also brought one more of the party belonging to the same company by the name of O'Brien who died in about an hour. The next morning two doctors belonging as they said to the Continental line having been down to the British lines with a flag of truce called and cleaned and dressed my wounds."

"I remained at Hart's for fourteen days-during that time had not been dressed, undressed or out of the couch on which I was first laid. Late in the night of the fourteenth day a detachment of British horse and foot commanded by the capt who made me prisoner came and put up to the house where I lay. He said it was more than he expected to find me alive and said something must be done or he would soon be off and fighting them again-Said he sound put me under parole and wrote two-each took one, the words of which I well remember. They were these "I Jonathan Nickerson, acknowledge myself a prisoner to the British army and do any thing prejudicial to the British army until exchanged and that I will come into the British lines as soon as able" signed by both-capt signed

"Frederick Williams Capt Commdr, Frog's Neck" The same morning the British marched off towards the American lines."

"About ten o'clock of the same day a party of militia commanded by capt Ichabod Doolittle of 25 or 30 men and a company of Continental troops commanded by Captain Fog belonging to New Hampshire it was said came to Harts house. I showed them my parole. They said they came purposely for me and I must go with them. They took and put me on a led horse and brought me to the American lines and from thence home to Ridgefield. I had not my own arms and accoutrements when taken and had to account for those taken. Soon after this I requested Ezra Nickerson to go to the lines and bring my equipments and clothing home and inquire of General Waterbury what I should do about answering my parole when able. Ezra told me that General Waterbury would see him and exchange soon and that I need not return for the remainder of my time."

Sources: 1. U.S. Pensioners 1818-1872. 2. Pension papers S28824.

****

Robert Nisbett age 12

Robert Nisbett was born in Ireland on 5 March, 1766, and he died after 1836 probably in Tennessee. His father came to this country when Robert was very young and they settled the Spartanburg District of South Carolina.

Robert states in his pension application of 1836, *"I served in various campaigns & various periods from the year 1778 to 1782. One of my old companions William Caldwell now resides in South Carolina...."* An enclosed statement shows services between those years amounting to 280 days as a Horseman & 82 days in the Infantry in the Companies of Captain John Berry, Colonel Andrew Berry, Captain John Collins, Captain John Nesbett & Captain Samuel Nisbett companies in the Regiment commanded by Colonel Roebuck.

Colonel Benjamin Roebuck commanded the Spartan Regiment in the militia. Captain Andrew Barry served as Captain of the 1st Spartan Regiment from 1777-1779 and the 2nd Regiment from 1779-1780. Captain John Nisbett served in the militia from 1780 to 1782 and was Robert's cousin. Captain Samuel Nisbett served from 1779 until 1780 and was Robert's uncle. Robert was probably able to join the militia at such a young age because of the influence of his relatives.

During Robert's time of service he would have taken part in the following battles: Ramsour's Mill 20 June, 1780, Musgrove's Mill 19 August, 1780, Kings Mountain 7 October, 1780, Cowpens 17 January, 1781, and Cunningham's Raid 1 August, 1781. Robert also served for two months as a spy under William Caldwell.

The Battle of Ramsour's Mill saw about 400 militia defeat 1,300 Loyalist militiamen. No regulars took part and many times it was neighbor against neighbor. Causalities were difficult to determine since no one was wearing uniforms. Because of a scarcity of ammunition the muskets were often used as clubs.

At the battle of Musgrove's Mill Robert Nisbett helped his 200 militiamen defeat nearly 500 hundred Loyalist militiamen. The patriots sent 20 men to attack the enemy, and then they pretended to retreat in confusion. The Loyalist's troops ran after them and into an ambush. After the battle Colonel Roebuck led his militiamen after Major Patrick Ferguson, a British officer who was recruiting men for the Tory militia.

On 6 October, 1780 Colonel Roebuck had caught up with Major Ferguson. The Colonel marched his South Carolina militiamen all night and faced Major Ferguson at the Battle of King's Mountain. Ferguson told the rebel militiamen to lay down their weapons or suffer the consequences. The patriots attacked and defeated a larger Loyalist force. Major Ferguson was killed in battle.

At the Battle of the Cowpens Robert and the rest of the South Carolina militia joined other militia groups and formed the center of the American line that was facing nearly 1,200 British regulars. Robert's militia company under the command of Colonel Roebuck was the first to be attacked by the British. Daniel Morgan, the American commander, knew that the militiamen had the reputation of running when facing a large number of British regulars. Morgan told the militiamen to fire two volleys at the British and then retreat and reform behind a hill. Behind the hill was Morgan's best troops, over 500 experienced troops. Morgan believed, correctly that the British would run after the retreating militiamen into the waiting trap. The cream of Cornwallis' army was completely defeated. The final battle at the end of the movie *The Patriot* drew inspiration from this battle. General Cornwallis present at the battle in the movie was not there.

Robert said in his application, *"I was with him (Roebuck) when he was wounded at Little River by the Tories & died of his wounds—I served 2 months as a spy with Caldwel (Captain William Caldwell)."*

Colonel Roebuck was wounded but did not die. He was captured and months later exchanged with other prisoners and he returned home. He died in 1788. This author could not find any information on Robert being a spy. It was not uncommon for young children to be used as spies. Robert moved to Tennessee around 1798.

Sources: 1. South Carolina Nisbets in Revolutionary War by Deborah Parks. 2. Roster of South Carolina Patriots in the American Revolution by Bobby Gilmer Moss. 3. Article in the Sunday Spartan Herald-Journal, Sunday Morning August 22, 1937. 4. A Guide to the Battles of the American Revolution by Theodore P. Savas and J. David Dameron. 5. Pension Application for Robert Nisbett S4617.

****

Gideon Noble age 13

Gideon Noble was born on 3 August, 1763 in Willington, Connecticut, and he died on 19 July, 1807 in Glastonbury, Connecticut. He married Lucy Wells on 18 February, 1787. His wife received a yearly widow's pension of $88.

Gideon enlisted as a fifer on 1 March, 1777 and served in captain Parker's Company in the 3rd Regiment under Colonel Comfort Sage. He later served under Colonel Webb. He fought at the Battle of Monmouth and suffered a ruptured Scrotum which left him disable and unable to serve.

Sources: 1. Connecticut Soldiers in the Revolutionary War. 2. Tombstone 3. D.A.R. Lineage Book, Vol. 23. 4. Pension Papers W24445.

****

Patrick Norris age 14

Patrick Norris was born in 1762 in Abbeville County, South Carolina, and he died on 12 February, 1840 in Greensboro, Alabama. He married Rachael Calhoun on 29 May, 1787 in South Carolina. He received a yearly pension of $80.

"At the age of about 14 years I served under Capt. Patrick Calhoun in Abbeville District South Carolina (in Nobles Fort) against the Cherokee Indians in 1776 for the space of 2 months. In 1780 after

Charlestown fell, volunteered under Col. Andrew Pickens Major Alex. Noble, and Capt. Robert Anderson in the month of November or December, I then marched and joined General Morgan who was encamped between Pacolet and Broad rivers, I was in the Battle of the Cow Pens with General Morgan, where Col. Tarleton was defeated."

At the Battle of Cowpens on 17 January, 1781 Patrick Norris was a militia rifleman in a brigade of four battalions of South Carolina Militia under the command of Colonel Andrew Pickens. He was place in the second line behind the main line of militia facing the British troops. Their job was to fire a couple of volleys and then retreat, while hoping to draw the British into a trap. The British fell for the ploy and as a result were defeated.

"I then went with Major Nobles (officer of the guard) who conducted the forge wagon with a considerable number of arms that were taken from Tarleton at his defeat to Gilbertstown in North Carolina, we then proceeded across the Catawba River and joined General Morgan & General Pickens where General Greene met us & held a council of war. Detachments were stationed at Sherrill's Ford, at Baties Ford and at Cowan's Ford, on the Catawba river, to intercept Lord Cornwallis, I was at Baties under General Pickens. General Davidson commanded at Cowan's Ford, where Cornwallis crossed the River. General Davidson was killed in the action."

Patrick took part in the Battle of Cowan's Ford on 1 February, 1781. As the British were crossing Catawba River, the militia opened fire. Once the British reached the river bank they formed a skirmish line and began to push the Americans back. Patrick makes note in his pension paper of General Davison being killed in action. The General was shot in his heart by a musket ball. That evening the Americans recovered his naked body, which had been robbed by British soldiers.

Superior British numbers and the fact that they had cannons forced to the Americans to flee during the battle. A patriot militiaman, Robert Henry wrote in a narrative of his retreat: *"I observed Beatty loading again; I ran down another load -- when I fired, he cried, 'it's time to run, Bob'"*. As Henry fled from the British, his friend, Beatty, was struck by British musket fire. He writes: *"I then ran at the top of my speed about one hundred yards".*

"I retreated with General Pickens on the road leading to Salisbury NC 6 miles, at Mrs. Tarrant's house, I was overtaken by Col.

Tarleton's Dragoons & light Infantry, an engagement ensued, in which some of both sides were killed, and some of the men taken prisoners. I then marched across the Yadkin, and above Moravian Town. The company was there dismissed for a few weeks & ordered to meet General Pickens at Baties' Ford, about the 25th of March, which order I obeyed; I then marched back to Spartanburg; in South Carolina under the officers before mentioned, and Col. McCall. I was then marched under Col. Clarke of Georgia & Col. McCall into the State of Georgia, on the Ogeechee where we had many skirmishes with Tories & Indians; many of the former were killed; the Indians were killed & Dispersed. I then marched back to Abbeville under Col. McCall who died of smallpox a few days after our return. I was constantly out, on scouting parties against the Tories & Indians for 3 or 4 weeks when General Greene besieged 96 a strong fortification commanded by Col. Cruger. I then joined General Greene, with Capt. Joseph Calhoun where I remained until the siege was raised, in consequence of a strong reinforcement under the command of Lord Rawdon coming to the besieged we returned and met 3 days afterwards near the place where Abbeville Court house now stands when we got there, we heard of a collection of Tories on long Cane Creek, a company of about 30 volunteered to go and disperse them; Capt. Joseph Calhoun was in command we came upon them unexpectedly, at daybreak, they fired upon us within 15 paces, when a shot killed my horse under me. William James Hutchison was killed by my side. The Tories fled in the swamp. I then went on a campaign with General Pickens, Major Capt. Noble & Capt. Calhoun, beyond Saluda river, down on the Congaree; below where Columbia now stands, in pursuit of the Tories; killing and dispersing them wherever we found them. We then returned and fell into the road leading from 96 to Orangeburg, behind the British, and had several skirmishes with their out guards, and took several prisoners. We then returned to the up country and I was constantly in the service of the United States against the Tories & Indians until about the last of October 1781. General Pickens, and Col. or General Clarke, undertook an expedition against the Cherokee Indians about this time. I marched with Col. Anderson & Capt. Calhoun into the State of Georgia, on its frontier, the first skirmish was at an Indian town called Sawta where we killed several and took some women & boys prisoners. We then went to another town Eschota 3 miles distant where we killed some and took others prisoners and both towns there was about 70 killed & taken prisoners. We burnt 2 other Towns about 15 miles distant. We then returned to Abbeville District; soon afterwards I was on a tour down on Edisto about a notorious Tory officer Bill Cunningham a blood stained desperado, we did not get *him; but we took others prisoners. On our return, the Tories intercepted our forage Wagons and killed John Pickens (a brother of General Pickens) and a few more; others were made prisoners, who were delivered to the Indians, and all massacred, by the Indians. We pursued them into the Nation, but were unable to recover our men. The same winter I was in 2 other expeditions against the Indians in one of which, I was in the frontiers of Georgia. After this General Greene called for aid from the up Counties when I volunteered again, as I always did, under cap Major Noble and marched from Abbeville to General Greene's Encampment near Charleston on Ashley River 2 miles below Bacon's Bridge. This was in April 1782. I remained there under General Greene until July from thence I returned to Abbeville and was on to expeditions again after the Indians. I was from time to time dismissed, but required to hold himself in readiness at all times and received no discharge until the end of the war."*

Sources: 1. Sons of the American Revolution Application. 2. South Carolina Marriage Index 1641-1965. 3. Pension Papers S15198. 4. Narrative of the Battle of Cowan's Ford-February 1st, 1781 by Robert Henry.

****

Mark Nowell age 14

Mark Nowell was born on 26 December, 1762 in York, Maine, and he died on 7 April, 1836 in North Berwick, Maine. He married Elizabeth Parker on 2 August, 1790 in York, Maine. He received a yearly pension of $82.

"I enlisted in the Navy of the United States in the year 1777 and served in the ship roll of thirty two guns under Thompson of Portsmouth N. Hampshire Captain. I served on board said ship [Raleigh] *about three months and was discharged on the petition of my widowed mother."*

"Soon after my discharge as aforesaid I shipped on board the ship "Minerva" of twenty guns commanded by Captain Grimes. I served on board this ship of the United States Navy about five months. Soon after I think in the year 1778 at Portsmouth I shipped on board the ship called the "Sullivan" of eighteen guns, Thomas Manning Captain. Soon after we sailed from Portsmouth harbor we fell in with an English ship bound to New York. After a battle of forty minutes we captured her and sent her back to Portsmouth then about two months afterward we fell in with a Kings packet called the Weymouth from Jamaica bound to London--after a battle of an hour we captured her there having been great slaughter on both sides."

"Soon after in the English channel were captured--I was put on board the captured brig. I was transferred to Ireland & remained a prisoner of Londonderry about one year, we were then transferred to the West Indies & soon after was exchanged. From the time & went on board the "Sullivan" until my return was about two years."

"In the year 1780 I enlisted in the Army of the United States for six months. I served the whole time in the first Massachusetts Regiment Commanded by Col. Joseph Voses and I was present at the execution of Major Andre the British Spy. I was discharged at West Point."

"Again in the year 1781 or 1782 I enlisted as a Soldier in the army of the United States for three years. I first went to West Point into Captain Hunt's light Infantry Company, Henry Jackson Colonel, in the ninth Massachusetts Regiment and served on that Company until after the peace."

"I was put into Capt White's Company of the fourth Regiment & in the company of light Infantry. I marched down to within fifteen or sixteen miles of New York to a place called East Chester & was then stationed to protect the inhabitants from being plundered by stragglers from New York—Toward the Autumn of 1783 I was revised to Capt Bawley's Company belonging to the only remaining Regiment of Massachusetts line. I was sent into New York to protect the city watch where I remained till the next Spring and then went by water to West Point and about July 1784 I was discharged."

Sources: 1. Sons of the American Revolution Application. 2. New England Historical & Genealogical Register Vol. 59, page 107. 3. Tombstone 4. Pension Papers S28827.

****

Jonathan Odgen age 14

Jonathan Odgen was born on 30 April, 1766 in Saratoga County, New York, and he died on 4 April, 1837 in Lawrence, Pennsylvania. He received a yearly pension of $31.66.

"In the year 1780 I resided in the town of Patent of Warren's Bush now the town of Florida Montgomery County in the month of May of that year I volunteered under Captain Jacob Gardenier. I was stationed at Fort Hunter and were employed in guarding buildings and making additions to said Fort and built two blockhouses. I was discharged the last of September having served four months and a half."

"In the year 1781 I volunteered under Capt Putman I rendezvoused at Fort Hunter, the last of April or the first of May where I was stationed to guard said Fort was discharged the last of September."

Sources: 1.The Bloodied Mohawk: The American Revolution in the Words of Fort Planks Defenders and Other Mohawk Valley Partisans by Kenneth D. Johnson. 2. Pension Papers S11154

****

Nathan Osborn age 13

Nathan Osborn was born on 14 July, 1763 in Woodbury, Connecticut, and he died on 21 November, 1845 in Windham, New York. He married Rebecca Mallory before 1796. He received a yearly pension of $80.

"On or about the fifteenth of July in the year 1776 enlisted in the Company Commanded by Captain Elkany Kimble for three months or more In the Continental wagon department carrying provisions and __?__ continental stores from the city of Hartford to Danbury and Fishkill at the expiration of the said time was discharged."

"I enlisted again at Woodbury of aforesaid sometime in the month of January 1777 according to the best of my remembrance In the Company Commanded by Captain Bissel Phelps In the wagon department Enlisted for Ten months I think for a longer time served until sometime in the month of December."

"In the same year was discharged at Litchfield Connecticut Enlisted again at Woodbury sometime about the month of January 1779 Enlisted in the company commanded by Captain Samuel Northam In the Continental wagon department and continued to serve under for 2 years during some parts of this time I was with General Knox drawing his common forage and provisions and baggage In New Jersey I think was discharged Woodbury."

"Previous to some of those Enlistments I served one month under Captain Ephraim Hinam drafted for one month or enlisted went to Middlesex in the county of Fairfield to guard the coast and then continued to serve out the said month and was discharged."

"I again Enlisted at the town of Waterbury New Haven County State aforesaid for two months under Captain Loomis went to the White Plains In the same wagon department carried the baggage for the French

army and there continued __?__ __?__ a number of days after my time Expired."

A Wagon Department was created in 1777 under the control of the Quartermaster's Department. Sometimes supplies had to be shipped over great distances and across rugged trail. At times the wagons were attacked by enemy troops or by highwaymen. There were never enough drivers and keeping them in the service was difficult. This is probably why they were willing to enlist 13 year old Nathan Osborn.

The life of a teamster was hard. Many times they drove the wagons for thirteen or fourteen hours a day in all kinds of weather. The roads were usually heavily rutted that would jar the spine of the driver. The enemy was always on the alert for these wagons. If the wagons were attacked it could result in death or prison for the driver.

Sources: 1. Census 1790, 1820, 1830, & 1840. 2. Connecticut Town Birth Records pre 1870. 3. U.S. Pensioners 1818-1872. 4. Pension Papers S11164.

****

John Osborne age 11

John Osborne was born on 16 March, 1769 in Massachusetts, and he died in 1842 in Michigan. He married Abigail McFarland. John enlisted as a marine in December 1780, and he received a monthly pension of $8.

"I was a marine in the revolutionary war with Great Britain in a frigate called the Deane and enlisted in the year 1780 December under Captain Nicholson and served in that station ten months."

Ads were placed in newspapers of Boston to encourage men to enlist aboard privateer ships. The ad below that ran in a newspaper may have been similar to the one that lured young John Osborne to go to sea.

An Invitation to all brave Seaman and Marines, who have an inclination to serve their Country and make their Fortunes

The grand Privateer ship DEANE, will Sail on a Cruise against the Enemies of the United States of America, by the 20th instant. The DEANE mounts thirty Carriage Guns, and is excellently well calculated for Attacks, Defense and Pursuit --- This therefore is to invite all those Jolly Fellows, who love their country, and want to make their fortunes at one Stroke, to repair immediately to the Rendezvous at the Head of His Excellency Governor Hancock's Wharf, where they will be received with a hearty Welcome by a Number of Brave Fellows there assembled, and treated with that excellent Liquor call'd GROG which is allow'd by all true Seamen, to be the LIQUOR OF LIFE

Sources: 1. America's Maritime Heritage by Eloise Engle and Arnold S. Lott. 2. Pension Papers S35022.

****

Edward Otis 14

Edward Otis was born on 6 April, 1766 in Lyme, Connecticut, and he died on 6 June, 1852 in LaPorte County, Indiana. He married Mary Merril in 1787 in Grange County, Vermont. He received a yearly pension of $36.66.

"I enlisted in the army of the United States in the year 1780 with Capt Lord and Served as a private in the first Regt. Continental line under the following named officers Col Stein and Capt Giles. I served at that time six months and had a regular discharge."

"In March 1781 in the Town of Lyme Connecticut I enlisted with Capt Ely as a private and entered the Service the company commanded by Capt Mills and served at that time five months."

"I was in an Engagement with the Enemy at Frogs Neck left the service."

Edward left the service because he was wounded at the battle of Frogs Neck. His great granddaughter wrote many years later, *"......carried an English bullet in his hip to his grave."*

After the war Edward moved to Vermont and got married. While living there he studied theology under the Reverend Fuller of the Baptist Church and became a minister. In 1809 he moved his family to Ohio and years later moved to Indiana. At the age of 75 he rode on horseback twelve hundred miles to his old home on Vermont and returned. He died in 1852, when on a trip his horse fell and injured him so serious that he later died from it.

The Battle of Frog's Neck is commonly called the Battle of Pell's Point fought on 18 October, 1776. In this battle a group of Americans ambushed a much larger British force and exchanged a few shots before they retreated. Edward was one of 13 Americans wounded.

Sources: 1. Lineage Book D.A.R. Vol. LXI, 1907. 2. Sons of the American Revolution Application. 3. U.S. Pensioners of 1835. 4. Pension Papers S32425.

****

William Overlin age 11

William Overlin was born on 12 December, 1765 and died on 24 December, 1837 in Spencer, Indiana. He married Letitia McKinney on 12 June, 1787 in Kentucky. She received his yearly pension of $80 and 200 acres of land.

"I enlisted in the Service of the United States in Westmoreland County & State of Pennsylvania in the company commanded by Captain Robert Beall of the 13th Virginia Regt commanded by Colonel John Gibson, and I was afterwards transferred to the 9th Virginia Regt and again transferred to the 7th Virginia Regt I was enlisted for a Fifer in which Situation I served part of the time I was in the Service, and then placed in the ranks, I enlisted in December in the year 1777 for during the War and I served till Some time in the Summer of 1783. I was honorably discharged at Pittsburgh Pennsylvania by General Irvin or Colonel Gibson which I do not recollect, but at the time I was discharged belonged to Captain Benjamin Biggs Company; I was in the Battle at German Town and I was in the baggage Guard at Battle of Brandywine."

William stated that he enlisted in December, 1777 and was present for the Battles of Brandywine and Germantown. Both of these battles were fought in the fall of 1776, so it is more likely that he really enlisted in December of 1776 which would make him at least 11 years old. Depending on what day in December he enlisted he could have still been 10 years old at enlistment. All three regiments he served in were present for both battles.

Sources: 1. Tombstone 2. Census 1830. 3. Kentucky Marriages 1802-1850. 4. U.S. Pensioners 1818-1850. 5. U.S. Headstone Applications for Military Veterans. 6. Pension Papers W9612.

****

James Owen age 13

James Owen was born on 6 August, 1762 in Dinwiddie, Virginia, and he died on 19 February, 1833 in Robertson, Tennessee. He married Anne Wilkes on 26 June, 1780 in Virginia. He received a yearly pension of $40.

Note: the person that took the statement of James was a very poor speller. Read with caution.

"I entered the Service of the united States under the following Nam'd officers and served as here in stated I was a substitute in my fathers place Valentine Owen in the latter part of May Seventeen hundred and Seventy Six and was placed under Capt William Snow to Charlestown South Carolina and there into Charlestown and staid there twenty or twenty five days and took the Oath of allegiance under Gov. Rutlge and from there to hadwells point and there we joined under Col. Orea and from there to Sulivans island and remained there until Sir Peter Parker came and attacked the fort and got completely drub'd and then back to hatwells point and from there to Charles town and there discharged in Charlestown and in the fall of seventeen hundred and seventy seven moved back to brunswic County State of Virginia then was called out in the millitia service and served about one month and returned home."

"I enlisted under Capt Joseph Greenhill and Charles Easley Lieutenant and from there we went to petersburg and ther we staid and Exercised our horses and under Barrel Stuvan and from there we went up to the long and there discharged."

"Then in the Spring one thousand seven hundred and Eighty one the militia was calld upon again then I substituted for Benjamin Lane then we march'd to Richard __?__ and there I listed under buck Stiff in the hors Service for the same term and served the tour out in dimwoody and brunswick and then discharged then in the fall of 1781."

"The militia was calld out agin out of brunswic County Virginia We marched out under Col Rich'd Eliot and Maj Thos Edmunds my Capt was Howel Eldridge we march'd down to Swans point upon James river will there we had a draft at Swans point and I drew to go to little york to face old Corn Wallis and we did face him and Col Merry Withers was our Col. We march'd from there up to Williamsburg and there got a discharge from under Col marry Withers hand."

Sources: 1. Sons of the American Revolution Application. 2. D.A.R. Patriot Index. 3. Virginia Marriages 1660-1800. 4. Pension Papers S5134.

****

William Owens age 13

William Owens was born in Frederick County, Virginia in 1762, and he died in Jackson County, Ohio in 1836. He married Nancy Creage (Craig) on 3 April, 1797. He enlisted as a volunteer at Fort Pitt in January of 1775 and served in Captain John Stephenson's Company and Colonel Muhlenberg's 8th Virginia Regiment.

"During this term of service I was in and fought at the engagement at Fort Moultrie, Sullivan's Island in South Carolina." This battle took place on 28 June, 1776 near Charleston, South Carolina. It resulted in an American victory.

"I marched from Pittsburg through Winchester Va to what was called the Big Bridge near Norfolk Virginia & remained there for a short time, and continued to march through North Carolina & South Carolina." When his enlistment was up William returned home.

In 1779 William joined the 9th Virginia Regiment as a substitute for William Batrup. He served under Captain Robert Beall and Colonels John Gibson and Richard Campbell. During this time he was engaged in garrison duty. For his three years of service he received a pension of $40.00 a year.

Sources: 1. 1820 & 1830 Census. 2. Abstract of Graves of Revolutionary Patriots. 3. The Official Roster of the Soldiers of the American Revolution Buried in Ohio. 4. DAR # A085365 5. U.S. Pensioners 1818-1872. 6. Tombstone of William Owens. 7. Pension Papers S4640. 8. Sons of the American Revolution Application. 9. West Virginia Marriage Index 1785-1971.

****

Asahel Packard age 13

Asahel Packard was born on 18 March, 1763 in Connecticut, and he died on 26 June, 1840 in Otsego, New York. He married Priscilla Williams on 26 March, 1812 in New York. It was probably a second marriage for both of them.

"I enlisted at Norwich in the State of Connecticut in the month of May 1776 in the company commanded by Capt. McCall in the Regiment commanded by Col. Rogers for the Term of one year. As a drummer. I marched with the said company to New London and from thence embarked on board of sloop in the month of August for New York but in the Sound

going we met a British Vessel of War which fired upon us and drove us back to New London."

"We went by land along the coast in Connecticut to Horse Neck on our way to New York but then learning that the British had taken New York we were ordered through various places in New York and Connecticut back to New London and to Norwich where we disbanded in the spring of the year 1777."

"Again in the month of May or June I was drafted into Capt Johnson's Company in Col Roger's Regt. and served about four months in guarding the Posts at New London."

"Again in the spring of 1780 I was called upon and rendered various services in Capt. Freemans Company in Col House's Regiment New Hampshire Militia."

"In April 1781 I enlisted and on the 1st of May was mustered and Joined Capt. Charles Nelson's Company in Col. Benjamin Wait's Regiment New Hampshire troops for the term of eight months as a Drummer."

Sources: 1. D.A.R. Lineage Book, Vol. 143. 2. Pension Papers W1312.

****

Hezekiah Packard age 13

Hezekiah Packard was born in Plymouth, Massachusetts on 6 December, 1762, and he died in Salem, Massachusetts on 25 April, 1849. He married Mary Spring in September of 1794.

He enlisted for five months in the summer of 1775 as a musician. He served under Colonel Paul Dudley Sargent of the 8th Massachusetts' Regiment. Hezekiah marched to Cambridge and served out his term.

"At or before the commencement of 1776, I enlisted for a year in the same capacity and was mustered under the same Regiment under Col. Sargent. Soon after the British left Boston, the Regiment was station'd there, & then for a time at Bunker Hill & afterwards at Castle William, now Fort Independence." Hezekiah served during the siege of Boston and the Battle of Bunker Hill. Castle William served as the main military base for the British. It was renamed Fort Independence in 1797.

"*By about June the regiment was ordered to New York & on reaching that place the Regiment was stationed _____*[could not read the next few words] *where I remained in service with the Regiment until the city was evacuated & then marched with the American Army to Harlem. I served out the full term of my enlistment but being sick in the hospital for several weeks. I returned to my native town Jan. 1777."*

Hezekiah served during the New York and New Jersey campaign which was a series of battles for control of New York City and New Jersey. The campaign lasted from July 1776 until March 1777. British gained control of New York City, and the Americans regained control of New Jersey. Just before his enlistment was up Hezekiah crossed the Delaware River with General Washington on the morning of 26 December, 1776 and defeated the Hessians at Trenton. After the battle, the Americans camped for the winter and Hezekiah went home.

"*In the summer of 1778 I again enlisted & volunteered for five months in the service of my country & I marched to Providence in the state of Rh. Island & was in a company commanded by Lieut. Watkins, as the company as for my recollection serves me was not full. It was not organized into a Regiment. I went with the division of the army ordered to the same place, in flat boats in the night & by moonshine to Newport, by direction as was understood of General Sullivan who, it was understood expected the aid of Counte de Grassa* [probably French Admiral d'Estaing] *in capturing that part of the Town occupied by the enemy. I serv'd the time for which I enlisted."*

General Sullivan had intended to work with the French fleet to assault Newport. Admiral d'Estaing's fleet was scattered by a storm, so he withdrew to Boston. Without the support of the French fleet, General Sullivan was then forced to retreat from a British force he could have defeated with the help of the French. Sullivan wrote a letter to the French Admiral protesting what he saw as treachery and cowardice on the Admiral's part. A few months after this, Hezekiah's enlistment was up and he returned home after serving a total of 2 years and 1 month. He was a veteran at the age of 15 and later awarded a yearly pension of $84.34.

After the war Hezekiah became a farmer and graduated from Harvard in 1787. The next year he was a principal of a grammar-school in Cambridge, and in 1793 he was an ordained pastor of the Unitarian Church in Chelmsford, Massachusetts.

Sources: 1. American Revolution: People and Perspectives, edited by Andrew Frank. 2. The Twentieth Century Biographical Dictionary of Notable Americans: Vol. IV. 3. Annals of the American Unitarian Pulpit by William Buell Sprague. 4. U.S. Newspaper Extractions from the Northeast, 1704-1930. 5. Society of Mayflower Descendants Applications, 1911-1929. 6. Sons of the American Revolution Application. 7. Pension Papers S20501. 8. U.S. Pension Roll of 1835.

****

Nehemiah Packard age 14

Nehemiah Packard was born on 27 October, 1760 in Bridgewater, Connecticut, and he died on 24 January, 1830 in Oakham, Massachusetts. He married Lucy Nye in 1780, and she received a yearly widow's pension of $61.88.

The following is a statement from James Conant, who was a fellow soldier to the pension bureau to support the service of Nehemiah Packard. *"I knew Nehemiah Packard and that said Nehemiah Packard served with me eight months in the Revolutionary War in the year 1775 in the same Regiment and Company. We were discharged the first day of January 1776."*

Nehemiah enlisted on 16 May, 1775 at the age of fourteen, and he served as a drummer in Captain Simeon Hazeltine's Company in Colonel Fellow's Regiment for eight months. This Regiment was formed as part of the right wing of the army under General Ward that besieged the British in Boston.

He marched with the Oakham Company on the Rhode Island alarm on 23 July, 1777. He served in a campaign to Bennington and Half Moon under Captain Edmund Hodges in Colonel Job Cushing's Regiment from 27 July to 29 August, 1777. For this campaign Nehemiah received 8 pounds from the town as pay.

He was also with Captain Cutler's Company which was raised in Western and Oakham and marched on 24 September, 1777 with Lieutenant Alexander Bothwell to join the army under General Gates. Nehemiah is also on a muster roll for May, 1778 dated at Valley Forge.

Sources: 1. Massachusetts Soldiers and Sailors in the Revolutionary War. 2. Soldiers of Oakham, Massachusetts, in the Revolutionary War by Henry Parks Wright. 3. Pension Papers W26833. 4. U.S. Pensioners 1818-1872.

****

William Paine age 14

William Paine was born on 9 April, 1762 either in Virginia or North Carolina, and he died in 1834 in Lawrence, Tennessee. He received a yearly pension of $20.

"I enlisted in the army of The United States in May 1776 in Pittsylvania County State of Virginia for <u>six months</u> under Captain Peter Perkins & Col. Christy in the ____ Regiment of the Virginia line that I served out my tour & was discharged in the Cherokee nation on Hiwassee River then North Carolina now Tennessee."

"I volunteered for one year under Captain William Underwood in Wilkes County State of North Carolina in the Spring of 1778 I served out my term & was discharged in the same County at the expiration of his term, I afterwards served as a minute man whenever I was needed, until the end of the War."

"I enlisted for six months in Virginia I marched against Lord Dunmore at pine top & drove him off & then marched against the Cherokees. In the second campaign I was engaged against the Tories & the only remarkable engagement I had was with the Tories at the Shallow Ford of the Adkin River, I was in the battle of <u>king's mountain</u> under the command of Colonel Cleveland."

The Battle of Shallow Ford took place on 14 October, 1780 in North Carolina. A company of 300 Tories were marching to join with British General Cornwallis. As they marched they plundered, killed, and burned the homes of the patriots. A group of 200 militiamen formed, including Edmund Paine, and waited for the Tories at the Yadkin River. As the Tories began to cross the river the patriots opened fire. The skirmish was short, and resulted in a patriot victory.

Edmund Paine was also at the Battle of Kings Mountain, which was fought on 7 October, 1780. He and 200 other Wilkes County militiamen were under the command of Colonel Benjamin Cleveland. According to legend, the Colonel had a great hunting horn that he blew to summon the militiamen into battle.

Sources: 1. One Heroic Hour at King's Mountain by Pat Alderman. 2. Wilkes County Bits and Pieces by Fay Byrd. 3. Twenty-four Hundred Tennessee Pensioners. 4. Pension Papers S3624.

****

Palmer age 11 or 12

What we know of this young boy was taken from the recollections of Captain Dring in 1824 and then published by H. B. Dawson in June, 1865. Dring served as a Masters-mate on board the privateer *Chance* when it was captured by the British in May of 1782. He was taken on board the prison ship *Jersey* along with the rest of the crew, including the young boy named Palmer.

Palmer was the first of the crew of the *Chance* to die, and he was the youngest of the crew. On the *Chance* Palmer served as a waiter to the officers and continued this duty on the prison ship. When the prisoners were taken aboard the *Jersey* they were inoculated for small pox and soon after Palmer became sick.

Dring said that during the night that Palmer died he held the boy during the lad's convulsions. When the boy died, Dring and another crewman sewed a blanket around the boy's body and the next morning the body was disposed of. Dring said the guards appeared to have no idea that the prisoners could feel any regard for each other.

Source: 1. American Prisoners of the Revolution by Danske Dandridge.

****

Abel Palmer age 14

Abel Palmer was born on 26 January, 1761 in Stonington, Connecticut, and he died on 8 April, 1813 in Otsego, New York. He married his cousin Lois Crow on 27 September, 1781 in Massachusetts. He enlisted in the 3rd company of the 6th Regiment of the Connecticut Militia under Colonel Samuel Parson. Abel served from 15 May, 1776 to 17 December, 1776. Later in his life he was an evangelical minister.

Sources: 1. Sons of the American Revolution Application. 2. Tombstone 3. D.A.R. Lineage Book, Vol. 54. 4. Obituary Connecticut Gazette Saturday June 19, 1813.

****

Daniel Palmer age 14

Daniel Palmer was born on 22 April, 1763 in Connecticut, and he died on 5 October, 1851 in Erie County, Pennsylvania. He received a yearly pension of $80.

"I entered the service of the United States under the following officers: Captain Story Lieut. Beckus Ensign Niles Col. Ely commanding officer at New London Connecticut. We marched from there to Dartmouth Rhode Island where I remained a few weeks and was marched back to New London and was from there marched to the White plains in the State of New York and remained there guarding the lines performing military duty and was discharged having served six months, this was the year 1777."

"Again in the summer of the year following served two months and was stationed at the fort near New London until discharged."

"Again in the summer of 1779 enlisted as a volunteer in the State of Connecticut in Capt. Robinsons Company and was transferred to Capt. Buels Company in Col. Dergys Regiment of the Connecticut Line. I was taken sick and was confined to my bed in the hospital for two or three months and joined the Regiment and crossed the Hudson river at Kings ferry and marched to the State of New Jersey near the town of Morristown when the Regiment went into winter quarters and remained there until my time had expired."

Daniel enlisted again as a substitute for Amos Dennison and served in Colonel Starrs Regiment in Springfield. After Daniel was discharged he served guarding the neighbor of Newark and then went into winter quarters. In 1781 he spent six months as a privateer on the *Hancock*.

Daniel's first pension application was rejected, because it stated that he was a deserter in 1782. He sent in a supplement to his service record to explain what happened: *"If I mistake not it was soon after the Burning of New London* [6 September, 1781] *that I engaged to serve and remained in the service until I think the next May or June. At this enlistment I engaged to serve for the period of three years, while the detachment to the Army to which I belonged was laying at Dobb's Ferry on the Hudson river I think about twenty miles from New York. One night by permission of the sentry I passed out of the camp for the purpose of obtaining some provisions as there was a lack in the camp at that time. After receiving the counter sign from Oliver Roure the sentry on duty I went to a house occupied by a Dutchman a short distance from the camp and saw a light burning. I went into the house and begged for provisions which I received and while eating a man followed by two or three others rushed into the room and seized me and told me that I was a prisoner. I asked him what I was a prisoner for, what I had down. He said nothing that I must go to New York and go into the British service to the regiment called the "Kings American light Dragoons."*

There were numerous Loyalists Regiments in the American Revolution. The King's American Regiment was led by Colonel Edmund Fanning. It was one of the most distinguished Loyalist units and was made up mostly of New Yorkers.

"This was marked on their caps. The men wanted me to enlist in the British service and offered two Guinee's bounty. I refused to enlist, I was taken before the General for examination and sent onto the prison ship. I made by escape from the prison ship by swimming to Blackman's Island from there I escaped to long Island where I was recaptured. I escaped a second time and went to Hampstead Plains on Long Island to the house of Peter Smith."

"I think he was a republican. He gave me a change of clothes. I laid off my soldiers coat. After searing me not to inform the British of his harboring me allured me to remain. I was at Smiths from the time I went there until peace was made which I think was about six months. I had no opportunity of getting off the Island it was closely watched by the British and escape was impossible."

Sources: 1. D.A.R. Lineage Book, Vol. 102. 2. Pension Papers S7298. 3. Tories Fighting for the King in America's First Civil War by Thomas B. Allen.

****

Isaac Parker age 14

Isaac Parker was born on 22 August, 1760 in Westford, Connecticut, and he died on 27 August in Bryon, New York. He married (1) Bridget Fletcher on 7 February, 1785 and (2) Catherine Wilson. He was a drummer in Captain Timothy Underwood's Company and William Prescott's Regiment, which marched from Westford on 19 April, 1775. He enlisted again in William Prescott's Regiment on 24 May, 1775 for 69 days. He served for 3 months in captain Reuben Butterfield's Company. Isaac enlisted in Captain Joshua Parker's Company, which was Colonel John Robinson's Regiment on 5 July, 1777.

He may have served at the Battle of Bunker Hill and in campaigns in Rhode Island and Connecticut in 1777. His father and three brothers also served in the Revolution.

Sources: 1. Sons of the American Revolution Application. 2. Year Book of the Sons of the American Revolution in the State of New York 1899.

****

Joseph Parker age 14

Joseph Parker was born on 9 September, 1762 in Methuen, Massachusetts, and he died on 22 September, 1828 in Henderson, New York. He married Abigail "Nabby" Whittier on 2 April, 1792 in Massachusetts. He enlisted in the militia one month before he turned fifteen years old. He received a monthly pension of $8.

"Sometime in the month of August 1777 I enlisted as a private in Captain Whittiers [this may have been Joseph's future father-in-law] *and was discharged the 8 day of December 1777."*

Joseph enlisted several more times over the next couple of years for short tours of duty. He was at the battle where Burgoyne surrendered and several small skirmishes.

Sources: 1. D.A.R. Lineage Book, Vol. 70. 2. Pension Papers S43796.

****

Israel Pearce age 14 (African American)

Israel Pearce was born in 1764 in Tyrrell County, North Carolina. He received a yearly pension of $88 for his service in the navy and army. Israel served aboard the *Caswell*, which in the spring of 1778 the North Carolina legislature purchased the ship from Virginia. That would make Israel's age of enlistment at 14. In the 1830 census for North Carolina Israel is listed as a "Free Colored Man"

The ship *Caswell* was purchased by North Carolina from Virginia to provide a joint defense of the Ocracoke Inlet, which was important for both states to maintain control of. The *Caswell* was commanded by Captain Willis Wilson and had a crew of one hundred and seventy men. During its time of service it laid off Ocracoke bar until it sunk there in 1779.

"I enlisted in the Naval Service of the United States, on board of the Ship Caswell Capt Wilson, in the early part of the War of the Revolution, but does not at this day recollect the exact period of my enlistment or of my discharges from said ship—as I am entirely an unlettered man & have no memorandums or writings whereby to refresh my recollection: but I state that the said ship was a Guard ship, mounting thirty six Carriage Guns and was stationed off Ocracok and that the period of my service on board of her under my enlistment was about twelve months."

"I furthermore state, that soon after my discharge from the said Ship, I enlisted in the Army of the United States (but does not recollect the exact date of his enlistment) under Captain Hall, and was afterwards transferred into the Company under the Command of Captain Goodman in the Regiment Commanded by Colo. Mebane under whom he fought at the Battle of Eutaw Spring, in which Battle my Captain was killed--and with my said Colo. was at the Siege of Charleston & at Gates' defeat, at the Hanging Rock & also at Polaskis defeat at Savannah. I do not at this day recollect the dates of any of my enlistments in the Army, nor the date of my discharge from the service, but state that that under my several successive enlistments my whole period of service in the Army was about five years. I was discharged at the High hills of Santee about six months before peace. My first enlistment was in the County of Tyrrell & state of North Carolina, under the Captain & Colo aforesaid, on the Continental establishment. Genl. Green Commander in Chief--and I was honorably discharged from the service at the place & time aforesaid."

The following statement was added to his pension application.

"He has not made an earlier application for a Pension – viz that he resides & has for a great many years resided in a thinly settled and uneducated part of the County and was not aware until within two or three years past, that any provision had been made for the relief of indigent Revolutionary soldiers & sailors:--and since he heard of it he has never been able until lately to find one of his associates in Arms by whom to establish his services or any part of them – and can only do so now by the Deposition of his old Comrade James Willie of Washington County in this state--and by his own oath."

Sources: 1. 1830 Census. 2. The Navy of the American Revolution, Its Administration, Its Policy, and Its Achievements by Charles Oscar Paullin, M.D., 1906. 3. Pension Papers S3660.

****

Martin Pease age 11

Martin Pease was born on 8 July, 1765 in Edgartown, Massachusetts, and he died on 22 January, 1852 in Clermont County, Ohio. He married Deborah Stewart on 27 May, 1795. In 1776 at the age of 11 he was at sea on a patriot ship and was captured by the British and taken to New York. After the war he commanded a whaling and merchant ship, and spent almost 20 years at sea.

In 1814 he moved his family to Ohio and settled on a 200 acre plot with five other Massachusetts families. He called the plot of land "Yankee Settlement." According to family lore, he was in France during the French Revolution, where he witnessed the execution of Louis XVI.

Sources: 1. Clermont County Genealogical Society, Record of Clermont's Illustrious Heroes Who Fought the British in 1776. 2. Census 1820, 1830, 1840, and 1850. 3. Tombstone 4. Official Roster of the Soldiers of the American Revolution Buried in the State of Ohio.

****

Abraham Peavy age 14

Abraham Peavy was born on 8 May, 1765 in Orange County, North Carolina, and he died on 15 May, 1837 in Butler County, Alabama. He married Lydia Seale on 6 September, 1784 in Georgia. She received a yearly widow's pension of $80.

"I was born the 8th of May in the year 1765 in Orange County North Carolina there is where volunteered in the year 79 or about that time under Captain Ned Guinn and Lieutenant William Guinn--Major Gholson, Colo O'Neal and General John Butler. I was excepted by the Captain aforesaid in the place or as a substitute for his father--and served for more than 2 years and when I was not in active service I was kept as a guard at the public Store House near Colonel O'Neal's in the said County -- I cannot recollect the exact time I was in service. My first march was down to Cox's mills in Chatham County North Carolina in search of Colonel Famin and his party Colo O'Neal commanded that march gone several weeks & returned to Orange. I was a number of skirmishes of slight character which I think it would be unnecessary to relate and I was discharged sometime after Wallace was taken not until the Tories all had ceased by Captain Guinn at the same County."

Sources: 1. U.S. Pensioners 1818-1872. 2. Pension Papers W10880.

****

Benjamin Peck age 10

Benjamin Peck was born on 11 April, 1770 in Massachusetts. He enlisted in 1780 as a drummer in Captain Jeremiah Putman's Company and Colonel John Lamb's 2nd Artillery Regiment. This regiment included 12 artillery companies from New York, Connecticut, and Pennsylvania. During the enlistment of Benjamin the regiment was at West Point. He is on the West Point muster rolls of February, March, and April, 1781 at West Point. Benjamin died in the poor house in 1844.

Sources: 1. Report of Daughters of the American Revolution Vol. 3. 2. Massachusetts Soldiers and Sailors in the Revolutionary War. 3. Massachusetts Town and Vital Records 1620-1988. 4. "The Music of the Army..." An Abbreviated Study of the Ages of Musicians in the Continental Army, by John U. Rees. Originally published in The Brigade Dispatch Vol. XXIV, No. 4, autumn 1993.

****

Peter Peck age 14

Peter Peck was born in 1766 in Rowan County, North Carolina, and he died on 10 April, 1851 in Claiborne County, Tennessee. His Wife Mary received a yearly widow's pension of $30.

"Sometime in the spring of 1780 I Resided in Roan County in the State of North Carolina where I was drafted to perform a 3 months Tour of duty and I belonged to Company commanded by Captain Lop which said company was attached to the Regiment commanded by Colonel Lock and we then marched to various places through the Country and then we marched to Salisbury and after my time of Service had Expired I received my discharge from Captain Lop."

"I then volunteered, my services in the Army of the United States for the Term of 9 months under the same Captain in the same Colonel and we then marched to the Fork of the ___?__ and from thence we marched to Abbott's Creek and from thence to Salisbury and various other places in search of the Tories and we took a great many of them prisoners and conveyed them to Salisbury and delivered them to Captain the Yarburry we marched into the County of Randolph and Mecklenburg County in the said State in pursuit of the Tories and took a great many more prisoners in the last above mentioned campaign I was in Engagement with the British and I had several skirmishes with the Tories did not receive any wounds while I was in the Army. He states he thinks it was sometime in the month of November 1781 that his time of service expired and that he then received his discharge from Captain Lop."

"I again volunteered my services in the Army of the United States for the term of 6 months under Capt Carr and I did not bear arms but I drove one of the Forage Waggons which supplied the Army which were then stationed at Salisbury and I performed said duty for the term of 6 months."

"I am a very poor man and very infirm and decrepit and I have no means by which I can be get a living except by labor and my constitution is so much impaired that I am scarcely able to perform any language and my wife is also very infirm so much so that she cannot contribute much towards a living."

"I enlisted a private in Rowan County North Carolina some time in February or March in the year 1782 or 83 under Captain Carr and Lieutenant Rickart for 5 years was marched against the Indians to where Knoxville in East Tennessee now stands from thence to Kentucky on the Ohio River near where Louisville now in was stationed the greater part my time there had some light skirmishes with the Indians and wounded one night while on guard in my right leg by an Indian from a canoe on the River the Main part of the Army was stationed further up the River I think I belonged to the 6th Regiment edit was commanded by Colonel or General __ Clark. I deem it unnecessary to give further details of his service as I supposes it is on the rolls of the department, but I was honorably discharged at the end of 5 years by his Captain or Lieutenant not now recollected which. That his discharge was wet & destroyed in crossing the Holston River. The true and only reason he did not make a statement of his regular service in his first declaration was the advice of his attorney to the contrary."

Sources: 1. U.S. Pension Roll of 1835. 2. Census 1840 & 1850. 3. Abstract of Pensions of North Carolina Soldiers of the Revolution, Vol 14. 4. Pension Papers W26296.

****

David Pembrook age 13

David Pembrook was born on 19 September, 1765 in Ulster County, New York, and he died on 2 December, 1836 in Gorham, New York. He married Leah and they had one child Martha. David enlisted in February of 1779, which was ten months before his fourteenth birthday. He received a yearly pension of $105, plus 500 acres of land in New York for his service. His wife died 18 months before his death, so his daughter applied for and received his pension in the amount of $100 a year.

He enlisted with his father David Pembrook (pension S43821) and his 10 year old brother James. David Jr. stated in a form letter found in his pension file that he was rendered incapable of performing the duty of a soldier, due to a wound and a loss of two toes on his left foot. This occurred during the War of 1812, as a member of the 5th Regiment.

"I enlisted with the army of the United States in the year 1779 with Captain Andrew Moody in Colonel John Lambs Regiment of New York Artillery, under General Knox, at West Point. It was on 1st February 1779 I enlisted as a Fifer in Captain Moody's company then went into the Ranks as a private after serving on this station about a year and a half Captain Moody was ordered to take his company to Fort __?__ on the Mohawk river, and I went with said company, and served there one year when Captain Stewart of Colonel Crane's Regiment came there and relieved us when we marched back to Albany and went from there to West Point, and there did duty—during this time Colonel Lamb went to the South, and was at the taking of Cornwallis as I was informed, and when Colonel Lamb returned we were joined to his Regiment again and remained in this Regiment until the 9th June 1783 when I was discharged."

"I was in one battle at Johnstown, where Colonel Willett commanded—when I entered the service at West Point in 1779 my Father David Pembrook and by brother James Pembrook belonged to the same company in which I enlisted under captain Moody (and whether any of them be now living, I do not know.)"

The Battle of Johnstown occurred on 25 October, 1781. The American militiamen engaged a raiding party of British soldiers near Johnstown. There were a series of skirmishes that took place and eventually the Americans were victorious. The news of the defeat of the British at Yorktown was received by the Americans after their victory at Johnstown.

Sources: 1. The Music of the Army, an Abbreviated Study of the Ages of Musicians in the Continental Army by John U. Rees, Originally Published in the Brigade Dispatch Vol. XXV, No. 2-12. 2. New York in the Revolution as Colony and State. 3. New York Pensioners 1835. 4. Pension Papers S22857.

****

James Pembrook age 10

James Pembrook was born in 1767 in Ulster County, New York. He enlisted as a drummer at West Point with his father and brother David. He served in Colonel Lamb's 2nd Regiment of New York Artillery. He was captured by the British on 6 October, 1777 and made his escape from them on 20 December, 1778. This could have happen at the Battle of Fort Montgomery on 6 October, 1777. Colonel Lamb had 100 men at this fort during the battle. It was located not far from West Point. The following is from his brother, David Pembrook's pension file S22857:

"I was in one battle at Johnstown, where Colonel Willett commanded--when I entered the service at West Point in 1779 my Father David Pembrook and by brother James Pembrook belonged to the same company in which I enlisted under captain Moody (and whether any of them be now living, I do not know.)" The story of David Pembrook is found in this book under the 13 year old soldiers.

Sources: 1.The Music of the Army, an Abbreviated Study of the Ages of Musicians in the Continental Army by John U. Rees, Originally Published in the Brigade Dispatch Vol. XXV, No. 2-12. 2. New York in the Revolution as Colony and State.

****

Lemuel Peterson age 12

Lemuel Peterson was born on 22 February, 1764 in Cumberland County, New Jersey, and he died in 1845 in Delaware County, Indiana. His pension was rejected.

"I left my home at my fathers home in Cumberland County New Jersey and on the 1st of March 1777 went on board a privateer vessel as a volunteer while said vessel lay in Little Egg Harbour commanded by Captain Samuel Seers to serve as a private. The name of the vessel by reason of the distance of time since escaped my youth at the time and age and consequence defect of memory at this time is not recollected but it cruised off between New York and Charleston to and from these places several times."

"We captured a brig south of the mouth of the Delaware River near cape Henlopen light house [it was destroyed by storm in 1925] *laden with Jamaica Spirits, wine, & Lemons being and arrived __?__ of eleven guns the name from the reasons as above mentioned in regard to the vessel on which I was a volunteer is not recollected. In attempting to take the brig we killed 10 or 11 persons had a hard fight in which she was by us dismasted & surrender with nine prisoners on board. This brig was under British colors. We towed her up Delaware River and thence Morris River in the State of New Jersey Cumberland County at Bells landing where she was considered by the proper authority as a lawful prize was __?__ and the proceeds distributed among said crew and they then disbanded on the 16th of June. When Samuel Seers was made captain of a new vessel just then being launched at Bells landing before __?__ and called the Morning Star which he took a cruise from which on his return in July he was chosen Colonel of the New Jersey militia under General Rose with Benjamin Thompson as Captain and Hans Peterson Lieutenant under him. I*

remained at my fathers house & residence as above described from the time of my release from the privateer in June above mentioned. I then on the first of August was drafted to serve under the last above mentioned officers and was first quartered at Bells landing above described and from thence under said officers was ordered to Mount Holly in New Jersey where we were stationed until after the 4th of July when I received a written discharge from Captain Thompson before mentioned. The British army in its passage from Philadelphia to New York passed through New Jersey while I was at Mount Holly but the soldiers at that place were not ordered at other portions of the New Jersey Militia to impede or intercept their march."

Some researchers believe that Lemuel left his wife and children in Delaware when he went west in 1803 to Ohio. He lived there for a few years, and then he moved to Indian Territory. He supposedly married an Indian named Ann "Whitehead" Dobbs, but there is no record to prove or disprove this. She was supposed to have been scalped and killed by her brothers who were upset with her marrying a white man.

Sources: 1. Revolutionary War Soldiers Buried in Delaware County Indiana by D.A.R. 2. Tombstone 3. Pension Papers R21900.

****

Gideon Petit age 13

Gideon Petit was born in Craven, North Carolina in 1765, and he died in 1842 in Obion, Tennessee. For his service he received a pension of $8.00 a month. At the time of his death he owned one slave.

He served as a fifer and when he was discharged three years later as a fife Major. Besides playing music that would help issue battle commands, a fife Major had to be a person of honesty because he would carry officer's letters to and from the post. Sometimes the letter would contain money. For this duty the fife Major might receive a penny for each letter he handled. He would also be expected to train the younger fifers in their duties. His appearance should be neat, since he would strut at the head of the other fifers who he commanded.

As the war continued the numbers of younger musicians declined. Beginning in 1777 the army began enlisting men for three years or the duration of the war. Many would trade the fife for a musket as they got older. As regiments consolidated, the need for musicians declined and also less young boys enlisted as the war dragged on.

"I enlisted on the 11th of April 1777 for 3 years with Jonathan Loomis Surgeon of the 8th North Carolina Regiment and was put into Captain Robert Raiford's company in the 8th North Carolina Continental Regiment commanded by Colonel Armstrong on the 11th of April 1780." Gideon served at the battles of Brandywine, Germantown, and Stono.

Sources: 1. The New Grove Dictionary of Music and Musicians, ed. Stanley Sadie, Vol. 8. 2. "The Music of the Army..." An Abbreviated Study of the Ages of Musicians in the Continental Army, by John U. Rees. Originally published in The Brigade Dispatch Vol. XXIV, No. 4, autumn 1993. 3. Census of 1790, 1810, 1830, & 1840. 4. North Carolina and Tennessee, Revolutionary War Land Warrants, 1783-1843. 5. Roster of Soldiers from North Carolina in the American Revolution, edited by Gertrude May (Sloan) May. 6. Pension Papers S41950.

****

Henry Pettit age 14

Henry Pettit was born on 22 January, 1763 in Essex County, New Jersey, and he died 12 October, 1838 in Rutherford County, North Carolina. He married Anna Pool on 7 February, 1783 in Spartanburg, South Carolina. Anna received a yearly widow's pension of $43.33.

"I entered the service of the United States under the following named officers and served as herein stated. To the best of my Recollection in the Year 1776 my Father was then living in South Carolina 96--now Spartanburg District on Lawson's fork of Pacolet we was __?__ on to build a fort known as Wofford's fort. I then volunteered myself in the place of my Father who was at Work on this fort. Col. William Wofford Commanded the fort. I was under the command of Capt. James Wood. This Service began about the 1st of June and lasted to the 1st of November. About that time the families generally went home. This Service was principally in endeavoring to keep the Tories & Indians from embodying. We had many a Chase after them."

"My next service was when Ferguson & Dunlap marched their Army through South Carolina into North Carolina. On their passage they was met by the Americans at Brown Oats fields. There were Several Killed. I was sent from that place with an express to Col. McDowell to Reinforce us. We pursued them after being reinforced to Musgrove's Mill on the Inoree River where we overtook them and defeated them In this service I was under Capt. James Smith, Col. John Thomas Commanded us. All returned home."

Major Patrick Ferguson was a Scottish officer in the British Army during the Revolution. According to legend, just before the Battle of Brandywine, he had the chance to shoot a high ranking American officer. He chose not to because it would mean shooting the man in the back. He was later told that General George Washington had been in the area during that time. Some historians believe that the man was not Washington but Count Casimir Pulaski.

Major James Dunlop of the Queen's Rangers was with Major Ferguson in South Carolina at this time, which Henry refers to in his pension application. Major Dunlop waged a harsh brutal style of warfare. The Americans held a deep hatred for both of these men.

"I was then placed under Capt. Henry Whitaker. We scouted through the upper parts of S. Carolina to the borders of North Carolina. We took a good many Tory prisoners on our arrival in the Neighborhood we were ordered on to meet the Main Army at Shiers Ferry under Genl. Sumter. When we came to that place they were in sight of us that is the British & Tories. There was some firing across the River. From that post we was ordered to Black Stock's where we had a Severe Battle. Genl. Sumter was wounded at that place. The volunteer part of the Army pursued after them under Col. Lacey to the mouth of Tyger River where we overtook a party and had an engagement. We went on down the River some Distance and crossed to the east side. In passing up the country we took a good many prisoners. We came on to the Main Army and gave the prisoners to them. I was then under Capt Trammell and Dickerson. We were ordered on then to join General Morgan. We joined him at the Grindal Shoals on Pacolet. We scouted on and met him again at Thicketty. We then kept with the Army until after the Battle of Cowpens. In that Battle I was wounded in my thigh which injured me very much at the time."

At the Battle of Blackstock's Farm on 20 November, 1780 Henry Pettit was among 1,000 militiamen under the command of General Sumter. Two days earlier they had taken Tarleton's British Legion of Dragoons by surprise at the Broad River. The British were bathing and watering their horses when the American fired upon them. Tarleton was outnumbered, but since he had never been defeated he later engaged the militia in a battle. It was at this battle at Blackstock's farm that he suffered his first defeat.

About two months later Henry and the South Carolina Militia faced Tarleton again at the Battle of Cowpens. Once again Tarleton was defeated and his dragoons had an 86 percent casualty rate which wiped them out as a fighting force.

"As soon as I was able I then enlisted in the Ten Month Service under Capt. William Smith, first under Col. Thomas then under the command of Col. Middleton. We was marched to the Country below Columbia kept in continual movements from one point to another from Savannah to the Congaree and near to Charleston. We had many Scrimmages with the Spys & foraging parties. Sometimes they had the better of us and sometimes we paid them back in their own houses. We joined the main Army some few day before the Battle of Eutaw Springs. I was placed as one of the Guard of the Baggage Waggons on that day. If I could have had a horse, I would have been in the battle in preference of my situation. After the Battle, we was ordered up the Country turned to Orangeburg. We had a Scrimmage near Orangeburg with some of them Rangers. We had to give the Ground to them we met another party above Orangeburg where we had an engagement. They fled to the Swamp we pursued them they escaped to Charleston about that time, the British began to leave their up Country posts and take to their strong hold in Charleston. We followed on after them occasionally Annoying them to the Four Holes where we made a stand for a few weeks to Search the Swamps between the Four Holes & Cypress. From there we was at the Round O then on to near Bacon's Bridge. From there to head Quarters. On the Congaree (before we went to Orangeburg we heard of the capitulation of Cornwallis) and our time that we enlisted for was expired and we returned home."

"In fact, for me to undertake to give in detail my service during the Revolutionary War is not in my power but one thing I do well know that from sometime of the Summer 1776--to the end of the War I was engaged in the defense of my Country. I then lived in the hottest part of the Tory Country on the Indian Boundary and a great place for the British to assemble. We that belonged to the Liberty party were compelled to be in readiness at all times. We were hunted after as for the Doe in the Woods. I am Wounded. I am Old. I am Infirm and in want of something to sustain me for the services I rendered my Country in the Revolutionary War."

The author has included the will of Henry Pettit, because it gave a good description of the disbursement of slaves during that time period.

"In the name of God Amen I Henry Pettit Sen of the County of Rutherford and State of North Carolina Being of Sound and perfect mind and memory Blessed be God do this twenty third day of August in the year of our Lord one thousand eight hundred and thirty eight make and publish this my Last will and testament in manner following. That is to say first all *my just debts Be paid. 2nd I leave my wife Anna Pettit my four Slaves also all my house hold and kitchen furniture also one horse and my Waggon & harnace also all my stock of cattle hogs and sheep during her life time or widowhood. At the death of my wife Anna Pettit I give and bequeth to my son Henry Pettit my negro Boy What commomally called Pompey; also to my son John Pettit I give and bequeath one negro Boy called Green; also all the farming tools. What property that remains at the Decease of my wife that is not herein otherwise disposed of Is to Be sold at public Sale on a twelve monthly credit out of the proceeds my daughter Elizabeth Mooney is to have twenty five dollars and also my daughter Hannah McDaniel is to have fifteen dollars the Remains is to Be Equally divided Between all my daughters; And I hereby make and ordain my son John Pettit Executor of this my Last will and testament and in case of death or inability William Taney In witnefs whereof I the said Henry Pettit have to this my Last will and testament set my hand and seal the day and year above written."*

Sources: 1. Tombstone 2. U.S. Pensioners 1818-1872 3. Will of Henry Pettit. 4. Pension Papers W5528.

****

Irby Phillips age 14

Irby Phillips was born on 20 May, 1762 in Richmond, Virginia, and he died on 10 August, 1838 in North Carolina. He married Elizabeth, when she was 15 at the house of Francis Bledsoe in May 1791. He received a yearly pension of $65. Elizabeth applied for a widow's pension, but it was rejected due to a lack of proof of marriage.

"I volunteered in the militia of that County as a minute man in the year 1776 (when I was about the age of 14 years) and continued enrolled in that capacity until the close of the war. I was first call'd out soon after my enrollment and marched under Captain Colyer Harrison to Hampton Virginia and joined the Regiment commanded by Colonel Peter Royster-- Major Stith Hardeman was also attached to the same Regiment-- during this tour I was engaged in watching Lord Dunmore, who was then lying with his ships in Hampton Rhodes and that my Company had frequent skirmishes with foraging parties from these vessels. In this tour I served as a private three months."

"My second tour was under Captain William Ryal also of Charles City County--in this tour ___?__ ___?__ Company was principally engaged in supporting __?__ __? insurrection of the Negroes and that and

571

the adjoining Counties and I served in this Company as a private three months."

"I was next call'd out under Captain Harrod and stationed at Charles City Court House under the command of Major Gregory, for the protection of that place, but was at length surrounded in the night by the British light Horse and owing to the Cowardice of Harrod and Gregory (both of whom was afterwards disgraced) most of them men was cut to pieces or drowned in a neighboring mill pond. In this Company I served as a private at least two months before its dispersion by the enemy as aforesaid."

"My next tour was in Captain Edward Maynard's Company which after joining Major William White's command at Charles City Court House, marched near to Burmuda Hundred to watch the British – in this Service I was occasionally marched into Henrico and prince George Counties and had frequent skirmishes with parties of the Enemy and on one occasion took two boats and kill'd and took 84 men – this affair took place __?__ it to Bermuda Hundred at a place called Shearly Hundred. I was afterwards taken prisoner by the British light Horse and placed on bord a prison ship at Bermuda Hundred from whence I made my escape in a small boat. In this tour including my imprisonment, he served as a private at least three months and a half."

"My next tour was under the same Captain William Ryal under whom I had formerly served, and was marched to Chesterfield Court-House where we joined General Nelson's Command and was then marched to Osborne's where we join'd Baron Steuben and then marched to Petersburg where we had a sharp engagement with the British under General Phillips--but had to retreat. In this tour I served as a private three months."

"My sixth and last tour I marched from Charles City Court-House to Little York under the command of Major Stith Hardeman, and there joined the Brigade of General Thomas Nelson and was before that place during the siege. After the Surrender of Lord Cornwallis I remained at little York a considerable time and was engaged in leveling the entrenchments, moving Garrison from on board British ships, filing ball &c. In this tour I served at least three months. "Besides these specified tours I served several others of shorter duration, one under Captain Ryal and marched to Sandy Point on James River and was engaged in guarding a vessel loaded with Flower intended for the American Army at Valley Forge. This vessel was blockaded by the enemy below who made many *attempts to cut her loose but was beat off nine or ten times in the vessel ultimately sailed and got out In this duty I served at least two months. I was frequently called out during the war to join various reconnoitering parties in which nothing particular happened by which this Service can be designated nor can he recollect the names of all the officers under whom I served while performing this duty."*

Sources: 1. U.S. Pensioners 1818-1872. 2. Pension Papers R8191.

****

John D. Piatt age 10

John Piatt was born on 17 March, 1766 in New Jersey, and died on 27 March, 1837 in Morris, New Jersey. He married Jane Henarie on 9 February, 1791. Jane applied for and received a widow's pension in the amount of $44.00 a year for her husband's service in the war.

Major Daniel Piatt, John's father, commanded the 1st Regiment in the New Jersey Line. Major Piatt was sent by George Washington to Somerset County, New Jersey in the frigid winter of 1779-1780 to plead with the people for food for the starving army. He accomplished his mission but due to exposure he developed pneumonia and died in April of 1780. John stated in his pension application of 1832 the following:

"I enlisted as a Fifer at the age of ten years in the Company of Daniel Piatt (who was my father) in the first New Jersey Regiment New Jersey Line as well as I can recollect at this time in the latter part of the year 1775.....I marched to Brunswick upper landing thence to Elizabethtown and joined the Regiment under Lord Stirling...marched thence to New York and lay in Barracks till the following spring opened then was ordered march to Long Island and from thence to Canada (the Regiment at this time was commanded by Colo. Win's) and proceeded toward Quebeck as far as the three rivers, there had an engagement with the British, and retreated to Ticonderoga and lay there till late in the fall, or beginning of winter and then returned to New jersey directly after my Father Capt. Danl Piatt recruited his Company again and was soon promoted to the rank of Major in the New Jersey line. The officers was in Pennsylvania recruiting a new Company at the time Genl Washington attacked the Hessians at Trenton, I attended the rendezvous as a musician. The Company was marched to the Delaware to aid Genl Washington in the battle—was prevented crossing the river till next day after the Capture of the Hessians—from thence was marched to Princeton— I saw the dead

and wounded in the college. The company quartered one Winter in Elizabeth, part of the 1ˢᵗ regt.—I think the regt. Was commanded by Col. Matthias Ogden—after that the regiment was marched to the Westward under Genl Sullivan—I was kicked by the horse of Col. Brearly and disenabled to continue the march with the regiment—The troops returned in the fall of 1779 and went into Winter quarters at Mendham near Morristown placed under the immediate command of Genl. Washington—where I joined my company and continued with them through the winter. The regiment was Marched to Camptown in the summer of 1780 at the time Genl Kniphausen marched the British army to Springfield on his way (as was supposed) to attack Genl Washington at Morristown—was then marched to Springfield was engaged in battle Young Ogden was killed a considerable number more killed and wounded I was in the house of Parson Coldwell saw his wife a corps shot by the British—at Springfield—was taken a prisoner at pluckemin [?] by British and released afterwards being a youth."

John served in the Battle of Springtown on 23 June, 1780 and he was taken prisoner for a short time. This was one of the last major engagements of the war in the north. Since most battles were taking place in the South this American victory at Springfield became known as the "forgotten victory."

Sources: 1. Pension Papers W1473. 2. U.S. Pensioners 1818-1872. 3. 1830 Census. 4. The New Grove Dictionary of Music and Musicians, ed. Stanley Sadie, Vol. 8. 2. "The Music of the Army..." An Abbreviated Study of the Ages of Musicians in the Continental Army, by John U. Rees. Originally published in The Brigade Dispatch Vol. XXIV, No. 4, autumn 1993. 5. Dearmyrtle's Joy of Genealogy by Pat Richley.

****

William Gabriel Pickens age 14

William Pickens was born on 18 October, 1760 in Camden, South Carolina, and he died on 2 May, 1835 in Marion, Kentucky. He enlisted several weeks before his fifteenth birthday, and he received a yearly pension of $80 for his service.

"About the first of October 1775 I first entered the service as a private in the District of Abbeville (formerly Ninety Six) and as a volunteer under Captain Robert Anderson (afterwards General). About the 2nd of July preceding my entering the service, the inhabitants along the frontiers and back settlements of Georgia and Carolinas, had generally forted up, in consequence of the Cherokee Indians, who were extremely troublesome

at this time; having been instigated by the British. To protect themselves from Indian warfare, and to defend the country as much as possible, the frontier inhabitants had constructed a line of forts along the Savannah river and had mustered themselves into companies, stationed principally at these forts. As soon as I joined the service, which was to aid in guarding the frontiers and in repelling the Indians, Captain Anderson, stationed himself at one of these forts called Fort Independence, situated on the Savannah, where we remained fourteen months in constant service against these Indians in scouring the country and protecting the inhabitants. In the latter part of the year 1777 (I think in December) General Williamson made a campaign into the Indian country and defeated the Indians first at Seneca and next at Tomassee, or some such name; which gave the frontier inhabitants an interval of peace, as the Indians were driven off. A fort was built at Seneca called Rutledge, which was afterwards left under the care of Captain John Moore, with a company of Independents, as they were called. I was not in this campaign, having been left with others under Captain John Pickens (my brother) to guard the fort. But the most of my company, under Captain Anderson was in this expedition. After the return of General Williamson, which I think was some time in January or February 1778, I was discharged by Captain Anderson as our services was not required any longer on the frontier. I think quiet certain that we were discharged in January 1778 having served from the month of October 1776 to January 1778, at least fifteen months."

"After my discharge, I immediately returned home (Abbeville) and engaged in waggoning for the American Army, and continued it until sometime in 1780, after the fall of Charleston, and the capitulation of Genl Lincoln but I am advised that this service (waggoning) gives no claim to a pension, and I pass over it. After the British entered Charleston, they soon established forts throughout the country and seemed to have subjected it to the British Crown. Resistance almost ceased, for the Tories and British together overrun the county. Indeed many of the Whigs found it necessary to take protection, it 'twas called under the British - this was a matter of necessity and many of the most devoted Whigs done so and particularly after the defeat of Gates at Camden in August of that year. Thus thing remained until the arrival of Genl. Green from the North. This gave encouragement to the Whigs, and they again began to take up arms under their several leaders, in defense of their country. If I am not mistaken, Green arrived late in 1780 or the first of 1781. Early in the spring of 1781 (I think in April) I, with many others, volunteered under Capt. Caruthers, Major Alexander Noble, and Col. Robert Anderson (the same who was

formerly my Captain) and joined General Green in May, then before Ninety Six. We continued here with Green, during the siege of this place, and until he was repulsed. Our regiment was actively employed during this siege, the particulars of which I could relate if necessary, but will only mention, that it was Green's first objective to approach cautiously and take the place by a regular siege, of which he had no doubt if time was allowed him. He pushed the siege rigorously until sometime in June, when he learned that a reinforcement under Rawdon was hastily advancing to the relief of the place, (then under Col. Cruger). This induced Genl Green to hazard an assault, as it would be impossible to succeed by a regular siege before the arrival of Rawdon. The troops were immediately disposed for the assault. Col. Lee succeeded in forcing the works assigned to him, but in other parts our troops were repulsed, after much hard fighting and considerable loss, Genl Green called off his troops. The next day he raised the siege, crossed the Saluda and encamped on Little river. In this siege, my brother in law, Captain Joseph Pickens (who was also a cousin) was killed. I served as a soldier in this siege, and remember the most of the particulars, but it is not necessary to relate them."

The Siege of Ninety-Six was from 22 May to 18 June, 1781. General Nathaniel Greene led 1,000 troops against 550 Loyalists in the fortified village of Ninety-Six. Much of the siege centered around a fortification called Star Fort. During the battle for the fort both sides fought hand-to-hand using bayonets and their muskets as clubs. When General Greene learned that British reinforcements were on the way, he called off the siege and retreated.

During the siege in May of 1781 an incident occurred involving two women, Grace and Rachel Martin, the wives of two brothers with the militia. The women learned that a courier would pass their way carrying important dispatches. It was late in the night and the two women dressed in their husbands clothes, gathered their weapons, and left to intercept the courier.

Soon the courier and his guards appeared on the road, and the women jumped from their hiding place and demanded the men to stop and turn over their dispatches. The men were taken by surprise and quickly obeyed the command. The women sent the dispatches by messenger to General Greene and they took shortcuts and arrived back home.

Soon the enemy courier and his guards arrived at the women's house and asked for accommodations for the night. One of the women asked the men why they had come back after having passed the house earlier. The men said that they had been taken prisoner by two rebel lads. The next morning the courier and guards departed, and had no idea that the two women who gave them hospitality were the same women who had captured them

"On the retreat of Genl Green the most of the militia dispersed for a few days, but re-assembled about fifteen miles above Ninety Six, and there joined Genl Pickens (another cousin to myself, being brothers' children, and with whom I had been raised.) After joining Genl Pickens, we marched toward North Carolina; crossed Broad River at Hamilton's Ford, and proceeded down towards the Congaree. Here I, with others, were sent out as spies to ascertain the situation of the enemy when on their march toward Charleston. We (the spy company) came up with the enemy's rear guard, and attacked it, in which we killed five. But we could do no more than harass their rear and flanks, to embarrass them in their march as much as possible, which we continued to do for ten miles. We were on horse, as were all now under the command of Genl Pickens. After this we marched up towards the Dutch fork, into a settlement almost entirely Tories, and who had embodied in considerable numbers near the line. After marching for sometime in search of them, I came to the determination of quitting the service for a while, as the support of an aged mother and widowed sister (the wife of Capt. Joseph Pickens, killed at Ninety Six) now devolved upon me and required my attention. But at this Captain Norwood called on me, and earnestly pressed me to join his company, and fill the place of one of his spies, who had been lately killed by Tories. Although it was almost absolutely necessary for me to quit the service at this time, and attend to the support of mother and sister, who were left quiet destitute, yet as my service as a spy was thought to be of considerable importance, I determined to forego the duty I owed at home, and immediately joined Captain Norwood as a spy, and continued in this service for the term of six months. Captain Norwood was principally stationed on the frontier, between the white settlements and Indian Nation. As well as I now remember, I joined Capt Norwood in the month of October 1781, having principally been under Capt Caruthers as before stated from April 1781 until October of the same year. I served full six months under Norwood as spy, and was discharged sometime in April or May 1782 as well as my memory serves me, and since my papers were sent back for want of dates, I have reflected much on the subject, and I do not think I am wrong in any of the dates I have mentioned. The length of the tours of duty mentioned, I have put down at least as short as they really were, as I do not desire to receive for more than I deserve."

"There is another circumstance which I omitted to mention in its right place. While I served under Colonel Anderson in 1781, we made an expedition to the frontiers of Georgia in search of the celebrated Bill Cunningham, who commanded a party of Tories and Indians, and who had done much mischief."

William "Bloody Bill" Cunningham enlisted in the Continental Army in 1775. His time of service was not a happy one, and in 1778 he switched sides and fought for the British. He earned the nickname "Bloody Bill" for being violent and ruthless in his raids on rebels and patriot civilians.

"After arriving towards the frontier, Capt. Robt. Maxwell and myself were sent forward to spy out the position, strength of the party. We discovered them encamped on Cane Creek on Tugaloo River. We immediately returned to our main body and gave the information. Colonel Anderson immediately planned the attack by dividing his force into three divisions, the right, left and Centre. The right and left were committed to the command of Maxwell and myself, and the centre he commanded himself. In this form we advanced, with the sanguine hope of surprising them, but unfortunately, just before reaching their camp, one of divisions accidentally met a party driving some cattle to the river, and fired upon them. This gave the alarm to the camp and they instantly fled. Thus our project was defeated, after we supposed they were within our power. In the year 1782 the Indians still continued troublesome on the Georgia frontiers. The inhabitants being weak and unable to protect themselves, dispatched messengers into South Carolina for assistance. I again volunteered to aid these people, and with a company of volunteers, marched to the Oconee River, and there had a battle with the Indians across the river—they were defeated and we took several prisoners. We were only about three weeks in this service, and I only mention it as a continuation of events in which I was concerned, not as a part of my service for which I claim a pension, as the term was so short as not to be worth mentioning. There are many other circumstances I could mention, but perhaps it is not necessary to mention them."

Sources: 1. Women of the Revolution: Bravery and Sacrifice on the Southern Battlefields by Robert M. Dunkerly. 2. U. S. Pension Roll of 1835. 3. 1820 Census. 4. Pension Papers S1244.

****

Eli Pierce age 14

Eli Pierce was born on 24 August, 1762 in Middleborough, Massachusetts, and he died on 26 December, 1852 in Watertown, Wisconsin. He married Polly Lyon on 29 April, 1798 at her father's house in Vermont. She received a yearly widow's pension of $96.

"I enlisted as near as I can recollect sometime in the year 1776 for 15 months in Massachusetts and served more than half of this time when I was taken sick and went home on furlough and was not able to refuse."

"I enlist about the first of May 1777 for three years in the State of Massachusetts in Captain Anasa Sopers Company in Col Tho. Marshal's Regiment in the Massachusetts line in the Continental establishment I served in said Corps till about the first of May 1780 when I was discharged at West Point in the state of New York."

Eli was at Valley Forge in the winter of 1777-78, and in June of 1778 he fought at the Battle of Monmouth. In this battle Eli was a member of the 10th Massachusetts Regiment and the 3rd Massachusetts Brigade under Brigadier General John Paterson. They made up the left wing of the battle formation led by Lord Stirling. The left wing faced the British 42nd, called the Black Watch, which was one of the best regiments in the world. The brigade Eli was in blunted the assaults of the 42nd several times and protected the left flank of Washington's army.

Sources: 1. Census 1820, 1830, 1840, & 1850. 2. Tombstone and Cemetery Sign. 3. U.S. Pensioners 1818-1872. 4. Pension Papers W4499.

****

Drura Pilkington age 14

Drura Pilkington was born on 3 April, 1762 in Amelia County, Virginia, and he died in 1843 in Willow Creek, South Carolina. He married Lydia Jane Lowery. In 1840 he owned 16 slaves. Drura received a yearly pension of $80.

"I was born in Amelia County & State of Virginia on the 3rd day of April 1762. I was called to perform was in the Militia Service when I was about 14 years of age. I march with a detachment of Militia from Amelia County to Valley Forge under the command of Lieut. Sam'l Cobb and upon my arrival was placed under the command of Capt. Wm. Taylor who I believe was of the regular Army -- Gen. Woodford commanded the

Brigade and all the army was under the Command of Gen. Washington, from thence the army marched to Monmouth and on the march I was taken sick and I remained in the Hospital not far distant from Valley Forge for about seven weeks and until after the battle at Monmouth."

When Drura became ill before the Battle of Monmouth he probably stayed at the Yellow Springs Hospital. This was located about 10 miles from Valley Forge and was the first military hospital to be built in the country. Hundreds of soldiers from the camp were cared for there.

Disease at Valley Forge was rampant. Sanitary condition were very poor and the men suffered from smallpox, typhoid fever, pneumonia and dysentery. About 2,000 troops died at Valley Forge that winter.

"I joined the Army near the White Plains and from thence the Army marched either to Philadelphia or the North river. I served in this service for the term of eighteen months and then enlisted under the aforesaid Capt. Williams Taylor and of the 2nd Regiment for three years. The Regiment was marched to West Point and stationed on the green near the forts. The regiment then marched (with others) marched under the command of Gen. Wayne to Stony Point and when the fort was stormed and taken -- this was the first Battle in which I was engaged. After the fort was taken the Army returned to West Point. That afterwards (as he was informed) an express was sent from Gen. Lincoln to Gen Washington for aid. That three Regiments were ordered on to Charleston So. Ca. and when the Brigade arrived at Fredericksburgh Va. Capt. Taylor resigned his commission and his Company was then commanded by Capt. John Stokes. Capt. John Stokes went home from Richmond Va. and did rejoin the Regiment -- I think the Regiments reached the City of Charleston So. Ca. early in May and was commanded by Gen. Lincoln and was soon afterwards taken by the British and soon afterwards I ran away and made my escape from the British and returned to Chesterfield County Va. where my Mother then resided. After Ld Cornwallis evacuated Charleston and had arrived in Virginia I was ordered out with the Militia and he went under the command of Capt. George Markham and joined the army at York under the Command of Gen. Washington and was present at the capture of Cornwallis and was soon afterwards disbanded -- and which was the last service he performed."

Drura took part in the nighttime attack on the fort at Stony Point on 16 July, 1779. He was assigned to the 1st Regiment commanded by Colonel Christian Febiger. They were a group of highly trained, selected group of men that successfully assaulted the south side of the fort.

Sources: 1. Census 1800, 1820, 1830, & 1840. 2. South Carolinians in the Revolution. 3. U.S. Pension Roll of 1835. 4. Pension papers S9458.

****

Robert Porter age 14

Robert Porter was born on 19 March, 1762 in Bridgewater, Massachusetts, and he died on 18 August, 1835 in Norfolk County, Massachusetts. He married Elizabeth Gay on 5 June, 1794. She received a widow's pension of $20 a year.

Robert served as a volunteer in Captain Wilser Company in the Regiment commanded by Col Nickolas Dike from 31 December, 1776 to 19 March, 1777. He later enlisted from 16 August, 1779 to about 15 September, 1779 in the Massachusetts Militia. The Regiment was commanded by Commandant Fish. His final enlistment was from 1 November, 1779 until the first of January, 1780. He served under captain Able Richards.

Source: 1. Pension Papers W1928.

****

Robert Porter age 11

Robert Porter was born on 10 January, 1768 in Philadelphia, Pennsylvania, and he died on 13 June, 1842. He joined his father in winter quarters in the Continental Army at Morristown, New Jersey in 1779. He served in Procter's 4th Regiment Pennsylvania Artillery. In 1781 he was commissioned a first lieutenant until the close of the war in 1783. At one time he served as an adjutant under the command of his father. Robert may have been present at the Battle of Bull's Ferry on 21 August, 1780. He received a yearly pension of $20.

At the close of the war Robert returned to Philadelphia and studied law. In 1810 he was appointed president-judge of the Third Judicial District of Pennsylvania. He married Mary Williams.

Sources: 1. Tombstone 2. History of Ohio: The Rise and Progress of an American State, Vol. 5 by Emilius Oviatt Randall & Daniel Joseph Ryan. 3. Year Book of the Sons of the Revolution.

****

Ptolemy Powell age 14

Ptolemy Powell was born in 1767 in Orange, Virginia, and he died in Spotsylvania, Virginia in 1843. He married a widow, Sidney Daniel Leavit, on 23 December, 1793. Ptolemy had a brother in the militia in service on the Gloucester side of the York River. His brother wished to see his family, so Ptolemy agreed to serve as his substitute for two weeks in the militia. He served for two weeks in the Battalion commanded by Major Campbell. This occurred just before the surrender of Cornwallis at Yorktown. According to the 1820 census, Ptolemy owned 17 slaves in Virginia.

Sources: 1. Tombstone 2. Virginia Militia in the Revolutionary War. 3. The Virginia Magazine of History and Biography, Vol XXVI 1918. 4. Sons of the American Revolution Application. 5. History of Virginians in the Revolution.

****

Samson Prescott age 13

Samson Prescott was born in Massachusetts in 1762, and he died in 1834. He was present at the Battle of Bunker Hill, fought on 17 June, 1775, with his older brother David who was wounded. They served in the Groton Company of militia in Colonel Prescott's Regiment. The night before the battle Colonel Prescott's men began to fortify the 75 foot Breed's Hill.

Source: 1. Massachusetts Society of the Sons of the American Revolution, 1893.

****

David Pressley age 13

David Pressley was born on 12 January, 1764 in Glasgow, Scotland, and he died on 11 May, 1834 in Anderson County, South Carolina. He said he came to this county in 1767 *"as an infant in the nurse's arms."* He married Ann Edmiston on 16 November, 1784, and they had 11 children. He received a yearly pension of $48.33.

David served in the War of 1812 with Youngblood's Regiment of the South Carolina Militia. In 1833 he founded Pressley's Station, later named Lowndesville, and became the station's postmaster.

"I entered the service of the United States at the age of thirteen years as a volunteer under Captain Andrew Hamilton early in the Autumn of the year Seventeen Hundred Seventy Six in the District of Ninety Six

now Abbeville district in the State of South Carolina. I was marched in this company to the Cherokee nation where a large body of troops all under the command of Major Williamson gave battle to and equal or superior force of Indians who in number were considered two thousand strong and who occupied the mountain heights above Major Williamson's Army in the valley orders were given to gain the heights above the Indians which were promptly done __?__ and the Indians being hard pressed were put to flight, their settlements laid waste and destroyed by Major Williamson's Army and the Army discharged or disbanded in October of the year Seventeen Hundred Seventy Six. My term of service during this Indian Campaign I estimate at least six weeks as well as I can recollect."

David Pressley was part of a 2,000 man force led by Colonel Andrew Williamson to fight the Cherokee Indians. In September of 1776 they walked into an ambush at a place called Black Hole. After a two-hour battle the Indians were forced to retreat, because they ran out of ammunition. Had it not been for this they might have won the battle.

"My subsequent service commenced in September in the year Seventeen Hundred and Eighty when volunteered as a private in Captain John McCawley's company under the command of General Marion in Williamsburg District in the State of South Carolina and continued in Captain John McCawley's for the term of thirteen months and attached to General Francis Marion's Brig maneuvering, marching, fighting, annoying & surprising the enemy from place to place on Black river in this State and elsewhere in that section of the country not now recollected under that able and energetic General, I was with General Francis Marion when he surprised and defeated Colonel Tynes a Tory officer who was more dreaded than any other enemy in that part of South Carolina where he carried on his military operations in the lower part of the State this surprise battle and defeat took place before day break between Georgetown & a place called Black Mingo the Tories were in number by report one hundred & fifty strong, thirty or forty of them were killed and wounded and the greater part of them taken prisoners including Colonel Tynes this surprise battle & defeat was in the year Seventeen Hundred and Eighty."

David Pressley was a member of the Kingstreet Regiment of Militia under Captain John McCauley, under the command of Colonel Francis Marion also known as "The Swamp Fox." Marion used hit-and-run guerrilla tactics to attack British or Loyalist supply line, patrols, and garrisons. He used small groups of men and chose the time and place of his attacks.

At the Battle of Black Mingo on 14 September, 1780 David was part of a force that surprised a group of Loyalists troops under the command of Colonel Ball. Sometime after midnight the Americans had their surprise attack spoiled, when the lead horses crossed the wooden plank bridge across Black Mingo Creek. The noise of the hooves alerted the Loyalists troops and the battle began. The Loyalists were disorganized, and in fifteen minutes the battle was over when the enemy retreated into the swamp.

Both sides were so close together in the battle that pieces of wadding from their guns struck on each other when fired. The Americans captured guns, ammunition, barrage, and horses. Colonel Marion took Loyalists Colonel John Ball's horse for himself and renamed it Ball. Colonel Marion learned from the battle to never cross a bridge in the night in a surprise attack without spreading blankets on the bridge to muffle the hooves of the horses.

Although a small victory when news of it spread, more men flocked to join Colonel Marion's unit. Some of the Loyalists were so impressed with the leadership ability of Colonel Marion, that they switched sides and joined him.

David Pressley also was part of the force that defeated the hated Loyalist Colonel Samuel Tynes on October 25, 1780. Tynes was camped near the Tearcoat Swamp when, at the stroke of midnight, Colonel Marion attacked from three sides. The Loyalist broke retreated into the swamp and Colonel Tynes managed to escape after losing more than forty men. A few days later Colonel Tynes was seen and captured.

"I was subsequently detailed with a few others under Captain Snipes & Serg't McDonald to reconnoiter and spie out the situation of the enemy near Georgetown this detachment way laid a rode all night, next morning went to the Whigs house to get refreshment & while there our sentinels fired and a body of British horse made their appearance Snipes detachment mounted their horses drew their swords & gave battle the British horse were defeated most of whom were killed, not a prisoner taken. I was not in any other battle or skirmish in the revolutionary war, but was actively engaged in General Francis Marion's brigade in Captain McCawley's company, and annoying the enemy until the close of the war,

& my whole term of service during the revolutionary war including his Indian Campaign I compute at fourteen & a half months service."

Sources: 1. Historical Dictionary of the American Revolution by Terry M. Mays. 2. Census 1830. 3. Roadside Plaque at Lowdesville. 4. U.S. Pensioners 1818-1872. 5. Sons of the American Revolution Application. 6. Pension papers W24917. 7. The Swamp Fox: Lessons in Leadership from the Partisan Campaigns of Francis Marion by Scott Aiken. 8. The Life and Times of General Francis Marion by Horatio Newton Moore. 9. The Chronology of the American Revolution: Military and Political Actions Day by Day by Bud Hannings.

****

Joshua Prewett age 13

Joshua Prewett was born in 1765 in Bedford County, Virginia, and he died on 27 January, 1843 in Trimble County, Kentucky. He married (1) Sarah Adams on 3 February, 1784 in Virginia. Sarah died in 1829. He then married (2) Mary Berkshire, a widow, on 12 July, 1829. He received a yearly pension of $80.

When a widow applies for her deceased husband's pension, she must show proof of death. This is usually achieved by having several people send a letter attesting to the fact that they attended the funeral of the person. Mary had a most unusual letter sent by John Stollstein as proof of her husband's death. John was a merchant, and he said he sold Mary several yards of material to use as shrouding for the funeral. The total cost was $2.10, and he would be happy to show his books of purchase as proof.

"I was born in Bedford County State of Virginia in the year 1765 where I remained until after I arrived at the age of thirteen years when my father married a second wife. I being unwilling to come under the government of a Step Mother deserted my father and in company with a family of Movers came to Kentucky, after being in Kentucky about six months I went to the Garrison at Louisville and in the month of March 1779 I did enlist under one Captain George of the Artillery, for a period of five years and was attached to General George Rodgers Clark's Regiment the day after I enlisted the Regiment under the command of General Clark left the Garrison and marched below the falls and got aboard some boats that had been pressed by General Clark; we then descended the Ohio River as low as its junction with the Mississippi where General Clark determined to ascend the Mississippi in pursuit of some Indians that had retreated up the River after having done some mischief in Kentucky. Here we had to leave some boats such as were not constructed foregoing up Stream with the balance of the crafts such as

Keel boats, Skifts &c. We proceeded up the Mississippi as high as its Junction with the Missouri on arriving at that place General Clarke ordered the Regiment ashore and proceeded after the Indians. After spending some time in a fruitless pursuit after these Indians __?__ Clark ordered the Regiment back to the landing. We then got aboard of their boats and descended the Mississippi River seven miles below the mouth of the Ohio River __?__ we landed their boats, and by __?__ of General Clark went ashore on the East shore of the Mississippi River, here General Clark ordered the erection of a fort and some __?__ houses. The Regiment __?__ under the direction of General Clark proceeded to build a fort and two Block Houses and sometime in the month of July 1780 – the fort was attacked by a numerous tribe of Indians I think that the number of Indians was about six times as many as Clark had in the fort, they demanded a surrender of the fort. Clark sent out Captain Helms and an interpreter to learn the terms upon which day demanded the Surrender. Helms was informed by the interpreter that the women and children that were in the fort should be spared but that officers and soldiers should be put to death. Helms through the interpreter replied that then they all would die together and returned with his flag to the fort. General Clark approving of Captain Helms' reply ordered the fort to prepare for a defense, in a short time the Indians made an attack upon the fort by firing upon the East side of the fort there fire was returned from the fort which was kept __?__ for the space of six days and nights with but little __?__ when the Indians finding their attack to be of little effect retreated during this engagement there were three or four in the fort killed and some few wounded – how many I do not now remember. When the Indians attacked the fort, the hunters were out in pursuit of provisions for the Regiments and that many of them were killed before they reached the fort, – after the Indians left the fort General Clark ordered a pursuit and in the pursuit they discovered that some of the Indians had been killed and appearance proved that the Indians had some wounded amongst them after pursuing the Indians a short time we returned to the fort where we remain until the fall of the year. General Clark then ordered that the Regiment should go up the Ohio River as high as Louisville accordingly we boarded our boats and some time later in the fall we reached Louisville. General Clark then ordered that we should proceed to build a fort for __?__ security and such buildings as would add to the comfort during the winter Season and after some time spent in laboring we erected a fort, block house __?__ . Here we remained until the summer of 1781. General Clark then ordered Captain George to take his Company of artillery and board a ___?__ and go up the Ohio River in order to give security to those that had settled near *the river and to afford some safety to those that were moving down said River. Accordingly Captain George with his Company of Artillery boarded said __?__ and ascended the Ohio River as high as the mouth of the Big Kentucky and in order to alarm the Indians he states that Captain George would frequently have his cannon discharged. We were alternately ascending and descending the Ohio River until the winter of 1781 when we went into the forts at Louisville and wintered with the balance of Clarke's Regiment. In the summer of 1782 General Clark ordered his Regiment up the Ohio River where a part of said Regiment went aboard on the boats and a part went by land. We united on the Ohio River where Cincinnati now stands. Here we built a block house and deposited some baggage and left some sick soldiers. General Clark thence ordered his Regiment to the upper __?__ towns on arriving at said towns the Indians made some defense in which engagement the Indians had 12 or 14 killed and some taken prisoner. General Clark remained at said towns until he ascertained that the Indians had dispersed, he then ordered a return to the block house. After reaching the block house it was ordered by General Clark that the Regiment proceed to the fort which we had built at Louisville. Accordingly some of the soldiers went __?__ the boats and some with some horses went by land, I was one that was sent by land and joined the Regiment at Louisville later on fall of 1782 –The Regiment under the Command General Clark was stationed at the Fort at Louisville and the men were frequently sent in small companies to the different forts in Kentucky for a pair defense. I remained in Captain George's Company of Artillery discharging my duty as a faithful soldier until the month of March 1784 when I was discharged in writing, which discharge was signed by his said Captain George."*

Sources: 1. U.S. Pensioners 1818-1872. 2. Pension Papers W27643.

****

Ephraim Price age 13

Ephraim Price was born in 1762 in Dinwiddie, Virginia, and he died in Butts, Georgia on October 31, 1846. He married Martha Williams on 18 October, 1791. According to an article in the Atlanta Constitution, Ephraim was a courier for George Washington, who later gave him a letter of recommendation in his own handwriting when he came to Greene County, Georgia. Ephraim joined the Virginia militia in 1775.

"I entered in the service of the United States in a volunteer company in the County of Sussex, Virginia, under the command of George

Reives sometime I think in September 1775. We were marched by Capt. Reives from Sussex Court House to Jamestown, Virginia to prevent meet the British under Gov. Dunmore, who had retired from the seat of Government at Williamsburg to this place when hostility had first commenced in this quarter of the country. When our company reached Jamestown we found that the British had left the place and we were marched back again home and discharged, after an absence from home in service about 3 weeks. I volunteered again under Captain Mgal (?) about the 1st of December of the same year 1775. Our company rendezvoused at Sussex Court House together with several other companies where Col David Mason took command of us and marched immediately to Norfolk where the British fleet had assembled. We arrived at Norfolk on this 24th day of December. On the first day of January 1776 the British set fire to the city. We remained at Norfolk about 3 weeks after the burning of this city and were then marched to a place called the Great Bridge, where we remained about 3 weeks longer, after which we were marched home and discharged, after a tour of about 10 weeks."

Colonel David Mason was the commander of the 15th Virginia Regiment. The burning of Norfolk occurred when British ships began shelling the town and landing parties came ashore to burn certain properties. A battle took place at Great Bridge on 9 December, 1775 before Ephraim's company arrived. The battle was an American victory and forced British Governor Dunmore out of Norfolk.

"I volunteered again under Capt George Reives sometime about the 1st of June 1776 and was marched by him to Little York where several companies had rendezvoused for the purpose of keeping the British from landing, I think. When we arrived we were taken command by Col John Ruffin. We remained at this place for about 3 months as well as I can recollect after which we were marched home and discharged."

Around the first of the year in 1777 Ephraim was drafted into the North Carolina militia (he had moved from Virginia) under the command of Captain John Power and Colonel Joseph Hawkins. He served in the lower part of North Carolina and was in a few skirmishes with Tories. He was discharged after three months.

According to pension records Ephraim served a total of seven months and one day, and he was awarded a pension of $30.11 per year for his service. Later in life he must have been very prosperous, because the census records of 1820 show that he owned 14 slaves.

Sources: 1. Census of 1820, 1830, & 1840. 2. Pension papers S31919. 3. Revolutionary War Pensioner Census 1841. 4. Roster of Revolutionary Soldiers in Georgia, Vol. I. 5. The Atlanta Constitution Oct. 31, 1915.

****

John Putnam age 12

John Putnam was born on 28 November, 1767 in Royalston, Massachusetts, and he died on 21 May, 1841 in Rome, New York. He received a monthly pension of $8 for his service.

"I enlisted in June or July 1780 at the town of Great Barrington, Berkshire County Massachusetts & served six months in the first Massachusetts Regiment. The winter following I enlisted in the Continental Establishment & the following spring joined the Massachusetts Regiment commanded by Col Smith, and served in that Regiment at West Point, which was afterwards consolidated with the 2nd Massachusetts Regiment until the fall of 1783."

Sources: 1. Register of the Pennsylvania Society of the Sons of the Revolution, 1888-1898. 2. Pension Papers S40306.

****

Thomas Rankins age 8

Thomas Rankins was born on 22 November, 1771 in Herkimer, New York and he died there on 5 February, 1833. He married Catharine Kessler on 22 November, 1791 in Herkimer, New York.

"I enlisted as a Fifer in the service of the United States, in the fall of the year 1779 or the summer of said year, in the company commanded by Cap't John Griggs, of Col. Van Shaick's Regiment, New York Line. I enlisted for and during the continuance of the war being then at Fort Stanwix. I continued in the same company and served in the same Regiment and Line, upon the Continental establishment, until the month of June 1783 as I believe. I served in various skirmishes at Fort Stanwix, and at Yorktown against Cornwalis, when I was taken. In June 1783 I was discharged at Newburg in New York, which discharge was signed by General Washington, but which is lost."

Sources: 1. Tombstone 2. New York Military in the Revolution. 3. Pension Roll of 1835. 4. Pension Papers.

****

George Palmer Ransom age 14

George Ransom was born on 3 January, 1762 in Connecticut, and he died on 3 September, 1850 in Pennsylvania. He enlisted in 1776 as a private in Captain Samuel Ransom's Company. George's widow received a yearly pension of $80.

George enlisted with his father, Captain Samuel Ransom, and brother-in-law into the 2nd Westmoreland Independent Company Militia. His first job with the unit was to bury the dead. On 20 January, 1777 George and his father fought in the Battle of Millstone.

In this engagement about 450 patriot militia waded through waist-deep icy water to defeat a group of British soldiers of equal size. The British did not expect that the Americans would cross except at the bridge. The Patriots captured men, horses, and 50 wagons filled with supplies. One of the British soldiers later said that the Americans were too well-trained to be militia.

George and his father also fought in the Battle of Bound Brook on 13 April, 1777. In this battle 500 American militiamen were defeated by 4,000 British troops and Hessians under the command of General Cornwallis. George and Captain Ransom also fought at the Battle of Brandywine and Germantown. They were also present for the Siege of Fort Mifflin from 26 September to 16 November, 1777. This defeat of the defending Patriots forced General Washington to retreat and take his army to Valley Forge for the winter. George celebrated his sixteenth birthday at Valley Forge.

In 1778 Captain Samuel Ransom, George's father, resigned his post when he heard that the Patriot forces in the Wyoming Valley were under threat of attack by Canadian Loyalists and their Indian allies. Captain Ransom's wife and several of the younger children lived in the area and were at risk. George remained with his unit and later learned of the death of his father. Tory militia and Iroquois Indians killed more than 300 Patriot defenders, including Captain Samuel Ransom on 3 July, 1778. Captain Ransom's body was slashed and his head was nearly decapitated in what became known as the Wyoming Massacre.

After learning of the death of his father, George and other men who had families in the area hurried back home. George identified the mutilated body of his father by the distinctive silver shoe buckles that his father wore. He stayed home through the winter to help take care of his family.

In 1779 George joined a company under the command of Captain Spalding. The Captain had served as a Lieutenant under Captain Samuel Ransom during 1777. George was present with Spalding at the Siege of Fort Mifflin. During that siege British bullets were tearing through the fort and men were falling on every side. A soldier in George's company threw himself on the ground and said, *"Nobody can stand this."* Spaulding looked at the man and calmly told him, *"Get up my good fellow, I should hate to have to run you through; you can stand it if I can."* The man got up and cheerfully returned to his duty.

In the summer of 1779 Spaulding's company, including George Ransom, joined the Sullivan Expedition and served as scouts. They were engaged at the Battle of Newtown on 29 August, 1779. This American victory was against a combined force of Tories and Iroquois' warriors. It successfully ended the threat of the Indians in upper New York. More than 40 Iroquois' villages were destroyed in the expedition. George later referred to this venture as *"bashing the Indians."*

Near the end of the war in December of 1780 George, who had been promoted to First Sergeant, returned to his home in Wyoming Valley. In December George visited the home of Benjamin Harvey, in order to court Benjamin's 17 year old daughter Elisha. During the evening Indians raided the house and took the five occupants, including George, as captives. The next morning the Indians released two of the captives, but they kept George, Elisha, and Benjamin.

After several days the Indians tied Benjamin to a tree and took turns throwing tomahawks at his head. The young braves missed every time, and the leader of the Indians thought that Benjamin must have been protected by the Great Spirit, so Benjamin was set free. They continued north with George and Elisha. George was later turned over to the British in Montreal and Elisha remained with the Indians through the winter. She was later traded to a Scotsman for a half barrel of rum. Two years later her father was able to get her release in a prisoner exchange, and she returned home.

In February of 1781 George was moved with other prisoners to Quebec to a place called Prison Island. The head guard was an 18 year old Scottish soldier, who would at times order the men to shovel snow. If a prisoner refused they were chained in irons. When George and another prisoner, William Palmeters, were asked they refused. The two men were placed in an open floorless house overnight in freezing temperatures. The next morning George was asked again to shovel the snow. He replied, *"Not by order of a damned Tory!"* The two prisoners were chained again and moved to another building, and they were subjected to various abuses throughout the winter.

In early June George and two other prisoners would at times sneak away during work detail and work on building a raft. On June 9 they escaped on the raft and crossed the St. Lawrence River. Exhausted and with little food mainly capturing snakes and frogs, they managed to reach Lake Champlain in two days. The men eventually reached the village of Putney, Vermont and split up. George walked south to Litchfield, Connecticut where he was born. The other two men walked to Albany, New York.

After George regained his health he rejoined the 1st Connecticut militia and remained with them until he was discharged at West Point in 1783. On 14 August, 1783 he married Olive Utley, and in 1786 they moved back to George's home in Luzerne, County, Pennsylvania and settled on his father's land. In 1787 George was promoted to Captain of the 7th Company and 3rd Regiment of the Luzerne Militia. Tragedy struck again in George's life when on 14 July, 1793 Olive died at the age of 33. George was then a widower with four small children. Six months later he married Elizabeth Lamoreaux, and together they had 13 children. George was 60 when his last child was born.

George continued to buy more land, and in 1799 he was promoted to Lt. Colonel in the Luzerne County Militia. For his service he earned the Badge of Merit, which was at that time the highest military honor, and his discharge papers were personally signed by General George Washington.

When George was an old man he overheard a young man criticize General Washington. Enraged, George took his cane and knocked the man down. George was taken to court and was questioned by Judge Hollenback. The judge asked the old man where he was in 1777, in July, 1778, in the summer of 1779, and in the winter of 1780. George said he was in Washington's army and heading back to Wyoming Valley to bury his father, with General Sullivan and a prisoner on the St. Lawrence. The judge then asked him, *"And did you knock the fellow down, Colonel Ransom?"* *"I did so, and would do it again under like provocation,"* said the Colonel defiantly. *"What was the provocation?"* *"The rascal abused the name of General Washington."*

Judge Hollenback had heard enough evidence and fined Colonel Ransom one penny and ordered the young man to pay the court costs. The people in the court room applauded.

Sources: 1. Sons of the American Application. 2. Register of the Pennsylvania Society of the Sons of the Revolution, 1888-1898. 3. Pension Papers W2694. 4. History of Westmoreland County, Pennsylvania, Vol. 1 by John Newton Boucher. 5. A Genealogical Record of the Descendants of Captain Samuel Ransom of the Continental Army by Captain Clinton B. Sears, 1882. 6. New England Families, Genealogical and Memorial, Vol 2, edited by William Richard Cutter.

****

Elisha Raymond age 14

Elisha Raymond was born on 9 November, 1761 in Gloucester, Rhode Island, and he died on 7 June, 1842 in Wisconsin. He married Abigail Inman, while he was still in the army on 25 April, 1781 in Gloucester.

"I entered the Service of the United States the later part of February 1776. I took the place of John Warner who had been drafted into the Militia. I served for one week at Providence Rhode Island under Captain Buslingame in Col Kimbells Regiment I think. Immediately I took the place of Tommy Ballard another Drafted man for one month served in the same company & under the same officers as first mentioned & then returned to Gloucester the place of my residence and immediately took the place of another Drafted man by the name of Joshua Matterson and marched immediately to Providence Rhode Island term of one month & then took the place of Thomas Raymond my brother who had been drafted for one month & served this month under Capt Stephen Winsor at Providence Rhode Island & then returned home to Gloucester about one month I took place of Daniel Barnes of Gloucester who had been Drafted. Marched too Providence Rhode Island and served one month under Capt Whipple. I think that in the month of November about the 15th day I was drafted at Gloucester aforesaid for one month & marched to Providence onto fields point and staid my time out under Capt Whipple & then returned to Gloucester."

"In the month of March or April 1777 I served as a substitute for my Father William Raymond one month in the Militia at Providence. About the first of July same year I served one month as a substitute for John Inman [this might have been his future wife's father or brother] *of Gloucester. I served this month at Providence Rhode Island."*

"I then enlisted for three months at Providence under Capt Caleb Sheldon and served the time of my engagement and was dismissed at Providence Rhode Island--Col Chad Brown was one of the officers. I returned to Gloucester in 1781. I enlisted at Gloucester Rhode Island in the light infantry for fifteen months under Capt Wilnorth of Gloucester & served about one year and then by __?__ I enlisted into the Regular Army for nine months which last __?__ was in the month of March following the capture of Cornwallis being in March 1782 the time which I enlist I think and Marched immediately to Providence & soon after marched to Philadelphia under Col Owney or Olney, belonged to a company Commanded by Capt Holden at Philadelphia in the last of April or first of May, was there inoculated for the small pox was confined for a short time & then marched back to Yarplanks point on the Hudson river and then Marched to Schyless Flats and staid through the summer & in November I went to Albany by water and from there to Saratoga where I arrived the last days of November there I received my discharge."

After peace was declared Elisha, his wife, and child moved to Stamford, Vermont. There they raised cattle, sheep and swine. Elisha was selected to serve as a Selectman for the county, and later he was appointed a highway surveyor. Around 1835 they moved to Racine County, Wisconsin. Elisha received a yearly pension of $80.

Sources: 1. Soldiers of the American Revolution Buried in Wisconsin. 2. Sons of the American Revolution Application. 3. U.S. Pensioners 1818-1872. 4. Pension Papers W26362.

****

Enoch Raymond age 14

Enoch Raymond was born on 25 September, 1763 in Bedford, New York, and he died 21 February, 1835 in Bedford. He married Susannah Lyon on 17 August, 1786 in Bedford. Enoch Raymond is found on the rolls of the 2nd Regiment of Westchester County Militia under the command of Colonel Thomas Thomas. Enoch received a yearly pension of $80.

"I entered as a private some time in the spring of the year 1778 in the company of minute man (volunteer) commanded by Captain Marcus Moseman in the regiment of the Militia of the county of Westchester aforesaid commanded by Col Thomas Thomas that said company was detailed from said regiment to serve in the American lines in the said county of Westchester. I did not take the service as aforesaid for any

particular term but I continued in actual service in said company from the spring of the year 1778 until the spring of the year 1781 when I was discharged During said term I was engaged with several skirmished with the enemy troops and in one six members of said company were taken prisoner and in another two of the members of said company were killed."

Sources: 1. U.S. Pensioners 1818-1872. 2. New York in the Revolution as a Colony and State, Vol. 1. 3. Pension Papers W17510. 4. Sons of the American Revolution Application.

****

John Readon age 13

John Readon was born in 1776 near Harris Ferry, which is now Harrisburg, Pennsylvania, and he died 12 February, 1835. He married Rachael Brooks in Alexandria, Virginia in 1792. For his service he received $64.00 per year. John said in his pension application that he had difficulty supporting his family due to the wounds he received from battle.

"I was attached to Col Abraham Buford's Regiment & General Scott's Brigade. I remained with Captain Wallace until the Battle of the Waxhaws of Buford's defeat at which time Captain Wallace was killed & most of his company wither killed or badly wounded among whom was me which happen on the 29th May 1780 when I paroled by Col Tarleton I then returned home."

The Battle of Waxhaws was fought near Lancaster, South Carolina against the British and they were led by Banastre Tarleton. When the Americans were attacked by the British Cavalry, many threw down their weapons to surrender. The British continued to kill the Americans, including the men who were not resisting. John was fortunate that he was captured and not killed. He was probably released due to his young age.

Sources: 1. Report to the National Society of D.A.R. Vol. 17. 2. DAR Magazine Vol. 54. 3. Records of the Revolutionary War. 4. Pension Papers S38330.

****

David Real (Reel) age 14

David Real was born in 1765 in Hampshear County, Virginia, and he died on 4 February, 1840 in Hardy, Virginia. He married Margaret

Moore in 1786 in Virginia. He received a yearly pension of $20 for his six months of service.

"*I Entered the Service of the United States under the following named officers and Served as himin stated that in the year 1779 in the first of August of that year I was drafted for a tower of three months and Placed under the Command of Captain James Parsons. Our first Rendesvous was at Morefields in the County of Hampshear from thence we marched by the most Direct Rout to Fort Pitt where we stayed about one month, thence to Wheeling on the Ohio River, at this last place we remained untill the Expiration of our Tower when we Returned home. We dispersed by the permit of Our Captain in the glades and Each found his way home his own way, with directions from Captain Parsons to assemble at his house on New years day to get our Discharge which a great proportion of us did and Received our Discharge from Captain Parsons, having served out my Tower of three months."*

"*Some time in the month of August I was again Drafted and placed in a company Commanded by Captain Stinson or Stevenson the Regiment was commanded by Col James Williams, Our Company again Rendesvous'd. at Morefields in the said County of Hampsheare and we marched by the most direct Rout to Winchester. It was the Intension of colonel Williams to March us direct to Yorktown where Lord Cornwallace lay Besieged by Our Army, but before our arrival Cornwallace had surrendered and Our Company was Detailed to guard the Prisonners at Winchester where we Remained the Remainder of Our Tower when I was Discharged having Served out my Tower of Three months.*"

Sources: 1. Census of 1830. 2. Pension Papers S15611.

****

Philip Reamer (Remair) age 13 or 14

Philip Reamer was born in 1763 in Pennsylvania, and he died on 15 March, 1815 in York County, Pennsylvania. He married Elizabeth Miller in York County in 1790. For some reason he changed his name to Barret Remair after he married. When his two daughters, Catherine and Christine, applied for his pension it was rejected, because there was no reason given for the name change. The pension bureau was not sure if the two names applied to the same person.

He served as a fifer in the 3rd Pennsylvania Regiment under Captain Samuel Kearsley and Colonel William Malcom. In 1780 he became a drummer. His two daughters gave the following account of his service in a letter to the pension bureau in 1851.

"He enlisted as a private in the service of the United States at Redding, Berks County Pennsylvania about the year 1776 first in the eleventh and afterwards in the second regiment in the Pennsylvania line. He was in the battles of Long Island, Brandywine, and Paola tavern. He was some of the time out of the service, but served in the whole about the term of five years and until the close of the war."

The 11th Pennsylvania was authorized on 16 September, 1776. The Regiment saw action at Brandywine, Paoli, Germantown, and Monmouth. During the winter of 1777-78 the Regiment was at Valley Forge. On 1 August the Regiment became part of the 2nd Pennsylvania Brigade.

The Battle of Paoli fought on 20 September, 1777 must have been a frightening experience for 14 year old Philip. The British launched a surprise attack on the camp of General Anthony Wayne. To make sure that the Americans were not alerted British commander Charles Grey had the flints removed from the men's muskets. This action later gave rise to the nickname "No Flint" Grey.

Nearly 300 Americans were killed, wounded, or missing during the rout. American troops fled in all directions, and there were reports that the British troops stabbed or mutilated Americans that tried to surrender. This would not be unusual because King George had declared that the colonists were rebels, which made them traitors in the eyes of the British. This means they would not be considered prisoners of war, and if captured they could immediately be executed.

Sources: 1. Pennsylvania Revolutionary War Battalions & Militia Index 1775-1783. 2. U.S. Revolutionary War Rolls 1775-1783. 3. "The Music of the Army..." An Abbreviated Study of the Ages of musicians in the Continental Army, by John U. Rees. Originally published in the Brigade Dispatch Vol. XXIV, No 4, Autumn 1993. 4. Pension Papers (no file number given).

****

David Reed Jr. age 12

David Reed was born 16 March, 1767 in Boothbay, Maine, and he died there on 28 March, 1841. He received a yearly pension of $30.

"In 1779 I enlisted into Capt Joseph Reed's company at Boothbay for the purpose of guarding the coast—was detached with the ten men to

now guard along the shore. In 1780 I enlisted at Boothbay into Capt Hinckley's company for five months—stationed at & near the harbor of Boothbay to guard the coast—Served the time out and was discharged. Afterwards in 1780 I enlisted at Boothbay for two months in Captain Tibbets company & served the time out guarding the coast."

Sources: 1. Pension Papers S18563.

****

William Reed age 14

William Reed was born on 10 December, 1762 in Caswell County, North Carolina, and he died on 15 January, 1843 in Hamilton County, Tennessee. He married Violett Brown on 4 January, 1789 in Pendleton County, South Carolina. He enlisted on 1 January, 1777, which was a month after he turned 14. William received a yearly pension of $31.66 and 640 acres of land in Tennessee for his service. In 1800 he owned 5 slaves.

"I entered the Service of the United States under the following named officers and served as herein Stated To Wit that on the first day of January Seventeen Hundred Seventy Seven I volunteered into the company of Capt. Waddy Tate under Lieutenants Davis & Poston as a private militia man for three months and marched through Salisbury in North Carolina to Camden in South Carolina to a Regiment under the command of Col. Shepherd where I remained until my term of service expired when I was discharged by Col. Shepherd and returned home to Caswell County, North Carolina."

"About the first of May Seventeen Hundred Eighty I volunteered again but my father being unwilling for me to leave home hired a Substitute by the name of Thomas Thaxton who served a tour of three months after crossing the South Carolina line."

"About the middle of August in the Same year there being another call or draft for men I volunteered again for a Three months tour as a private militia man (but was appointed Sergeant. in about Ten days) into the company of Capt. John Graves and Lieutenant Harold and marched to Lynches Creek crossing Pedee River at the mouth of Rocky River, at Lynches Creek I joined the Army under Genl Gates and was appointed Sergeant (as before stated) of the Pioneers to Cut a road from Lynches Creek to Rugeley's Mills and from the Mills I was marched in the night to the battle & place known as Gates defeat a distance of about Seven miles from the Mills; I recollect to have seen Capt. Porterfield who was badly *wounded in the engagement: from thence I returned to Hillsboro North Carolina and was marched from thence to a place called Lands ford on the Catawba River near the Waxhaw Meeting house, and from thence to a place called New Providence where I was discharged having been in Service four months though only called out for Three."*

A pioneer was a soldier, who would provide duties that included engineering in camp. Some of their duties might include digging latrines, clearing roads, or clearing an area for camp grounds. It was hard work but very necessary. In the British army it was usually assigned to blacks.

"I immediately volunteered again for Six weeks as a private Militiaman in Capt. James Wilson's Company which company belonged to a Battalion under the Command of Major Elijah Moore in the Regiment was commanded by Col. William Moore, General Smallwood having the command of the whole at this place, about this time Col. Rugeley and Maj Cook with the tories under their Command were taken by Col. Washington and I was appointed one of the Guard and marched with them to Salisbury North Carolina at which place I was discharged and returned to Caswell County my place of residence."

"In about three weeks I volunteered again under Capt. John Oldham as a private militia man for a tour of two months was attached to Col. William Moore's Regiment and marched to a place called Powels Race Paths joined the Army under General Pickens and defeated a body of Tories, my term of service having expired I was discharged and returned home."

In 1837 William added an amendment to his first declaration. In this new version he went into more detail on his last two tours of duty.

"I then Substituted in the place of a man (whose name I don't recollect) for one month and a half as a private in Capt. James Wilson's company and was attached to Col. William Moore's Regiment and Major Elijah Moore's Battalion and remained at New Providence until Genl Morgan & Col. Washington arrived on their way to Rugeley's Mills. We joined them but Col. Washington with his Regiment being in advance of us took Col. Rugeley & Major Cook with about one hundred & ten prisoners or tories, this was accomplished by a Stratagem of Col. Washington in a foggy morning by causing the Enemy to believe that a parcel of pine logs were Cannon. General Morgan placed the prisoners under the care of Col. Moore who took them to Salisbury where I remained

until my term of Service ended. I was then marched back to Caswell County and discharged."

William Reed fought in the battle took place at Rugeley's Mills on 4 December, 1780. In this battle the Americans were victorious. No one was killed, no one was wounded, and 115 Loyalists were captured. The patriots trapped 115 Loyalists in Rugeley's house and barn, and demanded that they surrender. When they refused, Colonel Washington had his men surround the buildings and they acquired a large, pine log and darken the color of the log. He then pointed this "Quaker Gun", as they are called, and told the Loyalist that if they did not give up he would open fire with the "cannon". Unaware that it was just a log, the Loyalists gave up. I would suspect that both sides had a good laugh when the deception was discovered.

"I omitted to name that on our march from the place where the prisoners were taken we met the Maryland Continentals at Charlotte at which place Genl Green took command of them. After being at home about two months Lord Cornwallis passed through our County in pursuit of General Greene. I then volunteered as a private under Capt. John Oldham and Major E. Moore's Battalion & Col. Wm Moores Regiment and marched down on the waters of Hyco Creek where we joined Genl Pickens and Col. Lee. We then crossed Haw River at General Butler's plantation and went on to Powels Race paths where we found and defeated a party of tories. We had with us at this place a party of the Catawba Indians. The next morning we chased Col. Tarleton across Haw River at the same ford we crossed at the previous evening, this was a two months tour from first to last at the end of which time I was discharged."

Sources: 1. U.S. Pensioners 1818-1872. 2. Census 1800. 3. Sons of the American Revolution Application. 4. Tennessee Genealogical Records. 5. South Carolina Marriage Index 1641-1965. 6. Pension Papers W5673. 7. A Military Journal during the American Revolutionary War, from 1775 to 1783 by James Thacher.

****

George Reese (Rees) age 14

George Reese was born on 8 February, 1763 in Dauphin County, Pennsylvania, and he died there on 13 August, 1828. He married Rebecca Cassel in 29 December, 1792. He received a yearly pension of $96. After he died, his wife received his yearly pension of $80. The family wrote letters to the Pension Office complaining that she should receive the same amount he did. Her pension amount did not change.

"I enlisted in Chester county in the State of Pennsylvania in the year 1777 in the company commanded by Capt. Joseph Prowell and subsequently served in the company commanded by Captain Abraham G. Claypoole in the eleventh Pennsylvania Regiment under the command of Colonel John Parron; I continued to serve in said corps or in the service of the United States until the month of January 1781 when I was discharged at Trenton in the State of New Jersey. I was at the battle of Brandywine and Germantown in the state of Pennsylvania."

George Reese said he was in the 11th Pennsylvania under the command of Colonel John Patton. The 11th Regiment was under the command of Colonel Richard Humpton. Colonel John Patton was commander of a Virginia Regiment, however, he did have in his regiment men from Pennsylvania, New Jersey, and Delaware. Captain Abraham Claypoole, commanded the 5th Company Patton's Regiment in 1779. Later, in 1781 he was Captain of the 3rd Company in the 11th Pennsylvania Regiment. Depending on the need. It was not uncommon for men to be moved around to different companies and regiments during the year

Sources: 1. Pension List of 1820. 2. Pension Papers W5692.

****

Ephraime Reynolds age 14

Ephraime Reynolds was born in 1765 in North Carolina. He enlisted twice in the North Carolina Militia and received a monthly pension of $8. His first enlistment was for 9 months in 1779. *"I was never engaged in any Battle being confined to the Hospital when the battle of Stono [1779] took place. I was discharged at Stono in the State of South Carolina."*

His second enlistment was for twelve months. *"I enlisted for twelve months under the aforesaid Capt. Samuel Jones in the Regiment commanded by Col. Little. I served the said time regularly and was discharged at Bacon's Bridge in South Carolina."*

The above information was written on a printed form used by the Pension Office. In his file was an addition letter written about his service but was too faint to read.

Sources: 1. U.S. Pensioners 1818-1872. 2. Roster of Soldiers from North Carolina in the American Revolution. 3. Pension Papers S38328.

****

John Richardson age 13

John Richardson was born in Louden, Virginia in 1765, and he died in Louden in 1822. He enlisted in the summer of 1778 in the Maryland Militia commanded by Captain John Rudolph, and he later served in the Virginia Continental line under Col Henry Lee. *"I was discharged from the service during inability in consequence of wounds received at the Battle of Eteau Springs in South Carolina".* He returned home and married Rebecca Davis.

Sources: 1. 1820 Census. 2. Pension Papers S46507.

****

Lysander Richardson age 14

Lysander Richardson was born on 30 March, 1763 in New Salem, Massachusetts, and he died on 3 April, 1813 in Woodstock, Vermont. He married Lois Ransom on 8 May, 1787.

At the age of fourteen Lysander enlisted as a waiter to his father Captain Israel Richardson. When General Burgoyne invaded the colonies from Canada in 1777 both father and son were summoned to the field. The Captain was sick so Lysander had to leave without him. He joined another boy named Joseph French, and the two boys took their knapsacks and muskets and marched together from New Salem to Stillwater. This was a distance of a little over a hundred miles.

Lysander enlisted on 11 July, 1777 in Captain Ebenezer Goodales's Company in the Regiment commanded by Lieut. Colonel Samuel Williams. He was discharged on 12 August, 1777, and he had a long walk back home. He enlisted again on 17 July, 1780 in Captain Seth Pierce's Company in the 6th Hampshire County Regiment commanded by Colonel Seth Murray. This tour was for three months, and he is listed on the rolls as 5'7" and with a dark complexion.

After the war Lysander was living in Woodstock and decided to enter the field of medicine. The town doctor Stephen Powers agreed to take him on as a student, if he would agree that if he obtained his license he would not practice within 10 miles of the doctor's home. When Lysander became a doctor he honored his agreement with Doctor Powers and moved to Barnard about ten and a half miles from Woodstock. He eventuality moved back to Woodstock and lived on a farm.

Sources: 1. D.A.R. Lineage Book, Vol. 54. 2. Sons of the American Revolution Application. 3. History of Woodstock by Henry Swan Dana, 1889. 4. Massachusetts Soldiers and Sailors in the Revolutionary War.

****

Alexander Ritchie age 11

Alexander Ritchie was born on 29 June, 1764 in Farmville, Virginia, and he died on 14 November, 1848 in Claiborne County, Tennessee. He married Elizabeth Doherty on 29 May, 1792. His pension application was rejected because he did not belong to any military unit.

"In the year 1776 I resided in the County of Montgomery and the State of Virginia and in what is now called Scott County in said State and I belonged to a Fort called Blakemore and in the month of May in said year I volunteered my services in the Army of the United States for the Term of six months under Captain Joseph Martain which said officer I understood was sent out from Henry County in Virginia to guard the Fintiers and shortly after I volunteered my Services that Captain Joseph Martain marched as I understood against the Cherokees under Colonel Christie and left Evan Shelby who was a Lout. in the command of the Fort and we ranged the country as Indian Spies until my term of service expired."

"In the month of April in the year of 1777 I again volunteered my service in the Army of the United States for the Term of six months under Captain James Gipson who then commanded the Fort at Blackmore's Station and also the Fort in the Ray cove and I was stationed Blackmore's Fort and we ranged the country as Indian Spies until my Term of service had expired and I received my discharge from Captain James Gipson."

"In month of April in the year of 1778 I again volunteered my services in the Army of the United States for the Term of six months under the same Captain James Gipson and I was again Stationed at Blakmore's Stationed and we ranged the country as Indian Spies until my Term of service expired."

"In November in the 1778 after the Expiration of the last above described Term of Service I moved with my father Alexander Ritchie Scr to his farm and I lived with my father until the 11th day of March 1779 and information came that the Indians had killed a family of the Phillipses

and eight of them in my father then moved immediately to Duncan's Fort at the Ford of Clinch River and I also accompanied him and together with others brought the dead down the River and buried them at the burying ground at the Fort."

"About the first of April next in the spring I again volunteered my services for the Term of six months in the Army of the United States under Captain John Snody who had the command of Duncan's Fort on clinch River William Cowe's Fort in Castle woods David Cowe's fort in the same neighborhood and William Mores Fort near Castel Run and I was stationed at Duncan's Fort and that they ranged all the County from one Fort to the other as Indian spies and after my Term of service had expired I received my discharge."

"I still lived with my father in Duncan's Fort during the hard winter of 1780 and in the month of March of said year we were again alarmed by the breaking out of the Indians who came near the Fort and killed Michor oglor family and about the first of April I volunteered my services in the Army of the United States for the Term of six months under Captain John Snoddy and this applicant further states that Captain Snoddy commanded at the forts as before described and that I was stationed at Duncan's Fort and that they ranged all the County as Indian spies as above described until my Term of service expired and I received my discharge."

Sources: 1. Census 1810, 1830, & 1840. 2. Some Tennessee Heroes of the Revolution. 3. Pension Papers R8784.

****

Judah Roberts age 14

Judah Roberts was born on 13 September, 1763 in Litchfield County, Connecticut, and he died on 12 June, 1839 in Windsor, Connecticut. He married Mercy Eno and he received a yearly pension of $80 for his service. He first enlisted in the service in May 1778.

"I entered as a volunteer & private in the state troops for the state of Connecticut in the later part of May 1778 in the company commanded by captain Joel Gillett & the Litenanunt was John Buser. I went to White Plains in the state of New York & from thence to Peekskill and from there to West Point in the state of New York & was employed in building the forts & the latter part of the year I went to Greenwhich in the state of Connecticut & was there stationed for the purpose of holding then enemy *in check and keeping them from plundering the country. I was under the command of the same officers during the whole of this service as when I entered the service & I served as a substitute & I left the service sometime in May 1779."*

"Sometime in September of 1779 I entered the service of the United States again at Horse neck in the town of Greenwhich as a militia man & private under the command of Major Davenport & belonged to the company commanded by Captain Benjamin Mills Lieutenant Samuel Banning. I was a substitute for John Walter. Went from Greenwhich to Stampford & was there placed as a guard over prisoners. I was in the service at this time three months."

"In March 1780 I was drafted for two months & sent to Horse neck from the town of Winchester in Litchfield County. I was in the Regt commanded by Col Mygatt & belonged to the company of which the Lieut. Was Goodwin."

"I volunteered at a place called Gitus Mills near Greenwhich in March 1781 as a private and served two months. General Waterbury commanded & in the company commanded by Capt Hatkiss & had been in a number of skirmished with the enemy."

"In 1781 I was drafted from Winchester and sent to New Haven Connt. As a private & belonged to the company commanded by Olmander Cattin & Lieut Goodwich to the tour of duty performed was two weeks."

"I enlisted in the Army of the United States in the last of March of 1782 & served in the third company regt. Continental line as a private under Col Samuel Webb."

Sources: 1. Lineage Book National Society of the D.A.R. Vol. 27, 1898. 2. Tombstone 3. Sons of the American Revolution Application. 4. Pension Papers S15622.

****

Stephen Robinson age 14

Stephen Robinson was born on 14 January, 1764 in Connecticut, and he died on 4 March, 1834 in Onondaga County, New York. He received a Badge of Merit signed by George Washington for his 5 years of service. He is listed on the rolls of the 2nd New York Regiment. He received a monthly pension of $8 for his service.

"Sometime in 1778 I enlisted as a private Soldier in the Company Commanded by Major Fisk in the second New York Regiment commanded by Colonel Van Cortlandt in the Continental army for the term of the war and served in the same __?__ as a drummer & was afterwards transferred to the company commanded by Colonel Walkins one of the aids of Baron Steuben in the same Regiment in which I served til the end of the war. I was discharged in June 1783."

Stephen was present at Sullivan's Expedition against the Tories and Indians in 1779 and at the Battle of Yorktown in 1781. At Yorktown the 2nd Regiment occupied the redoubt taken by the French. After the war Stephen served as a Captain of a company of light infantry militia in Washington County, New York.

His pension was suspended in April of 1823 based on a letter sent to the pension office in January. The letter was written by Martin Ford and several other neighbors in the area. Ford stated that Stephen became in debt for the sole purpose of obtaining a pension.

Stephen wrote to the pension office on 16 August, 1823, *"I demand a copy of all the information and documents which any person has sent into the war department that has authorized you to suspend by pension."* He wrote that he wanted this information for two reasons. First, he was going to prosecute the people who caused his suspension, and second he wanted to clear his name.

For the next couple of months several of his neighbors wrote to the pension office testifying to Stephen's honesty and good character. His pension was restored in November of 1823. In January of 1824 Martin Ford again wrote to the pension office stating that Stephen was *"unhonest"* and should not have a pension. No action was noted in the pension file of Stephen Robinson.

Sources: 1. Revolutionary Soldiers Resident or Dying in Onondaga County, N.Y., prepared by Rev. W.M. Beauchamp for the Onondaga Historical Association, 1863. 2. New York in the Revolution as Colony and State. 3. Pension Papers S43963. 4. Connecticut Town Birth Records pre 1870.

****

Archibald Rose age 14

Archibald Rose was born in 1764, and he died on 26 December, 1829 in Virginia. He served as a Sergeant in a Troop of Dragoons in the Continental Army. He received a monthly pension of $8.

"I enlisted in Major J. Nelson's Squadron in the State of Virginia in the company commanded by Capt William Armistead of the said State of Virginia sometime during the year 1778 as a private soldier by his merit was promoted to the rank of First Sergeant as per Captain William Armistead's Certificate I continued to serve in the said Corps, or in the service of the United States until the spring of the year 1783 when I was discharged from the service in Hampton in said state of Virginia, I was in the battles of ___ the Siege of York."

Sources: 1. U.S. Pensioners 1818-1872. 2. Pension Papers S39046.

****

Isaac Royal age 12

Isaac Royal was born maybe in Maine on 10 March, 1765, and died on 20 November, 1816 in Piscataquis County, Maine. He married Tabitha Nason in 1786. He served as a cabin boy to John Paul Jones during the Revolutionary War.

He joined the navy as a cabin boy in the fall of 1777. He served on the *Ranger,* which sailed from Portsmouth on 1 November, 1777. The *Ranger* had a crew of 140 men, 16 guns, and was built at a cost of $65,000 Continental dollars. Its mission, the first of its kind in the war, was to go to the Irish Sea and begin raids on British warships.

The crew became a problem for Captain Jones, because they wanted to be privateers and not be sailors looking for a fight with warships. When the *Ranger* reached France, Jones and Ben Franklin obtained French funds to refit the ship to make it faster and more maneuverable. The ship's gun ports were disguised, so that the ship and crew could easily be mistaken for a British ship.

Isaac Royal told the following account to his son John, and it was passed down through the family, *"At one time when I was a cabin-boy with John Paul Jones, we were cruising in English waters and fell in with an English merchant ship, at night, and anchored near her. I think we were flying the English flag. In the early morning Capt. Jones invited the English captain on board for breakfast. The Englishman accepted the invitation and came to our ship with several of his officers. While at breakfast, Jones, unknown to the Englishmen, ordered the American flag to be run up to the masthead. Breakfast over the visitors were escorted on deck and Capt. Jones, directing their attention to the colors, said, 'Look at the handsome flag at the masthead, the colors under which I sail.' They did so, and to their intense chagrin and wrath saw the stars and stripes. They were made prisoners, and their vessel was taken as a prize."*

This occurred in Carrickergus Harbor in Ireland. The prize made the crew of the *Ranger* a little happier about sailing with Captain Jones. During this voyage Captain Jones destroyed and captured several British Ships.

Isaac and his family settled in Dover, Maine around 1810. On his farm he and his wife raised 11 children. He was buried on his farm after dying of typhus fever in 1816. Unfortunately, he died before he was able to apply for a pension. This author is sure he would have had some wonderful stories to tell about his adventures on the high seas and in France.

Sources: 1. John Paul Jones: Finding the Forgotten Patriot by Robert L. Saunders. 2. Collections of the Piscataquis County Historical Society, Issue 1 by Piscataquis County Historical Society, Dover, Maine. 3. Census 1810.

****

Joseph Russ age 14

Joseph Russ was born on 19 December, 1762 in Bladen County, North Carolina, and he died after 1835. He received a yearly pension of $50.

"I was drafted in the Spring of the Year 1777, as a Private, at Elizabeth Town Bladen County, for a service of three months in a Company of which Joseph White was Captain, and William Jones (called Stuttering Bill Jones) was Lieutenant, and (as well as I recollect) in the Regiment of N. Carolina Militia called the first Regiment; and after having rendezvoused at Elizabeth Town, we were marched to Wilmington N. C., where I remained until the expiration of my term of service, and was then discharged. The Troops stationed at that place were under the command of General Robert Howe, who I believe belonged to the Continental Army."

"In a very short time after the above described Tour of duty (but the month or year, I cannot now recollect) there was another draft of Bladen Militia; when I became a substitute, at Elizabethtown, Bladen County, for one Isham Pitman a Private, for a service of five months, in a Company commanded by Captain John Yates, (the names of the other Officers not recollected). The Company rendezvoused at Elizabethtown and formed a part of the Regiment commanded by Col James Kenan of

Duplin County; were marched thence to Fayetteville (then Cross Creek), and stationed there until other Companies & Regiments of militia arrived at that place, to hold of whom were subsequently commanded by General Caswell, and were marched thence to Camden S. Carolina; thence down Santee River to a place called Cedar Creek, where we were joined by a Corps of Continentals under the command of Col Buford & Major Washington -- the whole Forced being destined to reinforce Charleston, then in a State of Siege; but information being received that that object could not be obtained owing to the place being too closely invested by the British-- they were countermarched to Camden--where Caswell & Buford with their respective commands, separated. The former, after the Troops under his command had suffered severely from privations & forced marches, returned to Fayetteville. On the march, information of the defeat of Colonel Buford's Command was received. My term of service having expired, I was discharged, at Fayetteville & returned home."

"In the summer of the year 1778, about the time of the great Eclipse of the sun, [this was the first total solar eclipse recorded in the United States] I became a substitute at Elizabethtown Bladen County North Carolina for one William Blackburn, a Private, in a Company of drafted Bladen Militia (the term of service not recollected)--we were marched to Fayetteville under the command of Capt Ephraim Mulford , where we were attached to the Troops under the command of General Harrington destined for the South; there were other Troops stationed at that place under the command of Col Thomas Owen of Bladen, destined for the upper part of the State: Before the Troops were marched off, I made an exchange with a man in Col Owen's Regiment, who had previously been under the command of General Harrington, and wished to go with him; and as Col Owen was from my neighborhood, I was desirous of going with him. -- the man with whom the exchange was made had four months to serve. From Fayetteville Captain Mulford returned home, and the Troops under the command of Col Owen proceeded to join the Troops under the command of General Jones, passing through Hillsboro in Orange County, and on their march were joined by a body of five hundred men, under the command of Col Parsley--we marched as far as the Shallow Ford of the Yadkin--where we had a skirmish with a body of Tories under the command of a man by the name of Bryan or Bryant, the morning after they reached the Ford. The Tories were defeated with the loss of 18 killed & 16 wounded. One of the Americans was killed. We were marched from the Shallow Ford to Salem; thence to Houser Town; and thence back again to the Head Quarters of General Jones; where I remained until I completed the term of service of the man, for whom I was substituted; was then discharged & returned home."

"In the year 1780 (time not precisely recollected except that it was a short time before the surrender of Cornwallis), I was drafted at Elizabethtown Bladen County, as a Private in Captain Ephraim Mulford's Company of Militia for a service of three months--the Company rendezvoused at Elizabethtown, where I was furloughed for a few days, and joined his company at the Head Quarters of General Butler at Rocky Point, on the North East River. The Troops were marched thence to the Big Bridge, about 20 or 25 miles above Wilmington -- thence to Swan's old Field, remained there 2 or 3 days, and while there received intelligence of Cornwallis' Surrender-- thence crossed the Cape Fear River, and down the same to Cobham's Bluff -- where I was stationed some time and discharged, having served not more than 5 or 6 weeks."

Sources: 1. U.S. Pension Roll of 1835. 2. Pension Papers S7435.

****

John Rutherford age 13

John Rutherford was born on 14 November, 1762 in Newburyport, Massachusetts, and he died there on 17 November, 1840. He married (1) Jane Davis on 28 January, 1796, and she died in 1814. He then married (2) Mary Wadleigh on 13 January, 1820. She received a yearly pension of $35 for his service.

"I first enlisted at Beverly in the year 1776 in the company commanded by Captain Putman in the regiment commanded by Colonel Hutchinson to serve as a private soldier thence for <u>one year</u> and marched with said company from Beverly to Winter Hill from thence to Cambridge, and afterwards to Dorchester to Norwich and to Fort Washington on Long Island. Before my term of service expired I was taken prisoner by the Enemy, carried to New York and there detained seven weeks and until exchanged."

John Rutherford was one of more than 2,800 American soldiers captured at the Battle of Fort Washington on 16 November, 1776. At the time of exchange John had to swear an oath not to enter the army again. He did not swear not to enter the navy, which he then did.

"I afterwards shipped and entered on board the private armed Schooner called the Glasgow commanded by Captain Parsons, Eight four *pound carriage guns and manned with about forty men commissioned by the Government of the United States as a privateer--sailed from Newburyport aforesaid in said schooner to the best of my present remembrance in the month of September AD 1777 on a cruise in which we captured the British armed ship Oxford of London mounting fourteen six pound carriage guns after a battle of seven __?__ and sent her into said Newburyport where she arrived safe. We fought on said cruise several battles with the enemy but made no other capture--on this cruise was on duty on board said schooner about Three months."*

"I also shipped and entered on board the private armed Schooner Hornet commanded by Captain Springer also commissioned by the Government of the United States mounting Ten four pound carriage funs and manned with about Forty men cruised in her off Halifax and on the Eastern Shore on which we captured the British Brig Success bound from London for Quebec mounting six carriage guns and maned with about Twenty men having on board Provisions and clothing for the British Army and arrived with said prize at Newburyport aforesaid after an absence of more than Two months."

"I also shipped and entered on board the privateer schooner Shark commanded by Captain Preston also commissioned by the government of the United States mounting Twelve large guns and maned with from Thirty to Forty men which I think was in the year 1778 and cruised in her off the Eastern Shore Two months during which we captured two British vessels laden with Fish and __?__ them __?__ to Newburyport aforesaid."

"I also shipped and entered on board the private armed Brig Gates commanded by Captain Newman who commissioned by the government of the United States mounting four six pound carriage guns and maned with from sixty to twenty men, was in a or on board said Brig of Halifax for which I think was in the year 1779 rather more than two months in which we captured a British Brig having on board Three hundred and sixty five pipes of Maderia wine and afterwards on the same cruise captured the British armed Schooner Rambler from Halifax both which got in safe."

"I also entered and shipped on board the private armed ship Monmouth commanded by Captain Paul Newman also commissioned by the government of the United States as a letter of Marque, mounting six carriage guns maned with about Thirty men and was in her on a cruise of the West Indies on which cruise we captured a British __?__ __?__ from

New York but finding she had persons on board diseased with small pox released her; on this cruise we were absent about Three months."

"I also shipped and entered on board the private armed Brig Adventure commanded by Captain John O'Brien also commissioned by the government of the United States as letter of Marque mounting six carriage guns and maned with about Twenty men; on this cruise sailed in company with the private armed Brig Hazzard commanded by John Foster Williams and on this cruise captured the British armed Brig Active mounting Eighteen carriage guns, after a serious engagement of Thirty Two minutes in which Nineteen of the enemy were killed also two of our own number—afterwards parted company from the Hazzard fell in with and had a smart engagement with a privateer British Schooner mounting ten guns and undermanned from our cruise haven been absent a few days over three months."

"I also shipped and served on board the private armed Letter of Marque Drake commanded by Captain Newman ship Mercury commanded by Captain Johnson Brig Congress commanded by Captain Wells ship General Stark commanded by Captain Fisher in one of which I was captured by the British and detained a prisoner on Antiqua Eleven months in the year 1783."

Sources: 1. Sons of the American Revolution Application. 2. 1840 Census. 3. Massachusetts Marriages 1633-1850. 4. Pension Papers W26422. 5. Sons of the American Revolution California Society.

****

John Ryker age 12

John Ryker was born on 18 January, 1764 in Closter, New Jersey, and he died on 22 November, 1848 in Jefferson County Indiana. He married (1) Mary Van Cleave on 16 June, 1784 in Lincoln County, Kentucky and (2) Amelia Littlejohn on 3 July, 1838 in Madison, Indiana. His pension application was rejected because he did not serve for six months.

"In the year 1776 met a party of British 300 in number, who ascended North River for the purpose of plundering, taking cattle or horses, had a skirmish below Dobbs Ferry in New Jersey, the British retreated. Went out under Captain Bell. Called from the company under the command of Captain Herrin, in which company I was a private from the latter part of the year 1776 to the latter part of the year 1777. My *service under Captain Herrin was for one year. Was in no engagement under his command, Was ordered to be always ready for services."*

"During this year in the month of June taken from the command of Captain Herrin and transferred to the command of the same Captain Bell who marched his company against a party of British who had plundered and had taken 40 head of cattle and horses. We fired on them at below Dobbs Ferry and this fire was exchanged. Our fire was made from the top of a cliff and had the desired effect. They retreated and we retook the cattle and horses. This service and the skirmish before stated under the same Captain Bell together amount to about 2 days service. This last service was in the month of July if I recollect right. My recollection of the dates is however very imperfect."

"The British then lay in New York — was __?__ in Rockland County New Jersey. Resided in Rockland County at this time. In 1778 moved to Virginia Beckly County, in 1779 left Beckly County Va. In the spring of 1780 landed at the falls of Ohio (Kentucky). On the first of July or thereabouts 1780, went on a campaign under the command of General Clark to the Miami Indian towns. Colonels Lynn, Logan & Slaughter has commanded under Clark. Colonel Slaughter had command of Transport Boats which conveyed stores & provision from Louisville to where Cincinnati now stands, Robert Johnson was Captain of my Company. We started from Bear Grass Floyd's Station, thence up the Ohio River. Some of the boats aforesaid on one & some on the other side the river. Men went on land except those who manned the boats. I was marched on the now Kentucky side the river. About 2 days march from Louisville boats on the opposite side were fired on by Indians, 2 men Killed 3 wounded who afterward died of their wounds. Captain Bunn was one of that number. We set out immediately to cross the river in our boats, fired on Indians & they dispersed. This was late in the evening. We arrived at the mouth of Licking, thence to Chillicothe, destroyed Indian town then. Town was in part fired by Indians upon our approach. We fired the balance and destroyed a large quantity of their corn. Thence to Piqua town when we had a battle with Indians, lossed 12 or 15 men. Killed a number of the Indians: took and destroyed town. Thence returned to Bear Grass same route. Campaign lasted two months & I think somewhat longer. Started in July about the beginning of the month. Returned home in September but the precise time I cannot recollect."

"In the spring of 1781 was called upon to work a tour of duty at Fort at Louisville for its defense & worked 30 days and soon after was

called upon to build Block house & __?__ some miles above the falls of Ohio. Worked 10 days as I believe."

"In the month of ___ 1781 went with a party of men under ___?___ to Bullets Lick to bring back families defeated & massacred by Indians (such as survived) while moving from Bear Grass to Harrodsburgh, massacre was at Clear Station. Went on 2nd trip to bury the dead, distance not now recollected, suppose it was 15 miles. Time occupied in going both trips was about 3 or 4 days."

"During Summer of 1781 Served as Indian Spy frequently went a distance of 20 or 25 miles. On the Ohio and up the River and in various directions, as occasion required (lived then on extreme frontier). Service as Spy here spoken of would amount to ___ days. In the spring of 1782 went out on scouting party under Captain Whitaker. Marched from Bear Grass to mouth of Kentucky River, distance 60 miles or thereabouts. Thence to Drinness Lick 15 or 20 miles, thence in a circuitous route to Floyd's Fork near where it empties into Salt River. Thence to Bear Grass. The whole distance of march about 150 or perhaps 160 miles not less: had no engagement or skirmish. This we performed in about 5 or 6 days or a week."

"In August 1782 went on expedition to the Indian towns of Miami under General Clark Col Slaughter, Logan, Floyd & Lynn: Richard Chinowith was my Captain. Marched from Bear Grass. Went up the Ohio River, army went on land & provisions were conveyed in boats. Boats now landed at Cincinnati where it now stands, and a Guard left with them, I was one of that Guard, The army went out against Indian towns: took one Indian town, destroyed some towns, and killed some warriors, Captain McCracken, captain of horses died at Cincinnati of wounds recd. in battle at Indian town, was buried close under the breastwork with the honors of war. Campaign lasted from August to last of October, about 2 months to the best of my recollection."

"Then was a spy sent out by Major Whitaker acted as such for 7 months, this was however after the year 1783. In 1782 went to Boone's Station from Bear Grass a distance of 25 miles, went to rescue families in the fort after it was attacked. Esq. Boon was wounded in the attack. Company was commanded either by Capt Hardy Hill or Whitaker. Service occupied 5 or 6 days."

Sources: 1. Indiana Marriage Index 1800-1941. 2. Sons of the American Revolution Application. 3. John Ryker Family Bible. 4. Roster of Soldiers and Patriots of the American Revolution in Indiana. 5. Pension Papers R9129.

****

John Sack age 13

John Sack was born in 1763, probably in England, and he died in 1831. By occupation he was a silk weaver. He enlisted for three years in 1776 in Virginia in a company commanded by Captain Bard and in the regiment commanded by Colonel Elbert in the Georgia Continental Line. He received $8.00 per month for his service.

"I continued to serve in said Corps until Savannah was captured, when & where I was taken prisoner of war & put on board the British ship Betsy they by consent of the Captain of said prison ship was allowed to go on board of a British privateer to help her weigh anchor, most of her crew having deserted which vessel took me to Sandy hook where I was pressed on board the British sloop of war Hunter. Then put on board the Vulture a British sloop of war. Then sailed up the North River then was put on board the Rainbow man of war about the time of General Arnold's defection, from which I deserted at the Eastern end of Long Island, went to the city of New York then apprehended as a British deserter & compelled to return on board the ship from which I deserted or to enlist as a soldier in the 84th Regiment of the British army, which last alternative I preferred & embraced."

It was not uncommon for American soldiers to join the British army or serve aboard a British ship rather than stay on a prison ship. Conditions on the prison ships were deplorable and in many cases were a death sentence. Over 10,000 American prisoners of war died from neglect.

"I then embarked with the British Army & landed at Suffolk in Virginia Where on the second night I deserted & joined the Army of my own Country, then commanded by General Eaton who gave me permission to go to North Carolina in Nov. 1781. That I was in a battle at Frederica Island. I was in the battles of Amelia Island & midway Meeting House & at the capture of Savannah."

Sources: 1. U.S. Pensioners 1818-1872. 2. Twenty-four Hundred Tennessee Pensioners. 3. Pension Papers S39062.

****

John Sample age 14

John Sample was born in 1760 in Ireland, and he died in 1835 in Jefferson, Alabama. He married Sarah Neely in South Carolina in 1783. John came to America with his parents to escape British oppression of the Irish. They came to South Carolina, because the state offered free land to any Protestants who settled the inlands and thus acted as a buffer against the Indians.

Statement made in 1833: *"That I entered the service of the United States under the following named officers and served as herein stated. Andrew Pickens was Colonel of the Regiment to which I belonged-- Armstrong Heard was Captain of the company to which I belonged when I first entered the service. I entered the Service when I was between 14 and 15 years old. I lived in Abbeville district in South Carolina when I entered the Service. I entered as a substitute in the first instance and place of one Robert Griffin. The first battle in which the Regiment to which I belonged was in between Col Pickens who commanded the Whigs and a Col Boyd who commanded a party of Tories at Kettle Creek. I was at the Siege of Savannah where General Williamson commanded the Brigade I was in Colonel Reed Commanded the Regiment and Armstrong Heard commanded the Company to which I regularly belonged, but at the storming of the Fort or the attempt to do so, I was in a Company commanded by Captain Burrow, I believe."*

The Battle of Kettle Creek was fought in Georgia on 14 February, 1779. Colonel Andrew Pickens had 200 South Carolina Militia, including John Sample, and an additional 140 Georgia militia engage Colonel Boyd who had 600 Tories. The Tories were camped at a bend in Kettle Creek, and the patriots attempted to mount a surprise attack at sunrise against them. The surprise failed and the battle raged on both sides of the creek for three hours. The Tories finally broke, and they retreated leaving Colonel Boyd dying on the field of battle.

Colonel Pickens approached the dying Boyd after the battle, the two men being from South Carolina, knew of each other. Boyd rejected Pickens offer of prayers instead he asked Colonel Pickens if he would deliver personal items to his wife and tell her of his fate, which Pickens eventually did.

"The next battle I was in was the Battle of Stono where General Lincoln Commanded. Andrew Pickens commanded the Regiment to which I belonged at Stono and I saw the horse of Col Pickens shot from under

him in the battle. Captain Samuel Moore Commanded the company to which I belonged at this time--The next principle engagement that I was in was at the Siege of Ninety Six in South Carolina where General Greene commanded the American forces. At this Siege I was again in Captain Samuel Moore's Company. At the raising of this Siege we were marched by Col Pickens across Broad River (General Greene with his forces having separated from him) and afterwards fell in the rear of the British at a place called Boggy Gully and killed Some of them and took Some prisoners."

"We then returned home and afterwards I joined a six months volunteer Company raised by the same Captain Samuel Moore and was engaged for some time against the Tories. In about two months after I joined Captain Moore's volunteer Company peace was made, and until the Tories were finally subdued. I was in many fights with the Tories which I have not enumerated--He was in the vicinity of <u>Bill Cunningham</u> who commanded the Troop of Tories & of Gen Robert Cunningham who also commanded a Brigade of Tories, and the history of the times when the test the difficulties, dangers and hardships encountered by the Whigs. I was almost constantly in the service from the time I entered it until the close of the war. I scarcely slept at home in my father's House during the whole continuance of the war in South Carolina, was constantly upon the alert, either in watching & fighting the Tories or upon the service enumerated."

Statement made on 21st day of June 1834: *"According to the best of my recollection I entered the service in 1773 or 1774. I arrived at this conclusion from a belief that I am now about seventy-four or seventy-five years of age, and I remember that I was between fourteen and fifteen years old when I entered the service. I lived when I entered the service in Abbeville district in South Carolina as stated in my first declaration--I entered as a private and as a substitute in place of one Robert Griffin. I served in a Company commanded by Armstrong Heard as before stated-- and was under Col Andrew Pickens as before stated. In my first service mentioned I served six weeks as the substitute of Griffin and was engaged in guarding the frontiers of Abbeville against the Cherokee Indians--when this term of service was out I again went as a substitute for a man whose name I do not now recollect for six weeks or two months I would not be positive which. In this second service I was again upon the frontiers against the Indians--When this Service was out I went into the service of my own account and was in the Battle at Kettle Creek under Colonel Pickens and fought against the Tories who were commanded by a Colonel Boyd. A large number of Tories were taken in this Battle as prisoners and were sent to Orangeburg and I was sent as one of the guard that went with* them--This term of service lasted six weeks or more. After this service was ended I went as a private in Captain Armstrong Heard's Company to the Siege of Savannah. I belonged to a Regiment commanded by Colonel Reed and was in a Brigade of Militia commanded by General Williamson. After the attempt to storm the Fort I was in a company Commanded by Captain Burrow as well as I remember."

"After this was over I joined a Company commanded by Captain Samuel Moore and was at the Battle of Stono where General Lincoln commanded. Col Pickens commanded the Regiment to which I belonged. I saw Colonel Pickens' horse shot from under him in this battle. In this Service I was engaged two months or more. The next service I was engaged in was the Siege of Ninety Six where General Greene commanded the American forces. At this Siege I was again in Captain Moore's Company. At the raising of the Siege we were marched by Col Pickens across Broad River (General Greene with his forces having separated from him) and afterwards fell in the rear of the British at a place called Boggy Gully and killed some of them & took some prisoners. We then returned home and afterwards I joined a volunteer Company raised by the same Capt Samuel Moore for six months and was employed against the Tories. In about two months after joining Captain Moore's volunteer Company he was killed by the Tories near __?__ Ferry on the Saluda. I then joined Captain Manfield's Company and served with him against the Tories. After this I was assigned to Capt John Calhoun's Company & served with him against the Tories. I served with Capt Calhoun till he was killed by the Tories near Swanseys Ferry on the Saluda in South Carolina. I then joined Capt Robert Maxfield's Company and served with him against the Tories. After this I was assigned to Capt John Calhoun's company and served with him in endeavoring to hold the Tories in check--I continued to serve with Captain Calhoun till after peace was made with Great Britain & until the Tories were finally subdued. I was in many fights with the Tories which he will not take the trouble to mention."

Sources: 1. The American Revolution in the Southern Colonies by David Lee Russell. 2. Tombstone 3. Census 1820 & 1830. 4. Alabama Revolutionary War Soldiers. 5. Pension Papers 32505.

****

James Sampson age 12

James Sampson was born on 11 April, 1764 in Duxbury, Massachusetts, and died 27 September, 1851 in Otisfield, Maine. He married Jemima Stetson on 12 January, 1786 in Maine. For his service he received a pension of $55 a year.

"*I entered the service of the United States at Duxbury County of Plymouth State of Mass on the first day of January AD 1777 and served <u>nine months</u> in the Company Commanded by Capt Andrew Sampson of Duxbury aforesaid, and was stationed during said months at the gurnet so called at the entrance of Plymouth Harbor.*"

The gurnet was also known as Gurnet Light or Plymouth Light. It was a lighthouse located on Gurnet Point at the entrance of the harbor. The light is accessible only by passing through the town of Duxbury.

"*Again I entered the service sometime in the winter of 1778 and served <u>three months</u> in a company commanded by Lieut Washburn and was stationed at the gurnet aforesaid. I commenced my service a short time after the Brig __?__ was cast away and was discharged the last part of the Spring or the first part of the summer.*"

"*Again I entered the service in the year 1780 on the first day of July and served three months and was discharged on the first day of November following on Butts Hill Rhode Island. The company to which I belonged was commanded by Capt Rider in the in the Regiment Commanded by Col Jacobs. I served in the whole <u>Sixteen and half months</u> as a private Soldier.*"

"*The first nine months I entered as a substitute for __?__ Sullivan and the three months service at the garnet I went as a substitute for a man by the name of Bartlett of Plymouth.*"

After the war James married Jemima and moved to Harrison, Maine. He purchased land and erected a log-house. He built mills on a stream in the area and carried on blacksmithing at the same time.

Sources: 1. Tombstone. 2. Sons of the American Revolution Application. 3. Maine Marriage Records 1713-1937. 4. Early Settlers of Harrison, Maine: with an Historical Sketch of the Settlement, Progress and Present Condition of the Town. 5. Pension Papers S18198.

****

Samuel Sanford age 9

Samuel Sanford was born on 15 April, 1766 in Milford, Connecticut, and he died on 27 September, 1858 in Ohio. He enlisted a few days before his 10th birthday and received a yearly pension of $26.66 for his service. He married Rhonda Atwater in November of 1795.

"I entered the service as an enlisted soldier on or about the 10th of April 1776 then on Long Island. After the battle of Long Island we retreated to Kingsbridge and thence to White Plains after the battle of White Plains we went to Fish Kill where I was discharged on or about the 9th of December 1776."

"I went to New York at the request of my father then a Lieutenant in the army and joined the troops on Long Island as before stated. I took the place of E___?__ Sanford who had served as a waiter for my father and he went into the ranks and served as other soldiers. When our army was about to cross the North River into New Jersey I was told by my officers that I was not old enough to endure a winter campaign and that I might return home. My father afterwards drew my wages and paid it to me in continental money."

Sources: 1. New England Families, Genealogical and Memorial, Vol. 1, Edited by William Richard Cutter. 2. D.A.R. Lineage Book, Vol. 14. 3. Pension Papers S4810.

****

John Schermerhorn age 13

John Schermerhorn was born on 23 January, 1764 in Schenectady, New York, and he died after 1834. He married Catherine Bradt on 4 March, 1788. He received a monthly pension of $20.

"In the year 1777 on the 10th day of August being to young to be enrolled in the Militia I volunteered for fourteen days & served with a party of Militiamen from the Regiment of Colonel Abraham Wimple to the Heldebergh in pursuit of Tories who reorganized there."

"In the year 1779 I served for the term of one month as a substitute for my father Jacob Schermerhorn. I also remained on duty at the same place as substitute for John Schermerhorn for the term of four weeks."

"In the month of January 1780 I was enrolled in Captain Abraham __?__ Company of Militia in the Regiment of Said Abraham Wimple was Colonel, and I continued to serve in said Company until the end of said war."

"I was often engaged in many scouting & patrolling parties. In the month of August of the tear last named I marched to Fort Plank, also

the same year with a party of 33 whites & 2 Indians to Ballston when that place was destroyed by the enemy. I was at Fort Herkimer on duty when Walter Butler was killed. I was with a detachment of Indians at Warren bush when that place was destroyed by the enemy."

Sources: 1. A History of Schenectady During the Revolution by Willis Tracy Hanson. 2. Pension Papers S23411. 3. Sons of the American Revolution Application. 4. Tombstone.

****

James Scott age 12

James Scott was born in June of 1764 in Augusta, Virginia, and died 5 July, 1848. While a baby his father David and mother Clarissa were among the very earliest settlers of Morgantown in Monongalia County, Virginia.

James stated in his pension files, *"I enlisted as a musician for three years, in the County of Monongalia aforesaid, in the fall of the year 1776 with my father Captain David Scott of the 13th Regiment of Virginia Continental troops."* The area was apparently in danger from Indians, because in 1777 two of James's sisters, Phoebe and Fannie, were killed in an Indian attack.

"I marched to Fort Kittanning on the Allegheny River about 50 miles from the present city of Pittsburgh, where we remained between 2 and 3 months. From that Fort we descended the Allegheny River to Pitt in bark canoes, where we remained during the residue of the latter year and following Spring---that during the summer of 1778 we left Fort Pitt under the command of Colonel John Gibson, the Army being commanded by General McIntosh, and descended the Ohio in boats to the mouth of the Big Beaver Creek, near which I assisted to build a Fort called McIntosh's Fort."

Fort McIntosh was built in Western Pennsylvania as a challenge to the British stronghold at Detroit. The purpose of the fort was to protect the western frontier from British and Indian attacks.

Captain David Scott retired 30 September, 1778 due to having his right arm amputated because of a wound to his hand. James wrote, *"About the month of November 1778 Lieutenant Colonel Richard Campbell of the same Regiment gave me a furlough to remain at home during the following winter—in the spring of the year 1779 my father hired and enlisted a man to serve as substitute in my place for the remainder of the term of my enlistment."*

For their service Captain David Scott was granted a pension of $100 a year (later raised to $240) and 4,000 acres of land and James received $88 a year. James married Amelia Daugherty in 1788 and they had 11 children. In 1800 James, former musician in the militia, became Major James Scott of the local militia.

Sources: 1. The Making of Morgantown, West Virginia by James Callahan. 2. The Sons of the American Revolution Application. 3. U.S. Revolutionary War Rolls, 1775-1783. 4. U.S. Pension Roll of 1835.

****

John Scott age 12

John Scott was born on 23 March, 1765 in Dublin, New Hampshire and he died on 21 December, 1847 in Peterbrough, New Hampshire. He married Bethia Ames on 18 February, 1788. He enlisted in his father's regiment as a fifer in July of 1777. He received a monthly pension of $8.

"In July AD 1777 I enlisted into Capt Scotts company as a musician for the term of three years and faithfully served said term part of it as a Musician and part of it as a Private Soldier in the __?__ Regiment, commanded by Col H Jackson in the Massachusetts Line in the Continental Service; and at the end of thereof was honorably discharged."

"On the 12th day of March AD 1781 I enlisted again as a private soldier for three years more and was attached to the 7th company in the 32nd Massachusetts Regiment and faithfully served in the said line as above mentioned till December 18th 1783."

John served under Colonel Henry Jackson in the Additional Continental Regiment which was predesignated the 16th Massachusetts Regiment in 1780. The regiment wintered at Valley Forge and in June of 1778 fought in the Battle of Monmouth and two months later at the Battle of Rhode Island.

Sources: 1. Tombstone 2. Census 1820, 1830, & 1840. 3. Massachusetts Marriages 1633-1850. 4. New Hampshire Death & Burial Records 1654-1949. 5. U.S. Pensioners 1818-1872. 6. Pension Papers W24918. 7. Suffering Soldiers by John Resch.

****

Christopher Seider age 10

Christopher Seider was born in March of 1758 in Braintree, Massachusetts, and he died on 22 February, 1770 in Boston, Massachusetts.

On 22 February, 1770 a large group of school boys and apprentices were picketing the shop of Theophilus Lilly, who was a merchant who had chosen not to boycott British goods. Local patriot leaders had organized the protest, and the names and addresses of merchants who would not support the boycott had been published in the Boston newspapers. Some merchants had been chased out of their shops and beaten, but the protest at Lilly's shop had been peaceful.

The group of boys began harassing Lilly by throwing rocks, snowballs, and ice at his shop and his customers. They even hanged Lilly in effigy in front of his store. Things began to get out of hand with the appearance of Loyalist Ebenezer Richardson.

Richardson was at one time a confidential informer for the Loyalist government and later for Customs officials. In the mid 1760's he became an official Customs employee, enforcing the laws against smuggling, and helping to collect hated taxes. He was a known and unpopular man in Boston.

Ebenezer Richardson lived nearby and rushed to Lilly's store to help the merchant disperse the crowd. Instead, the sight of Richardson aroused the crowd even more. More stones and other objects were thrown at Richardson, and one object caused a gash on his head. They chased him back to his home and began throwing objects at his house. Windows were broken, and Richardson's wife was hit in the head by an egg. Richardson was furious, and while standing in a second story window he aimed a musket filled with buck shot at the crowd below. He threatened to fire if the crowd did not disperse.

He fired his musket and later claimed that he intended the shot to be a warning, but he hit two boys. Sammy Gore who was nineteen years old, was struck in both thighs and a hand. Christopher Seider was hit by eleven pieces of lead shot described as the size of peas, and they struck the young boy in the breast and abdomen. Doctors attended to the boy, however, he died about 9 that night.

The following account of the event was published in the Boston Gazette three days later:

"On Thursday last in the forenoon, a barbarous murder extended with many aggravating circumstances, was committed on the body of a young lad of about eleven years of age, Son to Mr. Snider of this town. A number of boys had been diverting themselves with the exhibition of a piece of pageantry near the house of Theopolis Lillie, who perhaps at this juncture of affairs may be with the most propriety be described by the name of an IMPORTER. This exhibition naturally occasioned numbers to assemble, and in a very little time there was a great concourse of persons, especially the younger sort. One Ebenezer Richardson, who has been many years employed as an under-officer of the customs, long known by the Name of an INFORMER, and consequently a person of a most abandoned character, it seems, took umbrage at the supposed indignity offered to the importer and soon became a party to the affair. He first attempted to demolish the pageantry, and failing in the attempt, he retired to his house, which was but a few rods from the exhibition. Several persons passing by house, Richardson, who seemed determined to take this occasion to make a Disturbance, without the least provocation, gave them the most opprobrious language, charging them with perjury, etc. which raised a dispute between them. This, it is supposed, occasioned the boys to gather nearer Richardson's house, and he, thinking he had now a good colouring to perpetuate the villainy, threatened to fire upon them, and swore by god that he would make the place too hot for some of them before night, and that he would make lane through them if they did not go away. Soon after, a number of brickbats or stones were thrown among the people, from Richardson's house, but the witnesses, who were sworn before the magistrates, declared that it did not appear to them that till them any sort of stack was made by the people on the house. This, however, brought on a skirmish, and Richardson discharged his piece, loaded with swan shot, at the multitude, by which the unhappy young person above-mentioned was mortally wounded, having since died of his wounds. A youth, son to captain John Gore, was also wounded in one of his hands and in both his thighs, by which his life was endangered, but he is likely to soon recover of his wounds. We were assured that not less than 11 shot were found in the body of the unfortunate boy, who was inhumanly murdered by the infamous informer on Thursday last. It is hoped the unexpected and melancholy death of young Snider will be a means for the future of preventing any, but more especially the soldiery, from being too free in the use of their instruments of death."

After the shooting Richardson was hurried off to jail, but otherwise the man would have probably been beaten to death. Samuel

Adams always looking for some way to stir up more hatred against the British saw a golden opportunity with this tragic event. He paid for and helped organize the boy's funeral four days later, which turned out to be the largest ever held at that time in America. The people assembled at the Liberty Tree, where Samuel Adams had attached a board with the following message,

"Thou shalt take no satisfaction for the life of a MURDERER—he shall surely be put to death and

Though hand join in hand, the wicked shall not pass unpunish'd."

The funeral procession stretched more than half a mile with over 2,000 people in attendance. There were more than four hundred carefully groomed, very angelic schoolboys marching two by two, cloaked in white, and leading the coffin. Six boys carried the coffin followed by the boy's family and friends. The funeral and Samuel Adams speech fueled public outrage that peaked eleven days later with the Boston Massacre.

Ebenezer Richardson was convicted of murder in the spring, but the judges delayed his sentencing because they hoped he would receive a pardon from London. A pardon was received a few years later, and Richardson began a new job with the Customs service. The pardon was granted saying that Richardson acted in self-defense.

Phillis Wheatley, a young slave girl about 16 at the time of Christopher's death, later wrote a poem about the event entitled, *On the Death of Mr. Snider Murder'd by Richardson*. She became the first African-American woman to publish a book and the first to make a living from her writing.

Christopher Seider may have been a ten year old bystander on that cold day in February 1770. However, he became the first American causality of the forthcoming American Revolution. His death set into motion other events that would lead to war between England and her colonies.

Sources: 1. Discovering the American Past: A Look at the Evidence, Vol I: to 1877 by William Bruce Wheeler, Lorri Glover. 2. Founders: The People Who Brought You a Nation by Ray Raphael. 3. Bill O'Reilly's Legends and Lies: The Patriots by David Fisher. 4. In Pursuit of Liberty: Coming of Age in the American Revolution by Emmy E. Werner.

****

Howell Sellers age 14

Howell Sellers was born in March of 1762 in Chatham, North Carolina, and he died 17 October, 1832 in Chambersburg, Illinois. He and his wife Margaret moved to New Salem, Illinois in 1830 and were acquainted with Abraham Lincoln. Howell received a yearly pension of $30 for his service.

"I performed a tour of a little more than one month, as a volunteer militia man in the South Carolina Militia under Captain Arthur Simpkins in the year (I think) 1776--in May & June we marched from Edgefield County S.C. to East Florida against the British and Tories. Our General was __ Williamson our Cols Beard and Winn and Major Andrew Pickens. We were there marched to St Augustine but a disagreement took place between our General and the regular General and we were ordered back."

"I also in the fall of the same year entered the service again as a volunteer in the South Carolina Militia, under the command of Captain John Ryan, and remained in service under him until sometime in July of the next year, some more than six months. During this tour we marched from Edgefield County South Carolina (my residence during all my services) to Savannah in Georgia against the British, but before we arrived they had taken the place, and we met them on the way. We then turned back marched to Augusta Georgia, and then crossed the River Savannah into South Carolina and encamped opposite Augusta and saw the British enter the place. There we remained until General Ash of North Carolina came to the same place, when the British left the place, and Ash followed them to Brier Creek in Georgia and was there defeated by them."

The Battle of Brier Creek was fought on 3 March, 1779 in Georgia. General Ashe had about 1,300 men, including Howell Sellers, who was camped with Brier Creek between them and the British. General Ashe thought the British were miles away, and he was caught by surprise when the British attacked the rear of the American army. When the British charged with their bayonets flashing in the sunlight, the Americans broke and ran.

"During our encampment at this place I was one of a party of about 200 who were ordered against the Creek Indians in Georgia and we had a battle with them on a Creek called Rocky Comfort, in which 8 Indians were killed, in our Major Ross was wounded of which he died."

Howell Sellers was at the American victory against the Creek Indians at Rocky Comfort Creek on 29 March, 1779. The Americans under the command of Colonel Hammond were in pursuit of a party of Cherokee and Tory raiders. They overtook the raiders five miles east of Rocky Comfort Creek and engaged in a fierce hand-to-hand battle. Major Ross received a tomahawk wound in the abdomen and later died. Eight Indians were killed and scalped, and one of the soldiers rode back to camp carrying the Indian scalps.

"We then marched from this encampment back to Georgia, towards Savannah, and crossed into South Carolina again at Summerall's ferry, and from there to Stono ferry on Ashley River where the British were encamped. There a battle was fought by Genl Lincoln and Genl Williamson against the British, who were protected by breastworks and entrenchments and we had therefore to withdraw. At this place I was taken sick and sent home, I think in July 1777."

"I also performed 2 other tours one under Captain Nathan White, I think in the fall of 1777, of a little more than one month. During this tour we marched from Edgefield County South Carolina to Savannah and I was at the siege of that place by our troops while the British had possession of it. In an attempt to storm the place Genl Pulaski and the other under Captain James Corsey, in the year 1778 under him I continued in service for about one month. During this tour we marched in pursuit of the British to Ashley River in South Carolina where we joined General Greene's Army In this service we had no fighting."

General Pulaski was a Polish nobleman, who is one of the "Fathers of the American cavalry." He was killed during the assault at the Siege of Savannah in 1779. He is one of only eight people to be awarded honorary United States' citizenship.

Sources: 1. The American Monthly Magazine, August 1912. 2. Sons of the American Revolution Applications. 3. U.S. Pension Roll of 1835. 4. Pension Papers S31357. 5. Hucks Defeat and the Revolution in the South Carolina Backcountry May-July 1780 by Michael C. Scoggins. 6. Count Casimir Pulaski: From Poland to America, a Hero's Fight for Liberty by Ann Marie Francis Kajencki.

****

Josias Sessions age 13

Josias Sessions was born on 14 November, 1764 in Craven County, North Carolina, and he died in 1837 in Horry, South Carolina. In

1781 he married Elizabeth Tillman. In later years he must have been a prosperous farmer, because he owned 9 slaves according to the 1830 census. He received $50.00 a year for his service.

"That whilst I was at School in the Spring of the year 1777, being then but thirteen years old I was drafted to join the Company of Captain Daniel Murrell attached to the brigade of General Francis Marion, I was drafted to serve one month at a time, and in this way I served one year, making six months actual service under said draft. During this service the company to which I belonged was employed in guarding the Sea Coast on the Long Bay beach in All Saints Parish...after the expiration of one year Captain Daniel Murrell's Company to which I belonged subject to the same draft was ordered to join the main Army under General Marion then encamped on the Santee River..."

Captain Daniel Morrall commanded the Georgetown District Regiment. The regiment was under the command of General Francis Marion, who is considered one of the fathers of modern guerrilla warfare. Marion was known as the 'Swamp Fox."

"I was frequently detached to join skirmishing parties and one morning whilst on an expedition of this sort his party had a severe conflict with a party of the enemy near Georgetown who were driving some cattle to the town: that his party succeeded in repulsing the enemy & took the cattle from them: That Georgetown was at this time in the possession of the British and I marched with the main Army and after the town was surrounded the enemy were compelled to leave it, which they did I taking to their shipping. I served three months at this time and was then relieved and returned home."

While at home Josias said that he was constantly called out to join skirmishing parties against the Tories, who were very active in his area. He later joined with General Marion again, and served until the end of the war.

"I was in the Company of Captain Daniel Murrell in a severe battle with the Tories at called Bear Bluff in All Saints Parish the tories were commanded by Joshua Long after a very sharp conflict our company was under the necessity of capitulating but that sooner than be taken me and eight others swam the Waccamaw river and effected our escape." One of the legends of the area said that an old slave woman was in the house near the scene of the battle working at her loom. She was killed by a stray bullet. At night you can still hear the noise of her loom.

Sources: 1. Census of 1800, 1820 and 1830. 2. Roster of South Carolina Patriots in the Revolutionary War. 3. Pension Papers S18202. 4. South Carolina Revolutionary Battles by Terry Lipscomb.

****

Dudley Shackleford age 13

Dudley Shackleford was born in Virginia in 1765, and he was married to Winifred Witherspoon on 4 March, 1784. He received $80.00 a year for his service.

"I enlisted in the year 1778 in the service of the United States in a Company of Guards under the command of Captain John Robert at the Albemarle Barracks....The said Regiment was employed guarding General Burgoyne's Army while prisoners of war. I continued in the said service until sometime in the month of April 1781 when I was discharged."

Sources: 1. Historical Register of Virginians in the Revolutionary War. 2. Revolutionary War Records Section II. 3. Census of 1810 & 1830. 4. U.S. Pension roll of 1835. 5. Virginia Marriages 1600-1800. 6. Pension Papers S6084.

****

Thomas Shankland age 14

Thomas Shankland was born in 1764 in Cherry Valley, New York, and he died on 21 August, 1823 in Cooperstown, New York. His brothers Alexander and William (William is in this book) enlisted on the side of the patriots. Their father Robert was a rebel supporter. However, his wife Sarah and son Andrew were supporters of the Tories.

The family lived in Cherry Valley several miles from the village that was massacred by British, Tories, and Indians on 11 November, 1778. After the massacre of the people in Cherry Valley, Robert helped to bury them. Robert then took his family and fled to another settlement along the Mohawk River that he thought would be safer.

The following summer Robert and his 14 year old son Thomas returned to Cherry Valley and stayed in a cabin in the area. Just before sunrise one morning there was a heavy pounding at the cabin door. Robert and Thomas jumped from bed, and Robert took down their guns and told Thomas to load them as fast as they could be fired. Robert knew the intruders were Indians, and he began to hear them use their tomahawks to break down the cabin door.

Robert grabbed a spear and quickly opened the cabin door and charged the surprised Indians. Robert pierced the side of one Indian and the others fell back. He then jumped back into the cabin and shut the door. Robert and Thomas began firing at the Indians who returned the fire. Thomas managed to jump out of a window and began to run into the woods, while his father stayed and defended the house.

The Indians set fire to the house, however, Robert managed to escape through the cellar door into the woods. After the house burned down they left with their prisoner Thomas, and they took him into the western part of the state. The Indians later sold Thomas to a Frenchman who gave him his freedom at the end of the war. Thomas returned to his home and family.

In October of 1783 General Washington and other military officers visited the area and a reception was given in their honor. Washington and the others stayed up until late in the night listening to the wild border tales from the residents. It was said that Robert Shankland stood in the middle of the room telling of the fight he and Thomas had that summer day with the Indians.

Source: 1. History of Cherry Valley from 1740-1898 by John Sawyer.

****

William Shankland age 14

William Shankland was born on 15 August, 1762 in Cherry Valley, New York, and he died on 17 April, 1850 in Onondaga County, New York. He married Margaret Henry on 19 August, 1790. William's father was a supporter of the patriots, while his mother was a strong supporter of the Tories. Because his brother Andrew was a Tory and his mother supported the Tories, William changed his last name from Shanklin to Shankland. William received a yearly pension of $80.

William enlisted on the 11th of June, 1776 under the command of Captain Robert McKean as an Indian spy. He later served in Colonel Clyde's Regiment, which was probably the 1st Regiment of the Tryon County Militia.

"In the year 1778 as early as the first of July I entered as a volunteer into the company of Capt. Ballard who belonged to Col Aldens Regiment & was at Cherry Valley at the time the Indians & Tories attacked

& *Burned the settlement. Col. Alden was killed by the Indians at that time & I helped bury him."*

"The attack was made by Indians on the 11th of November 1778. I remained in Capt.Ballards Company until the Regiment to which I belonged joined Genl James Clinton at the head of Lake Sago or Otsego about the first of July 1799."

The Cherry Valley massacre occurred on 11 November, 1778 when the British, Tories, and Iroquois Indians attacked the village of Cherry Valley. American Colonel Alden had ignored warnings that an attack was planned, and he left the almost 300 men stationed there to defend the village against an enemy force of over 600 men.

Alden was killed during the attack, while he was running from a house to the fort. According to most accounts, Alden was nearly at the gate of the fort when he stopped and attempted to shoot his pursuer. His pistol was wet and misfired, and he was killed by a thrown tomahawk that hit him in the head. The enemy could not breach the walls of the fort, but they massacred over 30 people outside of the fort and took as captives an equal number.

An account of the attack on the Mitchell home describes how brutal the attack was. When the attackers reached the Mitchell house, he was outside and hid knowing that he could not aid his wife and children inside the house. When the attackers left the house, Mr. Mitchell went inside and found his wife and three of his children in a pool of blood. A fourth child, a girl of about 10, was still alive. While he was attending to her Mitchell noticed one of the attackers coming back, so Mitchell hid again. Mitchell saw the attacker, a Tory named Newberry, cleave with his hatchet the head of the wounded girl. Sometime later Newberry was caught and hanged for his crime.

In 1779 William volunteered about the 1st of August to follow a party of Indians who had attacked a settlement near Johnstown. He followed them as far as Albany and was then discharged. He was called out again that year and served at Fort Clyde for four weeks. He served several short tours in 1780 and 1781 as an Indian spy.

Sources: 1. A History of the Shankland Family Compiled by the Rev. Fr. V. John Shankland. 2. Revolutionary Soldiers Resident or Dying in Onondaga County, N.Y., prepared by Rev. W.M. Beauchamp for the Onondaga Historical Association, 1863. 3. Pension Papers W19015. 4. Diary of Captain Benjamin Warren at Massacre of Cherry

Valley by David E. Alexander, Originally Published in the Journal of American History, 1909. 5. History of Cherry Valley from 1740-1898 by John Sawyer.

****

Benjamin Sharp age 14

Benjamin Sharp was born on 23 January, 1762 in Lancaster, Pennsylvania, and he died on 1 January, 1844 in Warren, Missouri. He married Hannah Debough Fulkerson on 16 November, 1786 in Virginia. He received a yearly pension of $35.97.

"I entered the service of the United States under the following named officers and served as herein stated. In the month of June or July 1776 the whole country where I resided was broken up and driven into Forts by the Cherokee Indians. I then resided in what was the Fincastle County now Washington County Virginia. I volunteered and entered the service under the command of Captain Andrew Colville and did duty at Blacks Fort near where Abington now stands. I was then about 14 years of age. I was after some time marched to Shelbys Fort, then in North Carolina, now in Sullivan County and State of Tennessee, but I was generally employed in the defense of Blacks Fort for the defense of which the troops to which I was attached were raised. At this time most of the effective man in that part of the country had been, or were about to be, marched against the Cherokee Indians under Colonel William Christian and, commonly called Christian's Campaign. I was employed in this service, as I believe, somewhere between four and five months, but the precise length of time I am unable to say."

"Sometime after the above service was performed, but what year I cannot call to mind, but it was in the summer season, a report reached Washington County where I resided that the Glade Hollow Fort on Clinch River, then Washington County, but now Russell County Virginia was taken by the Indians and all the people killed. I volunteered under Captain James Dysart and I believe Samuel Newel was Lieut and James Vance, Ensign. The Glade Hollow Fort was about 35 or 30 miles from the Fort Blacks. We went to the Glade Hollow Fort and found it not taken, but the alarm had raised from the Indians' attacking and defeating a company of man commanded by Captain Smith in view of the Fort, two of Smith's men were killed, one was called Priest, and the other Little. I was employed in this service perhaps six weeks or more either guarding the forts or ranging. I served part of the time as a spy, and the balance as a private."

"In the year either 1778 or 1779 as I believe a report reached us that the Tories were embodying on New River in order to destroy the Lead Works in that quarter on which the Western country chiefly depended for their supply of that necessary article. I then volunteered under Captain James Fulkerson and I believe Nathaniel Dryden was Ensign. We marched under the command of Col William Campbell to New River and kept our headquarters in part of Peppers ferry and at Michael Prices five or six miles from thence, where detachments were constantly sent out in search of Tories, a good many of them we took, and among others, a Captain Britain who it was said held a Captain's commission among the Tories. I do not know how long I was employed in this service, some six weeks or more."

"In the year 1780 as I believe, Col. McDowell of North Carolina fled over the mountain from the head waters of the Catawba River, being driven from thence by a large body of British and Tories under the command of Major Ferguson, a British Officer. I then volunteered I think early in September under Captain Robert Craig, Lieut. William Blackburn and Ensign Nathaniel Dryden, and we marched for the Carolinas under the command of Col. William Campbell. On our way we were joined by the Cols. Shelby, Sevier, Cleveland & Genl. Williams, and their regiments. We overtook the British and Tories in South Carolina on Kings Mountain where Ferguson was killed and his whole army killed or taken. I was in the battle. Col. Campbell was appointed to Command & Genl. Williams and my commanding Lieut. and Ensign were killed in the action. The battle was fought I believe on the 7th or 8th of October and I think I returned home about the last of November."

"I left Col. Campbell by his permission, after the Company I served in had left him, he was then about two days march below Wilkes Courthouse on the Yadkin River in North Carolina. On this expedition we suffered greatly through hard duty and want of provision. A few weeks after my return from King's Mountain information was received that the Indians were coming in force against the settlements. I then volunteered under the command of Captain Andrew Cowan, and by the courtesy of the superior officers, I commanded as Ensign in said company but as there was no other subaltern officers in the company, I did the duty of lieutenant during the whole of that expedition, but was not commissioned. We marched for the Cherokee towns under the command of Colonel Arthur Campbell. The advance of the Army met the Indians on their way to the settlements, killed seven or eight of them and caused them to retreat. I was in Several Skirmishes with the Indians this campaign, one of which was very warm while it continued. This service as well as I can remember continued about six weeks or two months. It was in the dead of winter. We were in the town on Christmas day. We destroyed a great deal of corn, and other provisions, burned 16 or 17 towns; killed a good many Indians; took 30 or 40 women and Children Prisoners; and took a good many cannon; we sent the prisoners and cannon up the river to Fort Henry at the Long Island on Holston River. This is the last service I recollect of performing in the war of the revolution."

"I was prepared at another time to march for the defense of Kentucky against an army of British and Indians advancing from Canada, but before we started, intelligence was received that they had taken Ruddles and another Fort the name of which I do not now remember and had made good their retreat with the prisoners to Detroit, in consequence of which the expedition did not proceed."

The following letter was written by Benjamin Sharp about the Battle of King's Mountain. The letter was published in 1843 in *The American Pioneer*.

"We then moved on, and as we approached the mountain the roll of the British drum informed us that we had somwthing to do. No doubt the British commander thought his position a strong one, but the plan of our attack was such as to make it the worst for him he could have chosen. The end of the mountain to our left descended gradually to a branch; in front of us the ascent was rather abrupt, and to the right was a low gap through which the road passed. The different regiments were directed by guides to the ground they were to occupy, so as to surround the eminence on which the British were encamped; Campbell's to the right, and so on, till last the left of Cleveland's to join the right of Campbell's, on the other side of the mountain, at the road."

"Thus the British major found himself attacked on all sides at once and so situated as to receive a galling fire from all parts of our lines without doing any injury to ourselves. From this difficulty he attempted to relieve himself at the point of the bayonet, but failed in three successive charges. Cleveland, who had the farthest to go, being bothered in some swampy ground, did not occupy his position in the line till late in the engagement. A few men, drawn from the right of Campbell's regiment, occupied this vacancy; this the British commander discovered, and here he made his last powerful effort to force his way through and make his escape; but at that instant Cleveland's regiment came up in gallant style; the colonel, himself, came up by the very spot I occupied, at which time his horse had received two wounds, and he was obliged to dismount. Although fat and unwieldy, he advanced on foot with signal bravery, but was soon remounted by one of his officers, who brought him another horse. This threw the British and tories into complete disorder, and Furguson seeing that all was lost, determined not to survive the disgrace; he broke his sword, and spurred his horse into the thickest of our ranks, and fell covered with wounds, and shortly after his whole army surrendered at discretion. The action lasted about one hour, and for most of the time was fierce and bloody."

"I cannot clearly recollect the statement of our loss, given at the time, but my impression now is that it was two hundred and twenty-five killed, and about as many or a few more wounded; the loss of the enemy must have been much greater. The return of the prisoners taken was eleven hundred and thirty-three, about fifteen hundred stand of arms, several baggage wagons, and all their camp equipment fell into our hands. The battle closed not far from sundown, so that we had to encamp on the ground with the dead and wounded, and pass the night among groans and lamentations."

"During the whole of this expedition, except a few days at the outset, I neither tasted bread nor salt, and this was the case with nearly every man; when we could get meat, which was but seldom, we had to roast and eat it without either: sometimes we got a few potatoes, but our standing and principal rations were ears of corn, scorched in the fire or eaten raw. Such was the price paid by the men of the Revolution for our Independence."

"Here I might conclude, but I cannot forbear offering a small tribute to the memory of our commanding officers. Col. Williams; CLEVELAND, I have already spoken of; SEVIER, I did not see in the battle, but his bravery was well attested; three times my eye fell upon our gallant commander [CAMPBELL], calm and collected, encouraging the men, and assuring them of victory. At the close of the action, when the British were loudly calling for quarters, but uncertain whether they would be granted, I saw the intrepid SHELBY rush his horse within fifteen paces of their lines, and commanded them to lay down their arms, and they should have quarters. Some would call this an imprudent act, but it showed the daring bravery of the man. I am led to believe that three braver men, and purer patriots, never trod the soil of freedom, than CAMPBELL, SHELBY and SEVIER."

Sources: 1. Tombstone 2. Pension Papers S17086. 3. U.S. Pension Roll of 1835. 4. The American Pioneer A Monthly Periodical, Vol. II, 1843.

****

John Shaw age 14

John Shaw was born on 29 January, 1763 in Baltimore, Maryland, and he died in 1827 in Shelby, Alabama. He married Mary Margaret Irwin on 11 August, 1788 in Georgia. He received a yearly pension of $43.33. Mary filed for a widow's pension, but it was rejected because she needed a new declaration and proof of marriage.

"On or about the year One thousand seven hundred seventy seven I entered the Service of the United States in the month of June to the best of my recollection of said year as a Substitute for one Hethcoat Picket in Captain George Adams's company of the 4th Regiment of the North Carolina militia commanded by Col Williams attached to Gen Caswell's Regiment and I served about six months in this Tour & during which period Gates defeat took place"

"Shortly after my discharge I was drafted for a three months Tour and served under Nathaniel Dickerson as Captain in Col Moore's Regiment commanded by Gen Butler during this tour I was in no engagement."

"Shortly after my term of service was expired I Volunteered for a term of service partly as mounted Infantry and partially as a militia man of the North Carolina line under the command of Captain Dudley Reynolds and part of the time Reynolds was under the command of Nathaniel Dickerson a regular officer."

"Soon after this term of service expired I Volunteered under the command of Captain Reynolds again who was commanded by Col William Moore of the North Carolina line this term of service was for a shorter period than was usual but how long I cannot recollect."

"Soon after this service ended I was drafted for a 3 months tour under the command of Lieutenant __ until we reached Head Quarters when we were attached to Captain Dickerson's Company and Col Moore's Regiment we were marched to Wilmington in North Carolina where we remained until after Cornwallis surrendered. Soon after which we were honorably discharged."

Sources: 1. Census 1800 & 1810. 2. Tennessee State Marriages 1780-2002. 3. Pension Roll of 1835. 4. Pension Papers R9443.

****

Samuel Shelly age 11

Samuel Shelly was born on 20 January, 1766 in Stratford, Connecticut, and he died on 17 March, 1838 in Jefferson County, New York. Town records indicate he was born in 1766. However his death date on his tombstone is 1765. It would not be unusual for a family member to have the wrong date of birth placed on a tombstone.

He enlisted as a fifer in May 1777 in Captain James Eldridge's Company in the 3rd Regiment commanded by Colonel Samuel Prentiss. He was present at the surrender of Cornwallis at Yorktown.

Sources: 1. Connecticut Town Birth Records, Pre 1870. 2. U.S. Pensioners of 1835. 3. Pension Papers S36306. 4. D.A.R. Lineage Book, Vol. 23.

****

Andrew Sherburne age 14

Andrew Sherburne was born on 30 September, 1765 in Rye, New Hampshire, and he died on 27 November, 1831 in New York. He received a monthly pension of $8.

"So time in the month of April 1779 being then a lad, I entered the United States service on the continental establishment on board the Continental Ship of war Ranger, mounting 18 carriage guns, then laying in Portsmouth harbour in Newhampshire commanded by Thomas Simpson Esq."

Andrew's father was against the practice of privateering so he gave permission for Andrew to join the navy. Two of Andrew's half uncles were also on board the ship. He was employed as a waiter to Charles Roberts, the boatswain.

"Shortly after I entered on board said ship she sailed and joining in company with the frigate Providence and ship Queen of France of 20 guns proceded on a cruise in quest of the British Jamaca fleet, and on the banks of Newfoundland fell in with, and captured the sail of the said fleet and then returned to Boston"

Many on board the *Ranger* were taking their first voyage, and when the sea became rough some of them including Andrew became seasick. The old sailors enjoyed making fun of the sick recruits. During the voyage Andrew was kept busy with his job, which included practice with the cannons.

They captured a British ship called the *Holderness,* which had 22 guns but did not have enough men to manage all the guns. The captured ship was loaded with cotton, coffee, sugar, rum, and allspice. The *Ranger* then set sail for Boston and arrived the last of July 1779.

"Several of our prizes having been recaptured--from Boston the said ship Ranger returned to Portsmouth discharged part of her crew and shiped others and immediately proceded to Nantuckett rode, rejoined her old consort and proceded on a second cruise on the coaste of the southern states and went into Charlston harbour S.C. and after obtaining some fresh provisions water & went cruising on the coast of Florida took several small transports of but little consequence, and were chased and driven into Charlston harbour by a vastly superior British fleet which for many weeks blocaded the harbour; in which interval the British armey pressed on, and beseaged the town in every part by land. While in this town, the Ranger drawing the last water of any of the ship, was sent on several expeditions against batteries which, the British had erected on James's Island and on the margin of the rivers When the crewes of said ships could be no longer serviceable on board, a large proportion of the men were taken out to man the forts."

"After sustaining a hard siege in all the month of May 1780 and our provisions being entirely expended, the town and shiping by capitulation were surendered to the British abot the last of May 1780. I have therefore served on board the aforesaid ship Ranger in the service of the United States more than nine months in continuation viz. from April 1779 until the last of May 1780 and never was formally discharged from said ship. While a prisoner in Charlston, I had the small pox and having had no medical assistance, the foundation of ill health was here laid from which I have never fully recovered The circumstance of the ship having changed a considerable part of her crew and there being but few living, I am not able to say whether any one now surviving belonged to the said Ship all the time that I did."

After the fall of Charlestown in May of 1780 Andrew was taken prisoner by the British. The officers were paroled and allowed to keep their waiters, and Andrew and some of the men from the *Ranger* were sent to

Portsmouth. During the voyage Andrew and several of the men became ill with small pox.

Andrew recovered from the smallpox in Portsmouth, and he learned that his father had died and the family was in need of money. Andrew decided the best way to acquire money was to become a privateer. He shipped out on the *Greyhound* under the command of Captain Jacob Wilds. Captain Wilds promised that Andrew would receive a full share of what they captured.

After being at sea for several weeks the *Greyhound* was taken captive off Newfoundland. Andrew and the captured Americans were put on board the *Fairy*, a British sloop of war, and they arrived in Plymouth, England the end of November 1781. Andrew was taken before a court of Admiralty to be questioned for determination if he was a prisoner of war or a pirate. When the questioning was over for the men, the verdict was read and they were, *"severally and individually committed to Old Mill prison, for rebellion, privacy, and high treason on his Britannic Majesty's high seas, there to lay during his Majesty's pleasure, until he saw fit to pardon or otherwise dispose of you."*

Andrew found some prisoners he knew from Portsmouth, New Hampshire, and he was given clothing and he was sent to a school which was kept in the prison. There he learned to read and write, navigate, and do ship building. Conditions were harsh and food was scarce, in fact the American prisoners were given less food than the French or Spanish prisoners. In time Andrew became very ill and was sent to the prison hospital.

After the war had ended Benjamin Franklin, who was in France, negotiated to set the prisoners in England free. The prisoners were told that several ships would take them back to America once they were discharged by the doctor. Andrew who was still in the hospital had been recovering, but the doctor refused to discharge him. Andrew pleaded with the doctor to let him leave, but the doctor said he was too weak and would not survive the trip.

Andrew's half uncle Lawrence was one of the prisoners, and he promised the doctor that he would watch over and take care of Andrew on the voyage home. The doctor finally agreed, and he told Lawrence that if Andrew died the *"blood will be on your hands and not mine."*

After being away for over a year Andrew finally returned home in 1782, and he was reunited with a family that had given him up for dead. Once back at home Andrew needed to work to help support the family, so he joined on a privateer called the *Scorpion* a brig of eight guns getting ready to sail to the West Indies. The *Scorpion* was returning from the West Indies in November of 1782, and it was captured by the British. Once again Andrew was a prisoner of the British, and he was taken to New York Harbor and put aboard the prison ship the *Jersey*.

Andrew was taken aboard the *Jersey* the last of November in 1782, and he later wrote in his memoirs, *"I had now commenced a scene of suffering almost without a parallel. The ship was extremely filthy, and abounded with vermin. A large proportion of the prisoners had been robbed of their clothing. The ship was considerably crowded, many of the men were very low spitited; our provisions ordinary, and very scanty. They consisted of worm eaten ship bread, and salt beef. It was supposed that this bread and beef had been condemned in the British navy. The bread had been so eaten by weevils, that one might easily crush it in the hand and blow it away. The beef was exceedingly salt, and scarcely a particle of fat could be seen upon it."*

Sometime in January of 1783 Andrew was taken sick and placed aboard one of the hospital ships, and he was placed in a bunk where the wind and snow would blow across him from openings in the ship's hull. One morning after a snowstorm, the snow was up to four inches deep on Andrew's bed. Remarkably, Andrew became well enough to return to the *Jersey*. After a day or two Andrew was again sick and returned to a hospital ship.

Back aboard a hospital ship Andrew recalled in his memoirs, *"A man who lay next to me had been a nurse, but was taken sick, and had his feet, and even his legs, frozen. I had several times seen them dressed: at length, while they were dressing his feet, I saw the toes and bottom of his feet cleave off from the bone, and hang down by the heel."*

Before the Treaty of Paris was signed in September 1783 officially ending the American Revolution, groups of prisoners were being released from the *Jersey*. One day a small schooner was sent from Rhode Island to take some of the prisoners home. Andrew was one of the men chosen, and in a few days he was once again a free man. For the next several years Andrew again went to sea, and he finally settled down in 1788. He became a very religious man and became a Baptist minister.

"In the winter of 1788 I traveled to the city of New York and settled for my wages with Col. Benj. Walker and received a final settlement so called of about 73 Dollars which at that time was not worth ten dollars. I am now 53 years of age in poor health and in reduced circumstances, have no real estate and am much dependent on my friends for a living and absolutely need the assistance of my country for support."

Sources: 1. U.S. Pensioners 1818-1872. 2. Memoirs of Andrew Sherburne; a Pensioner of the Navy of the Revolution, Written by Himself, 1828. 3. American Prisoners of the Revolution by Danske Dandridge. 4. Pension Papers S42275.

****

Daniel Shields age 14

Daniel Shields was born on 14 February, 1766 in Scotland, and he died on 20 September, 1835 in Albany, New York. He married Elizabeth Fenn on 16 April, 1807. He received a yearly pension of $80.

Daniel enlisted as a drummer in 1780 at the age of fourteen at Fishkill, New York. He was so small he could not pass muster in New York City. He is found on the roll of the 1st New York Regiment under Colonel Goose Van Schaick and in the Company commanded by Captain George Sytez. He was at the surrender of Yorktown under Lafayette and was discharged when peace was declared.

According to a letter in Daniel's pension file, he had apparently been given a cane that belonged to General Washington. When Lafayette visited Washington D.C. in 1825, Daniel presented the cane to his old commander. Unfortunately, the cane was later lost on a steamboat on the Mississippi.

Sources: 1. D.A.R. Lineage Book, Vol. 14. 2. Pension Papers W2339.

****

John Shreve age 13

John Shreve was born on 6 April, 1762 in Burlington County, New Jersey, and he died on 8 September, 1854 in Mt. Union, Ohio. He married Abigail Ridgway on 9 September, 1786 in New Jersey. He received a yearly pension of $320.

He served with his father, Colonel Israel Shreve, and they were both at the Battle of Brandywine. Colonel Shreve had two horses shot from under him and was wounded. His son John took charge of his father and nursed him until he recovered. When the British marched through New Jersey they burned the home of the Shreve family and destroyed their crops because Israel was an American officer.

"I entered the army of the United States in the year 1775 as a cadet or volunteer and served in the 2nd New Jersey Regiment which was raised for one year, commanded by Col William Maxwell and Israel Shreve was his Lieutenant (who was my father) I marched with said Regiment for Canada in the winter following & arrived before the Walls of Quebec the later part of April 1776. General Thomas of New England commanding at that time, on the retreat from that place, General Thompson of Pennsylvania arrived and making a stand at Mount Independence, I was on or about the 12th day of July appointed Ensign by General orders and annexed to Capt joseph Brailey's Company said Regiment after the expiration of said term Col Maxwell was appointed Brigade General, and Lit Col Israel Shreve was appointed Col of the 2nd N.J. Regiment, which was raised for three years or during the war. I was appointed first Ensign in our Regt and annexed to Capt John Hollingshead's Company their recruiting Warrants were dated in December 1776. I think we were mustered the first of February 1777 & I received a commission as Ensign soon after, signed by John Hancock, President."

John Shreve and his regiment arrived with the American army at Quebec on 25 March, 1776 and began a siege of the city until 5 May, 1776. They then retreated and went back to New York, and they remained there until November when they returned to New Jersey.

"The New Jersey Brigade being stationed near Amboy where the enemy lay, having several engagements at the short hills, and I received a Lieutenant commission soon after, I was sick absent in July, but Joined the Regt in August."

The Battle of Short Hills, also known as the Battle of Metuchen Meetinghouse, was fought on 26 June, 1777. The fight was between the American General "Lord Stirling" and British Generals William Howe and Cornwallis. The Americans fought hard, but they were outnumbered and outgunned and were forced to retreat toward Westfield.

While following the American retreat, Lord Cornwallis was near Westfield when he approached a farm house. The woman of the house, known in the area as "Aunt Betty" Frazee, was baking bread for the hungry American troops. Cornwallis approached her and said, *"I want the first loaf of bread that next comes out of that oven."* He then turned and sat under a large shade tree.

When the bread was done "Aunt Betty" took the bread to Cornwallis and told him, *"Sir, I give you this bread through fear, not in love."* Cornwallis was moved by her spirit and courage and told his men that none of them were to touch a single loaf of her bread.

"In September of that year marched with the N. Jersey Brigade to the state of Delaware, we and Gen Connaway's Brigade (of the Pennsylvania Line) formed Gen Stirling's Division, and was on the right wing of the army at the battle of Brandywine on the 11th of that month, Col Shreve was wounded that day when the enemy got possession of Philadelphia the New Jersey line wintered at the Valley-forge."

At the battle of Brandywine on 11 September, 1777 Colonel Israel Shreve's Regiment caught the full force of British General Howe's army. The fight lasted about 45 minutes and the Americans were forced to retreat. Colonel Shreve was wounded in the thigh and his son, John, would take care of his until he returned to duty in November.

"In the spring the 2nd Regiment marched into New Jersey and remained in and about Haddonfield seven miles from that city until the British crossed the Delaware river and marched towards New York, said Regt being Joined by the whole N. Jersey line retreated before them having frequent engagements with their advance parties until they reached the neighborhood of Monmouth court house then fell into their rear and joined the main Army. After the battle of Monmouth in 1778 the N Jersey line took part at Elizabethtown & Newark for some time then was with the main Army on the west side of the North river until General Arnolds elopement then marched to West Point and remained there until the beginning of winter then after making a foraging excursion on the East side of the river toward New York, returned to New York and Elizabethtown and remained there during the winter, having several engagements with small parties of the enemy, at one time they came in force sufficient to take possession of Elizabethtown for a short time and they burnt the Barracks at that place, in June 1779 the enemy commanded by General Knyphausen, with 6 or 8 thousand men took possession of Elizabethtown and penetrated as far as Springfield they burnt the most of the town General green with 1500 regulars including the N Jersey line and the militia of the neighborhood opposed them at several passes from morning until near night."

While the main army was at Valley Forge preparing to march the 2nd New Jersey Regiment under Colonel Shreve, along with his son John, foraged for supplies, and with the aid of local militia they skirmished with the British and Tories during April and May. In June at the Battle of Monmouth the 2nd Regiment covered the retreat of General Charles Lee's men, and they were in reserve for the rest of the battle.

The 2nd New Jersey Regiment fought at the Battle of Connecticut Farms on 7 June, 1780. This took place after the British had crossed from Staten Island and invaded Elizabethtown, New Jersey. Colonel Shreve wrote later that it was the warmest action for his brigade since he enlisted. The Regiment later fought the British at Springfield on June 23 and forced the British to retreat back to Staten Island.

"September of that year the N Jersey Brigade joined General Sullivan and marched up the Susquehanna and Tioga rivers in pursuit of Indians and had several engagements with them, after returning from this expedition the N Jersey line passed the winter and the most of the summer of 1780 on or near the lines toward New York. I think we wintered in huts on Bound Brook the winter of the following after the revolt of the Pennsylvania and New Jersey lines toward the close of this winter, one of the N Jersey Regiments was reduced and the officers and privates were redistributed among the other Regiments, my father (Col Shreve) being a very fleshy man, retired on half pay. I went home with him on furlough, I wrote to camp informing that I wished to retire from the army as my father had done, if they did not accept that or my resignation I should wait for orders to join the Regiment."

John Shreve wrote that his father was a fleshy man and retired at half pay. Colonel Shreve's weight had ballooned up to 320 pounds, and he could not get a horse that could carry him faster than a walk. So he did the sensible thing and retired. I suspect that John also left the army, although willing to come back if needed, because his father did and he was needed around the farm. Also, John had been in the army for nearly six years.

The following is a letter written by John Shreve at the age of 91 that was published in *The Mirror* a local newspaper. This copy is from *The Genealogy and History of the Shreve Family from 1641*, page 347.

"I was born on the 8th day of the 4th month (April), in the year 1762, in Burlington Co., New Jersey. My mother died when I was about

nine years old. My father married again in about three years after. In the year 1775 the war of the Revolution commenced. Soon after the battle of Bunker Hill, the Provincial Congress ordered four regiments to be raised in New Jersey to serve one year. My father thought it was his duty to assist in liberating his country from British tyranny and he was appointed Lieutenant-Colonel of the second regiment, which was raised and equipped and marched in February, 1776, for Canada. My father thought it was not proper to leave me with a stepmother, and took me with him in the army. I was appointed an ensign in the regiment the 15th of July, and returned to Philadelphia and went to school to fit me better for the next campaign. When the regiment was discharged in December, a new regiment was ordered to be raised. My father was appointed Colonel, and I was appointed First Ensign in the regiment. We lost a Captain killed in the battle at the Short Hills in New Jersey, in the month of June. I was promoted to the rank of Lieutenant the first of July. My father was wounded in the battle of Brandywine, the 11th of September, 1777. I went with him through Philadelphia to New Jersey—then took him to the town of Reading, in Pennsylvania, when the British entered Philadelphia—and I joined the regiment at White Marsh. Shortly after we went into winter quarters by building huts at Valley Forge, where we suffered for want of provisions and clothes. After a partial supply of the latter, my father was ordered with his regiment to cross the river Delaware and take a stand at the town of Haddonfield, seven miles from Philadelphia, to watch the motions of the enemy. In March, 1778, General Washington thought they were preparing to make their escape through New Jersey to New York. When the British were moving their army over the river, General Maxwell was ordered with the other two regiments (the first and third) to join the second; and joined us at Mount Holly. When the enemy evacuated the city and crossed over the river, Washington moved the army and crossed the Delaware at Corell's and Howell's ferries above Trenton. I was ordered, with a guard, to take the baggage of the brigade to the northeast of Trenton, and stay which they met at Monmouth Court House. I followed our army and was at English Town, three miles from the battle ground. The day after, when the enemy had moved off in the night and left their dead and most of their wounded, I joined the brigade with the baggage; this was in June, 1778. The enemy made their escape to Sandy Hook and New York. Our brigade was ordered on the lines at Elizabeth Town and Newark, where we remained through the winter following. We had many skirmishes and engagements with the British and Tories that winter and spring. They came out with eight or nine thousand men and thirty wagons in June, 1779, intending to take our stores of provisions at Morris Town.

We stopped them at the town of Springfield. The people said when they returned, the thirty wagons were full of dead and wounded. In September of that year, our brigade was ordered to join General Sullivan, to chastise the Indians and Tories, towards the Susquehanna, and their towns in Genesee county, now west of New York. On our return we wintered near Morris Town, in New Jersey. In 1780 we were on the lines of our former station, near Newark, when the British ship brought Major John Andre (the English spy) and laid at the head of Tappan Bay, about seven miles below West Point Fort. General Greene was ordered with several brigades to lay at the little town of Orange our brigade was one. I was ordered to take a stand with twenty-six men near to where the ship lay to watch her motions. While there I saw General Arnold, the traitor, go on board the ship when he made His escape—and saw Major Andre, the spy, hung at Orange Town. In the year 1781, my father being very fleshy, weighing three hundred and twenty pounds, he could not get a horse that could carry his weight faster than a walk, and he retired from the army on half pay. We then had but little property, except our public securities, which could not be turned into money. We thought it best for me to leave the army also, and help to support his family. That year ended the war. I stayed and assisted the family until the year 1786. Then I was married and remained in New Jersey until the fall of 1787, then removed with my wife and one child to the west side of the Alleghany Mountains, and purchased 100 acres of land, with but two or three acres cleared, and a small cabin without a nail or any sawed board, on Little Red Stone Creek, a branch of the Monongahela river, about thirty-three miles south of Pittsburg, where I remained thirty-eight or forty years and raised a family of nine children. I cleared about sixty acres of the land, mostly with my own hands. I served the township a great part of the time in all the public offices. A county commissioner three years—five different times a commissioner for laying graded roads—and times in the State Legislature. I went once to the Falls of Ohio and returned by the wilderness through part of Tennessee, and part of Virginia. I went three times with flour down the rivers Monongahela, Ohio and Mississippi, to New Orleans, and took flour from New Orleans to the West Indies, one time to Havana, in the Island of Cuba; one time to Kingston in the Island of Jamaica. Took sugar from Cuba and rum from Jamaica to New York and paid six thousand seven hundred dollars duty to the United States on the sugar and rum. I was concerned with a company in a manufactory, after the close of the last war with England, and lost the most of my savings from my fifty years' toil. I surveyed land occasionally for more than thirty years. I had the rheumatism in my limbs, which prevented me from following the compass, and I moved to the State of Ohio, where I have remained with my children about twenty-seven years. Congress acknowledged to be indebted to services rendered to the United States and I am now receiving an annuity which enables me to provide a comfortable living in mv old and declining age. JOHN SHREVE."

Sources: 1. History of Union County, New Jersey by Frederick William Ricord, 1897. 2. The Pennsylvania Line Munity, its Origins, and Patriotism by Charles S. Yordy III. 3. The Genealogy and History of the Shreve Family from 1641 by L.P. Allen, 1901. 4. New Jersey Marriage Records. 5. Tombstone 6. Pension Papers S3890.

****

Joshua Simonds age 13

Joshua Simonds was born on 11 October, 1767 in Hancock, Massachusetts, and he died on 14 February, 1837 in New Berlin, New York. He married Lois Graham on 20 May, 1793 in Greenbush, New York. He received a yearly pension of $21.66.

"In the year Seventeen hundred & Eighty one (1781) I enlisted under my father Joshua Simonds who was a Lieutenant for three years. I enlisted in the month of April of that year not being quite 14 years of age. I mustered about the first of May in 1781 by Genl Rossetter and we marched down to Albany when we were put under Captain Abraham Livingston. The company staid in Albany about two or three weeks when we marched down to Schoharie and staid about two weeks. We marched down to Fort Plain on the Mohawk River when we were stationed with other troops the command of Colonel Willet. I remained there at Fort Plain until the said October until we hear of the capture of <u>Genl Cornwallis</u> then we went to German Flats to "Fort Herkimer" where we remained until about the middle of November. We were discharged by Colonel Willet."

Sources: 1.The Bloodied Mohawk: The American Revolution in the Words of Fort Planks Defenders and Other Mohawk Valley Partisans by Kenneth D. Johnson. 2. Pension Papers W19365. 3. U.S. Pensioners 1835.

****

Samuel Sinclair age 14

Samuel Sinclair was born on 10 May, 1762 in Nottingham, New York, and he died on 8 February, 1827 in Sinclairville, New York. He married Sally Perkins in 1795, and when she died in 1804 he married Fanny Edson a year later. He received a monthly pension of $8.

At age fourteen Samuel was in the army as a waiter to his uncle, Colonel Joseph Cilley. Barely one year later he enlisted in Captain Amos Morrill's Company of the 1st New Hampshire Regiment under the command of Colonel Cilley. His older brothers Bradbury and John also joined the same company. Samuel was at the Battles of Bemis Heights, Saratoga, and Monmouth. He was also present at Valley Forge. His brother Bradbury died at Valley Forge. Samuel was also a member of the Sullivan Expedition against the Indians in 1779. He was discharged from the army on 20 June, 1780.

After the war he married, and in the early 1800's he and his family lived in New York. While there he was appointed a Major in the state militia. The village of Sinclairville was named after him.

Sources: 1. Sons of the American Revolution Application. 2. The History of the Sinclair Family by Leonard Allison Morrison. 3. Pension Papers S43142. 4. D.A.R. Lineage Book, Vol 33, 1900.

****

John Singer age 13

John Singer was born on 11 March, 1763 in Lancaster, Pennsylvania, and he died on 13 May, 1829 in Philadelphia. He married Anna Maria Musser on 20 June, 1793. He received no pension because he died in 1829, and his wife died in 1828. Most did not apply for a pension until 1832 or later.

On account of his young age he feared rejection at home so he traveled to Philadelphia to enlist. *"I was accepted as a drummer boy in Captain Andrew Graff's Company. I was mustered in at Philadelphia July 16th 1776."*

Tradition says that on one occasion on a march he was too tired to walk, and he was carried on the strong shoulders of one of the men. While being carried he still kept the men in step with the beat of his drum. He was taken with other prisoners and held on the prison ship *Jersey* in New York Harbor. He later escaped and returned to enlist as a private on 24 August, 1778 in the 8th Battalion of Lancaster County commanded by Colonel Alexander Lowrey in Captain Roberts MacKay's Company. He served until October 1781.

John was probably taken prisoner at either the Battle of Brandywine or Battle of Germantown in 1777. He later joined the 8th Pennsylvania, and he may have seen action near Fort Laurens and in the Sullivan Expedition.

Sources: 1. Sons of the American Revolution Application. 2. Yearbook of the Sons of the American Revolution in the State of New York, 1909.

****

Josiah Singletary age 14

Josiah Singletary was born on 24 October, 1765 in Bladen County, North Carolina, and he died there on 18 October, 1844. He married Sarah Harrison on 9 July, 1780 in Bladen County. He received a yearly pension of $43.33.

"In the fall of the year 1777 (as well as now recollected) I became a Substitute for my Uncle Benjamin FitzRandolph, who had been drafted into a Company of Bladen Militia commanded by Captain Charles Bullock and Lieutenant William Dye called into service by order of Col Thomas Brown commanding the Bladen Militia, on an expedition against the Tories who had collected in considerable numbers on and near the South Carolina line, in Robeson, then a part of Bladen County, the County being formed from different parts of the County, rendezvoused at Fair Bluff in the County of Columbus then a part of Bladen--thence we marched to Ashpole, thence to a place called the Goose Pond--thence to Bear Swamp. The Tories continued to retire and finally dispersed. At Bear Swamp, the Company was relieved by another portion of Bladen Militia under the command of Col James Richardson, and were discharged, having performed one months tour of duty."

"In the beginning of the year 1778 (as well as recollected) Captain Jared Irwin raised a Troop of Light Horse, in the County of Bladen, in which I became a Volunteer, and which Company continued in service, tho' not constantly till the close of the War. Col Thomas Robeson, who, at an early period of the war, had been Colonel of the County, but had resigned, also raised a Troop of cavalry, the two Companies sometimes acted together, and whenever that was the case Colonel Robeson commanded--a man by the name of McDaniel commanding my Company; but most generally, he and Captain Irwin took the field alternately with their companies sometimes for one – two, or three weeks, and occasionally for a longer period."

"I was in an expedition against the Tories, who had collected in the County of Robeson (then Bladen) under the famous Col Hector McNeill. On this occasion, we were accompanied by Col Robeson's Company, and a Company of Light Horse from Cumberland County under Captain Patrick Travis. We approached the Tories so near being separated only by a small swamp that the sentinels on each side conversed which each other. The object being to surprise the Tories, but being defeated in that, and they being more numerous, (as was soon ascertained) than the Whigs--Colonel Robeson concluded to retire, and marched to Stewart's Mills near Rockfish Creek, seven or eight miles below Fayetteville. Within a day or two after arriving there, the Tories under McNeill, made an attacked in front and rear. The Whigs broke through their front, and effected a retreat with the loss of a private William Strong killed. My Brother Joseph Singletary was severely wounded, and my horse was also wounded."

Josiah's brother Joseph was wounded by a broadsword in several places and he was disabled in one leg. Joseph lay wounded three or four months at his mother's home.

"The Company collected again on the Cape Fear River, and the next day, me and several others under Colonel Robeson returned to Stewart's Mill to see what had become of the Tories. They had gone off; upon ascertaining which, the Company returned home. I was in another expedition against the Tories, in the same Company. They had collected at Sterlings Mills on Drowning Creek or Lumber River. Irwin's Company surprised, and defeated them as they were crossing the Mill dam. In their precipitate flight, they left a considerable number of their horses, which were taken."

"I was engaged in various other expeditions under Captain Irwin in different parts of the Country, but how often, when and the other circumstances I do not recollect. The County of Bladen then embraced a large extent of territory, and within its limits, the Tories, being mostly emigrants from the Highlands of Scotland, were numerous, active, and loyal to the British Government. The Head Quarters of Irwin was at Elizabeth Town, except when obliged to retire before superior numbers of the enemy. On one occasion the Tories emboldened by the march of Lord Cornwallis's Army down the Cape Fear River towards Wilmington, collected to the number of three or four hundred in Elizabethtown, the Company owing to inferiority of force, being obliged to retire across the Cape Fear--Colonel Robeson, who took command of the Company, in consequence of Captain Irwin's being disabled by a severe attack of the Small Pox, caught from a British deserter, took command of the Company, and being of opinion that it would not be prudent to remain near so large a force of the enemy, conducted the Company over Neuse River, but immediately returned. On our countermarch from Lisbon to Sampson County between Colley Swamp and the Cape Fear, about nine miles from Elizabeth, we were met by Mrs. McRee, the mother of Major Griffith J. McRee of the Continental Army, who left home for the purpose of apprising them of the situation of the Tories. By that time we had been joined by Cols Brown, and Owen, and Capt Peter Robeson, and several other Whigs, and in consequence of the information received from Mrs. McRee, an attack on the Tories was determined on--although the whole force of the Whigs did not exceed Eighty men. We accordingly marched to the Cape Fear, and forded it at night, about half or three quarters of a mile below the village--attacked the Tories at a point called Tory Hole-- drove them to the upper end of the Village; where the ammunition of the Whigs having been expanded, we were under the necessity of retiring: after having killed or mortally wounded their commanding officer Col Slingsby, Captain David Godwin and a private named Edward Harrison- -Lieutenant Baldwin and several privates were severely wounded. Of the Whigs none were killed, and only two privates James Singletary, and James Cain slightly wounded. The Tories were so severely handled, that they dispersed the next Morning. I was in active service, in Irwin's Company, at least twelve months. For it was notorious, that there was not in this part of the Country, a more zealous, active and intrepid partisan Officer in the Whig service, then Captain Irwin, and no one did more in sustaining, within his limited sphere of action, the common cause. His men were held ready for service at a moment's warning, and for a period of more than three years, they were for a considerable portion of the time, in the field, exposed to every species of hardships and privations."

The Battle of Tory Hole was fought on 27 August, 1781 between the patriot militia of Bladen County and the Troy militia of Bladen County. The patriots were not sure of how many of the enemy they faced so Sally Salter, the young wife of a local man, offered to enter the enemy's camp and find out.

She took a basket of eggs and took the ferry across Cape Fear River and entered the camp of the Tories. She walked around the camp selling her eggs and making mental notes of what she saw. After acquiring what she needed, she went back across the river to report her findings.

That night, because the Tories had taken all the boats, the patriots crossed the river naked with their clothes tied in bundles on top of their heads. Once across they got dressed and at daybreak took the Tory camp by surprise. The patriots outnumbered began to shout out commands to fictitious units, and many of the men also yelled out "Washington". The Tories thinking they were under attack by a large force panicked and ran. Many of the enemy ran into a deep ravine where they were easy to shoot at. This site became known as Tory Hole. Nineteen of the enemy were killed with no loss of patriot lives. Some Tory survivors of the battle reported that they were attacked by Washington's whole army.

Sources: 1. Dictionary of North Carolina Biography: Vol. 5, P-S, edited by William S. Powell. 2. Historical Sketches of North Carolina from 1584 to 1851 by John H. Wheeler. 3. U.S. Pension Roll of 1835. 4. Pension Papers W6064.

****

Eli Skinner age 14

Eli Skinner was born on 30 July, 1760 in Colchester, Connecticut, and he died on 7 February, 1841 in Brookfield, Massachusetts. He married Lucinda Nims on 28 August, 1783 in Massachusetts. He served as a fifer in the militia at the age of 14.

"About the first day of May 1775 I was enlisted into the army of the Revolution for the term of Eight months. I was enlisted by Jacob Poole of the said Shelburne. I a few days after visiting with several others who had enlisted stared from Shelburne under said Lieutenant Poole & marched to Cambridge in Massachusetts, near Boston where we arrived in the said May but do not recollect the day. When we arrived at Cambridge we joined a company commanded by Capt Agnippa Wills. I served out my eight months and was discharged."

"In December 1776, still residing at Shelburne, a call was made for Militia to serve three months—I volunteered for and in that service I was mustered at Greenfield Mass Dec. 26th 1776, my Capt was John Well, of said Shelburne. Capt Wells company was organized at Greenfield on said 26th day of Dec 1776 being composed of Militia troops (volunteers & drafted) from the towns of Shelburne, Charlemont, Greenfield, Benardston & Colerain. Marched to Northampton Mass--When Capt Wells received orders to report with his company to Ticonderoga--me and my said company left Northampton the next day & marched the way Chesterfield, Pittsfield & Greenbush to Albany N.Y. from Albany by Fort Miller & Fort Anne to Skenesboro and from there to Ticonderoga, where we arrived the

7th or 8th *day of Jan 1777. On marching to Ticonderoga Capt Wells company was attached to Col Robinsons Regiment. Me and my company remained at Ticonderoga doing Garrison duty till our three months expired and was dismissed at Ticonderoga and returned back to Shelburne."*

After the war Eli and his wife lived in Massachusetts, Vermont, and Illinois. He worked as a blacksmith, and he worked a farm with two of his brothers. He held several town offices and was a respected citizen. He received a yearly pension of $36.60 for his service.

Sources: 1. Sons of the American Revolution Application. 2. Massachusetts Marriages 1633-1850. 3. Tombstone 4. Monument erected by Illinois Society of the Sons of the American Revolution. 5. U.S. Pension Roll of 1835. 6. Pension Papers S31366.

****

Charles Smith age 14

Charles Smith was born on 2 June, 1763 in Frederick County, Virginia, and he died on 12 May, 1846 in Sherman West Virginia. He married Jane Morton on 19 June, 1783 in Orange County, Virginia. He received a yearly pension of $40.

"In the month of December in the year 1777 as well as I recollect and in Battletown in the County of Frederick and State of Virginia I volunteered as a private under the command of Capt Trueston but I do not recollect the names of the subalterns--we marched from Battletown in the county of Frederick in the state of Virginia to Winchester Va thence to Frederick town in the state of Maryland thence to Lancaster in the state of Pennsylvania leaving Philadelphia to the right owing to the small pox being there, thence to the neighbourhood of Morristown in the state of New Jersey and were there incorporated into a regiment but does not recollect the names of the field officers. I was engaged in guarding the garrison and fought in the battle against British at Morristown aforesaid and was discharge in the latter end of March and returned home after having served six months as a private soldier."

"In the month of May in the year 1779 he volunteered and march under Capt Heiskill, Lieut. Calimese and ensign Catlet to Harpers ferry across the Potomac River--crossed into Maryland, thence to Fredericktown in the state of Maryland thence to Lancaster in the State of Pennsylvania and was employed in guarding the prisoners taken from Winchester in the State of Virginia and was discharged in the month of

August 1779 after having served three months as a private soldier and returned home again to Battletown in Frederick County and State of Virginia"

"In May in the year 1781 I volunteered and marched under Capt. Calimese and Lieut Calimese through the Counties of Fauquire Culpeper and Caroline and went through Richmond Va. thence to New Castle Va. at which place I was incorporated into Gen Layfayett's Regiment but shortly after was selected __?__ served as flying light infantry and as such marched under aforesaid Capt and Lieut Calimese to yorktown Va. and was there engaged principally in tracing the __?__ lines __?__ purpose of makeing discoveries and bringing on an attack frequently marching fifteen miles at night and returning before day. I fought in the battle at yorktown and witnessed the Surrender of Lord Cornwallis. was discharged in October 1781 and returned home after having served six months as a private soldier."

In June of 1835 Charles provided additional information on his service, including the reason he enlisted at a young age. *"The cause of my volunteering young as I was was by being urged by my friends after the death of my father to go into the service of his Country, that men were hard to raise and I having been taught to believe it was better to die than live under the government of Great Britton, I therefore volunteered my services. Concerning my age Captain Trustons company consisted of several young men of my own age, that I say, was another inducement for me to volunteer my services."*

Sources: 1. U.S. Pension Roll of 1835. 2. Pension Papers S15649.

****

Edward Smith age 13 or14

Edward Smith was born on 10 May, 1762 in Augusta County, Virginia, and he died on 6 December, 1852 in Owsley County, Kentucky. He married Hannah Crabtree on 6 September, 1787 in Virginia. He received a yearly pension of $60.

"I entered the service as a volunteer in the spring of the year 1775 under Captain James Dysart by order of Col Arthur Campbell who was the Col. Commandant of Washington County, and was continued in this service to guard the frontier inhabitants of the said County against the indians for six months and was then discharged by the said Captain Dysart."

"In the spring or early part of the summer of 1776 I again volunteered and was placed under the same Captain and served another six months in the same service and was again honorably discharged by the same officer."

"In the year 1777 I volunteered & performed a six weeks tour of service under Ensign Andrew Kincannon in pursuit of Tories in that part of the country bordering on New river and was after the performance of said service honorably discharged."

"In 1778 I volunteered under Captain James Dysart and marched to the Rocky Station in Powell's Valley. There we joined Captain Martin and served two months when I was honorably discharged."

"In the fall of the year 1780 I again volunteered under Captain Andrew Colville on the expedition under Col. William Campbell to the South which terminated in the capture of Major Furguson at King's Mountain in South Carolina and that I was in that battle. After the capture of Ferguson me and William Snodgrass were sent by Col Campbell to meet that part of the militia who were following on foot and to direct them to halt which service we performed. We were then permitted to pass down the Catawba and approach the lines of Cornwallis. In this service we were near being taken by Tarlton's horse--After surmounting many difficulties we joined the troops under the command of General Davis and Sumpter and they sent us as an express to Col Campbell whom we came up with at the Moravian towns--we remained with him some time and were then permitted to return home and on this tour I faithfully served four months. I performed other small tours of duty which I will not name."

Sources: 1. U.S. Roll of 1835. 2. Pension Papers W9301.

****

Levi Smith age 14

Levi Smith was born in 1761 in Amherst, Massachusetts, and he died on 11 September, 1828 in Hamilton, Ohio. He was wounded by a musket ball during the war. He first served as a private when he answered the Lexington Alarm of 19 April, 1775. He served for two days in Colonel Porter's Regiment.

He served two tours as a fifer with Captain Dickerson's Company, under the command of Colonel Woodridge's 25th Massachusetts' Regiment. The first tour was for three months starting on 8 May, 1775.

Levi was with the regiment at the Battle of Bunker Hill on 17 June, 1775. The regiment arrived just before the start of the battle and were deployed on the right flank. Some of the regiment were at the breastwork on Breed's Hill. The regiment helped to cover the retreat after the British had taken the hill.

Levi's second tour with the same regiment began on 28 September, 1775 as a fifer. He was stationed for three months at Prospect Hill outside of Boston.

On 7 May, 1777 Levi enlisted for one month as a fifer in Captain John Thompson's Company under Colonel Leonard's Regiment. He marched to reinforce the Northern Army. He served a one month tour on 21 July, 1779 at New London under Colonel Elisha Porter. He was a Fife Major in Colonel Ezra Wood's Regiment from 1 September, 1779 to 1 November, 1779. In 1780 he enlisted for 3 years and appeared on the Descriptive list of enlisted men. He was described as fair complexion and 5' 9" tall.

Sources: 1. Sons of the American Revolution Application. 2. Year Book of the Society of Sons of the Revolution in the State of Illinois, 1913.

****

Jesse Smith age 14

Jesse Smith was born on 16 April, 1765 in Montgomery County, North Carolina, and he died on 11 April, 1842 in Franklin, Georgia. His second wife was Anna Mitchell who he married on 31 January, 1832. She received a yearly widow's pension of $43.33.

"I entered the service of the United States in the Militia of Camden South Carolina in Camden District, I was drafted under Capt John Steel for three months in the month of May or June 1780 & was marched & joined Genl Sumter at Chester South Carolina & was in the Regiment commanded by Col Bratton, and was in an engagement at Henderson's Ford on Catawba River 18th of August 1780, were defeated & dispersed had served a few days over the three months Tour."

Jesse Smith said he was at an engagement at Henderson's Ford on 18 August, 1780. This was called the Battle of Fishing Creek, also known as the Battle of Catawba Ford. American General Thomas Sumter was camped and at posted guards some distance away. While the general was sleeping under a wagon, British Lieutenant Colonel Banastre Tarleton with a force of 350 troops captured the American guards before they could alert the camp. The British then managed to place themselves between most of the militia and their weapons and forced the Americans to flee.

The unprepared Americans had 150 men killed, 300 captured, lost their supplies, and 100 British prisoners were freed. Jesse was lucky to be among the 400 soldiers to escape. General Sumter escaped into the forest on horseback, but he was knocked from his horse when he struck an oak limb. When he came to, he found his horse and road to safety. This British victory, combined with others in the area, gave hope that the Carolinas and Georgia would be under their control. British General Clinton summed up the feelings, when he referred to the control of the trio of states as, "three stripes...of the detestable thirteen."

"In the month of May 1781 was again drafted in Camden aforesaid & was put under command of said Capt Steel and was under command of Col Lacey & General Sumter & was marched to Rocky Mount & from thence to Camden where we joined the Regulars under Genl Green and was marched to Ninety Six & was ordered with Lacey's command at Orangeburg during the Battle of Ninety Six from Orangeburg we again joined General Green and was marched to Eutaw Springs where we fought the British there and where our major O'Neal was killed. After the battle a few days I received a discharge from Captain Steel having served three months."

"In the month of January 1782 I volunteered myself for seven months in Camden aforesaid, under Capt Cook and Col Taylor and was marched from Orangeburg to the For Holes, Thence to Bacon's Bridge, thence to Moncks Corner, all in South Carolina, & was then discharged by Captain Goode, Captain Cook having become sick & returned home, had no fighting in this last campaign except we took one Colonel more & 60 & 70 Tories & hung him & four of his men at Orangeburg."

Sources: 1. Historical Dictionary of the American Revolution by Terry M. Mays. 2. Roster of Revolutionary Soldiers in Georgia, Vol. III. 3. U.S. Pensioners 1818-1872. 4. U.S. Pensioners 1818-1872. 5. Pensioner Papers W2450.

****

Michael Smith age 14

Michael Smith was born in 1762 in Virginia, and he died in 1840 in Rush County, Indiana. He received a monthly pension of $8.00.

"I enlisted for the term of three years in the month of February in the year 1777 in the state of Pennsylvania in the company commanded by Captain U. Springer in the regiment commanded by Colonel John Gibson in the line of the state of Pennsylvania on the continental establishment. I continued to serve in the said corps until the month of June 1783 when I was discharged from the service in Pittsburgh in the state of Pennsylvania."

Sources: 1. U.S. Headstones Application for Military Veterans 1925-1963. 2. Pension Papers S40448.

****

Thomas Smith age 12

Thomas Smith was born in 1766 in Virginia. In 1778 he enlisted for three years in the Convention Guard Regiment. He said in his pension application, *"I enlisted in the year 1777 or 1778. I was stationed at the Albemarle Barracks afterwards I marched to Peaked Mountain I was then marched to Winchester Barracks where I was afterwards discharged."*

Thomas said he served under Captain John Roberts and Colonel Francis Taylor. John Robert was appointed a Captain in 1779 and Francis Taylor was placed in command of the regiment in March of 1779.

The Convention Guard Regiment was raised by the Virginia governor in December of 1778. The 600 man regiment was raised to act as a guard for captured British troops. The regiment served from January 1778 until June of 1781.

Albemarle Barracks was a prisoner of war camp for British soldiers. Hundreds of British soldiers escaped from the barracks due to the lack of an adequate number of guards. The barracks was located outside of Charlottesville, Virginia. As the British army moved north from the Carolinas in the later part of 1780 the prisoners were moved to several places, one was Winchester.

In addition to his three years of guard duty, Thomas also served a tour of 40 days and one tour of three months in the Virginia militia under Captain Green. Thomas received $80 a year for his service.

Sources: 1. Pension Papers for Thomas Smith. 2. The Magazine of Albemarle County History Vol. 41, 1983. 3. Records of the Revolutionary War by William Thomas Roberts Saffell.

****

William Smith age 14

William Smith was born on 22 July, 1763 in Augusta County, Virginia, and he died on 26 January, 1842. He married Hannah Snead on 22 January, 1793. He received a yearly pension of $21.66.

"In the first tour of duty I was drafted for one month to guard a large number of British and Hessians who were Captured at Saratoga and brought to Charlottesville in the County of Albemarle, State of Virginia for safe keeping, I think this was in the latter part of the year 1777 or early in the year 1778. My Captain was David Shelton of the County of Amherst Virginia from which place I marched. At the expiration of one month I was discharged and returned home."

"Some few months after the expiration of the first tour I was again drafted for one month and marched from the County of Amherst to Charlottesville to guard the same British and Hessian prisoners who were still detained there in Custody. I do not now recollect who my officers were upon this second tour; on this second tour I served one month and was discharged."

"The manner in which troops were detailed to guard the prisoners at Charlottesville was as follows, two militia companies were drafted and marched at the same time from the County of Amherst to serve one month when they were relieved by two other companies, and I suppose and believe that the same rule was observed towards other Counties in furnishing their quotas of the guard."

"I was again drafted for three months and marched early in the year 1781 from the County of Amherst under the command of Capt James Barnett & Lieut John Woodruff Charles Dabney of the County of Hanover in Virginia was Colonel of the Regiment. The Company to which I belonged was in the first place stationed at Williamsburg but was at short intervals marched to several other places to keep watch upon the British whose foraging parties were continually roving about the Country to the great alarm of the people and destruction of their property. whilst stationed at the halfway house about twelve miles from Yorktown, one of the American Soldiers who had been riding in the Country, came into Camp with information that he had seen a number of British a few miles from the Camp; the Company to which I belonged was with several other companies immediately marched out in pursuit of them and captured

about seventy who surrendered without making any resistance. I was one of the guard detailed to escort these prisoners to Williamsburg where they were delivered to Gen'l Steuben. At Williamsburg I was discharged and returned home, having served in this tour three months and two or three weeks."

"I had not been at home more than a week or ten days to the best of my recollection when owing to the unsettled state of the time I was again called out for twenty days and marched from the County of Amherst That part of it now called Nelson County, Virginia, under the command of Capt. Richard Taliaferro and Lieut Charles Eides company officers; the name of Colo was Meriwether and Gen'l. Stevens commanded the Brigade, in this tour declarant was present and engaged in the Battle of Hot water, I was with the troops that were stationed at a place called Malbams Hill and was marched to reinforce Gen'l Wayne at Hot water. the reinforcement arrived at the latter ground during the fight. this tour was for twenty days as before stated, but the Company to which I belonged was detained more than twice that length of time for I recollect that I marched from home late in the month of April and was not discharged until after harvest."

The Battle of Hot Water, near Williamsburg, Virginia took place on 26 June, 1781. American troops attacked British foragers and regained cattle taken, and they then were forced to retreat when Cornwallis and his army approached.

Source: 1. Pension Papers W2629.

****

William Smith age 14

William Smith was born on 17 February, 1762 in Lunenburg County, Virginia, and he died in 1840 in Lincoln, Tennessee. He married Phoebe Denton on 4 September, 1792 in Tennessee. He is listed on the 1820 census roll owning 6 slaves. William received a yearly pension of $100.

"Sometime in the spring of 1776, I being then but fourteen years of age, I volunteered my services to the then Capt John Sevier and was received under the following circumstances. Men being called for, me, with others, went from a Settlement on Watauga River, where I then resided with my widowed mother, to Wammas fort to be inspected by an officer whose name I do not now remember. But I recollect that during

our ride I killed a buck; and that on the inspector objecting to me, on the ground of my youth, one of my companions, more advanced in years, related that incident, the inspector thereupon received me; remarking that "if the boy can kill a deer, he certainly can bring down an Indian." I was then placed, as a private, under the command of Capt Sevier, whose lieutenant was Jonathan Tipton, and served a term of three months, in Garrison, at Fort Watauga. The then <u>Capt</u> James Robinson, with a small company, were also in Garrison during the same time, and at the same place. And while there the fort was attacked by Cherokee Indians, who were, repelled without loss to the Garrison. I would here state that for this service I was paid in money by my Captain; but for all the services subsequently rendered his country, by me, I have never received anything whatever. And that ever after, I furnished my own equipment, viz. arms and horse; for, after this, I was always mounted, and myself and comrades provided our own subsistence in the best way we could, there being at no period of my service any commissary attached to the troops with whom I served."*

William Smith served under Captain John Sevier, and William was present when the Americans defended Fort Watauga against an attack, by the Cherokee Indians in July of 1776. Before the Indians launched their attack a group of settlers raced to get inside the fort. The gates were closed when Captain Sevier saw a tall young woman running toward the front gates with the Indians in persuit. Sevier managed to reach over the palisades and pull the young girl to safety. The girl was Catherine Sherrill, who the captain would later fall in love with and marry. After the war, Sevier would serve six two-year terms as Tennessee's governor.

"During the summer and autumn of 1779 I served from four to six months (the precise time I cannot tell; because, having no documentary references, I have to depend solely upon my memory which I dare not rely upon to furnish me with particular dates,) as a lieutenant under the immediate command of Capt, (afterwards General) Landon Carter. I was appointed to office by the then Col John Sevier, who was the commander of the forces raised in Washington County (then North Carolina) or by his recommendation, I cannot say which. The troops, under command of Col Sevier, rendezvoused at Lick Creek on Nolichucky River; at which place we were to have been joined by Col Campbell of Virginia; but there learning that hostile Indians were on their march towards the settlements, we marched to Big-creek of French broad, up Long-creek, to Boyd's creek, & after crossing it and proceeding about three miles, we met the Indians, gave them battle & defeated them. We then returned to Great Island (since

called Sevier's Island) in French-broad river, and there staid about eight days, subsisting principally upon hickory-nuts, Walnuts and grapes. At the expiration of that time we were joined by Col Campbell, who took the command, and we then marched back to the battle ground, up Boyd's creek, thence to Little river etc. to the Tennessee, & crossed at the Virginia line and entered Chota,--where they remained several weeks--thence through sundry Indian towns, & back home and were disbanded."

"Sometime in the Summer of 1780, Capt Valentine Sevier appointed me an ensign in his company, and we joined Col Isaac Shelby, who was then on his way from Sullivan County to unite with Col McDowell. We marched in a few days and joined that officer at a ___?__ house where me & my troops lay encamped near a Creek, the name of which I do not remember. Shortly after I was detached under Shelby & Col (since General) Clarke, of Georgia, to surprise an enemy's post, in front, which was accomplished after marching all night. The post I remember was commanded by Capt Patrick Moore, who surrendered it without resistance in a very short time after it was demanded. There was with me a volunteer called Capt William Cocke, who was sent to the fort with the flag, and who soon after left the detachment. In a short time after this affair, Shelby & Clark, with their commands, were detached to observe the movements of the enemy, who was in force in the country under the command of Major Ferguson."

The battle of Fort Thicketty occurred in the summer of 1780, when Patriot Colonel Shelby captured the fort from Tory Captain Patrick Moore without firing a shot. Colonel Shelby used a fake cannon, commonly called a "Quaker cannon", to convince Moore to surrender.

"It was some time while roasting ears were plenty that we had a battle with a portion of that officers troops near Wofford's Iron-works; and that on the whole of the enemy's forces coming up, the Americans retreated. I remember that in this action Col Clarke was wounded in the neck by a sword, lost his hat and returned to McDowell's camp bareheaded; and that a Major Burrell Smith of Virginia, who along to Clark's command, was killed."

At the Battle of Wofford's Iron Works, fought on 8 August, 1780, William Smith was under the command of Colonel Shelby of the Sullivan County North Carolina Militia. There was a skirmish between the Patriot and Tory militia units. When Tory reinforcements under Major Ferguson approached the battle, the Patriots retreated. As noted in William's pension application, Patriot Colonel Clarke received two sabre wounds, one on the back of his neck and the other on his head. His neck stock stopped the neck wound from being fatal.

"*A week or two later I was engaged in the battle of Enoree, at Musgrove's mill, in which action the British Col Ennis was said to be shot in the shoulder. In about one month after this event I returned to his home, and while preparing to again join the Army was thrown from his horse, badly hurt, and never again served under Colonel Shelby.*"

William Smith also fought at the Battle of Musgrove Mill, an American victory, on 19 August, 1780. In this battle a smaller force of patriot militiamen defeated a larger Tory Militia. During the battle one of the Tory commanders, Colonel Clary, mounted his horse to escape. Two patriot militiamen seized the bridle bit of the horse to stop his escape. Because there was confusion and the militia were not in uniforms, Colonel Clary yelled at the two patriots, "Damn you, don't you know your own officers?" He was instantly released and was able to escape.

"*Another term of service I rendered in the spring of the year 1780 as follows. I volunteered as a private, under the above named Colonel Clarke, in a company commanded by a Captain Dooly, in Washington County North Carolina, and marched through the upper parts of North & South Carolina, and crossed the Savannah River about sixty or seventy miles above Augusta in Georgia thence proceeded to Augusta, and were principally employed in harassing, taking and killing known tories whenever they could be found; from thence we returned home, through the upper parts of Georgia & South Carolina; being at this time, to the best of my recollection, in service about two months.*"

"*In March 1781 I joined Col John Sevier, at the greasy cove of Nolichucky River, in the capacity of an Ensign, in a company commanded by Capt Valentine Sevier, Alexander Greer Lieutenant, and marched into the middle settlements of the Cherokees, on the headwaters of Little Tennessee river and entered Tuckasejah town, where we took a number of prisoners, and thence proceeded to a number of adjacent towns, burnt the houses, and destroyed all the grain we could find. I was in service, as I believe, about two months at this time.*"

"*Soon after my return from the last mentioned expedition--either in April or May 1781 as I think--I again joined Col Clarke on Watauga River, Washington County, as a private under a command of Captain Dooley as before, and marched through the upper parts of North, & South Carolina into the upper part of Wilkes County Georgia, recruiting men on* the way as opportunity offered,--the object of Clarke being to take Augusta from the English troops, under command of Colonel Brown, who had it in his possession. Thence, after some weeks delay, we proceeded to invest Augusta, and finally took it. During the siege the American Capt Price was shot through the thigh, and died of the wound. We remained after the surrender of the Fort and place, about one month, and then returned home."

William was a member of the militia at the Siege of Augusta between 22 May and 6 June, 1781. Fort Cornwallis, which was the main defense of the town was forced to surrender to the patriots. The Americans built a thirty foot tower and placed a cannon on top to fire down into the fort. The enemy was defenseless and were forced to surrender on 6 June.

"I think that it was in September 1782 that I again joined the standard of Col John Sevier for another expedition against the Cherokees. We were joined by a party of men under the command of Col Anderson of Sullivan County (then North Carolina) and after the junction, we marched to the Big--island in French Broad River; at which place it appearing that there were forty-two men without any Capt--a lieutenant being the highest officer among them I was appointed, by Colonel Sevier, to command them, and I acted as their Captain during the residue of the campaign; which to the best of my knowledge and belief was a term of about two months. From Big Island we marched to the upper Cherokee towns,--the Indians of which were then friendly--and procured to guides, John Watts, a halfbreed Indian, and an Indian called Noonday, to conduct them to the towns of the hostile Indians. In this expedition some Indians were killed, & some of their towns burned. A white woman named Jane Ireland, who had some time before been taken captive, on Roan's Creek Washington County North Carolina, was brought in and delivered to Sevier, by the guide John Watts. A white man by the name of Samuel Martin, who had been taken prisoner at Nashville, was also brought in and surrendered to the commanding officer. After visiting various towns they proceeded to Chota, on the Tennessee River, where the friendly Indians and whites had a talk, and from there the troops returned home."

Sources: 1. U.S. Pension roll of 1835. 2. Sons of the American Revolution Application. 3. Census 1820. 4. Pension Papers S1723. 5. The Delineator, Vol. 63, edited by R.S. O'Loughlin, 1904. 6. Colonial and Revolutionary History of Upper South Carolina by John Belton O'Neall Landrum. 7. Traditions and Reminiscences Chiefly of the American Revolution in the South by Joseph Johnson.

****

William Smith age 13 or 14

William Smith was born in 1762 in Massachusetts, and he died on 25 February, 1835 in Rome, New York. He married Elizabeth Hopkins on 4 January, 1785 in Rowley, Massachusetts. He received a yearly pension of $40.

"I entered the service of the United States as a private soldier in the Continental establishment in the spring of 1775 under Captain Thomas Mighill in a Regiment of Infantry Commanded by Samuel Gerrish in the Massachusetts line; continued in the same Regt till the expiration of eight months which was the term of my enlistment then I immediately enlisted again under Capt Joseph Pettingills in a Regiment of Infantry commanded by Col Baldwin (do not recall his given name) for a term of one year, after the expiration of said term I enlisted another term of six weeks and was discharged in February 1777."

In 1775 Colonel Samuel Gerrish commanded the 25th Regiment. William Smith joined the regiment in the spring of 1775 and was probably at the Battle of Bunker Hill fought in June. William's enlistment was up at the end of the year, and he joined the 9th Massachusetts' Regiment under the command of Colonel Loammi Baldwin. William probably participated in the American victories at the Battle of Assunpink Creek (also known as the Second Battle of Trenton) on 2 January, 1777 and the Battle of Princeton the next day. William may have been discharged before Valley Forge.

Source: 1. Pension Papers W22264.

****

Daniel Southerland age 13

Daniel Southerland was born in 1764 in Prince William County, Virginia, and he died on 22 February, 1838 in Habershaw County, Georgia. There is confusion about how many times he may have married and who the women were. According to his pension papers he did marry Isabella Haygood in 1819, and she received a yearly widow's pension of $40.

"I volunteered & entered the service of the United States in 1777 at Guilford Court house in the State of North carolina where I then resided, under Capt John Nelson, Cols Paisley & Martin, Major Owen &

Gen Rutherford were all commanding officers--was marched from Guilford Court house to the head of the Catawba River to a place called the Pleasant Gardens in the indian nation where we were stationed for some time. From there I was marched to what was called the big Town house on the Tennessee River, which place we burnt together with several other Towns & killed some of the Indians. I was then marched to the Valley Towns on Valley River, which Towns we also burnt & cut down & destroyed the corn & everything else we could find belonging to the Indians. I was then marched back to the Pleasant Gardens where I was discharged. Served this tour three months."

"*In April 1778, I again volunteered in Guilford County, N. Carolina under Capt John Dooly & was marched to Fort Dooly in Wilkes County in the State of Georgia, where I remained for some time. I was then marched to Fort Heard, I think in the same County. I was then marched to the head of Long Creek, where I was Stationed some time, during which time we had a skirmish with the indians, when my Captain Thomas Dooly was Killed (Capt John Dooly being promoted to Col—Thomas Dooly was put in his place)--I was then marched back by Fort Dooly to Guilford County, N. Carolina where I was discharged. Served this tour, three months."*

"*I again entered the service at Guilford Court house in May or June 1779* [this should be 1780 because the battle of Camden took place in 1780] *under Capt Oniel or Brashear & was marched into South Carolina to join Gen Gates, which we did about a day's march from Camden, was in the Battle of Camden, or Gates' Defeat. Before I joined Gates' army, I was marched to Salisbury & to the mouth of the Rocky River, at which place we had a skirmish with the Tories. From Gates' Defeat I was marched back to Guilford County, N. Carolina, where I was discharged, having served this time three months."*

Daniel Sutherland was part of the North Carolina militia that made up the left flank of the main body of the army. As the British attacked, American units began to panic and flee. This soon spread to the North Carolina militia, and some of them began to break and run.

"*I again entered the service at Guilford Court house, N Carolina in the fall or winter of 1780, under Captain May or Moore, but from some circumstance, Captain May or Moore did not march with us, when I was appointed by Col Martin to take the command of the company, which I did during this tour. We marched from Guilford down into Randolph & Chatham Counties after the tories, Col Fannin being at their head. Had several skirmishes with the Tories, after which I returned back to Guilford & was discharged by Colonel Martin, having served this time three months-- Served in all 12 months, nine months as a private, and three months as a Captain."*

Sources: 1. Sons of the American Revolution Application. 2. North Carolina Marriage Index 1741-2004. 3. Pension Papers W66081.

****

William Spain age 13

William Spain was born on 28 September, 1763 in Pitt County, North Carolina, and he died there on 23 October, 1841. He married Nancy Church on 25 February, 1797 in Pitt. She received a yearly widow's pension of $80. William served as a fifer during the war.

"I enlisted in the County of Pitt and the State aforesaid on the 10th of March 1777 in the Company commanded first by Captain May afterwards by Captain Tartanson of the 8th Regiment of North Carolina and I continued to serve in the said Regiment until its reduction in 1778 when I continued to serve in the 2nd Regiment of North Carolina until the surrender of Charleston South Carolina to the British on the 12th of May 1780 when I was carried to Nova Scotia & remained a prisoner during the continuance of the war. I was in the Battles of Brandywine, Germantown and at the Siege of Charleston."

William is listed on the roll of Captain Francis Tartanson in the 8th North Carolina Regiment. At the Battle of Brandywine the 8th Regiment was placed in the main body of the army under the command of Brigadier General Francis Nash. At the battle of Germantown they were held in reserve. The Regiment became the 3rd at Valley Forge and was later captured at Charleston in 1780.

The above pension statement by William was written in 1818. After William was captured, he volunteered to enlist in the British army in order to get free from the prison ship he was on. Some Americans chose to do this because of the horrible conditions they endured as prisoners.

William did not include this information in his pension statement, and some people in the area where he lived wrote to Washington that he should not receive a pension since he deserted and joined the British. The following statement was written by William to explain his actions.

"State of North Carolina Pitt County William Spain of the County & State aforesaid maketh answer to the charges preferred against him in the War Department and saith as follows: "That on the 10th day of March 1777 I enlisted as a soldier in the 1st Regiment of Continental line, commanded by General Nash and on the day of April in the same year, then 13 years of age offered myself as a substitute for my father and was received in his place. -- I continued in the service of the United States until 1780 and was posted in the aforesaid time at the places as follows -- I first marched to Alexandria in Virginia and cont' there for 6 or 7 weeks for the purpose of being vaccinated, then marched to Philadelphia, from there to Trenton from there back to Philadelphia, thence to the head of Elk River, I was present at the Battle of Brandywine, on the 11th of September, on the 12th, retreated to Philadelphia, thence to Germantown and was present there on the 4th of October when the Battle was fought. I then took winter quarters at Valley Forge about 20 miles from Philadelphia -- thence marched to Monmouth New Jersey and was present at the Battle of Monmouth on the 28th of June 1778 & from thence to Brunswick New Jersey, thence to White Plains New York, thence marched to Continental Village and there remained for nearly two months, thence marched to Haverstown on Hudson the liver from thence to West Point & remained there until orders were rec' for the N.C., & Virginia troops to march South,-- then marched to Charleston S. Ca where I arrived 3rd day of March 1780, and remained there and was present at the different skirmishes and at the time of surrender on the 12th May 1780, the whole of which time I remained an American soldier, I remained a prisoner in Charleston five months was then taken on board a British ship where I remained for five other months a prisoner when becoming destitute of clothing and money and not receiving any help from the United States, I enlisted in March 1781 with the British for the sole purpose of getting clothing, the conditions of my enlistment was that I should either go the Spanish main or to Jamaica and not with a view to fight against the United States and had I have been brought back to fight against the United States, I would have deserted and joined the flag of my Country, I remained in Jamaica until peace was made and received nothing but my wages & clothing – that I received no Bounty lands from the British Government nor wished none my only object being as above stated of providing myself with clothing -- that after my discharge I proceeded to Nova Scotia for the purpose of getting to my Country, there being no American vessel in the ports of Jamaica -- I further saith that there is no person, by whom I can prove the latter part of the above facts by as there is no person in this country nor on any of the adjoining counties to my knowledge who was *confined with me, -- I further saith that during the last war, I used my exertions to encourage volunteers, I attended the musters and acted as a musician for the about purpose of encouraging the use, volunteer their services to their Country."*

While William was in Jamaica, peace was declared and he received his release. There were no American ships in port, so he took a British ship to Nova Scotia. There was no information available on how he got back to Pitt County.

A neighbor, John Anderson, wrote two letters to the pension office that was not in support of William. Anderson served with William and years earlier William had written a letter in support of Anderson's receiving a pension. John Anderson worded his letter very carefully. Below are parts of the two letters he sent.

"Honored Sir: it is my wish that every Revolutionary Soldier should have the pension who is entitled to it & it is not my wish for the Government to be wronged. I shall make the statement of Wm Spain services in: he entered in the American Service about the 1st of May 1777 in May 1780 he was taken a prisoner at Charleston S. C. & then enlisted with the British & served with them to the end of the War & then was carried to Novisiolia [Nova Scotia] & discharged by lord Montague which discharge I have seen likewise he received 50 acres of land and a town lot I have seen the place of it several good Citizens of Pitt County don't think he ought to draw the pension"

"I have understood there have been many defrauds committed on Government & I think it the duty of every Honest man to detect them if he can. Honored Sir I am your most obedient & very humble servant August 1, 1835   John Anderson"

"Sir I received your letter dated the 16th of instant & what Spain says respecting never bearing arms against the United States is true. He never bore arms in either Army but was a fifer in both & was discharged as Such by lord Montague at the end of the war you wrote he deems bearing arms against the United States a very poor excuse he played the fife for them that did he was Stationed on Island of Jamaica to protect the island from being taken by our allies the French & our best friends & many of our American vessels were captured & carried there & the Regiment he belonged to had the seamen prisoners....."

"....from his own acknowledgment he enlisted with the enemy they did not enlist him for to answered no purpose but they enlisted them to bring the United States into Subjugation..." December 30, 1835   John Anderson.

It became clear to many of the prisoners that being set free was not likely to happen during the war, and at least 75% of the men held on prison ships died. So, some Americans were persuaded to save themselves by enlisting with the British. They were promised they would not have to fight against their countrymen and were given food, clothing, and money. They would then be sent to the East Indies, Jamaica, or even Africa to fight the enemies of the British. Many did made it back home. If they did get back, they were considered deserters and might be refused a pension by the government.

William did have several people writing letters in support of his service. One letter identified John Anderson and Henry Barnwill as *"informants"*, and that the character of William was just as good as John Anderson. William kept his pension, perhaps due to his youth at the time, and after his death his wife received it.

Sources: 1. Census 1830 & 1840. 2. U.S. Pensioners 1818-1872. 3. Pension Papers W6148.

****

Michael Spatz 14

Michael Spatz was born on 4 April, 1764 in Reading, Pennsylvania, and he died there on 1 September, 1851. According to his obituary eight companies of men attended the burial. He received a monthly pension of $8. He married twice, Elizabeth Smith in 1787 and Catherine Knarr in 1826.

"In 1778 I entered at Reading Pennsylvania on the 2nd day of October for the Wyoming service against the Britons & Indians in the Company of Musketry commanded by Christian Madera & Ensign Hartman Leightheiser and in a Regiment commanded by Col. Valentine Eckert. I continued to serve at Wyoming in the same company & Regiment from the 2nd day of October AD 1778 to the 2nd day of April AD 1779 when I was then Honorably discharged for 6 months service."

"I was in above mentioned duly Enlisted for the term of 6 months & as such honorably discharged as aforesaid General Sullivan had Cut a

Road over the pine mountains to get his Troops to & over the mountain having heard that the Enemy lay in many places on the in roads from said road in ambush we procured a trusted person as our guide who made use of a compass & by this means we avoided said Sullivan's road & arrived safe to Wyoming."

Michael took part in the Sullivan Expedition against the Tories and the Iroquois Indians during the summer of 1779. The troops destroyed more than 40 Indian villages and much of their winter food supply.

"I served 18 months as a Marine, and was on the ship South Carolina; was taken prisoner and confined on a prison ship in the North (or Hudson) rivers; was subject to many hardships during my imprisonment."

Sources: 1. West Virginians in the American Revolution. 2. Federal Pensioners in 1820. 3. Pension Papers S3957.

****

Orange Spencer age 14

Orange Spencer was born on 30 July, 1764 in Richmond, Massachusetts, and he died on 10 January, 1843 in Pennsylvania. He married Sarah Bostwick on 4 December, 1767. He received a monthly pension of $30.17, and at the time of his application he was a Baptist minister. The children of Orange applied for his pension after the death of their mother Sarah in 1845. Their claim was rejected.

"In the winter of 1778 and 1779 I volunteered to go in the militia as a musician to go to Johnstown. I went to the Fort at Johnstown and served as a musician in the company commanded by Capt Lytte. This time I was about ten or twelve days and was dismissed and went home."

"In the next summer (1779) I volunteered again to go as a musician to serve in the Fort at Johnstown three or four times to serve in the same fort. I served aforesaid for the period of about two months. The fort at Johnstown was garrison by the Militia and I was frequently called out on alarms occasioned by the Indians and Tories."

"In the summer of 1780 I was called out in the militia to go to Sacondago block house under the command of Capt Putman. I was called out at several different times at Sacondago in that year and __?__ that during that year I served as a militiaman at that place at least for a period of two months."

"In the year 1781 in the month of May or June I was called out again in the militia to serve at the block house and help build the block house at Warrens brush. The company in which I served was under the command of Capt Yeoman the block house was sometimes under the command of an orderly sergeant. In this year and the succeeding year 1782 I performed a duty at this Place for a period at different times according to about six months."

"In the month of February 1782 I went as a volunteer in the company under the command of Captain Harrison in Col Willet's regiment on an expedition in Oswego we were about fourteen days on this expedition and then returned home. My feet were frozen all this expedition which disabled me for labor or business for some months aforesaid and I still feel the effects of it."

Sources: 1.The Bloodied Mohawk: The American Revolution in the Words of Fort Planks Defenders and Other Mohawk Valley Partisans by Kenneth D. Johnson. 2. Tombstone 3. U.S. Pensioners 1818-1872. 4. Pension Papers R9985.

****

Nicholas Spink age 13

Nicholas Spink was born on 6 December, 1763 in Rhode Island, and he died on 17 March, 1849 in Little Falls, New York. He served as a drummer in the 1st Rhode Island Regiment. He received a monthly pension of $8.

"I enlisted as a Musician in Captain Peckham Company in Colonel Christopher Greenes Regiment in the Spring of 1777 for the term of three years and continued as said Musician till the Spring of 1780 when I was discharged. I was in the Battle of Monmouth in New Jersey in the summer of 1778 and in a great number of small engagements and being often exposed to the fire of the enemy during the time I was in the service."

The 1st Rhode Island Regiment was also known as the "Black Regiment" because it had several companies of African American soldiers. The commander was Colonel Christopher Greene who was a cousin of General Nathaniel Greene.

Nicholas was probably at the Battle of Red Bank on 22 October, 1777. At that battle 600 Americans repelled 900 Hessian troops who were trying to take Fort Mercer. During the battle Mrs. Whitall was in a room in her home inside the fort. She was on the second floor spinning on her wheel trying to pass time during the battle. A British cannon ball entered the attic just above her. The cannon ball rolled across the floor and down the stairs landing at the foot of the stairs no more than 10 feet from where she was sitting. She got up, took her spinning wheel to the basement, and continued her spinning.

Nicholas was also present for the Battle of Rhode Island which took place on 29 August, 1778. He is listed at the rank of Corporal in the Valley Forge muster roll. After spending the winter at Valley Forge he fought in the Battle of Monmouth on 28 June, 1778.

During the battle the 1st Rhode Island Regiment was under the command of Major General Charles Lee who ordered his men to retreat. General Washington, angered at the retreat, relieved Lee and ordered the men back into the fight. The men now under the command of Layfette were kept in reserve for the main American army.

Sources: 1. D.A.R. Lineage Book, Vol. 34. 2. Pension Papers S42363. 3. Forty Minutes by the Delaware "The Battle of Fort Mercer" by Lee Patrick Anderson.

****

Amos Spofford age 14

Amos Spofford was born on 28 August, 1765 in Bradford, Massachusetts, and he died on 6 September, 1838 in Sharon, New Hampshire. He married Mary Taggart on 1 January, 1794. He received a yearly pension of $80.

When his father was drafted Amos at the age of 14 went as his substitute and served for three years. Before he left home he and his mother sheered a sheep and from the fleece she made useful garments for Amos to wear. Amos marched away with the men through "Spoffords Gap" with the tune *Over the Hills and Far Away*, an old traditional British song. One version is:

Tommy was a Piper's Son,
And fell in love when he was young;
But all the Tunes that he could play,
Was, o'er the Hills, and far away.

Sources: 1. Sons of the American Revolution Application. 2. Descendants of John Spofford and Elizabeth Scott by Dr. Jeremiah Spofford, 1888. 3. Pension Papers W22292. 4. D.A.R. Lineage Book, Vol. 41.

****

Abraham Sprague age 13

Abraham Sprague was born on 8 February, 1764 in Providence County, Rhode Island, and he died on 1 March, 1847 in Decatur, Illinois. He married Celestia Freelove Hubble. His pension was rejected, because he did not satisfy proof of service.

"In the Spring after I was <u>thirteen years old</u> I think in May I volunteered for a tour of Six Months under Captain Jonathan Brooks in the Massachusetts Militia. I was born in Providence Rhode Island but was principally raised in Lanesborough Berkshire County in Massachusetts."

"I entered the Service at the time aforesaid at Lanesborough. I think the Regiment to which I was attached was the Second Regiment of Massachusetts Militia."

"About 2 or three days after I entered said service me and my company marched to a place called Stone Arabia I recollect that we commenced our march from Lanesborough on Sunday; me and my company kept garrison at Stone Arabia or Stony Arabia till my tour Six Months was out."

"I was in the Battle fought at Stone Arabia; that Col Brown was killed in said Battle—I think Colonel Brown was killed at the first fire of the enemy—I lived when at home within five miles of Col Brown. I was discharged in October (last of it) I suppose the cause of my getting into the Service while so young was owing to the influence and exertion of one Solomon Cole or Coal at whose suggestion I volunteered."

The Battle of Stone Arabia, also known as the Battle of Klock's Field or the Battle of Failing's Orchard, was fought on 19 October, 1780. Sir John Johnson led his Loyalist troops and Indians toward Fort Paris under the command of Colonel John Brown. Colonel Brown took his 300 troops, including Abraham Sprague, out of the fort to meet Johnson. Early in the morning of the 19th the two sides clashed. Colonel Brown, mounted on his conspicuous black horse, was killed immediately. He fell in battle on his 36th birthday.

The Indians gathered around his body, stripped it of all clothing, except for his ruffled shirt, and then scalped him. In all 45 Americans were killed before the Americans withdrew. After the British and Indians were out of sight, four young militiamen, Abraham being one of them, came out of their hiding places and took the body of Colonel Brown to safety at Fort Keyser.

Sources: 1. Pension Papers R1006. 2. Colonel John Brown: His Services in the Revolutionary war, battle of Stone Arabia by Garret L. Root, 1884.

****

Abraham Sprague age 13

Abraham Sprague was born on 19 October, 1764 in Dutchess County, New York, and he died on 21 November, 1838 in Delaware County, New York.

"In the year 1778 I enlisted in the army of the United States under Capt. Campbell at Peekskill in Westchester Co. N.Y. in the month of June between 13 and fourteen years of age, I enlisted for three years…"

"…I soon marched from Peekskill to White Plains from thence to Danbury in Connecticut from thence to Hartford from thence to Danbury for winter quarters. About this time Capt Campbell (who had but an arm) was promoted and succeeded in command of the company by Capt Hughs from the State of Maryland. On the 20th day of March 1779, I marched with Gen. Poors Brigade from Danbury for Old Springfield thence to Northampton thence to Northfield thence to Charlestown thence to Hanover to Hanover Hill when I with the Regiment was employed during the summer in constructing a road from __?__ toward Canada and in the fall went winter quarters in Morristown New Jersey and joined Gen Howe's Brigade while there during the winter a detachment of which I was one were ordered to destroy some huts wood which belong to the enemy on Staten Island which we affected without loss."

"About this time I was chosen as one of the foot guards to Gen. Washington by Major Livingston that in the month of June (I think) the guard in which I served was in the Battle of Elizabethtown N.J. We were engaged with the right wing of the enemys army. There was fighting at intervals and __?__ portions for two or three days, a great many of my comrades in the guard were killed I helped carry Major Livingston from the field wounded and as I suppose mortally as I saw him no more. I received a slight wound in the engagement—the guard as much reduced in __?__ of numbers but were not disbanded until the fall of 1780."

"I joined my former regiment and went into winter quarters at Fishkill Burroughs Dutchess County, N.Y. in the spring of 1781 about the first of April I received a furlough for sixty-days to visit my family for the first time since joining the army—I having heard that my father had been killed by the Indians which I afterwards found to be true. I went home and

while there and before the expiration of my furlough the regiment marched for the south and was at the taking of Cornwallis as I understand at the expiration of my furlough I knew nothing of the fate of my regiment where to join it, and that my 3 years was expired before I saw any of my officers or knew where to find them."

"I received 3 dollars of bounty money having 17 dollars due as they told me and that then was fifteen months pay due me when my term expired."

The purpose of Washington's guards was to protect the General and the official papers of the Continental Army. The strength of the guard was increased from 180 men to 250, when Washington was encamped with his army at Morristown near the British army.

Abraham was at the Battle of Elizabethtown fought on 7 June, 1780. On that day Elizabethtown was attacked by British forces, which caused great damage to the town's property. The British hoped to advance to Morristown. The two armies clashed at Connecticut Farms and Springfield. Near Connecticut Farms is where General Washington sent his personal guard, Abraham and 153 members, to charge a Hessian unit. The next day the British troops began their retreat.

Abraham's pension application was rejected as stated in a letter sent to him from the pension office on 18 May, 1833. *"Claim not allowed as it appears from the rolls that he deserted and never after joined his regiment."* His desertion date is shown as 5 February, 1781.

This is Abraham's obituary in the Army and Navy Chronicle. *"At his residence in Hancock, Delaware County, N.Y. on the 21st November, of apoplexy, ABRAHAM SPRAGUE, in the 74th year of his age. At the age of 13 years enlisted in the service of his country, and continued there until the termination of the war. He was a member of General Washington's life guard the year it was principally cut off. He was engaged in several battles, and saw the blood flow at Elizabethtown. After the war he returned to this county, and purchased him a place, where he resided until his death. His mind was strong and intelligent, and his hand was always to assist such as were in need. He left a large circle of relatives and friends to mourn his loss."*

You decide after reading about Abraham Sprague...does he sound like a man that would desert at the end of his term of duty?

Sources: 1. Army and Navy Chronicle, and Scientific Repository, Vol. 8 by William Quereau Force. 2. Pension Paper R10005.

****

John Stephens age 14

John Stephens was born on 30 January, 1763 in Orange, Virginia, and he died on 31 March, 1842 in Franklin, Kentucky. He married Martha Faulkner on 21 May, 1785 in Kentucky. He received a yearly pension of $60.

"In the year 1777 I was drafted in the County of Orange & State of Virginia in Capt Benjamin Johnson's Company of drafted militia, and went to Fauquier Court house as a guard, and took possession of the prisoners at that place, and shortly afterwards went to the Barracks at Charlottesville in the County of Albemarle where I staid two months the period for which I was drafted."

"I served two other tours of two months each as a drafted militia man at the same place but cannot now recollect with certainty the name of the officers under whom I served these two tours--After this and prior to the year 1781 I served another tour of two months low down in the Pamunkey River which I think was in the spring of the year--the name of my officers not recollected."

"After this in the summer season the year not recollected I served another tour of two months and one in the winter season of two months low down in Virginia near to Williamsburg --One of the two last tours I do not recollect which, I served under Captain Hankins. I then served a tour of two months between Richmond & Williamsburg under Colonel Matthews, and I think I was in Captain Waugh's Company, I well recollect a false alarm in the Army in Dandridge's old field--one of the two last mentioned tours I served as a substitute for man named Collins, who lived as I understood near the Bull-run Church in Fauquier County Virginia."

"In the summer of 1781, I again entered the service as a substitute and Joined Lafayette at Richmond Virginia a day or two before the burning of Manchester, and on the evening after Manchester was burnt I was detached from the main Army & was marched to the Mobbin hills below Richmond under Captain George Waugh & Lieutenant Jamison, and did not join the main Army again until I was discharged which was just below Williamsburg a day or two after the arrival of General Washington at Williamsburg. This was called the Marquis' Retreating

tour, and Major Long of Culpeper commanded the Battalion to which I belonged at the time I was discharged."

"*After this a reinforcement was called for from Orange County and I was again drafted and met the main Army at or near Can't Courthouse just after the surrender of Lord corn Wallace and from thence I was detailed and marched as a guard to Winchester Virginia where I remained until I was discharged which was in the winter season."*

"*I may not have named the different tours which he served exactly in the order in which they occurred but supposes that it is not important, provided the department shall be satisfied that the services were faithfully performed. During all of which time I lived about three miles from what is called the Orange Springs, in Orange County Virginia and removed to Kentucky in the fall of 1782. And in October of that year I joined Captain Robert Johnson's Company of which Cave Johnson was Lieutenant and then joined General George Rodgers Clark's expedition against the Shawnee Indians. I think I left Bryant's Station in Kentucky about the 23rd day of October and returned home in the early part of December having served about 6 weeks on this last expedition."*

Sources: 1. Sons of the American Revolution Application. 2. U.S. Pension Roll of 1835. 3. Pension Papers S31392.

****

Barney Stewart age 14 (African American)

Barney Stewart was born in 1762 in Brunswick County, Virginia, and he died on 18 February, 1839 probably in Summer County, Tennessee. He received a yearly pension of $30.

"*On this 14th day of May personally appeared in open Court before the County Court of Sumner Barnet Stuart a free man of color being about 70 years of age being first duly sworn according to law makes the following declaration in order to obtain the benefit of the act of Congress passed June 7th 1832. That sometime during the Revolution I think about the year 1776 I was drafted for the term of three months under Captain John Clayton commanded by Col Richard Elliott--was marched from Brunswick County Virginia, where I was born and raised and drafted to Norfolk Virginia. There remained during my term of service, acting as cook after my arrival at Norfolk having borne arms until that time-- I was then discharged and returned home to Brunswick."*

"After about four years after my first term of service was again drafted for three months under Captain Henry Walton commanded by Col Wilkins was marched to a little town called Cabin Point on James River--was marched up and down to James River--was frequently in camp having Pine huts--I again served in the capacity of a cook. After my three months expired I was discharged and returned home."

"I was again drafted under Captain William Vaughn commanded by Colonel Watson some time before the surrender of Lord Cornwallis [October 19, 1781] for the term of three months – was marched from Brunswick to several places not recollected--finally to Little York--was there, but on the opposite side of the River, when Cornwallis surrendered. After my term expired I was discharged-- having served again as cook."

Sources: 1. U.S. Pension roll of 1835. 2. Pension Papers S1724.

****

John Stewart age 13

John Stewart was born in June 1763 in Dobbs County, North Carolina, and he died on 7 May, 1838 in Darlington, South Carolina. He enlisted in the army around August 1776 at the age of 13. He received a yearly pension of $46.66. In the Census of 1800 it was recorded that he owned one slave.

"About two months after the battle at Fort Moultrie, [this occurred 28 June, 1776] I was drafted & served in the militia service three months at Charleston South Carolina under Captain George King. The American Army was stationed there, as I was informed, for the purpose of protecting the town from the British and were then lying out in their ships meditating an attack upon it. Generals McIntosh, Lincoln and Pinckney were there but I do not know which of them had command of the American forces though who I believe that it devolved upon one or the other of them."

"At the taking of Charleston by the British: at this time and place I served three months under the same officers. When the British were surrounding the town, I was stationed on the breastworks at a place called the Sugar House and on the Surrender of the town, was taken prisoner & discharged on my parole for one-year."

"In the year 1781 (before my parole was out) I volunteered under Captain Daniel DuBose & served one month under that officer at Wadboo:

during this term of Service nothing occurred worthy of being noticed & when that term expired I returned to Darlington."

"In the same year I served <u>one</u> month at Combee under Capt Andrew DuBose instead of Capt Bacot Colonel Swinton was there as also Marion who first in command. At this place the British attempted to surprise the Americans, who after a few scattering shots compelled them to retire. In this term I was a volunteer & at the expiration of it he returned to Darlington."

"I served <u>one</u> month at the High Hills of Santee under Capt Samuel Bacot: I remained stationed there until the month expired. I think Genl Sumter was there & had command of the forces. There was no engagement this year, or other circumstance worthy of notice."

"In the latter part of the same year I was drafted again & served one month at Wadboo under Capt David Dubose. Genl Marion being the officer in command of Col Swinton was also there. At this place there was a small skirmish between a party of the British & the Americans in which the British lost a few of their men, but the Americans sustained no injury except to loss of a wagon containing their ammunition."

"In the year 1782 I served <u>one</u> month at McCord's ferry under Capt John Norwood--There was no engagement here the British came to the edge of the Swamp but did not advance near enough for an attack."

"In the same year I served one month on the northern side of Great Ped Dee under Capt John Norwood in pursuit of the Tories. I had no regular engagements but was often concerned in skirmishes with them & spent the whole of this term in that manner."

"In the same year I served another tour of <u>one</u> month under the same officers & in the like manner. In the latter part of 1782 under Capt Connel, I served one month at Jeffries Creek Bridge, Colonel Baxter being the highest officer; we were stationed at this place & only left there in scouting parties. Thus making an actual service of fourteen months as a private in the War of the Revolution. I also served at various times on scouting parties where the __?__ of the Tories upon the property & lives of the citizens rendered his interference necessary. On all these occasions during the whole of the war I was ready & willing to offer my services & at one time in this service was wounded in the left side by a ball which went through that part of my body & from which I feel considerable pain *(like the cramps) to this day. In the year 1831 I became blind which together with the palsy has rendered me utterly helpless."*

Sources: 1. Census 1800. 2. Pension Papers S7621.

****

Samuel Stickney age 13

Samuel Stickney was born on 15 May, 1762 in Rowley, Massachusetts, and he died on 9 January, 1835 in Brownville, Maine. He married Irene Rawlings who died in 1787 and he married Polly Atwood on 29 April, 1792 in Bradford, Massachusetts. The Rev. Ebenezer Dutch performed the ceremony for the last marriage. He received a yearly pension of $65. On Samuel's tombstone it said he also served as a sergeant.

"I enlisted in the company and regiment as a fifer in February 1776 for two months which period I fully served out at Cambridge Mass. In December 1776 I enlisted as a Fifer for three months in Capt Howel's company of Newburyport, I served out the full period of my enlistment at Providence, R.I. where I was discharged in February 1777."

"The first of July 1778 I enlisted as a fifer for six months in Capt Simeon Brown's company in Col Wade's regt of the Massachusetts troops. I was discharged the first of January 1779. In June 1780 I enlisted as a "six month man" for the town of Bradford Massachusetts I joined the army at Fishkill & adjutant Bowles put me in as Fife Major of Col Turner's Massachusetts regiment. I served as Fife Major of said Regiment for six weeks. In April 1783 I enlisted as a fifer for two months in Capt Robinson's company in Col Titcomb's regiment of the same troops."

During his last enlistment he was described as eighteen years old and 5'9" with a ruddy complexion. He had a total of 13 children from both marriages. He was known as a man of strong physique, although not of great stature. There were numerous stories told of his great endurance and strength.

He was the first mail-carrier between Brownville and Bangor, and some of the tales of the great loads carried by him are remarkable. On one of his trips he carried on his back from Sebec to Brownville (a distance of 7 miles) an old fashioned hand-loom. On one occasion as he started to step over a fallen tree, an old bear rose up on the other side and was about to attack him. Samuel had nothing to defend himself, but on his shoulder he was carrying a bag of potatoes. He threw the bag of potatoes striking the bear in the head causing the animal to retreat. Samuel gathered up the potatoes and continued his journey.

Sources: 1. U.S. Pension roll of 1835. 2. Maine Society Sons of the American Revolution. 3. Pension Papers W25159. 4. Tombstone 5. Historical Collections of Piscataquis County, Maine pages 192-194.

****

Asa Stiles age 14

Asa Stiles was born on 21 March, 1766 in Hebron, Connecticut, and he died on 14 August, 1836 in West Chazy, New York. He married Olive Rood on 15 September, 1785 in Connecticut. He received a yearly pension of $50. Olive's widow's pension was rejected, because there was a problem proving the date of their marriage.

Asa's date of birth was in question. Some researchers show it at 1768. Asa once stated that he entered the Revolutionary War at the age of 12. Different times during his life Asa gave different dates of his birth. This author has listed his date of birth as 1766 based on Connecticut birth records.

Asa also enlisted with his son in the War of 1812. He enlisted on 18 February, 1813 in the 11th Regiment of the Infantry. In August of 1813 he transferred to the 29th Regiment. On 20 May, 1813 he was unloading a wagon near Burlington, Vermont, and a barrel of provisions fell and struck him dislocating his right knee. Due to the injury he was discharged on 20 October, 1813. He received a monthly pension of $4.

"I enlisted as a volunteer at Lebanon Connecticut in the month of June 1780 (the summer before Cornwallis was taken) into Capt Days Company don't recollect Lieut name Ensign William Bull, Col Hezekiah Wylly's Regiment Continental Militia for three months, marched to Middletown, then called Chatham Conn. Staid there about a month then marched to New London County remained there about two weeks and then marched to ___?___ where I remained until the time for which I enlisted."

"In the fore part of June 1782 (next year after Cornwallis was taken) I again enlisted at Hebron Connecticut as a volunteer into Capt John Gilberts Company Col Samuel Gilberts Regiment Continental State Troops. I served in that Company and Regiment for one year when at the close of the war in June 1783 I was discharged."

Sources: 1. Registry of District of Columbia Society of the Sons of the American Revolution. 2. Sons of the American Revolution Application. 3. U.S. Pension Roll of 1835. 4. Pension Papers R10182.

****

John Stoddard age 14

John Stoddard was born on 18 July, 1767 in Woodbury, Connecticut, and he died on 15 September, 1849 in Peru, New York. He married Phebe Northrup on 11 September, 1786 in Connecticut. He enlisted on 1 April, 1781 in Captain Nathaniel Edward's Company in General David Waterbury's Brigade of the Connecticut Militia.

Sources: 1. Year Book of the Sons of the American Revolution in the State of New York, 1899. 2. Connecticut Men in the Revolutionary War. 3. Connecticut Town Marriage Records pre 1870.

****

Isaac Stone age 14

Isaac Stone was born on 30 June, 1764 in Norton, Massachusetts, and he died on 27 April, 1844 in Muskingum County, Ohio. He married Chloe Morey on 1 December, 1792 in Norton. He received a yearly pension of $50.

"In the latter part of November or December 1778 there was an alarm and I marched from Norton Massachusetts where I resided to Warnick State of Rhode Island, I went as a substitute for one Nathan Perry for three months when I was discharged."

"In the month of June 1779 I enlisted as a volunteer at Norton, aforesaid for the share of six months, under the command of Captain Franklin, Lieutenant Bates. The said company was raised for the purpose of defending Providence a city in Rhode Island. I marched and served at providence for the whole enlistment which was six months. The company marched during said six months once to Rhode Island to guard som hay, we were gone about six weeks."

"In the month of June 1780 I enlisted in the continental army under the command of Capt Abner Howard Lieutenant Michell for six months at Newton. We marched to Springfield and were then mustered from there we marched to West Point where we joined the Regiment, the Colonels name was Bailey, the Brigade was commanded by Gen Learned

who soon left the Brigade and after that it was commanded by Colonel Bailey."

"We marched down the North River and crossed over into the state of New Jersey. While we were in New Jersey we did not stay more than two or three weeks in a place. We were at Orangetown English neighborhood. In November we marched back to West Point, we were stationed in Fort Arnold, afterwards called Fort Clinton. I remained for a few weeks in January 1781 I was discharged."

"I enlisted for six months Baron Steuben commanded the left wing of the army, the Baron used frequently to give the word of command to regiment. General Washington was there I saw him and quite frequently Gen Learned Brigade was on the left Gen Paterson next, __?__ next & then Lafayette. I was in no engagement."

Isaac Stone served in the 2nd Massachusetts Regiment or Bailey's Regiment. The regiment stayed in New York during most of the tour by Isaac. By the time the regiment began to move south toward Yorktown, Isaac had been discharged.

Sources: 1. Massachusetts Town & Vital Records 1620-1988. 2. U.S. Pensioners 1818-1872. 3. Lineage Book D.A.R. Vol. 38, 1902. 4. Pension Papers W6182.

****

William Stone age 13

William Stone was born in Pennsylvania in 1763, and he died there on 4 December, 1831. He married Dorathea on 13 November, 1786 in Germantown, Pennsylvania. He was at the Battle of Trenton in December of 1776.

"I was enlisted by Capt. Mullen of the United States Marine corps to serve on board the Delaware Sloop of war under the command of Capt. Alexander, I was in the Battle of Trenton under the command of Gen. Washington in Capt. Mullens company after the Hessians was taken."

"At the time the British attempted to retake Trenton and was in the battles the next day at Princeton from thence I marched to the city of Philadelphia and served the remainder of my term of service on board the Delaware sloop of war."

The Continental Marine's Commandant was Captain Samuel Nicholas. He commanded a battalion made up of three companies.

William and about eighty other men belonged to the second company commanded by Captain Robert Mullan. At the Battle of Trenton the Marines were added to a brigade of Philadelphia militia also dressed in green. At Trenton the Brigade was unable to land only a few men due to the ice in the river. This prevented the Marines to participate in the Battle of Trenton.

A few days after the capture of Trenton the Marines helped to defend the Assunpink Bridge, which ran through Trenton from the attacking British army. At the Battle of Princeton on 3 January, 1777 they reinforced the retreating army and charged into the British line. This forced the British to retreat and gave the Americans another victory. After the battle, William's company took twenty-five British prisoners to Philadelphia and then returned to the sloop *Delaware*.

Sources: 1. Pension Papers W3122. 2. Semper Fidelis: The History of the United States Marine Corps by Allan Reed Millett.

****

Naphtali Streeter age 14

Naphtali Streeter was born in 1763 in Gloucester, Rhode Island, and he died on 15 September, 1839 in Gustavus, Ohio. He married his second wife Elizabeth Reynolds on 17 February, 1798 in New Jersey. They were married by the Baptist preacher Peter Wilson. In 1859 Elizabeth applied for Naphtali's pension after his death. She said that he had left her 10 to 15 years before he died for "parts unknown," and that she had recently learned of his death in Ohio. Naphtali's son John wrote that his father and his step-mother were not happy together, and his father left her and the children to go to Ohio. The couple never divorced. She received a yearly widow's pension of $80.

"I entered the service of the United States in the spring of 1777 as a volunteer and served three months. The Regiment was commanded by Colonel Reed. I was engaged in the battle fought at New Port, Rhode Island. I marched from Gloucester to Providence from thence to New Port."

"I again entered the service in the spring of 1778 as a volunteer and served for the period of six months. The Regiment was commanded by the same Colonel Reed."

"In the spring of 1779 I removed from Gloucester in Rhode Island to Land off in the state of New Hampshire. I there joined the Company of Rangers commanded by Captain Luther Richardson. The Regiment was commanded by Major Whitcomb. I was frequently engaged with Indians."

Sources: 1. Yearbook of Sons of the American Revolution in the State of New York, 1909. 2. Pension Roll of 1835. 3. Pension Papers W3617.

****

William Sturman age 13

William Sturman was born in 1763 and died after 1823. He married a woman named Delpha in Virginia.

"I enlisted for the term of two years on the 15th day of January in the year 1776 in Bedford County in the state of Virginia in the company commanded by Capt. Henry Terril of the Regiment commanded by Col. Josiah Parker and Lieutenant Col William Davis in the Line of the State of Virginia on the Continental establishment that he continued to serve in the said Court and in the Service of the United States until the two years the term of my enlistment expired when I was discharged from Service at the Valley Forge Camp in Pennsylvania on the ___ day of February 1778 that I was in the battle of Brandywine and Germantown and marched as far north as Morristown in New Jersey."

The enlistment of many soldiers expired at the end of 1777, while the army was in winter camp at Valley Forge. William received $27.35 per year for his service.

Sources: 1. Pension Papers S39093. 2. Twenty-four Hundred Tennessee Pensioners.

****

John Suddarth age 13

John Suddarth was born in Amherst County, Virginia on 16 February, 1765, and he died after 1839 in Kentucky. He married Mary Wells.

"I volunteered in the army of the United States about the last of June 1778 as a substitute for my brother James Suddarth under the command and in the company of Capt. John Burley or Burliegh and in the Regiment of Col Bland of the Virginia Troop but I can not state whether of the state or Continental line. Under the command of these officers I was engaged as a Private in guarding Prisoners in the County of Albemarle

Va which Prisoners had been taken by Gen Gates in the defeat of Gen Burgoyne. I continued in this service until the last of September (a period of three months). I was relieved by the return of my brother for whom I had substituted."

"I again joined the army of the Revolution from said County of Albemarle & state of Va about the middle of July 1781 in the company of Benjamin Harris and joined a portion of the main Army at Williamsburg while to the best of my recollections was under the command of Major Merryweather. I will not say that Merryweather was the highest officer in command there but from my _____recollection it now seems to me to have been so. From Williamsburg we marched to Travis Point at the mouth of Queens Creek into Yorktown where we remained a few days guarding a member of _____?____ to belonging to the American Army. From there we were marched down to the main encampment before Yorktown."

"We were post on duty during the time at 8 o clock in the morning & not relieved until the succeeding morning at 8 o clock only taking our time to eat our meals. We then rested the succeeding 24 hours & so until the works were finished. I was present the taking of two British outpost the one stormed by the French the other by the Americans. I was not a participant in the storms. I was drawn out with a larger Body of other troops to render such <u>aid</u> as might become necessary. Each man of the troops with him had a _____?____ and so soon the redoubts had surrendered they were thrown down on the work of ____?____ was commenced."

The outpost that John refers to is a redoubt. A redoubt or fort system usually consisted of an enclosed defensive emplacement outside a larger fort. On October 14 the American trenches were within 150 yards of British redoubts 9 and 10. Four hundred French troops took redoubt 9. With their bayonets fixed the Americans charged toward redoubt 10. After heavy fighting the Americans overwhelmed the British. During this battle John states that he was being held in reserve to render aid if necessary. With the capture of these two redoubts the Americans placed their artillery in them, and they could now shell the town from three directions. The next day Cornwallis turned his cannons on an American position and attacked it with 350 British troops. French soldiers aided the Americans and drove the British back. It is after this that John was an eyewitness to the courage of General Washington.

"During the process of there works I witnessed a deed of personal daring & coolness in General Washington to which I never saw equaled.

During a tremendous cannonade from the British in order to demolish our Breastworks a few days prior to the surrender, Gen Washington visited that part of our fortifications behind which I was posted and whilst here discovered that the enemy were destroying their property & drowning their horses (they were killing their horses to preserve their food). *Not however entirely assured of what they were doing, he took glass & mounted the highest prominent & most exposed point of our fortifications, and there stood exposed to the enemy's fire where shot seemed flying almost as thick as hail & were instantly demolishing portions of the embankment around him for ten or fifteen minutes, until he had completely satisfied himself of the purposes of the enemy. During this time his aids were demonstrating with him with all their earnestness against this exposure of his person and once or twice drew him down. He severely reprimanded then & resumed his position. I continued at Yorktown till the surrender of Cornwallis. I then marched as a guard with the prisoners as far as Nolan's ferry on the Potomac where we delivered them to MaryLand troops. Thence I returned and was discharged about Christmas of that year. Making the period of my service five months & a half this making the entire period of my service eight months & a half."*

John Suddarth applied for his deserved pension. On 25 November, 1839 a letter was written to him rejecting his pension claim. It stated that the Virginia militia called at Yorktown was called to serve only three months and not six months. Because of this his total service was 5 ½ months, and 6 months was need to receive a pension.

Sources: 1. Pension Papers R10293. 2. Sons of the American Revolution Application. 3. The Revolution Remembered edited by John C. Dann. 4. General George Washington: A Military Life by Edward G. Lengel.

****

John Summers age 13

John Summers was born on 26 May, 1762 in Fairfax County, Virginia, and he died on 23 September, 1833 in Cobb, Georgia. On 2 July at Caswell, North Carolina he married Mary Gimboe. For his service John received $80.00 per year.

He did not know when he enlisted, but he remembered that he enlisted after he heard that the British had ascended the Potomac and burnt some houses. This was probably Royal Governor Lord Dunmore doing this in July of 1775. This caused the militia to be called out. *"......I was* with them & went down to prevent further depredation, & I was out on this occasion about two or three weeks."

After this John moved to Caswell County, North Carolina for the remainder of the war. He served a nine month tour under Captain David McFarland. The unit marched to Wilmington in pursuit of the British and Tories. He was in no engagements, but his unit did capture a few prisoners.

"After staying at home a short time, the troubles increasing, the Captain, by the name of Meshack Turner, of the Militia Company to which I belonged beat up for volunteers to be organized & remain in service for twelve months & promised that we should be paid the same as regulars. We marched to Savannah river just opposite to Augusta in Georgia, & thence turned down the river & joined Gen Lincoln's army at a place called Dorchester the army maneuvered about until the battle of Stono in which I was engaged."

Soon after the battle John returned home and his father was later drafted for nine months. John took his father's place and served under General Caswell. He then marched with the army to Camden and fought the Battle of Camden, where the American General Gates was defeated.

"...I was in that engagement & was wounded in the left hand, having my fore finger where it joined the hand shattered & nearly shot off. After this battle I returned home, having served about six months of the nine month tour & remained till my wound got well & then tories having risen & done considerable mischief, killing Col Maybirn the neighborhood rose in arms & I volunteered to go against them under our Capt Runnells & served three months. This service was principally in pursuing & fighting the tories. We had an engagement with the tories commanded by a Col Piles & totally defeated them killing a good many. The battle was fought at a pair of race paths, but I do not well remember the Country & it was for notoriety called Piles defeat. Gen Pickens was head commander & my Col was one William Moore. We had another engagement at Whites or Whiteses Mill on the reedy fork of the Haws river with the British & Tories united, but their force was so superior to the American troops, the latter being not more than three hundred they were obliged to retire. That completed my service which uniting all the tours makes about thirty three months & a half."

Sources: 1. Census 1820 & 1830. 2. North Carolina Marriage Index 1741-2004. 3. Revolutionary War Pensioner Census 1841. 4. Pension Papers S31999.

****

George Sutherland age 13

George Sutherland was born at Prince Edward County, Virginia in 1762, and he died in January 1847 in Fluvanna, Virginia. He married (1) Jane (Johnson) Shores on 15 September, 1791, and he married (2) Mary Herndon on 18 October, 1822 by the Rev. Isaac Tuckadoo. He settled first in Virginia and shortly before the revolution he moved to North Carolina. He was a very successful farmer, because it was reported in the 1830 census that he had seventeen slaves.

George enlisted in the 1st North Carolina Regiment under the command of Colonel Thomas Clark in the fall of 1775. He agreed to enlist as a drummer for three years.

"Early in the following spring I was marched to the North thro' Virg'a to George Town in Maryland where the said troops were inoculated and from thence was march to Philadelphia and from thence to Trenton in Jersey and the troops to which I was attached were marched to & stationed at a place then called the half Moon, and were there at the time of the engagement at Trenton the 25th Dec'r. Thence said Regiment was marched back to George Town where we had been inoculated and in the summer or fall of that year said troops were marched to the northward again, and stationed on the Schulkill River near Philadelphia."

In the spring of 1777 George was placed in a hospital at Trenton, and after he recovered he rejoined his regiment and was discharged in August of 1777. George was promoted to Sergeant in October of 1777. He had served for more than two years. In the fall his regiment would be part of the Battles at Brandywine and Germantown. They would later be at Valley Forge during the winter of 1777-1778.

In the fall of 1780 he again enlisted on 5 October, 1780 and served in the Virginia Militia Brigade commanded by General George Weedon. General Weedon was a seasoned military officer, but he had resigned his commission in 1778 after a dispute with the Congress over Seniority. While back home in Virginia, Weedon agreed to lead a brigade of Virginia Militia at the request of Governor Thomas Jefferson.

George Sutherland served in the Virginia Militia in a company commanded by Captain Samuel Eddins of the 1st Regiment of Continental Artillery. Just before the siege of Yorktown in the fall of 1781 he was discharged. He was suffering pain and swelling of one of his knees. He applied for a pension stating that he had been, *"laboring under the deep affliction of blindness for several years past."* Because of this he was unable to undertake a trip to find any of his old comrades to prove his service.

His first application for a pension was rejected in a letter on 8 July, 1837 from J. L. Edwards for two reasons. (1) He was so young when he claimed to have entered the service. (2) There was no record that he served in the Artillery, as he stated. In a review of his petition it was found that he was in the Infantry rather the Artillery as he had previously stated. On 15 February, 1843 George was granted a pension of $100.00 per year for his 12 months service as a private and 12 months service as a Sergeant.

Sources: 1. The Sutherland's in America, A Journal of American Ancestry, Vol E, No. 2, New York Feb. 1913. 2. Census of 1810, 1820, and 1830. 3. Virginia Marriages 1660-1800. 4. Sons of the American Revolution Application. 5. DAR patriot Index P66OX. 6. U.S. Pensioners 1818-1872. 7. Pension Papers S7667. 8. Roster of Soldiers from North Carolina in the American Revolution by North Carolina DAR.

****

William Tapscott age 14

William Tapscott was born on 24 January, 1764 in Cumberland County, Virginia, and he died in 1834 in Green Kentucky. He received a yearly pension of $23.33 according to the 1800 census he owned 11 slaves but by the 1830 census he had no slaves.

"I entered the service of the United States in the Army of the Revolution and served as hereinafter stated under the following named officers to wit I entered to serve three months in the militia in a company commanded by Captain Benjamin Jordan, as a substitute for my father Henry Tapscott, who had been drafted to serve in said company for said tour of three months, to guard the prisoners, then stationed at the Albemarle Barracks; at the time I entered the service this tour I lived in the County of Buckingham State of Virginia, the year I served this tour I do not recollect very certainly that think it was in the year 1778 and in the fall season of the year, this tour I served out until I was discharged by my Captain and went home. My service was exclusively at the Albemarle Barracks in guarding the British prisoners, stationed there at the time."

"My second tour I served when I resided in Cumberland County State of Virginia and was drafted to serve in the militia for three months, this was in the year 1781 as best I well remember it was the year Cornwallis surrendered, I served this tour in a company commanded by Captain Creed Haskins, my Lieutenant was of the name of Blanks or

Blankenship I am not positive which, this company was in a Regiment commanded by Colonel Mathis I joined the troops of the United States on this tour a short distance above Richmond Virginia when the enemy were pursuing and the United States troops were on the march up the country on James river, and after I joined them they continued the march, until they reached what was called the Point of Fork on James River, here we made a very short halt, the British then returned down the country, and we continued the march down the River in the rear in pursuit, and ultimately marched to a place called the Maubin Hills at that place there were a good many men under command of different officers amongst the number I remember General Stephens very well, at the Maubin Hills, I remained until his time expired, I was discharged by his officers and returned home."

"I remained only five days when I again on the 3rd tour ended to serve three months more from the same County in a company commanded by a Captain whose name I have forgotten & who was unwell as it was then said & did not march with the company, but the company went on to the Maubin Hills under the command of the Lieutenant who was by the name of William Daniels, who continued to command the company until I was detached to serve in the Infantry, when I was put in the company then commanded by a Lieutenant of the name of Joseph Coleman, whether the Captain had resigned or not I do not remember, I never knew him in the service--Lieutenant Daniels Company was attached to the Regiment commanded by Colonel Mathis, the Company of Coleman was attached to the same Regiment, from the Maubin Hills the troops marched on in a direction to Richmond and from thence marched to a small town called New Castle, from thence down James River, and ultimately to what was called the Burnt chimneys, while here one morning information was received that the enemy were preparing to give us battle when the Army was formed, and in a short time thereafter Colonel Mathis the commander of our regiment came riding by us in a great hurry & told us to take care of ourselves the best way we could, & he continued his flight in a hurry-- some of the men fled & some remained, and a detachment of the enemy's horse came up & took some men of our Regiment prisoners--I was in no engagement with the enemy on those tours, but had some scouts, on several occasions--I continued to serve this tour, which I was drafted to serve for three months, until his time expired & requested leave to go home, but was required to stay a month longer, which I did and was discharged at the end of that time at old Williamsburg in Virginia having served in this tour four months."

"I was discharged from his last tour 3 days before the surrender of Cornwallis to General Washington at Little York. I was acquainted with General Washington when in the service, at least I saw him with his life guard where he was on his way to little York this was at I recollect to have seen Genl Lafayette, Genl Stephens & Genl Wayne, with many others of the Continental officers."

Sources: 1. Census 1810 & 1830. 2. U.S. Pensioners 1818-1872. 3. Pension Papers S38416.

****

David Taylor age 13

David Taylor was born on 25 December, 1763 in Orange, New Jersey, and he died on 17 April, 1840 in Bloomfield, New Jersey. He married Cornelia Van Brockle on 4 August, 1794 in New Jersey. David enlisted in the spring of 1776 at the age of 13. He received a yearly pension of $80.

"The first service which I performed in the Revolutionary War was when in the fourteenth year of my age (being in the year 1776) I volunteered my service in a company of militia commanded by Capt. John Peck. I think Major Clark commanded the Battalion and Col. Vancortland commanded the regiment, at this time I think I was out five or six days in the month of March or April. I remember that I went with the company from Newark to Aequackananck in the county of Essex aforesaid for the purpose of taking a quantity of Iron from a gang of refugees who were furnishing the enemy with Iron and other articles. I distinctly remember we getting the Iron and conveying it to Newark."

"In the same year (1776) in June I went out as a substitute in the militia for Benjamin Stockman for a period of one month in the same company under Captain Peck, at this time we were stationed at Bergain in the county of Bergen and state of New Jersey where I remained one month. I remember while I was on this tour of duty the British landed on Long Island. From this time until the fall of the year 1779 I performed several tours of duty in the militia in cases of alarm which were very frequent."

"I think to the best of my recollection I was out five months, but cannot be particular as to the time but remember that during this time I was under Capt Peck part of the time Capt. Thomas Williams and Capt. Samuel Parsons, at this time I was within the age of sixteen years and therefore was not obliged to bear arms. [I suspect he meant to say he was obligated to bear arms. At the age of sixteen they could be drafted.] *In*

November or December in the year 1779 I went out as a substitute in the militia for Samuel Sigler in a company commanded by Capt Abraham Speers for one month at this time we were stationed at Second River in the county of Essex aforesaid where I remained one month."

"In January in the year 1780 I enlisted in the service of the State of New Jersey for a period of three months in a company commanded by Capt Wheeler James Medden was Major of the battalion and Col Vancorthance commanded the Regiment, at this time we were stationed at Elizabeth Town in the County of Essex aforesaid during this tour of duty we were employed a part of the time in digging entrenchments & after the term of three months had expired I enlisted immediately again under the same officers for another period of three months and remained in the service of the State aforesaid at the second term of three months during which time there were two engagements with the Americans and British. The first of which I was in at this time of the other I was sick and unable to turn out. When the second tour of three months expired we were marched to Newark and there discharged."

"In the month of August or September in the year 1780 I enlisted in the service of the State of New Jersey aforesaid for a period of six months in a company commanded by Capt John Craig Major Clark commanded the battalion and Col Crane commanded the regiment. In a short time after I enlisted the company to which I belonged was marched to Rhaway where we joined the regiment from thence we marched to Princetown and Trenton and from place to place from Trenton to Elizabeth Town in the State of New Jersey guarding this line and eventually after serving out the term of six months was discharged. We were employed in guarding the lines from Acquackanach to Elizabeth Town in the county of Essex."

"I remember that on one of these tours of monthly service under Capt Williams I was in the battle of Springfield in the county of Essex aforesaid and after the battle when the enemy were dispersing, me and three or four of my companions perused the enemy and on the road near Newark we came in contact with several of the enemys horsemen and several shots were exchanged at which I was wounded by a pistol ball passing the front of my right thigh which caused me to lay by about ten weeks during which time doctor Caleb Lindsley attended me. About seven months before the close of the war I enlisted in the service of the State of New Jersey for a period of nine months in a company commanded by Isaac Morrison. Major Peatt commanded the battalion and Colonel Matthias

Odgen commanded the Regiment. I continued in active service until the close of the war being about seven months during which time we were employed in guarding the lines from Elizabeth Town to Trenton."

At the Battle of Springfield fought on 23 June, 1780 David Taylor was a member of the militia company under the command of Captain Thomas Williams, which was part of the 2nd New Jersey Regiment under the command of Colonel Philip Van Cortlandt. Their job was to hold the second bridge in Springfield in case the American troops needed to retreat. After the American victory at Springfield, General Washington praised the role of the New Jersey Militia.

"At the close of the war I was discharged at Newark in the county of Essex aforesaid. I remember of being at the battle of Monmouth and in several other skirmishes but cannot be particular in dates."

The Battle of Monmouth was fought on 28 June, 1778. The temperature was consistently above 100 degrees during the battle. Years after the battle David Taylor would tell his children, *"It was a terrible hot day."* After the battle 37 American soldiers were found to have died of heat-stroke.

Sources: 1. Lineage Book National Society D.A.R. Vol. 27, 1898. 2. Tombstone 3. Sons of the American Revolution Application. 4. New Jersey Pensioners. 5. Pension Papers S762.

****

James Tenney age 14

James Tenney was born on 21 December, 1766 in Deerfield, Massachusetts, and he died on 30 December, 1841 in Lewis County, Virginia. He married Thankful Shippee on 14 April, 1785 in Massachusetts. He received a yearly Pension of $80.

"I was born on the 21st December 1766, and not having any documents to assist my memory which has become somewhat frail I am unable to specify dates with perfect accuracy--I enlisted in the Town of Shelburn where I then resided, in the State of Massachusetts under Lieut Shepherd in the year 1780, in the month of December, I think, and marched to Springfield in the same State where my company was enrolled and drilled by Lieut Shepherd until the Soldiers there were ordered to West Point. At West-Point I was placed in the 1st Regiment of Massachusetts, Commanded by Col Joseph Vose or Voss. The Field Officers were, Col. Jos. Vose and his brother Elijah Vose Leiut Col., and Maj'r. Pettingill and

adjutant Bowles, and I was placed under the immediate command of Capt Green. During the time I was in the service I was detached from Headquarters which was at West-Point on several occasions, but cannot specify the dates. I marched to Verplank's Point and thence to Croton and back to West-Point. At another time I was placed on board of a Gun-boat in the Hudson river below West Point and opposite Fort Montgomery, at the point of Antony's Nose, where the old chain had been stretched across, and thence I was ordered back to West-Point"

This chain is called the Great Chain, and was across the Hudson River in 1778. The links were 12 inches wide and 18 inches long, and the chain weighed over a hundred tons.

"At another time I was sent down the Hudson to the Spy-boats under Lieut Shaler (he cannot remember the Captain's name) to Sing Sing opposite Terry Town and after remaining there some time was ordered (amongst those who never had had the Small-pox) to the York huts to be inoculated, and passed through West Point again on their way to the Yorkhuts where I was inoculated and remained the Winter, and thence was marched back to the Flats above, and near to, West-Point where I was stationed for some time."

Smallpox was a serious problem in the American army. General Washington felt all troops should be inoculated, and all troops who came from the south were ordered by Congress to be inoculated. The inoculated soldiers were placed in huts that were ordered to be kept clean with lots of straw for the mattresses.

"I am not certain that these services were performed in the order they are stated; but the last winter of my service I was stationed at Snake Hill (West of New Windsor and about 5 miles, he thinks, from West Point) I had enlisted for three years, and as my term had not expired when Peace was proclaimed, I was detained until the __ day of __ 1783, and before I was discharged the brigade to which I was attached were ordered to March to Philadelphia, under Col. Vose aforesaid, and Captain Kilham was the Capt. of my company. My brigade was marched to Philadelphia for the purpose of quelling a mutiny or insurrection, which had broken open the Treasury."

There was growing frustration and anger in the army at the end of the war, because Congress was behind in paying the men. The army was disbanded, and the soldiers were each given three months pay and issued notes to pay what was owed each man. Because Congress was short of money, they also could not honor their promise to repay the men for the food and clothing the men provided for themselves during their service. An assembly of officers met and there was fear of a revolt. Washington spoke to the men and was able to quell the anger.

"From Philadelphia the 1st Reg't. of Massachusetts regulars, to which I was attached was marched back to West Point and there (at West-Point) I received my discharge from General Knox which is dated on the __ day of __ I was a substitute, I believe, for my Father; but I am not certain whether his class was drafted or volunteered or either. My Father Josiah took from my my bounty money, but allowed me to keep my wages or pay. I was not (by a few days) 15 years old at the time I enlisted, and I served nearly three years."

Sources: 1. Massachusetts Marriages 1633-1850. 2. U.S. Pensioners 1818-1872. 3. Tombstone 4. West Virginians in the American Revolution. 5. Pension Papers W3888. 6. Medicine and the American Revolution: How Diseases and Their Treatments Affected the Colonial Army by Oscar Reiss, M.D.

****

Joseph Terry age 14

Joseph Terry was born on 27 July, 1761 in Chesterfield County, Virginia, and he died on 23 May, 1838 in Virginia. He received a yearly pension of $80.

"I enlisted in the army of the United States in the year 1775 the October after I was fourteen years of age with Capt. John Mosby who was attached to the 2nd. Regiment Commanded by Col. Alberd. I was a resident at the time of enlistment of the County of Buckingham and State of Virginia, and in December following I with other recruits marched to Cumberland old Courthouse. Jacob Winfree was 1st. Lieutenant, John Clark 2nd. and Robert Mosby ensign to the said Company. About three weeks after that the Company marched from Cumberland Old Courthouse through the State of North Carolina & South Carolina to the Town of Savannah within the State of Georgia, and was there attached to the 2nd. Regiment above stated under the Command of Col. Elberd and to the Brigade of General Howe where we remained in and about 12 months when this 2nd Regiment was ordered by the commanding general to march to Florida in order to dislodge the British from St. Augustine which they then held possession of. We pursued their march till we arrived within sight of St. Johns river, where we were met by an express informing them that the provision ships which had been sent on to meet the Regiment were

all captured by the enemy. We then retreated back to Savannah and suffered very seriously for provisions having to pass through wilderness Country where rations could not be procured. We however got back. Some two or three months after our return there was a call for Volunteers from the Regulars to go upon sea after the British ships, that me with about 30 more turned out and went on board of a Galley called the Washington commanded by Capt. John Wingate, after cruising some time we captured three British vessels. One ship, one sloop and one snow, and returned into port with the prises. Some time after that the exact day I do not now recollect but think it was about two years & better after my enlistment in the month of December a battle took place between Gen'l Howe's Brigade and the enemy, in which the Americans were defeated and me among the rest was taken prisoner, and put on board the prison ships where I remained until the last day of August following when I was induced to enlist in the British service in order to save my life being almost worn out by the privation incident to my situation. After enlisting I was sent on shore, where I availed himself of the first opportunity that offered and deserted their service, and resided in the State of Georgia and performed Militia duty till the end of the war. My being taken prisoner is the cause that I have no discharge or other documentary evidence of my services as before the war ended nearly all the officers with whom I served were dead or so dispersed that I have yet to see either of them."

Sources: 1. U.S. Pension Roll of 1835. 2. Pension Papers S7701.

****

Eliphaz Thayer age 14

Eliphaz Thayer was born on 14 March, 1762 in Braintree, Massachusetts, and he died on 31 December, 1848 in Quincy, Massachusetts. He married his cousin Deliverance Thayer on 14 March, 1782 in Braintree. He received a yearly pension of $61.44.

Eliphaz enlisted as a substitute for Jacob Turner on 1 December, 1776 and served until 1 March, 1777. He served the entire tour under Captain Stephen Penniman at Dorchester Heights. *"I did duty in the company the whole term except when I was attached as a waiter to the Deputy Commissary Thomas Durant at Boston also when I was detached with several others from said company to do duty on the Castle in Boston Harbor."*

The Deputy Commissary was an appointed position, whose function was to acquire provision for the army. Eliphaz served on Castle Island, which was a fortification in Boston Harbor.

Eliphaz served four more tours of duty from April 1777 until October 1780. Most of the time was spent on guard duty, and he also was a guard on the prison ship *The Rising Empire*. He was also serving at West Point during Arnold's treason.

Sources: 1. Massachusetts Society of the Sons of the American Revolution 1893. 2. Pension Papers S6235. 3. Tombstone 4. Massachusetts Town and Vital Records 1620-1988.

****

Joseph Thomas age 14

Joseph Thomas was born on 11 January, 1763 in Fauquier, Virginia, and he died on 13 July, 1844 in Russellville, Alabama. He married (1) Mary Morgan who died in 1826 and (2) Mary Lindsey in 1826. She received a widow's yearly pension of $80.00.

"I enlisted in the Army of the United States in the year 1777 on the 11th or 12th day of February with Simon Morgan in Farqui County State of Virginia & served in the 13th Regiment of the Virginia line under the following named officers to wit Simon Morgan Lieut Robert Bell Capt Crawford Col, that at Pittsburgh or Fort Pitt Col Gibson took the command of the Regiment who continued in command until the spring or __?__ after the battle of Germantown when Col McIntosh took the command of the Regiment & continued it until the expedition against the Misisha & Mingo Towns when Col Broadhead commanded, George Washington was commander in chief at Brandywine & Germantown & at Camps at Valley Forge."

"I enlisted for three years & served out my time & was discharged the last of February or first of March 1780 at Pittsburgh or Fort Pitt Pennsylvania, I lived in Fauquier County State of Virginia when I entered the service & returned there after my discharge, I received a discharge but has lost it I was on the baggage Guard during the Battle of Brandywine & was in the Battle of Germantown."

Joseph served in the 13th Virginia Regiment and 1st Company under Captain Robert Beall. At the battle of Brandywine Joseph was assigned to baggage guard. This was important, because this baggage included all the supplies, food, and extra ammunition needed to sustain the army.

At the Battle of Germantown, Joseph was part of the 1st Virginia Brigade under Brigadier General Peter Muhlenberg and in the division commanded by Major General Greene. Joseph was part of the troops that fought against British pickets at Luken's Mill in savage fighting. Smoke and heavy fog then threw the Americans into confusion and finally into a retreat.

"I marched from Virginia to Pittsburgh, State of Pennsylvania, from there to Philadelphia where I joined the Grand Army under Washington from there to Trenton in the State of New Jersey, thence to Brandywine where the battle was fought, thence to the Battle of Germantown thence to Valley Forge where we took up winter quarters, thence to Pittsburgh, thence down the Ohio River about thirty miles where we built a Fort called it Fort McIntosh in honor of our Colonel, thence we marched back & up the Allegheny River about twenty-five miles and built Fort Crawford; thence to the mouth of New River where we __?__ Garrison during the winter & returned to Pittsburgh in the spring, thence to the Minisha & Mingo __?__ __?__ we destroyed, thence back to Pittsburgh where I was discharged a short time after the expiration of three years, from the commencement of my term of service."

"I was drafted and turned out volunteer to avoid being drafted about the month of October 1780 in Fauquier Virginia for six months & served under Captain Winn Major Triplett, & joined Colonel afterwards General Morgan in South Carolina and was at the taking of the Tories at Rugeley's Mill that he served out my term."

Sources: 1. North Carolina Index to Marriage Bonds 1741-1868. 2. Tennessee State Marriages 1780-2002. 3. U.S. Pension Roll of 1835. 4. Pension Papers W9518.

****

William Thomas age 14

William Thomas was born on 20 January, 1763 in Culpeper County, Virginia, and he died on 27 November, 1835 in Franklin, Georgia. He married Agnes (Nancy) Carruthers on 19 January, 1792 in Georgia. He received a yearly pension of $33.33.

"I entered the service of the United States in the militia in the state of North Carolina in the month of April 1777 in Guilford County as a

volunteer under Capt. John Leek, Col James Martin commanded. The regiment was marched to Guilford Courthouse thence to Cross creek and defeated the Scotch at that place."

The battle that William describes is the Battle of Moore's Creek. At this battle Colonel Martin commanded the 1st Regiment of the North Carolina Militia and defeated sword-wielding Loyalist Scotsmen. This battle, however, occurred on 27 February, 1776 which was a full year before the battle William describes. There was no other battle that fits William's description occurring in the area in 1777. If William was at the battle, then he enlisted at the age of 13.

In August of 1778 William volunteered for the same regiment and marched on the Cherokee Indian nation. They burned down 17 Indian towns and destroyed their supplies during this three months tour. William later joined the regiment again, and during the tour he was taken ill and placed in a hospital. When he was strong enough to travel, he was sent home to recover. He joined twice for several months in 1781 to defend against the Tory threats.

Sources: 1. Tombstone 2. U.S. Pensioners 1818-1872. 3. Pension Papers W6279.

****

George Thomason age 13

George Thomason was born in Prince Edward County in 1763 and died in Davidson, North Carolina on 28 November, 1849 after a five day illness. He married Mary Smythe, and he received $60.00 a year for his service.

He first enlisted as a volunteer from Caswell County in the North Carolina militia commanded by Colonel Sheppard in the winter of 1776. He was stationed near Camden in South Carolina to observe, if there would be another attack upon South Carolina. After serving for four months he was discharged. He served several more short tours in Caswell County, until he and his parents moved to Surry County.

"....in the winter of 1778 or 1779 I entered a company of militia for a five months tour as a substitute for _____?_____ the company being commanded by Capt James Sheppard, that to the best of my recollection my company in this service was attached to a Regiment commanded by Colonel Brevard, that we were marched south to the Savannah river, Georgia being then in the possession of the British, that

if I recollects right we were proceeding to reinforce Gen Ash but did not get in the action of Briar Creek, that having served out this five months tour I was discharged."

Colonel Hugh Brevard had seven brothers that served in the revolution. His parents' house was burned to the ground by the British army. The reason the house was destroyed was given to Hugh's mother by a British officer, *"You had eight sons in the rebel army."*

"In the year 1779 if I recollect the year right I volunteered in a company of militia for three months in a company commanded by Captain James Colonel Joseph Williams being Colonel, that whilst in this duty, I was detached with his company together with two other militia companies perhaps 3 to guard and protect the commissioners in running the boundary line between N Carolina & Virginia, that if I recollect right that the commissioners names in the part of North Carolina were Richard Henderson, John William and perhaps in truth that in the part of Virginia I recollect Doct Walker, that I recollect which in this service one of the companies from Wilkes County not his own revolted and had to be kept on duty by own means and martial law, that having served three months I was discharged."

"In the winter of 1780 & 80 I again entered upon a three months tour as a substitute for a person whose name I do not now recollect that I recollect this substitution very well from the circumstances that the person for whom I substituted had belonged to a party of Tories who were defeated at the Station fort by a party of Whigs and either taken prisoners or dispersed and upon being promised pardon upon serving a tour of three months of the Whig side, they __?__ __?__ and the person for whom I substituted (not ___?___ ___?___ acquainted with him) being afraid that for his officer he may then in some battle be placed in the front rank he got me as a substitute for him. That this company was commanded by Capt B Humphreys Joseph Philips being Colonel of the Regiment and was detached for southern duty and marched towards Head Quarters but was turned back at Salisbury and they were employed in guarding prisoners, having served out my three months I was discharged."

George said that he served six tours from the County of Caswell and 4 months in the winter of 1776, 1777, 1778 and 1779. He also served a five month and a three month tour in 1780 and a three month tour in the winter of 1780. His final tour was for three months in 1781. He stated that in his first three months tour he acted as a drummer and a private in all the other tours.

Sources: 1. U.S. Pensioners 1818-1872. 2. U.S. Federal Census Mortality Schedules 1850-1885. 3. Census of 1840. 4. U.S. Revolutionary War Rolls 1775-1783. 5. Pension Papers S7712. 6. Colonial Men and Times by Lillie Dupuy Van Cullen Harper.

****

Alexander Thompson age 14

Alexander Thompson was born on 26 September, 1762 in Cherry Valley, New York, and he died after 1834. He served with his brother William on many tours. The family home was destroyed in November 1778 by the enemy. Alexander's pension was rejected, because he did not provide proof of at least six months of service.

"I enlisted the Army of the United States as a private soldier in the Militia of the State of New York in the year 1776 as a volunteer under Captain Thomas Whitaker & Capt Robert MeKeen of Cherry Valley, then the county of Tyron & State of New York, the Regiment was commanded by Colonel Samuel Campbell & Lt. Col Samuel Clyde both of said Cherry Valley. Lt John Campbell belonged to Capt McKeens Company Sergeant John Thompson, my brother, belonged to the same company Capt Whitaker after Capt Keen took command."

"Cherry valley was a frontier town in the state of New York in the time of the Revolution I was called out I think on or before the tenth day of May, as I volunteered, to keep Guard & help build a Breast work around Col Campbell's house in said Cherry Valley. I was kept on duty til Four Weeks. Then in a few days, say four days after I was again called out as Volunteered, to help build Fort Alden, in the 23 of June after went out on said Fort there three weeks til the 13th of July after. In July 1776 I went out on a Scout to the Butternuts under Capt Keen was gone Twenty one days til the Fourth of August after then in the same Month of August I was called out again, went to the Butternut again and was gone twelve days. There on the 24th of the same month I went out on a Scout under Ensign Benjamin Dickson, to Middlefield after Tory's we took some Torys recollect one by the name of Chamberlain, Michael McDermitt and Hector Southerland, which we brought to Fort Alden was gone Nine days. On the Tenth of September Same year I was called out to do Garrison duty in Fort Alden & on the 1st of November after I was again called out, did garrison duty Five Weeks, and on the 18th of November, in said Fort & at Col Campbells I think I was sent Twenty days til into December after I furnished my own provisions I went out Scouting aforesaid."

"In the year 1777 on the 2nd of May in said year I was called out under Capt McKeen to do garrison duty in Fort Alden and repair & enlarge said fort, did duty in Fort til the 2nd of June after one month I went out in Scouting parties under Lt John Campbell & Ensign Dickerson three times."

"I volunteered under Capt Ballard of the Continental line in the Army of the Revolution in July to go on a Scout to the Butternuts about 30 or 40 miles from said Cherry Valley, after Indian & troys were gone twenty three days--In October of the same year I again volunteered under Capt Ballard aforesaid to go to the Butternuts after the Indians & Troy's I was gone at least Fourteen days."

"On the 7th of November after was called out to garrison Fort Alden under Capt McKeen was in the action on the eleventh of November 1778 in and about Fort Alden was present when Col Alden was killed. His Guard were mostly killed and 20 or 30 of the inhabitants of Militia of Cherry Valley were killed. Hugh Mitchell's wife and his five children; Robert Wells; John Wells; Jane Wells; Catharine Murphy; and Jane Ferguson. Were amongst those taken prisoner were: Betsy Dunlap; Old Misses Dunlap; the Reverend Dunlap; and Lieutenant Colonel Stacia."

On 11 November, 1778 British and Iroquois forces attacked the fort at the small village of Cherry Valley. The defenders in the fort were unprepared resulting in a large loss of life. Forty- four soldiers and settlers were killed and forty-one were captured. Alexander Thompson was a defender inside the fort and a member of the 7th Massachusetts Regiment commanded by Colonel Ichabod Alden. The fort was taken, but the defenders could do nothing to prevent the enemy from destroying the village. The enemy burned every building in the village and carried off the cattle and some of the inhabitants. Most of the captives were later set free.

"In the month of January 1779 I was drove off from Cherry Valley, I joined a company of Militia commanded by Col Marinus Willet. Col Willet commanded the militia along the Valley of the Mohawk til the end of the Revolutionary War."

For the next year Alexander served numerous tours of guard duty. During this time he saw no action. On 12 August, 1781 was a skirmish with the British at Bowman's Creek. *"I commanded a party of six soldiers I was gone three days and was in action with the Indians at Bowmans Cree. I was wounded with a Rifle Ball, in the right leg below the knee, by the Indians in the said action."*

For the rest of 1781 and all of 1782 Alexander was called out several times to serve. Much of the time he served as an orderly sergeant in the regiment. His last service was in the summer of 1783.

Sources: 1.The Bloodied Mohawk: The American Revolution in the Words of Fort Planks Defenders and Other Mohawk Valley Partisans by Kenneth D. Johnson. 2. Pension Papers R22005. 3. The Complete History of the United States of America: Revolutionary War by John Clark Ridpath.

****

Benjamin Thompson age 14

Benjamin Thompson was born on 26 March, 1761 in Chester, New Hampshire, and he died on 6 March, 1842 in Boscawen, New Hampshire. He married Abigail Hazeltine on 28 February, 1842 in New Hampshire. She received a widow's yearly pension of $80.

"I enlisted at Concord County of Merrimack and State of New Hampshire about the month of March A.D. 1775 under Capt Joshua Abbot in Col Scammell Regt in the New Hampshire line for one year. Marched directly to Winter Hill from there to West Point there served out the full time of one year."

"I enlisted at Concord in the now county of Merrimack and state aforesaid the first of May A.D. 1776 under Col Aaron Kingsman for six months and put into Capt Daniel Livermore's company in Col Dearborn's Regt in New Hampshire line. Marched to New Jersey there was drafted out and marched to White Plains from thence marched to a place called Soldier's Fortune for winter quarters, then served out the full time of nine months from the time of my enlistment owing to my being drafted served three months more and then discharged."

In Benjamin's first tour he was in the 3rd New Hampshire Regiment commanded by Colonel Alexander Scammell. He may have participated in the Battle at Bunker Hill in June of 1775. In William's second tour he was in the 1st New Hampshire Regiment commanded by Colonel Henry Dearborn.

Sources: 1. U.S. Pensioners 1818-1872. 2. Sons of the American Revolution Application. 3. Pension Papers W26518.

****

James Thompson age 13

James Thompson was born on 18 December, 1763 in Pennsylvania, and he died in July 1851 in Madison County, Georgia. In later life he was a very rich man, because the 1820 census states that he owned 15 slaves.

He first volunteered for the service in March of 1776 and served in the militia company commanded by Captain Cain under Colonel Charles McDowell. This six month tour provided protection of the frontier from the Indians. His second frontier tour was for three months under the command of Captain Thomas Kennedy. His third tour was from July to October 1778 under Captain Smith. James served a three month tour at Templeton's Station and a year later under the command of Captain John McDaniel. He served a two month tour in the summer of 1779 under Captain John McDaniel.

"The next tour of duty of three months commencing in May seventeen hundred & eighty and continued in service until August following, making the three months aforesaid, under Capt Camp the whole under the commands of Generals Charles McDowell and Rutherford. While in this service the British light horse & tories fell in with this detachment of troops then under the command of Gen Charles McDowell at the house of Hampton on Green River in South Carolina and killed three Americans and wounded several. I with several others were ordered as a scout to proceed the morning before this skirmish and make what discovers we could in regard to the British and Tories and did not return until after the engagement."

The skirmish that James is referring to occurred on 15 July, 1780 in South Carolina and very close to the border with North Carolina. A Loyalist spy was sent into the American camp to gather information. The spy returned with the information and the Loyalist Captain James Dunlap was sent to attack the camp commanded by Colonel Charles McDowell. The Americans were able to repel the attack but suffered a loss of eight men.

"The next was a tour of duty of three months under Capt Samuel Woods & Gen Charles McDowell at the battle of Kings Mountain and also Major joseph McDowell who commanded as a Major in this engagement. I commenced this service in August of seventeen hundred & eighty and continue until November following making the term last aforesaid and was first of my company that fired a gun in said battle."

Major Joseph McDowell is usually spoken of as the hero of the battle who led the Burke County militia. He is also known as Joseph "Quaker Meadows" McDowell to distinguish him from his cousin Captain Joseph "Pleasant Gardens" McDowell, who was also at the battle. Descendants of "Pleasant Gardens" Joseph was quick to point out that he was the one that really led the Burk County militia up the mountain.

"My next was a tour of duty of three weeks under Major Joseph McDowell against the Cherokee Indians. I commenced this tour in May seventeen hundred & eighty one and served as last aforesaid. In this expedition the party, consisting of about eighty men, preceded into the Cherokee Nation burned two of their towns & killed five Indians. The whole of this service I performed as a private."

Sources: 1. Tombstone. 2. Census of 1800, 1820, and 1830. 3. U.S. Pension Roll of 1835. 4. Pension Papers S32014.

****

Samuel Thompson age 14

Samuel Thompson was born on 14 March, 1765 in North Carolina, and he died on 22 May, 1842 in San Augustine, Texas. He married Precious Wolford in Louisiana in 1787. Her father was a Tory during the war. Samuel received a yearly pension of $80.

"In 1778 or 1779 I served under Captain Joseph Worford of South Carolina a tour of four or six months, a part of which was for my elder brother and a part for myself. The company served under Colonel Thomas also of South Carolina in the district of Ninety Six. I then resided in the said District of Ninety Six in said State of South Carolina."

"This tour was served under a draft. I marched to Princes Fort, in the said District, where I was stationed until the British took the City of Charlestown. There were no regular officers or soldiers with me at this time to my knowledge. I have no documentary evidence and I know of no person whose testimony I can procure who can testify to his service, except Bailey Anderson."

"After the fall of Charlestown I went out to a Fort called Goings Fort and remained there forted against the Indians--Tory hunting and Indian scouting, for a year or two. During the time I belonged to Captain Parsons Company-- Captain Parsons was the commanding officer--But

Colonel Roebuck was chosen for our Colonel but whether he was ever commissioned or not, I do not __?__."

"In the year 1779 or 1780 I volunteered under Colonel Roebuck and carried an express from him to General Morgan to inform him of the advance of Colonel Carlton to attack him--I remained with General Morgan until after the battle of the Cowpens in which battle I was engaged."

The letter Samuel Thompson carried to General Morgan warned the General of an attack by Colonel Banastre Tarleton. At the beginning of the battle on 17 January, 1781 Samuel was under the command of Colonel John Thomas, and he was placed in the second line of militia in the center of the front battle line.

Brigadier General Daniel Morgan had asked the militia to fire three volleys and then retreat. This would draw the British into the waiting Continental regulars in the back ranks. Morgan always told his sharpshooters in the first line to *"aim at the epaulettes, and not at the poor rascals who fought for sixpence a day."* Many British officers were killed that day.

"I was then sent back to Goings' Fort--Colonel Roebuck called for men to go and attack the Fort Tories called "Williams Fort"--I volunteered & went with Colonel Roebuck and was out to the best of his recollection about 2 weeks. But I was out frequently & almost constantly but I cannot recollect the length of time precisely. From 1778 or 1779 I was constantly engaged in the cause of the revolution, and a great part of the time I was a refugee from my own home, and carried arms against the Enemy. I did nothing else but defend myself & friends against the British--Tories & Indians."

In 1826 Samuel and his family sailed to Texas and was part of the group of settlers brought in by Stephen F. Austin. By this time Samuel was a physician and owned eighteen slaves. He held various offices in San Augustine, and Thompson Academy was founded in 1839 on land donated by Samuel.

Sources: 1. Tombstone 2. Biography from "The Handbook of Texas" online. 3. Pension Papers S31420. 4. Library of American History Containing Biographical Sketches.

****

Baze Thurman age 13

John Thurman was born on 24 January, 1763 in Prince William County, Virginia, and he died on 6 May, 1836 in Spencer, Kentucky. His pension application was rejected, because it required more proof. He owned 2 slaves in 1820 and 1 slave in 1830.

"I entered the Service in the Regiment commanded by Colonel Lee in the month of May in the year 1776." Baez served for five months and was discharged after marching to Philadelphia. He was drafted as a pioneer to assist opening roads along the Potomac River. The roads were used to transport provisions of General Washington's army.

"I entered the service as a private soldier as a substitute for John Thurman and was mustered into service at Dumfries." He was discharged after four months after guarding British prisoners. He was later drafted into the service in the fall of 1780 as a private soldier in the Virginia Militia.

Sources: 1. Census 1820 & 1830. 2. D.A.R. #A203627. 3. Pension Papers R10583.

****

Richard Tice age 14

Richard Tice was born on 28 September, 1762 in Gloucester, New Jersey, and he died on 27 August, 1848 in Independence, Texas. He married Letitia Bates on 12 January, 1790 in Pennsylvania.

He served as a fifer in a company commanded by Captain Jonathan Williams at the age of 14. He later served as a private at the Battles of Trenton, Princeton and Monmouth. He lived in Philadelphia and Long Island in New York. He came to Texas October 1842 to live with his daughter and son-in-law. His grave is marked by the DAR and the SAR.

Sources: 1. Tombstone 2. Pennsylvania Marriage Records 1700-1821. 3. Sons of the American Revolution.

****

Arthur Toney age 14 (African American)

Arthur Toney was born in 1765 in Dinwiddie County, Virginia, and he died 19 July, 1847 in Caswell, North Carolina. He married Elizabeth Edwell in December, 1779 in Caswell. When Elizabeth was five she was owned by John Williams of Caswell County. Arthur received a yearly pension of $29.19. He enlisted as a substitute for his brother John.

In the 1820 Census the ten members of his family were listed as Free Colored. In the 1840 Census there are 2 Free Colored, which are probably Arthur and his wife and one slave listed.

"I entered in the Service of the United States during the Revolutionary war I think in the Spring of 1779-- & I enlisted in the State of South Carolina at Bacon's bridge near Charleston under Captain William Litle a Regular officer of the United States Army and I was attached to Colonel Henry Dixon's Command in the 3rd Regiment of North Carolina Commanded by General Sumner and I marched from Bacon's Bridge in South Carolina to Hillsboro in North Carolina and from there I was marched to Halifax in North Carolina & then to Edenton from there to Camden in South Carolina--& from there to Bacon's Bridge & there we Remained until the end of the war. I was in no battles in Consequence of me being Kept with the baggage Wagons—generally—I am well acquainted with Captain James Burton and Captain Benj. C. West--of Caswell County aforesaid."

When Arthur joined the 3rd North Carolina Regiment it was so depleted that it had been sent home to recruit new men. It was the first North Carolina regiment to march to protect Charleston, South Carolina in late 1779 or early 1780. On 12 May, 1780 162 men of the regiment surrendered to the British Army at the fall of Charleston.

A letter in Arthur's pension file mentions that in 1792 his brother John received twenty six pounds, four shillings, and eight pence for his services as a soldier in the army. It also states that Arthur received twenty three pounds, seven shillings, and eleven pence for his service. In another letter Daniel Walker verified the date of date for Arthur saying that he was there when he died, and he made Arthur's coffin.

Sources: 1. 1820 and 1840 Census. 2. Pension Papers W4835.

****

William Toomes age 10

William Toomes was born on 8 May, 1768 in Albemarle, Virginia. His pension application was rejected because of his extreme youth.

"In the spring of the year 1778 in the County of Albemarle and the State of Virginia I entered the service in the militia Company

commanded by one Captain John Martin as a substitute for my father John Tombs. The Company rendezvoused at Charlottesville and marched from thence to Hobbs Hole the Company to which I belonged was joined by others on its march to Hobbs Hole, after being stationed some length of time at said Hobbs Hole the troop was marched to Williamsburg at which place I was discharged after serving three months as a musician in said Captain Martin's Company."

"In the Spring of the year 1779 I again entered the service under Captain Smyth (Christian name not recollected) as a musician and as a Substitute for one Robert Page and served as well as recollected six months. The company rendezvoused at Charlottesville and joined the army near Petersburg commanded as I believe by General Lafayette. From Petersburg the army marched in great haste and under much alarm as this petitioner then believed, the route the army pursued I cannot now state with any degree of certainty I discharged in an old field not near to any place of notoriety known to me."

"In the year 1780 I again entered the service in a militia company as a Substitute for John Massie commanded by the aforesaid Captain John Martin. The Company rendezvoused at Charlottesville and marched from thence and joined the army near Baltimore. I cannot recollect the movements of the army after I joined it but think there was some skirmishes by parts of the army. I served as a musician and was discharged after a six months tour somewhere near the Delaware River."

"In the year 1781 I again entered the service in a militia company as a subject to my father Commanded by one Captain Dohority (christian name not recollected). The company rendezvoused at Charlottesville early in the month of February and joined the Army I think that was commanded by General Greene not far from the Eastern shores of Maryland, I again served as a musician the different routes taken by the army or the different places touched upon by the army I cannot relate but believe the army was at Richmond Virginia but the army ultimately came near to Yorktown and guarded some baggage during the siege that terminated in the capture of Cornwallis"

"I as will be seen was only about 10 years old when I first entered the service I cannot therefore recollect distinctly who were the field officers I served under during the several tours above mentioned nor what particular officer commanded each tour, but I recollect that Colonel Linsey commanded one of the tours in that capacity & Colonel Henderson another -- I also recollect that Generals Lee, Greene, Lafayette and

Washington commanded at different times while I was in service but in what particular tours I do not recollect."

Source: 1. Pension Papers R1036.

****

Israel Trask age 10

Israel Trask served both in the Army and Navy. Much is known and written about him, because he recorded his adventures in his pension application in such detail. The account covers 20 pages in his own handwriting which is not too difficult to read.

Israel was born on 5 February, 1765 in Gloucester, Massachusetts, and he died there on 4 October, 1854. He married Judith Somes on 26 September, 1790, and they had at least 8 children. At the age of 10 he served two tours with his father, which started in May of 1775 in the Massachusetts line and lasted about a year.

He describes his enlistment, *"I volunteered in the service of the United States as a soldier in a company by Capt. John Low…I believe took place in Gloucester, as Lieutenant Trask, my father, procured a number of recruits there as well as other places, and Beverly was assigned for their meeting, and from thence we marched to headquarters."*

Captain John Low's Company was under Colonel Mansfield's 19th Regiment, which was commanded by Lieut. Colonel Israel Hutchinson. During the summer and fall they slept under light tents. During the winter of 1775 they quartered on Winter Hill. Israel wrote, *"When cold weather set in we were put under barracks and quartered on Winter Hill during this period. I had various duties assigned me such as the care of the Baggage and the property of the mess. When the officers were called on duty, which was daily, either to Mount Guard, or Fatigue duties in fortifying the camp, the entrenchment of which had a line of continuity from winter Hill to Watertown when finished, my duty was alternately was to take The edibles prepared at the mess to the officers on duty, which in some instance miles apart."*

He goes on to describe some of the officers, *"My knowledge of the General Officers of the Army during this first term of service was quite limited. General Greene I knew well, mounted on a white horse, made frequent visits of inspection to our regiment, from which I infer I was attached to the brigade he commanded. Major General Lee I also knew, from the circumstance of his angry threats to cane an officer of considerable grade in the army for unsoldierly conduct and the high excitement the fact created among the officers of the army."*

Nathanael Greene was a private when the war began and was promoted to Major General of the Rhode Island Observation in May of 1775. The next month he was again promoted as a Brigadier General of the Continental Army. Major General Charles Lee was a British officer before the war. When the revolution began he expected to be named Commander-in-Chief of the Continental Army. Instead the command was given to George Washington, who Lee grew to despise. Lee was noted for being coarse in his language.

Israel's term of service expired on 31 December, 1775. *"If a certificate of discharge was given, Lieutenant Trask, my father, must have received it, as he did my rations as well as wages, whatever may have been paid. Personally I never received either. The day immediately following the expiration of my first term of service, I recommenced my duty in the service of the United States for another term the first day of January, 1776..."*

The company Israel enlisted in was under the command of Captain John Banker, Lieutenant Pearce, Lieutenant Trask, and Ensign Cooper. This was the 5th Massachusetts Regiment, which was also known as the 27th Continental Regiment under the command of Colonel Israel Hutchinson. Sometime before the winter ended the regiment was ordered to Cambridge. Once there the officers were quartered in the second story of the college buildings, which were also called the Harvard Yard.

While quartered at Cambridge Israel sees General George Washington for the first time. An event occurred that impressed upon Israel the General's physical as well as mental power. It also revealed how low the state of discipline was in the army and how difficult it would be to raise it. The incident was between troops from Virginia and troops from New England.

This is the account of the incident as told by Israel Trask, *"A day or two preceding the incident I am about to relate, a rifle corps had come into camp from Virginia, made up of recruits from the backwoods and mountains of that state, in a uniform dress totally different from that of regiments raised on the seaboard and interior of New England. Their white linen frocks, ruffled and fringed, excited the curiosity of the whole army, particularly to the Marblehead regiment, who were always full of fun and mischief."*

It should be noted here that the Marblehead Regiment commanded by John Glover was the 14th Continental Regiment. It was composed of seafaring men from the area around Marblehead. They manned the boats at the crossing of the Delaware River before the Battle of Trenton.

"(They) looked with scorn on such rustic uniform when compared to their own round jackets and fishers' trousers, directly confronted from fifty to an hundred of the riflemen who were viewing the college buildings. Their first manifestations were ridicule and derision, which the riflemen bore with more patience than their wont, but resort being made to snow, which covered the ground, these soft missives were interchanged but a few minutes before both parties closed, and a fierce struggle commenced with biting and gouging on the one part, and knockdown and they then opened with as much apparent fury as the most deadly enmity could create.

Reinforced by their friends, in less than five minutes more than a thousand combatants were on the field, struggling for the mastery."

"At this juncture General Washington made his appearance, whether accident or design I never knew. I only saw him and his colored servant, both mounted. With the Spring of a Deer he leaped from his saddle, threw the Reins of his bridle into the hands of his servant and rushed into the thickest of the Melee with an iron grip seized two tall, brawny, athletic, savage looking Riflemen by the throat keeping them at arm's length alternately shaking and talking to them. In this position the eye of the Belligerents caught sight of the General. Its effect on them was instantaneous flight at the top of their speed in all directions from the scene of conflict. Less than fifteen minutes time had elapsed from the commencement of the row before the general and his two criminals were the only occupants of the field of action. Here bloodshed, imprisonment, trials by court martial were happily prevented, and hostile feelings between the different Corps of the Army extinguished by the Physical and Mental Energies timely exerted by one individual."

American troops fortifying Cambridge during the siege of Boston needed places to stay. Harvard President Samuel Langdon offered his campus to the troops. The five Harvard buildings were used to house 1,600 troops. Tents and barracks were assembled in Harvard Yard. The Harvard students moved their studies to Concord. Unfortunately, when the soldiers left it was discovered that they tore off the metal roof of Harvard to melt into bullets. They also stripped brass doorknobs and box locks from the buildings, along with pieces of interior woodwork. The Massachusetts House of Representatives later reimbursed Harvard for the damages.

In March the British left Boston, and the troops at Harvard moved into the city. Before Israel's regiment left Boston and moved to Dorchester, a mutiny broke out in the army. It was quickly quelled and the leaders were arrested, convicted, and condemned by court-martial. Two of the men to be shot belonged to the Marblehead regiment.

Israel visited the men in jail, *"The criminals were heavily ironed and strongly guarded and were by the sentence to be kept until the day of execution. The door of the prison by order was left open during the daytime with free permission to receive the visit of all, whether drawn by friendship or curiosity. Of the latter nearly the whole army availed themselves of the liberty given. When I visited them, I learned they were both natives of Marblehead and both married men and their wives, respectable looking women had taken up their temporary abode in the same prison with their husbands. The ghastly countenances of the latter on which the deepest contrition portrayed, the tears of penitence coming down their rough cheeks made impressions on a young mind not easily effaced. The stern purposes of Washington were inflexible to the prayers and supplications of the friends of the criminals. He continued to receive in silence all solicitations in their favor until those purposes were attained. He then freely granted the unexpected pardon."*

During the summer the regiment left Dorchester and they marched to New York. There were no real fights with the British during this time, just an occasional exchange of small fire. It was during this time that Israel witnessed public punishment inflicted in the regiment.

"Five or six soldiers were condemned to be flogged for the crime, I believe, of being concerned in the mutiny at Boston. This incident was impressed on my memory with increased force from the interest made to exonerate Major Putman's son from his share of the duty of applying the cat to the naked backs of the criminals that fell to him as a drummer in the regiment. A hear or two older than myself he was however obliged to submit, and take his share of the unpleasant duty with his colleagues."

When orders came for the regiment to march, Israel's father directed his son to return home and be ready for further orders. This was in the late summer about the time his enlistment was up. Later his father became ill and quit the army and never enlisted again. His father received all the pay due to Israel while he was in the army. In the early part of 1777 twelve year old Israel entered the navy.

"In the early part of the year 1777 I entered the sea service Privateer Schooner Speedwell Philemon Haskell commander. Cruised in and about the Banks of Newfoundland and captured four prizes all arrived safe at Gloucester. The latter part of the same year, was fitted and commissioned as a letter of marque the same vessel and same commander went to Martinique."

The schooner *Speedwell* had 3 guns and 12 men and was owned by David Peirce of Gloucester. It captured three fishing brigs: the *Dolphin*, *George*, and *Phoenix*. The salt taken from the fishing ships brought a high price. The "letter of marque" was a government license authorizing the privateers to attack and capture enemy ships.

"Early in the year 1778 I entered on board the ship Black Prince of Salem Captain Elias Smith, Lieutenants Bordman and Nathaniel West. A few days out captured after smart action brig of sixteen guns commanded by a lieutenant of the British Navy."

Israel's family was facing financial hardship due to the illness of his father, so Israel signed on as a cabin boy for the *Black Prince*. As the cabin boy he would receive a one-half share of the ship's take. The captain received three shares, and most of the crew received one or one and one-half shares. After the war he returned home with an excess of $20,000 in gold and goods.

His first captain, Captain Smith, was only five feet tall and probably not much taller than Israel. Under Captain Smith the ship was very successful, which resulted in the capture of several prizes. Smith was later replaced by Captain Nathaniel West. The *Black Prince* joined with a fleet on 30 June, 1779, an event that would prove to be disastrous.

"On board this ship I entered a volunteer. I believe in April 1779, and sailed from Salem the forepart of summer of said year and arrived at an Eastern Port I believe called Townsend, where we lay many days waiting the arrival of other armed vessels and transports destined for the expedition to Penobscot. I continued on board this ship until she was blown up at the head of Navigation on Penobscot River, from whence, with many others, I escaped to the dense forests and traveled through the wilderness about three hundred miles with a pack on my shoulders containing a light blanket, a small piece of rusty Pork, a few biscuits, a

bottle wine, and one shirt wending my way across streams and through underbrush until the second days march my shoe gave way. The rest of the way I performed on my bare feet until I reached home which I infer from the following incident was the month of September /79."

In 1779 the British sent an expeditionary force to the Penobscot River to remove the American presence there. They were to establish a fort which would provide them with a naval base. The American fleet was sent to stop them. The British attacked the American fleet capturing nine ships and running several others ashore. Early on 16 August, 1779 the privateers began scuttling their vessels. One of the first ships burned was the *Black Prince.*

"Late in October, 1779 I again volunteered in the ship Rambler, twenty guns of Beverly, Capt. Benjamin Lovett commander, Nathaniel Swazy, first lieutenant. Cruised on the Atlantic, Bay Biscay, and entered Bilboa (in Spain) *in December, where the ship was visited by the Honorable John Adams and his son John Quincy on their way through Spain to Paris. Sailed from thence the latter part of January, 1780. In one of the heavy gales of that severe winter, we were partially dismasted, lost main yard and mizzenmast. Arrived at Beverly the following March."*

The *Rambler* was a schooner of 200 tons, 20 guns, a crew of 50 men, and insured for $15,000. In the *Works of John Adams* Vol. 3 the future President mentions that on Wednesday January 19, 1780 he visited the schooner *Rambler* and received two 13 gun salutes.

"1780. Early in April, I again sailed in the brig Wilkes of Gloucester, fourteen guns commanded by Capt. Job Knight. Took two prizes and sent home. Afterwards captured by the Ferry (Fairy), *sloop of war. Carried into St. John's Newfoundland, where I was forced from the prison ship at the point of the bayonet on board the Vestal frigate and compelled to do duty until the arrival of Admiral Edwards, whose humanity, at the instances of a pathetic petition, ordered that I should with fourteen others be returned to the prison ship. Soon after, an exchange of prisoners took place. I returned home under the cartel."*

The *Wilkes* was a 160 ton schooner with 16 guns and a crew of 75. Captain Knight was commissioned on it on 21 April, 1780. When it was captured by the British ship *Fairy*, it was renamed the *Prince Edward.* In the fall of 1782 the *Prince Edward* was captured by the Americans and returned to Gloucester. British Admiral Edwards, who removed Israel from the British ship back to the prison ship, was noted for his humane treatment toward American prisoners. Moving Israel back to the prison ship and then later to be exchanged may have saved his life.

"In the winter of 1781 I sailed in the brig Garland of Newburyport, letter marque, Captain Knap, for Martinique. On the return voyage captured and carried into Bermuda. After some months detention under the cartel flag of exchange. In the summer of 1781 I served in making two voyages in safety to Martinique and back first in the brig Ranger, Captain Knight, letter of marque, second in small brig from Gloucester, Captain Hough."

A brig was a sailing ship with two square-rigged masts. They were fast and maneuverable and used as a warship and merchant ship. A cartel flag identified to all that a cooperative arrangement between two groups had been arranged. It might fly on a ship that carried prisoners that were exchanged.

"In the spring of 1782 I entered on board the ship Betsy eighteen guns of Gloucester, Petty officer Capt. Joseph Porter commander. Second day out captured by the Perseverance and Ceres frigates the former rated forty-four the first of that class ever launched from the Navy yards of Great Britain. Here we experienced the full force of the insolent Pride and lofty arrogance so prevalent in the Navy and Army of Great Britain at that period. On board the Perseverance the Prisoners were driven down under the haulup deck their only beds large ironbound water casks with a stifled, impure air to respire. Only four in the daytime and one at night were allowed to leave this dungeon to catch the pure air or answer the calls of nature. In about a fortnight we were relieved from these impurities to be thrust into a filthy prison ship at Halifax a large old condemned East Indiaman. On her three decks were housed or entombed some hundreds of our countrymen, many of whom many of had been her occupants for three long years. The gloomy aspect of the ship preferable to a lengthy abode in this horrific Avernus. With spirits and energies unrelaxed the eighth day of confinement, two of our intrepid companions and expert swimmers swam in ice cold water two miles to a fortified island and brought off, in the obscurity of a foggy evening, two boats within breath hearing of a sentinel. The smaller of the boats unperceived reached the ship into which I was the last to enter. At that moment the alarm was given to the guard, and a volley of about forty muskets was poured in us before we had pulled a stroke. Only one ball entered the boat. Before a recharge could be made, we were hid in the obscurity of the night and succeeded by hauling our boat on uninhabited islands in the daytime and embracing the night for *progressions, in making good our escape. After a fortnight of great suffering, we got on board of an American cruiser and reached our home a little over a month from the time we left it."*

"1782 I afterwards sailed in the brig Congress, letter marque, Captain Clark. Latter part of the same year I sailed in the ship the Ruby, Captain Babson both strongly armed the latter eighteen funs both voyages to West Indies and both return safe with valuable cargoes. In the winter of 1782 again sailed on the Ruby Captain Babson to Guadeloupe where the news of peace reached and where we lay until it took effect in those latitudes."

Israel Trask had been in the war off and on from 1775 until it ended in 1783. In 1800, the year his wife died, he was still living in Gloucester, Massachusetts. According to the census his real estate was worth $12,000. Israel died in 1854.

Sources: 1. Voices of the American Revolution: Stories of Men, Women, and Children who Forged Our Nation by Kendall F. Haven. 2. In Pursuit of Liberty: Coming of Age in the American Revolution by Emmy E. Werner. 3. Massachusetts Soldiers and Sailors in the Revolutionary War. 4. U.S. Revolutionary War Pension and Bounty-Land Warrant Applications Files 1800-1900. 5. Pension Application for Israel Trask S30171. 6. The Revolution Remembered: Eyewitness Accounts of the War for Independence Edited by John C. Dann. 7. Tombstone &. 1810 & 1810 Census. 8. Harvard's Year of Exile, Harvard Gazette by Corydon Ireland. 9. American Maritime units and Vessels and Their supporters During the Revolutionary War 1775-1783 by Grandville W. Hough. 10. History of the Town of Gloucester, Cape Ann: Including the Town of Rockport by John James Babson. 11. Beverly Privateers of the American Revolution by Octavius Thorndike Howe, M.D. 12. The Penobscot Expedition Archaeological Project: Field Investigations 2000 and 2001, prepared by Naval Historical Center Underwater Archaeology Branch. 13. Works of John Adam Vol. 3 by John Adams. 14. Massachusetts Town and Vital Records 1620-1988. 15. U. S. Census.

****

Josiah P. Tucker age 14

Josiah Tucker was born on 5 August, 1766 in Salisbury, New Hampshire, and he died on 9 November, 1845 in Oswego, New York. He married Lucy Dougherty in New York on 31 January, 1794. He received a yearly pension of $42.42.

"I enlisted in July 1779 for Six Months *mustered at Amherst New Hampshire in Capt Ezekiel Worthings Co Col Mooney Regt. Of New Hamps. Regt. Col Schammel in Capt Isaac Farwells Company. The portion of the 2nd Regt which Farwells Co was attached was commanded*

by Major William Scott. The Regt lay at Peekskill and near there until winter quarters when we went to <u>Highlands or Hampshire huts</u> on North River and was discharged in December having served <u>Six Months</u>."

"Volunteered in 1782 in Capt Ebenezer Websters Co I went west to Block house at East Oxbow in Newbury port under command and Gen Bailey & scouted against Indians <u>Three Months</u>."

Sources: 1. Tombstone 2. DAR #10653. 3. Sons of the American Revolution Application. 4. Pension Papers W2026.

****

<u>Mangnus Tullock</u> age 13

Magnus Tullock was born in Kirkwall, Scotland on 8 February, 1764, and he died in Blount, Tennessee on 27 October, 1845. His family sailed to the colonies on the ship Marlborough in 1775 and arrived at Savannah, Georgia. They were indentured servants to Thomas Brown in Richmond County, Georgia until 1783. He married Nancy Logan in South Carolina in 1784. His pension papers amounted to thirty-three pages, for which he received $88.00 per year for his service.

"I enlisted in Abbeville County in the State of <u>South Carolina</u> in a place called White Hall fort on the Hard labor Creek at the residence of one General Williamson on the ___ day of ___ in the year 1777 in the 13th year of my age. I enlisted for three years under the command of Captain John Bowie commander of the 2nd independent Company as it was at that time called and was not attached to any regular Regiment, myself with a certain Sanders Moore to beat the drum & myself to <u>play the fife</u>....."

Captain John Bowie, 5th South Carolina Regiment, was commandant at Fort Independence sometime between May and November 1777, and he took orders from the militia leaders at Ninety Six.

"....we remained at Charleston and on the command of Captain Conyer when the six months had expired we obtained permission for Moore & myself to go to Charleston 3 miles or thereabouts from the Island, we went, as Colonel Huger of the 5th Regiment on the Island for us to Join him & sent me back to the Island for that purpose I obtained the orders to Join my old captain Bowie & done so,, I played the Fife & was a musitioner during the three years of my service. Captain Bowie remained with us some days in Charleston in order to obtain some Clothing for the Company. We were then marched to fort Independence in

Abbeville County, now but at that time in 96 District on Rocky River. I do not recollect how long I remained at fort Independence however, we were then marched through the State of Georgia to the Cherokee Nation to a place called the Standing Peace Tree or near to that place we were then alternately marched through the upper part of Carolina & Georgia for some time. Some times we were under the command of General Williamson a militia General but most commonly we had no officer of a higher grade that our Captain John Bowie. Fort Independence being our head quarters we were marched to that place again on the ___ day in the year ___."

"*We were marched to the State of Georgia to a ferry at New Richmond the next down opposite to Augusta the British at that time was in possession of the town, we were stationed on the opposite side of the River where we threw up a Battery no officer higher in Command than captains there were a part of three companies one Captain Martin's company a militia man the others were what they called independents. We remained there until the British evacuated Augusta we were then marched through the town & on down to Bear Creek & Joined Gen Lincoln or rather below the Creek. We after remaining under the command of the General & marching through the States of Georgia and Carolina we left them & were marched back to fort Independence in the State of South Carolina and remained there some time & then early in the Spring of I cannot recollect the date of the year, Joined General Lincoln & was marched through the Country until the <u>Battle of Stono</u> in the State of Carolina when I was marched to that place & was in the Battle at that place under the command of Major General Lincoln after the Battle we were marched to Governor Bull's Country seat under the Command of our Captain Bowie we remained there some time & was sent back to fort Independence. We remained there some time guarding the frontiers & in November we were marched to Savannah in the State of Georgia and was in the Battle at that Place the siege at that place continued 3 weeks. The British at that place kept their stand and we lost hundreds of man & were defeated. We were then marched back to fort Independence to guard the frontiers and after scouting about there some time we were ordered back to the Cherokee Nation under the command of General Williamson in search of a British agent by the name of Cameron. We found him in the Nation but he fled and made his escape.*"

Alexander Cameron was a British Indian agent who had great influence with the Cherokee Indians. When the revolution started, he fled his plantation and took up residence with the Overhill Cherokees. He wanted the Indians to remain neutral, but the colonists kept pushing into their land. The Indians took up arms to drive the settlers out of their lands. Cameron led the Indians on some of these raids making him a hated man in the territory. Meanwhile, some men in the area forged a letter to show that Henry Stuart, Cameron's brother, had written a letter to Cameron to instigate a Cherokee insurrection against the colonists. Then, Cameron became a hunted man.

Major Williamson instructed James McCall to lead a 33 man expedition for the purpose of getting the Indians to return land taken in recent raids. The true purpose of the mission was given to James in a sealed package of orders. After the mission was under way James opened the orders and informed the men that the real mission was to capture Cameron.

Cameron was forced to flee into Creek Indian country to avoid capture by the Americans. For a period of time he lived with David Taitt, a British deputy for the Creek, and he later fled to safety in the fall of 1777.

After the escape of Cameron, Mangus and his troop marched back to Fort Independence and spent their time hunting Tories. The North Carolina Militia was later captured at the Siege of Charleston.

"We give up our arms & went to a place called Cow head & took protection, we however at this time discharged [since they were British prisoners they were paroled which meant that they upon release they promised not to take arms again for a specific period of time] *& were not to lift arms again for a year and a day. I was discharged in July of 1780 to the best of my recollection."*

"I then in the Spring of 1781 volunteered under the command of Captain Bushelo a French officer *man Regiment of Colonel Anderson in the State of South Carolina. We then were scouting about between the Savannah and Saluda Rivers until the siege of Ninety Six & Joined Gem Green & Gen Pickens & was at the Siege of Ninety Six. Lord Rhoden came up a British man and Gen Greene that it most prudent to give back & done so. General Pickens covered Gen Greens retreat & marched to Congaree River and stopped. as we had come down from Ninety Six to that place we had taken some prisoners. Captain Bushelo was then ordered to take 11 man & march & to guard them to Camden about 32 miles distance to Colonel Armstrong. Colonel A. then heard that some Tories were coming down the River and ordered us to Scout about &*

ordered Captain Bushelo & his men to guard some empty Wagons down to General Greene. We done so. I was stationed not far from Eutaw Springs. We were marched back to Abbeville County & put again under the command of Colonel Anderson & General Pickens & was commanded by them until the close of the war. Some time in the year 1782 to the best of my knowledge I was for this last Term of two years no written discharge."

In all, Mangus served three years as a fifer, and 18 months he was a volunteer soldier. For his service in the revolution he received $69.00 a year.

Sources: 1. Tombstone. 2. U.S. Headstone Application for Military Veterans 1925-1963. 3. Census 1790, 1800, and 1830. 4. U.S. Pension Roll of 1835. 5. U.S. & Canada, Passenger & Immigration lists Index 1500-1900. 6. Pension Papers S6273. 7. Roster of South Carolina Patriots in the American Revolution. 8. Tennessee Early Tax List Records 1783-1895. 9. Twenty-four Hundred Tennessee Pensioners. 10. Scottish & English Immigrants to the Georgia Frontier 1774-1775, National Genealogical Society Quarterly Vol. 70:3, Sept. 1982, by Robert Scott Davis, Jr. 11. Alexander Cameron, British Agent among the Cherokee, 1764-1781 by John L. Nichols.

****

Bishop Tyler age 13

Bishop Tyler was born in Preston City, Connecticut on 22 January, 1767, and he died on 12 April, 1844 in Griswold, Connecticut. He married Alice Morgan on 29 November, 1797. Bishop later became a surgeon and served in the War of 1812 in the 8th Regiment (Belcher's) Connecticut Militia.

He wanted to enlist at the age of twelve, but he could not get his father's permission. Just before he turned fourteen his father gave him permission to join and serve as a waiter and play the fife with a family friend, Captain Charles Miles. Bishop Tyler enlisted on 1 March, 1781 into a company of state troops commanded by Captain Charles Miles for one year. He served Captain Miles as a waiter. Bishop wrote the pension board about his service on 22 November, 1833.

"……we marched to New Haven and was there mustered, marched to Horseneck in the state of New York and there joined the army and was engaged in actual military service there & in that vicinity for the term of one year during which time we had many skirmishes with the enemy and the Captain of our company with about thirty of the company went out on an exploring excursion and were taken prisoner and carried

prisoner to New York and after being detained there a number of weeks were exchanged and rejoined the army at the expiration of the term of my enlistment on the first day of March 1782."

In one of the letters Bishop sent to the pension board he gave an account of a skirmish that he was in during the summer of 1781 under Captain Miles. Simeon Hewitt also told of the skirmish in a letter he wrote in support of Bishop Tyler's pension. The skirmish took place at a place in New York called "Frog's neck". The author was able to find an earlier skirmish that occurred there in 1776. Bishop Tyler reported the following account:

"I was in one battle at Frog's neck...We were trapped with Delaney's corps & considerable number were Killed & wounded & afterwards at or near the same place we were again engaged with the same corps under Delaney & a considerable number of French troops were killed. In the first engagement our troops retreated & at the last we succeeded. I there saw Genl Washington for the first time."

"In the year 1782 in the spring of the year in the month of April or May I think May, I again entered into the service of my country at Fort Griswold in Groton in Connecticut opposite of New London for the term of two months, as a substitute for Joseph Belcher deceased who was draughted for said term, and was appointed a corporal and did a corporal's duty it being the year after the destruction of the Fort by Arnold, our duty was to repair and guard the prisoners on board the prison ship, was there when the prisoners rose and took the guard and thence I lost my gun and all my military apparatus for which I have received nothing."

"I was in the company of Capt. John Cobb of Stonington attached to Colonel McClellan's regiment and the whole of this time was devoted to military service at the end of two months I was discharged"

Colonel Samuel McClellan led men at the Battles of Lexington and Concord and played an important role at Bunker Hill. He was later appointed to oversee troops at Groton Heights and New London in Connecticut. His great-grandson was George B. McClellana a Major General during the Civil War.

"On the 24th day of September in the year 1782 I again entered the service of the same Fort as a substitute for Barton Cooke deceased, as appears by the pay roll of Captain Elisha Prentice's company Col.

McClellan's Regiment., my Captain gave me the offer to serve as a corporal or to be his waiter, I chose to be his waiter, and preformed that duty, nothing unusual occurred in this tour of service."

Bishop had several people write to the pension bureau to give proof of his service. For some reason he felt compelled to write a letter to them on 5 December, 1833, and explained why he joined the army at such a young age when he was not required to do so. It is a very moving and patriotic account given to Judge John Hyde, who wrote down what Bishop said. Fortunately, the Judge had beautiful handwriting that was very easy to copy.

"Bishop Tyler of the town of Griswold in the county of New London, being called to explain why a youth of the tender age of fourteen should be engaged in the service of his country, when the militia laws did not require those under sixteen years to be enlisted in the militia feels no small mortification at being called upon to answer such a question to obtain the small sum which the tardy justice of his country has seen fit bestow as testimony of its estimation of these services____mortification that when he has not only made solemn oath to those services, but proved them by most respectable witnesses_____He feels however some gratification that at the time when this question comes to him from Washington to be answered, he has been & is sitting in a respectable Court of Justice as foreman of a very respectable Query deciding the causes of his fellow citizens. That he is a practicing Physician in his native town in which town he has represented in the Legislature of the State & was employed as a surgeon in the last war at New London."

"But the question recurs, why at the under age of fourteen, he engages in the service of his country when the law did not oblige him to do so? The answers, because he loves his country____Because he was born and educated in New England_____In Connecticut____in the Parish of Pachang in the town of Preston, In a Parish where he was accustomed to attend Public worship on the Sabbath, where the Parish Minister was an ardent friend of his country & taught his people to pray for the success of the righteous cause in which it was engaged, where the people at his recommendation on one Sabbath & information of the distresses of the soldiers of the revolution came laden on the next Sabbath with blankets, mittens, shoes, & stockings & other necessaries for their relief filled the broad aisles with them & which was dispatched for their use as soon as the Sabbath & its holy services had ended____where Mothers, or one at least on helping her young son to pit on his knapsack to join the army, took

him by the hand----bid him Adieu---prayed God to help & preserve him but charged him whatever might happen to him never to let her hear that he "died of a wound in his back."

"Because finally he was the son of Colonel Samuel Tyler a member of the same Parish & himself an officer of the revolution: liberty, and finally yielded to the importunity of a son whose juvenile order had been unkindled by his own spirit to take part in avenging its wrongs----If more be necessary, he adds, that he well recollects when he was twelve years old a company of soldiers Commanded by Capt. Carr were passing from Rhode Island to join the continental army tarried at his father's house one nighty and noticed him playing on a fife made from a stalk of elder bush & urged him to enlist as his fifer, he agreed to do so, if his father's consent could be obtained____it was applied for & refused, but from that time he continually importuned his father to enlist, to which he finally consented when he could place him under the charge & as the waiter of his friend & neighbor Capt. Charles Miles with whom he served as stated in his original declaration and before that service expired had occasion to use other weapons than a fife & preform other service that those of a waiter to his captain who was a prisoner to the enemy."

"Having had a good common school education and being a boy of size, he acquired a knowledge of Stuben's manual exercise equal, as he supposed to any of his fellow soldiers & so much so that on the journey of the troops in his next service, he was appointed by his officers a corporal and employed in drilling new recruits and volunteers to the duties of a corporal until ten days before his term expired when on a vacancy occurring the same officers appointed him a sergeant the duties of which he performed for the residue of his tour. The first period of service was one year from March 1781 to March 1782 under Captain Miles_____the second at Fort Griswold for a period of two months as above stated during the duties of a corporal for all the time excepting ten days & that time as a sergeant according to his best knowledge & belief as to the division of time. The third service was in the same fort two months as well be proved by a copy of the pay roll herewith transmitted. Having also written to the commissioner of Pensions & been informed by letter that his papers, which were transmitted in July 1832 were not to be found, he has furnished, as advised a new set of papers & all the additional evidence in his power in relation to his service accompanies by his first papers----his new declaration having been made before the old ones were returned from Washington."

Bishop said he had a knowledge of Steuben's manual. This manual was a drill manual that Baron von Steuben used to train American troops at Valley Forge. The Prussian drill techniques he taught were far more advanced than those of other European armies. The book reduced the motions in the manual of arms to ten and the number of motions to reload from nineteen to fifteen. He also implemented a standard pace and cadence and to keep pace in a march without the use of a drum. The book had instructions on every aspect of operating a military organization. Once Washington's army was trained used the Baron's book it gave the men the confidence that they could defeat the British.

"He respectfully suggest that he had fully proved his services & believing those services to have been meritorious as well as useful to his country & in the performance of which he feels a proud satisfaction whatever the results of this application which he hopes will be granted, but if rejected he hopes it will not be done because it was of an age to tender to perform such services while the Hero of two wars presides over the destinies of his country."

Dated at Norwich the 5th day of December A.D. 1833

Bishop Tyler

Bishop Tyler was granted a pension of $33.99 a year on 8 April, 1834. He wrote back to the pension board and complained that it was too low for his service. He was later granted a pension of $53.99 per year.

Sources: 1. Report of the National Society of the DAR Oct. 11, 1900. 2. Tombstone. 3. Pension Papers S30377. Connecticut Town Marriage Records pre-1870. 4. 1840 Census. 5. U.S. Pensioners 1818-1872. 6. U.S. Revolutionary War Rolls 1775-1783. 7. Children & Youth in a New Nation edited by James Marten.

****

<u>Comfort Tyler</u> age 14

Comfort Tyler was born on 27 February, 1764 in Ashford, Connecticut, and he died on 5 August, 1827 in New York. He married (1) Deborah Wemple who died in 1785 and (2) Elizabeth Brown.

Comfort tried to enlist at the age of 13 but was turned away. At the age of 14 he got his parent's permission and enlisted in 1778. He mainly served light duty at West Point. As a young man he taught school and then became a successful land developer. At times he would bend the law somewhat to get what he wanted.

Sources: 1. History of the Town of Onondaga by Dwight H. Bruce, Onondaga's Centennial, Vol 1, 2. Tombstone 3. Connecticut Town Birth Records pre 1870.1896. 4. Onondaga's Soldiers of the Revolution by the Onondaga Historical Society, 1895.

****

Frederick Unsell age 14

Frederick Unsell was born on 25 August, 1765 in Frederick County, Maryland, and he died on 11 September, 1835 in Marshall, Illinois. He married Jane Masters on 6 December, 1789 in Pennsylvania. He received a yearly pension of $80.

"In the month of August I think in the year 1779 my step Father Peter Kitchens went to Catfish when he was requested to Enlist in the Service of the State of Pennsylvania & he Kitchen did enlist according & requested the officer who had enlisted him to enlist me his step-son also-- accordingly the next day the Recruiting officer came to the field in which I was at work & asked me to enlist. I refused to Enlist without the consent of my mother--Captain Hughes had brought with him for the purpose of aiding him in persuading me to Enlist one Jacob Wolf upon a part of whose farm my step-father live--Hughes told me to enlist and take the bounty & then we would go to the house and See my Mother & if she would not consent that I should go he, Hughes would take back the bounty money & let me off from my engagement upon these conditions. I enlisted as a private soldier & took the bounty money which to the best of my recollection was Ten Dollars. Captain Hughes & myself then went to the house of my Mother to obtain her consent to my enlistment but she would not consent to it being my extreme youth till Captain Hughes informed her that he, Hughes, had enlisted my step Father when she consented that I should go--accordingly the next day I repaired to Catfish to join my company agreeably to my orders from Captain Hughes."

"At Catfish I found a company of about 70 men--I staid at this place a few days & we were then marched from there to, about 30 of us to Caldwell's mill & the rest to fort Wheeling--Caldwell's mill is about 15 or 20 miles from Catfish. I think at Shinter creek there was a small fort there called Caldwell's station. We had been sent to guard this fort & we staid at it Eight months as well as I remember under the command of Lieutenant Morrison from Caldwell's station we were sent to guard a small station the name of which I cannot at this moment remember but I think it was called Ryenson's station. It was on Wheeling creek about 14 miles from Fort Wheeling--at this Station Ryenson's we found the balance of the

company 70 which had Separated at Catfish—at Ryenson's we staid Six months—2nd Lieutenant__(I cannot remember his first name but I think it was Isaac) Peterson was commander at Ryenson's when there, From Ryenson's 30 of us were Sent to Fort Jackson a distance of 20 or 25 miles from Ryenson's on the south fork of Ten mile creek. The officers of the company to which I belonged I can recollect but not having been under the command of any others I can now say the officers were Captain Hughes Lieutenant Morrison & 2nd Lieutenant Isaac Peterson--I was all the time under the command of Lieutenant Morrison at fort Jackson we staid fourteen & fifteen months making a period in all of 28 months all that time I was not at any time engaged in any civil pursuits but was engaged with the spying the situation of & guarding the settlement against the Indians & were not marched against the British at all--we had several of our men killed by the Indians during my service & had frequent skirmishes with them."

"Late in the month of October 1781 or early in the month of November of that year we were marched from Fort Jackson to Catfish where I think we found two hundred men waiting for their discharge. After waiting here over two days my term of Service having expired, I go my Discharge & went home to my parents & served as a private Soldier and duty as such."

Most pension information in other applications end here. The service is described, officers named, and dates are given. Frederick continues with information that is interesting but not necessary for determination of his pension.

"I was entitled to I think 100 acres of land besides the bounty for enlistment we __?__ our provisions regularly from Pittsburg. We got all our clothing also from Pittsburg & was furnished I supposed by the state of Pennsylvania. We had __?__ or very short blue coats trimmed with white & the button holes worked in with white thread--our clothing & provisions were Sent to us from Pittsburg to the different Stations at which were stationed. I was to get $8 I think per month--I drew my pay as did also the rest of the company to which I belonged to from Lieut. Morrison."

"However I took up a part of my pay from one ___Marshall who sold goods had a kind of Store--I took it in goods of him & I suppose he got his pay from Morrison. I think that Catfish (which if I remember right is something like a village) derived its name from an Indian of the name of Catfish who by some reservation perhaps owned the land & who after was sold it to one Hugh Wilson. I was well acquainted with colonel or

General Gibson--He was a large fair-haired man & was married to or at least had an Indian woman of the Decanane tribe for a wife by whom he had Several children whom I have often Seen--I have thus given as full an account of my service as I can & told all I know about the matter."

John Gibson was appointed a General and placed in command of the militia in the Western frontier. In 1763 he and several other men was captured by Indians along the Ohio River. Some of the captives were put to death and Gibson was saved by an Indian squaw. He spent the next year as a captive, and according to some sources may have married an Indian that was the sister-in-law of a Mingo warrior. Frederick Unsell's information may have verified the rumors. Gibson later became governor of the Indian Territory.

Sources: 1. U.S. Pensioners 1818-1872. 2. American Revolutionary Soldiers of Franklin County, Pennsylvania. 3. Pension Papers W22472. 4. Encyclopedia of American Biographies.

****

John Van Auken age 12

John Van Auken was born in October, 1765 in Pennsylvania and he died on 19 March, 1854 in New York. Some researchers give his birth year as 1767 but John gives it as 1765 in is pension application. He was married to Margaret Westfall in June 1788 in Pennsylvania. John received a yearly pension of $88.

"In the year 1778 I served 6 months as a Drummer from the first of April to the 1st of October.

In the year 1779 I served 4 months as a Drummer from the first of May to the first of September.

In the year 1780 I served 4 months as a Drummer from the first of April to the first of August.

In the year 1781 I served 8 months as a Drummer from the first of March to the first of November.

In the year 1782 I served 8 months as a Drummer from the first of March to the 1st of November."

"In the year 1778 I volunteered as a Musician in Captain Jacob DeWells Company of Minute Men in Col Strouds Regiment, think the Brigade Commanded by General Van Horn of Pennsylvania Militia—

resided at that time in the town of Upper Smithfield now called New Milford in the State of Pennsylvania—From the year 1778 I continued in the Service until the year 1782. During Said Service I was in actual Service guarding the Frontier along the Delaware River in the Vicinity of then Upper Smithfield in Said State of Pennsylvania—a Term not less than Thirty Months was engaged in one warm skirmish with the Indians (our common enemy) who during my whole service were very troublesome. Plundering and burning property and killing the inhabitants, and needing the most vigilant watching—I assisted in building our fortifications in the Town then called Upper Smithfield along the Delaware River. During the whole of my service I was in one Regular fought Battle but was concerned in one skirmish equally Dangerous, with the Indians and was during the whole term above mentioned, much exhaustion, and suffering great fatigue."

Sources: 1. Lineage Book D.A.R. Vol. LXI, 1907. 2. Sons of the American Revolution Application. 3. Pension Papers S25827.

****

Peter Van Driesen age 14

Peter Van Driesen was born on 4 May, 1763 in Schenectady, New York, and he died on 13 July 1844 in New York. He married Anna on 24 October, 1793. His pension was suspended after his death, because of his young age when he enlisted and for further proof of service.

"In the year 1777 I served as a private in the New York Militia at least Nine Months *in the Regiment commanded by Colonel Jacob Block in the company commanded by Captain Christian House. In the month of April 1777 I volunteered for one year. I served Seven months as above and then by reason of the illness of my father I procured a substitute by the name of William Pepper who performed my duty for the term of three months. I then returned to his post and served the remaining two months of my engagement."*

Peter also served short tours in 1778, 1779, 1780 and 1781. *"In the summer of 1778 (I think) I was detached with many others as a reinforcement under Lieutenant Tindermand or Tinderman and marched there to Fort Stanwix that while there the Fort was attacked by the Indians in which a private by the name of Nicholas Brown was wounded by a musket ball passing through his body after which said Brown drew a pension."*

Sources: 1. A history of Schenectady During the Revolution by Willis Tracy Hanson. 2. Pension Papers R10859.

****

Cornelius Van Dyck age 14

Cornelius Van Dyck was born on 27 February, 1763 in Schenectady, New York, and he died there on 31 August, 1832. He married Maria Van Petten on 11 March, 1787 in Schenectady. He received a yearly pension of $40.

He enlisted in March 1777 under Captain Abraham Othout of the 2nd Albany County Militia. During the fall and winter he performed three months service at Saratoga, and it is believed that he served throughout the campaign against Burgoyne. During the year 1778 he was twice on duty at Schoharie, and in the fall he served one month at Stone Arabia. He performed considerable service from 1779 to 1781 under various officers.

Sources: 1. A History of Schenectady During the Revolution by Willis Tracy Hanson. 2. New York Pensioners 1835. 3. Pension Papers W26612. 4. Tombstone.

****

Peter Van Dyke age 13

Peter Van Dyke was born in 1767 in Kinderhook, New York, and he died there on 14 October, 1810. He served as a drummer boy in the New York Levies in 1780 in the company of Captain Isaac Bogart. Their assignment was to guard the frontier. He was a member of Van Rensselaer's 4th Regiment of Militia. The unit could not be deployed outside of New York for more than three months at a time.

Source: 1. D.A.R. Lineage Book, Vol. 17.

****

Catherine Van Winkle age 13

Catherine Van Winkle was born on 1 June, 1763 in Hudson County, New Jersey, and she died there on 5 December, 1863. The following occurred on 15 September, 1776 and is from her obituary in the *American Standard*, Jersey City 16 December, 1863:

"From the steeple of the old church at south Bergen, she beheld the British fleet take possession of the city of New York, and not long after, she saw King George's army march past her father's house on its way to

Philadelphia. About this time the British took possession of her father's house—converting it into an arsenal, and they made an attempt to hang her father, because he would not disclose the whereabouts of money which he was supposed to be possessed of. After swinging him from a beam in the house, they left him for dead; but, fortunately, the last spark had not fled, and his life was saved by being cut down by the daughter who is the subject of this notice. While the British were operating in this vicinity, she performed one of those heroic acts for which the women of those trying times were celebrated, in carrying a message, under perilous circumstances, to a section of the American army encamped at Belleville, informing the commandant of a designed night attack upon his forces by the British, and thus giving him time to frustrate the designs."

Catherine and her younger sister Maria often carried messages from Lafayette to General Washington at Belleville, which was a distance of about 7 miles. On one occasion they walked there in the night to warn Washington of a British plot to surround and capture him.

The quick wit of the two girls saved the life of an American soldier one time. The soldier was at their father's house, when a party of British soldiers surrounded their house in search of him. The girls quickly hid him between the feather and straw beds of their own beds, and then they went to bed. When the British soldiers entered their room the girls pretended to be asleep. The soldiers entered their room to search for the soldier. They poked under the bed with their bayonets and searched other areas of the room. Convinced that the American soldier was not in the house they left.

Over the years Washington, appreciative of the loyalty of the family, would visit Catherine's father's house for dinner. On 26 August, 1782 Catherine married George Shepherd who had served in the New Jersey Militia.

Sources: 1. Jersey City and Its Historical Sites by Harriet Phillips Eaton by James Langston
2. Women Patriots of the American Revolution: a Biographical Dictionary by Charles E. Claghorn.

****

John Vanasdal age 13

John Vanasdal was born on September 1763 in Somerset County, New Jersey, and he died in 1826 in Greenbrier, West Virginia. In 1790 he married Ester Shanklin. He received a pension of $35.80 a year for his service. He enlisted in September of 1776, which would make him either twelve years old or just turned thirteen.

"In the month of September in the year 1776 I served one month tour of Militia duty, as a Drummer for Captain Vanbrights company. Vanerster was Lieutenant, immediately after the commencement of this tour the British took possession of New York--our company was then stationed at Bergen, but on the arrival the British retreated to Newark. the Colonels name as well as I can recollect was Nelson. During this service our Regiment marched to Elizabeth town and thence to Staten Island, where we intended to attack a Small fort at Coxtown, on the Island, but was met by an express, who informed our party that another party of Militia were ahead of us for the same purpose—were beaten back—and we retreated to Newark."

John then served several short tours as a drummer in the militia. He served two weeks in May of 1777 under Lieutenant Stocton, one month in May/June in 1777 under Captain Lot, two months in the summer of 1777 under the command of Captain Cumpton, and in September of 177 under the command of Captain Babcock.

"In the spring of the year 1778 (particular months not remembered, but Know that it was the spring of the year after the British left Brunswick) served two months under the command of Capt'n Cornelius Lot, as a Drummer, in Col Wine's Regiment of Jersey Militia. This service was performed at Elizabeth town, in Jersey."

"In the month of June 1778 I served ten days, as a Drummer, in the company commanded by Capt. Lott in Col. Vromes regiment and was in the Battle at Monmouth---this service was an immediate call on the Militia in the neighbor of Monmouth where I resided."

Since John was called for short periods of time, you could assume that he was called when there was a chance of a battle. This would show how important the drummer was in the battle. The Battle of Monmouth had many people killed and was fought in stifling heat. It must have been a real physical and mental test for the teenager.

Source: 1. West Virginians in the American Revolution. 2. U.S. Pension Roll of 1835. 3. Pension Papers S11611.

****

John Vanderburg age 14

John Vanderburg was born on 15 March, 1762 in Poughkeepsie, New York, and he died on 8 December, 1840 in Norway, New York. He received a yearly pension of $30.

"In the Spring, I believe, of the year 1776 I enlisted as a volunteer for nine months into the service of the United States and went to Fishkill on the Hudson river to Muater, where I entered into a company of which one John McKuister was captain and one Joel Wix was Lieutenant one Harry Dodge was I believe, Adjutant of the Regiment to which this company belonged Col Wilson Well commander of the regiment."

"The first move of the regiment was to West Point, where it remained for some time, but the precise length cannot recollect, next the regiment went to White Plain and from thence to Fort Plain in Montgomery County."

"At this place Colonel DuBois commanded the regiment and one Captain White, and I believe Andrew White was Captain of the company to which I belonged, the former Captain John McKuister having been superseded in the __?__ either by death or other causes unknown to me."

"The Regiment or a part thereof including the company to which I belonged pursed the indians tories northerly up the Mohawk. There was a battle about this time a short distance from Fort Plains in the North side of the Mohawk river. I was in that battle, and took 30 or 36 prisoners and three pieces of cannon."

"From this station I went as one of the guard to take the 30 or 36 prisoners before alluded to Poughkeepsie. I think that the regiment was disbanded at Poughkeepsie and that each company returned to the place of residence. I took from a savage the scalp of Colonel Brown who had been killed & scalped at Stone Arabia. I was 14 years old when I entered the service of the United States."

Colonel John Brown was killed on his 36th birthday at the battle of Stone Arabia on 19 October, 1780. The remains of most of the soldiers, including Colonel Brown, were taken back to Fort Keyser and buried together in a pit.

"In the spring of the year 1776 I again listed as a Volunteer for six months and went to Fishkill again where we mustered. The name the Colonel who commanded the regiment was DuBois the name of the

Adjutant was Tollch but I cannot give his Christian name. The name of the captain of my company was Andrew White, the same as the year before. The Regiment went to West Point and thence to Saratoga. I was one of the detachment sent out to destroy the bridges between Fort Edward and Saratoga to prevent the approach of Gen Burgoyne & his army--and this detachment took a spy from Burgoynes Army by the name of Thomas Loveless who was afterwards tried condemned and hung. The company to which I belonged was with several others drawn off from Saratoga to a little before the battle of Saratoga and went to West Point to keep Garrison, and remained there until disbanded again which I think was in the winter, the forepart of the winter of 1777 & 8."

Thomas Lovelace was employed by British General Burgoyne as a spy. Lovelace was a Tory and was hanged for treason from an oak tree.

After the war John lived in Poughkeepsie for about 10 years. In June of 1789 the County Grand Jury indicted him for *"an assault on Margaret Rynders with an intent to ravish her."* He pleaded not guilty to the charge. After several appearances in court over a number of months the action was dropped.

<small>Sources: 1. Vanderburgh/Cook Families Early Settlers of Norway, Herkimer County, New York by William J. Powers, Jr. 2. The Pictorial Field Book of the Revolution Vol 1, 1851 by John Lossing Benson. 3. U.S. Pension Roll of 1835. 4. Pension Papers S16279.</small>

****

Frederick Vaughan age 12

Frederick Vaughan was born 26 November, 1767 in Lebanon, Connecticut, and he died on 10 August, 1845 in Kane County, Illinois. He married (1) Margaret Lucy Blodgett c. 1793 and (2) Catherine Cornett in 1806 after the death of his first wife.

"I entered the Service of the United States under the following named officers as served herein as stated.—I declare that ___?__ to orders issued by Governor Trumbull of the state of Connecticut in a call for volunteers and militia I enlisted and turned out on the 13th day of October 1780 for the term of nine months in the company commanded by Capt Whitiny Backus and in the Regiment commanded by Col. Daniel Tilden after my enlistment as aforesaid I was march'd to New Lebanon from thence to Windham, thence to Colchester and from thence to Norwich Landing where the company took up their quarters from some weeks in the connution with the main part of the Regiment, we were then march'd to

New London near the town where we had our winter quarters and on the opening of 1781 were employed for some time as guards and scouts upon the coast, we were then march'd to Norwich Landing where on the 14th of July 1781 I was discharged having served out the said term of nine-months for which I volunteered."

Colonel Daniel Tilden was a friend of Thomas Jefferson. Tilden commanded a company of men at the Battle of Trenton in which the future president James Monroe served. Years later President Monroe would visit Connecticut and he would visit his old commander where they would reminisce of the early campaigns.

"On the first day of September 1782 I volunteered and enlisted for the Term of three months in the company commanded by Capt John Vaughan [Frederick's father] *in the Regiment commanded by Col Canfield in the Connecticut Troops. Immediately on my enlistment as aforesaid I was march'd to Fishkill on the Hudson River in the State of New York, thence crossed over with the said company to West Point where I was stationed on Garrison duty during the whole of the said tour of three months, was discharged on the first of December 1782 and went home making one years Service in the whole."*

An article was published about Frederick in the Aurora Beacon-News. His grandson, A. Beebe, was interviewed and he stated, *"......grandfather was an old man when I was a youngster. I often heard him speak of his war experience and of General Washington whom he knew personally."* Frederick received a pension of $40 a year for his service.

Sources: 1. Tombstone. 2. Aurora Beacon-News 1959. 3. Pension Papers S32565. 4. Census of 1800, 1820, 1830, & 1840. 5. Revolutionary Soldiers Buried in Illinois.

****

John Vaughan age 13

John Vaughan was born on 13 March, 1763 in Boston, Massachusetts, and he died on 16 April, 1860 0n Amelia Island, Florida. He married Rhonda Miller in 1797 in Georgina. He enlisted on 2 January, 1777 and gave his age as sixteen. He received a yearly pension of $80.

"I enlisted into Capt. Wiley's company of the 8th Massachusetts regiment in the early part of the year 1777 to serve during the War. I continued to serve in the revolutionary army until December, 1780."

He served under Colonel Michael Jackson at the Battle of Saratoga in the fall of 1777. At this battle John's Regiment was in the Brigade under the command of Brigadier General Ebenezer Learned of the right wing of Major General Horatio Gates.

John was discharged at the end of the war and later rejoined the army and fought in the Indian War in Colonel Hamer's Regiment. In 1795 he was a Lieutenant of the Department of the Militia at Burnt Fort in Georgia. There he met his future wife Rhonda Miller. They later made their home on a sea cotton plantation on Amelia Island. It was reported that he may have owned hundreds of slaves. He again joined the army and served in Georgia in the War of 1812.

Sources: 1. The Beville Family by Agnes Beville Vaughn Tedcastle. 2. Tombstone 3. U.S. Pension Roll of 1835. 4. Pension Papers S46292.

****

John Waddill age 11 or 12

John Waddill was born on 1 November, 1764 in Pennsylvania, and he died in 1855 in Hot Springs, North Carolina. His father came to the colonies from Ireland and also served in the war. John married three times. His first wife was Rebecca Sevier the daughter of his Captain, John Sevier, who later became a general and governor of Tennessee. When Rebecca died John married Maria Blanchard, and after her death he married Nancy Haywood. His pension application was rejected, because he needed more proof for his service. He claimed he needed the money, because he was very poor and had a large family to support. He had a total of 16 children.

"At the age of 12 years, being very short for my age, in the year 1776 I did service in Fort Hopson on the North Blank of Nolichucky River, in what was then Washington County, North Carolina. Forty or fifty men guarded the Fort under Captain James Robertson. I was not attached at this time to Captain Robertson's company and do not claim for this Service--I was engaged only in the duty of hawling and in fatigue duty and an occasional sentry duty-- not being on the Service of a Scout. In the summer of 1776 we evacuated the Fort, being too weak to hold it against the Body of Indians, that were advancing to its attack. We retreated to the Sycamore Shoals Fort on Watauga River. We here remained until the 10th of November 1776. Captain Robertson had left the Fort. There were two companies formed at the Sycamore Fort. John Sevier was made a Captain when Captain Robertson left. The Fort fell under the command of J. Sevier. Shortly after we evacuated Fort Hopson. The Indians, of whose

approach we had been warned while in Fort Hopson on Nolichucky attacked us in Fort Sycamore Shoals. The Indians were said to be 600 strong. There were 80 men in the Fort. The Indians attacked us first from the North side, a small part having crossed the River. The others immediately attacked from the South side. Twenty Indians were said to be killed, we lost no man. The Indians commenced attacked in the morning about 9 o'clock. They retired about a mile and there remained for two or three weeks. Some of them went up Holston. They killed three men and a boy, and took a boy prisoner, whom they afterwards burnt. In about two or three weeks they moved off, spreading themselves along the Frontiers, and continued infesting them until Colonel Christian's Expedition. On the 10th of November 1776 I was verbally discharged by Captain Sevier after a Service of four months."

The battle with the Indians that John Waddill describes took place on 21 July, 1776. The Indians reached Fort Caswell and the fort had only 75 defenders. Just before the Indians attacked, a few settlers raced to get inside the fort before the gates closed. Catherine Sherrill, who was Captain John Sevier's future wife he would marry in 1780, was pulled to safety by the Captain just before the Indians captured her.

During the attack James Cooper and a young boy, Samuel Moore went out of the fort after some boards to cover a hut. The Indians attacked them killing and scalping Cooper. Samuel was captured and taken to an Indian town, and there he was burnt at the stake. After a two week siege the Indians retreated.

"When the two companies were formed at the Sycamore Fort, I became a volunteer under Captain Sevier early in the month of July 1776. In December 1776 I volunteered for six months under Captain William Clark in Fort Sevier on the South side of Nolichucky River, Samuel Williams was a Lieutenant and Frances Hughes Ensign. (The officers under Captain Sevier in declarant's first service under Captain Sevier were George Hart, Lieutenant, Elijah Robertson Ensign Joseph Lusk Orderly Sergeant, William Tatum commissary). There was a company of Horsemen under Captain Thomas Price, who were connected with our company in the Fort. There were 40 men in our company and 80 men in Captain Price's. The whole were commanded by Colonel John Sevier. In June 1777, day not recollected, Fort Sevier was evacuated and we were verbally discharged by Captain Clark after a service of six months in Fort Sevier."

"The company of Horsemen was still kept up. I immediately, in the month of June 1777, date not recollected, volunteered for 12 months under Captain Price. Each man was promised five shillings in North Carolina money. Each man found his own horse. We still kept Sevier's Fort as a point of meeting. We ranged from Sevier's Fort to French Broad River, near the Indian trails, to the upper and lower War fords, on French Broad, the Lick Creek and the Big Bend of Chucky. The Indians kept quiet during this time. They made several attempts, but always finding that we were on the look out, they retired. Christopher Cunningham was our Lieutenant; Charles Young Ensign, Southey Nelson was the Orderly Sergeant. In September 1777 we evacuated Fort Sevier and made a Station at Camp Creek, Brown's Treaty line, then the Indian Border line of Washington County, Greene County not being yet struck off. At Camp Creek, we continued our station, until ordered to meet at Fort Sevier in January 1778, when we were discharged. I served under Captain Price seven months as a horseman. Captain Price verbally discharged us and told us, that he would give us written discharges on application. My Father received my discharge and received the pay from Colonel Carter or Colonel Sevier on the delivery of the discharge."

"In the course of the year 1780 I volunteered as a Substitute for my Father under Captain Robert Sevier, C. Cunningham Lieutenant in three short tours against Tories on Holly Creek in Washington County and on Limestone in the same County. I was engaged in this service one month. We disarmed the Tories and found them to the Court held by County Magistrates. Col. Clarke had come over from Georgia with his men to the Battle of King's Mountain in the year 1780 and he was about to return in November 1780. Colonel Clarke came into Washington County and was about 10 miles from Brownborough."

"I volunteered under Captain James McLane one of the Captains under Col. Clarke, in the month of November on the second or third day, 1780, near Brownsborough, Washington County, N. C. at Samuel Sherrell's house. Captain McLane was a Brother in law of Mr. Sherrell and being on a visit to him there met me. Hugh McGill was a Lieutenant of our company. I volunteered for six months under Captain McLane. I joined Colonel Clarke's Corps of about 500 men, and was marched across the Iron Mountain--passing out at the Limestone Cove and through the Rock Creek Gap. We were marched through the country, which is now Burke and Rutherford--crossing the head waters of Catawba and Green rivers and Broad River into South Carolina. In this State we marched through what is now Greenville and Pendleton district, crossing Saluda and Rock rivers. We had occasionally to separate and divided into parties for provisions. We were reunited at Clarke's Station on the South Side of Savannah River, on Pistol Creek, where we remained for several days. Thence we marched towards Augusta on the South Side of Savannah River, recrossing the Savannah below where the Town of Washington in Wilkes County now stands. Thence we marched to Liberty Hill opposite to Augusta about 25 miles from Liberty Hill we were joined by near 200 Carolinians. We killed several Tories in the course of this expedition, and destroyed their property. The Georgians, who had been driven from their homes and whose families and relations had been murdered by the Tories and their property destroyed, were so much exasperated, that they could not be restrained from retaliation. We made an unsuccessful attack upon Augusta, which was garrisoned by Colonel Brown with a body of Tories and Indians. In the attack, we lost a few men, among whom was Captain Price. We remained before Augusta for seven days and then withdrew up to Clarke's Station upwards of 50 miles above Augusta. From this Station we kept the Indians, Creek and Cherokee, in check. We killed some Indians up Savannah River in Pendleton District. The whole body of men under Colonel Clarke were lying near the Quaker Springs. At this place I was discharged verbally by Captain McLane in the month of June 1781, date not recollected – after a Service of seven months. From this place I returned home."

"After the close of the revolution in 1783, viz in the year 1788 I served a tour as a horseman against the Cherokees of the term of three months, commencing in the last days of September or first of October under Captain Samuel Henley and served on the frontiers, in now Blount County."

"My next service was performed under Captain Jacob Tipton, Lieutenant John Lyle and Charles Robinson Ensign, Major Mathews Rhea commanding three companies, called six months levies, I marched under Captain Tipton from Washington County, Territory of the United States, in June 1791, to the North Western territory, and was joined to the Army under General St. Clair—I marched with the company an Army into the Indian Country about 30 miles North East or North of Port Jefferson, where the Army was attacked by the Indians on the fourth day of November 1791 and was totally defeated with a severe loss in killed--wounded and otherwise. After which defeat I returned to his home in Washington County aforesaid after having served from the time of his enrollment in May 1791 to December 1791 a period of nearly 7 months."

"The Indians being troublesome about this time in what is now middle Tennessee, a company of drafted militia was raised in Washington & Sullivan counties under Captain Jacob Brown and Lieutenant John Skiltern in which Company I acted as Ensign for the term of six months or thereabouts the commencing in May 1792 and ending in November of the same year which service was performed as a footman and Ensign in Middle Tennessee--that on the return of the company to their homes, near Knoxville and East Tennessee, I fell in company with a body of soldiers under General John Sevier destined for the frontiers, and joined the company of Captain Greer from Washington, taking the place of Ensign, marched to South West Point on the Tennessee River and assisted in erecting four block houses, which service continued from about the first of November to the last of December a period of near two months. I merely state this last service, after 1783, to show that I belonged to that class called Indian fighters, and doubt not that my name can be found upon the rolls in the War Department of Washington City."

Source: 1. Pension Papers R10977. 2. Life of General John Sevier by Francis Marion Turner.

****

David Wade age 14

David Wade was born on 22 February, 1763 in Elizabethtown, New Jersey, and he died on 22 July, 1842 in Cincinnati, Ohio. He married Mary Jones on 20 June, 1786. His pension was rejected, because it needed to be more specific and have more proof of service. David's son became a Brigadier General for the union in the Civil War.

"I entered the service of the United States under the following named officers and served as herein stated viz Captain William Britton, Lieutenant Jonathan Tenson, Barney Ogden Ensign, Field officers Col Spencer Oliver the names of my Major and General I do not recollect at Connecticut Farms in the state of New Jersey in the month of June 1777 and remained there until we were attacked by the enemy and still remained there three or four weeks after the skirmish and then marched to Chatham and Springfield and was then discharged having served three months."

"I again entered the service under the following officers Captain Matheus Potter, Aaron Tate Lieut or Ensign at Connecticut farms aforesaid and marched to Elizabeth Town and remained there one month and was discharged."

"I again entered at Connecticut farms aforesaid under Captain Craig and marched to the lines between Hackensack and Amboy and remained there one month and was again discharged."

"I entered the company commanded by captain Little and again marched to the lines aforesaid and there remained Guarding and preforming other military duty one month and was again discharged."

"I continued in said company serving in monthly tours not less than twelve months serving at different places sometimes on the lines between Hackensack and Amboy at other times at Richway Elizabethtown Newark and Second River during which time I was in the battle of Springfield and was then wounded in the wrist in the year 1780 and again entered the service soon after under Captain Thomas Clark and sailed from Brunswick for the purpose of taking a British vessel called the Swan loaded with arms, provisions, and clothing and after capturing her was driven by the Storm to Brookleface when me and my party were taken prisoners and taken to New York and was detained on board the prison ship seven months and fifteen days--and was liberated by an exchange of prisoners and again entered the service soon after my exchange under Captain Brookfield and again marched to the lines between Hackensack and Amboy and served one month and was discharged. I again entered the service and served under Captain Townly and served on this line aforesaid one month."

Sources: 1. Sons of the American Revolution Application. 2. Official Roster of the Soldiers of the American Revolution Buried in the State of Ohio. 3. Pension Papers R10981.

****

James Walker age 12

James Walker was born on 8 July, 1762 in Ashford, Connecticut, and he died on 25 December, 1849 in Becket, Massachusetts. He married Sarah Flint on 14 June, 1787 in Connecticut. His father Lieutenant Ebenezer Walker was at the battle of Lexington. James received a monthly pension of $8.

"I entered the Army of the United States as private soldier in the latter part of April in the year 1775 and served seven months in a company by Captain Stephen Knowlton in the first Regiment of the Continental Line (called Genl. Putnam's Regiment) and was discharged on the first day of December of the same year."

James enlisted in February of 1776 for one year in the 2nd Regiment of the Continental Line under the command of Colonel Robert Durgey. He served again in June 1777 under Colonel Samuel Willis in the 4th Regiment, and he was transferred on 8 January 1779 to a regiment of Light Infantry under Colonel Jonathan Miegs in the Pennsylvania Line. He was discharged on 8 January, 1780. His final enlistment was from April 1781 to the close of the war. He was in a company of Light Dragoons in the 2nd Regiment under Colonel Sheldon.

"I was in the engagement at Bunker's Hill on the 17th June 1775. I was at Trenton at the taking of the Hessians on the 25th Dec, 1776. I was at the battle of Stoney Point on the 15th July 1779. I was at the taking of Fort __?__ on Long Island near the close of the war. I was at the battle of __?__ Frog's Neck and many others, the dates of which I do not recollect."

James was at the Battle of Bunker Hill and was probably serving in the 3rd Connecticut regiment under the command of Colonel, later General, Israel Putnam. He may have been the officer who gave the order *"Don't fire until you see the whites of their eyes."* However, these words are also attributed to several other officers.

At the Battle of Trenton James was a member of the 2nd Regiment of the Continental Line and a part of St. Clair's Brigade. This brigade entered the lower end of town near the bridge, and engaged the Hessians on King Street. The Hessians under the command of Colonel Johann Rall formed at the lower end of King Street and tried to advance. The Americans held their line forcing the Germans to retreat to an orchard. By 9:30 in the morning the fighting was over and the Hessians were captured.

At the Battle of Stony Point James was under the command of Colonel Return Jonathan Megis who had been given to the 3rd Connecticut Regiment. The plan was to attack the fort at Stony Point at midnight under complete silence. Four regiments, one under the command of Megis, would carry out the attack.

General Wayne had told the men that if anyone attempted to retreat or sulk in the face of danger, the officer next to him was to put him to death. To keep the element of surprise the soldiers were ordered not to speak or load their muskets and risk a discharge. Any man that broke the rule would be put to death.

One officer later reported that one man disobeyed the order. *"The column was ascending the hill. The man left his station and was loading his musket. I ordered him to return and desist from loading his musket. He refused, saying he did not understand fighting without firing. I immediately ran him through the body."*

Sources: 1. Washington's Immortals: The Untold Story of an Elite Regiment Who Changed the Course of the Revolution by Patrick O'Donnell, Chapter 24. 2. Pension Papers S43231. 3. D.A.R. Lineage Book, Vol. 20.

****

Peter Walker age 14

Peter Walker was born on 13 December, 1765 in Massachusetts, and he died on 17 April, 1838 in Ohio. He married Dianna Brower on 20 April, 1788. She received a yearly widow's pension of $88. He served as a fifer in the 8th Massachusetts Regiment under Colonel Michael Jackson. He enlisted on 27 October, 1780 two months until his 15th birthday, and he served until December 1783.

Sources: 1. Pension Papers W4371. 2. Official Roster of the Soldiers of the American Revolution Buried in the State of Ohio.

****

William Walker age 12

William Walker was born 23 September, 1763 in King & Queen County, Virginia. He stated in his pension application that in May of 1775 he was first drafted into the militia, *"and marched to Yorktown, for the purpose of securing and guarding the Military Stores there deposited, and prevent the forces under Lord Dunmore from taking possession or removing them."*

John Murray, fourth earl of Dunmore, was Virginia's royal governor. Tensions between the colony of Virginia and Great Britain had increased, so he removed gunpowder from storage in Williamsburg in April of 1775. This caused Lord Dunmore to lose his already weakened support of the colonists in Virginia. He fled to Hampton Roads in the summer and declared martial law. His troops lost the Battle of Great Bridge in December, and his fleet later shelled Norfolk. Soon after that he fled to England.

William Walker reported, *"...about the time of the battle of Great Bridge and Norfolk was burnt, I was drafted for a third time in the militia...and marched to Yorktown for the purpose of guarding the town*

American forces I believe was between fifteen & sixteen hundred this battle was fought in the month of October 1780 in two or three days after the Battle was fought 12 or 15 of the Tories that had been notorious for killing many of Whigs, was executed by hanging them, the prisoners were marched off I believe for Charlottesville in Virginia."

"In the month of March 1781 I volunteered under the command of Captain William Cabell, Tilman Walton (my brother) Lieutenant, mustered in service at Lovings Gap, marched from thence to Charlottesville Cabells Company were put under the command of Baron Steuben, Marched to Point Fork, driven from thence with great loss of Stores some were killed, others wounded with the loss of Prisoners, retreated to Albemarle old Court House Joined the Army of Lafayette marched to Richmond soon after Williamsburg where soon after Joined the combined forces of the American Army under the command of Genl Washington and other Distinguished Officers of the American Revolution which Resulted in the Capture of Cornwallis on the last of October 1781. I returned to my father's in Amherst County about the first of the year 1782. I served by Country two years and six months for which I never received one dollar found my own Clothing and Horse."

An American arsenal was located at Point Fork, Virginia where the James River and Fluvanna River meet. In May of 1781 Baron von Steuben relocated at the arsenal with the 5th Virginia and groups of the militia. British General Cornwallis sent a force under the command of Lt. Col. Simcoe to capture Point of Fork. When Von Steuben saw Simcoe's troops he believed that the entire army under Cornwallis was near, so he abandoned the arsenal leaving it to the British.

The Virginia General Assembly ordered an investigation into Von Steuben's conduct and blamed him for the loss of supplies. Von Steuben defended his decision to abandon the arsenal based on the knowledge he had. The Baron was exasperated with the General Assembly and their questioning of his decision. He later said, *"Every farmer is a general...but nobody wishes to be a soldier."*

Sources: 1. Fluvanna County, Virginia Order Book, 1779-1782. 2. Lineage Book National Society of DAR Vols. 61-62. 3. Tombstone. 4. South Carolina Marriage Index 1641-1965. 5. Walton Family Papers 1804-1910. 6. Revolutionary Soldiers in Alabama. 7. U.S. Pension Roll 1835. 8. Pension Papers S17184

****

Israel Warner age 9

Israel Warner was born on 27 May, 1768 in Bennington, Vermont and he died on 22 January, 1862 in Aurora, Illinois. He married Esther Bartholomew in 1801 and they had a son and two daughters. He served as a waiter and messenger for his father Colonel Seth Warner.

Colonel Warner was 6'3" with brown hair and blue eyes and he was a very experienced woodsman and leader. He began his military career as a teenager in the French and Indian War. This might explain why he had no problems with his 9 year old son being in the military. Colonel Seth Warner took part in the capture of Fort Crown Point, the Siege of Quebec, and the Battles of Hubbardton and Bennington.

Before the war he was a co-founder, along with Ethan Allen and Remember Baker, of the Green Mountain Boys. Before the revolution the Green Mountain Boys, also known as the Bennington Mob, became a militia organization that helped the settlers in New Hampshire defend themselves against New York. The two colonies were at odds over who owned certain grants of land.

New York Justice of the Peace John Munro made the mistake of trying to arrest Seth's cousin Remember Baker. Colonel Warner struck the New York official with the flat of his cutlass. This resulted in the Colonel being outlawed by the authorities in New York, who hunted him but never captured him.

When the revolution began, the Green Mountain Boys became the nucleus of the Vermont militia and they selected Seth as their leader. Other members of the militia stayed with Ethan Allen. In 1777 Seth Warner enlisted his 9 year old son Israel to serve in his command.

"I was a private in the company commanded by Capt Gideon Bronson in Col. Warner's regiment of the army of the revolution."

"I enlisted and was enrolled at Manchester Vermont, in the year 1777 and was in actual service during the whole of the war of the revolution and was discharged at West Point in 1783."

The above statement is all Israel put in his pension papers about his service. Years later he wrote a letter to Henry Stephen, a Vermont historian, *"Gen Stark and my father consulted to send a letter to Gen Stafford on Stafford Hill and father said, "Put Israel on a horse, and told me not to spare horse flesh, and not to speak to anyone but tell them that the enemy was just into Bennington. When I got to Gen Stafford, he came out and I gave him my father's letter. He wanted me to stay until the next morning but I told him I must go back to give information and rode the best part of the night but the volunteers did not arrive until the next day at evening..."*

This crucial message enabled the militia to be reinforced and meet a detachment of British General Burgoyne's army in battle on 16 August, 1777. The victory was a decisive one by the Americans. Nearly all of the 900 Hessian force was killed or captured. General Burgoyne's main army was now reduced by 1,000 men which helped to lead to his defeat at Saratoga. Colonel Warner's brother, Daniel, was killed during this battle. The United States issued a commemorative stamp in 1927 in honor of the battle.

Young Israel stayed in the army until 1783 and after his discharged he was 15 years old and a 6 year veteran. His father had already left the army and was in poor health due to several battle wounds. Israel returned home and in 1784 his father, at the age of 41, died leaving the family in financial trouble. Harper's Monthly magazine publish an anecdote (below) in December of 1864 and it was re-published several times after that. Some historians have serious doubts if the story is true. If it is not true, it should be.

"When Colonel Warner died just after the revolution, his farm was heavily mortgaged. Seth had spent all his energies supporting the Revolution, and the family finances had suffered. Seth's untimely death left his family facing a certain loss of their farm. George Washington, who held Seth Warner in high regard as a Patriot, personally rode to the Warner farm in 1789 and counted out the silver coins to the exact sum required to retire the mortgage and save the farm. Washington wanted this act of Generosity kept a secret."

After the death of his father Israel help to support his mother as a land surveyor in Whitehall, New York. This is probably why Israel waited until the old age of 33 to marry. In 1853 he moved his family to Illinois and in his old age he lived with his daughter Esther Kenyon. Israel died at 94 in 1862 and was among a few of the surviving soldiers of the Revolution. He received $6.33 a month for his service.

Sources: 1. Tombstone. 2. Historical Memoirs of Colonel Seth Warner, from the Natural and Civil History of Vermont, Vol. 2. 3. Sons of the American Revolution Fox Valley Patriot Profile. 4. Plaque at the Big Wood Cemetery. 5. Census of 1790, 1810, 1830, and

1840. 6. U.S. Pensioners 1818-1872. 7. Sons of the American Revolution Application. Pension Papers S42610.

****

Nathaniel Warner age 13

Nathaniel Warner was born on 4 July, 1767 in East Haddam, Connecticut, and he died on 16 April, 1847 in Chautauqua County, New York. He married Ruth Colier on May 20, 1795 in Bristol, Connecticut. They had thirteen children. He enlisted in the 5th Regular Connecticut Line in January of 1781.

He applied for a pension on 11 October, 1832, *"I was born at East Haddam in the State of Connecticut, at which last mentioned place I entered the service of the United States in the Revolutionary War in or about the month of January 1781, for three years. That I enlisted under Capt. Richards, in Col. Sherman's Regiment, and Genl Huntington's Brigade. In the spring of the same year, I was mustered at New Haven & there marched off to the Highlands where I joined the army. Went from thence to Pine's Bridge and stayed about six weeks & then returned under Capt. Richards to the Highlands and from thence I crossed the river to West Point, where I remained the principal part of the time (being the whole time in service) until I was discharged at Westpoint, in September 1783, having served about two years & eight months on Continental establishment that in consequence of my cutting wood for the use of the army, I was discharged before my tour of service expired."*

When Nathaniel first wrote to the pension bureau he mistakenly gave his birth date as 1769, which would have made him 11 years old when he enlisted. This young age resulted in red flags thrown on his application. As a result his pension was rejected. He did send a letter stating the mistake and that the real year of his birth was 1767. Unfortunately, he would have to send another statement of his service and his witnesses would have to again write him letters of support.

One witness of support, Cornelius Philips, was a soldier that served with him. Cornelius wrote on 20 June, 1836, *"At the time he (Nathaniel) enlisted he was a stout rugged boy of sufficient age & capacity to bear arms as much as any man..."*

Nathaniel's pension was finally granted nearly five years after he first applied. He received $80.00 a year for his service. His wife applied for and received his pension after his death in 1847. She had to submit proof of marriage, his service, and statements from people that knew Nathaniel. His final pension file consisted of 141 pages.

Sources: 1. Children & Youth in a New Nation edited by James Marten. 2. Tombstone. 3. Census of 1800, 1830, & 1840. 4. History of Chautauqua County, New York. 5. U.S. Pensioners 1818-1872. 6. U.S. Revolutionary War Rolls 1775-1783. 7. Records of the Massachusetts Volunteer Militia. Pension Papers S23990.

****

Simpson Warren age 13

Simpson Warren was born in 1762 in Halifax County, Virginia, and he died after 5 February, 1834. For his service of six months he received $20.00 a year.

"I entered the service of the United States under the following named officers & served as herein stated: I resided in Halifax County in Virginia where I enlisted, I enlisted under Captain Rogers, Lieut Street & Ensign Shackelford in the Virginia line & was marched through Petersburg Williamsburg & Yorktown to Groyn Island where the British were then stationed for three months, but served out six months. I served three months against the Indians at the Long Islands of Holston."

Sources: 1. U.S. Pension Roll of 1835. 2. Pension Papers S18262.

****

Bildad Washburn age 12

Bildad Washburn was born on 24 August, 1762 in Kingston, Massachusetts, and he died there on 18 September, 1832. He married Lucy Adams on 12 September, 1784 in Massachusetts. He received a yearly pension of $88.

"I enlisted in April 1775 soon after the battle of Lexington for eight months as Drummer in the company under the command of Capt. Peleg Wadsworth belonging to the Regiment of Col. Theophilus Cotton."

"I enlisted in the Spring of the year 1776 in the company under the command of Capt. William Weston which company was stationed at the Gurnet in the outer harbor of Plymouth to garrison the Fort. I served as Drummer in said company for the space of two years."

Sources: 1. D.A.R. Lineage Book, Vol. 45. 2. Pension Papers W14113.

****

Mason Watts age 13

Mason Watts was born in 1765 in Frauquier County, Virginia, and he died on 122 March, 1850 in Jennings County, Indiana. He married Deborah Ryler on 18 June, 1793, and they had 13 children. For his service he received $100.00 a year.

"I enlisted in the armey of the United States in the year 1778 with Elias Edmunds and served in the second state Regiment of Artillery of the Virginia line under the following named officers Lieut Blackwell, Capt Edmunds & Col Thomas Marsahall, the names of the other officers I do not recollect in Fauquire County Virginia and marched from there to York & remained there guarding the fort, erecting breast works & performing other military duty two years & six months—and was then marched to South Carolina and arrived within fifteen miles of the Hanging Rock where Bluford was defeated by Tarlton and from there retreated back to near Guilford Court House where the army under Genl Gates came up, and was then ordered on with his army to Deep river & remained there a few weeks, and was then marched back to Richmond Virginia and discharged having served three years the time for which I enlisted."

Sources: 1. Census of 1820 & 1830. 2. Kentucky Marriage Records. 3. Roster of Soldiers and the Patriots of the American Revolution Buried in Indiana. 4. U.S. Pensioners 1818-1872. 5. Tombstone. 6. Pension Papers S17760.

****

Edward Wayland age 12

Edward Wayland was born in May of 1763 in Fairfield County, Massachusetts, and he died there on 9 May, 1833. He married Mary Bennet on 2 August, 1786. He received a yearly pension of $58.33.

"I enlisted in the service of the United States in the War of the Revolution in January 1776 at Stratford in Fairfield County for three weeks in the company commanded by Zachariah __?__ and the Regt was commanded by a Col. Ward. I with the rest of the company marched from said Stratford the place of my enlistment to New Haven & took shipping & crossed into Long Island & continued on the Island & served in said company for two months and a half."

Edward served numerous other short tours for the next few years. In April of 1777 he was drafted and served for six months in a guard house on a beach. In December of 1777 he enlisted and marched to Sawpits in New York, where he guarded the Lines.

"I marched to Sawpits in the state of New York to guard the lines so called which was infested by the British & Tories who were constantly making incursions into the country to murder & plunder its inhabitants."

In 1778 Edward was a substitute for Isaac Nickels for three months in the state militia. In July 1779 after the burning of Fairfield he served for one month doing guard duty. In 1780 he served two months guard duty on the coast of Long Island Sound.

Sources: 1. D.A.R. Lineage Book, Vol. 63. 2. Pension Papers W18242.

****

Sheffield Weaver age 12

Sheffield Weaver was born on 18 November, 1763 in Swansey, Massachusetts, and he died on 26 July, 1836 in Fall River, Massachusetts. He married Lydia Reade on 23 August, 1792. He received a yearly pension of $80.

"Sometime in March of the year 1776 my father & brother Nathan Weaver, returned to Freetown where we then resided. My brother Nathan Weaver was taken sick with a malady called the "Kings evils" which caused him to return home."

The King's evil is a tuberculous swelling of the lymph glands. It was once believed that it was curable by the touch of royalty. Once the person was touched the monarch would present a gold coin to the person. This amulet that contained the monarch's healing power would be worn around the neck on a ribbon, which would keep the condition from returning.

"My father remained at home some two or three days. I then went with my father as a substitute for my brother Nathan Weaver to Newport in Rhode Island and joined the company commanded by said Jonathan Brownwell in Colonel Lippitts Regiment."

"I remained there doing duty as a soldier & creating a Fortification now called Fort Adams, until the British Fleet have in sight off Newport. When the British fleet have in sight we were ordered to & did disperse & collected & drove to the north end of the Islands of Rhode Island all the cattle & sheep we could find & finally got all or nearly all

the cattle & sheep so collected on the Main. We then mounted three or four cannon on the hill to the eastwards of the Ferry so called. By aid of these cannon we prevented the British, who had followed us, from coming onto the Neck, so called & prevented them from procuring any cattle or sheep so far as we could learn."

Sheffield served again in 1778 for nine months guarding prisoners. He served for several months in 1779 and in 1780 he served as a driver for supply wagons.

Sources: 1. D.A.R. Lineage Book, Vol. 37. 2. Pension Papers S29539.

****

Isaac Webb age 14

Isaac Webb was born on 11 October, 1766 in Williamstown, Massachusetts and he died on 16 August, 1847. He received a yearly pension of $30.

"I entered the service of the United States in the latter part of the month of February in the year 1781. I enlisted in Sunderland in the county of Bennington in the State of Vermont for nine months in Capt Daniel Comstocks company Colonel Fletchers Regiment and General Roger Enos's Brigade of the Vermont troops. I joined the company when I enlisted and we marched to Pittsford Fort in Rutland County Vermont, about 25 miles from Ticonderoga Captain Comstocks company and Capt Whites company of the same Regiment were the only two companies stationed at Pittsford Fort and Major Armstrong commanded the Head Quarters of the Regiment at Castleton Fort about 20 miles distance where General Roger Enos had his head Quarters: I served in Captain Comstocks company at Pittsford Fort ads aforesaid private for 5 when I was transferred to Captain Brookins company of the same Regiment at Castleton Fort."

"In the Spring of 1782 I again enlisted at Williamstown in Massachusetts in the Massachusetts line for three years but was not called out."

Sources: 1. Pension Papers S11703. 2. Rolls of the Soldiers in the Revolutionary War, 1775 to 1783 in Vermont by Chauncey L. Knapp.

****

Isaac Webb age 14

Isaac Webb was born on 5 March, 1761 in Stamford, Connecticut, and he died on 11 May, 1840 in Clearfield, Pennsylvania. He married Mary Weed on 2 October, 1791 by the justice of the Peace Charles Webb (possibly his father). He received a yearly pension of $80. Some researchers report that Isaac was born in 1766. In his pension statement Isaac says it is 1761.

"I was born of the fifth day of March 1761. In the year 1775 in the month of July to the best of my recollection. I then resided in the town of Stamford entered as a private in captain Edward Shipmans company of Connecticut troops in Col Chas Webbs regiment. Then being about fourteen years of age and marched to Boston. In the Spring in the month of March 1776 to the best of my recollection I set out with the troops on their way to New York and accompanied them as far as Stamford, when, Col. Charles Webb, my father gave me a leave of absence and I did not join the army in New York."

Isaac served in Colonel Webb's 7th Connecticut Regiment. The Captain of the 3rd Company was Captain Nathan Hale. Hale was captured by the British and hanged as a spy on 22 September, 1776. His final words were reported to be, *"I regret that I have but one life to lose for my country."* There is no proof that he ever said this.

This author found it strange that right after he joined, his father would send him home. One possible reason is that spring was the planting season. Isaac's father could not be home to tend to the planting and the oldest brother was serving in the army. There were several more kids at home younger than Isaac. It is possible that his father sent him home to be the man of the farm and get the crops planted. Isaac's older brother would be killed in the war in 1780.

"I think until the month of July where I resumed till the first of November 1776, when I obtained leave to return home. In the Spring of 1777 I had the small pox and did not rejoin the army nor did I serve with any regular force during this year in the following 1778 but remained at home at Stamford was engaged for one half my time in doing voluntary duty as coast and town guard & repelling the invasion of the enemy from Long Island & New York and was in several warm engagements with the enemy during these incursions in one of which fifteen men were killed."

"In the month of March 1779 I entered a company commanded by Captain Jesse Bell and stationed as a Town guard at the town of Stamford and Greenwich. The company was raised to serve one year from the first of January 1779 and I about the first of March took the place of one George Finchely & served out his time till the first of January 1780. During this time Captain Bells company had several skirmishes with the foraging parties of the enemy, one of which I particularly remember, in the town of Stamford in which three of Captain Bells men were killed & one wounded and one of the British taken prisoner being wounded-------."

"In the year 1780 & 1781 I had the fever and again remained at home in Stamford but was engaged a number of times in repelling parties of the enemy and one occasion I was with a party that captured a gun boat from the enemy---."

"In January & February 1782 to the best of my recollection I believe I served a two months tour under Captain Samuel Lockwood at Greenwich and Horseneck, during which time I marched with Capt Lockwoods company to Pennsylvania, West Chester County of New York and captured several British officers, after a firm resistance after setting the house on fire the company retreated and were harassed on our return by the enemies horse [troops]."

"On the ninth of July 1782 I was drafted under Capt Amos Smith of the Connecticut militia, and under Major Lawrence at Stamford doing light duty as a guard at Greenwich & Stamford & repelling the incursion of the enemies foraging parties from New York. I entered on this duty about the first of August to the best of my recollection & remained on duty until the news of peace in the spring of 1783."

The Connecticut coastline and Long Island was separated by only a few miles. Connecticut was largely under the control of the patriots, and Long Island was firmly in control of the British. Connecticut offered supplies of food and lumber the British needed for their army. Sometimes the British would raid on land, and other times they would raid using whaleboats. These whaleboats were shallow-draft boats ideal for shallow water, much like the Vikings in Europe used centuries earlier.

One time a British foraging party came back from a raid in Connecticut bringing some needed cows. The local newspaper mocked them by publishing the following poem:

*"In days of yore the British troops
Have taken warlike kings in battle;
But now, alas! Their valor droops,
For Gage takes naught but—harmless cattle."*

Sources: 1. Connecticut Town Birth Records pre 1870. 2. Sons of the American Revolution Application. 3. U.S. Pension Roll of 1835. 4. Pension Papers W4851. 5. The American Revolution: A Very Short Introduction by Robert J. Allison.

****

Elijah Weeks age 12

Elijah weeks was born on 23 August, 1764 in Brookfield, Massachusetts, and he died on 24 June, 1834 in Cayuga County, New York. He married Sarah Batchelder on 24 March, 1793 in Massachusetts He received a yearly pension of $42.64 for his service. Elijah served in the 10th Massachusetts Regiment.

"I enlisted in the army of the United States in the fall of the year 1776 in a regiment of Massachusetts line into Capt. Josiah Smiths company Col. Thomas Marshalls regiment and General Pattersons Brigade for the term of three years."

"I marched to Mount Independence, retreated from there to Skenesborough. I was with the baggage was fired upon by the British, Indians, & Tories at Skenesborough & forced to retreat. The building in which the baggage was placed was destroyed together with the baggage, continued to retreat to Fort Ann had a skirmish at Fort Ann & continued to retreat before Burgoyne until I arrived at Stillwater or Bemis Heights where I found the main army. I was a waiter to my father Thomas Weeks was transferred to the Commissioner Dept. After the taking of Burgoyne I marched with the army to the south and joined General Washington at Valley Forge and went into winter quarters. My father and I were discharged the winter of 1779."

Elijah was part of a small body of troops that left Fort Independence and sailed up Lake Champlain to Skenesboro. This group of about 600 men moved into Fort Anne and were attacked by troops from Burgoyne's army. The Battle of Fort Anne, called a skirmish by Elijah, was fought on 8 July, 1777. The battle lasted for nearly 2 hours until the Americans finally abandoned the fort and retreated. The Americans later joined up with the main army and defeated Burgoyne at Saratoga in the fall of 1777.

Sources: 1. Genealogy of the Family of George Weeks of Dorchester, Massachusetts by Robert D. Weeks, 1885. 2. D.A.R. Lineage Book, Vol. 31. 3. Sons of the American Revolution Application. 4. Pension Papers W29774.

****

Joshua Wells Jr. age 13

Joshua Wells was born on 19 January, 1763 on Long Island, New York, and he died on 10 October, 1855 In New York. He married Hannah Finch c. 1785 on Long Island.

He served as a private at the Battle of Long Island on 27 August, 1776 in Captain Paul Reeve's Company in Colonel Josiah Smith's Suffolk County 1st Regiment of Minute Men. Joshua's father, Corporal Joshua Wells age 34, served in the same company. Both men are listed on the company rolls.

The New York militia was under the command of General Greene, who gave orders to Colonel Smith to march to Brooklyn. General Greene arranged his regiments to defend against a frontal attack by the British. The British unexpectedly attacked on Greene's left flank. After many skirmishes the Americans began to retreat. In a show of goodwill the British allowed the Americans to retreat to Manhattan. When the Suffolk 1st Regiment returned home it was disbanded.

Sources: 1. New York in the Revolution as Colony and State by New York Comptroller's Office, James Arthur Roberts. 2. Sons of the American Revolution Application. 3. Lineage Book of the D.A.R. Vol. LXI, 1907.

****

Nathan West age 13

Nathan West was born on 22 March, 1763 in Newport, Rhode Island, and he died on 1 April, 1835 in Minerva, New York. He married Martha Titus on 16 July, 1787 in Vermont. Martha, or Polly as she was called, is said to have killed a bear which came into their barnyard to kill a sheep. A wax statue of her killing the bear with a club is said to have stood in the Educational Building in Albany, until that part of the building burned many years ago.

Nathan served as a fifer from early 1777 to 1783 in the Rhode Island Line. He received a yearly pension of $96 for his service.

"I enlisted in January or February 1777 in the company of Capt. William Allen in the regiment commanded by Col. Jeremiah Olney in the Rhode Island Line of Troops."

Nathan belonged to the 2nd Rhode Island Regiment under the command of Colonel Olney. They fought in the Battle of Red Bank on 22 October, 1777. At this battle the Americans successfully defended Fort Mercer against 2,000 Hessian soldiers. The unit also fought at the battles of Monmouth and Springfield.

On 1 January, 1781 the regiment was consolidated with the 1st Rhode Island Regiment and re-designated as the Rhode Island Regiment under the command of Colonel Olney. The Regiment fought at the Siege of Yorktown in 1781.

Sources: 1. D.A.R. Lineage Book, vol. 41. 2. Pension Papers W19596.

****

Ezekiel Whaley age 12

Ezekiel Whaley was born in 1765 in Lenoir, North Carolina, and died in 1830 in Lenoir, North Carolina. He married Nancy Ann Jarman around 1784.

He enlisted 20 July, 1777 as a fifer, *"In the company commanded by Captain John Sheppard in the 10th Regiment of the United States and I continued to serve in the said Corps or in the service of the United States until the 4th day of July 1783 when I was discharged from service of the United States on James Island that I was at the siege of Charleston and taken prisoner."*

The 10th Regiment was organized during the summer and fall of 1777 at Kinston, North Carolina as a unit of the North Carolina Troops named Sheppard's Regiment. The regiment was assigned to the main Continental Army as Sheppard's Additional Continental Regiment. They did not see any action.

The small regiment was depleted due to desertions and illnesses. The small number that made it to the winter quarters at Valley Forge in 1777 were disbanded and attached to the 1st and 2nd North Carolina

Regiment. Ezekiel was placed in the 2nd Regiment under Major Hardy Murfree and Colonel John Patton.

Ezekiel saw action at the Battle of Monmouth and the Siege of Charleston. At Charleston the regiment was captured and taken prisoners by the British. He remained a prisoner of war from 12 May, 1780 until his release on James Island on 4 July, 1783.

For his service Ezekiel received 1,000 acres and $8.00 per month. According to the census he lived on a farm in Lenoir for the rest of his life. The 1830 census shows that Ezekiel was in possession of one young female slave.

Sources: 1. U.S. Census 1790, 1810, 1820, and 1830. 2. U.S. Pensioners 1818-1872. 3. U.S. Revolutionary War Rolls 1775-1783. 4. A Guide to the Battles of the American Revolution by Theodore P. Savas and J. David Dameron. 5. Pension Application for Ezekiel Whaley S42064.

****

Reynolds Whaley age 14

Reynolds Whaley was born on 5 October, 1762 in North Kingstown, Rhode Island, and he died in October of 1844 in Attica, New York. He married Elizabeth Odell and he received a yearly pension of $28.33.

"In the month of March in the year 1777 at North Kingstown in the state of Rhode Island I enlisted as a private soldier and as a substitute for one James Martruss who was drafted as one of the Rhode Island Militia for the term of Forty Days. I joined the company of Militia under the command of Captain Rathbone Lieutenant Sweet and no ensign. I was discharged in the month of April 1777. I and the said company were stationed there to guard the Sea Shore."

Reynolds continued to enlist for short tours while guarding the shore and the military store house in the area. He served in August of 1777, March of 1778, April of 1779 and his last tour was in July of 1782. He was in no battles or skirmishes during his tours of duty.

Sources: 1. U.S. Pensioners of 1835. 2. Sons of the American Revolution Application. 3. Pension Papers S11771. 4. Register of the Pennsylvania Society of the Sons of the Revolution, 1888-1898.

****

Leonard Wheatley age 14

Leonard Wheatley was born on 15 December, 1765 in Prince William County, Virginia, and he died in Kentucky in 1855. He received a yearly pension of $20.

"I entered the service in the Militia of Virginia in the month of May 1780. I entered as a substitute for John Wheatley under Captain Evans and served a tour of three months. I lived in Prince William County Virginia when I entered the service. I was first marched to a little town called Dumphries on Quantico Creek and remained there about a month and then marched to Falmoth, then to Hunters Works, and guarded there 3 or 4 weeks. I was then marched to Dumphries and was there dismissed."

"I again entered the service as a substitute for Charles Cappage in the month of July 1781. The company was collected at Dumphries and remained there some time. I was then ordered to March up to Colchester a little town between Dumphries and Alexandria. On the march up to Colchester, we met General Washington with the Army coming down to Yorktown and then received orders to return and Started expecting to go to Yorktown by way of Rackoon ford. Before we reached Rackoon ford we were ordered to halt and not to march on to Yorktown."

"I was dismissed about the time Cornwallis surrendered and then marched home. After I had been at home a few days the brother of Alexander Mcdonnold came to me and requested me to go and take the place of his brother Alexander McDonnall who was then sick in service. I then started and met the British prisoners near Falmouth, where I took the place of Alexander McDonnall, and marched up to the Barracks about six miles above Winchester, and after remaining at the Barracks Some time I was discharged by Captain Ballard who was my Captain during the time I was a substitute for Alexander McDonnall."

Sources: 1. Tombstone 2. U.S. Pensioners 1818-1872. 3. Census 1820, 1830, and 1840. 4. Pension Papers S20783.

****

Benjamin Wheeler age 13

Benjamin Wheeler was born on 7 February, 1764 in Rehoboth, Massachusetts, and he died on 6 February, 1836 in Bloomfield, New York. He married Celia Buffinton on 28 July, 1782. He received a yearly pension of $95.

"I entered the service in the Spring of the year 1777 my brother Simeon Wheeler was drafted in Captain Simeon Cole's Company and I was a substitute for my brother Simeon and was a waiter to Captain Cole for the term of three months."

Immediately after he was discharged, Benjamin enlisted Captain Nathaniel Carpenter's company in Colonel Lane's Regiment and served as a waiter to Captain Carpenter.

"In the Spring of 1778 was a volunteer in captain Israel Hicks Company and served three months, and after this was in Captain Israel Nichols Company for four months and believe the Regiment was commanded by Colonel Slack. I was on Rhode Island when General Sullivan retreated and was in the picket guard."

For the next two years he served four tours of several months each. During this time he served in and around Rhode Island.

"In the Spring of 1881 I enlisted in Captain Jabez Barney's Company for five months and was marched to Providence, Suffield, and Sitchfield to Fishkill and then to West Point and joined Colonel Jacksons Regiment and done duty at West Point and was fourth Sergeant in said company and was discharged at West Point. The same day I again enlisted for four months in captain Olneys company at West Point and soon after went to verplanks point and soon after to Jersey and went with the Army to Yorktown in Virginia and was there at the capture of Cornwallis. I saw General Washington at Providence, at West Point and at Yorktown. After the Battle at Yorktown was sent back to west Point and was there discharged and went home. It was near the last of December when I got home."

Source: 1. Pension Papers S15484.

****

Hezekiah Wheeler age 14

Hezekiah Wheeler was born on 30 April, 1763 in Stafford Springs Connecticut, and he died on 31 October, 1833 in Rowe, Massachusetts. He married Meribah Muler on 29 July, 1788. He received a yearly pension of $80.

"I served in the Revolutionary War about 16th March 1778 during the war in Col. Henry Sherburne Elijah Blackman Capt Continental line. I was transferred and I was discharged I think under Col Webb &

discharged in 1783. I was in Col Hasnitter (?) Regiment at the Taking of Cornwallis."

Hezekiah belonged to Sherburne's Additional Continental Regiment, which was formed on 12 January, 1777 with men from Rhode Island and Connecticut. At Yorktown Hezekiah was under the command of Lt. Colonel Alexander Hamilton. Hezekiah finished his service in 3rd Continental Regiment in the Connecticut Line under the command of Colonel Samuel Batchley Webb. The Regiment was disbanded in June 1783.

Sources: 1. Lineage Book National Society of the D.A.R. Vol. 27, 1898. 2. Tombstone 3. U.S. Pension roll of 1835. Pension Papers W6486.

****

Isaac Wheeler age 14

Isaac Wheeler was born in 1764 in New York, and he died on 12 September, 1846 in Dearborn, Indiana. He married Eleanor Johnson on 16 January, 1787. He received a monthly pension of $8. He served as a drummer in the 1st New York Regiment and was present when the regiment fought against the Onondaga Indians in April 1779. He was also present at the Battle at Yorktown.

"I enlisted during the war in the month of November 1778 at Johnstown in now Montgomery County in the State of New York in a company by Captain Van Reasselar of the first regiment commanded by colonel Goose Van Schaick on the Continental establishment. I continued to serve until the 8th day of June 1783 when at the close of the war I was discharged at West Point."

Source: 1. Pension Papers S40681.

****

Isaac Wheeler Jr. age 8

Isaac Wheeler Jr. was born on 6 June, 1768 in New London County, Connecticut, and he died there on 11 May, 1856. He married Hannah Holmes in March 1790 and they had seven children. After her death he married Olive Lisson in March 1810 and they had four children.

Isaac Wheeler at the age of 29 re-enlisted in 1776 and took with him into the army his two slaves, Enoch, Caesar, and his oldest son eight year old Isaac Jr. Young Isaac was made a fifer in the same company of his father. They served under Lieutenant Colonel Christopher Lippitt in Lippitt's Rhode Island Regiment State Troops.

Isaac Jr. had a desire for a uniform and told his father he would not play his fife without a proper uniform. His father employed a Newport shoemaker to make a pair of red topped high boots for his son and he told Isaac Jr. that this was the uniform for boy fifers. The boy was pleased with his uniform and played his fife.

Once during camp the young Isaac contracted camp fever, and his father carried him in his arms on a pillow by horse back to their home. Isaac Sr. was given a 20 day pass to go home and nurse his son back to health. Once recovered the two rejoined the regiment. Isaac Jr. was a great favorite with the rest of the troops. They taught him to dance and to sing their camp songs. One of the favorites that Isaac sung was,

> "I have been beat and I have been banged,
> And all for desertion;
> If ever I enlist for a soldier again,
> The devil may be my surgeon."

Isaac Jr. was at the Battle of Rhode Island on 29 August, 1778. During the American retreat from Newport he was brought off the island on the back of Jim Freeman, who was an Indian of the Charlestown Tribe and in later years he made an annual visit to see the boy he had saved.

Near the end of the war, being large for his age, he engaged in privateering. The ship on which he served was captured by the British. The captured Americans were placed below decks on the British ship except for Isaac. Because of his young age he was permitted to be on the upper deck. A British Lieutenant who had a pompous attitude and was prone to drink too much took a dislike toward the young boy. Toward the evening the Lieutenant gave the boy a kick and with a curse told Isaac to get out of his way. This anger caused Isaac to knock the man down with a single swing. Isaac was immediately seized and taken below with the promise that in the morning he would be placed in yardarms. Fortunately, during the night the French retook the ship and Isaac was set free in Chesapeake Bay. Isaac later saw the surrender of Cornwallis at Yorktown.

In Isaac's later years he was described as a large strong man of athletic build and given to boxing, wrestling, and jumping. It was said that he never weighed less than two hundred pounds and often two hundred and fifty pounds. He applied for a pension late in his life but failed to obtain one. The person he entrusted with his papers lost most of the important ones.

Sources: 1. Chapter Sketches: Connecticut D.A.R. 2. D.A.R. Magazine, Vol 7, July-December 1897.

****

William Wheeler age 14

William Wheeler was born in 1763 in South Carolina, and he died on 28 December, 1832 in Hall, Georgia. He married Nancy Davis on 16 November, 1785 in South Carolina. She received a yearly widow's pension of $96.

"I Enlisted for the term of three years sometime in the winter of (say January or February) 1777 in the State of South Carolina in the company commanded by Captain Montgomery in the 6th Regiment commanded by Colonel Henderson in the line of the State of South Carolina on the Continental Establishment--that soon after my Enlistment Captain Montgomery resigned his commission and Captain Warley took the command of the said company under whom I continued to serve (to wit Captain George Warley) attached to the 6th Regiment commanded by Colonel William Henderson line in the State of South Carolina until just before the surrender of Charleston to the common Enemy in 1780 when I was discharged from the service in the State of South Carolina."

Sources: 1. U.S. Pensioners 1818-1872. 2. Pension Papers W6485.

****

John Skinner Whitcomb age 12

John Whitcomb was born on 10 June, 1766 in Colchester, Connecticut, and he died on 8 December, 1858 in Mehoopany, Pennsylvania. He married Sarah Marsh in 1789 in New York. She received a yearly widow's pension of $80.

In 1811 John moved his family to Pennsylvania near Laceyville. There he built a frame house from logs that he cut, and he rafted them 60 miles to the nearest sawmill. Once cut he loaded them into a boat and poled back up the river. He ground his own paint using an old kettle and a cannon ball. He raised his own apple orchard from seeds he brought from Connecticut.

"On the 11th day of March 1779 I entered the service of the United States as a substitute for Eli Catlin in the wagon department, in a company raised by Capt Simion Catlin for three years service and during service was commanded by Capt Bonds and attached to the department commanded by Col Hay & remained in that service as a substitute until the 25th day of June 1780."

"In the fore part of July in the same year I enlisted into the United States service under Capt Sloper for three months, was mustered in Farmington & marched to Horse neck where we remained for some time engaged in small scouting parties against the refugees & cowboys & remained there until the expiration of the said term of service."

"In the month of May 1781 I again entered the wagon department as a substitute & remained in that service eight months under command of Capt Hughes & stationed at Fishkill & was discharged the first of January 1783."

"In the later part of April 1782 I enlisted for eight months among those that enlisted to fill vacancies in the standing or regular army. Was mustered at Fishkill to the Highlands opposite West Point & was there attached to a continental Regiment commanded by Col Growner & in a company commanded by Capt Durkee in the first Regt. & 1st Brigade commanded by General Huntington. We lay at the highlands through all the summer & in the fall went over to West Point for winter quarters. At the expiration of eight months was discharged."

"In April 1782 I entered the service as a substitute for Timothy Catlin in a company commanded by Capt Nichols in a Regt commanded by Col Willet. I was stationed in the Mohawk River at Fort Plain for the defense of the frontier of New York. I remained there five or six months when another substitute by the name of Marshal was sent to take my place & I returned home."

John Whitcomb belonged to the first Connecticut Regiment under General Jedediah Huntington. It was formed in 1776 and disbanded at West Point on 15 November, 1783.

Sources: 1. U.S. Pension Roll of 1835. 2. Tombstone 3. Pension Papers W3377. 4. The Whitcomb Family in America: a Biographical Genealogy by Charlotte Whitcomb, 1905. 5. Lineage Book D.A.R. Vol. 53, 1905.

****

Abraham White age 14

Abraham White was born on 21 June, 1762 in Washington County, Maryland, and he died on 22 June, 1853 in Vermillion County, Indiana. He married three times, (1) Elizabeth Morse in June of 1777, and she died 2 years later. (2) Abigail White, his first cousin, in 1800, and she died in 1807. (3) Amelia "Molly" Hopewell in 1808 in Kentucky. Abraham's father was also a soldier, and he died in 1777.

"I entered the service of the United States under the following named officers & served as herein stated, that is to say, 1st in the month of January (day of month not recollected) in the year 1777 I entered as a volunteer & served as a private under Captain Zadoc Springer & served two months on the west fork of the Monongahela at Pricketts fort, Garrison a Captains command & under said Captain Springer."

"In the month of September (day of the month not recollected) in the year 1778 I was drafted into a company under command of Captain James Daugherty. My Colonel's name Evans, Major Zadoc Springer Corps under command of Genl. McIntosh on an expedition against the Indians West of the Ohio river. While on this expedition the Corps to which I belonged built fort McIntosh on the Ohio River & fort Lawrence on a branch of the Muskingum, served four months (4 months) dismissed in January 1779 at Fort McIntosh."

"In the month of August 1781 (day of month not recollected) I entered as a volunteer under Captain Ichabod Ashcroft, in a Regiment under command of Col. McLeary, whose Corps commanded by Genl. Clarke as an expedition to the falls of Ohio the term for which I engaged was six months to which I belonged was dismissed near Wheeling on the Ohio River."

"In the month of March 1782 I engaged as a volunteer to keep guard at a station called Bans fort in the Conemaugh a branch of the Allegheny River in the term there was only a guard of ten men under John Ashcroft a Sergeant, dismissed at said fort sometime in May."

"Immediately after being dismissed from Bans Fort I engaged as a volunteer in a company commanded by Capt. Thomas Carr on an expedition against the Indians under Capt. Crawford to Sandusky plains & was in the action at said plains commonly called Crawford's defeat the names of field officers which I recollect on said expedition were David Williamson 2nd in command Thomas Gaddis 3rd in command."

The Crawford Expedition took place between 25 May, 1782 and 12 June, 1782. The soldiers were attempting to destroy the Indian town of Sandusky, which was the headquarters of the hostile Indian tribes. The Indians were aware of the soldier's mission and had moved to another village about 8 miles away. The Indians also sent runners to other tribes and to the British seeking their help.

Crawford and his men were attacked by the combined forces of the Indians and British. The Americans found themselves surrounded, and their retreat turned into a rout. Numerous soldiers, including Crawford, were captured and later tortured to death. Most of the Americans, including Abraham White, managed to find their way back to safety. (This author's 5th great-grand uncle, Captain Thomas Ogle, was killed in this battle.)

Sources: 1. Census 1840 & 1850. 2. Tombstone 3. Pension Papers W6473.

****

Goven White age 13

Goven White was born on 4 January, 1766 in King George County, Virginia, and he died on 4 January, 1835 in Robertson County, Tennessee. In his pension application Goven gives his birth date as 4 January and his wife gives his death date as 4 January. He married Ann Fergusson in June 1786. She received a widow's yearly pension of $43.33.

"I volunteered, and entered the service of the United States as one of the State Troops of the State of Virginia, in the year 1779, and served about Ten months under the following named officers to wit Captain Langhorn Dade, who was in a short time Succeeded by Capt William Bombray (Major not recollected) Colonel Stith, General Weaden, that at the time I entered the service he resided in the County of King George State of Virginia (does not recollect the time when he left service after his first tour of Ten months,) I remained at home some time, how long does not recollect, and was drafted, and again entered the service of the United States, and marched to York Town served three months was at the siege of Little York, was disbanded at Albemarle Barracks."

Sources: 1. U.S. Pensioners 1818-1872. 2. Twenty-four Hundred Tennessee Pensioners. 3. Pension Papers W1014.

****

James White age 14

James White was born on 8 September, 1763 in Culpeper County, Virginia, and he died in 1843 in Rapides, Louisiana. His pension was rejected due to lack of proof of service.

"I entered the service at the County of Culpeper in the State of Virginia in the Company commanded by Captain John Slaughter Robert Covington was Ensign of said company, John Roberts was the Major of the Battalion to which said company was attached, and that I cannot say with certainty who was the Colonel who commanded said Company but thinks it was Colonel __ Thorn from the fact that he was sometimes with them. We rendezvoused at Culpeper Court House and were marched from thence to Albemarle Barracks for the purpose of guarding a body of prisoners, who were called Hessians and kept and guarded at that place for the term of two years and nine months, I cannot now say whether said Company was of volunteers or regular soldiers, I think we were generally in uniform. That it was as well as I can now remember in the year 1778 that I so entered the service as aforesaid, I recollect that it was through the persuasion of an uncle of mine that my father permitted me to enter the service, and whether my father ever received any Compensation for my services I do not know--I was with said Company during all the time aforesaid and served as above stated."

Source: 1. Pension Papers R11417.

****

Howell Whitmore age 14

Howell Whitmore was born on 25 December, 1765 in Brunswick County, Virginia, and he died on 2 January, 1847 in Gilmer County, Georgia. He married Nancy Smith on 24 March, 1801 in Orange County, North Carolina. She received a yearly widow's pension of $34.33.

"I entered the service as a private soldier sometime in the month of August in the year Seventeen hundred eighty by volunteering under the command of Captain William Watson Major Peyton Skipper & Col Tucker was marched to Taylor's Ferry on the Roanoke River in the State of North Carolina where I joined Colonel Butler's Regiment and was marched from thence to Guilford Court house North Carolina and joined the Army commanded by General Greene and was in the engagement fought at that place saw at that place Generals Lawson & Stephens Cols Mumpford, Washington & Lee the two latter having the command of the Cavalry. I

marched from thence to Ramsey's Mill in Chatham County North Carolina the company to which I belonged being then disbanded I returned to Virginia Greenville County the place where I lived."

Brigadier General John Butler commanded Howell Whitmore and the rest of the members of the North Carolina Militia at the Battle of Guilford Courthouse on 15 March, 1781. Howell and his comrades were placed along a split-rail fence that faced the road the British were expected to use to reach the battlefield. General Greene rode along the fence, which offered the men no protection, and asked the militia to fire two volleys and then they could withdraw. Unfortunately, once the battle began the North Carolina boys withdrew early and many without firing a shot.

Days after the battle General Greene was very critical of the North Carolina militia. He blamed the defeat of the Americans on *"the shameful waste which prevails among the N. Carolina Militia."* Greene's criticism of the militia became so intense that his friend Joseph Reed cautioned him on what he said in public, because it could cause serious problems between the Continental regulars and the bulk of the country. He suggested for Greene to develop an attitude toward the militia that he should hold toward his wife: *"Be to their faults a little blind, and to their virtues very kind."*

"I entered the service having served seven months I remained at home a few days when I was called out again by my Captain joined Col Tucker's Regiment and marched to Surry Court house in the State of Virginia remained there a few days and was marched from thence to James town where I remained there 4 or 5 weeks and was discharged by my Captain."

Sources: 1. U.S. Pension Roll of 1835. 2. Pension Papers W509. 3. The North Carolina Continentals by Hugh F. Rankin.

****

Alexander Williams age 14

Alexander Williams was born in 1762 in Augusta County, Virginia, and he died after 1832. He received a yearly pension of $50. According to the 1820 census he owned 4 slaves.

"I was drafted as one of the Malitia of the said County of Augusta in or about August 1776 and attached to the company under the command of Capt Henderson of said County, and with other men marched under the command of Col William Bowyer of Augusta to join the army under the

command of Gen'l McIntosh to the Western frontier for its protection against the Indians--I joined the army at Fort McIntosh where I remained for some months the precise time I do not recollect, that from Fort McIntosh, I marched with other troops to Fort Laurence where I remained but a short time, and was then with other troops discharged and reached home in the month of Jan'y 1777."

"In March 1777 I engaged to serve as a substitute for a certain Archibald Lockridge who was one of the drafted Malitia of Augusta County, and marched as such substitute from the Town of Staunton in the County of Augusta to the protection of the whites on the western frontiers of Virginia against the Indians, under the command of Capt William Kincaid of the Augusta Militia I was stationed for some time at a Block House called Louders on the Western fork of the Monongalia river that while there I volunteered with other men to go to another Block house under the command of Ensign James Steele of the Augusta Malitia, the name of this latter Block house I do not now remember, that after remaining at the last named place for a short time, I was with other troops regularly discharged."

"In the month of February 1781 I volunteered as one of the Malitia of Augusta County, and marched with other troops from the County of Augusta to the State of North Carolina, I marched in the company commanded by Capt Thomas Smith of the Augusta Malitia, and under the command of Col George Moffett of the Augusta Malitia, I joined the american army near Guilford Ct House, and was enlisted among other troops as a rifleman and placed under the command of Col Campbell of the rifle Corps--I was attached to the troops under the command of said Campbell in the battle of Guilford in March 1781. I received no wound, I was regularly discharged with the other malitia with whom he marched from Augusta."

Alexander was a member of the Augusta County Militia at the Battle of Guilford Court House fought on 15 March, 1781. His commanding officer, Colonel George Moffett, became ill and had to leave the field that day. Alexander was a Virginia rifleman, and he was placed in the first line on the left flank. Captain Thomas Smith led the rifle company, and he was under the command of Colonel William Campbell.

Many of the riflemen were local men that heard there was going to be a battle. One man was home plowing when he heard the firing of cannons. He grabbed his gun and jumped on his horse to join the fight. Another man, a local Irishman called John Larkin, arrived in time with a "spit of meat in one hand and his rifle in the other." He was told he could join the men, so Larkin calmly "sat down and striking his spit into the ground beside him. He ate from the meat while preparing his rifle for the oncoming battle."

As the British advanced upon the Americans, the sharp-shooting Virginia rifleman began taking targets of opportunity rather than firing in synchronized volleys. At first the Americans were pushed back on the left flank, until the encouragement of Lt. Colonel Lee and Colonel Campbell resulted in their men taking the fight back to the British.

"I next marched as one of the drafted Militia of Augusta County under the command of the same Capt Thomas Smith with whom I had marched to North Carolina the spring previous, I rendivouzed at the Widow Teese's and marched from their under the command of Col Samuel Lewis to Richmond I think about August 1781 from Richmond I marched to various points in the lower part of Virginia, the names of which I do not now recollect, I remember of being station for a few weeks near Williamsburg, and from thence I marched with the troops attached to Gen'l Mulenburgs brigade to York Town. I was present at the Siege of York and remained there untill after the capture of Cornwallis in October 1781 when I was discharged."

Sources: 1. U.S. Pension Roll of 1835. 2. 1820 Census. 3. Pension Paper S6410. 4. Long, Obstinate, and Bloody: The Battle of Guilford Courthouse by Lawrence E. Babits & Joshua B. Howard.

****

Caleb Williams age 14

Caleb Williams was born on 12 April, 1767 in Glastonbury, Connecticut, and he died on 20 December, 1854 in Troy Pennsylvania. He received a yearly pension of $46.66, and after his death his wife received a yearly pension of $112.

"I enlisted regularly in the service of the United States under Captain Bissel Phelps, and was put in charge of a tem, employed for the purpose of carrying the baggage of the French, in the year 1781. The team was the property of an individual by the name of Blush. I took the team at Hartford Conn. I was employed in the continental service, drawed pay as a soldier, and considered myself as such, and was not engaged by the owner of the team. The team was hired by the government as I supposed. After arriving at Annapolis where the baggage was shipped, the team

returned. I was the journey changed the first team to another, which I was in charge of until they returned to Connecticut. Both teams were ox teams, the first had one horse before the wagon. The last team I drove (during the whole of the last term of service) was the property of the government."

"I was employed in first drawing the magazines, from Fishkill Barracks to Fishkill __?__ Afterwards in drawing timber at West Point to repair the fortifications, afterwards in drawing forage, for Sheldon's light horse until discharged at Horse Neck."

Fishkill Barracks was established in 1776, and it became the largest of the Continental army depots. Beside the supplies it was also a barracks for 2,000 soldiers. It contained a prison, hospital, storehouse, armory, and powder magazine.

Sources: 1. D.A.R. Lineage Book, Vol. 117. 2. Pension Roll of 1835. 3. Pension Papers W9165.

****

Hickman Williams age 13

Hickman Williams was born on 21 or 22 February, 1763 in Franklin, North Carolina, and he died in March 1826 in North Carolina. He married Winna Clifton who died in 1837. Winna never applied for the widow's pension of $80 a year, so her children applied for it after her death. Their claim was rejected.

Hickman joined the Wake County, North Carolina Militia the last of May 1776. He served in the 3rd Regiment commanded by Colonel Jethro Sumner. Hickman was discharged in the summer of 1777, which was several months before the regiment went into battle.

Sources: 1. U.S. Pensioners 1818-1872. 2. Pension Papers R11629.

****

Lew Williams age 14

Lew Williams was born on 19 June, 1763 in Dinwiddie County, Virginia, and he died on 22 November, 1838 in Rutherford County, Tennessee. He married Winfred Sovell in November 1803 in Virginia. He received a yearly pension of $36.50.

"I was born 19th of June 1763 Dinwiddie County State of Virginia, and in the year 1777 at Brunswick Court in said State I entered the service of the United States as a substitute for Henry Harrison, under Capt John Williams,--Maj Williams commanded the Corps--and there was two other companies of militia under the same Officers. I was marched from Brunswick down to Hick's Ford now called Ball ford and then to Sea Cay old fields to South Hampton County and at this place the Corps was encamped, three or four weeks, and news reached the commanding officer from Norfolk, that the services of the Corps was not then wanted, and I was discharged."

"In the same year I became a substitute for Jehu Peoples, and joined the service under Capt James Marshall Col Richard Elliott then commanded, and there was then in service several other militia companies--Elliott marched the Court to Hick's Ford and to Cabin Point on James River, and I was stationed at this place until discharged."

"In the latter part of 1777, at Brunswick Court house I again entered the service as a volunteer under Captain Turner Benun & rendezvoused at the long Ordinary two miles above Petersburg--At this place Gen Muhlenberg and Col Rolly Dowman commanded. There were other Troops than the Corps of which I was attached at the long Ordinary. I was marched to the Chuckytuck Mills, and there Major Boys took the command, for here Gen Muhlenberg and Col Dowman left the Corps and were stationed at or near Suffolk,--at this place I remained in camp until the expiration of his three months Tour, and I was discharged."

"In the year 1778 I again joined the service at Brunswick Court house, in a troop of light horse, under Captain Peter Jones, and was marched by South Hampton Courthouse to near Norfolk-- and here I was in a skirmish and was wounded by a British trooper in the knee, which has disabled me up to the present moment--General Muhlenberg commanded at the time at that section of Country--I did not recover from my wound until my term of three months service had expired and then I was discharged."

"In Brunswick County 1781, I volunteered under Capt James Harrison, and was marched to near Petersburg, where Gen Robert Lawson and Maj John Holcomb took the command of the Corps. I was marched to Poutry Fork, and there joined Baron Steuben--from here we retreated to Prince Edward and then to Charlotte--and at this point, Gen Lawson marched his Corps to James River and crossed at Carter's Ferry, and after one day's March, he joined the Marquis de Lafayette, and marched with him towards York. The time for which I had joined the service having expired on the March, declarant was discharged."

Sources: 1. U.S. Pensioners 1818-1872. 2. Pension Papers W1344.

****

John Willis age 14

John Willis was born in Virginia in 1766, and he died probably in Tennessee after 1833. He received a yearly pension of $24.44.

"In the fall of 1780 about the first of September, I entered the service of the united States as a volunteer under Captain Shelton in the County of Henry State of Virginia, and was marched under said Shelton to a place called the Hollow otherwise, flower gap under the Blue Ridge against the Tories, who were very numerous in that part of the country at one time my company was stationed at __?__ a considerable time then again at a place called Hedgepeth's near the blue ridge, and was on duty at different points guarding the Settlements against the incursions of the Tories--the Lieutenants name attached to said company was Francis Barret. after continuing three months, me with the other volunteers were marched home and arrived at home about the tenth of December 1780."

"Again about the first of January 1781 hearing that Lord Cornwallis had Entered North Carolina in pursuit of General Greene, and that volunteers were much needed to aid Genl. Greene in repelling the Enemy from the country me with Several others residing in my neighborhood in the county of Henry, volunteered a Second time under Captain Shelton, and marched from home with the Regiment commanded by Col. Lyon about the 18 of January 1781 towards Guilford Court House and when the troops got within about twenty miles of Guilford Court House in North Carolina, the said Col. Lyon after having loitered on the way--He determined to return home, and would not march any farther alledging that his force was too weak to oppose the Enemy and that his retreat might be cut off should he proceed any farther, and accordingly I was marched home under Col. Lyon--which we reached about the 1st of april having been out on duty other three months."

"Again about the first of October 1781 I marched as a volunteer under Captain Shelton to York Town in Virginia to aid in the capture of Cornwallis--but upon reaching the head quarters of General Washington, and when within about a days march of York Town, information reached Captain Shelton that Lord Cornwallis had surrendered, me with the company commanded by Capt Shelton returned back, and reached home

about the first of November having served fully one month on that march--making in the whole seven months and ten days."

Sources: 1. U.S. Pension roll of 1835. 2. Pension Papers S1603.

****

Godfrey Williston age 14

Godfrey Williston was born in 1763 in Springfield, Massachusetts, and he died on 23 December, 1832 in Onondaga County, New York. He married Lydia Smith in February 1793. She received a yearly widow's pension of $79.45.

He was sometimes called Joseph because his uncle, who he lived with after the death of his father, asked if he could call Godfrey by the name Joseph. This was the name of Godfrey's father and his uncle's brother.

"I enlisted in the Army of the United States in the year of 1777 in the month of April with Captain Charles Colton & served in the third Regiment of the Massachusetts line under the following officers Colonel Greaton & Major Oliver Capt. Charles Cilton. At the time I enlisted as aforesaid for the term of three years."

"After I enlisted I joined the army & was stationed at Springfield until sometime in the summer of 1777 when I was marched with Captain Coltons Company from thence to at or near Stillwater to escort General Gates on his way to join the northern Army until the surrender of Burgoyne & the day of his surrender was marched to Albany with Capt. Coltons Company where I remained with said Company until the spring of the year 1788."

"In the spring of 1778 was marched to West Point & staid a short time & was marched from there to White Plains where I remained with said company until late in the fall of 1778 when I was marched to Roxbury in Connecticut where I remained a short time from thence to a station between Fishkill & Peekskill where I remained during the winter with said company during the winter with said company & the succeeding summer was stationed at different places a long the lines, at ___?___ & went into winter quarters at a place near Peekskill & was discharged the next April."

Godfrey was at the Second Battle of Saratoga and the Battle of Bemis Heights fought on 7 October, 1777. The 3rd Massachusetts Regiment was under the command of Major General Benjamin Lincoln and part of the right wing of the army in Brigadier General John Nixon's Brigade.

After the war there was great unhappiness among many people in Massachusetts about the depreciation of the paper currency. Riots occurred around Springfield and Northampton in May and June of 1782. One of the leaders, Rev. Samuel Ely, was arrested and placed in jail. On June 12 Ely was rescued by a mob from the Springfield jail. Godfrey was called out to join the militia for six days to retake Ely. Ely later surrendered, and after much discussion over several days everyone dispersed and went home.

Sources: 1. Revolutionary Soldiers Resident or Dying in Onondaga County, N.Y., prepared by Rev. W.M. Beauchamp for the Onondaga Historical Association, 1863. 2. U.S. Pensioners of 1835. 3. Early Days in New England by Henry Martyn Burt & Silas Wright Burt. 4. Massachusetts Soldiers and Sailors in the Revolutionary War.

****

Payson Williston age 14

Payson Williston was born on 12 June, 1763 in Orange, Connecticut, and he died on 30 January, 1856 in Easthampton, Massachusetts. He married Sarah Birdseye on 12 September, 1790. He received a yearly pension of $33.33.

"In the month of March 1778 I entered the company of Infantry commanded by Capt. Silas Kimberly as a substitute for some person whose name I cannot recall to mind. While serving in that company the same was ordered and marched into Newhaven on my way from Hartford. I served as a private in said company for the term of two months. We were employed in keeping guard on the shore of Long Island."

"In the month of March AD 1779 I again entered the service as a private in the company commanded by Capt. Phinehas Bradley of Newhaven. The company was divided into four sections or detachments two of which were stationed at Easthaven in the state of Connecticut and at Newhaven and the other at Westhaven. This was a company of Artillery in the Connecticut State Troops I served in the company stationed at Westhaven."

"I was the __?__ guard every third day. Then on each of the nights of the first and second and third of July 1779, I was on guard all night. On the morning of the fourth of July about sunrise the British landed on the shore of Long Island in Westhaven. While returning from guard that morning I met the section of my company with the Field piece and joined them. We fired once upon the enemy then retreated before their superior force to Newhaven from the west. The company found the enemy entering Newhaven on Broadway so called and retreated before them to Easthaven where we remained until the enemy left Newhaven on tuesday night. The enemy fired upon us as we left the harbor. The company were then ordered to hold themselves in __?__ to march in half an hours warning to Fairfield when the enemy next landed but were not sent for."

"I returned in the company as a private until the first of November 1779. I entered Yale college as a member of the Freshman class. I well remember on the day that I entered college returning to Westhaven and finishing my tour of duty and keeping guard the remainder of that day and night. I entered college after the regular term had commenced and said term commenced six weeks after the second Wednesday of September of that year."

In 1779 Payson went to Yale College and graduated from there in 1783 as a minister. One man who remembered him years later as a teacher wrote about Payson, *"I have heard of instances in which young men who went to study with him were so unpleasantly impressed by his abrupt and dogmatical manner, that they refused to remain with him a single day."*

Sources: 1. Biographical Sketches of the Graduates of Yale College. 2. Pension Papers S17787.

****

William Wills age 14

William Wills was born on 16 April, 1765 in Virginia, and he died on 10 August, 1834 in Kentucky. He married Mary Ballard on 22 May, 1787 in Virginia. He received a yearly pension of $60.

"I was born in the State of Virginia on the 16th day of April 1765 in the County of Albemarle. My father Entered the service of the US in the year 1779 sometime in the summer of that year but cannot say with certainty what month. I was very young. I am also unable to say what were the names of the officers but I well remember of having to convey to my Father some money soon after he commenced his march. I recollect I

overtook the Army somewhere near Richmond and my Father offered me if I would take his place he would give me a Negro girl. I declined having been so young not exceeding 14 years. My father however told me that I should stay and perform the duty assigned him. But my father's conducting me to Major Muchelwain and asking him if he would accept of me in the room of my father for the term for which he was drafted which I think was under a draft for 18 mons. The Major immediately observed he would. That he would not give me for two of him. I was then taken by the Major as his cook & I so continued sometimes cooking for him and at other times for General Washington until the Term had expired for which my father was drafted."

"I then continued with the Army marching through Virginia and Pennsylvania. I well remember the time the American Army lay siege at York I then was a cook for the same Major which took place in 1781 sometime in the fall. I then staid at the Barracks for two months and was discharged by my Major But have lost it."

Sources: 1. D.A.R. Ancestor #127133. 2. U.S. Pensioners 1818-1872. 3. Tombstone 4. Pension Papers S31484.

****

Cornelius Wilson age 11

Cornelius Wilson was born c. 1766 in Mecklenburg, Virginia, and he died on 22 June, 1822. He married Anney Stephens. Cornelius was the youngest of four orphaned boys. The two middle boys enlisted in the army and the oldest stayed home with Cornelius. The two boys that enlisted were later killed in the war. In October of 1777 Cornelius ran away and joined the 5th Virginia Regiment and he served as a fifer in Captain William Fowler's Company part of Colonel Josiah Parker's Regiment. The older brother went after Cornelius and tried to talk him into returning home. Captain Fowler said Cornelius would be taken care of so the older brother also enlisted.

Cornelius received a split lip from a sword so he then became a drummer. He served at Valley Forge in the Commander-in-Chief's Guard as a drummer. He probably was present at the Battle of Monmouth and the Siege of Charleston. The name Cornelius Wilson is listed in the Valley Forge muster roll project. Company pay rolls show that he received $7 and 1/3 dollars per month while he was in the army.

Sources: 1. Obion Company History Book Vol. II by William Herrell Wilson. 2. Let the Drums Roll. Veterans and Patriots of the Revolutionary War Who Settled in Maury County Tennessee. Bicentennial Publication of the Maury County Historical Society by Marise Parish Lightfoot. 3. U.S. Revolutionary War Rolls 1775-1783. 4. The Commander-in-Chief's Guard Revolutionary War by Carlos E. Godfrey, M.D.

****

Robert Wilson age 12

Robert Wilson was born on 1 April, 1763 in New York City, and he died on 30 May, 1811 in New Hartford, New York. He died of a fever while traveling from his home to Utica, New York. Robert married Amelia Dunham at her father's home on 9 January, 1803. Amelia applied for a widow's pension under the name Amelia Hickcox, Her second husband, Mr. Hickcox, died before she applied for the pension. She received a widow's yearly pension of $240.

Robert's father died when he was young and Robert was trained in the duties and hardships of military life by his mother's brother Captain James Gregg. Robert enlisted at the start of the war at the age of 12 as a fifer under the command of his uncle, Captain Gregg. Robert was commissioned as ensign on 9 June, 1781 making him at the age of 18 the youngest ensign in the army. He served as ensign in Captain John Graham's Company, 1st Regiment in the New York Line.

At the surrender at Yorktown Cornwallis, feigning illness, sent General O'Hara with his sword, to lead the beaten army to the field of humiliation and surrender. Having arrived at the head of the line, General O'Hara advanced toward Washington, and, taking off his hat, apologized for the absence of Cornwallis. The American commander-in-chief pointed him to General Lincoln for directions. Lincoln escorted the royal troops to the field selected for laying down their arms.

There were twenty-eight British Regiments and each were to surrender their flag. The British had twenty-eight captains, each with their regiment's flag facing twenty-eight American Sergeants ready to receive the flags. American Colonel Alexander Hamilton was the officer of the day and had appointed Ensign Robert Wilson to conduct the ceremony. The British captains refused to present their flags to non-commissioned officers. Hamilton, to spare the feelings of the British captains ordered Ensign Wilson to receive the flags and then hand them to the American Sergeants. The scene is depicted in an engraving in the *Pictorial Field*

Book of the Revolution, Vol. II by Benson J. Lossing. There is also a detailed account of the ceremony.

Robert's pension information was made by his wife in 1853. He had apparently given her a detailed account of his service.

"He entered the service as a Fifer in the company commanded by Captain James Greigg who was his mothers brother & which company belonged to General Clintons Brigade as I was informed & believes at the age of about twelve years & served under his said Uncle as such musician until he was commissioned an Ensign which commission I have had in my possession from the time of my marriage with said Robert Wilson until about eight years since I gave it to my son James G. Wilson & who has since died & the said Commission is not to be found among any of his papers & I have made diligent Enquiry for the same & search where it would be most likely to have been Kept & it is lost & cannot be found – I know the commission bore date June 9th 1781 at which time the said Robert Wilson was but about eighteen years of age & he entered the service as I was informed & believes about the commencement of the war & served until the close of the war when he was regularly discharged he at the time of his discharge holding the said commission as Ensign as aforesaid I was informed by her said husband & __?__ to be true that he served under his said Uncle James Griegg in the battles fought in the Vally of the MowHawk River in the State of New York against the British & Indians & that he was the Ensign who was appointed by Colonel Hamilton the officer of the day to conduct the ceremony of receiving the Brittish Flags at the surrender of Lord Cornwallis at Yorktown; he (Wilson) being then the youngest Ensign in the army and that he performed that service as such Ensign & received the colours of twenty eight Regiments from twenty eight Brittish Captains & handed them over to twenty eight American Sergeants under the directions of Col. Hamilton I had often talked over with said Wilson the __?__ & hardships he had passed through while a soldier & officer in the army of the Revolution & well remembers the accounts given by him of the same & which said accounts have been often repeated to others by him in her presence the truth of which I never doubted I have no record of the age of said Robert Wilson he was an old Batchelor when I married him & called himself about thirty nine years of age I have never seen the record of his birth & cannot give his age or the time of his entering & leaving the army except from his statements to me."

Sources: 1. Pictorial Field Book of the Revolution, Vol. II by Benson J. Lossing, 1850. 2. Year Book of the Sons of the Revolution in the State of New York, 1899. 3. Pension Papers W7746.

****

Zaccheus Wilson age 14

Zaccheus Wilson was born in November 1765 in Mecklenburg, North Carolina, and he died on 21 October, 1842 in Henderson, Tennessee. He married three times and had nine children. His mother Eleanor stated that he was in the service in October of 1780 making him 14 since his birthday was in November.

Zaccheus had six brothers and a father that also served during the revolution. His brothers Robert and Joseph were taken prisoners at the surrender of Charleston and were later allowed to return home. Once at home rather than be forced to join the Tory militia they enlisted again in the American army. In one battle Joseph encountered a Tory militiaman that he knew in hand-to-hand combat. He killed the Tory after a severe struggle and carried off the dead man's rifle. Zaccheus's father Robert and his brother John were later captured and placed in jail in Camden. One of their jail mates was Andrew Jackson, the future president.

In October of 1780 General Cornwallis and his troops stopped at the Wilson plantation and began stealing provisions. Cornwallis soon learned that he was at the home of a patriot leader who had seven sons in the rebel army. Cornwallis encouraged Mrs. Wilson to have her husband and sons join the British army. He offered them rank, honor, and wealth if they joined.

Mrs. Wilson replied, *"I have seven sons who are now, or have been bearing arms. Indeed my seventh son, Zaccheus, who is only fifteen years old, I yesterday assisted to get ready to go and join his brothers in Sumter's army. Now sooner than see one of my family turn back from the glorious enterprise, I would take these boys* [pointing to three or small sons] *and with them would myself enlist under Sumter's standard, and show my husband and sons how to fight, and if necessary to die for their country."*

The cruel Lieutenant Colonel Banastre Tarleton turned to General Cornwallis and sneered, *"Ah! General! I think you've gotten into a hornet's nest! Never mind, when we get to Camden, I'll take good care that old Robert Wilson never comes back again!"* He apparently knew that Robert Wilson was in jail at Camden.

The next day the British army moved out, and a group of scouts captured Zaccheus who was found on the flank of the British with his rifle. It appeared that he was preparing to lie in wait and ambush some of the enemy. He was taken to Cornwallis, who demanded that the boy act as a guide. He wanted the young boy to show him the best place to cross the Catawba River. When the British reached the river, Zaccheus showed them the best place to cross. Some of the British troops were half way across, when they found themselves in deep water and were swept down river by the strong current.

Cornwallis, red with rage, drew his sword and said he was going to cut the boy's head off for his treachery. Zaccheus faced him and replied, *"I have no arms and I am your prisoner. You have the power to kill me."* He then added, *"But Sir, don't you think it would be a cowardly act for you to strike an unarmed boy with your sword. If I had but half of your weapon, it would not be so cowardly, but then you know you would not be so safe."* If this exchange had taken place between Zaccheus and Colonel Tarleton, the young boy would have likely been killed on the spot.

Cornwallis was impressed with the lad's courage and said to him, *"You are a fine fellow, and I would not hurt a hair on your head. Go home and take care of your mother and tell her to keep her boys at home."*

Later sometime in November Cornwallis had Robert, his son John, and several other men released from jail in Camden and had them safely transported to a prison in Charleston. Before the guards arrived, Robert organized the men to escape. When the prisoners overpowered their guards, Robert Wilson made the guards swear never again to bear arms against the rebels and sent them on their way with a warning, *"If I ever find a single mother son of you in arms again, I will hang you up to a tree like a dog."* With people like the Wilsons it is no wonder that the rebels won their freedom from Great Britain.

By the time of his death in 1842 he was the owner of eight slaves, which he left to his wife and several children.

Sources: 1. Women of the Revolution, Vol. III, Chapter XX, 1852 by Elizabeth F. Ellett. 2. Women of the Frontier by Billy Kennedy. 3. Women of the Century by Phebe Ann Hannaford. 4. Will of Zaccheus Wilson.

****

Jacob Wisner age 14

Jacob Wisner was born in August of 1762 in Pennsylvania, and he died 26 December, 1846 in Chester County, Pennsylvania. He married Sarah Olivine on 10 November, 1811 in Reading, Pennsylvania in a ceremony conducted by the Reverend Muhlenburg. Sarah received a widow's pension of $96 a year. Jacob served as a fifer in Company A of the 4th Pennsylvania Regiment from June 1777 until 18 January, 1781. He enlisted nearly two months before his 15th birthday.

"I enlisted in the year one thousand Seven hundred and Seventy Seven as a fifer about the month of June in Captain Soull's Company in the fourth Pennsylvania Regiment Commanded by Col Butler. I continued to serve in the said corps or in the Service of the United States as a fifer until the 18th day of January 1781 when I was discharged home. I served at Trenton in the State of New Jersey by General Anthony Wayne. I was in the Battle of Brandywine at the Battle of Monmouth and was with General Sullivan against the Indians."

At the Battle of Brandywine Jacob and the 4th Pennsylvania were in the main body that that was positioned to the left of Char's Ford. The British assaulted the position and drove the Americans from it. The American defeat took place on 11 September, 1777.

On 20 September, 1777 Jacob was in the Battle of Paoli. As General Washington was retreating from Brandywine, they left General Anthony Wayne and the Pennsylvania Regiments behind to harass the British troops that were preparing to advance on Philadelphia. Wayne's troops were surprised by an attack by the British near Paoli Tavern. Claims by the Americans were made that the British took no prisoners and gave no quarter. Later the battle was referred to as the "Paoli Massacre." Lt. Colonel Hubley of the 10th Pennsylvania later claimed to witness the cruelty of the British. *"I with my own Eyes, see them, cut & hack some of our poor Men to pieces after they had fallen in their hands…"*

The retreating American army next met the British at the Battle of Germantown on 4 October, 1777. The 4th Pennsylvania Regiment were under the command of Major General John Sullivan. Many of Sullivan's troops began to run short of ammunition and began to pull back. Due to a heavy fog, the group that Jacob was with began trading fire with another group of Americans. Once again the American forces were defeated by the British.

Jacob and his regiment spent a cold winter at Valley Forge. After the first of the year in 1778 they began to receive training from the Baron von Steuben. In late spring of 1778 the British began to evacuate Philadelphia, and General Washington had his army break camp at Valley Forge and go after them. The two great armies met in battle on 18 June, 1778 at the Battle of Monmouth. Jacob's regiment under General Anthony Wayne had engaged the British, and the American commander Major General Lee pulled three of Wayne's regiments out of the fight. Seeing this the British commander focused more men on attacking Wayne's Pennsylvania troops.

Major General Lee sensing a full scale attack panicked and ordered a full retreat. General Washington saw the men retreating from the battlefield and ordered the men back into the fight. He then removed Lee from his command. The battle ended in a draw, when the British troops pulled out of the fight. The Americans had at last engaged the British and were not defeated.

In the summer of 1779 Jacob became involved in his last battle. He was part of the Sullivan campaign against the Iroquois Indians. The Americans destroyed at least forty Indian villages in western New York, and thus putting an end to Indian raids in the area.

Sources: 1. "The Music of the Army..." An Abbreviated Study of the Ages of Musicians in the Continental Army, by John U. Rees. Originally published in The Brigade Dispatch Vol. XXIV, No. 4, autumn 1993. 2. Pennsylvania in the War of the Revolution: Battalions and Line 1775-1783. 3. DAR Magazine Vol. 25. 4. The Wisners in America & Their Kindred by George Franklin Wisner. 5. Pension Papers W26040.

****

John Witderstein age 14

John Witderstein was born in 1763 in New York, and he died there on 19 June, 1835. He married Margaret Kesler on 2 August, 1786. He received a yearly pension of $80.

When John was at winter quarters at Valley Forge his mother had made him a buckskin suit which protected him from the cold. He served in the 2nd Company of the 3rd Regiment of the New York Line.

"I did enlist on the eighth day of June 1777 in the army of the United States in the New York line of the Continental establishment into Captain Thomas De Witts Company in Colonel Peter Gansevoorts Regiment. I was at Fort Stanwix while it was besieged twenty one days by

the common enemy and went in the expedition against the Indians under General Sullivan. Was in a skirmish on Staten Island and was engaged in the taking Cornwallis besides various other engagements and skirmishes."

The siege of Fort Stanwix took place from 2 August to 22 August, 1777. The fort was attacked by British troops, Tories, and Indians. According to folklore when the Americans raised the flag over the fort on 2 August, 1777 it was the first time that the flag of the United States was flown in battle.

Sources: 1. Sons of the American Revolution Application. 2. U.S. Pension Roll of 1835. 3. D.A.R. Lineage Book, Vol. 33. 4. Pension Papers W8341.

****

Solomon Witherington age 14

Solomon Witherington was born on 4 October, 1761 in Lenoir County, North Carolina, and he died on 28 June, 1840 in Craven County, North Carolina. He married (1) Mary Moore who died in 1822 (2) Susan Davis he married on 20 September, 1823 in North Carolina. He received a yearly pension of $37.76.

"When about fourteen years of age I Served as a Substitute for John Dismal who was drafted by Captain Menan Patrick at Kinston Lenoir County North Carolina but at what precise time I entered the Service I am unable to State, being now advanced in years, and very young when I enlisted--We were ordered to rendezvous at Kinston, and thence under the command of Genl William Bryan, Col William Caswell, Capt John Stringer McIlwaine, Lieutenant Thomas Shute, together with Blarney Harper ensign Isler Kilpatrick first Sergeant, James Cowaid second Sergeant and Elijah Johnson corporal, we marched through North Carolina and South Carolina without the occurrence of any occurrence worthy of mention, until we reached a place called the White House, on the Savannah River which divides the State of So. Ca. from Georgia--at that place they __?__ a party of British soldiers on the opposite side and thereupon immediately fired upon them, we then marched to Augusta Old Field, about a mile below the town of Augusta, and lay there one week, until the British evacuated Augusta, whereupon the Americans entered the town. After remaining at Augusta a very short time, we marched from the town of Augusta, to Brier Creek in Georgia, where we engaged with the British. The engagement took place between one and two o'clock and

resulted in the defeat and dispersion of the American forces--our light horse fared very badly, and were nearly all destroyed."

Solomon fought at the Battle of Brier Creek on 3 March, 1779 in eastern Georgia. He was fortunate to survive, because over one third of the American forces were killed or taken prisoner. On 3 March the Americans were warned that a British force was approaching. The militia had a shortage of ammunition and the camp was in disarray. As the Patriots formed a battle line, Solomon was among the troops on the left flank.

When the Americans saw the British charging them with bayonets fixed, the American militia broke and ran and many without firing a shot. The American troops in the Continental Army held their ground but were soon overwhelmed by the British.

"In the general dispersion which ensued I fell in with sixteen of the American forces, and we agreed to make James Noble, one of our number, captain of the Sixteen; after wandering about in the woods for Some time, on their way home we reached the Savannah River, where it was quite broad, and found in the River an old raft of plank, all of the Sixteen immediately got upon it, but we were unable to carry it across the Stream--this we therefore abandoned, and perceiving an old canoe on the opposite side of the river, we all agreed to give Dick Johnson, one of our number, one hundred dollars, to swim across and bring over the canoe; after some hesitation he agreed to make the attempt, and pulled off his clothes, and jumped into the stream, but after Swimming twenty or thirty yards, he returned to the same bank, whence he Started, and refused to go. All the surrounding country being alarmed by the victory of the enemy and our situation growing more and more dangerous, I swam across the River, obtained the canoe, and thus the whole party gained the opposite bank; after reaching this side of the river, we traveled upon the banks of the same, until we came to a house called the Two Sisters which was occupied by two women, and where there was a ferry. They informed us that the British had just passed, and gave us some Hominy, of which we partook very heartily. We then retraced our steps down the River, and ultimately reached the White House, where we found our baggage, wagons & of which we took possession, nobody having them in charge, and remained there three days--on the third day, the remnant of our light horse came up; and on the fourth day the brigade came up and we marched down to a small place called Purryburg, where we continued to remain until our time was out. Colonel William Caswell, here took command of our Regiment and under him we marched on to Charleston, thence through Georgetown,

and Wilmington (North Carolina) to Kinston in North Carolina having served five months, which added to the time consumed in traveling home, made five months & eighteen days."

"About two years after the discharge, (when I was 16 years of age) at Purrysburg in So Ca, I was drafted at Kinston No Ca, as well as I can recollect under the command of General Richard Caswell, Col. Benjamin Axum, and Col Richard Caswell, I marched to Cross Creek (now Fayetteville) thence up to Hillsboro, and from the latter place, we took up our line of march for South Carolina, we crossed the Yadkin River, and near Lynches Creek were joined by General Gates; under the general command of General Gates we proceeded on to Camden, but before we reached the latter place, we were met by the British, and an engagement took place, which resulted in the complete __?__ of the Americans. I was not present in the engagement but was left a short distance from the battleground on the road, quite Sick--the first person I saw after the defeat was "Tory John Cox," as he was afterwards called, he informed me, of the complete overthrow of the American Army; this man was a very valiant soldier, and much attached to the camp of the Whigs, but Subsequently became a rank tory. Col. Benjamin Axum came up and informed me that all was lost, and I must take the best care of myself that I could, and I accordingly made my escape, and after a long and tedious journey finally Succeeded in reaching Kinston in North Carolina. Upon this tour of duty, I served three months."

Solomon was ill and did not participate in the Battle of Camden on 16 August, 1780. His unit, under the command of Major General Richard Caswell, was placed on the left flank. Once again the North Carolina militia broke and ran when the British charged with their bayonets.

George Watts was a member of the North Carolina militia and was present at the battle. Many years later he recalled his memories of the battle, *"...I fired without thinking except that I might prevent the man opposite from killing me. The discharge and loud roar soon became general from one end of the lines to the other. Amongst other things, I confess I was amongst the first that fled. There was no effort to rally, no encouragement to fight. Officers and men joined in the flight."*

"I was engaged, as a substitute afterwards, for Christopher Taylor, to guard the magazine of arms & ammunition which was kept in Kinston, under Captain Samuel Caswell and General William Caswell, and served three months."

"I next volunteered in August 1780, under Genl Lillington, and marched with Captain Matthew Mosely and Maj William Shepard from Kinston, to intercept Major Craig, who at the ahead of some British forces, was reported to be on his way from Wilmington to New Bern N Ca. The Americans fell in with him at Harget's in Jones County, and after a smart brush, he retreated & came to New Bridge over Trent River, where on picket guard, engaged with his light horsemen, we again retreated, and finally succeeded in reaching New Bern without any further molestation. I then went to Trenton where after serving the 10 days out for which we enlisted, we were relieved and marched back to Kinston under Major Shepard. I never received any formal discharge for this service."

"I again served as a substitute for Nathan Witherington, who was drafted by Captain Ezeriah Moore, and ordered to rendezvous at Kinston; thence under the command of Captain Thomas Gatlin, we marched to Wilmington, and whilst on our way, having received the news that peace was proclaimed between this and the mother country; we were disbanded & returned home."

Sources: 1. North Carolina Marriage Index 1741-2004. 2. Tombstone 3. U.S. Pensioners 1818-1872. 4. Pension Papers S7936. 5. Revolutionary War by Robert Grayson.

****

Joseph Wood age 14

Joseph Wood was born in 1762 in Scituate, Rhode Island, and he died after 1848. He received a yearly pension of $40.

"I was born in the town of Scituate in the county of Providence and State of Rhode Island on the first day of September, 1762, according to the family record of births kept by my father of the births of several children. When I was fourteen years old (in my fifteenth year), I entered the service of the United States in the Revolutionary army as a waiter for Capt. Nathan Olney and continued in such service as waiter for Captain Olney one year. It was in the Spring of the year I think when I entered the service, but the month or the particular part of the spring it was when I so entered the service I cannot now state, for I do not recollect. From the time of my birth till I so entered the service, I resided in the said town of Scituate."

"During the time while I so served as waiter for Captain Olney. I was stationed in Bristol in the state of Rhode Island. I think that there was only one Regiment stationed at Bristol during the year while I was there

and I think that the Regiment stationed there was commanded by Colonel Angell, but I am not certain. I do not recollect how many companies there were in the said Regiment, nor the names of the captains, except Captain Olney and one whose name I think was Knight, called Capt Knight. That I do not now recollect the names of any of the members of Capt Olney's company except one, whose name was Thomas Eldredge, whom I knew in Scituate before I entered the service and who entered the service about the same time when I did, and I think it was in the spring of 1777 when I so entered the service. I enlisted that time for one year and served faithfully that length of time as waiter for Capt Olney."

Joseph was in Captain Stephen Olney's Company under the command of Colonel Israel Angell of the 2nd Rhode Island Regiment. At the Battle of Princeton Captain Olney saved the life of the future United States President James Monroe.

"Before my time of service as waiter for Capt Olney had expired, my father had removed with his family from the said town of Scituate to the town of Colchester in the county of New London and State of Connecticut. When my time of service as waiter for Capt Olney expired and when I was discharged therefrom in the spring of I think 1778, I went immediately to my father's in Colchester. I remained there at home with my father till the first of March, 1781, when I again entered the service of the United States in the Revolutionary Army as a private in the company commanded by Capt Simeon Allen and was stationed at Fort Griswold in the town of in the state of Connecticut. Col Ledyard then commanded Fort Griswold. I remained in the service in the fort till the next September, when the fort was taken by the British."

"At the time the fort was taken, there were in the forts as I understood about seventy-five. I made my escape from the fort. A man by the name of Avery, whose Christian name I do not remember, also made his escape from the Fort. I never heard of any others having made their escape from the Fort at that time, but all who did not make their escape were put to death. Col Ledyard and Capt Simeon Allen were killed."

"When Col Ledyard found that he was not able to withstand the attack upon the Fort, he opened the gate to surrender. As he did so, the British commander asked, "Who commands this Fort?"

"Col Ledyard answered, "I did, but you do so now," and presented to the British commander his sword."

"The British commander took the sword and thrust it through Col Ledyard. This I heard and saw. Upon that, Capt Allen, who was standing nearby in the act of presenting his sword to surrender, drew it back and thrust it through the British officer who had thus killed Col Ledyard. Captain Allen was then immediately killed the British. This I also saw. I then leaped the walls and made my escape."

The Battle of Groton Heights, also known as the Battle of Fort Griswold, was fought on 6 September, 1781. Benedict Arnold was ordered by the British to attack the Port of New London. Arnold landed with about 1,700 men and burned the town, and he then turned his attention to Fort Griswold located across the river in Groton. About 800 British troops attacked the fort that was defended by 150 American troops, including Joseph Wood, led by Colonel William Ledyard.

After a 40 minute battle Colonel Ledyard was forced to surrender, and he opened the gates to the British. As the Colonel attempted to hand a British officer his sword as a sign of surrender he was killed. This led to about 70 other American troops shot, stabbed, or bludgeoned to death. In all about 80 Americans were killed during the battle and 30 were wounded. One American survivor of the battle said that only one American was killed before the British entered the fort. British losses were reported to be 51 killed and 141 wounded. Most British records do not mention the death of Colonel Ledyard or the killing of the other Americans after the surrender.

What caused the British troops to go on killing after the surrender by the Americans? One account reports that during the battle the fort's flag was shot down and later raised again. Some of the British troops may have thought that the colors had been struck and the battle over. Yet the Americans kept on fighting. Also, the Americans were accustomed to shooting at and trying to kill British officers during fighting, which the British considered to be a breach of battlefield etiquette. So, the death of many British troops and officers may have led to the British officer killing Colonel Ledyard after he offered his sword in surrender.

Historians have not agreed on how Colonel Ledyard was killed and who killed him. Other eyewitness accounts of the surrender support what Joseph Wood described in his pension application. An eyewitness account by George Middleton, a twelve year old local boy that was in the fort, claims that British Captain Bloomfield killed Colonel Ledyard.

"After I had made my escape from the Fort, I met a fellow soldier by the name of Avery, but whose Christian name I do not remember, and who had also made his escape. Avery and myself traveled up the river together a short distance, I think about a mile, when we found a boat. We then got into the boat and rowed across to the other side of the river. We there met large numbers of the militia on their way to New London. It was near night when we got to New London. It was before dark. When we got there, Arnold had burned the town the town and left with his forces."

"I recollect that among those killed in Fort Griswold there were a number by the name of Avery, but how many there were of that name, or what were their Christian names, I do not now remember [there were nine killed and three wounded], I also recollect that a fellow soldier with whom I was well acquainted and whose name was Jehiel Judd was killed in the Fort. I also recollect that a man by the name of Frink, another by the name of Allen, and another by the name of Miner were killed in the Fort, but I cannot recollect either of their Christian names. There were two men in the Fort by the name of Miner, one a drummer and the other a fifer, and I suppose they were both killed."

"I stayed in New London overnight, and on the next morning I crossed over the river in a ferryboat and went to Fort Griswold. The dead were still lying in and about the Fort, and the People were just then coming in to bury the dead. A man by the name of Ebenezer Averill went from New London across the river to the Fort with me. We did not stay long at the Fort. I did not then look about to ascertain whether I knew any of the dead. I felt much too sorrowful & gloomy to do so then. I showed Averill where I made my escape. After remaining at the Fort a few minutes I, in company with Averill, crossed the river in the ferryboat back to New London. I left Averill, in New London and went home to my father's house in Colchester, where I arrived that night. I stayed at home that night, the next day, and the next night. On the Next morning, Lieutenant Fox called for me to go with him to Fort Waterbury at Horseneck, and I went. I arrived at Fort Waterbury with Lieutenant Fox in some three or four days after we started from Colchester. When I arrived at Fort Waterbury, I entered the service in the company commanded by Capt Charles Miles. Gen Waterbury commanded there. Mead was the colonel when I entered the service there, as I then understood."

"I continued in the service the principal part of the time at Horseneck, where we built Fort Waterbury, till I was discharged about the first of March, 1783. After the first of March 1783 we were marched to Stamford and there discharged."

"I refer to my affidavit made on the 24th day of September 1847 before Aaron Chatfield a justice of the peace. Beside the names of my fellow soldiers which I mentioned in that affidavit I now recollect the following--Sergeant Ellis, Serg. Starr--a man by the name of Wist, and another by the name of Blakesley from the service in March 1783 I returned home to my father's in Colchester County."

"After the close of the war, there was a man and fellow soldier who served with me during the whole of the last year named Willcox, his Christian name I cannot recollect, but I think it was John. One of our sergeants name was Benedict, but I cannot now recollect his Christian name, nor from what place in Connecticut he came. There were two brothers by the name of Gifford, but their Christian names I am not now able to recollect. I well recollect z soldier by the name of Dana, but his Christian name I do not now recollect, but I do recollect that he did not serve in the same company with me, but served in one of the other companies and I think in Capt Allen's. I recollect four of the captains in our regiment, viz., Capt Miles, who commanded our company, Capt Allen, Capt Stoddard, and Capt granger. I recollect that during some part of the time Dana was engaged with the officers, but in what capacity I do not recollect."

"I well recollect that, while I was at Horseneck, we had a great battle of snowballing. The men were regularly paraded on each side and had a regular fight of snowballing. The battle became very animated. The snow was wet and would pack very hard. Many of the soldiers got hurt, and the blood ran freely, and the battle became so warm and so much in earnest that the officers interposed and stopped it."

"I also recollect well the man who was called "Potpie." He was called Potpie because he had, as it was said, stolen a potpie and been caught with it. I think the name by which I first knew him was Palmer. He deserted from our army and went over to the British. He, as I understood, deserted from the British, and while skulking about the country, was captured by our men and brought in and confined in prison. I was informed that he run the gauntlet, though I was absent on duty at the time and did not see it. I saw him receive three hundred lashes, one hundred each morning for three successive mornings. It was after that when he was sent away to prison."

"I recollect that young Dana, Sergeant Benedict, and the two brothers Gifford served with me in the army during the last year. I would also name, among the many others who served with me, Bishop Tyler, Elijah Taylor, Daniel Thompson, Wilmot Tobias, and John Tobias, a man by the name of Babcock, and one by the name of Munroe, but I cannot recollect their Christians names. I recollect the surnames of many more. I recollect that young Dana was an active and smart young man and a good and courageous soldier."

"I recollect that in February 1782, that one hundred of the British light horse came up to Palmer's Hill, a little east of Titus River, and had collected about one hundred head of cattle which they were about to drive off. We, while at the fort, heard of it, and Ensign Allen with fifty men, myself among them, started, intending to intercept them at the bridge over Titus river which they had to cross. When we got to the bridge, we found that the British light horse had passed the bridge with the cattle. We pursued them and overtook them at the top of the hill where Genl Putnam rode down the steps. We attacked them there and they charged upon us, and we repulsed them and continued our attack. We followed them on about six miles to Byram river. Within that time and distance, the British light horse charged upon us twice more, and we each time repulsed them. We recovered the cattle, the last of them on the bridge over the Byram river. The British killed six of the cattle and cut many more of them. After the British passed the Byram river, they kept on and made no more defense. We took one horse from them, with the saddle, bridle, holster, and one pistol. The horse was wounded but recovered. I and two others shot at the man when the horse which we took fell."

"I state this occurrence, believing that my companions, if any of them are still alive, will remember it. I cannot not recollect the names of any who were with me except Ensign Allen and a man by the name of Marshal and another by the names of Haskins. Marshal, Haskins, and myself were the three who shot at the British soldier whose horse we wounded and took."

"After the first March, 1783, we were marched to Stamford and there discharged."

Sources: 1. Surrender, Then Massacre at a Fort in Connecticut, published in the New York Times 29 June, 1990, by Nick Ravo. 2. The Battle of Groton Heights: A Collection of Narratives, Official Reports, Records, Etc., 1882, by Charles Allyn. 3. Pension Papers S23084.

****

Samuel Wood age 14

Samuel Wood was born in Massachusetts in 1767, and he died there after 1848. He enlisted in the 4th Regiment of the Massachusetts Line and served under Colonel William Shepard. The Regiment disbanded in November of 1783 at West Point.

"I enlisted for three years service into Capt Holbrooks Company and Col. Shepards Regiment in the Massachusetts line in the month of April in the year 1781. I immediately went to Boston where I staid for one month to guard prisoners on board the guard ship. After which I went to West Point. I faithfully served two years and eight months."

Sources: 1. Massachusetts Society of the Sons of the American Revolution, 1920. 2. Pension Papers S33945.

****

Samuel Wood age 14

Samuel Wood was born on 6 April, 1765 in Newburgh, New York, and he died on 11 May, 1853 in Dexter, New York. He married Elizabeth Smith in January of 1789. He received a yearly pension of $23.40.

"In September 1779 my Father timothy Wood was drafted to perform a tour of duty in Capt. Christian Van Deuson Colonel Jesse Woodhull's New York State Troop of Infantry. I took his [lace as substitute and served in the capacity as Drummer. I immediately marched in said company to a place about two miles below West Point called Cons Hook. After about two weeks marched to Buttermilk Falls and Fort Montgomery which was back of said Falls and then continued about two weeks longer and then marched to Haverstraw Bay when after more than two weeks we were dismissed. This expedition was called for by an alarm from the British and were kept out that long to prevent Tory's cowboys from driving cattle to the British."

"In June 1780 as part of the same Capt. Van Deuson company to the number of about twenty five were drafted to perform another tour of duty. I went as a Drummer a Substitute for Andrew Sherwood and marched from New Windsor to Ringwood Furnace in the State of New Jersey. I believe this was when the castings were done for the army and it was supposed the British would attempt to burn it. At Ringwood Furnace we met detachments from other companys and were now organized into a full

company in Capt. Daniel Tuttle of the same Regt. took the command of the whole. Having ascertained the Furnace to be in no danger we were marched to Crompond and were there divided into small parties for patrolling or scouting in various directions and took up a number of cowboys with cattle and sheep which they were driving to the British. We remained at this place until we had severed one month and were dismissed and returned home."

Ringwood Furnace was important to the American war effort because it supplied hardware for the army.

"About the first of August in the same year 1780 another draft was made upon the same company Capt. Van Deuson Woodhull's Regt and I took the place of Peter Lowrie a substitute for him and was enrolled a Drummer in said company and marched under the command of Lieut. Andrew Southerland our Capt. did not go, he having just preformed a tour, to Crompond when our party being a part of Van Deuson only sent a part of the company of Capt. Kleaser Woodhull belonging to the same Regt. Woodhull not being there Lieut. Southerland took command of the whole and soon after marched to Tappan Bay and then did duty in patrolling or scouting parties, had several skirmishes with scouts from the British but lost no lives."

"My next tour of duty commenced about the middle of October the same year 1780 and was performed as the capacity of Drummer as Substitute for my Father Timothy Wood who was drafted for a months tour in Capt. Kleaser Woodhull's company Colonel Jesse Woodhull's Regt. marched immediately to old Fort Montgomery and patrolled in that neighborhood and back in the county almost of Crompond the whole month without accomplishing anything more than to quit the fears of the inhabitants respecting depredations of Troys Cowboys."

"1781 in the middle of July I volunteered as Drummer in Capt. Asa Deans Company Col. Jesse Woodhull's Regt. for a half months tour and marched immediately to Sterling Furnace 18 or 20 miles southwest from West Point. We remained there two weeks and were dismissed and returned home."

Sterling Iron Works, about 25 miles from West Point, made the iron links for the Hudson River Chain. This chain weighed 186 tons and was made and delivered in six weeks in April of 1778. The chain stretched across the Hudson River and was used as a defense in keeping British ships from traveling up the river. It served to protect West Point from the British Navy.

"1781 September my older Brother Thurston Wood was drafted for a half month's tour and I went as a substitute for him, did duty as a Drummer. Was marched to Hackensack New Jersey and then did duty in patrolling til the time expired."

"1781 about the 10th November I volunteered as a Private in Capt. David Sand's Company in Colonel McClaughry Regiment for one month. Marched to the North River crossed it at Fishkill landing and marched across the mountains to Peekskill. Lay there a while and marched up the river to Robinson's House. Did nothing this tour except watch the movements of the British on the River."

Sources: 1. Sons of the American Revolution. 2. D.A.R. Lineage Book, Vol. 22. 3. Pension Papers S28955.

****

Moses Woodburn age 14

Moses Woodburn was born on 2 October, 1764 in Stonington, Connecticut, and he died on 30 December, 1836 in Pennsylvania. He married Asenath Wright and he received a yearly pension of $50.

"I first served as a substitute for my Brother John Woodburn for about eight or nine months in a sergeants guard of about 17 or 18 men. William Clark was the sergeant on this duty Capt. Rathbone had the chief care. We had the charge of a number of pieces of cannon in a battery facing the harbor & all kept two guards constantly stationed on the battery and one at the point. I was discharged in May or June 1780."

"Soon after being discharged I enlisted under a Major Petus a recruiting officer and went with thirty or forty others was mustered at Danbury Connecticut by Col. Canfield & marched to Peekskill & joined the regular army and General Washington & was attached to Capt. Douglass Company in Col. Starrs 1st Connecticut Regiment I think in June 1780 & was drilled for three or four weeks and the army crossed over the Kings ferry on the west side of the river & remained eight or ten days. Marched from there to Orangetown opposite Tappan Bay & staid there for about two or three weeks and then went to a place called Paramus between __?__ and Hackensack & staid a few days. Then back to fort Lee where we were __?__ under Baron Stuben--remained there I think 4 or 5

weeks during this time some Indians came along with Gen. Washington some treaty having been made with them--from there went back to Hackensack & built small chimneys to our tents & remained encamped about 6 weeks then marched to Orangetown & remained two weeks or more during which time Major Andre was executed at Orangetown west of the stone church & I was one of the guards who conducted him from the stone church to the place of execution & was near him when he was executed this I think was in November or December 1780—from there we marched and crossed the river at Kings ferry __?__ into the Highlands about two miles east of West Point & encamped for winter and built huts until sometime in January 1780 when I was discharged. I was kept until within about two years about which time my house was burnt."

"In February 1781 I entered as a volunteer in the armed brig called Marquis Lafayette at New London & was absent on a cruise under Capt. Peter Richards off New York & off Charlestown South Carolina & took three prizes one a ship bound from Charleston to Dublin which was retaken, one a sloop from Bermuda to New York loaded with rum which we sent to New London where it arrived—and a brig from Charleston to Liverpool loaded with ten __?__ which was burnt after taking out some of the cargo we returned to New London in June 1781."

"Went on another cruise under Capt. Elisha Hierman in the same vessel off Halifax & the mouth of St. Lawrence & was __?__ about three months. I did not return till shortly after New London was burnt & arrived there I think in November 1781. Took no Prize--went on another cruise in the same vessel under Capt. Nicholas Fosdick about the 1st of December 1781 and went off Jamaica & the West India islands & took one brig loaded with salt which was sent into Bedford where I arrived--was absent about 4 months I think I returned in March 1782 to New London."

"Went on another cruise in the armed sloop Randolph under Capt. Prince in April 1782 & __?__ off New York. Took three prizes near __?__ Island by the aid of a ship called the Confederacy & went back to New London. The first day we sailed send them __/__?__ the cruise went off Sandy Hook & took a brig some distance from the Hook—the brig from New York to Quebec was chased by the British sloop Adamant of 50 guns & was obliged to throw our guns overboard & return to New London after an absence of about two months."

Sources: 1. D.A.R. Lineage Book, Vol. 49. 2. Pension Papers S22605.

****

James Wooldridge age 14

James Wooldridge was born on 26 November, 1760 in Chesterfield County, Virginia, and he died on 11 October, 1839 in Prince Edward County, Virginia. He received a yearly pension of $47.77.

"I entered the service of the United States as well as I recollect the 1st of April 1775, as a private under the command of Captain James Dixon and Ensign John Roper, I met at Thompson's run the Long mountain in Bedford (now Campbell) and marched through the County of Franklin &, and into the lead mines in the County of Montgomery where Colonel Lynch commanded, me with twelve or eighteen men under the command of Ensign Roper were sent down to Red Island River to guard the powder mill where we remained four or five weeks, I was then ordered back to the lead mines and after our tour of three months had expired, he was discharged."

"In the spring of 1776 I again volunteered and marched as a private under the command of Capt. Robert Adams and Lt Thomas McReynolds, I met at Thompson's in Bedford (now Campbell) marched direct along the main Western Road to the lead mines where I joined Colonel Lynch still in command, I remained at that place three months and was discharged."

James served under Colonel Charles Lynch of the Virginia Militia. Colonel Lynch and his men were ordered to guard the lead mines in Wythe County. The mines were an important source for the making of ammunition. The lead was mined by slaves, and it was an attractive target to the British.

"I served a third tour, I volunteered & marched the last of March or the first of April 1777 under the command of Captain James Dixon, Lt Christopher Irvine and James Russell Ensign, I met at Donelson in the County of Bedford, now Campbell, and marched from thence to Goose Creek in the same County, where we remained a few days until joined by Capt. Henry __?__ Company, and then both Companies marched in company with each other to the Big Island on the Holston River where we joined the main Army commanded by Colonel Shelby after remaining there a short time Capt. Dixon's company were ordered to the Rye cove on Clinch River, where there was a garrison, and families of the frontier settlers had come in there for protection against the Indians; here I saw Major Martin who had command of the Fort at that place, we remained at that place until ordered back to the big Island to the treaty and was present

at the treaty I saw several of the Indian Chiefs among them Sconsto or a name resembling it, and the Little Carpenter we remained there until after the Treaty and were discharged after serving a tour of six months."

"I served a fourth tour substituted for man by the name of Joel Ferguson, that I met at Buckingham Courthouse as well as I now recollect the latter part of November 1778 and marched as a private under the command of Captain William Duiguid, Lt. John Burke, I do not recollect the name of his Ensign, to the Albemarle Barracks, where Colonel Cole had the command, I served in this tour three months, and was discharged."

Sources: 1. U.S. Pensioners 1818-1872. 2. Pension Papers S11884.

****

Phineas Wright age 12

Phineas Wright was born on 3 February, 1763 in Lebanon Connecticut, and he died on 25 December, 1842 in Richford, Vermont. He received a monthly pension of $8.

"I enlisted in the month of March 1776 under Captain Sloans Company in Colonel Patersons Regiment in the Massachusetts Line. I served the same until the first of January 1777."

Phineas served under Colonel John Paterson in the 15th Continental Regiment. The Regiment was in New York City in April 1776. It was later ordered to reinforce the American Army in Canada, and in November of 1776 he rejoined the main army. Phineas may have taken part in the Battle of Trenton on 26 December, 1776.

Sources: 1. Connecticut Town Birth Records, Pre 1870. 2. Vermont Men in the Revolutionary War. 3. D.A.R. Lineage Book, Vol. 19. 4. Pension Papers S45472.

****

Stephen Wright age 12

Stephen Wright was born on 18 May, 1764 in Westford, Massachusetts, and he died on 16 February, 1857 in Shelburne, Massachusetts. He married Sarah Prescott on 4 December, 1788. He received a yearly pension of $40. His pension application is very difficult to read.

"In 1776 in the month of December I entered the service of the United States in a military company commanded by Capt. Seth Murray to

a Regiment commanded by Col. Seth Pomeroy. I marched with my company to Fishkill in the state of New York for about six weeks. The __/__ of the time at Morristown in the state of New Jersey."

Stephen served again in the New York area in the first part of 1777. In the spring of 1777 he joined a regiment commanded by Colonel Wells and marched to Vermont and then to Fort Ticonderoga. After the surrender of the fort he was discharged. In July of 1780 he served at West Point under Colonel Sprout.

Sources: 1. Sons of the American Revolution Application. 2. D.A.R. Lineage Book, Vol. 28. 3. Pension Papers W14202.

****

Mary "Polly" Wyckoff age 6

Polly Wyckoff was born in February of 1770 in Allentown, New Jersey, and she is buried there. On the night of 19 November, 1776, three Tories guided the British forces across the Hudson River and up the Palisades in an attempt to attack the American soldiers at Fort Lee in New Jersey. Polly was visiting friends in Bogartsfield and spotted the British troops on the morning of 20 November. The troops had just climbed the Palisades and were marching southward toward Fort Lee.

Polly ran into the friend's house and told her mother what she had seen. Her mother passed the warning on to Peter Bogart, who rode to warn the American troops that the British were going to attack. The next day 2,000 American troops retreated across the Hackensack River and made their way to Hackensack. They took all the boats and destroyed bridges on their retreat. The Americans lost their supplies at Fort Lee, but the British failed to capture Washington and the American troops. It was during this retreat that Thomas Paine wrote *The American Crisis*, which began, *"These are the times that try men's souls."*

Sources: 1. Historical Collections of the State of New Jersey by John W. Barber and Henry Howe, 1844. 2. Women Patriots of the American Revolution: a Biographical Dictionary by Charles E. Claghorn.

****

Henry Yeager age 13

Henry Yeager was born on 15 March, 1763 in Philadelphia, Pennsylvania, and he died after 1839.

"I volunteered as a drummer in a company commanded by Capt. Weed towards the close of October or beginning of November 1776. The regiment to which my company was attached was commanded by Col Ayres or Eyre and Major Boyd. The regiment went up to Delaware in boats from Philadelphia to Trenton, where we encamped. General Washington with the army, was on towards Princeton and Col Ayres or Eyres regiment had drawn three days provisions and raised their tents to march onward in pursuance of orders, when we were directed to Philadelphia, Genl Washington having determined to retreat in consequence of the British, in a large force under Cornwallis marching upon him from New Brunswick. Col Ayres or Eyre with his regiment therefore retired to Philadelphia in boats and encamped in the District of Kenington, in the county of Philadelphia where we remained under orders for about ten days, when we were dismissed in December about the middle of the month 1776."

"Upon Washington's retreat as herein mentioned, he crossed the Delaware from New Jersey and destroyed the bridges, and removed all boats to prevent the British, who were very close upon him from following."

"I again entered the service of the United States and volunteered as a drummer, in Philadelphia, in a company commanded by Capt Ashton, in the month of February as near as I can state; 1776. I went with the company to the Fort at Billingsport, with this company at this time Col Bradford commanded the Fort. I remained there two months, when my term expired I returned to Philadelphia."

"In a few days after my return, I volunteered again as a drummer in a company commanded by Captain Esler. I went again to the Fort at Billingsport with my company, and remained two months with Capt Esler, who at the expiration of that time returned to the city with my company. I remained at the Fort and volunteered as a drummer, in the reliving company which arrived there at that time commanded by Capt Peale Col Will of the 3rd (I think) Regiment Pennsylvania Volunteers, then commanded the Fort. Some time after I had joined Capt Peale, a superior British force from below that point, approached the Fort to attack it and Col Will retreated, having first spiked the cannons. The troops under Col Will went over to Fort Mifflin from Billingsport, but we could not be, or at all events, were out, received there. We then crossed to Red Banks, in Gloucester County New Jersey and from thence marched up through New Jersey as far as Burlington, Burlington County in the last named state, where we encamped."

"We had been there but a short time when information of hostilities at Germantown was received and we immediately marched under Col Will toward that point for the purpose of joining the army there, but on our way we were met by some scattered portions of American troops who informed us of the unfortunate termination of the battle at the last named place. Col Will therefore marched his troops on to White Marsh, in the county of Montgomery, Pennsylvania where we encamped for about then days or two weeks, when our term having expired were dismissed."

"Upon being discharged as above stated, I in Company with one George Lechler who was also in Col Wills Regiment when it was dismissed at White Marsh, returned to Philadelphia but a few days when we were both arrested by British Authorities (the British having in possession of Philadelphia) and taken to Genl Howe's quarters in 2nd street below Spencer opposite Little Dock street, in Philadelphia. I was accompanied by my mother and when we arrived at the Generals quarters, a Major Bedford asked if I was here son, and having answered affirmatively, he remarked that I would be hanged. I was put in a Guardhouse at the corner of 2nd & Little Dock Street. Lechler was confined separately in another, in Little Dock Street."

"The next day we were taken to the house at the N.W. corner of 2nd & Spencer streets, for trial. I was taken before the Judges first. I was charged with having brought letters from the American Army and I was asked if it was true. I answered in the negative. I was asked if I belonged in the Rebel Army. I answered that I belonged to Washington's army. I was then charged with having come into the city as a spy, and was asked if such was not the fact. I answered no, but I came to see my parents. I was examined for a length of time when similar matters without eliciting more than is herein stated. After a short conference, one of the Judges asked me my name and upon giving it the former said to me "You are to be hanged by the neck until you are dead, dead, dead." I was then conducted from the room, in the entry or hall, I met Lechler who inquired what had taken place, and I informed him that I was to be hanged."

Lechler was then conducted before the judges, and I was afterwards told by him that similar proceedings occurred and a like sentence was pronounced on him. We were then both taken to the Walnut Street prison. Soon after we had been there Provost Marshall Cunningham in my hearing, directed the "Spies" to be brought before him. I and Lechler were accordingly conducted to him, when he said to us "I'll give you half an hour and no longer," and ordered us to be confined in separate *dungeons. At the expiration of the half hour (to me a very short one) we were again taken before Provost Marshall Cunningham who ordered a negro to bring two halters. The marshal asked who was the oldest. Lechler answered that he was the youngest. The Marshall then directed that all the other prisoners should quit the yard, and the gates be closed. He directed the negro to place one halter on Lechler's neck and the other on mine, to back both against the gate, and to draw the ropes through the top of it, which was done. At this moment a man came in and gave a paper to the Marshall, who read it, and then ordered the ropes to be loosen from the gate and wound around the prisoners bodies. I and Lechler were then ordered to our dungeons where we were taken. The next morning we were brought before the Marshall's room, when the ropes were taken off us, and we were put into the yard among the other prisoners. After this I remained in prison eight weeks and three days before I was released."*

"Soon after the British evacuated Philadelphia, to wit in the month of June 1778 I volunteered again as a private. In Philadelphia in the 7th company of an Artillery Regiment. The company I was attached to was commanded by Capt Samuel Neeves or Neebs who being __?__ was deprived of his command and succeeded by Capt Andrew Boyd. Part of the Regiment was stationed at Fort Mifflin and part at Billingsport, according to the best of my recollection. I belonged and remained attached to this company more than two years."

"Soon after leaving the Artillery Regiment above mentioned I shipped in Philadelphia on board the privateer ship Rising Star, Capt Samuel Carson. We sailed in a cruise which was to have been for six months, but at the expiration of about five months, having taken several valuable prizes, the Capt broke it up and returned home. During the cruise we captured the British privateer brig _Rattlesnake_ not long after I returned from this voyage I shipped with the merchant ship _Franklin_, Capt John Angus, freighter with five hundred hogshead of tobacco bound to a port in France. The ship carried twenty two long g's. On the voyage we took on an English brig, but about a week afterwards were captured by the British frigate New Adventure. Me and the others on board were taken to Weymouth, England thence to Plymouth in the Dublin seventy four, and were imprisoned nearly two years until exchanged about six weeks after in 1763."

Unfortunately Henry's pension was rejected. He had letters to prove that he served in 1776 but no proof of any other service. If he could have proved the two years in the artillery regiment it would have given him a full pension. He probably died before he could gather the needed evidence.

Sources: 1. Pension Papers R11929.

****

Jean York age 14 (African American)

Jean York was born in 1771 in South Carolina, and he died on 16 June, 1787. He was a member of the "Black Hessians." This group was made up of former slaves in South Carolina, Virginia, Georgia, New Jersey, and New York. They were recruited for Hessian Regiments to serve as drummers and fifers.

From the start of the war the British sought slaves by offering them freedom. This was never the official government policy, but done by local commanders without sanction by their government. About 20,000 slaves joined with the British, because they believed that if the rebels won their status as slaves would not change.

In 1785 Jean enlisted as a drummer in Major Goebel's Company. The Hessians welcomed the blacks into their ranks as equals and without racial stigma. In all, around 150 blacks served as "Black Hessians" and about 47 of them were from South Carolina.

Most of the "Black Hessians" were drummers and tended to be very young. Caesar Ferguson of Newport and Peter Savannah were only eleven, London of Charleston was twelve, and March and Isaac were thirteen. Some of the slaves were later reclaimed by their owners. This happened to Isaac, who at the age of 13 enlisted and was reclaimed at the end of August. Many of these young boys enlisted with one or more of their friends.

The military life sometimes did not appeal to the boys and some deserted. If they were captured they might be flogged or in some rare cases put to death. A thirteen year old drummer from Flatbush named Jacob enlisted and two years later he deserted at the age of fifteen. He was caught and forced to run the gauntlet of two hundred men on two successive days. When the punishment had ended he was allowed to enlist again. Four years later, on 25 May, 1783, he again deserted with his uniform and equipment. London of Charleston deserted at the age of twelve with his uniform and his weapon.

These boys that joined with the Hessians did so not out of love for the British, but for several other reasons. Some were looking to gain their freedom, some needed work because their masters had fled and their farms were destroyed, some may have been attracted to the gaudy uniforms that the Hessians wore. Some might have enlisted because the British paid more, and their money was much sounder than the Continental currency.

After the war a number of the black soldiers went back with the troops to live in Germany. One of the blacks died and was the first black man autopsied in Europe. The German scientist were very surprised to learn that his internal organs were the same as the whites.

Sources: 1. The Black Hessians; Negroes Recruited by the Hessians in South Carolina and Other Colonies by George Fenwick Jones, printed in the South Carolina Historical Magazine, Vol. 83, #4. 2. Best Little Stories from the American Revolution by C. Brian Kelly with Ingrid Smyeer. 3. In Pursuit of Liberty Coming of Age in the American Revolution by Emmy E. Werner.

****

Elizabeth Zane age 16

Elizabeth Zane was born on 19 July, 1765 in Berkeley County, Virginia, and she died on 23 August, 1823. Her bravery is immortalized in a book written in 1903 by her descendant, Zane Grey, entitled *Betty Zane*.

Elizabeth and her family moved into the area that is now Wheeling, West Virginia. The family and several others established Fort Henry in this wilderness. It was surrounded by thick woods and the Indians in the area were very much pro-British. On 11 September, 1782 Fort Henry was attacked by British and their Indian allies.

The fort had only about 16 fighting men and the rest were women and children. During the attack Elizabeth occupied the sentry box with her brother Jonathan and John Saltar. Her job was to load the guns for the two men. The people inside the fort were facing over 300 enemy fighters. The supply of powder soon dwindled to just a few loads left.

Elizabeth's brother Ebenezer remembered that he had carelessly left a keg of gunpowder back at their home, which was about 60 yards from the fort's gate. Colonel Zane, Elizabeth's father, called the men together and said that someone who was a fast runner would need to go for the powder. He reminded them of the danger of journey, and said there would be a good chance the runner would be shot down by the enemy.

Several of the boys volunteered. However, the Colonel was hesitant to let them leave. They could not afford to lose any of the fighting men, and Elizabeth knowing this volunteered. She told her father she was aware of the danger but should she fall her loss would be less important than if a fighting man was to fall. She told her father, *"You have not one man to spare; a woman will not be missed in the defense of the fort."*

The men opened the gate, and Elizabeth stepped outside and began walking at a fast pace. The Indians looked at here and did not consider her any threat, and several of them yelled, *"Squaw, Squaw"* as she passed by. She quickly made it to the house and tied a tablecloth around her waist and poured the powder in it. As she started back to Fort Henry the enemy realized what this girl was up to and began firing. Ball after ball whizzed past her as she ran back to the fort. She entered the fort unharmed with only one musket ball hole in her dress. About two days later a relief force was sent, and the Indians and British retreated. Her feat is even more impressive, because she had gone without sleep for the past 40 hours.

Sources: 1. Young and Brave: Girls Changing History. 2. The Women of the American Revolution, Vol. 2 by Elizabeth Fries Ellet. 3. Elizabeth Zane Chapter, West Virginia State Society, D.A. R. 4. Some Pennsylvania Women During the War of the Revolution, edited by William Henry Egle.

****

Bibliography

1. Bracken, Jeanne Munn, *Women in the American Revolution*. Boston, Massachusetts: History Compass, 2009.
2. Buchanan, John, *The Road to Guilford Court House: The American Revolution in the Carolinas*. New York, New York: John Wiley & Sons, 1999.
3. Burrows, Edwin G., *Forgotten Patriots, The Untold Story of American Prisoners During the Revolutionary War*. New York, New York: Basic Books, 2010.
4. Clagborn, Charles E., *Women Patriots of the American Revolution: a Biographical Dictionary*. Lanham, Maryland: Scarecrow Press, 1991.
5. Cohn, Scotti, *Liberty's Children*. Bloomington, Indiana: Xlibris Corp., 2004.
6. Dann, John C., editor. *The Revolution Remembered: Eyewitness Accounts of the War for Independence*. Chicago, Illinois: University of Chicago Press, 1977.
7. Dandridge, Danske. *American Prisoners of the Revolution.* Charlottsville, Virginia: Michie Company, 1911.
8. Frank, Andrew, *American Revolution: People and Perspectives*. Santa Barbara, California: ABC/CLIO, 2008.
9. Garden, Alexander, *Anecdotes of the American Revolution: Illustrative of the Talents and Virtues of the Heroes and Patriots, Who Acted The Most Conspicuous Parts Therein, Vol. 2*. Charleston, South Carolina: A.E. Miller, 1828.
10. Haven, Kendall, *Voices of the American Revolution*. Westport, Connecticut: Greenwood Publishing, 2000.
11. Johnson, Kenneth D., *The Bloodied Mohawk: The American Revolution in the Words of Fort Planks Defenders and Other Mohawk Valley Partisans*. Rockport, Maine: Picton Press, 2000.

12. Kelly C. Brian and Ingrod Smyer, *Best Little Stories from the American Revolution*. Chicago, Illinois: Cumberland House, 1999.
13. Marten, James, *Children and Youth in a New Nation*. New York: New York University Press, 2009.
14. Nell, William C., *The Colored Patriots of the American Revolution*. Boston, Massachusetts: Robert F. Wallcut, 1855.
15. Rose, Alexander. *Washington's Spies, The Story of America's First Spy Ring*. New York, New York: Bantam Books, 2007.
16. Savas, Theodore P., and J. David Dameron. *A Guide to the Battles of the American Revolution*. New York, New York: Savas Beatie, 2010.
17. Savas, Theodore P., and J. David Dameron. *The New American Revolution Handbook: Facts and Artwork for Readers of All Ages, 1775-1783*. New York, New York: Savas Beatie, 2010.
18. Stover, Allan, *Underage and Under Fire Accounts of the Youngest Americans in Military Service*. Franklin, North Carolina: McFarland and Company, 2014.
19. Taylor, Alan, *The Divided Ground, Indians, Settlers, and the Northern Borderland of the American Revolution*. New York, New York: Random House, 2006.
20. Sutherland, Jonathan D., *African Americans at War, An Encyclopedia Vol. 2*. Santa Barbara, California: ABC/CLIO, 2004.
21. Werneer, Emmy E., *In Pursuit of Liberty: Coming of Age in the American Revolution*. Westport, Connecticut: Potomac Books, 2009.
22. Zall, P.M., *Becoming American Young People in the Revolution*. New Haven, Connecticut: Linnet Books, 1993.

Ancestry.com has digitized copies of the Census, Revolutionary Pensions, and Bounty-Land-Warrant Application Files. On occasions reading the applicant's handwriting will prove to be a challenge. They also have on file Sons of the American Revolution Applications.

NAME INDEX

A

Addison, William..............1

Albee, Obadiah...............3

Allen, Cyrus...................19

Anderson, Andrew............5

Anderson, James................5

Andreson, James.............5

Andrews, Elkanah............8

Anthony, Israel................9

Applegate, Asher............10

Applegate, Daniel............10

Armstrong, Archibald......11

Arnold, Isaac..................12

Ash, John.......................15

Ashcraft, Daniel..............17

Atwood, Ebenezer...........19

Ayres, James..................12

B

Baldwin, John.................21

Ballard, Robert................21

Bailey, George................22

Bain, Casparus................23

Baker, Jeremiah..............24

Baker, Jonathan..............24

Ballou, Asa....................25

Barber, Edward...............25

Barker, Josiah..................26

Barnes, Shadrack..............28

Barron, James..................29

Bartol. Samuel..................31

Bassett, Joseph.................32

Bates, William..................32

Baugh, Henry...................33

Beals, Nathan..................34

Beck, William..................36

Bedinger, Daniel...............331

Beebe, Constant................39

Beekman, William.............40

Beeler, Jacob....................41

Benedict, Isaac..................43

Benjamin, Ebenezer............43

Benjamin, Nathan..............44

Besse, Jabez....................44

Bicker, Adam..................45

Bissell, Daniel..................46

Bivens, John....................47

Black, David...................48

Blackleer, William.............49

Blair, John......................49

Bonney, Ezekiel................49

Boom, Nicholas................50

Boone, Jemima.................51

Booz, Richard..................52

Borders, Peter..................54

Bosworth, Nathaniel...........55
Bovee, Jacob.......…..………..55
Bowles, Charles...............56
Boyd, James....................57
Bradley, Ariel..................59
Bradley, Richard..............59
Brasher, John….....………….60
Brazil, Byrd..................…62
Breckenridge, George.….......63
Breden, Andrew…….……....63
Breton, Adam...................65
Brewer, David…................67
Brewer, Henry.................69
Brewester, William.............69
Bridges, George...............70
Briggs, Abner..................71
Briggs, Benjamin.............72
Brister, Aaron..................73
Broach, Charles................75
Brooks, Reuben................76
Brown, Austin.................78
Brown, John...................78
Brown, Joshia..................80
Brown, Reuben................81
Bulkley, Eleazer................82
Bull, Gurdon...................88
Burbank, David................88

Burbank, Eleazer...............88
Burdick, Gideon……...........90
Burkes, Samuel.................90
Burney, Samuel................94
Burns, John.......…..……...95
Butler, Medad…....……….96
Butler, Nancy.........…........96

C

Caldwell, William…...…......96
Campbell, Thomas................98
Cannday, John.............…...99
Canterbury, John..............100
Carr, Caleb....................102
Carr, James....................102
Carter, Isaac...................103
Carter, Philip.............…....106
Carey, Absalom................107
Case, Isaac....................109
Casler, Richard................109
Cassel, Ephrain................111
Caster, Richard................112
Cathcart, James................114
Chambers, Benjamin..........115
Chambers, Edward............117
Champman, Isaac..............117
Champlin, George.............118
Chandler, James.........…....119

812

Chandler, Martin..............120
Child, James...................121
Child, Thomas.................121
Child, Salmon..................122
Childers, Isom..................122
Chisham, James...............123
Christian, Daniel..............125
Christopher, Henri............126
Cilley, Jonathan................127
Clark, Burgess..................129
Clark, John.....................131
Clarke, Christopher...........134
Clarke, Nathaniel..............135
Clayton, Peter..................136
Clearman, John................138
Clements, Benjamin..........139
Cleveland, William............140
Cliborne, William..............141
Clute, Bartholomew..........142
Coates, William................143
Cogswell, Ferris...............145
Cole, John......................145
Cole, John......................146
Cole, Henreitta................147
Coleman, Daniel..............147
Coleman, Edward............148
Coleman, Robert..............151

Collinsworth, John............159
Conaway, John................154
Congleton, Moses............156
Cook, John.....................160
Cook, John.....................162
Coons, Frederick.............164
Copland, Joel..................166
Crane, Mayfield...............167
Crawford, Alexander.........168
Creemer, William.............168
Croft, Ezekiel..................169
Cronk, John....................172
Cross, William.................173
Curtis, Felix....................174
Curtis, Solomon...............174
Cushing, Charles.............176

D

Dabney, Austin................176
Dains, Asa.....................179
Dale, Adam....................181
Danforth, Samuel.............181
Darrow, John..................182
Davidson, Catherine.........183
Davis, Ann.....................184
Davis, David...................185
Davis, Joseph.................186
Davis, Samuel.................187

Davison, Paul....................189
Day, Solomon...................189
Deake, Charles..................190
Deets, Adam.....................191
De Forest, Gideon...............192
Denny, Absalom.................193
Denney, John....................194
Dickey, William.................195
Dixon, Jeremiah.................195
Doak, Benjamin.................196
Dodge, Richard.................197
Donelson, Rachel...............198
Donnell, Thomas................199
Dowdy, Betsy...................200
Downing, Stephen..............201
Drake, Benjamin................202
Drake, Phoebe..................204
Driskill, David..................205
Drone, William.................206
Duesler, Marcus................207
Dunham, Nathaniel............208
Dunlavy, Francis...............208
Dunston, Almon................215
Duprey, William...............216
Durand, Fisk...................217

E

Eakin, William.................218

Eddins, William................218
Edgman, William..............224
Eggleston, Eliab................225
Ellis, Robert....................229
Evans, Edward.................229
Evans, Joseph..................231
Everly, Simeon.................232

F

Fain, Ebenezer.................234
Falls, William..................237
Fairchild, Abijah...............240
Farmer, Ezekiel................241
Farrar, Leonard................242
Field, Pardon...................244
Field, Pardon...................244
Files, Adam.....................246
Findley, Paul...................248
Flansburgh, William..........251
Flower, Zephon................251
Fones, William.................252
Foote, Asahel..................254
Forbes, James..................256
Force, Silas.....................256
Ford, Augustus................257
Ford, John......................258
Forten, James..................259
Foscue, Frederick.............261

Fosdick, William..............262
Fox, Daniel....................262
Fox, John......................263
Frazer, Jeremiah...............265
Frazier, James.................267
Freeman, Sampson...........272
Friend, Nathaniel..............273
Fulmer, John...................274
Futrell, Nathan................274

G

Gage, Reuben..................275
Gale, Robert...................276
Garris, Bedford................277
Gates, Jonathan...............277
Gault, Andrew.................278
Geiger, Emily..................279
Geiger, John...................280
Geohegan, Anthony..........281
Gilbert, Joseph................282
Gill, John......................284
Gillett, Asa....................285
Glascock, Robert.............. 287
Goff, Richard..................288
Godwin, Abraham............289
Godwin, David................289
Gore, Thomas.................290
Gorin, John....................291

Gorton, Hannah...............292
Gotham, Henry................293
Granger, Daniel...............293
Green, Paul....................297
Green, William................298
Greenwood, Bartlee..........299
Guest, William................299
Gundy, Jacob..................302
Gunn, Gabriel.................303
Guyer, John Peter.............303
Gwin, John....................305

H

Hair, Robert...................305
Hallock, William.............306
Hannah, Robert...............307
Hannaman, William..........310
Haptonstall, Abraham........312
Hardesty, Hezekiah...........313
Hardy, Thomas................314
Harmon, Jehiel................315
Harper, Joseph................316
Harrington, John..............317
Hart, Ebenezer................317
Hart, Henry....................318
Harwell, Lowden.............319
Haskell, Stephen..............322
Hatch, Herman................323

Hatch, Jeremiah.............323	Hooker, Increase............351
Hauser, Jacob...............324	Hooks, Charles...............351
Hauver, Andrew..............325	Hooper, Absalom...............352
Hawkins, Christopher........326	Horne, Nicholas...............354
Hawkins, Samuel.............328	Hudson, John....................355
Hawkins, William............329	Hudson, Samuel...............365
Hayward, Benjamin..........330	Hughes, Benjamin............366
Head, James..................331	Hull, James......................368
Head, James..................331	Hulldereman, John.............368
Heath, William...............322	Hunt, Abijah....................369
Hemstead, Hallam............333	Hunt, Davis......................371
Hesser, Frederick.............333	Hurst, Richard..................372
Hewitt, Simeon...............335	Hutt, John.......................374
Hicks, Jabez....................337	Hyde, Irvine....................378
Hill Henry.....................337	**I**
Hill, Nicholas..................338	**J**
Hillard, Joseph................340	Jackson, Andrew...............379
Hitchcock, Gaius..............341	Jackson, Matthew.............381
Hoadley, Culpeper............342	Jenkins, Enoch..................383
Hodges, Nathaniel............342	Jenks, John......................384
Hogan, Prosser................343	Johnston, Nicholas.............385
Hoisington, Veline............344	Jones, Epahras..................386
Holcomb, Jonathan...........348	Jones, Horatio..................387
Holland, John..................349	Jones, Reuben..................393
Hollaway, Thomas............349	Jones, Richard..................394
Holly, Justus...................350	Jones, Richard Lord............395
Holmes, James.................350	Justice, Simeon................397

K

Kelly, Jared.....................398
Kennedy, David.................399
Kennelly, John...................399
Kenner, Rodham................400
Kercheval, John..................402
Kern, Nicholas...................406
Kidd, James.......................407
Kidd, James H...................408
Kidd, William....................410
Kincaid, James...................412
Kincaid, Samuel.................417
King, Lemuel....................418
King, Lemuel....................419
King Thomas....................421
Kinsley, David..................421
Kirkland, William..............422
Kitchen, Benjamin..............215
Klumph, Jeremiah..............426
Knapp, James....................426
Knight, Richard.................427
Koons, Peter.....................428
Kuhus, George..................429

L

Lacey, Elijah....................429
Lackey, Andrew................431
Land, Lewis.....................433
Langston, Dicey................434

Larkins, Presely.................436
Latham, William................440
Lee, Samuel......................441
Leman, Jeannette...............4443
Lemmon, James................443
Lester, Joshua...................444
Levering, Jeremiah.............109
Lewis, Timothy.................444
Liddell, William................446
Light, John.......................448
Lightfall, Francis...............450
Linton, Isaac.....................452
Livesay, George................453
Livingston, Henry..............454
Logan, Drury....................458
Lord, Richard...................459
Love, Marc......................460
Loving, Christopher...........461
Ludington, Sybil...............462
Lusk, Jacob......................464
Lusk, Michael...................467
Lusk, William...................468
Lyman, Elisha..................468
Lynch, Elijah....................470

M

McA, Eliezer....................471
McAlister, John.................472

McBrayer, Hugh..............474	Micheller, Jacob...............518
McCaw, James.................475	Middleton, John..............519
McClung, Samuel.............477	Miller, Valentine..............519
McCord, John..................480	Mills, George..................521
McDonald, Hugh..............481	Mitchell, Benjamin...........521
McGaughy, Samuel...........487	Montgomery, Alexander.....521
McKinzie, Isaac................490	Montgomery, John............523
McMeans, James..............491	Moody, Lemuel...............524
Madeira, Nicholas.............492	Moore, Behethland...........525
Magee, James...................495	Moore, Robert.................526
March, James....................498	Morris, Daniel.................527
Martin, Nathaniel..............498	Morris, David..................529
Martling, Daniel...............499	Morris, David 531
Mason, Isaac....................500	Munson, Joseph................532
Mason, Jeremiah...............501	Myers, Samuel.................532
Mason, Peter....................503	**N**
Massey, John...................503	Nail, Reuben....................534
Matthews, Peter................504	Newton, Jason..................535
Matthews, William............507	Newton, Moses................536
Mattlock, Jacob................509	Nickerson, Johnathan.........537
Maxwell, James................511	Nisbeth, Robert................540
Meek, Alexander............... 513	Noble, Gideon..................542
Meek, Basil.....................514	Norris, Patrick..................542
Meeker, Caleb..................514	Nowell, Mark..................545
Meeker, Obed..................516	**O**
Merrill, Asa.....................516	Odgen, Jonathan...............546
Merriman, Charles.............517	Osborn, Nathan................547

Osborne, John...................548
Ottis, Edward......................549
Overlin, William.................550
Owen, James......................550
Owens, William..................552

P

Packard, Asahel..................552
Packard, Hezzekiah.............553
Packard, Nehemiah..............555
Paine, William...................556
Palmer...............................557
Palmer, Abel.....................557
Palmer, Daniel...................557
Parker, Isaac.....................559
Parker, Joseph...................560
Pearce, Israel....................560
Pease, Martin....................561
Peavy, Abraham.................562
Peck, Benjamin..................562
Peck, Peter.......................563
Pembrook, David................564
Pembrook, James................565
Peterson, Lemuel................566
Petit, Gideon....................567
Pettit, Henry....................568
Phillips, Irby....................571
Piatt, John.......................573

Pickens, William................574
Pierce, Eli........................579
Pilkington, Drura...............579
Porter, Robert...................581
Porter, Robert................... 581
Powell, Ptolemy.................582
Prescott, Samson................582
Pressley, David..................582
Prewett, Joshua..................585
Price, Ephraim...................587
Putnam, John....................589

Q

R

Rankins, Thomas................589
Ransom, George.................590
Raymond, Elisha.................593
Raymond, Enoch.................594
Readon, John....................595
Real, David......................595
Reamer, Phillip..................596
Reed, David.....................597
Reed, William...................598
Reese, George...................600
Reynolds, Ephraime.............601
Richardson, John................602
Richardson, Lysander...........602
Ritchie, Alexander..............603
Roberts, Judah..................604

Robinson, Stephen.............605
Rose, Archibald...............606
Royal, Isaac...................607
Russ, Joseph...................608
Rutherford, John..............610
Ryker, John...................612

S

Sack, John....................615
Sample, John..................616
Sampson, James..............618
Sanford, Samuel..............619
Schermerhorn, John..........620
Scott, James..................621
Scott, John...................622
Seider, Christopher........... 623
Sellers, Howell...............626
Sessions, Josias..............627
Shackleford, Dudley..........629
Shankland, Thomas..........629
Shankland, William..........630
Sharp, Benjamin..............632
Shaw, John...................636
Shelly, Samuel...............637
Sherburne, Andrew...........637
Shields, Daniel...............641
Shreve, John..................641
Simmonds, Joshua...........647
Sinclair, Samuel..............647
Singer, John..................648

Singletary, Joshia.............649
Skinner, Eli....................652
Smith, Charles................653
Smith, Edward................654
Smith, Levi....................655
Smith, Jesse..................656
Smith, Michael...............657
Smith, Thomas................658
Smith William.................659
Smith, William................660
Smith, William................665
Southerland, Daniel..........665
Spain, William................667
Spatz, Michael...............670
Spencer, Orange..............671
Spink, Nicholas...............672
Spofford, Amos...............663
Sprague, Abraham...........674
Sprague, Abraham...........675
Stephens, John................677
Stewart, Barney..............678
Stewart, John.................679
Stickney, Samuel.............681
Stiles, Asa....................682
Stoddard, John...............683
Stone, Isaac...................683
Stone, William................784
Streeter, Naphtall............685
Sturman, William............686

Suddarth, John..................686
Summers, John.................688
Sutherland, George...........:..690

T

Tapscott, William..............691
Taylor, David..................693
Tenney, James..................695
Terry, Joseph...................697
Thayer, Eliphaz.................698
Thomas, Joseph...............699
Thomas, William..............700
Thomason, George............701
Thompson, Alexander.........703
Thompson, Benjamin.........705
Thompson, James.............706
Thompson, Samuel...........707
Thurman, Baze.................709
Tice, Richard...................709
Toney, Arthur..................709
Toomes, William...............710
Trask, Israel....................712
Tucker, Josiah..................719
Tullock, Mangnus..............720
Tyler, Bishop...................726
Tyler, Comfort..................727

U

Unsell, Frederick...............728

V

Van Auken, John..............730

Van Driesen, Peter............731
Van Dyck, Cornelius..........732
Van Dyke, Peter...............732
Van Winkle, Catherine.......732
Vanasdal, John.................733
Vanderburg, John.............734
Vaughan, Frederick...........736
Vaughan, John.................737

W

Waddill, John..................738
Wade, David....................742
Walker, James.................743
Walker, Peter..................745
Walker, William...............745
Walton, William...............746
Warner, Israel.................749
Warner, Nathaniel............751
Warren, Simpson..............752
Washburn, Bildad............752
Watts, Mason..................753
Wayland, Edward.............753
Weaver, Sheffield.............754
Webb, Isaac....................755
Webb, Isaac....................756
Weeks, Elijah..................758
Wells, Joshua..................759
West, Nathan..................759
Whaley, Ezekiel...............760
Whaley, Reynolds.............761

Wheatley, Leonard...........762
Wheeler, Benjamin...........762
Wheeler, Hezekiah............763
Wheeler, Isaac.................764
Wheeler, Isaac.................764
Wheeler, William..............766
Whitcomb, John................766
White, Abraham................768
White, Goven...................769
White, James...................770
Whitmore, Howell.............770
Williams, Alexander..........771
Williams, Caleb................773
Williams, Hickman............774
Williams, Lew..................774
Willis, John.....................776
Williston, Godfrey............777
Williston, Payson..............778
Wills, William..................779
Wilson, Cornelius..............780
Wilson, Robert.................781
Wilson, Zaccheus..............783
Wisner, Jacob...................785
Witderstein, John..............786
Witherington, Solomon.......787
Wood, Joseph...................790
Wood, Samuel..................796
Wood, Samuel..................796
Woodburn, Moses.............798

Woodridge, James............800
Wright, Phineas................801
Wright, Stephen...............801
Wyckoff, Mary.................802

Y

Yeager, Henry..................802
York, Jean......................806

Z

Zane, Elizabeth................807